Introduction to Mathematical Programming

Russell C. Walker

Carnegie Melon University

PRENTICE HALL, Upper Saddle River, New Jersey 07458

Library of Congress Cataloging-in-Publication Data

Walker, Russell C.
    Introduction to mathematical programming / by Russell C. Walker.
        p.   cm.
    Includes bibliographical references and index.
    ISBN: 0-13-263765-0
    1. Programming (Mathematics).   I. Title.
    QA402.5.W334   1999
    519.7—dc21   98-51415
                                                  CIP

For Susie, Dana, and Robbie

Acquisition Editor: George Lobell
Editorial Assistant: Gale Epps
Editorial Director: Tim Bozik
Editor-in-Chief: Jerome Grant
Assistant Vice President of Production and Manufacturing: David W. Riccardi
Editorial/Production Supervision: Richard DeLorenzo
Managing Editor: Linda Mihatov Behrens
Executive Managing Editor: Kathleen Schiaparelli
Manufacturing Buyer: Alan Fischer
Manufacturing Manager: Trudy Pisciotti
Marketing Manager: Melody Marcus
Marketing Assistant: Amy Lysik
Creative Director: Paula Maylahn
Art Director: Jayne Conte
Cover Designer: Bruce Kenselaar

Cover credit: Vasily Kandinsky, "Rising Warmth (Sufsteigende Warme)," *September 1927. Watercolor, wash,
india ink and pencil on paper, 25.3 x 346 cms (9 15/16 x 14 3/16 inches). Solomon R. Guggenheim Museum, New York.
The Hilla von Rebay Foundation. Photo by David Heald. Copyright The Solomon R. Guggenheim Museum Foundation,
New York. (FN 1970.42); © 1998 Artists Rights Society (ARS), New York/ADAGP, Paris.*

©1999 by Prentice-Hall, Inc.
Simon & Schuster / A Viacom Company
Upper Saddle River, New Jersey 07458

Printed in the United States of America

10 9 8 7 6 5 4 3 2 1

ISBN 0-13-263765-0

Prentice-Hall International (UK) Limited, London
Prentice-Hall of Australia Pty. Limited, Sydney
Prentice-Hall Canada Inc., Toronto
Prentice-Hall Hispanoamericana, S.A., Mexico
Prentice-Hall of India Private Limited, New Delhi
Prentice-Hall of Japan, Inc., Tokyo
Simon & Schuster Asia Pte. Ltd., Singapore
Editora Prentice-Hall do Brasil, Ltda., Rio de Janeiro

Contents

Preface

Introduction

This is a text written for an audience of business students with the mathematical background and the interest to appreciate an occasional departure from a main emphasis on applications. A student can begin this text following a calculus course at a level comparable to that taught for engineering and science students. Only differential calculus is required, and the key elements of calculus needed for optimization are recalled at the beginning of Chapter 5. The needed background on vectors and matrices is found in Chapter 2.

There is enough material for a two semester course. It could serve as the text for a variety of courses with titles such as linear programming, optimization, quantitative methods for management, or operations research.

Software can be used productively in solving many of the problems proposed. Examples using the optimization packages LINDO and LINGO appear in several chapters as well as in Appendix A. The symbolic mathematics package *Maple* is also used in the chapters on vectors and matrices and on nonlinear optimization. An appendix on *Maple* indicates how to use it to do curve fitting, solve network problems, and to solve linear programs. There is also an appendix introducing the TI-82 and TI-92 graphing calculators.

Objectives

The first objective is to provide the needed background to begin to employ mathematical programming as a tool. While managerial applications are the primary focus, mathematical techniques can prove useful in many areas. The key step is to acquire the mind-set that allows one to recognize when a mathematical model can be useful. Even for a person who does not expect to use mathematics him or herself, it is certainly desirable to be familiar with the ideas when working with or supervising others who do the actual analysis of problems. So the ultimate objective is to acquire an attitude that appreciates the potential of the methods to be presented, and then to develop an understanding and ability to apply them.

The second objective is to achieve some appreciation and understanding of the mathematics associated with the applied techniques. There are some proofs here and there, and also an occasional excursion into topics such as basic graph theory, linear algebra, analysis, properties of algorithms, and combinatorics. While these side-trips can be largely ignored by those solely interested in applications, they could also be pointed out and amplified by the instructor who wants a course that emphasizes the mathematics.

The following summary indicates both the key applications and the mathematical highlights.

Chapter 1: Introduction to the Problems

The first chapter provides a survey of problem types to be considered to give an early view of the applications possible with the tools to be studied. In some cases the effect of the solution of a problem on an organization is indicated to emphasize the relevance of these skills. The sample problems in the third section suggest the linear structure involved in most models we consider and some of the issues associated with model formulation. The concluding section presents a graphical approach to solving two variable linear programs. This introduces a key managerial tool and also motivates the need for algebraic methods to solve problems involving more variables.

Chapter 2: Vectors and Matrices

This chapter develops the ideas needed to treat linear problems and serves two purposes. First, it contains the prerequisite material for the study of linear programming. Second, it can be viewed as a brief introduction to matrix algebra in its own right. The reader or instructor might choose to omit certain sections depending upon his or her goal.

For instance, matrix inverses are discussed twice: a brief introduction of the 2×2 case in Section 2.4 and a more detailed discussion including the $n \times n$ case in Section 2.7. Beyond Chapter 2, inverses are actually needed only in the Exercises of Section 3.3. Hence, Section 2.7 could be omitted if the reader is not specifically interested in inverses.

Section 2.6 is the key section because the row operations used there are the same as those needed later in the simplex algorithm.

Section 2.5 is important later because of the linearly independent set of vectors corresponding to each basic solution in the simplex algorithm. We take advantage of the discussion of linear independence to discuss some basic mathematical reasoning which should be understood by any student who has studied mathematics. These ideas are then used in proving several propositions concerning linear independence.

Chapter 3: Linear Programming

The central topic in the text is linear programming. Sections 3.2 and 3.3 develop the simplex algorithm. In Section 3.4 we establish that the simplex algorithm is correct. Section 3.5 discusses the formulation of problems and is therefore of particular importance to those most motivated by applications. Section 3.6 extends the simplex algorithm to problems with nonstandard constraints. Section 3.7 discusses the solution of minimization problems by using an associated maximization problem. Example 3.7.8 illustrates some of the power of linear programming as a managerial tool, and helps to motivate the coming discussion of sensitivity analysis in Section 3.8.

Chapter 4: Network Models

Chapter 4 treats four network problems: the transportation problem, the critical path method, the shortest path problem, and minimal spanning trees. Sample models in LINGO or LINDO are provided.

The discussions of shortest paths and minimal spanning trees require some introduction to graph theory. The effectiveness and correctness of an algorithm are also introduced and considered for minimal spanning tree algorithms.

Chapter 5: Unconstrained Extrema

In this chapter we discuss classical optimization techniques. Some knowledge of differential calculus is required. Convexity is discussed in connection with the economic order quantity problem and inventory management. A section is devoted to the application of least squares curve fitting. There is a discussion of the theory underlying optimization and also an introduction to the use of *Maple* to solve optimization problems.

Chapter 6: Constrained Extrema

This chapter extends the discussion begun in the previous one to problems in which the solution is subject to constraints. The key theorem is the Karush-Kuhn-Tucker theorem for solving convex problems. The main applications presented are the minimization of the cost of a cardboard box, the maximization of utility, the minimization of the cost of equipment replacement, and choosing an investment portfolio to achieve an acceptable return at minimum risk. The chapter concludes with a look back at linear programming as a special case of convex programming.

Chapter 7: Integer Programming

Integer programming is introduced after first discussing the dual simplex algorithm. The dual simplex algorithm is needed to facilitate the addition of a constraint to a linear program for which an optimal solution has been obtained without having to resolve the problem. This then forms the basis of a branch-and-bound approach to solving integer programs. The chapter considers the knapsack problem to introduce the branch-and-bound method, and then develops a general branch-and-bound algorithm. A variety of integer programming models is then discussed, and the chapter concludes with an approach to the traveling salesman problem.

Chapter 8: Introduction to Dynamic Programming

Certain problems to which a solution can be defined through a succession of steps are approachable by dynamic programming. The first example is the longest path problem, which is quite similar to the determination of earliest times in the CPM method. We then consider two extensions of problems considered earlier – the fixed cost transportation problem and a variation of the knapsack problem called the cargo loading problem. We also return to the traveling salesman problem and indicate some of the computational challenge of such problems. Dynamic programming relies on recursion, so it is necessary to introduce some of the key ideas associated with recursive functions. This leads the reader on a brief excursion through the Towers of Hanoi, Fibonacci numbers, and the binomial expansion.

Chapter 9: Case Studies

Chapter 9 presents several more open-ended problems suitable for longer assignments and possibly group projects. Solutions to the cases and suggestions for their class use are available for instructors.

Appendix A: Introductions to LINDO and LINGO

The linear programming package LINDO is extremely useful in solving the linear programs formulated in Chapter 3 as well as the integer programming models of Chapter 7 and the critical path problems of Section 4.3. Examples of its use are presented here along with the use of the basic commands. Other examples of the use of LINDO can be found in Sections 3.5, 3.8, 4.3, 7.1, and 9.1.

Appendix A also contains a brief introduction to LINGO, a related package allowing the solution of nonlinear problems. As a modeling language, LINGO is particularly useful for its ability to efficiently express problems with repetitive constraints. Examples of its use can be found in Section 4.3 in conjunction with critical paths and in Section 4.5 where it is used to determine a minimal spanning tree. It is also used in Chapter 6 in conjunction with nonlinear optimization.

Appendix B: Introduction to *Maple*

The symbolic computation package *Maple* can be very useful, particularly in solving classical optimization problems such as are presented in Chapters 5 and 6 as well as in doing matrix computations, curve fitting, solving linear programs, and solving network models. *Maple* is also briefly introduced in Sections 2.7, 5.4, and 5.6.

Appendix C: Introduction to Texas Instruments Graphing Calculators

A calculator can be of great value in some of the problems to be considered. Solving an equation to determine a critical point is an obvious example. Less obvious are curve fitting discussed in Section 5.5 and dynamic programming in Chapter 9. This appendix provides brief introductions to the TI-82 and TI-92 and their use for such applications. A sample program to solve a cargo loading problem is included.

Appendix D: Selected Answers and Hints

The answers to many of the problems, chiefly the odd ones, are provided here. In some cases a hint is provided instead of the answer. While it is useful to have answers to some of the problems, students should also seek to develop their ability to monitor the correctness of their own work.

Suggestions for instructors

At Carnegie Mellon, the first mathematics course taken by business majors is an adaption of the first calculus course taken by science and enineering majors that emphasizes business and economics applications. Then Chapter 2 and topics from Chapters 5 and 6 are in their next course along with additional calculus from another text. Compound interest is also discussed to form the mathematical basis for subsequent work in accounting and economics. Their third course is applications oriented, and usually includes Chapter 1, Chapter 3 except that Section 3.4 is just touched lightly, much of Chapter 4, and much of Sections 7.1, 7.2, 7.6, and 7.7.

The instructor interested in the mathematics associated with the applications should devote some time to the bit of mathematical reasoning and its use to discuss linear independence in Section 2.5. Indirect proof is next used in Section 3.4 in relating extreme points and basic solutions and again in Section 4.5 in discussing trees. The correctness and effectiveness of algorithms are touched on in Sections 4.4 and 4.5. Chapters 5 and 6 also include several proofs and an introduction to convexity. Section 8.1 introduces recursion, combinations, permutations, and the binomial expansion.

An instructor seeking an emphasis on the development of algorithms will want to emphasize Sections 3.4, 4.4, and 4.5 as suggested above, as well as the branch-and-bound methods developed in Sections 7.2 – 7.5, and 7.7. Additionally, the dual simplex algorithm is discussed in Section 7.3 and an analysis of a dynamic programming approach to the traveling salesman problem is presented in Section 8.4.

Chapter summaries are provided including lists of specific learning objectives. For most of the objectives an illustrative example is suggested along with a typical exercise. This makes describing the content of a test especially straight forward. One simply observes that the test will cover a particular set of objectives.

Dependencies among topics

The chapters are organized so that many of the later topics are largely independent to allow variety in the selection of course content. The only essential topic is linear programming. To provide a guide in choosing a path through the text we first identify the essential material on linear programming, and then discuss what is needed for each of the later topics.

A basic introduction to linear programming should include at least some of the material from the first three sections of Chapter 1 to provide an appreciation of the context in which these techniques developed and the scope of their application. Then the fourth section presents the graphic solution technique. To make the transition to the simplex algorithm Sections 4 – 6 of Chapter 2 are needed. The section on linear independence can be largely omitted if the course is to have little focus on the mathematical foundations of the techniques.

Chapter 3 contains the essentials of linear programming. Section 3.4 can be omitted if no effort is to be made to verify the simplex algorithm. The first exposure to LINDO to solve linear programs is in Section 3.5.

In the subsequent discussion we will refer to these sections – Sections 1.2 – 1.4, 2.4 – 2.6, 3.1 – 3.7 – as the *essential core*.

Chapter 4 on network models can be discussed immediately following the essential core material on linear programming. Since equality constraints and duality arise the material from Sections 3.6 and 3.7 is particularly important.

The discussion of classical non-linear optimization in Chapters 5 and 6 is largely independent of any prior material although the notions of constrained extrema and the set of feasible solutions from a discussion of linear programming would certainly be helpful. Knowledge of differential calculus is also essential for these chapters.

One could take any of several approaches to selecting topics from Chapter 7 on integer programming. Beyond the essential core it is helpful to also first do Sections 4.1 and 4.2 for the introduction to networks and the transportation algorithm as an example in which integer values for the variables are automatic. Considering just the knapsack problem and the traveling salesman problem is one approach. For a course interested only in formulating problems and relying on a software package for their solution one can omit the development of the branch and bound process in Sections 7.3 – 7.5. Doing the entire Chapter provides both an introduction to the models and to the solution process.

Chapter 8 revisits models developed previously from the standpoint of dynamic programming. It builds on the discussion of the transportation problem in Section 4.2, the knapsack problem in Section 7.2, and the traveling salesman problem in Section 7.7.

The cases in Chapter 9 require varying backgrounds, although Chapters 3 and 4 and the ability to use a linear programming package will suffice for most.

Website

Supplementary information, including data files for some of the problems, and an assortment of helpful links are provided at the author's homepage:

$$\text{http://www.math.cmu.edu/}{\sim}\text{rw1k/}$$

Acknowledgments

The author wishes to thank his colleagues Deborah Brandon, Vipul Jain, Anthony Kearsley, Darren Mason, Reha Tütüncü, Nathan Richey, Steve Shreve, John Tolle, and Bill Williams for their contributions and helpful comments. The contributions of students Eric Hanover, Chris Knorr, Dan Rosenberg, Timothy Stoudt, and Bill Walton also deserve mention. Thanks are also due to Florin Manolache for his technical support.

The author would also like to acknowledge the many suggestions of the reviewers: Sanjo Zlobec (McGill University), Ognian B. Enchev (Boston University), John E. Mitchell (Rensselaer Polytechnic Institute), Margaret M. Wiecek (Clemson University), Irwin S. Pressman (Carleton University), Antonio M. Lopez, Jr. (Loyola University), Yuen-Fat Wong (DePaul University), and James Calvert (University of Idaho). Their comments were extremely helpful.

This book was completed while the author was a Faculty Fellow at the Center for Innovation in Learning at Carnegie Mellon. He would like to thank the center for its support.

The author would also like to thank Rick DeLorenzo, Bob Lentz, George Lobell and the rest of the staff at Prentice-Hall for their encouragement, support, and advice.

Russell C. Walker

Pittsburgh, PA

Chapter 1

Introduction to the Problems

1.1 Introduction

As computing has made possible the analysis of increasingly complex situations, modern decision making has come to rely more and more upon mathematics. The discipline which has evolved to serve the needs of decision makers is *operations research*–the process of formulating and solving a problem to reach a decision affecting the operation of an organization.

Operations research as a discipline had its beginnings during World War II, although some of the underlying mathematical ideas are much older. The problems presented by troop movements, antisubmarine warfare, crew scheduling, radar deployment, and other aspects of warfare led British military leaders to employ teams of scientists to seek solutions. Their clear success motivated other nations to adopt a similar approach.

The emergence of operations research continued as mathematicians and managers sought nonmilitary applications after the war. Large corporations competing for profits were among the first to employ the new techniques.

Gradually the problems to be addressed were classified into types, as discussed in the next section. Among the tools that emerged to solve them is *mathematical programming*. This approach builds a mathematical model to reflect the range of managerial options, and a solution is obtained by a programmable process called an *algorithm*.

This young discipline took advantage of the increasing power of computers. Advances in computing and developments in algorithms for solving mathematical programming problems proceeded in tandem.

A major milestone [6] was achieved in 1947 when George Dantzig introduced the simplex algorithm. This approach, which promptly assumed a major role in the solution of linear problems, will be the central topic in Chapter 3. Dantzig wrote a comprehensive introduction to the discipline of linear programming in [7].

Today mathematical programming is an important tool employed by operations research staffs in most large organizations and by academic departments in many universities.

Our objective here is to provide the essential background for anyone who may need to employ mathematical programming. A basic understanding of the fundamentals will prove valuable whether the manager does his or her own problem analysis or relies on the work of others.

The basic understanding to be gained can be summed up in four goals:

- The ability to recognize a problem appropriate for solution by mathematical programming.

- The ability to formulate a managerial problem as a mathematical program.

- An understanding of the mathematics underlying the methods of mathematical programming.

- Mastery of the algorithms used and familiarity with their computer implementation.

We will address all four of these goals – minimizing, however, our attention to the actual computer implementation of algorithms. The Appendices provide introductions to some useful software, and some of the examples and exercises will require computing for their solution.

We do not consider the actual use of the information gained from the mathematical treatment of a problem. However, the managerial value of these methods should become evident, particularly in the discussions of duality theory and sensitivity analysis in Chapter 3, of the critical path method in Chapter 4, and of integer programming in Chapter 7. Chapter 9 offers the reader experience with more open-ended problems where the appropriate method of solution is not apparent from the location of the problem in the text.

The implementation of any conclusions reached can often be expected to require personal leadership characteristics of management – an area that is clearly beyond our scope here.

1.2   Types of problems to be considered

Solution of the examples in this introductory chapter must await mastery of the underlying mathematical foundations. However, the sample problems serve to indicate the types of application possible, and many will be revisited as the bases of exercises in later chapters.

In reading over the examples, the reader should try to identify examples of some of the most common types of problem, as described below: allocation, sequencing, routing, blending, scheduling, project management, network, and knapsack.

Allocation problems

The solution of an *allocation problem* allows an organization to allocate resources in order to optimize some measure of success. The most frequent objectives are to maximize profit or to minimize cost. Resources might include such things as land, money, manufacturing time, or raw materials. Often an allocation problem results in a decision involving how many of each of several possible products to produce. We call this a *product mix problem*.

A good example is discussed in [4]. That model considers the production process from the availability of raw materials through manufacturing to the demand for the products. The analysis of the process led to an altered inventory policy, a reduction in the number of products offered, and an increase in profit. As a result of the improved utilization of the existing production facilities management concluded that a planned expansion would probably not be needed.

Because of the easy accessibility of the language of the applications, we will occasionally consider allocation problems drawn from farming. However, accessibility is not our only motivation, since [19] indicates that such models can be of considerable value to the small farmer.

Sequencing problems

The objective of a *sequencing problem* is to schedule multistage operations in the most efficient manner. Examples include ordering the way in which different products are manufactured on the same equipment or the sequence in which several cities are visited on a sales trip. The latter, called a *traveling salesman problem*, will be considered at length in Chapter 7.

While the model is introduced in terms of a salesman, among the important applications is guiding an automated drill [15] to drill holes for mounting components on a circuit board. A few minutes, or even seconds, saved in a repetitive operation such as this becomes highly valuable over the product's total production.

Routing problems

The goal of a *routing problem* is to plan the movement of goods in an efficient manner. Here efficient usually means lowest cost, but in special instances, such as those involving a perishable good, efficient may mean fastest.

The trucking industry comes to mind in this connection. Besides improving the profit margin and efficient movement of goods, the routing application can help reduce employee turnover. The scheduling technique known as swap and drop [37], where two drivers meet midway, trade loads, and then return to their starting points, serves driver morale by giving them more time at home as well as enhancing the movement of goods.

Blending problems

A *blending problem* occurs when two or more resources are combined to produce a product having certain characteristics – for instance, to produce a wine with a given alcohol content by mixing several other wines, or to achieve certain characteristics by mixing paints. A problem is seldom purely a blending problem, and often it includes other requirements.

A complex mix of chemical, economic, managerial, and technological issues made blending in the oil industry an early fruitful application of mathematical programming. The discussion in [5] shows the importance of the problem as well as the influence of policy and government regulation on the solution.

Scheduling problems

A *scheduling problem* involves planning production to meet customer demand within capacity and supply constraints in an optimal fashion. Objectives may include minimizing costs such as overtime, shipping, storage, and back orders. We will see that some scheduling problems share many of the mathematical characteristics of routing problems with physical destinations replaced by points in time.

In an interesting scheduling application, the manager of four McDonald's franchises developed a scheduling algorithm [26] for his employees. The result was to cut the time needed to make out the schedule by at least 80% while lowering costs by reducing staff at slack times. Another result was to improve employee morale by being able to schedule more people at their preferred times.

A special type of scheduling problem has as its goal the determination of the optimal order quantity to achieve efficient inventory management. Such a problem is often referred to as an *economic lot size problem.*

A significant application of such a model [1] was achieved by a group of seniors at the Air Force Academy. Their project dealt with a 250,000 item spare parts inventory. The pilot project saved $600,000 with a forecast total savings of $7 million.

Project management problems

The goal of a *project management problem* is to plan the tasks to be accomplished so that the project is completed on time. Issues that might be considered include keeping the cost within budget and allocating additional resources to tasks to shorten the time required for their completion.

A critical issue in many industries is the shutdown of production facilities for maintenance and inspection. The loss of production is expensive, and every day saved in the process can be valuable. In the example discussed in [31], the cost of each day of shutdown at a Weyerhaeuser paper production facility was pegged at $500,000. One tool used to improve their use of shutdown time is the critical path method to be discussed in Chapter 4.

Network problems

A *network problem* is one that seeks to in some way link locations in an efficient manner. Reliable and efficient communication are among the central objectives of connection problems. It is not an accident that one of the fundamental papers on the subject [29] appeared in a journal related to the telephone industry. The application suggested there and to be discussed in Chapter 4 is stated in terms of secure communication within an underground group, but has obvious parallels in telephone connections and computer networks.

Some network problems involve the selection of the location for critical components in a network. In a model [14] designed to improve its overall production and inventory management, the Agrico Chemical Co. also considered the location of facilities as well as the production and shipping. The result was an estimated savings of more than $18,000,000 in the first three years.

Knapsack problems

The *knapsack problem* takes its name from the process of choosing items to take on a back-packing trip. The goal is to take items which will have the maximum utility but will not exceed the weight limit that you are willing to carry. The solution is a set of decisions as to whether or not each item should be included in the knapsack.

Among the applications is the choice of tax strategies that a small business or individual professional might employ. This model, discussed in [13], has the goal of maximizing the tax savings within the constraint of the cash-flow budget.

1.3   Sample problems

Listed below are examples of some of the types of problems we have discussed. The reader should try to classify the problems according to type. In a few cases we consider the first steps toward a solution: the identification of the variables and the formulation of the equations or inequalities that express the circumstances.

Nearly all the expressions associated with these problems will be *linear*, i.e., they will be of the form

$$4x_1 + 2x_2 + 3x_3$$

where $x_1, x_2,$ and x_3 are variables. Such an expression might represent the profit of a company or the number of units of a resource required. Frequently the variables will represent the number of units to be produced of each of the products made by a company. The coefficients will be drawn from the data given in the problem. Thus, an equation using this expression would have the form

$$4x_1 + 2x_2 + 3x_3 = 50$$

and an inequality the form

$$4x_1 + 2x_2 + 3x_3 \leq 150.$$

Such an inequality might express a limitation on a raw material such as iron with the coefficients 4, 2, and 3 representing the units of iron required for a unit of each of the corresponding products. Note that with these units assigned to the coefficients and the variables x_j, each term in the sum has the same units – the number of units of iron – as a result of the cancellation:

$$4 \, \frac{\text{units of iron}}{\text{unit of product 1}} \cdot x_1 \text{ units of product 1} = 4x_1 \text{ units of iron}$$

This is a critical observation since meaningful addition of several such terms requires that they all have the same units.

The next section will be devoted to the geometric interpretation of such expressions. Their algebraic manipulation will be introduced in Chapter 2.

Our first example involves farming and is taken from [10] with the permission of my late friend and colleague Richard Duffin. Because the resources and terminology of such examples are readily accessible, we will often return to this and similar examples in introducing new aspects of linear programming.

Example 1.3.1. Farmer Brown is planning his planting for the coming year. He expects to raise two crops: potatoes and wheat. He has 100 acres of land available for planting and will be able to devote 160 days of labor to his crops. He expects an acre of wheat to require four days of labor, while an acre of potatoes requires only one day.

He has \$1,100 that he can use for the start-up costs of planting and cultivating. It costs \$10 an acre to plant and cultivate potatoes, while the corresponding costs for an acre of wheat are \$20.

If Brown expects a revenue of \$40 per acre for potatoes and \$120 an acre for wheat, how many acres of each should he plant in order to achieve the maximum possible revenue?

Note that the expression for the revenue

$$40x_1 + 120x_2$$

where x_1 and x_2 are the number of acres of potatoes and the number of acres of wheat, respectively, does not include any measure of the ability of Farmer Brown to sell his crops. Thus, the assumption that all crops can be sold at the given price is built into the resulting model. This is a common assumption in such problems. ∎

In Farmer Brown's problem, it would be acceptable to have the variables assume noninteger values in the solution since it is conceivable to plant a fractional number of acres of a crop. In the next example, the variables will represent numbers of people, and thus must be integers. We will see that in some cases the structure of the problem will automatically yield integer values. In other cases we will need to use special techniques to explicitly impose the integer requirement. This will be discussed in Chapter 7.

Example 1.3.2. The Metropolis City Hospital has the minimal daily requirements for nurses shown in Table 1.3.1.

Table 1.3.1

Time of day (24-hour clock)	Period	Minimal number of nurses required during period
2-6	1	20
6-10	2	64
10-14	3	72
14-18	4	68
18-22	5	44
22-2	6	32

Note that Period 1 follows immediately after Period 6 on a 24-hour clock.

Each nurse works eight consecutive hours, i.e., two consecutive periods. The hospital seeks to obtain a daily schedule that requires the minimum number of people, provided each of the above minimum requirements is met.

For this problem, we will let x_i represent the number of nurses starting at the beginning of period i. Note that, unlike the previous example, the constraints for this problem set forth minimum requirements rather than maximum supplies available. Such constraints are expressed as inequalities in the opposite direction. For instance,

$$x_3 + x_4 \geq 68$$

represents the nursing staff requirement for Period 4. ∎

The next several examples deal with various aspects of production involving either scheduling or determining an optimal product mix.

Example 1.3.3. The Miller Tool and Die Company makes five products: v, w, x, y, and z, which require time in four departments: blanking, forming, drilling, and assembly, requiring the following per-unit processing times:

Table 1.3.2

Product	Time required (hours)			
	Blanking	Forming	Drilling	Assembly
v	1	1	.5	1
w	1	0	.25	2
x	2	3	0	1
y	0	2	1	2
z	.5	1	.5	1

The marginal contribution of a unit of each product to the company's profit is:

Table 1.3.3

Product	Profit contribution
v	$64 per unit
w	$72 per unit
x	$104 per unit
y	$120 per unit
z	$56 per unit

The time available in each of the four departments and the estimated incremental costs of idle time are given below:

Table 1.3.4

Department	Time available	Cost of idle time per hour
Blanking	120 hrs	$12.00
Forming	120 hrs	$8.00
Drilling	80 hrs	$9.00
Assembly	160 hrs	$12.00

Determine the product mix that will maximize the profit while operating within the production limitations. ∎

In this problem, data is supplied to take into consideration the cost of having equipment stand idle. This information can be incorporated into the objective function in a manner suggested in the exercises.

Example 1.3.4. Comet Manufacturing makes three products – A, B, and C – and in doing so utilizes four processes: stamping, turning, assembly, and testing. The required processing times in minutes per unit of each product are as follows:

Table 1.3.5

	Stamping	Turning	Assembly	Testing
A	4	6	18	6
B	1	4	12	5
C	2	12	15	5

The available processing capacities in hours per month are:

Table 1.3.6

Stamping	960
Turning	3,800
Assembly	6,800
Testing	2,940

The minimum requirements to meet existing orders are:

Table 1.3.7

A	8,500 units
B	9,000 units
C	5,800 units

The profit per unit sold of each product is 75 cents for A, 60 cents for B, and 45 cents for C. Comet anticipates that each unit produced above the minimum can be sold for the same amount. What quantities of each product should be produced next month for maximum profit? ∎

Example 1.3.5. A company with two plants must meet the following needs of four of its customers during the next week:

Table 1.3.8

Destination	Units	Shipping cost/unit	
		From Plant 1	From Plant 2
A	500	$1.00	$5.00
B	300	$2.00	$3.00
C	1,000	$3.00	$2.00
D	200	$4.00	$1.00

Each unit of product must be machined and assembled. The costs, requirements, and labor availabilities in the two plants are as follows:

Table 1.3.9

	Hours/unit	Cost/hour	Hours available
Plant No. 1:			
Machining	0.10	$16	120
Assembling	0.20	$12	260
Plant No. 2:			
Machining	0.12	$15	120
Assembling	0.22	$12	240

In which plants should these orders be manufactured in order to fill the orders at minimum total cost? ∎

Example 1.3.6. The Sure-Start Battery Co. makes six models of battery. The models differ in three respects: case size (Small or Large), duration of warranty (30 or 48 months), and whether or not the batteries are permanently sealed or will require maintenance of the water level. Only the 48-month batteries are sold in a sealed model.

The models have been given the following designations according to the length of warranty, case size, and whether or not they are sealed (SE): 30S, 48S, 30L, 48L, 48S-SE, 48L-SE.

The six models are produced on the same production line with downtime being required for a change of model.

Altering the production line for a model change requires several types of changes, the costs of which are independent of each other. A change in case size costs $400. The cost for changing the plates varies, chiefly because of the different metals required in sealed (SE) models.

Table 1.3.10

Plate change costs	
From 30 to 48	$600
From 48 to 30	$500
From non-SE to SE, an additional	$300
From SE to non-SE, an additional	$400

Because the SE models use a different electrolyte and also require different caps on the cells, there is an additional charge incurred in changing to or from an SE model:

Table 1.3.11

Cap change costs	
To an SE model	$500
From an SE model	$300

Determine the order in which the Sure-Start company should manufacture its six lines so that the total downtime cost between production runs is minimized. ∎

Example 1.3.7. The Elite Kitchen Co., which produces customized kitchen cabinets, finds that it has heavy commitments for a month in which employees have already scheduled vacations. Thus, meeting its customer demands on time may require overtime work and possibly building some units in advance, which entails holding costs.

The demands and single-shift capacities for the four weeks are shown in Table 1.3.12.

Table 1.3.12

	Weeks			
	1	2	3	4
Demand in units	16	17	18	20
Capacity in units	12	9	14	17

Overtime labor can be hired at a per-unit cost. The available overtime capacity varies because not all workers will accept overtime during the summer. The respective weekly overtime capacities are 7, 5, 8, and 9 units. Because the personnel available differ in seniority, the per-unit overtime costs also vary with the week and are, respectively, $140, $130, $150, and $140. For each week of storage, the holding cost in terms of space and tied-up capital is $50 per unit.

How should Elite schedule its production for the month in order to meet all demands on time while minimizing the total overtime labor and holding costs? ∎

Example 1.3.8. A salesperson needs to visit five cities on a regular basis and wishes to minimize the total cost of the round trip. He figures that it costs $0.20 per mile to operate his car. Table 1.3.13 gives the distances in miles between the cities. Between certain cities the only reasonable routes utilize a system of toll roads on which the toll is $0.04 per mile, rounded up to the nearest $0.05. An * indicates toll roads.

Table 1.3.13

	1	2	3	4	5
1	–	55	45	90*	45
2	60	–	55	20	75
3	40	55	–	35*	120*
4	90*	20	35*	–	25
5	50	80	120*	30	–

How should the round trip be scheduled to minimize his costs? ∎

Example 1.3.9. An auto company produces three lines of cars, Subcompact, Mid-sized, and Grand Luxury, with respective miles-per-gallon ratings of 32, 24, and 17. It must produce a total of at least 100,000 cars in the coming market year, and in order to satisfy federal legislation the average miles per gallon of the cars produced must be at least 25.

Because of the high profit margin, the company would like to make at least 20,000 of the Grand Luxury line. The capacity of their engine plant for the smaller models limits production of Subcompacts and Mid-sized cars to a total of 90,000.

The respective prices for the lines of cars are $14,500, $19,000, and $23,000. At the end of the model year, the recent experience has been that 10% of the Subcompacts and the Mid-sized cars are sold at a 15% discount, and 20% of the Grand Luxury line are sold at a 20% discount.

Determine how many of each line should be manufactured in order to achieve the maximum sales revenue. ∎

Example 1.3.10. Production scheduling. Excelsior Electric Co. makes custom motors for a variety of applications. Its two plants ship their production to three dealers. The production hours available in the plants for the second quarter vary because of downtime for scheduled maintenance on equipment:

Table 1.3.14

Plant	April	May	June
A	400	360	360
B	425	350	375

Plant A requires 20 hours to produce a motor; Plant B requires 25. Because B is older and less efficient, production costs are $100 more per motor in B than in A.

Shipping costs from the plants to the dealers and orders for the quarter are shown in Table 1.3.15.

Table 1.3.15

Dealer	Monthly orders			Shipping costs from	
	April	May	June	A	B
1	12	9	11	45	60
2	10	12	8	50	70
3	8	11	12	75	40

Building ahead and stockpiling of motors is possible with a cost of $55 per month; orders that are not shipped in the month requested are subject to a contractual penalty of $80 per month.

Determine a production schedule to meet the demands for motors with the minimum total of shipping, storage, penalty, and production differential costs. ∎

The expression for the ordering cost in the next example will not be linear as in the examples considered so far. We will find that the solution of such problems will require calculus techniques as developed in Chapters 5 and 6.

Example 1.3.11. Dolphin Speedboats expects to produce 1,000 boats in the next year. Dolphin buys engines from a subcontractor and must regularly replenish its supply of engines in order to keep pace with production. Aside from the costs of the engines themselves, two costs are associated with maintaining the needed inventory: the supplier charges $100 to process an order, and it costs Dolphin $15 to store each engine. Dolphin wishes to place regular orders for a fixed number of engines. How many engines should Dolphin order each time? ∎

Managing a complex activity requires scheduling interdependent tasks and allocating resources for their timely completion. The following example illustrates the simplest version of such a problem. We will use a graph to depict dependence among the tasks in Chapter 4. There we will also refine the problem by using variable times for the completion of tasks and the allocation of additional resources to assure completion of the project on time and within budget.

Example 1.3.12. Consider the following tasks involved in building a frame house. Given the relationships among the tasks and the estimated time in days required for each, determine the shortest time required to complete the construction.

Table 1.3.16

	Task	Immediate predecessor	Expected duration
A.	Excavate for foundation		2
B.	Pour foundation	A	3
C.	Install sewer and water lines	A	2
D.	Frame in walls	B	6
E.	Brick chimney and fireplace	D	2
F.	Install roof	D	3
G.	Install wiring and ductwork	F	3
H.	Insulate	E, G	2
I.	Install windows and siding	H	5
J.	Install wallboard	H	3
K.	Connect utilities	C	2
L.	Paint interior	K	4
M.	Clean site	L	1

∎

The next example requires that a decision be made for each of five experiments. Each of these decisions is represented by a variable that can assume only two values: the value 0, indicating "no," or a value 1, indicating "yes." Problems involving integer variables will be considered in Chapter 7.

Example 1.3.13. NASA must make a decision regarding which experiments should be flown on a deep-space probe that can accommodate a total payload of 140 pounds. A panel of experts has assigned numerical values to each of the experiments. The assigned values and the weights of the experiments are shown in Table 1.3.17. Determine which experiments should be selected for the probe in order to achieve the greatest total value.

Table 1.3.17

Experiment	Weight	Value
1	35	60
2	45	70
3	55	80
4	42	90
5	35	50

■

Curve fitting is a highly useful application of the classical optimization techniques to be discussed in Chapter 5. The following problem is a typical example.

Example 1.3.14. Alvin Manufacturing has noticed what seems to be a steady growth in the number of customers for a new product line it introduced five years ago. The number of customers is given in Table 1.3.18.

Table 1.3.18

Year	1	2	3	4	5
No. customers	5	8	9	12	14

Assuming that the growth in the number of customers is linear, predict the number of customers in each of the next two years. ■

Exercises

1. Farmer Brown's problem, Example 1.3.1, involves three constraints, one for each resource, of the form $ax_1 + bx_2 \leq c$. Determine the constraints.

2. Suppose that Farmer Brown of Example 1.3.1 can borrow $300 at 10% interest. If he decides to go ahead and borrow, he must then decide if he should use the amount borrowed to make more available for start-up costs or to hire additional labor at $20/day. Formulate the two sets of constraints that help him decide if he should borrow, and if so, how much, and how he should use the borrowed money.

3. Determine the cost of a transition from a 48S to a 48L-SE model in Example 1.3.6.

4. Letting the number of units of products v through z be $x_1, x_2, \ldots, x_5$, respectively, write the constraints imposed by the limited hours available in the blanking and forming departments of Example 1.3.3.

5. Using your answers to the previous exercise, determine an expression for the cost of the unused hours, if any, in the blanking department.

6. Determine the objective function for Example 1.3.3 by subtracting the costs of idle time in all the shops from the profit.

7. The formulation of the problem in Example 1.3.6 will be seen in Chapter 7 to depend only on the table of costs of changing from one model battery to another. Form the required table by calculating the 36 costs.

8. The calculation of production capacities is a part of some problems. In Example 1.3.10 it is a matter of dividing the number of production hours available by the number of hours required for a motor. However, in Example 1.3.5, there are two processes, and the capacity in each plant is the minimum capacity for the two processes. Calculate the capacities for the two plants in Example 1.3.5.

9. Example 1.3.13 involves two linear functions – the scientific value to be maximized and the total weight, which is limited to 140 pounds. Formulate the objective and the single constraint.

10. Match each of the examples with the corresponding problem type:

A.	Example 1.3.9, Auto company	1.	Knapsack
B.	Example 1.3.12, House construction	2.	Inventory
C.	Example 1.3.7, Elite Kitchen Co.	3.	Product mix
D.	Example 1.3.13, Deep space probe	4.	Sequencing
E.	Example 1.3.11, Dolphin Speedboats	5.	Project management
F.	Example 1.3.6, Sure-Start Battery Co.	6.	Scheduling

1.4   Graphical solution of linear programs

In stating the problems in the previous section, we noted that several involved only linear expressions. In particular, if x_i represents the quantity of the ith product in Example 1.3.3, then the expression

$$z = 8x_1 + 9x_2 + 13x_3 + 15x_4 + 7x_5$$

expresses the profit. Because the company's objective is to maximize this expression, we call it the *objective function* of the problem. A similar linear expression expresses the number of hours of assembly time required, and since only 110 hours of assembly time are available, the following inequality describes that limit on the plant's production:

$$x_1 + 2x_2 + x_3 + 2x_4 + x_5 \leq 110.$$

Such an inequality is called a *constraint*. The combination of a linear objective function and a set of linear constraints expressing the restrictions on the values that the variables can assume is called a *linear program*. A linear program is solved by determining the optimal value of the objective function subject to the constraints. Here we consider a graphical method of solution that is useful when there are only two variables.

Applications of linear programming occur in many areas of business and government. The method of geometric solution will be illustrated by the following problem. The initial example is again drawn from farming since the units and terminology are easily understood.

Example 1.4.1. Farmer Jones has 100 acres of land to devote to wheat and corn and wishes to plan his planting to maximize the expected revenue. Jones has only $800 in capital to apply to planting the crops, and it costs $5 to plant an acre of wheat and $10 for an acre of corn. Their other activities leave the Jones family only 150 days of labor to devote to the crops. Two days will be required for each acre of wheat and one day for an acre of corn. If past experience indicates a return of $80 from each acre of wheat and $60 from each acre of corn, how many acres of each should be planted to maximize his revenue?

With x assigned to denote the number of acres of wheat and y the number of acres of corn, the expected revenue is given by $z = 80x + 60y$. The number of days of labor that will be required is then given by $2x + y$, and the limit of 150 days leads to the constraint

$$2x + y \leq 150.$$

Adding the capital and acreage restrictions and the requirement that the variables be nonnegative yields the following linear program:

$$
\begin{aligned}
\text{Maximize}: \quad & 80x + 60y \\
\text{Subject to}: \quad & x + y \leq 100 \\
& 2x + y \leq 150 \\
& 5x + 10y \leq 800 \\
& x \geq 0, \; y \geq 0
\end{aligned}
$$

When graphed, each of the constraints is represented by a *half-plane*, i.e., the points on a straight line plus all the points on one side of the line.

A half-plane is graphed by first graphing the line obtained by replacing the "$\leq$" or "$\geq$" with an equals sign. When graphed, this line forms the "edge" of the half-plane. When the line does not pass through the origin, the quickest way to graph it is usually to determine the points where the line intersects the axes and connect them. Then, by testing points on either side of the line in the original inequality, one determines on which side of the line the points satisfy the original inequality.

In Figure 1.4.1, the dollar constraint from Farmer Jones's problem has been graphed by connecting the intercepts $(160, 0)$ and $(0, 80)$ and then determining that the origin satisfies the constraint, so that the half-plane lies on the same side of the line as the origin.

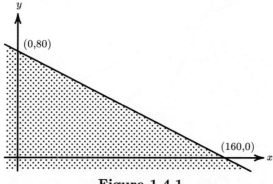

Figure 1.4.1

When the three resource constraints and the two nonnegativity constraints are graphed on the same axes, their intersection yields the set of feasible planting combinations for Farmer Jones. This is illustrated by the shaded area common to all five half-planes in Figure 1.4.2.

Note that the x-intercept $(160, 0)$ of the dollar constraint does not belong to the set of feasible solutions since land availability limits planting to 100 acres, and labor limits the number of acres of wheat that can be planted to 75.

The corners on the set of feasible solutions are obtained by solving simultaneously pairs of equations obtained by making the constraints equalities. For instance, the corner $(40, 60)$ is the solution of the system

$$
\begin{aligned}
x + y &= 100 \\
5x + 10y &= 800.
\end{aligned}
$$

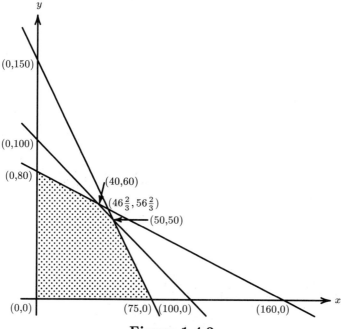

Figure 1.4.2

In terms of Farmer Jones's problem, that corner represents the result of planting all 100 acres and spending all available capital while working

$$2 \cdot 40 + 1 \cdot 60 = 140$$

days, leaving 10 of the 150 days available unworked.

Note that the corner $(46\frac{2}{3}, 56\frac{2}{3})$ obtained from the system

$$
\begin{array}{rcrcl}
2x & + & y & = & 150 \\
5x & + & 10y & = & 800
\end{array}
$$

is not a feasible solution since it would require $103\frac{1}{3}$ acres, i.e., $3\frac{1}{3}$ more acres than are available. This is expressed graphically in Figure 1.4.2 since the point $(46\frac{2}{3}, 56\frac{2}{3})$ lies outside the half-plane representing the acreage constraint.

The solution to the problem is determined geometrically by drawing level curves of the objective function on the same set of axes as the set of feasible solutions. For a given revenue of $\$z_0$, the level curve is obtained by solving $z_0 = 80x + 60y$ for y, which yields the line

$$y = -\frac{4}{3}x + \frac{z_0}{60}.$$

Thus, the family of curves representing points producing the same revenues are straight lines having slope $-\frac{4}{3}$ and having the property that the line corresponding to the largest possible revenue will have the greatest y-intercept. This is illustrated in Figure 1.4.3.

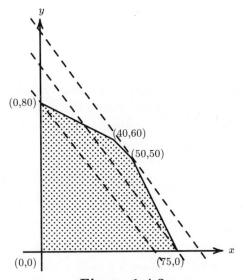

Figure 1.4.3

The significant geometric fact is that the line representing the highest obtainable revenue intersects the set of feasible solutions at a corner. Here, the corner producing the greatest revenue is $(50, 50)$.

The geometric method of solution based on these observations includes three steps:

1. Draw the set of feasible solutions.

2. Determine the corners of the set.

3. Choose the corner producing the maximum (or minimum) value of the objective function.

Evaluating the objective function at the corners confirms that the maximum occurs at $(50, 50)$:

$$
\begin{aligned}
z(0,0) &= \$0 \\
z(0,80) &= 80 \cdot 0 + 60 \cdot 80 &= \$4800 \\
z(40,60) &= 80 \cdot 40 + 60 \cdot 60 &= \$6800 \\
z(50,50) &= 80 \cdot 50 + 60 \cdot 50 &= \$7000 \\
z(75,0) &= 80 \cdot 75 + 60 \cdot 0 &= \$6000
\end{aligned}
$$

Thus, Farmer Jones should plant 50 acres of wheat and 50 acres of corn to obtain a maximal revenue of $7000. These activities will use all of his acreage and require his family to devote all of the allotted 150 days of labor. However, since the input costs are only

$$5 \cdot 50 + 10 \cdot 50 = \$750$$

he will have $50 of capital remaining. ∎

In Farmer Jones's problem Figure 1.4.3 showed that the level curve corresponding to the optimal solution intersected the set of feasible solutions in a single point, $(50, 50)$, thus yielding a unique solution. It can happen that the level curves are parallel to an edge of the set of feasible solutions, leading to a solution that is not unique. Also in the example the set of feasible solutions was bounded, indicating a bounded solution. The cases leading to nonunique solutions and unbounded solutions are illustrated in the exercises.

The next chapter will develop the necessary techniques with vectors and matrices to approach problems involving more than two variables. The main linear programming tool, the simplex algorithm, will be developed in Chapter 3.

Exercises

1. Determine the inequality from Example 1.3.1 expressing the limitation on capital and draw its graph.

2. Draw the graphs of $x_1 + 2x_2 \leq 30$ and $3x_1 + x_2 \leq 40$ on the same set of axes. Shade the area common to both half-planes.

3. Draw the portion of the graph of the plane $4x_1 + 3x_2 + 6x_3 = 24$ that lies in the first octant.

4. Solve the following linear program graphically:

$$
\begin{array}{rrcrcl}
\text{Maximize:} & x_1 & + & 3x_2 & & \\
\text{Subject to:} & x_1 & + & x_2 & \leq & 40 \\
& x_1 & - & 2x_2 & \leq & 10 \\
& x_1 & & & \leq & 20 \\
& \multicolumn{5}{c}{x_1 \geq 0, \quad x_2 \geq 0}
\end{array}
$$

5. Solve the following linear program graphically:

$$
\begin{array}{rrcrcl}
\text{Maximize}: & 5x_1 & + & 4x_2 & & \\
\text{Subject to}: & -4x_1 & + & 2x_2 & \leq & 8 \\
& x_1 & & & \leq & 7 \\
& 3x_1 & + & 2x_2 & \leq & 29 \\
& \multicolumn{5}{c}{x_1 \geq 0, \quad x_2 \geq 0}
\end{array}
$$

6. Solve the following linear program graphically. Note the effect of the constraint involving a $\geq$ inequality.

$$
\begin{array}{rrcrcl}
\text{Maximize}: & 3x_1 & + & 2x_2 & & \\
\text{Subject to}: & 2x_1 & + & 5x_2 & \geq & 20 \\
& -2x_1 & + & x_2 & \leq & 10 \\
& x_1 & + & x_2 & \leq & 13 \\
& \multicolumn{5}{c}{x_1 \geq 0, \quad x_2 \geq 0}
\end{array}
$$

7. A minimizing example. Solve the following linear program graphically. Note the different nature of the set of feasible solutions brought about by reversing the direction of the inequalities.

$$
\begin{array}{rrcrcl}
\text{Minimize}: & 2x & + & 8y & & \\
\text{Subject to}: & 3x & + & 4y & \geq & 15 \\
& 2x & + & 5y & \geq & 24 \\
& x & + & 10y & \geq & 27 \\
& \multicolumn{5}{c}{x \geq 0, \quad y \geq 0}
\end{array}
$$

8. Consider the linear program:

$$
\begin{array}{rrcrcl}
\text{Minimize}: & 40y_1 & + & 30y_2 & & \\
\text{Subject to}: & 2y_1 & + & y_2 & \geq & 14 \\
& 3y_1 & + & 2y_2 & \geq & 24 \\
& 2y_1 & + & 3y_2 & \geq & 21 \\
& \multicolumn{5}{c}{y_1 \geq 0, \quad y_2 \geq 0}
\end{array}
$$

(a) Draw the graph of the set of feasible solutions and label the feasible corners.

(b) Draw the level curves of the objective function corresponding to the objective function values $w_0 = 340$, $w_1 = 310$, and $w_2 = 250$.

(c) Determine the solution of the linear program.

9. Consider the linear program:

$$
\begin{array}{rrcrcl}
\text{Maximize}: & 3x_1 & + & 2x_2 & & \\
\text{Subject to}: & 5x_1 & + & 2x_2 & \geq & 20 \\
& 2x_1 & - & x_2 & \leq & 12 \\
& x_1 & + & x_2 & \leq & 12 \\
& \multicolumn{5}{c}{x_1 \geq 0, \quad x_2 \geq 0}
\end{array}
$$

    (a) Draw the set of feasible solutions and label the feasible corners.

    (b) Draw two level curves of the objective function, one corresponding to the optimal value and one corresponding to a value smaller than the optimal value.

    (c) Determine the solution of the linear program.

10. **Formulation exercise.** A company manufactures two lines of its product. It is planning production for a week in which it has available only 80 of a particular component needed for both lines. Inventory levels indicate that at most 50 of the first line should be made. The product lines require two hours and four hours of labor, respectively, and 280 hours of labor are available. If the contributions to profit of the two lines are $60 and $80, respectively, formulate and solve the linear program to determine how many of each line to make to maximize their potential profit from the week's production.

11. **Formulation exercise.** A hardware store owner plans to diversify her business by renting out equipment as a sideline. Initially she plans to handle rug scrubbers, floor sanders, and chainsaws. A distributor estimates the respective monthly incomes from these items at $150, $100, and $90. The distributor also advises that she should buy at least as many scrubbers as her total of sanders and saws and no more than three saws. Scrubbers, sanders, and saws, together with the necessary supplies, cost $700, $650, and $500, respectively. In addition, she plans to buy a service contract on each item for an additional charge of $25 each. She has $9000 available. Her floor space is limited, and she can commit only 45 square feet of space to her rental operation. The three machines require 3, 2, and 2 square feet of space, respectively, for their storage.

If her objective is to maximize income, formulate a linear program to determine the number of each type of equipment to buy.

12. **Minimization formulation.** A kennel owner has a choice of two dog foods to buy in bulk quantities to feed the dogs under her care. The average dog needs eight ounces of protein, eleven ounces of carbohydrate, and 100 milligrams of iron a day. A pound of Dog Grub includes three ounces of protein, five ounces of carbohydrate, and 30 milligrams of iron. A pound of Canine Chow includes four ounces of protein, 12 ounces of carbohydrate, and 35 milligrams of iron. If Dog Grub and Canine Chow cost $1.10 and $.90 a pound, respectively, how much of each should she buy to meet the daily needs of the average dog at a minimum cost?

13. **Nonunique solution.** Show that the following linear program does not have a unique solution. Determine a solution which does not occur at a corner,

and describe the set of optimal solutions:

$$
\begin{array}{rrcrcl}
\text{Maximize}: & 30x & + & 15y \\
\text{Subject to}: & 2x & + & y & \leq & 20 \\
& x & & & \leq & 8 \\
& -x & + & y & \leq & 10 \\
\end{array}
$$
$$x \geq 0,\ y \geq 0$$

14. Show that the following linear program does not have a unique solution. Describe the set of optimal solutions:

$$
\begin{array}{rrcrcl}
\text{Minimize}: & 4y_1 & + & 2y_2 \\
\text{Subject to}: & y_1 & + & 3y_2 & \geq & 18 \\
& y_1 & + & & \geq & 4 \\
& 2y_1 & + & y_2 & \geq & 20 \\
\end{array}
$$
$$y_1 \geq 0,\ y_2 \geq 0$$

15. Solve the linear program:

$$
\begin{array}{rrcrcl}
\text{Maximize}: & 10x_1 & + & 30x_2 \\
\text{Subject to}: & 5x_1 & + & 10x_2 & \leq & 300 \\
& -5x_1 & + & 15x_2 & \leq & 100 \\
& 4x_1 & + & 3x_2 & \leq & 180 \\
\end{array}
$$
$$x_1 \geq 0,\ x_2 \geq 0$$

16. **Unbounded solution.** Show that the set of feasible solutions to the following problem permits the objective function to assume arbitrarily large values:

$$
\begin{array}{rrcrcl}
\text{Maximize}: & 2x & + & 5y \\
\text{Subject to}: & 3x & - & 2y & \leq & 6 \\
& 5x & - & 4y & \leq & 8 \\
\end{array}
$$
$$x \geq 0,\ y \geq 0$$

1.5 Summary and objectives

Operations research is the process of formulating and solving a problem whose solution leads to a decision affecting the operation of an organization. In this brief introduction, several types of problems were introduced that can be solved by the mathematical programming methods to be developed. Several specific examples cited indicate the potential value of mathematical programming to an organization.

We saw that models of most of the problems involve linear functions, i.e., expressions of the form

$$c_1x_1 + c_2x_2 + \cdots + c_nx_n$$

where the c_j's are constant coefficients. The chapter concluded with the formulation and graphical solution of the most common type of problem – a linear program.

   We solved a simple linear program by a graphical method in Section 1.4. Most of the abilities that the reader should have acquired are related to the method introduced in that section.

Objectives

Following completion of this chapter, the student should be able to accomplish the objectives listed below. For each objective a typical example and/or exercise is suggested.

1. Recognize the type of a problem as classified in Section 1.2. Exercise 10 in Section 1.3.

2. Recognize linear expressions that occur in problems. Example 1.3.1, Exercises 1 and 4 in Section 1.3.

3. Graph the intersection of a set of half-planes and determine the coordinates of the corners of the intersection. Example 1.4.1, Exercise 2 in Section 1.4.

4. Formulate the linear program to solve an elementary problem. Example 1.4.1., Exercise 7 in Section 1.4.

5. Solve a two variable linear program by the geometric method used in Section 1.4. Example 1.4.1, Exercise 4 in Section 1.4.

6. Identify graphically a two variable linear program having a non-unique solution. Exercise 13 in Section 1.4.

7. Identify graphically a two variable linear program in which the objective function is unbounded. Exercise 16 in Section 1.4 .

Chapter 2

Vectors and Matrices

2.1   Introduction

As the examples in Chapter 1 indicate, we will be dealing with problems involving a large number of variables. Most of the calculations in such problems can be expressed in terms of vectors and matrices. The central problem will be the solution of systems of linear equations.

To put the problems to be considered in a familiar context, recall what was probably the first algebra problem you saw – solving the equation

$$ax = b.$$

The solution can be completely discussed in three lines:

- A unique solution exists if and only if $a \neq 0$, and the solution is $x = \dfrac{b}{a}$.

- Infinitely many solutions exist if and only if both $a = 0$ and $b = 0$.

- There is no solution if and only if $a = 0$ and $b \neq 0$.

The central objective of this chapter is to develop the analogous statements when a single equation in one variable is replaced by a system of m equations in n variables. In the example below, $m = 3$ and $n = 4$:

$$
\begin{array}{rcrcrcrcr}
3x_1 & + & 2x_2 & + & x_3 & - & x_4 & = & 8 \\
x_1 & - & x_2 & + & 4x_3 & - & 2x_4 & = & 5 \\
2x_1 & + & x_2 & - & 5x_3 & & & = & -2.
\end{array}
$$

The first step toward solving this problem is to develop notation in which this system of equations can be expressed as

$$Ax = b.$$

The notation will involve a rectangular arrangement of numbers A, to be called a *matrix*, and a column of numbers b, to be called a *vector,* formed from the coefficients and the right-hand-side constants, respectively, of the equations:

$$A = \begin{bmatrix} 3 & 2 & 1 & -1 \\ 1 & -1 & 4 & -2 \\ 2 & 1 & -5 & 0 \end{bmatrix} \quad \text{and} \quad b = \begin{bmatrix} 8 \\ 5 \\ -2 \end{bmatrix}.$$

After defining vectors and matrices and exploring the necessary algebraic operations, we will develop a solution procedure paralleling the three cases suggested above for $ax = b$.

The solution to $ax = b$ involved recognizing if either a or b were zero, taking the reciprocal $\frac{1}{a}$ of a if a were not 0, and multiplying $\frac{1}{a}$ and b. The formation of the reciprocal will be replaced by the inversion of a matrix. The determination of the existence of an inverse will rely on the concept of the linear independence of a set of vectors. The entire solution process will use a method called Gaussian elimination. This process will reduce the solution of a system of linear equations to the solution of a sequence of linear equations, each involving a single variable.

The development will be intuitive, drawing heavily on two- and three-dimensional examples. However, the concept of linear independence underlies the theory of this and subsequent chapters, and its understanding requires some knowledge of logical reasoning. We will take the opportunity to introduce some basics of mathematical reasoning in the context of a discussion of linear independence.

2.2   Vectors

A *vector* is a column of numbers of the form

$$v = \begin{bmatrix} 5 \\ -2 \\ 4 \end{bmatrix}.$$

The individual numbers in a vector are called *components*. Components of the vector v are referred to individually by using subscripts to indicate their position within v, e.g., here $v_3 = 4$. We will generally use lower-case letters – v, x, y, etc. – to identify vectors and the corresponding letters subscripted to identify individual components. The set of all vectors having n components will be denoted by R^n and referred to as *n-dimensional space*, or simply as *n-space*. The *zero vector* in *n*-space, written 0, is the vector whose every component is 0.

Two vectors are said to be *equal* if their corresponding components are equal.

We will think of vectors in column form as in the example above. Frequently it is convenient, if only for typographical reasons, to be able to express a vector as a row. Then the example above would be expressed as

$$v^T = [5, -2, 4].$$

The expression v^T is read as the *transpose* of v.

It is often necessary to consider vectors with a large number of components, and to do this we will study vectors having n components where the integer n is unspecified. To illustrate vectors geometrically, however, we are limited to the examples of R^1, R^2, and R^3. In these more familiar spaces, we can represent vectors geometrically as points or arrows, whichever is more appropriate for the application at hand.

For example, if $x^T = [2, 3]$, we can measure the components $x_1 = 2$ and $x_2 = 3$ along coordinate axes as shown below and think of x as the plotted point.

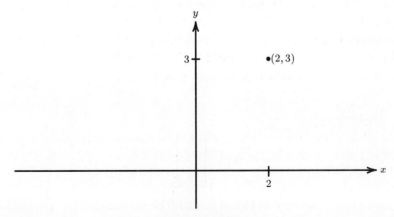

Figure 2.2.1

We could also think of x as any arrow in the plane which is parallel to, and as long as, the arrow originating at the origin and terminating at $(2,3)$. A sample of arrows, all representing the same vector, appears in Figure 2.2.2. The end with the arrowhead is referred to as the *terminal end* of the vector and the other end as the *initial end.*

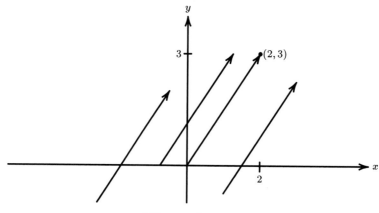

Figure 2.2.2

Similarly, a vector in R^3 can be represented as an arrow originating from the origin and ending at a particular ordered triple in R^3.

The *vector sum* of two vectors in n-space is the vector formed by adding the corresponding components. Thus, if u and v both belong to R^n, and their sum is w, then

$$w_i = u_i + v_i \quad \text{for} \quad i = 1, \ldots, n.$$

For instance, if

$$u = \begin{bmatrix} 3 \\ 5 \\ 2 \end{bmatrix} \quad \text{and} \quad v = \begin{bmatrix} 2 \\ -1 \\ 4 \end{bmatrix}$$

then

$$w = \begin{bmatrix} 5 \\ 4 \\ 6 \end{bmatrix}.$$

Geometrically, the sum of two vectors is the diagonal of the parallelogram formed by the two vectors added as illustrated in Figure 2.2.3.

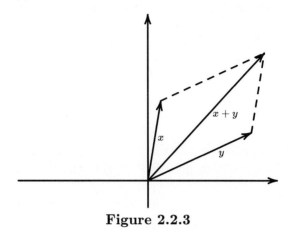

Figure 2.2.3

To distinguish a number c in R from the vector $[c]$, we refer to numbers as *scalars*. The operation *scalar multiplication* consists of multiplying all components of a vector by the same scalar. Thus, if w is the result of multiplying a vector v by a scalar c, components of w are given by $w_i = cv_i$.

Scalar multiplication is most frequently interpreted geometrically as changing the length and/or reversing the direction of a vector. This is illustrated in Figure 2.2.4.

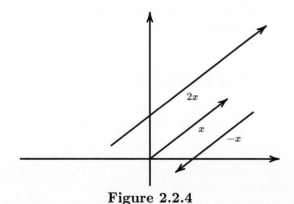

Figure 2.2.4

As the figure indicates, the set of all scalar multiples of a vector is the set of vectors parallel to the given vector, including those which point in the opposite direction. Note that if the initial ends of all the scalar multiples of x were placed at the origin, the vectors would all lie in the same line through the origin. This observation will be important in the next section.

As a less geometric interpretation, if a vector $p^T = [p_1, p_2, \ldots, p_n]$ consists of the prices for a particular n items, then the scalar multiple

$$1.1p^T = [1.1p_1, 1.1p_2, \ldots, 1.1p_n]$$

is the vector consisting of the prices following a 10% increase in prices.

The problems in Chapter 1 frequently required that we formulate an expression for quantities such as cost or profit. Here is an example.

Example 2.2.1. Express the profit in Example 1.3.4 from the sales of three items which produce per-item profits of 75, 60, and 45 cents, respectively.

Letting $x_i, i = 1, 2, 3$, represent the respective sales levels, we obtain

$$\text{profit} = 75x_1 + 60x_2 + 45x_3. \qquad \blacksquare$$

The calculation of profit above combined two vectors $p^T = [75, 60, 45]$ and $x^T = [x_1, x_2, x_3]$ to produce a scalar. This is an important type of calculation, and we now define it in general. Let $x^T = [x_1, x_2, \ldots, x_n]$ and $y^T = [y_1, y_2, \ldots, y_n]$ be two vectors in n-space. The *dot product* of x and y is

$$x \cdot y = \sum_{i=1}^{n} x_i y_i = x_1 y_1 + x_2 y_2 + \cdots + x_n y_n.$$

Note that the product of two vectors is a number, not a vector. For this reason, the dot product is often called the *scalar product*.

If the dot product is used to define a function by defining

$$f(x) = v \cdot x$$

for a constant vector v, we find that the function has two important properties:

$$\begin{aligned} f(x + y) &= f(x) + f(y) \\ f(cx) &= cf(x). \end{aligned}$$

A function which satisfies these properties is called a *linear function*. *Linear algebra* is the study of such functions.

The profit function defined above is an example of a linear function, and the properties above can be interpreted in a profit context. If x and y are the sales figures for two quarters, then the first simply says that the profit function is additive, i.e., that the profit over the two quarters is the sum of the two quarterly profits. If sales increase by 20%, then the second property in the form $f(1.2x) = 1.2f(x)$ says that profit will increase proportionally.

Exercises

1. Vector addition is *associative*, that is, when three vectors are to be added, it does not matter whether the first or the last two are added first, e.g.,

$$u + (v + w) = (u + v) + w.$$

Demonstrate this property with the vectors

$$u^T = [3, -2, 5], \ v^T = [4, 7, 8] \ \text{and} \ w^T = [-1, 3, 5].$$

2. Vector subtraction is a combination of scalar multiplication by -1 and vector addition. With u and v as in the preceding problem, calculate $u - v$.

3. Vector addition and scalar multiplication are frequently combined by first carrying out scalar multiplications and then adding the resulting vectors. With u and v as in the previous problems, calculate $3u + 2v$.

4. Carry out the vector addition of $u^T = [2, 3]$ and $v^T = [-1, 4]$ and draw a figure to illustrate the parallelogram law of vector addition.

5. The difference $x - y$ of two vectors is the vector that must be added to y to obtain x. Thus, from the parallelogram law of vector addition, the initial end of $x - y$ must be at the terminal end of y and the terminal end of $x - y$ must be at the terminal end of x. With $x^T = [1, 4]$ and $y^T = [3, -2]$, calculate $x - y$ and draw a picture to illustrate this definition of vector subtraction.

6. **Sigma notation.** Verify each of the following calculations:

   (a) $\sum_{i=1}^{5} i = 15.$

   (b) If $x^T = [2, 3, -4, 1]$ and $y^T = [4, -2, 6, 5]$, then $x \cdot y = -13$.

   (c) $\sum_{i=1}^{5} i(5 - i) = 20.$

   (d) If $z^T = [4, -2, 1, 3]$ and x and y are as in (b), then $z \cdot (y - x) = 30$.

7. Suppose that the four products of a company earn profits of \$8, \$10, \$12, and \$7 per unit, respectively. If the vector x in 4-space represents the sales of the products, use a dot product to express the company's profit as a linear function.

2.3   The span of a set of vectors

It is important to be able to determine which vectors can be formed from a given set of vectors by combining the operations of addition and scalar multiplication discussed in the previous section. From Figure 2.2.4 we can see that, given a single nonzero vector, the only vectors we can obtain are those that are parallel to the given vector. If the set contains more than one vector, the key construction will be the linear combination.

Given a set $\{v_1, v_2, \ldots, v_n\}$ of vectors, and a set $\{c_1, c_2, \ldots, c_n\}$ of scalars, the vector

$$w = c_1 v_1 + c_2 v_2 + \cdots + c_n v_n$$

is called a *linear combination* of $\{v_1, v_2, \ldots, v_n\}$.

Example 2.3.1. Determine the linear combination $3v_1 - 2v_2$ given the vectors $v_1 = [3, 1, -2]^T$ and $v_2 = [2, -2, 1]^T$.

$$3 \begin{bmatrix} 3 \\ 1 \\ -2 \end{bmatrix} + (-2) \begin{bmatrix} 2 \\ -2 \\ 1 \end{bmatrix} = \begin{bmatrix} 9 \\ 3 \\ -6 \end{bmatrix} + \begin{bmatrix} -4 \\ 4 \\ -2 \end{bmatrix} = \begin{bmatrix} 5 \\ 7 \\ -8 \end{bmatrix} \quad \blacksquare$$

The set of all linear combinations of $\{v_1, v_2, \ldots, v_n\}$ that can be formed is called the *span* of $\{v_1, v_2, \ldots, v_n\}$.

From the discussion of scalar multiplication and Figure 2.2.4, we can easily describe the span of a nonzero vector.

Example 2.3.2. Determine if the vector $w^T = [3, 6]$ belongs to the span of the vector $v^T = [4, 2]$.

Since the linear combinations that we can form using only v are the scalar multiples of v, then w must satisfy the equation

$$w = cv$$

for some scalar c. In terms of components, this means that c must satisfy the two equations

$$3 = 4c \quad \text{and} \quad 6 = 2c.$$

Since only $c = \frac{3}{4}$ satisfies the first and only $c = 3$ the second, no single value of c can be found that satisfies both equations, and we conclude that w does not belong to the span of v. $\blacksquare$

The following proposition summarizes the situation with regard to the span of a single vector.

Proposition 2.3.3. *The span of a nonzero vector is the set of all scalar multiples of the vector. Interpreted geometrically, the span of a nonzero vector is the set of vectors lying in the line through the origin containing the vector.*

If there are two or more vectors, the situation is more complicated but can still be given a graphical interpretation using the parallelogram law of vector addition illustrated in Figure 2.3.1. Consider two nonparallel vectors v_1 and v_2 and a third vector w as shown.

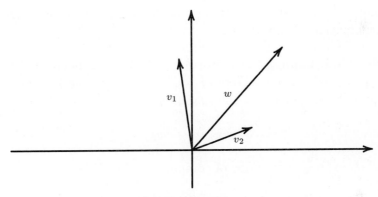

Figure 2.3.1

The geometric process of showing that w lies in the span of $\{v_1, v_2\}$ consists of describing how a linear combination is formed geometrically:

1. Generate the individual spans of v_1 and v_2 by drawing lines through the origin.

2. Draw lines parallel to each of these through the terminal end of w.

3. The terminal ends of the required scalar multiples of v_1 and v_2 lie on the two sides of a parallelogram as shown in Figure 2.3.2.

Note that if v_1 and v_2 were parallel, they would lie in the same line through the origin and the construction just described would only work if w were also in the same line.

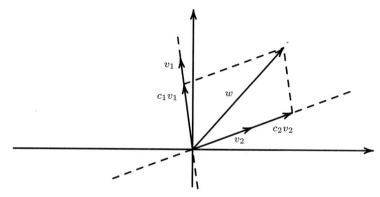

Figure 2.3.2

We now consider an algebraic approach to expressing one vector as a linear combination of two others.

Example 2.3.4. Express the vector $w^T = [8, 7]$ as a member of the span of $\{v_1, v_2\}$, with the given vectors $v_1^T = [2, 3]$ and $v_2^T = [4, 1]$. The equation expressing w as an element of the span of $\{v_1, v_2\}$ is

$$w = av_1 + bv_2$$

which, when expressed in terms of components, becomes:

$$
\begin{array}{rrrcr}
2a & + & 4b & = & 8 \\
3a & + & b & = & 7.
\end{array}
$$

We recognize this as the problem of determining the point of intersection of two lines in the plane, and we solve the pair of equations by subtracting a multiple of one from the other to obtain a new equation involving a single variable. In this instance, subtracting $\frac{2}{3}$ of the second equation from the first will eliminate the variable a leaving an equation in b:

$$\left(2 - \left(\frac{2}{3}\right)3\right)a + \left(4 - \left(\frac{2}{3}\right)1\right)b = 8 - \left(\frac{2}{3}\right)7$$

which leads to

$$\frac{10b}{3} = \frac{10}{3} \text{ or } b = 1.$$

Now substituting $b = 1$ into the second equation yields $a = 2$. Hence, we have determined that

$$w = 2v_1 + v_2$$

or, in component form,

$$\begin{bmatrix} 8 \\ 7 \end{bmatrix} = 2 \begin{bmatrix} 2 \\ 3 \end{bmatrix} + \begin{bmatrix} 4 \\ 1 \end{bmatrix}. \quad \blacksquare$$

Like the geometric construction above, the algebraic solution can fail. If the vectors v_1 and v_2 are parallel, then one is a scalar multiple of the other. Thus, attempting to eliminate one variable by subtracting a multiple of one equation from the other will fail because both variables will drop out. Try repeating the above process with v_2 replaced by $2v_1$ to see exactly what will happen.

The description of spans in 2-dimensional space is provided in the following theorem.

Theorem 2.3.5. *If v_1 and v_2 are nonzero vectors in R^2, then the span of $\{v_1, v_2\}$ is R^2 unless v_1 and v_2 are parallel. If v_1 and v_2 are parallel, the span is the line through the origin that contains both vectors, and any vector in the span can be expressed as a scalar multiple of either v_1 or v_2.*

We will call a pair of nonzero vectors in R^2 which are not parallel a *linearly independent* pair. In Section 2.5 we will generalize the idea of linear independence to sets of vectors in R^n.

Exercises

1. Determine a so that $y^T = [5, a]$ is in the span of the vector $x^T = [2, -3]$.

2. Calculate the linear combination $3u - 2v + w$ where

$$u^T = [2, 4, -7], \ v^T = [1, 2, 3], \text{ and } w^T = [-4, 2, 0].$$

3. Express the vector $w^T = [3, -2]$ as a linear combination of the two vectors $u^T = [3, 5]$ and $v^T = [1, -3]$.

4. Repeat the previous problem with u replaced by $u^T = [-2, 6]$. Describe what happens.

5. If the sales (in thousands of units) of a company are given by the vector $x^T = [1.3, 5.4, 3.7, 1.9, 4.5]$ for their five products, use scalar multiplication to determine their sales if sales increase by 20% for each product.

6. If the sales (in thousands of units) of the company in the previous problem in three successive years are given by $x^T = [1.4, 5.2, 6.1, 4.3, 2.4]$, $y^T = [1.6, 5.1, 5.8, 3.7, 2.5]$, and $z^T = [1.2, 4.8, 5.7, 3.9, 2.6]$, use vector addition to determine their total sales for the three years.

7. If the per-unit profits for the five products of the company in the preceding exercise are given by $p^T = [10, 7, 8, 11, 12]$, decide whether the company's profits increased between years 1 and 2 and between years 2 and 3.

2.4   Matrices

A *matrix* is a rectangular array of numbers. An $m \times n$ matrix, where $m \times n$ is read "m by n," has m rows and n columns. A vector is a matrix with one column, i.e., an $m \times 1$ matrix. We will generally use italic capital letters like A to denote matrices, and the corresponding lower-case letter, doubly subscripted, to denote individual entries of the matrix. Thus, if

$$A = \begin{bmatrix} 0 & 2 \\ -1 & 3 \end{bmatrix}$$

we would have $a_{11} = 0, a_{12} = 2, a_{21} = -1$, and $a_{22} = 3$. Note that the first subscript refers to the row of the entry and the second to the column.

If

$$A = \begin{bmatrix} a_{11} & a_{12} & \cdots & a_{1n} \\ a_{21} & a_{22} & \cdots & a_{2n} \\ & & \vdots & \\ a_{m1} & a_{m2} & \cdots & a_{mn} \end{bmatrix} \quad \text{and} \quad B = \begin{bmatrix} b_{11} & b_{12} & \cdots & b_{1n} \\ b_{21} & b_{22} & \cdots & b_{2n} \\ & & \vdots & \\ b_{m1} & b_{m2} & \cdots & b_{mn} \end{bmatrix}$$

are two matrices of the same size, then their sum is formed as for vectors – by adding corresponding components. Thus,

$$A + B = \begin{bmatrix} a_{11} + b_{11} & a_{12} + b_{12} & \cdots & a_{1n} + b_{1n} \\ a_{21} + b_{21} & a_{22} + b_{22} & \cdots & a_{2n} + b_{2n} \\ & & \vdots & \\ a_{m1} + b_{m1} & a_{m2} + b_{m2} & \cdots & a_{mn} + b_{mn} \end{bmatrix}.$$

The difference $A - B$ of two matrices is defined similarly.

Multiplication of a matrix by a scalar is also performed componentwise as for vectors. Thus, we have

$$5 \begin{bmatrix} 0 & 2 \\ -1 & 3 \end{bmatrix} = \begin{bmatrix} 0 & 10 \\ -5 & 15 \end{bmatrix}.$$

Matrix multiplication is the most complicated, and probably the most useful, of the matrix operations that we will consider. Its importance follows from its central role in systems of equations.

In introducing this chapter, we noted that our main objective was to be able to solve problems of the following type:

$$\begin{array}{rcrcrcrcr} 3x_1 & + & 2x_2 & + & x_3 & - & x_4 & = & 8 \\ x_1 & - & x_2 & + & 4x_3 & - & 2x_4 & = & 5 \\ 2x_1 & + & x_2 & - & 5x_3 & & & = & -2. \end{array}$$

With the matrix of coefficients A, the vector x of unknowns, and right-hand side b,

$$A = \begin{bmatrix} 3 & 2 & 1 & -1 \\ 1 & -1 & 4 & -2 \\ 2 & 1 & -5 & 0 \end{bmatrix}, \quad x = \begin{bmatrix} x_1 \\ x_2 \\ x_3 \\ x_4 \end{bmatrix}, \quad b = \begin{bmatrix} 8 \\ 5 \\ -2 \end{bmatrix}$$

the system of equations is written $Ax = b$.

We now consider matrix multiplication in order to understand the product Ax. In order for the product of two matrices to be defined, the number of columns in the left factor must equal the number of rows in the right factor. Consider the matrices A and B below:

$$A = \begin{bmatrix} a_{11} & a_{12} & \cdots & a_{1n} \\ a_{21} & a_{22} & \cdots & a_{2n} \\ & & \vdots & \\ a_{m1} & a_{m2} & \cdots & a_{mn} \end{bmatrix} \quad \text{and} \quad B = \begin{bmatrix} b_{11} & b_{12} & \cdots & b_{1r} \\ b_{21} & b_{22} & \cdots & b_{2r} \\ & & \vdots & \\ b_{n1} & b_{n2} & \cdots & b_{nr} \end{bmatrix}$$

The matrix product $C = AB$ is an $m \times r$ matrix where the element in row i and column j is defined by

$$c_{ij} = \sum_{k=1}^{n} a_{ik}b_{kj} = a_{i1}b_{1j} + a_{i2}b_{2j} + \cdots + a_{in}b_{nj}.$$

Hence, the element in row i and column j of the product of A and B is the sum of the products of the corresponding entries of row i of A, the matrix on the left, and of column j of B, the matrix on the right.

Example 2.4.1. The product of two 2×2 matrices is shown below:

$$\begin{bmatrix} 0 & 2 \\ -1 & 3 \end{bmatrix} \begin{bmatrix} 4 & 5 \\ -2 & 6 \end{bmatrix} = \begin{bmatrix} (0)(4)+(2)(-2) & (0)(5)+(2)(6) \\ (-1)(4)+(3)(-2) & (-1)(5)+(3)(6) \end{bmatrix}$$

$$= \begin{bmatrix} -4 & 12 \\ -10 & 13 \end{bmatrix}. \quad \blacksquare$$

The product of two matrices will have as many rows as the left matrix and as many columns as the right matrix. Hence, we must pay attention to the order in which the product is taken. It may happen that the product AB is defined but BA is not. For instance, if A is a 3×4 matrix and B a 4×5 matrix, then AB is defined and is a 3×5 matrix, but the product BA is not defined.

Even if the product is defined in both orders, the two need not be equal. We describe this behavior by saying that matrix multiplication is not commutative. This is shown in the next example.

Example 2.4.2. We multiply the two matrices of the previous example in the reverse order to show that the results are different.

$$\begin{bmatrix} 4 & 5 \\ -2 & 6 \end{bmatrix} \begin{bmatrix} 0 & 2 \\ -1 & 3 \end{bmatrix} = \begin{bmatrix} (4)(0)+(5)(-1) & (4)(2)+(5)(3) \\ (-2)(0)+(6)(-1) & (-2)(2)+(6)(3) \end{bmatrix}$$

$$= \begin{bmatrix} -5 & 23 \\ -6 & 14 \end{bmatrix}. \quad \blacksquare$$

To further illustrate the extent to which matrix multiplication fails to be commutative, the following example shows that when both products AB and BA are defined, they need not even have the same dimension.

Example 2.4.3. Consider the products of a 1×2 matrix and a 2×1 matrix:

$$\begin{bmatrix} 1 & 2 \end{bmatrix} \begin{bmatrix} 3 \\ 4 \end{bmatrix} = [(1)(3)+(2)(4)] = [11]$$

$$\begin{bmatrix} 3 \\ 4 \end{bmatrix} \begin{bmatrix} 1 & 2 \end{bmatrix} = \begin{bmatrix} (3)(1) & (3)(2) \\ (4)(1) & (4)(2) \end{bmatrix} = \begin{bmatrix} 3 & 6 \\ 4 & 8 \end{bmatrix}. \quad \blacksquare$$

When three matrices are multiplied together, they can be grouped in two different ways, and the answer is unaffected. In symbols,

$$A(BC) = (AB)C.$$

This is called the *associative property* of matrix multiplication. Similarly, there are two *distributive properties* that apply when matrix multiplication and matrix addition are combined:

$$
\begin{aligned}
A(B+C) &= AB + AC \\
(A+B)C &= AC + BC.
\end{aligned}
$$

Of course, in the above equations we assume that all the matrix multiplications are defined.

There is no cancellation property for matrix multiplication, i.e., if we are given

$$AB = AC$$

we cannot generally cancel A to obtain $B = C$. The next example demonstrates the absence of a cancellation property.

Example 2.4.4. One can easily verify that

$$
\begin{bmatrix} 1 & 2 \\ 2 & 4 \end{bmatrix}
\begin{bmatrix} 2 & -4 \\ -1 & 2 \end{bmatrix}
=
\begin{bmatrix} 1 & 2 \\ 2 & 4 \end{bmatrix}
\begin{bmatrix} 0 & 0 \\ 0 & 0 \end{bmatrix}
$$

but clearly

$$
\begin{bmatrix} 2 & -4 \\ -1 & 2 \end{bmatrix}
\neq
\begin{bmatrix} 0 & 0 \\ 0 & 0 \end{bmatrix}. \quad \blacksquare
$$

The transpose of a matrix has a definition similar to that of a vector defined earlier. If

$$
A =
\begin{bmatrix}
a_{11} & a_{12} & \cdots & a_{1n} \\
a_{21} & a_{22} & \cdots & a_{2n} \\
& & \vdots & \\
a_{m1} & a_{m2} & \cdots & a_{mn}
\end{bmatrix}
$$

then the *transpose* of A is the matrix

$$
A^T =
\begin{bmatrix}
a_{11} & a_{21} & \cdots & a_{m1} \\
a_{12} & a_{22} & \cdots & a_{m2} \\
& & \vdots & \\
a_{1n} & a_{2n} & \cdots & a_{mn}
\end{bmatrix}
$$

obtained from A by turning the columns into rows. In terms of individual entries, if C is the transpose of A, then $c_{ij} = a_{ji}$, i.e., the entry in row i and column j of the transpose is the entry from row j and column i of the original matrix. For example,

$$\begin{bmatrix} 3 & 2 & -1 \\ 2 & -1 & 1 \end{bmatrix}^T = \begin{bmatrix} 3 & 2 \\ 2 & -1 \\ -1 & 1 \end{bmatrix}.$$

In setting up problems such as those introduced in Chapter 1, we will need to understand the behavior of units under matrix multiplication. Consider the following example.

Example 2.4.5. A company produces two lines of decorative metal paper-weights – A and B – for which the principal resources required are iron, brass, and labor. The amounts of each needed per paperweight are tabled below:

Table 2.4.1

	A	B
Iron (oz)	12	16
Brass (oz)	2	3
Labor (min)	20	12

The resources needed to make 50 of line A and 75 of line B are then obtained by the matrix multiplication below:

$$\begin{bmatrix} 12 & 16 \\ 2 & 3 \\ 20 & 12 \end{bmatrix} \begin{bmatrix} 50 \\ 75 \end{bmatrix} = \begin{bmatrix} 1,800 \\ 325 \\ 1,900 \end{bmatrix}.$$

The reader should examine this product to be certain that the units are those of the needed resources, e.g., to see that the appropriate units on 1,800 are ounces of iron. ∎

A matrix is *square* if the number of rows equals the number of columns. A square matrix A is *symmetric* if $A = A^T$. If the i, j component of A is a_{ij}, then the i, j component of A^T is a_{ji}, so in terms of components, symmetric means $a_{ij} = a_{ji}$.

A square matrix A is a *diagonal matrix* if all entries not on the main diagonal are zero, i.e., A is diagonal if $a_{ij} = 0$ for $i \neq j$. Every diagonal matrix is symmetric. The $n \times n$ *identity matrix I* is the $n \times n$ diagonal matrix with ones on the diagonal.

I is called the identity matrix because it serves as the multiplicative identity element for matrix multiplication as 1 does for the real numbers. Thus, for any $n \times m$ matrix A, $m \times n$ matrix B, and vector $x \in R^n$, we have

$$IA = A, \ BI = B, \text{ and } Ix = x.$$

The $m \times n$ *zero matrix* 0 is the $m \times n$ matrix whose every entry is zero.

If A is a square matrix, it may be possible to determine another square matrix, denoted A^{-1}, called the *inverse* of A, such that

$$AA^{-1} = A^{-1}A = I$$

where I is the $n \times n$ identity matrix. For any matrix A, there will be at most one such inverse matrix, and it is helpful to note that either of the equalities

$$AB = I \text{ or } BA = I$$

is sufficient to conclude that $B = A^{-1}$, i.e., we need not check that both equalities hold. In Section 2.7 we will develop a method to determine the inverse A^{-1} for an $n \times n$ matrix based on the first of these equations. In this section we consider only the trivial case of a 1×1 matrix and the simple case of a 2×2 matrix.

If a matrix has an inverse, it is said to be *nonsingular*; otherwise, it is called *singular*. If A is a 1×1 matrix, i.e., if A has a single entry, then A is nonsingular if its entry is nonzero, and A^{-1} is the matrix whose only entry is the reciprocal of the entry of A. In this case, the identity matrix I is the matrix whose only entry is 1.

One approach to the calculation of the inverse of a nonsingular 2×2 matrix A involves the *determinant* of A, defined below:

$$\det(A) = \begin{vmatrix} a_{11} & a_{12} \\ a_{21} & a_{22} \end{vmatrix} = a_{11}a_{22} - a_{12}a_{21}.$$

When this quantity is zero, we will see that A^{-1} is not defined and A has no inverse.

The following algorithm provides a convenient way to calculate the inverse of a 2×2 matrix:

1. Calculate $\det(A)$. If $\det(A)$ is zero, stop. A is singular.

2. Interchange the entries on the main diagonal.

3. Change the signs of the off-diagonal entries.

4. Scalar multiply the resulting matrix by the reciprocal of $\det(A)$.

If the vectors forming the columns of A are parallel, i.e., if one is a scalar multiple of the other, one can easily see that no inverse will exist because $\det(A)$ is zero.

Determination of the inverse of a larger matrix must wait until Section 2.7. However, before leaving this section, let us consider an example of the use of the matrix inverse.

Recall that at the beginning of the chapter we saw that a system of linear equations could be expressed as

$$Ax = b$$

where A is the matrix of coefficients, x a vector of unknowns, and b a constant vector. If we multiply this equation by A^{-1}

$$A^{-1}Ax = A^{-1}b$$

and use the definition of matrix inverse, we obtain

$$Ix = A^{-1}b \text{ or } x = A^{-1}b$$

since I is the identity matrix.

Example 2.4.6. Use an inverse to determine the solution to the following system of equations:
$$\begin{array}{rcl} 2x_1 & + & 3x_2 & = & 4 \\ 2x_1 & + & 4x_2 & = & 5. \end{array}$$

The matrix of coefficients is

$$A = \begin{bmatrix} 2 & 3 \\ 2 & 4 \end{bmatrix}.$$

Then $\det(A) = (2)(4) - (3)(2) = 2$ and the inverse of A is

$$A^{-1} = \frac{1}{2} \begin{bmatrix} 4 & -3 \\ -2 & 2 \end{bmatrix}.$$

Thus, the solution is

$$x = A^{-1}b = \frac{1}{2}\begin{bmatrix} 4 & -3 \\ -2 & 2 \end{bmatrix}\begin{bmatrix} 4 \\ 5 \end{bmatrix} = \begin{bmatrix} \frac{1}{2} \\ 1 \end{bmatrix}.$$

Hence, $x_1 = \frac{1}{2}$ and $x_2 = 1$. ∎

While here we used determinants only in obtaining the inverse of a 2×2 matrix, determinants of larger matrices will useful in Chapters 5 and 6. For that reason we will investigate the determinant of a 3×3 matrix and discuss the evaluation of the determinant of an $n \times n$ matrix in the exercises.

The determinant of an $n \times n$ matrix is expressed in terms of n determinants of $(n-1) \times (n-1)$ matrices. In the case of a 3×3, this is

$$\begin{vmatrix} a_{11} & a_{12} & a_{13} \\ a_{21} & a_{22} & a_{23} \\ a_{31} & a_{32} & a_{33} \end{vmatrix} = a_{11}\begin{vmatrix} a_{22} & a_{23} \\ a_{32} & a_{33} \end{vmatrix} - a_{12}\begin{vmatrix} a_{21} & a_{23} \\ a_{31} & a_{33} \end{vmatrix} + a_{13}\begin{vmatrix} a_{21} & a_{22} \\ a_{31} & a_{32} \end{vmatrix}.$$

We illustrate with an example.

Example 2.4.7. Evaluate the determinant of

$$\begin{vmatrix} 2 & 4 & 3 \\ 3 & 2 & 4 \\ -1 & 3 & 5 \end{vmatrix}.$$

$$\begin{vmatrix} 2 & 4 & 3 \\ 3 & 2 & 4 \\ -1 & 3 & 5 \end{vmatrix} = 2\begin{vmatrix} 2 & 4 \\ 3 & 5 \end{vmatrix} - 4\begin{vmatrix} 3 & 4 \\ -1 & 5 \end{vmatrix} + 3\begin{vmatrix} 3 & 2 \\ -1 & 3 \end{vmatrix}$$

$$= 2(2 \cdot 5 - 3 \cdot 4) - 4(3 \cdot 5 - 4 \cdot (-1)) + 3(3 \cdot 3 - 2 \cdot (-1))$$

$$= 2 \cdot (-2) - 4 \cdot 19 + 3 \cdot 11$$

$$= -47. \quad ∎$$

In Section 2.6 we will develop a method of solving systems of equations that does not require determining an inverse, and we will extend the process to larger systems. But before we can do that, we first must investigate the concept of linear independence, which is the generalization of the condition, mentioned above in conjunction with the existence of the inverse, that two vectors not be scalar multiples of each other.

Exercises

1. Carry out the indicated matrix operations:

(a.) $\quad 3\begin{bmatrix} 2 & -4 \\ 3 & 6 \end{bmatrix} - 3\begin{bmatrix} 4 & 1 \\ 2 & 0 \end{bmatrix}.$ (b.) $\quad 4\begin{bmatrix} 2 & 4 & -1 \\ 3 & 2 & 3 \end{bmatrix} + 2\begin{bmatrix} 1 & 3 \\ 2 & 4 \\ -1 & 2 \end{bmatrix}^T.$

2. Carry out the indicated matrix multiplications:

(a.) $\begin{bmatrix} 2 & -3 \\ 4 & 1 \end{bmatrix}\begin{bmatrix} 2 & 3 \\ 4 & 6 \end{bmatrix}.$ (b.) $\begin{bmatrix} 2 & 3 & 5 \\ 4 & 1 & 3 \end{bmatrix}\begin{bmatrix} 2 & 3 & -1 \\ 1 & -4 & 3 \\ 2 & 0 & 2 \end{bmatrix}.$

3. Multiply each pair of matrices in all orders for which a matrix product is defined:

(a.) $\begin{bmatrix} -2 & 3 & -2 \\ 1 & 2 & 4 \end{bmatrix}\begin{bmatrix} 6 & 3 \\ 1 & 0 \end{bmatrix}.$ (b.) $\begin{bmatrix} 2 & 6 \\ 4 & -3 \end{bmatrix}\begin{bmatrix} 5 & 4 \\ -1 & 3 \end{bmatrix}.$

(c.) $\begin{bmatrix} 2 & -1 & 3 \\ 4 & 5 & 6 \end{bmatrix}\begin{bmatrix} 2 & 6 & 4 \\ -1 & 5 & 2 \\ 4 & 3 & 1 \end{bmatrix}.$

4. Set up the matrix for Farmer Brown's problem, Example 1.3.1, and carry out the matrix multiplication similar to that of Example 2.4.5 to determine the resources needed to produce 30 acres of potatoes and 50 acres of wheat.

5. Set up the matrix for the minimization formulation problem from Exercise 12 in Section 1.4 and determine the protein, carbohydrate, and iron content of a combination of eight pounds of Dog Grub and ten pounds of Canine Chow.

6. Using an inverse, determine the solution of the system of equations

$$\begin{cases} 3x & + & 4y & = & 3 \\ 2x & + & 2y & = & 1. \end{cases}$$

7. Determine the inverses of the matrices A and B below and calculate the product $B^{-1}A^{-1}$. Use these matrices to confirm the following identity: $(AB)^{-1} = B^{-1}A^{-1}$.

$$A = \begin{bmatrix} 2 & 2 \\ 4 & 5 \end{bmatrix} \text{ and } B = \begin{bmatrix} 3 & 4 \\ 4 & 5 \end{bmatrix}.$$

8. Evaluate the determinant of each of the following matrices:

(a.) $\begin{bmatrix} -2 & 2 & -2 \\ 1 & 2 & 4 \\ 3 & 0 & 5 \end{bmatrix}.$ (b.) $\begin{bmatrix} 2 & -1 & 2 \\ 4 & -3 & 4 \\ 1 & 2 & 3 \end{bmatrix}.$

9. **Determinant of an** $n \times n$ **matrix.** For an $n \times n$ matrix A, let A_{ij} denote the matrix obtained by deleting row i and column j from A. Then the determinant of A is given by

$$\det(A) = \sum_{j=1}^{n} (-1)^{i+j} a_{ij} det(A_{ij})$$

It can be shown that the choice of row i does not affect the value of the determinant, and can be made in such a way as to simplify the calculation. Show that this definition with $n=3$ and $i=1$ yields the definition given earlier for a 3×3 matrix.

10. Evaluate the determinant of each of the following matrices:

(a.) $\begin{bmatrix} -2 & 3 & -2 & 4 \\ 1 & 0 & 4 & 5 \\ 3 & 0 & 5 & -1 \\ 2 & 2 & 6 & 1 \end{bmatrix}$. 　　(b.) $\begin{bmatrix} 1 & -1 & 2 & 4 & 2 \\ 4 & 0 & 4 & 0 & 1 \\ 1 & 2 & 3 & -2 & 6 \\ 2 & 3 & -1 & 2 & 5 \\ -1 & 2 & 3 & 0 & 4 \end{bmatrix}$.

11. The determinant of a submatrix located in the upper left-hand corner of a matrix is called a *principal minor*. Determine the three principal minors of the matrix in Exercise 10 (a.) above.

12. A matrix A is *positive definite* if $\det(A)$ is positive and all its principal minors, as defined in the previous exercise, are positive. Determine if each of the following matrices is positive definite:

(a.) $\begin{bmatrix} -2 & -2 & 0 \\ -2 & 6 & 3 \\ 0 & 3 & 4 \end{bmatrix}$. 　　(b.) $\begin{bmatrix} 1 & 3 & 4 \\ 3 & 2 & 0 \\ 4 & 0 & 2 \end{bmatrix}$.

2.5 Linear independence

In Section 2.3 we saw that a plane is spanned by any two nonzero vectors belonging to the plane that were not parallel. In the preceding section we saw that a 2×2 matrix has an inverse precisely when the vectors forming its columns are not parallel.

In this section we will extend the property of two vectors in R^2 not being parallel to the corresponding property for a set of vectors in R^n. We will find that the concept of linear independence discussed here is of great importance in determining solutions to systems of equations and the existence of matrix inverses. In Chapter 3 it will be used in discussing the nature of solutions to a linear program.

Because this section is more conceptual, the presentation will require an understanding of some of the ideas underlying mathematical reasoning. We will therefore pause, where necessary, to discuss these ideas.

Let $\{v_1, v_2, \ldots, v_k\}$ be a set of nonzero vectors in R^n. This set is *linearly independent* if and only if the only solution to the equation

$$c_1 v_1 + c_2 v_2 + \cdots + c_k v_k = 0$$

is the trivial solution $c_1 = 0, c_2 = 0, \ldots, c_k = 0$.

Since the concept of linear independence is introduced to generalize the statement that two nonzero vectors are not parallel, let us first consider the example of two vectors in two dimensions.

Example 2.5.1. Show that the following pair of vectors is linearly independent:

$$v_1 = \begin{bmatrix} 1 \\ 4 \end{bmatrix} \text{ and } v_2 = \begin{bmatrix} 3 \\ 5 \end{bmatrix}.$$

We must solve the system of equations

$$c_1 v_1 + c_2 v_2 = 0$$

which, when the vectors are substituted, becomes

$$c_1 \begin{bmatrix} 1 \\ 4 \end{bmatrix} + c_2 \begin{bmatrix} 3 \\ 5 \end{bmatrix} = \begin{bmatrix} 0 \\ 0 \end{bmatrix}.$$

Then in component form the system is

$$\begin{array}{rcrcl} c_1 & + & 3c_2 & = & 0 \\ 4c_1 & + & 5c_2 & = & 0. \end{array}$$

Subtracting 4 times the first equation from the second yields an equation in c_2 alone

$$(4 - (4)(1))c_1 + (5 - (4)(3))c_2 = 0$$

which leads to

$$-7c_2 = 0 \quad \text{and hence} \quad c_2 = 0.$$

Substituting into the first equation yields $c_1 = 0$. Therefore, the set $\{v_1, v_2\}$ is linearly independent. ∎

The linear independence of the set of vectors forming the columns of a matrix has important consequences for equations involving the matrix. The linear independence demonstrated in the above example will be seen to show that for the matrix V below whose columns are v_1 and v_2,

$$V = \begin{bmatrix} 1 & 3 \\ 4 & 5 \end{bmatrix}$$

the inverse V^{-1} exists, and for any vector b in R^2 the system of equations $Vx = b$ has a unique solution.

A set of vectors which is not linearly independent is said to be *linearly dependent*. Thus, to express linear dependence, we need to express the opposite, or *negation*, of linear independence. This requires a look first at mathematical reasoning.

For a sentence P, the sentence denoted by $\neg P$ is called the *negation* of P and is its logical opposite.

Example 2.5.2.

(a) The negation of "$x < 0$" is the inequality "$x \geq 0$."

(b) The negation of

> "The vector x has a unique representation as a member of the span of $\{v_1, v_2, \ldots, v_k\}$."

is

> "The vector x either can be represented in more than one way as a linear combination of $\{v_1, v_2, \ldots, v_k\}$ or is not a member of the span." ∎

Since linear independence requires that a certain type of linear combination does not exist, its negation, linear dependence, can be expressed as the assertion that such a linear combination does exist. This definition is useful in arguments in that it produces a nonzero constant as a consequence of linear dependence.

The set $\{v_1, v_2, \ldots, v_k\}$ of vectors in R^n is *linearly dependent* if there exists a linear combination

$$c_1 v_1 + c_2 v_2 + \cdots + c_k v_k = 0$$

in which for some i, $c_i \neq 0$. This definition will be useful in proving the next theorem. But before proceeding, we consider an example.

Example 2.5.3. Show that the following set of vectors is linearly dependent:

$$\left\{ \begin{bmatrix} 1 \\ 3 \\ -2 \end{bmatrix}, \begin{bmatrix} 3 \\ -1 \\ 3 \end{bmatrix}, \begin{bmatrix} -2 \\ 4 \\ -5 \end{bmatrix} \right\}.$$

Note that the third vector is the difference of the first two vectors. Thus, the following linear combination, with nonzero coefficients, yields the zero vector:

$$1 \begin{bmatrix} 1 \\ 3 \\ -2 \end{bmatrix} + (-1) \begin{bmatrix} 3 \\ -1 \\ 3 \end{bmatrix} + (-1) \begin{bmatrix} -2 \\ 4 \\ -5 \end{bmatrix} = \begin{bmatrix} 0 \\ 0 \\ 0 \end{bmatrix}. \quad \blacksquare$$

We will see that a linearly independent set of vectors in R^n has properties similar to a pair of nonzero, nonparallel vectors in R^2. To see how the next theorem expresses this similarity, recall that a pair of parallel vectors in R^2 failed to span R^2 because one is a scalar multiple of the other, i.e., one lies in the span of the other.

Theorem 2.5.4. *The set $\{v_1, v_2, \ldots, v_k\}$ of nonzero vectors in R^n is linearly independent if and only if no vector in the set is in the span of the other vectors in the set.*

The "if and only if" in the theorem means that each of the two conditions implies the other. In such a case, we say that they are *equivalent*. Thus, the theorem is saying two things:

Proposition 2.5.5.

(a) *If the set $\{v_1, v_2, \ldots, v_k\}$ of nonzero vectors in R^n is linearly independent, then no vector in the set is in the span of the other vectors in the set.*

(b) *If no vector in the set $\{v_1, v_2, \ldots, v_k\}$ of nonzero vectors in R^n is in the span of the other vectors in the set, then the set is linearly independent.*

Before considering a proof of (a) above, we need to discuss the relationship between statements (a) and (b). Note that both parts of the proposition have the form

$$\text{If } P, \text{ then } Q,$$

and that one can be obtained from the other by interchanging P and Q. Two propositions related in this way are said to be *converses* of each other.

Example 2.5.6. The converse of

$$\text{"If } x < 0, \text{ then } x \text{ is not positive."}$$

is

$$\text{"If } x \text{ is not positive, then } x < 0." \qquad \blacksquare$$

In a proposition of the form

$$\text{If } P, \text{ then } Q,$$

P is called the *hypothesis* and Q is called the *consequence*. Thus, the converse of a proposition is formed by interchanging the hypothesis and the consequence.

In Example 2.5.6, although the first statement is true, the second is false, since a number that is not positive need not be negative, but could be zero. Thus, a proposition and its converse are not logically related, i.e., either one or both may be false. The exercises at the end of the section will provide further examples showing the absence of a logical relationship between a proposition and its converse.

To prove Theorem 2.5.4, now seen to be a statement and its converse, one needs to prove both parts of Proposition 2.5.5. We will prove one of them here and leave the proof of the other to the exercises. To simplify the proof, however, we will first need to introduce the contrapositive of a proposition.

The *contrapositive* of the proposition

$$\text{If } P, \text{ then } Q$$

is the proposition

$$\text{If } \neg Q, \text{ then } \neg P.$$

Hence, the hypothesis of the contrapositive is the negation of the original conclusion, and the conclusion is the negation of the original consequence. The contrapositive of the first proposition in the above example is

"If x is positive, then $x \geq 0$."

Unlike the relationship between a proposition and its converse, a proposition and its contrapositve are equivalent. Thus, one has the option of proving a proposition or of proving its contrapositive. In this instance, we will find it easier to prove the contrapositive.

Proposition 2.5.7. (Contrapositive of Proposition 2.5.5 (a)) *If a vector in the set $\{v_1, v_2, \ldots, v_k\}$ is in the span of the other vectors of the set, then the set is linearly dependent.*

Proof. Let v_i be a linear combination of the other vectors in the set, so that

$$v_i = c_1 v_1 + \cdots + c_{i-1} v_{i-1} + c_{i+1} v_{i+1} + \cdots + c_k v_k.$$

Then by subtracting v_i from both sides, we have

$$c_1 v_1 + \cdots + c_{i-1} v_{i-1} - v_i + c_{i+1} v_{i+1} + \cdots + c_k v_k = 0.$$

But this is a linear combination of the vectors belonging to the set that equals 0, but in which not all the coefficients are zero, since $c_i = -1$. Hence, the set of vectors is linearly dependent. $\square$

Linear independence could be rephrased as "The set $\{v_1, v_2, \ldots, v_k\}$ of nonzero vectors is *linearly independent* if and only if the zero vector 0 has a unique expression as a linear combination of the vectors in the set." The following proposition shows that the uniqueness carries over to all vectors in the span of a linear independent set.

Proposition 2.5.8. *The set $B = \{v_1, v_2, \ldots, v_k\}$ of vectors is linearly independent if and only if every vector in the span of B has a unique representation as a linear combination of members of B.*

Proof. One direction of the proof is clear since a unique representation for all vectors implies a unique representation for 0.

The other direction is proven by contradiction. Suppose that we have distinct representations for a vector x in the span of B. Then

$$x = c_1 v_1 + c_2 v_2 + \cdots + c_k v_k$$

and

$$x = d_1 v_1 + d_2 v_2 + \cdots + d_k v_k$$

where for some i, $c_i \neq d_i$. Then

$$x - x = (c_1 - d_1)v_1 + (c_2 - d_2)v_2 + \cdots + (c_k - d_k)v_k = 0.$$

However, 0 must have a unique representation as a linear combination of vectors from B in which each coefficient is 0, and here, $c_i - d_i \neq 0$. Hence, a contradiction has been reached. $\square$

Exercises

1. Give the negation of each of the following statements:

   (a) Every equation with one unknown has a solution.

   (b) There is at least one solution to the equation $x + 1 = x$.

   (c) There is at most one solution to the equation $x + 1 = x$.

   (d) There is no solution to the equation $x + 1 = x$.

2. For each part of Exercise 1 above, decide whether the given statement or its negation is true.

3. State the converse of each of the following propositions, and decide for each whether both the statement and its converse are true, both are false, or one is true and the other false:

   (a) If n is a multiple of 4, then n is a multiple of 2.

   (b) If n is a prime integer, then n is odd.

   (c) If $a^2 = b^2$, then $a = b$.

4. State the contrapositive of each statement in Exercise 3 above, and decide for each whether both the statement and its contrapositive are true, both are false, or one is true and the other false.

5. Complete the proof of Theorem 2.5.4 by stating and proving the contrapositive of Proposition 2.5.5 (b).

6. Show that the set $\{[2,3]^T, [4,1]^T\}$ is linearly independent.

7. Show that the set $\{[2,4,-4]^T, [-3,2,1]^T, [-2,4,-1]^T\}$ is linearly dependent.

has scalar product of zero

8. A set of nonzero vectors $\{v_1, v_2, \ldots, v_n\}$ is *mutually orthogonal* if it satisfies $v_i \cdot v_j = 0$ for $i \neq j$. Use the fact that the dot product distributes over vector addition and scalar multiplication to show that

$$c_1 v_1 + c_2 v_2 + \cdots + c_3 v_n = 0$$

has only the trivial solution. Hence, show that a mutually orthogonal set of vectors is linearly independent.

2.6   Systems of equations

The main objective of this chapter is to be able to solve systems of equations such as the one from the beginning of the chapter:

$$
\begin{array}{rrrrrrr}
3x_1 & + & 2x_2 & + & x_3 & - & x_4 & = & 8 \\
x_1 & - & x_2 & + & 4x_3 & - & 2x_4 & = & 5 \\
2x_1 & + & x_2 & - & 5x_3 & & & = & -2.
\end{array}
$$

In Example 2.5.1, we solved such a system with two equations in two unknowns, and now we generalize that method to m equations in n unknowns by developing an algorithm, called *Gaussian elimination*. First we will consider the case where m and n are equal. We will then use the algorithm to investigate spans of vectors in dimensions other than two. Finally, we will consider the case where there are more variables than equations. In the course of the investigation, we will discover that Gaussian elimination can be used to investigate various properties of a matrix.

The fundamental operations used in Gaussian elimination are called *row operations*. We have used these operations in Section 2.3 to express a vector as a member of the span of a pair of vectors in R^2 and again in Section 2.5 to test a pair of vectors for linear independence. The essential property of row operations is that they can make the solution of a system of equations more nearly apparent without changing the solution.

The three basic row operations are:

1. Multiply a row by a nonzero scalar.

2. Subtract a nonzero multiple of one row from another row.

3. Interchange two rows.

Although we have not yet used the third operation, we will find it essential in certain cases to avoid division by zero, and helpful in others to simplify calculation.

In introducing these as "row operations," we are thinking of applying them to matrices which will represent a system of equations. However, they can also be applied to systems of equations directly, thinking of each equation as a row. We will do examples using both approaches.

Example 2.6.1. Solve the following system of equations:

$$
\begin{aligned}
2x_1 + x_2 + x_3 &= 7 \\
4x_1 + 4x_2 + 3x_3 &= 21 \\
6x_1 + 7x_2 + 4x_3 &= 32.
\end{aligned}
$$

The objective of Gaussian elimination is to simplify a system of n equations each involving n variables to a system in which there is one equation in a single variable, one in two variables, and so on to one equation in n variables. If this is accomplished properly, each equation can then be used to determine a value for one variable.

The first step in this simplification process is to multiply the first equation by $\frac{1}{2}$ in order to obtain a 1 as the coefficient of x_1:

$$
\begin{aligned}
x_1 + \tfrac{1}{2}x_2 + \tfrac{1}{2}x_3 &= \tfrac{7}{2} \\
4x_1 + 4x_2 + 3x_3 &= 21 \\
6x_1 + 7x_2 + 4x_3 &= 32.
\end{aligned}
$$

Having a coefficient of 1 in the $(1, 1)$ place facilitates the elimination of x_1 from the other equations. In this example, we must subtract 4 times equation 1 from equation 2, and then subtract 6 times equation 1 from equation 3 to obtain:

$$
\begin{aligned}
x_1 + \tfrac{1}{2}x_2 + \tfrac{1}{2}x_3 &= \tfrac{7}{2} \\
2x_2 + x_3 &= 7 \\
4x_2 + x_3 &= 11.
\end{aligned}
$$

Now we continue the process by dividing the second equation by 2 to obtain 1 as the coefficient in the $(2, 2)$ position:

$$
\begin{aligned}
x_1 + \tfrac{1}{2}x_2 + \tfrac{1}{2}x_3 &= \tfrac{7}{2} \\
x_2 + \tfrac{1}{2}x_3 &= \tfrac{7}{2} \\
4x_2 + x_3 &= 11.
\end{aligned}
$$

Subtracting 4 times equation 2 from equation 3 will now complete the desired reduction:

$$
\begin{aligned}
x_1 + \tfrac{1}{2}x_2 + \tfrac{1}{2}x_3 &= \tfrac{7}{2} \\
x_2 + \tfrac{1}{2}x_3 &= \tfrac{7}{2} \\
- x_3 &= -3.
\end{aligned}
$$

The Gaussian elimination process is now complete. It has reduced the system to one having an equation in a single variable, an equation involving two variables, and one involving all three variables. The solution is now determined by the technique of *back substitution,* using each equation in turn to determine a value for one of the variables.

We quickly determine that $x_3 = 3$.

From equation 2 we have

$$
x_2 = \frac{7}{2} - \left(\frac{1}{2}\right) x_3
$$

which yields, since $x_3 = 3$,

$$
x_2 = \frac{7}{2} - \left(\frac{1}{2}\right) 3 = 2.
$$

Similarly, by substituting $x_3 = 3$ and $x_2 = 2$ in the first equation we obtain

$$
x_1 = \frac{7}{2} - \left(\frac{1}{2}\right) x_2 - \left(\frac{1}{2}\right) x_3 = \frac{7}{2} - \left(\frac{1}{2}\right) 2 - \left(\frac{1}{2}\right) 3 = 1.
$$

Thus, the solution is $x^T = [1, 2, 3]$.   ■

In the preceding example, the system of equations was reduced by Gaussian elimination to one associated with a *triangular matrix,* i.e., a matrix A in which $a_{ij} = 0$ for $i > j$. This will be more apparent in the next example where we replace the system of equations by a matrix.

Systems of equations in which this occurs and a unique solution is obtained are said to be *consistent*.

Example 2.6.2. Determine whether $w^T = [7, 2, -1]$ belongs to the span of the set of vectors below:

$$v_1 = \begin{bmatrix} 2 \\ -1 \\ 2 \end{bmatrix}, \qquad v_2 = \begin{bmatrix} 3 \\ 2 \\ -4 \end{bmatrix}, \qquad v_3 = \begin{bmatrix} 2 \\ 2 \\ -1 \end{bmatrix}.$$

To decide whether w belongs to the span of the set of three vectors, we must try to determine values for $x_1, x_2,$ and x_3 such that

$$w = x_1 v_1 + x_2 v_2 + x_3 v_3.$$

Thus, we must solve the corresponding system of equations

$$\begin{array}{rrrrrr} 2x_1 & + & 3x_2 & + & 2x_3 & = & 7 \\ -x_1 & + & 2x_2 & + & 2x_3 & = & 2 \\ 2x_1 & - & 4x_2 & - & x_3 & = & -1. \end{array}$$

We will solve this system by representing it by the matrix below in which each equation has a row, each variable a column, and the right-hand side is added as the last column on the right. This matrix is referred to as the *augmented matrix* for the system.

$$\left[\begin{array}{rrr|r} 2 & 3 & 2 & 7 \\ -1 & 2 & 2 & 2 \\ 2 & -4 & -1 & -1 \end{array} \right]$$

We now perform row operations. Divide the first row by 2 to obtain a 1 in the (1, 1) position:

$$\left[\begin{array}{rrr|r} 1 & \frac{3}{2} & 1 & \frac{7}{2} \\ -1 & 2 & 2 & 2 \\ 2 & -4 & -1 & -1 \end{array} \right].$$

We now add rows 1 and 2 to place a 0 in the (2, 1) position and subtract twice row 1 from row 3 to place a zero in the (3, 1) position:

$$\begin{bmatrix} 1 & \frac{3}{2} & 1 & \bigg| & \frac{7}{2} \\ 0 & \frac{7}{2} & 3 & \bigg| & \frac{11}{2} \\ 0 & -7 & -3 & \bigg| & -8 \end{bmatrix}.$$

The combination of row operations that resulted in a 1 in the $(1, 1)$ position and zeroes below it is called *pivoting*. We continue by pivoting on the $(2, 2)$ position: multiply row 2 by $\frac{2}{7}$, and then add 7 times the new row 2 to row 3 to produce the next matrix:

$$\begin{bmatrix} 1 & \frac{3}{2} & 1 & \bigg| & \frac{7}{2} \\ 0 & 1 & \frac{6}{7} & \bigg| & \frac{11}{7} \\ 0 & 0 & 3 & \bigg| & 3 \end{bmatrix}.$$

Finally, we divide by the last row by 3:

$$\begin{bmatrix} 1 & \frac{3}{2} & 1 & \bigg| & \frac{7}{2} \\ 0 & 1 & \frac{6}{7} & \bigg| & \frac{11}{7} \\ 0 & 0 & 1 & \bigg| & 1 \end{bmatrix}.$$

We now have obtained a matrix involving a triangle of zeroes below the diagonal of one's. Rewriting with variables, we can complete the solution by back substitution:

$$
\begin{aligned}
x_1 \; + \; (\tfrac{3}{2})x_2 \; + \; \quad x_3 \; &= \; \tfrac{7}{2} \\
x_2 \; + \; (\tfrac{6}{7})x_3 \; &= \; \tfrac{11}{7} \\
x_3 \; &= \; 1.
\end{aligned}
$$

Thus, the solution is:

$$
\begin{aligned}
x_3 \; &= \; 1 \\
x_2 \; &= \; \tfrac{11}{7} - \left(\tfrac{6}{7}\right)1 = \tfrac{5}{7} \\
x_1 \; &= \; \tfrac{7}{2} - \left(\tfrac{3}{2}\right)\left(\tfrac{5}{7}\right) - 1 = \tfrac{10}{7}
\end{aligned}
$$

We can conclude that w is in the span of the three vectors, and that

$$w = \left(\frac{10}{7}\right)v_1 + \left(\frac{5}{7}\right)v_2 + v_3. \quad \blacksquare$$

In the example just finished, $w^T = [7, 2, -1]$ could have been replaced on the right-hand side by the zero vector, resulting in a solution of all zeroes. We would thus have shown that the given set of vectors is linearly independent, as we did earlier in Example 2.5.1. Alternatively, we could have chosen an arbitrary vector b from R^3 as the right-hand side and concluded that the given set of vectors spans R^3.

In general, if Gaussian elimination can be applied to determine a unique solution to $Ax = 0$ for an $n \times n$ matrix A, then the columns of A form a linearly independent set. Application of Gaussian elimination to the system of equations $Ax = b$ for such a matrix will always result in a unique solution independent of the choice of b. Verifying these observations in R^n would prove the following theorem.

Theorem 2.6.3. *Any linearly independent set of n vectors in R^n spans R^n and any vector in R^n can be expressed as a linear combination of the vectors for a unique set of coefficients.*

A linearly independent set of vectors which spans R^n is called a *basis* for R^n. Thus, the preceding theorem implies that any linearly independent set of n vectors in R^n is a basis.

In the examples considered thus far the number of equations and the number of variables have been equal. Further, the columns of the matrix involved have been linearly independent, and the solutions have thus been unique, with each equation being used to determine the value of one of the variables. We now consider systems of equations for which this will no longer be the case, i.e., where either the solution is not unique or no solution exists.

The case in which no solution exists, called an *inconsistent system,* is recognized by reaching a contradiction in the Gaussian elimination process in which zero is equated to a nonzero number. We will consider such systems in the exercises at the end of the section.

In Chapter 3 and beyond, we will devote much effort to seeking an optimal solution among the set of solutions to a system with a nonunique solution. Thus that is the key case.

To solve a system $Ax = b$ which has a nonunique solution, it will be helpful to also consider the related system $Ax = 0$, where b has been replaced by the zero vector. This system of equations is called the associated *homogeneous system.* The set of solutions to $Ax = 0$ is denoted by N_A and is called the *nullspace* of A. If n is the number of variables, we will see that N_A is a vector subspace of R^n.

The next theorem describes the set of solutions to the system $Ax = b$.

Theorem 2.6.4. *The set of solutions to $Ax = b$ has the form $p + N_A$, where p is any solution to $Ax = b$ and N_A is the set of solutions to the homogeneous system $Ax = 0$.*

In systems such as those of Examples 2.6.1 and 2.6.2, in which the solution is unique, N_A consists of the single vector 0. In systems of equations such as those to follow, where the solution is not unique, the Gaussian elimination and back-substitution process will generate a set of vectors which spans N_A.

In a system where the solution is not unique, we will see that at least one of the variables can be assigned an arbitrary value. The *nullity* of a matrix A is the number of variables than can be assigned arbitrary values in the solution of the system of equations $Ax = b$. For each variable to which we can assign an arbitrary value in the solution, we say that we have a *degree of freedom*. We will find that the number of degrees of freedom will be the number of vectors needed to span N_A.

The *rank* of a matrix is the number of vectors in the largest linearly independent set of vectors that can be formed from the columns of the matrix. The sum of the column rank and the nullity of A is equal to the number of variables in the system of equations $Ax = b$.

Three reasons may make it impossible for each equation to be used to determine a value for one of the variables. They are:

1. There may be more variables than equations.

2. The number of variables and the number of equations may be equal, but one equation may be a combination of other equations and therefore may not make a requirement on the solution beyond those made by the other equations.

3. There may be no solution.

The following system of equations is an example of the first case:

Example 2.6.5. Determine all solutions of the system of equations:

$$
\begin{array}{rcrcrcrcrcr}
x_1 & + & x_2 & - & 2x_3 & + & x_4 & + & 3x_5 & = & 2 \\
2x_1 & - & x_2 & + & 2x_3 & + & 2x_4 & + & 3x_5 & = & 7 \\
3x_1 & + & 2x_2 & - & 4x_3 & - & 3x_4 & - & 10x_5 & = & -5.
\end{array}
$$

Since there are two more variables than equations and each equation can determine a value for only one variable in terms of the others, there will be at least two variables for which no value can be determined. We will make an arbitrary choice of value for those variables.

We proceed with Gaussian elimination and allow the process to reveal which variables can be determined. Subtracting twice the first equation from the second and three times the first from the third produces the following system:

$$
\begin{aligned}
x_1 + x_2 - 2x_3 + x_4 + 3x_5 &= 2 \\
- 3x_2 + 6x_3 \qquad - 3x_5 &= 3 \\
- x_2 + 2x_3 - 6x_4 - 19x_5 &= -11.
\end{aligned}
$$

Divide the second equation by -3 to obtain a 1 in the $(2,2)$ place. Then, adding the new second equation to the third equation yields the following system:

$$
\begin{aligned}
x_1 + x_2 - 2x_3 + x_4 + 3x_5 &= 2 \\
x_2 - 2x_3 \qquad + x_5 &= -1 \\
- 6x_4 - 18x_5 &= -12.
\end{aligned}
$$

The objective in forming the system above was to eliminate x_2 from the third equation, however, x_3 also dropped out. We will therefore use the third equation to determine x_4, which is now the first variable in the equation with a nonzero coefficient.

We proceed with back substitution as before, with the only change being that the values obtained for $x_1, x_2,$ and x_4 will depend on x_3 and x_5, which can be assigned arbitrary values. In general, for each equation we determine the value of the first variable having a nonzero coefficient in the equation in terms of the variables in the equation which do not appear first in any equation.

$$
\begin{aligned}
x_4 &= 2 - 3x_5 \\
x_2 &= -1 + 2x_3 - x_5 \\
x_1 &= 2 - x_2 + 2x_3 - x_4 - 3x_5 \\
&= 2 - (-1 + 2x_3 - x_5) + 2x_3 - (2 - 3x_5) - 3x_5 \\
&= 1 + x_5
\end{aligned}
$$

If we make arbitrary choices for x_3 and x_5, $x_3 = a$ and $x_5 = b$, we now have values for the five variables which depend on the arbitrarily chosen values a and b:

$$
\begin{aligned}
x_1 &= 1 &&&+ &\ b \\
x_2 &= -1 &+\ 2a &- &\ b \\
x_3 &= &\ a \\
x_4 &= 2 &&- &\ 3b \\
x_5 &= &&&\ b.
\end{aligned}
$$

The structure of the set of solutions to the system becomes apparent when we express these equations in vector form:

$$
\begin{bmatrix} x_1 \\ x_2 \\ x_3 \\ x_4 \\ x_5 \end{bmatrix} = \begin{bmatrix} 1 \\ -1 \\ 0 \\ 2 \\ 0 \end{bmatrix} + a \begin{bmatrix} 0 \\ 2 \\ 1 \\ 0 \\ 0 \end{bmatrix} + b \begin{bmatrix} 1 \\ -1 \\ 0 \\ -3 \\ 1 \end{bmatrix}.
$$

With $p^T = [1, -1, 0, 2, 0]$, $u^T = [0, 2, 1, 0, 0]$, and $v^T = [1, -1, 0, -3, 1]$, we have the expression

$$ x = p + au + bv $$

for a solution x to the original system of equations. The vector p is called a *particular solution* and is a specific solution to the system of equations. The vectors u and v are solutions to the homogeneous system $Ax = 0$ and span the nullspace N_A. The nullity of the matrix A is two, and the rank is three. ■

After the next example we will relate the rank of a matrix to the number of nonzero components in a solution to a system of linear equations.

Example 2.6.6. Determine a vector representation for the set of solutions of

$$
\begin{aligned}
x_1 &- &x_2 &+ &2x_3 &= &3 \\
2x_1 &- &x_2 &+ &x_3 &= &3 \\
-3x_1 &+ &2x_2 &- &3x_3 &= &-6.
\end{aligned}
$$

Unlike the previous example, here the number of variables equals the number of equations. Thus, we expect that it will be possible to use each equation to determine a value for one of the variables.

We again apply Gaussian elimination.

Since the coefficient of x_1 in the first equation is already a 1, to pivot on the $(1, 1)$ position, we need only subtract twice the first equation from the second and add three times the first equation to the third:

$$\begin{array}{rcrcrcr} x_1 & - & x_2 & + & 2x_3 & = & 3 \\ & & x_2 & - & 3x_3 & = & -3 \\ & & -x_2 & + & 3x_3 & = & 3. \end{array}$$

Now we add the second and third equations to eliminate x_2 from the third:

$$\begin{array}{rcrcrcr} x_1 & - & x_2 & + & 2x_3 & = & 3 \\ & & x_2 & - & 3x_3 & = & -3 \\ & & & & 0 & = & 0. \end{array}$$

The unexpected elimination of x_3 from the third equation and the appearance of a zero on the right-hand side indicates that the third equation was redundant, i.e., that it is a linear combination of the other two. In fact, had we suspected such a thing, we might have noticed that in the original system the third equation is the negative of the sum of the first two. Such a system of equations is called *redundant* since at least one equation depends on the others. Thus, the rows of the system form a linearly dependent set.

When the equation $0 = 0$ is encountered, it is discarded, and we continue to solve the system consisting of the remaining equations. Here we will be able to determine x_1 and x_2 in terms of x_3.

$$\begin{aligned} x_2 &= -3 + 3x_3 \\ x_1 &= 3 + x_2 - 2x_3 \\ &= 3 + (-3 + 3x_3) - 2x_3 \\ &= x_3. \end{aligned}$$

As in the previous example, we make an arbitrary choice for x_3, $x_3 = a$, and obtain a vector expression for the set of solutions:

$$\begin{array}{rcrcr} x_1 & = & & & a \\ x_2 & = & -3 & + & 3a \\ x_3 & = & & & a \end{array}$$

or in vector notation,

$$\begin{bmatrix} x_1 \\ x_2 \\ x_3 \end{bmatrix} = \begin{bmatrix} 0 \\ -3 \\ 0 \end{bmatrix} + a \begin{bmatrix} 1 \\ 3 \\ 1 \end{bmatrix}. \qquad \blacksquare$$

In the example above, we could set $a = 0$ and have a solution with only one nonzero variable, and in Example 2.6.5 we could set two variables to zero and have a solution with only three nonzero variables.

One way to view the number of nonzero variables required in a solution is through the concept of rank. Recall that the *rank* of a matrix is the number of vectors in a largest linearly independent set of columns of the matrix. One can show that it is also equal to the number of vectors in a largest linearly independent subset of rows of the matrix.

Note for example that in the matrix of Example 2.6.5, which has rank 3, columns 3 and 5 are linear combinations of the other three columns:

$$\begin{bmatrix} -2 \\ 2 \\ -4 \end{bmatrix} = 0 \begin{bmatrix} 1 \\ 2 \\ 3 \end{bmatrix} - 2 \begin{bmatrix} 1 \\ -1 \\ 2 \end{bmatrix} + 0 \begin{bmatrix} 1 \\ 2 \\ -3 \end{bmatrix}$$

and

$$\begin{bmatrix} 3 \\ 3 \\ -10 \end{bmatrix} = - \begin{bmatrix} 1 \\ 2 \\ 3 \end{bmatrix} + \begin{bmatrix} 1 \\ -1 \\ 2 \end{bmatrix} + 3 \begin{bmatrix} 1 \\ 2 \\ -3 \end{bmatrix}.$$

Columns 3 and 5 are the columns that correspond to the variables that can be set to zero in our solution. We will see in the proposition below how such linear combinations can be used to show that the number of nonzero variables needs to be no greater than the rank.

The following result is useful in linear programming, particularly in the context of the transportation problem in Chapter 4.

Proposition 2.6.7. *If the system of equations* $Ax = b$ *has a solution and the rank of* A *is* m, *then there is a solution with at most* m *nonzero coordinates.*

Proof. Assume that A has n columns denoted by a_j, $j = 1, \ldots, n$, $n \geq m$, and that the first m form a linearly independent set. If $m = n$, then the proposition obviously holds. Otherwise, let y be a solution to $Ax = b$, and suppose that $y_j \neq 0$ for some j, $m < j \leq n$. Since the first m columns are the largest linearly independent subset, we can write a_j as a linear combination of the first m columns:

$$a_j = c_1 a_1 + \cdots + c_m a_m.$$

The system of equations $Ay = b$ can be expressed in terms of the columns of A:

$$y_1 a_1 + \cdots + y_m a_m + \cdots + y_j a_j + \cdots + y_n a_n = b$$

and we can replace $y_j a_j$ by

$$y_j a_j = y_j c_1 a_1 + \cdots + y_j c_m a_m.$$

The system of equations $Ay = b$ can then be rewritten without the vector a_j by collecting terms:

$$(y_1 - y_j c_1)a_1 + \cdots + (y_m - y_j c_m)a_m + \cdots + y_n a_n = b.$$

Continuing in this way, we can eliminate all nonzero coordinates of y with subscripts greater than m.□

Exercises

1. Solve each of the following systems of equations:

$$\text{(a)} \quad \begin{array}{rcrcrcr} 2x_1 & - & x_2 & + & 2x_3 & = & 2 \\ 4x_1 & - & x_2 & + & 3x_3 & = & 5 \\ x_1 & + & 2x_2 & + & x_3 & = & 4. \end{array}$$

$$\text{(b)} \quad \begin{array}{rcrcrcr} 3x_1 & - & 2x_2 & + & x_3 & = & -3 \\ x_1 & + & 2x_2 & + & 2x_3 & = & 10 \\ 4x_1 & - & x_2 & - & x_3 & = & -14. \end{array}$$

$$\text{(c)} \quad \begin{array}{rcrcrcr} & & x_2 & + & 3x_3 & = & 7 \\ -x_1 & + & 3x_2 & - & x_3 & = & -10 \\ 2x_1 & + & x_2 & + & 4x_3 & = & 12. \end{array}$$

2. Determine if the set of vectors $\{[1,3,1]^T, [2,5,-4]^T, [4,11,-2]^T\}$ is linearly independent.

Systems of equations in which the number of variables is less than the number of equations arise less frequently than those in which the number of variables is higher, but they can be of interest in examining spans. A solution exists only when the extra equations are redundant and can be reduced to the equation $0 = 0$ by Gaussian elimination. The next two problems demonstrate the two possibilities.

3. Is $[6,7,0]^T$ in the span of $\{[1,2,-1]^T, [4,3,2]^T\}$?

4. Is $[3,-1,4]^T$ in the span of $\{[1,2,-1]^T, [4,3,2]^T\}$?

5. Solve the system of equations from the beginning of the chapter:

$$\begin{array}{rcrcrcrcr} 3x_1 & + & 2x_2 & + & x_3 & - & x_4 & = & 8 \\ x_1 & - & x_2 & + & 4x_3 & - & 2x_4 & = & 5 \\ 2x_1 & + & x_2 & - & 5x_3 & & & = & -2. \end{array}$$

6. Solve the following systems of equations. Determine the rank and the nullity of each coefficient matrix.

(a)
$$
\begin{aligned}
x_1 + 3x_2 + x_3 + 2x_4 &= 0 \\
x_1 - x_2 + 2x_3 &= 1 \\
2x_1 + 2x_2 + 3x_3 + 2x_4 &= 1 \\
3x_1 + x_2 + 5x_3 + 4x_4 &= 4.
\end{aligned}
$$

(b)
$$
\begin{aligned}
x_2 + 2x_3 + x_4 &= 1 \\
x_1 - 2x_2 - 3x_3 + x_4 &= 0 \\
x_1 - 2x_2 + x_3 + x_4 &= 1.
\end{aligned}
$$

(c)
$$
\begin{aligned}
x_1 + 3x_2 + x_3 &= 1 \\
5x_2 - 6x_3 &= 0 \\
2x_1 + x_2 + 8x_3 &= 3.
\end{aligned}
$$

7. Inconsistent system. The following system of equations is from Example 2.6.6 with the constant in the third equation changed. Use Gaussian elimination to show that no solution exists.

$$
\begin{aligned}
x_1 - x_2 + 2x_3 &= 3 \\
2x_1 - x_2 + x_3 &= 3 \\
-3x_1 + 2x_2 - 3x_3 &= 8.
\end{aligned}
$$

8. Determine all solutions to each of the following systems of equations:

(a)
$$
\begin{aligned}
3x_1 + 2x_2 + 5x_3 &= 19 \\
-4x_1 + 3x_2 - 4x_3 &= -23 \\
5x_1 + x_2 + 3x_3 &= 18.
\end{aligned}
$$

(b)
$$
\begin{aligned}
3x_1 + 12x_2 - 6x_3 &= 9 \\
5x_1 - 8x_2 + 2x_3 &= 2 \\
6x_1 - 4x_2 &= 5.
\end{aligned}
$$

(c)
$$
\begin{aligned}
4x_1 + 6x_2 - 4x_4 &= 6 \\
3x_1 - 9x_2 + 6x_3 &= 12 \\
3x_1 + 2x_3 - 2x_4 &= 7 \\
2x_1 + 12x_2 - 4x_3 - 4x_4 &= -2.
\end{aligned}
$$

9. Determine the equation of the plane spanned by the following set of vectors:

$$
\left\{ \begin{bmatrix} 1 \\ 3 \\ 2 \end{bmatrix}, \begin{bmatrix} -4 \\ 3 \\ 1 \end{bmatrix}, \begin{bmatrix} -2 \\ 9 \\ 5 \end{bmatrix} \right\}.
$$

Hint: Let $y = [y_1, y_2, y_3]^T$ and apply Gaussian elimination to the system $Ax = y$, where A has the given vectors as its columns. The required equation is the linear equation that the components of y must satisfy in order for $Ax = y$ to have a solution.

10. Determine the equation of the plane spanned by the following pair of vectors:

$$\left\{ \begin{bmatrix} 1 \\ 3 \\ -2 \end{bmatrix}, \begin{bmatrix} 2 \\ -1 \\ 4 \end{bmatrix} \right\}.$$

11. A plane makes a 400-mile flight in two hours going with the wind. On its return it flies against the same wind, and the trip requires two and a half hours. How fast can the plane fly in still air, and how fast is the wind blowing?

12. Three fractions have 4 as their sum. The first fraction is double the second, and the second is double the third. Determine the fractions.

13. A man and his two sons worked for a neighbor for 10 days and received $360. On another occasion the man and his older son worked for 5 days and received $135. On a third occasion the two sons worked 8 days and received $168. What were the daily wages of each?

14. You have 40 coins including pennies, nickels, and dimes. The value of the coins is $2.00. But if the pennies became dimes, the nickels became pennies, and the dimes became nickels, you would have only $1.62. How many of each kind of coin do you have?

15. Suppose that a company produces two products that rely on parts A and B purchased from another company. The first product requires two of part A and three of part B; the second requires one of part A and two of part B. They have 69 of part A on hand and 110 of part B. How many of each product can they make?

16. Consider the following system of equations:

$$\begin{array}{rcrcrcrcr}
-x_1 & + & x_2 & & & + & x_4 & = & 4 \\
3x_1 & & & + & 3x_3 & + & 3x_4 & = & 3 \\
& & 2x_2 & + & 2x_3 & + & 4x_4 & = & 10 \\
x_1 & + & x_2 & + & 2x_3 & + & 3x_4 & = & 6.
\end{array}$$

The vectors $x^T = [-3, 1, 4, 0]$ and $y^T = [-5, 0, 7, -1]$ are both solutions to the given system. Determine an expression for the difference $x - y$ as a linear combination of elements of the nullspace of the matrix of coefficients.

17. On occasion we have referred to "a" largest linearly independent subset of a set of vectors, implying that such a subset is not unique. Determine at least two different largest linearly independent subsets of the following set of vectors:

$$\left\{ \begin{bmatrix} -2 \\ 4 \\ 6 \end{bmatrix}, \begin{bmatrix} 3 \\ 1 \\ -2 \end{bmatrix}, \begin{bmatrix} 2 \\ 3 \\ 1 \end{bmatrix}, \begin{bmatrix} 7 \\ -7 \\ -14 \end{bmatrix} \right\}.$$

18. Determine two different solutions to the following system of equations, each having only two nonzero components:

$$\begin{array}{rrrrrrrr} x_1 & - & 5x_2 & + & 4x_3 & - & x_4 & = & 6 \\ 2x_1 & - & 4x_2 & + & 7x_3 & - & 3x_4 & = & 11 \\ 2x_1 & + & 2x_2 & + & 6x_3 & - & 4x_4 & = & 10. \end{array}$$

19. **Inconsistent systems.** Apply Gaussian elimination to the following system of equations until a contradiction is reached in which 0 is set equal to a nonzero number:

$$\begin{array}{rrrrrrr} x_1 & + & 5x_2 & + & 4x_3 & = & 3 \\ 2x_1 & + & 2x_2 & & & = & 2 \\ -3x_1 & + & .x_2 & + & 4x_3 & = & -7. \end{array}$$

Note that the third column of the matrix of coefficients is the second column minus the first, i.e., the set of columns is not linearly independent.

2.7   The inverse of a matrix

In Section 2.4 we investigated a quick way to determine whether a 2×2 matrix has an inverse and to determine the inverse if it exists. Here we will develop a general method to determine the inverse of a nonsingular $n \times n$ matrix. The process will involve solving several systems of equations at the same time. Failure of the method will imply that the matrix is singular, i.e., has no inverse. Inverses are needed primarily for a few exercises in Chapter 3.

Gauss-Jordan elimination is an extended version of Gaussian elimination in which the matrix of coefficients is reduced beyond a triangular matrix to a diagonal matrix. It is particularly well adapted to solving several systems of equations simultaneously.

Consider the following example.

Example 2.7.1. Solve the following system of equations:

$$
\begin{aligned}
2x_1 &- x_2 + 2x_3 = 1 \\
3x_1 &+ x_2 - 5x_3 = 9 \\
-x_1 &+ 2x_2 + x_3 = 4.
\end{aligned}
$$

The augmented coefficient matrix is given by

$$
\left[\begin{array}{ccc|c}
2 & -1 & 2 & 1 \\
3 & 1 & -5 & 9 \\
-1 & 2 & 1 & 4
\end{array}\right].
$$

For our first pivot, we divide row 1 by 2 to obtain a 1 in the $(1,1)$ position, and then use this 1 to eliminate the coefficients below it. As with Gaussian elimination, this produces the matrix below:

$$
\left[\begin{array}{ccc|c}
1 & -\frac{1}{2} & 1 & \frac{1}{2} \\
0 & \frac{5}{2} & -8 & \frac{15}{2} \\
0 & \frac{3}{2} & 2 & \frac{9}{2}
\end{array}\right].
$$

We now pivot on the $(2,2)$ position. To do this, we divide the second row by $\frac{5}{2}$ to obtain a new second row. As with Gaussian elimination, we then use the pivot element to eliminate the $\frac{3}{2}$ in the $(3,2)$ position. But now we also use the pivot element to eliminate the $-\frac{1}{2}$ in the $(1,2)$ position. This yields the matrix below:

$$
\left[\begin{array}{ccc|c}
1 & 0 & -\frac{3}{5} & 2 \\
0 & 1 & -\frac{16}{5} & 3 \\
0 & 0 & \frac{68}{10} & 0
\end{array}\right].
$$

Finally, we divide row 3 by $\frac{68}{10}$ to obtain a new row 3 with a 1 in the $(3,3)$ position. We use this pivot element to eliminate the coefficients in the $(1,3)$ and the $(2,3)$ positions. This gives the matrix

$$
\left[\begin{array}{ccc|c}
1 & 0 & 0 & 2 \\
0 & 1 & 0 & 3 \\
0 & 0 & 1 & 0
\end{array}\right]
$$

which represents the equations

$$x_1 \qquad\qquad = \quad 2$$
$$x_2 \qquad\quad = \quad 3$$
$$x_3 \quad = \quad 0. \quad \blacksquare$$

Thus, we have found the solution to the system of equations. The difference between this method and Gaussian elimination is that back substitution has been replaced by additional row operations.

The advantage of this method for solving several systems of equations which share the same matrix of coefficients will be demonstrated next.

Example 2.7.2. Solve the following systems of equations by Gauss-Jordan elimination.

$$\begin{cases} x_1 + 2x_2 = 2 \\ 3x_1 + 4x_2 = 1, \end{cases} \qquad \begin{cases} x_1 + 2x_2 = 1 \\ 3x_1 + 4x_2 = 0, \end{cases}$$

$$\begin{cases} x_1 + 2x_2 = 0 \\ 3x_1 + 4x_2 = 1. \end{cases}$$

Note that the three systems have the same matrix of coefficients. We form an augmented matrix as in the previous example, except that now we include the vectors from the right-hand side of all three systems of equations:

$$\left[\begin{array}{cc|ccc} 1 & 2 & 2 & 1 & 0 \\ 3 & 4 & 1 & 0 & 1 \end{array}\right].$$

Now we apply Gauss-Jordan elimination as in the previous example, extending the row operations over all five columns, to reduce the first two columns to the identity matrix.

Here we need only subtract 3 times the first row from the second in order to reduce the first column:

$$\left[\begin{array}{cc|ccc} 1 & 2 & 2 & 1 & 0 \\ 0 & -2 & -5 & -3 & 1 \end{array}\right].$$

Now we divide the second row by -2 and then subtract twice the new second row from the first to reduce the second column:

$$\left[\begin{array}{cc|ccc} 1 & 0 & -3 & -2 & 1 \\ 0 & 1 & \frac{5}{2} & \frac{3}{2} & -\frac{1}{2} \end{array}\right].$$

Checking will now show that we have determined the solution to each of the three systems of equations, and that the solutions are located in the positions of the respective right-hand sides of the systems of equations. Thus, they are:

$$\begin{cases} x_1 & = & -3 \\ & x_2 & = & \frac{5}{2}, \end{cases} \qquad \begin{cases} x_1 & = & -2 \\ & x_2 & = & \frac{3}{2}, \end{cases} \qquad \begin{cases} x_1 & = & 1 \\ & x_2 & = & -\frac{1}{2}. \end{cases}$$

The last two of the three systems solved in the example above are of particular significance to the question of determining the inverse of a matrix. To demonstrate, let A be the matrix of coefficients common to the systems of equations above and let B be the matrix whose columns are the respective solutions to the last two systems. Then consider the matrix product AB:

$$AB = \begin{bmatrix} 1 & 2 \\ 3 & 4 \end{bmatrix} \begin{bmatrix} -2 & 1 \\ \frac{3}{2} & -\frac{1}{2} \end{bmatrix} = \begin{bmatrix} 1 & 0 \\ 0 & 1 \end{bmatrix} = I.$$

Thus, by solving the two systems of equations

$$\begin{cases} x_1 & + & 2x_2 & = & 1 \\ 3x_1 & + & 4x_2 & = & 0, \end{cases} \qquad \begin{cases} x_1 & + & 2x_2 & = & 0 \\ 3x_1 & + & 4x_2 & = & 1. \end{cases}$$

and using the respective solutions as columns in a matrix, we have determined the inverse of the matrix of coefficients. ∎

The process used in the example is the general process that we will use to determine an inverse and is summarized below:

To determine the inverse of an $n \times n$ matrix A or determine if the inverse fails to exist:

1. Form the augmented matrix $[A \,|\, I]$ where I is the appropriate identity matrix.

2. Apply Gauss-Jordan elimination to the augmented matrix until the first n columns have been reduced to those of the identity matrix or until division by zero occurs.

3. If division by 0 occurs, the matrix A fails to have an inverse. Stop.

4. If Gauss-Jordan elimination can be completed, then A^{-1} exists and is the matrix derived from I by Gauss-Jordan elimination.

We illustrate with an example.

Example 2.7.3. Determine the inverse of the matrix A below:

$$A = \begin{bmatrix} 2 & 1 & -1 \\ 2 & -1 & 2 \\ 1 & 0 & 0 \end{bmatrix}.$$

We begin with the augmented matrix formed by placing the columns of the identity to the right of the matrix A:

$$[A \,|\, I] = \begin{bmatrix} 2 & 1 & -1 & 1 & 0 & 0 \\ 2 & -1 & 2 & 0 & 1 & 0 \\ 1 & 0 & 0 & 0 & 0 & 1 \end{bmatrix}.$$

Pivot on the $(1,1)$ position to obtain

$$\begin{bmatrix} 1 & \frac{1}{2} & -\frac{1}{2} & \frac{1}{2} & 0 & 0 \\ 0 & -2 & 3 & -1 & 1 & 0 \\ 0 & -\frac{1}{2} & \frac{1}{2} & -\frac{1}{2} & 0 & 1 \end{bmatrix}$$

Now pivot on the $(2, 2)$ position. Since we are using Gauss-Jordan elimination, we eliminate both the $(1, 2)$ and $(3, 2)$ entries:

$$\begin{bmatrix} 1 & 0 & \frac{1}{4} & \frac{1}{4} & \frac{1}{4} & 0 \\ 0 & 1 & -\frac{3}{2} & \frac{1}{2} & -\frac{1}{2} & 0 \\ 0 & 0 & -\frac{1}{4} & -\frac{1}{4} & -\frac{1}{4} & 1 \end{bmatrix}.$$

Finally, pivot on the $(3, 3)$ position and eliminate the $(1, 3)$ and $(2, 3)$ entries:

$$\begin{bmatrix} 1 & 0 & 0 & 0 & 0 & 1 \\ 0 & 1 & 0 & 2 & 1 & -6 \\ 0 & 0 & 1 & 1 & 1 & -4 \end{bmatrix}.$$

Therefore,

$$A^{-1} = \begin{bmatrix} 0 & 0 & 1 \\ 2 & 1 & -6 \\ 1 & 1 & -4 \end{bmatrix}. \quad \blacksquare$$

When we are given a single system of equations to solve, it is usually not worthwhile to compute the inverse of the coefficient matrix to solve the system. However, if we must solve several systems, all having the same coefficient matrix, the computation of the inverse can be done once and the inverse then used to solve all the systems.

The following theorem relates the existence of the inverse to linear independence.

Theorem 2.7.4. *The inverse of a square matrix exists if and only if the columns of the matrix form a linearly independent set.*

Proof. We prove only the "if" portion. Let A be an $n \times n$ matrix. From Proposition 2.5.8, if the columns of A are linearly independent, every vector in R^n has a unique representation as a linear combination of the columns of A. In particular, if e_k is the kth column of the identity matrix I, then the system of equations

$$Ax = e_k, \ k = 1, 2, \ldots, n,$$

has a unique solution. Then A^{-1} is the matrix having the solution to the system $Ax = e_k$ as column k. $\square$

The determination of a matrix inverse, as well as other matrix operations discussed in this chapter, can obviously become tedious computationally. For this reason, we provide an example of the use of the symbolic mathematics package *Maple* to calculate a matrix inverse in Listing 2.7.1. More information can be found in Appendix B.

To use the linear algebra capabilities of *Maple*, one must first load a package called `linalg` containing the linear algebra functions. The first command loads that package. When you load `linalg`, you will get a list of the available commands. That list is omitted here. Listing 2.7.1 exhibits two key features of *Maple* – the prompt is a > and each command is terminated by a ; or a :. The : prevents display of the output.

Next a matrix M is entered. A bracketed sequence of entries, [...], is called a *list* within *Maple*. Thus, the command in which a matrix is entered shows that a matrix is a list of lists, with each individual list making up a row of the matrix. *Maple* displays the matrix in response to the command to confirm that it has been entered.

In the three commands following entry of the matrix, we change the matrix entry in row 3 and column 2, then display the matrix to confirm the change, and then calculate the inverse of M and assign it to M2.

Listing 2.7.1

```
> with(linalg):
```

```
> M:=matrix([[2,1,3,1],[2,6,5,2],[4,-1,5,2],[2,0,1,5]]);
```

$$
M := \begin{bmatrix} 2 & 1 & 3 & 1 \\ 2 & 6 & 5 & 2 \\ 4 & -1 & 5 & 2 \\ 2 & 0 & 1 & 5 \end{bmatrix}
$$

```
> M[3,2]:=2;
```

$$
M[3, 2] := 2
$$

```
> evalm(M);
```

$$
\begin{bmatrix} 2 & 1 & 3 & 1 \\ 2 & 6 & 5 & 2 \\ 4 & 2 & 5 & 2 \\ 2 & 0 & 1 & 5 \end{bmatrix}
$$

```
>M2:=inverse(M);
```

$$
M2 := \begin{bmatrix} -\dfrac{46}{21} & -5/42 & \dfrac{61}{42} & -2/21 \\ -\dfrac{23}{21} & 4/21 & \dfrac{10}{21} & -1/21 \\ 2 & 0 & -1 & 0 \\ \dfrac{10}{21} & 1/21 & -8/21 & 5/21 \end{bmatrix}
$$

Note that if the entries in the original matrix are not floating point numbers, i.e., do not involve decimals, then the result is given in fractions and is exact.

Exercises

1. Use the matrix inverse computed in Example 2.7.3 to solve the system of equations

$$
\begin{array}{rcrcrcr}
2x_1 & + & x_2 & - & x_3 & = & 5 \\
2x_1 & - & x_2 & + & 2x_3 & = & -2 \\
x_1 & & & & & = & 1.
\end{array}
$$

2. Determine the inverse of each of the following matrices:

(a) $\begin{bmatrix} 0 & 2 \\ 2 & 0 \end{bmatrix}.$

(b) $\begin{bmatrix} -1 & 0 & 5 \\ 0 & -2 & 4 \\ 1 & 2 & 4 \end{bmatrix}.$

(c) $\begin{bmatrix} 1 & -2 & 3 \\ -2 & 5 & -6 \\ 2 & -3 & 6 \end{bmatrix}.$

(d) $\begin{bmatrix} 1 & 0 & 1 & 1 \\ -1 & 1 & 0 & 1 \\ 0 & 1 & -1 & 1 \\ 1 & 1 & 1 & 1 \end{bmatrix}.$

3. Determine the third column of the inverse of the matrix:

$$
\begin{bmatrix}
2 & 4 & 3 & 2 \\
3 & 6 & 5 & 2 \\
2 & 5 & 2 & -3 \\
4 & 5 & 14 & 14
\end{bmatrix}.
$$

4. Use Gauss-Jordan elimination to solve the following two systems of equations:

$$
\begin{cases}
2x_1 & + & 5x_2 & = & 18 \\
-x_1 & + & 3x_2 & = & 13.
\end{cases}
\qquad
\begin{cases}
2x_1 & + & 5x_2 & = & -4 \\
-x_1 & + & 3x_2 & = & -10.
\end{cases}
$$

5. **Elementary matrices** The three basic row operations can be carried out by multiplication by matrices, called *elementary matrices*, that differ only slightly from an identity matrix and have easily obtained inverses. For each of the pairs of matrices below, verify that the first one carries out the indicated operation and that the second is its inverse:

(a) Multiply row three by k, $k \neq 0$:

$$
\begin{bmatrix} 1 & 0 & 0 \\ 0 & 1 & 0 \\ 0 & 0 & k \end{bmatrix}.
\qquad
\begin{bmatrix} 1 & 0 & 0 \\ 0 & 1 & 0 \\ 0 & 0 & \frac{1}{k} \end{bmatrix}.
$$

(b) Interchange rows one and two:

$$\begin{bmatrix} 0 & 1 & 0 \\ 1 & 0 & 0 \\ 0 & 0 & 1 \end{bmatrix}. \qquad \begin{bmatrix} 0 & 1 & 0 \\ 1 & 0 & 0 \\ 0 & 0 & 1 \end{bmatrix}.$$

(c) Add c times row three to row two:

$$\begin{bmatrix} 1 & 0 & 0 \\ 0 & 1 & c \\ 0 & 0 & 1 \end{bmatrix}. \qquad \begin{bmatrix} 1 & 0 & 0 \\ 0 & 1 & -c \\ 0 & 0 & 1 \end{bmatrix}.$$

2.8   Summary and objectives

In this chapter we discussed essential aspects of vectors and matrices that we'll need later. The central problem was the solution of a system of linear equations.

Gaussian elimination is the main tool used in solving systems of linear equations. Gaussian elimination was used both to determine a unique solution, if it existed, and to determine the structure of the set of solutions if a system of equations does not have a unique solution. A modification of Gaussian elimination, Gauss-Jordan elimination, was used to determine the inverse of a nonsingular matrix.

The main concept underlying the solution of systems of equations and the existence of an inverse is linear independence. In this concluding section we summarize the use of Gaussian elimination and the role of linear independence.

Both Gaussian and Gauss-Jordan elimination are accomplished by careful application of the following three row operations:

1. Multiply a row by a nonzero scalar.

2. Subtract a nonzero multiple of one row from another row.

3. Interchange two rows.

Examples 2.6.1 and 2.6.2 demonstrate the application of Gaussian elimination to systems having a unique solution.

A set $\{v_1, v_2, \ldots, v_k\}$ of vectors in a vector space is *linearly independent* if

$$c_1 v_1 + c_2 v_2 + \cdots + c_k v_k = 0$$

implies that $c_i = 0$ for $1 \leq i \leq k$. The theorem below describes the role of linear independence in the solution of systems of equations and the existence of inverses.

Theorem 2.8.1. *Let $S = \{v_1, v_2, \ldots, v_n\}$ be n vectors in R^n and let A be the $n \times n$ matrix having the vectors of S as columns. Then the following are equivalent:*

(a) *S is a linearly independent set.*

(b) *A^{-1} exists, i.e., A is nonsingular.*

(c) *The system of equations $Ax = b$ has a unique solution for any vector $b \in R^n$.*

(d) *Each vector in R^n has a unique representation as a linear combination of the vectors in S.*

Hence, the linear independence of the set of columns of a square matrix A guarantees the existence of a unique solution to the system of linear equations $Ax = b$ for any $b \in R^n$.

The solution is obtained by applying Gaussian elimination to reduce the system of n equations in n variables to a system having one equation in a single variable, one in two variables, and so on, that allows the solution to be determined by back substitution.

If the columns of A are not linearly independent but b is in their span, then a solution exists, but is not unique. In this case, Gaussian elimination shows that the set of solutions is the set of all vectors that can be formed by adding a solution to the homogeneous system $Ax = 0$ to any solution to $Ax = b$. Expressing this set of linear combinations in vector form allows the determination of a basis for the set N_A of solutions to the homogeneous system. Theorem 2.6.4 expresses this result, and Examples 2.6.5 and 2.6.6 demonstrate the solution procedure.

A square matrix A having linearly independent columns has an inverse, i.e., a matrix denoted by A^{-1} such that

$$AA^{-1} = I$$

where I is the identity matrix. Column k of A^{-1} can be seen to be the solution of the system

$$Ax = e_k$$

where e_k is the vector having its kth component equal to 1 and all others equal to 0. Thus, to determine A^{-1} for an $n \times n$ matrix having an inverse, one must solve the n systems of equations

$$Ax = e_k, \ k = 1, 2, \ldots, n.$$

   We used Gauss-Jordan elimination to efficiently solve this set of equations. Gauss-Jordan elimination is a modification of Gaussian elimination that lends itself to the solution of several systems of equations that have the same matrix of coefficients. Example 2.7.2 demonstrates Gauss-Jordan elimination, and Example 2.7.3 demonstrates its use to determine an inverse.

Objectives

The following objectives describe what the student should be able to do at the conclusion of the chapter. For most objectives a typical example and exercise are indicated.

1. Perform the vector operations of addition, scalar multiplication, and formation of a linear combination. Example 2.3.1. Exercise 2 of Section 2.3.

2. Use summation notation. Exercise 6 of Section 2.2.

3. Use the scalar product to describe linear functions. Example 2.2.1. Exercise 7 of Section 2.2.

4. Perform the matrix operations of addition, multiplication by a scalar, multiplication, and transpose. Examples 2.4.4 and 2.4.5. Exercises 1 and 2 of Section 2.4.

5. Determine the inverse of a 2×2 matrix and use it to solve a system of equations. Example 2.4.6. Exercise 6 of Section 2.4.

6. Define linearly independent set of vectors and determine if a set of vectors is linearly independent. Example 2.5.3. Exercises 6 and 7 of Section 2.5.

7. Form the negation of a given sentence, or the converse or contrapositive of a given proposition. Examples 2.5.2 and 2.5.6. Exercises 1, 3, and 4 of Section 2.5.

8. Be able to demonstrate understanding of the proofs in Section 2.5 Linear Independence. Exercise 5 of Section 2.5.

9. Solve a system of n linear equations in n unknowns for $n = 2, 3, 4$ by Gaussian elimination. Examples 2.6.1, 2.6.5. Exercise 1 of Section 2.6.

10. Classify a system of linear equations as consistent, inconsistent, or redundent. Section 2.6.

11. Determine the rank and nullity of a matrix, and know their definitions. Example 2.6.5. Exercise 6 of Section 2.6.

12. Determine if a given vector lies in the span of a given set of vectors. Example 2.6.2. Exercise 4 of Section 2.6.

13. Determine the set of all solutions to a system of linear equations having a nonunique solution and express the set in vector form. Example 2.6.5. Exercise 8 of Section 2.6.

14. Use Gauss-Jordan elimination to solve several systems of linear equations having the same matrix of coefficients. Example 2.7.2. Exercise 4 of Section 2.7.

15. Determine the inverse of an $n \times n$ matrix, $n = 2, 3, 4$, or show that the inverse does not exist. Example 2.7.3. Exercise 2 of Section 2.7.

16. Determine a specific column of the inverse of a given matrix. Example 2.7.2. Exercise 3 of Section 2.7.

17. Discuss the role of linear independence of a set of vectors as related to systems of linear equations and the existence of a matrix inverse. Theorem 2.8.1.

Chapter 3

Linear Programming

3.1   Introduction

In this chapter we consider one of the most important and versatile managerial tools: linear programming. Several problems from Chapter 1 are of this type, so you have already been exposed to some areas in which linear programming is frequently applied, as well as the graphical solution method.

The most common objectives of linear programming are to maximize some measure of profit or to minimize a cost. Correspondingly, there are fundamentally two types of problems to consider – one maximizing an objective and one minimizing an objective.

These two problems are stated below in general form:

$$
\begin{aligned}
\text{(MLP)} \quad \text{Maximize}: \quad & z = c_1 x_1 + c_2 x_2 + \cdots + c_n x_n \\
\text{Subject to}: \quad & a_{11} x_1 + a_{12} x_2 + \cdots + a_{1n} x_n \;\leq\; b_1 \\
& \qquad\qquad\qquad \vdots \\
& a_{m1} x_1 + a_{m2} x_2 + \cdots + a_{mn} x_n \;\leq\; b_m \\
& x_1 \geq 0, \; x_2 \geq 0, \; \ldots, \; x_n \geq 0
\end{aligned}
$$

Aside from the change of objective, the key difference between the problems is the direction of the inequalities in the constraints.

$$
\begin{aligned}
\text{(mLP)} \quad \text{Minimize}: \quad & w = d_1 y_1 + d_2 y_2 + \cdots + d_m y_m \\
\text{Subject to}: \quad & e_{11} y_1 + e_{12} y_2 + \cdots + e_{1m} y_m \;\geq\; f_1 \\
& \qquad\qquad\qquad \vdots \\
& e_{n1} y_1 + e_{n2} y_2 + \cdots + e_{nm} y_m \;\geq\; f_n \\
& y_1 \geq 0, \; y_2 \geq 0, \; \ldots, \; y_m \geq 0
\end{aligned}
$$

81

As we saw in Chapter 1, the term *linear* in *linear programming* follows because all the expressions involved are linear. The term *programming* indicates that the problems can be solved by an algorithm that will terminate in finitely many steps. The main goal in this chapter is to study the fundamental algorithm for linear programming, called the simplex algorithm. The simplex algorithm will employ the row operations used previously in Gaussian elimination.

In Chapter 1 we used a geometric approach to solve the linear program below to decide how many acres of wheat and corn Farmer Jones should plant to maximize revenue:

$$
\begin{array}{rrcrcl}
\text{Maximize}: & 80x & + & 60y & & \\
\text{Subject to}: & x & + & y & \leq & 100 \\
& 2x & + & y & \leq & 150 \\
& 5x & + & 10y & \leq & 800 \\
& \multicolumn{5}{c}{x \geq 0, y \geq 0}
\end{array}
$$

We concluded that he should plant 50 acres of each crop and would have $50 left. However, since the geometric method is limited to problems having only two variables, we could not have solved it if more crops had been involved.

As a first step toward the simplex algorithm to be used in larger problems, in the next section we will reexamine Farmer Jones' problem and introduce variables to account for excess resources like the extra $50 in cash.

Principal emphasis will be on the maximization problem (MLP). We will see that minimization problems of type (mLP) are solved by solving an associated maximizing problem.

Later in the chapter we will develop extensions of the simplex algorithm to problems in which the variables are not required to be nonnegative or in which the constraints are equalities or inequalities in a direction opposite to that found in (MLP) or (mLP).

A key tool is the analysis of the effect of changes in the problem, such as in the resources or in the objective function coefficients. This analysis will follow from the interplay between a pair of problems of type (MLP) and (mLP) and has great value in managerial planning.

Later, in Chapter 7, we will consider the addition of a constraint in the context of solving linear programs with variables constrained to be integers. We will see that the use of integer variables greatly expands the scope of the applications.

3.2 Slack variables

This section begins development of the method of algebraic solution of linear programs. The step taken here is to introduce a type of variable which aids both in the understanding of the significance of the solution and in the solution process itself. A *slack variable* is one that is introduced into a constraint to represent unused resources and to allow inequality constraints to be replaced by equalities. To illustrate, recall Farmer Jones' problem from Example 1.4.1.

Example 3.2.1. Farmer Jones has 100 acres of land to devote to wheat and corn and wishes to plan his planting to maximize the expected revenue. Jones has only $800 in capital to apply to planting the crops, and it costs $5 to plant an acre of wheat and $10 for an acre of corn. Their other activities leave the Jones family only 150 days of labor to devote to the crops. Two days will be required for each acre of wheat and one day for an acre of corn. If past experience indicates a return of $80 from each acre of wheat and $60 from each acre of corn, how many acres of each should be planted to maximize his revenue?

With x_1 denoting the number of acres of wheat and x_2 the number of acres of corn, we saw that this problem leads to the linear program below of type (MLP):

$$
\begin{aligned}
\text{Maximize}: \quad & 80x_1 + 60x_2 \\
\text{Subject to}: \quad & x_1 + x_2 \le 100 \\
& 2x_1 + x_2 \le 150 \\
& 5x_1 + 10x_2 \le 800 \\
& x_1 \ge 0, \; x_2 \ge 0
\end{aligned}
$$

Although the problem appears to involve only two variables, the solution is fully described only when, besides concluding that 50 acres of each crop should be planted, we note that there will be $50 unspent, all days will be worked, and all acres will be planted. Thus, three other quantities are involved in the problem – the unused resources, such as the unspent $50. These quantities will be represented by slack variables.

If a nonnegative slack variable s_i is introduced into the ith constraint of the problem and the constraint made an equality, then the problem becomes:

$$
\begin{aligned}
\text{Maximize}: \quad & 80x_1 \;+\; 60x_2 \\
\text{Subject to}: \quad & x_1 \;+\; x_2 \;+\; s_1 \qquad\qquad\qquad\;\; = \;\; 100 \\
& 2x_1 \;+\; x_2 \qquad\quad\; +\; s_2 \qquad\qquad = \;\; 150 \\
& 5x_1 \;+\; 10x_2 \qquad\qquad\qquad +\; s_3 \; = \;\; 800 \\
& x_1 \geq 0,\; x_2 \geq 0,\; s_1 \geq 0,\; s_2 \geq 0,\; s_3 \geq 0
\end{aligned}
$$

We observe a very important characteristic in the resulting system of equations. In each equation there is a variable which occurs in only that equation and has 1 as its coefficient. We call these *isolated variables*, and will find them useful in determining a first solution.

Dropping the variables and labeling the columns by the corresponding variables, we obtain the following matrix:

$$
\begin{array}{ccccc|c}
x_1 & x_2 & s_1 & s_2 & s_3 & \\
1 & 1 & 1 & 0 & 0 & 100 \\
2 & 1 & 0 & 1 & 0 & 150 \\
5 & 10 & 0 & 0 & 1 & 800
\end{array}
$$

The inclusion of the slack variables enables us to easily obtain solutions of a very special type. These solutions have only three nonzero variables, one for each constraint, and at all times the nonzero variables are isolated variables and therefore correspond to columns of an identity matrix. Such solutions are called *basic solutions*, and the corresponding set of isolated variables is called the *basis*.

The first basic solution is obtained by setting each isolated variable equal to the corresponding right-hand-side entry in the matrix above and setting the remaining variables equal to zero:

$$
x_1 = 0,\; x_2 = 0,\; s_1 = 100,\; s_2 = 150,\; s_3 = 800.
$$

Here the basis is the set $\{s_1, s_2, s_3\}$. This solution corresponds to the origin in Figure 3.2.1 and reflects the situation where no crops are planted.

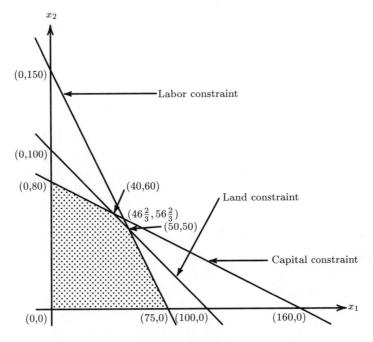

Figure 3.2.1

Notice that in the figure the point $(75, 0)$ is obtained by increasing x_1 until a constraint – here the days of labor available – is encountered. The result is that in the corresponding solution, 75 acres of wheat will be planted and all days will be worked. Thus, $s_2 = 0$. In terms of the matrix, this is accomplished by a pivoting operation to transform the column $[1, 2, 5]^T$ corresponding to the number of acres of wheat into $[0, 1, 0]^T$, the current column associated with the number of days unworked. Hence, we pivot on the 2 in the first column in order to replace it by a 1, and obtain the matrix below:

$$
\begin{array}{ccccc|c}
x_1 & x_2 & s_1 & s_2 & s_3 & \\
0 & \frac{1}{2} & 1 & -\frac{1}{2} & 0 & 25 \\
1 & \frac{1}{2} & 0 & \frac{1}{2} & 0 & 75 \\
0 & \frac{15}{2} & 0 & -\frac{5}{2} & 1 & 425
\end{array}
$$

The new basic solution

$$x_1 = 75, \ x_2 = 0, \ s_1 = 25, \ s_2 = 0, \ s_3 = 425$$

reflects the situation when 75 acres of wheat and none of corn are planted, leaving 25 acres unplanted, using all the labor, and leaving \$425 of capital unspent. The basis here is the set $\{x_1, s_1, s_3\}$.

Geometrically, the next basic solution is obtained by following the labor constraint along the edge of the set of feasible solutions until another constraint – here the acreage constraint – is encountered. Thus, the next solution is obtained by letting x_2 become positive and setting s_1, the number of unplanted acres, to 0. This requires that we pivot on the entry in the column of x_2, the variable to become positive, and in the row of s_1, the variable being set to zero, which is the $\frac{1}{2}$ in the $(1, 2)$ position:

$$
\begin{array}{ccccc|c}
x_1 & x_2 & s_1 & s_2 & s_3 & \\
0 & 1 & 2 & -1 & 0 & 50 \\
1 & 0 & -1 & 1 & 0 & 50 \\
0 & 0 & -15 & 5 & 1 & 50
\end{array}
$$

The new solution

$$x_1 = 50, \; x_2 = 50, \; s_1 = 0, \; s_2 = 0, \; s_3 = 50$$

reflects the situation when 50 acres of each crop are planted, all acres are planted, all days allotted are worked, and \$50 of capital remain. Figure 3.2.2 indicates how to determine graphically that this is the optimal solution.

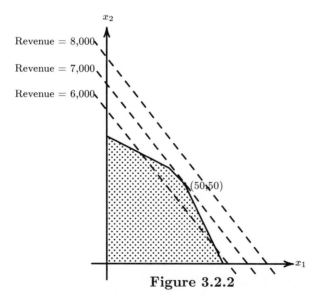

Figure 3.2.2

The three broken lines in the figure are lines of equal revenue corresponding to revenue levels of \$6,000, \$7,000, and \$8,000. Since the \$6,000 and \$7,000 lines both intersect the set of feasible solutions, both represent attainable levels of revenue. Note that the \$7,000 line meets the set of feasible solutions in a single point – the point $(50, 50)$ corresponding to the current basic solution. All lines corresponding to higher levels of revenue miss the set of feasible solutions. Thus, the point $(50, 50)$ corresponds to the highest possible level of revenue. ∎

A constraint is said to be *slack* in a solution if the corresponding slack variable is positive; otherwise, a constraint is said to be *tight.* A tight constraint is affecting the solution, while a slack constraint is not. Here, the first and second constraints are tight in the optimal solution, and the third constraint is slack since \$50 is left over.

The selection of the pivots in this example was made possible by the geometric insight gained from Figure 3.2.1. The conclusion that the solution was optimal also relied on geometric evidence from the lines of equal revenue. In order to use this method when such geometric insight is not present, the simplex algorithm to be introduced in the next section will rely on a series of rules to determine the succession of pivots and to decide when an optimal solution has been reached.

Exercises

1. Consider the linear program:

$$
\begin{aligned}
\text{Maximize}: \quad & 12x_1 \ + \ 20x_2 \\
\text{Subject to}: \quad & 2x_1 \ + \quad x_2 \ \le \ 100 \\
& -3x_1 \ + \ 5x_2 \ \le \ 240 \\
& x_1 \qquad\qquad \le \ 40 \\
& x_1 \ge 0, \ x_2 \ge 0
\end{aligned}
$$

Draw the set of feasible solutions and relate the "corners" to basic solutions.

2. Consider the linear program:

$$
\begin{aligned}
\text{Maximize}: \quad & 40x_1 \ + \ 15x_2 \\
\text{Subject to}: \quad & x_1 \ + \quad x_2 \ \le \quad 100 \\
& \qquad\qquad x_2 \ \le \quad 75 \\
& 20x_1 \ + \ 15x_2 \ \le \ 1{,}900 \\
& x_1 \ge 0, \ x_2 \ge 0
\end{aligned}
$$

Draw the set of feasible solutions and relate the "corners" to basic solutions.

3. Consider the following linear program:

$$
\begin{array}{rlrcr}
\text{Maximize}: & 5x_1 & + & 2x_2 & \\
\text{Subject to}: & x_1 & - & x_2 & \leq & 10 \\
& x_1 & + & 2x_2 & \leq & 40 \\
& & & x_2 & \leq & 15 \\
\end{array}
$$
$$ x_1 \geq 0, \quad x_2 \geq 0 $$

(a) Draw the set of feasible solutions and label the feasible corners.

(b) Determine the solution.

(c) Draw level curves of the objective function, including one corresponding to the optimal value, one corresponding to a value higher than the optimal value, and one corresponding to a value lower than the optimal value.

4. Consider the linear program:

$$
\begin{array}{rlrcr}
\text{Maximize}: & 10x_1 & + & 12x_2 & \\
\text{Subject to}: & x_1 & + & x_2 & \leq & 150 \\
& x_1 & + & 2x_2 & \leq & 100 \\
& 8x_1 & + & 4x_2 & \leq & 320 \\
\end{array}
$$
$$ x_1 \geq 0, \quad x_2 \geq 0 $$

Insert slack variables. By using a pivoting operation, determine a basic solution in which the resource in the third constraint is exhausted, the other two constraints are slack, and x_1 has a positive value.

5. Consider the linear program:

$$
\begin{array}{rlrcr}
\text{Maximize}: & 5x_1 & + & 4x_2 & \\
\text{Subject to}: & -4x_1 & + & 2x_2 & \leq & 8 \\
& x_1 & & & \leq & 7 \\
& 3x_1 & + & 2x_2 & \leq & 29 \\
\end{array}
$$
$$ x_1 \geq 0, \quad x_2 \geq 0 $$

Insert slack variables. By using a pivoting operation, determine a basic solution in which the resource in the second constraint is exhausted, the other two constraints are slack, and x_1 has a positive value.

6. Insert slack variables in the linear program of the previous problem. By pivoting, determine a basic solution in which the second constraint is tight, the other two constraints are slack, and x_2 has a positive value.

7. In the example, we moved from the solution $(75, 0)$ to $(50, 50)$ by proceeding along the labor constraint until the acreage constraint was encountered. Show that, had we ignored this constraint and gone on until the capital constraint was encountered by pivoting on the $\frac{15}{2}$, then the nonfeasible solution $(46\frac{2}{3}, 56\frac{2}{3})$ would have been obtained.

Capital Constraint: $5x_1 + 10x_2 \leq 800$

8. In our solution process for Example 3.2.1 we considered only three points: $(0,0)$, $(75,0)$, and $(50,50)$. However, ten points are identified in Figure 3.2.1. For each of the other seven, determine the values of the slack variables and decide which constraints, if any, are violated. Which of these points correspond to feasible plantings of crops by by Farmer Jones?

3.3   The simplex algorithm

The solution of a maximizing linear program of type (MLP) is determined by generating a sequence of basic feasible solutions corresponding to increasing values of the objective function. Section 3.2 showed that such a sequence can be generated by Gauss-Jordan pivoting operations. In the next section we will establish that we need consider only basic solutions.

In this section we add the objective function to the system of equations as studied in the previous section and develop a set of rules to select the pivots. This set of rules is the central topic of the chapter and will also influence the material in the next chapter. In Section 3.6 we will modify these rules to allow for the solution of any maximizing linear program.

The process is illustrated by the following example.

Example 3.3.1. Consider Farmer Jones' problem from Sections 1.4 and 3.2:

$$
\begin{aligned}
\text{Maximize}: \quad & z = 80x_1 + 60x_2 \\
\text{Subject to}: \quad & x_1 + x_2 \leq 100 \\
& 2x_1 + x_2 \leq 150 \\
& 5x_1 + 10x_2 \leq 800 \\
& x_1 \geq 0, \; x_2 \geq 0
\end{aligned}
$$

The first step is to restate the problem with slack variables and with all variables of the objective function written on the left side with the value of the objective function last:

$$
\begin{aligned}
-80x_1 - 60x_2 \qquad\qquad\qquad + z &= 0 \\
x_1 + x_2 + s_1 \qquad\qquad\qquad &= 100 \\
2x_1 + x_2 \qquad + s_2 \qquad\qquad &= 150 \\
5x_1 + 10x_2 \qquad\qquad + s_3 \qquad &= 800
\end{aligned}
$$

We next drop the variables and consider the matrix of coefficients. We single out the objective row – which we now move to the bottom – and the column of constants because they will require special treatment.

x_1	x_2	s_1	s_2	s_3	z	
1	1	1	0	0	0	100
2	1	0	1	0	0	150
5	10	0	0	1	0	800
-80	-60	0	0	0	1	0

This matrix is called the *simplex tableau.* Having described it, we can set down the rules of the simplex algorithm. ■

In studying the rules of the simplex algorithm, it is helpful to recall that the negative entries in the last row were derived from the revenues, so they represent opportunities to increase the value of the objective function.

THE SIMPLEX ALGORITHM

Rule 1. Obtain the **initial basic solution** by setting each slack variable equal to the corresponding resource and setting the other variables equal to zero.

Subsequent solutions are obtained by a succession of pivoting operations to make positive a variable that had been zero and vice versa. The variable becoming positive is called the *entering variable*, since it is entering the basis, and the one becoming zero is called the *departing variable*.

Rule 2. Choose the **entering variable** from among those having negative coefficients in the objective row. Usually the one having the most negative coefficient is selected; in case of a tie, choose arbitrarily from among those tied.

Selection of the departing variable depends upon the *replacement quantities*—the nonnegative quotients that can be formed by dividing the resource by a positive entry in the column of the entering variable. *Note that only a row having a positive entry in the column of the entering variable will produce a replacement quantity.*

Rule 3 identifies the departing variable by examining the replacement quantities. This rule also maintains nonnegativity by selecting the value of the entering variable from among the replacement quantities so that no variable will be negative in the next solution.

Rule 3. Choose the **departing variable** to be the basic variable in the row producing the smallest replacement quantity.

Having chosen the entering and the departing variables, pivot on the entry in the row of the departing variable and the column of the entering variable.

The remaining rules determine when the algorithm should terminate and identify the status of the solution. In particular, the algorithm must recognize an unbounded problem, when an optimal solution has been reached, and when alternative optimal solutions exist.

Rule 4. There is **no upper bound** on the objective function when one column has entirely nonpositive coefficients above a negative coefficient in the objective row.

The absence of an upper bound is detected when applying Rule 3. Where no replacement quantities can be found there is no upper bound. Geometrically, the replacement quantities represent points where the increase in the value of the entering variable is limited by constraints. When no replacement quantity exists the value of the variable can be increased without bound.

Rule 5. The solution is **optimal** when all entries in the objective row are nonnegative.

Rule 6. If all basic variables are positive, an optimal solution is **not unique** if in the optimal tableau a zero occurs in the objective row in a column corresponding to a nonbasic variable and including a positive entry.

A second optimal basic solution with the same optimal objective function value can be obtained by pivoting in a column identified by Rule 6. We will consider the the complications arising from a basic variable being zero in the solution, called a degenerate solution, in Example 3.3.2.

An example illustrating a combination of Rules 4 and 6 is presented in the final exercise at the end of the section.

The implementation of these rules is summarized in the flowchart in Figure 3.3.1.

SIMPLEX ALGORITHM FLOWCHART

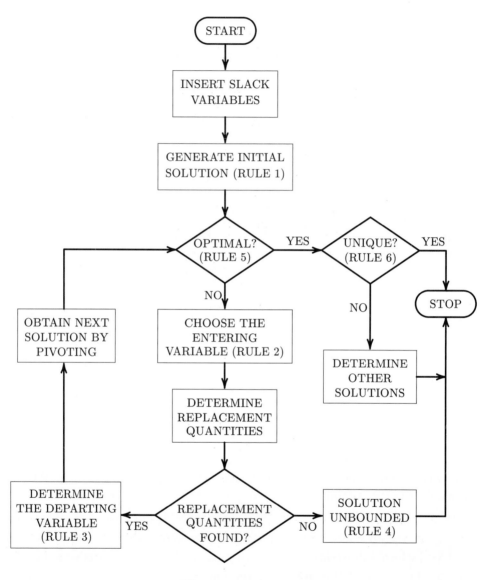

Figure 3.3.1

Now recall the initial simplex tableau for Farmer Jones' problem:

x_1	x_2	s_1	s_2	s_3	z	
1	1	1	0	0	0	100
2	1	0	1	0	0	150
5	10	0	0	1	0	800
-80	-60	0	0	0	1	0

According to Rule 1, the initial solution is

$$x_1 = 0, \ x_2 = 0, \ s_1 = 100, \ s_2 = 150, \ s_3 = 800, \ z = \$0.$$

Since no revenue is produced with this solution, the value of the objective function in the lower right-hand corner is 0.

Since there are two negatives in the objective row, Rule 5 indicates that this solution is not optimal. Rule 2 implies that x_1 should enter the basis, i.e., x_1 should become positive. The replacement quantities are

$$\frac{100}{1} = 100, \quad \frac{150}{2} = 75, \quad \frac{800}{5} = 160.$$

Since the smallest of these is the 75 obtained from the second row, the 2 in row 2 and column 1 will be the pivot. As a consequence, the basic variable appearing in the second row, s_2, will become 0 and nonbasic. This yields the tableau below

x_1	x_2	s_1	s_2	s_3	z	
0	$\frac{1}{2}$	1	$-\frac{1}{2}$	0	0	25
1	$\frac{1}{2}$	0	$\frac{1}{2}$	0	0	75
0	$\frac{15}{2}$	0	$-\frac{5}{2}$	1	0	425
0	-20	0	40	0	1	6,000

in which the basis is $\{x_1, s_1, s_3\}$. Assigning each right-hand-side value to the basic variable having coefficient 1 in the corresponding row yields the new solution:

$$x_1 = 75, \ x_2 = 0, \ s_1 = 25, \ s_2 = 0, \ s_3 = 425, \ z = \$6,000.$$

This corresponds to the x_1-intercept $(75, 0)$ in Figure 3.2.1. The -20 in the objective row indicates that the solution is not optimal (Rule 5) and that x_2 should enter the basis in the next solution (Rule 2). The replacement quantities are

$$\frac{25}{\frac{1}{2}} = 50, \quad \frac{75}{\frac{1}{2}} = 150, \quad \frac{425}{\frac{15}{2}} = 56\frac{2}{3}.$$

Since the smallest value occurs in the first row, Rule 3 indicates that we should pivot on the $\frac{1}{2}$ in row 1 and column 2:

x_1	x_2	s_1	s_2	s_3	z	
0	1	2	-1	0	0	50
1	0	-1	1	0	0	50
0	0	-15	5	1	0	50
0	0	40	20	0	1	7,000

The new basis is $\{x_1, x_2, s_3\}$ and the new solution is

$$x_1 = 50, \; x_2 = 50, \; s_1 = 0, \; s_2 = 0, \; s_3 = 50, \; z = \$7,000.$$

Since the objective row contains no negative entries, we see from Rule 5 that this is the optimal solution. Further, since none of the entries corresponding to the nonbasic variables (here s_1 and s_2) in the objective row are zero, the solution is unique (Rule 6).

Note that no change has occurred in the column corresponding to z. No change can ever occur in the z column because all entries except the objective row entry are zero. Thus, this column can be omitted. The last entry in the last column will remain the current value of the objective function.

Rule 2 of the simplex algorithm indicates that the entering variable can be chosen arbitrarily from among those having negative coefficients in the objective row, but that usually the variable with the most negative entry is selected. In particular, in case of a tie, it does not matter which variable is chosen.

The case in which there is a tie in Rule 3, i.e., in which two or more rows yield the smallest replacement quantity, is more serious. The result is a basic feasible solution in which one of the basic variables is zero. The following example illustrates this situation.

Example 3.3.2. Solve the linear program:

$$
\begin{aligned}
\text{Maximize}: \quad & 50x_1 \;+\; 40x_2 \\
\text{Subject to}: \quad & 3x_1 \;+\; 2x_2 \;\leq\; 120 \\
& x_1 \;+\; 6x_2 \;\leq\; 120 \\
& 2x_1 \;+\; x_2 \;\leq\; 80 \\
& x_1 \geq 0, \; x_2 \geq 0
\end{aligned}
$$

Figure 3.3.2 shows the graph of the set of feasible solutions.

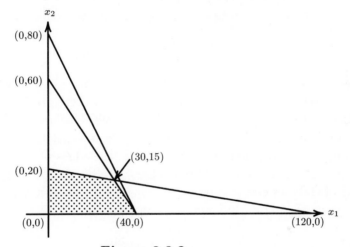

Figure 3.3.2

By introducing a slack variable s_i into constraint i for each of the constraints, we obtain the initial simplex tableau:

x_1	x_2	s_1	s_2	s_3	
3	2	1	0	0	120
1	6	0	1	0	120
2	1	0	0	1	80
−50	−40	0	0	0	0

Making x_1 positive will lead directly to a tie for the smallest replacement quantity. The replacement quantities are:

$$
\frac{120}{3} = 40, \quad \frac{120}{1} = 120, \quad \frac{80}{2} = 40.
$$

There is a tie between the first and third rows; we arbitrarily choose the third and pivot on the 2 in row 3 and column 1, producing the tableau:

x_1	x_2	s_1	s_2	s_3	
0	$\frac{1}{2}$	1	0	$-\frac{3}{2}$	0
0	$\frac{11}{2}$	0	1	$-\frac{1}{2}$	80
1	$\frac{1}{2}$	0	0	$\frac{1}{2}$	40
0	-15	0	0	25	2,000

The tie for smallest replacement quantity has produced a basic solution

$$x_1 = 40, \ x_2 = 0, \ s_1 = 0, \ s_2 = 80, \ s_3 = 0$$

in which there are only two positive variables: x_1 and s_2. The third basic variable, s_1, is zero. Such a basic solution, in which there are fewer positive variables than constraints, is called a *degenerate basic solution.*

Figure 3.3.2 indicates what has occurred. We see that the point $(40, 0)$ corresponding to the degenerate solution lies on the edges of the half-planes representing three constraints. Stated algebraically, the point lies at the intersection of three lines:

$$
\begin{aligned}
3x_1 &+ 2x_2 &=& \ 120 \\
2x_1 &+ \ x_2 &=& \ 80 \\
&\ \ \ x_2 &=& \ 0
\end{aligned}
$$

The result has been to simultaneously exhaust two resources; i.e., s_1 and s_3 have both been set to zero. The variable s_3 was intentionally set to zero by the choice of the pivoting operation which made x_1 the new basic variable in the third row. However, s_1 became zero because the edge of the half-plane corresponding to the first constraint happened to pass through the point $(40, 0)$.

An immediate possible consequence of a degenerate solution is that the next replacement quantity may be zero, as happens when x_2 becomes basic in the next tableau:

x_1	x_2	s_1	s_2	s_3	
0	1	2	0	-3	0
0	0	-11	1	16	80
1	0	-1	0	2	40
0	0	30	0	-20	2,000

The variable x_2 is now basic, but is zero. The new solution remains degenerate and, like the previous one, corresponds to the point $(40, 0)$. Since the value of the objective function did not change as a result of the iteration, there is a miniscule possibility that the simplex algorithm could now enter a sequence of iterations with the same objective function value that would lead it back to this one. The result would be to put the simplex algorithm into an infinite loop and prevent it from reaching the optimal solution. Such behavior, called *cycling*, rarely occurs in practice. In most instances the simplex algorithm goes on to determine an optimal solution. Here, s_3 becomes basic in the next iteration:

x_1	x_2	s_1	s_2	s_3	
0	1	$-\frac{1}{16}$	$\frac{3}{16}$	0	15
0	0	$-\frac{11}{16}$	$\frac{1}{16}$	1	5
1	0	$\frac{3}{8}$	$-\frac{1}{8}$	0	30
0	0	$\frac{65}{4}$	$\frac{5}{4}$	0	$2,100$

Note that in selecting the row of the pivot, row 1 was not considered because the -3 in row 1 and the column of s_3 prevented a replacement quantity from being calculated in row 1. Thus, 0 was not a replacement quantity.

This solution is not degenerate, and the value of the objective function has increased, so cycling has been avoided. In fact, it has reached its optimal value at the point $(30, 15)$. ∎

While cycling is rare, E. Beale in [2] concocted an example in which it does occur.

Exercises

1. Solve by the simplex algorithm:

$$
\begin{array}{rrrrl}
\text{Maximize}: & 20x_1 & + & 30x_2 & \\
\text{Subject to}: & x_1 & + & x_2 & \leq 4 \\
& -x_1 & + & x_2 & \leq 1 \\
& 2x_1 & + & 4x_2 & \leq 10 \\
& \multicolumn{4}{c}{x_1 \geq 0, x_2 \geq 0}
\end{array}
$$

2. Solve by the simplex algorithm:

$$\text{Maximize}: \quad 10x_1 \;+\; 12x_2$$
$$\text{Subject to}: \quad x_1 \;+\;\;\; x_2 \;\le\; 150$$
$$x_1 \;+\; 2x_2 \;\le\; 100$$
$$8x_1 \;+\; 4x_2 \;\le\; 320$$
$$x_1 \ge 0, x_2 \ge 0$$

3. Solve by the simplex algorithm:

$$\text{Maximize}: \quad 20x_1 \;+\; 6x_2 \;+\; 8x_3$$
$$\text{Subject to}: \quad 8x_1 \;+\; 2x_2 \;+\; 3x_3 \;\le\; 400$$
$$4x_1 \;+\; 3x_2 \qquad\qquad \le\; 200$$
$$x_3 \;\le\; 40$$
$$x_1 \ge 0, x_2 \ge 0, x_3 \ge 0$$

4. Consider the following smplex tableau:

x_1	x_2	s_1	s_2	s_3	
-2	0	1	$-\frac{3}{2}$	0	2
1	1	0	$\frac{1}{2}$	0	4
3	0	0	$\frac{1}{2}$	1	9
-1	0	0	$\frac{1}{2}$	0	4

(a) Determine the basic feasible solution corresponding to this tableau.

(b) Determine the next tableau.

(c) Is the solution corresponding to the tableau you calculated optimal? Why or why not?

5. Consider the following simplex tableau:

x_1	x_2	x_3	s_1	s_2	s_3	
-2	1	4	$\frac{1}{2}$	0	0	24
3	0	3	$-\frac{3}{2}$	1	0	9
2	0	-1	-1	0	1	8
-4	0	-5	3	0	0	64

(a) Determine the basic feasible solution corresponding to this tableau.

(b) Determine the next tableau if x_1 is made a basic variable.

(c) Does the tableau that results from (b) above represent an optimal solution?

6. Using the simplex algorithm, determine two optimal basic feasible solutions to the problem. Draw a graph of the set of feasible solutions, including the level curve of the objective function corresponding to the optimal value, to indicate the situation graphically.

$$\begin{array}{rrrrr}
\text{Maximize}: & 30x_1 & + & 40x_2 & \\
\text{Subject to}: & 2x_1 & + & 5x_2 & \leq & 90 \\
& 3x_1 & + & 4x_2 & \leq & 100 \\
& \multicolumn{4}{c}{x_1 \geq 0, x_2 \geq 0}
\end{array}$$

7. Solve by the simplex algorithm:

$$\begin{array}{rrrrrrr}
\text{Maximize}: & 4x_1 & + & 5x_2 & + & 2x_3 & \\
\text{Subject to}: & x_1 & + & 2x_2 & + & x_3 & \leq & 10 \\
& x_1 & + & 3x_2 & + & 2x_3 & \leq & 18 \\
& \multicolumn{5}{c}{x_1 \geq 0, x_2 \geq 0, x_3 \geq 0}
\end{array}$$

8. In any simplex tableau, consider the matrix formed by the entries in the columns of the slack variables and the rows of the constraints. The right hand side of the tableau is the product of that matrix with the right-hand side from the initial tableau. Confirm this for the three tableaux of Example 3.3.1.

9. **Inverses and the simplex algorithm.** The entries in the columns of the slack variables above the objective row form the inverse of the matrix formed from the columns in the original tableau corresponding to the variables which are basic in the current tableau. To confirm this observation, examine the matrices below associated with last two tableaux of Example 3.3.1. Note that the position of the original columns is determined by the row in which the variable is basic; i.e., in the optimal tableau x_2 is basic in the first constraint and its original simplex column is first, while x_1 is basic in the second constraint and its original column appears second. Confirm that:

(a) $\begin{bmatrix} 1 & -\frac{1}{2} & 0 \\ 0 & \frac{1}{2} & 0 \\ 0 & -\frac{5}{2} & 1 \end{bmatrix}$ is the inverse of $\begin{bmatrix} 1 & 1 & 0 \\ 0 & 2 & 0 \\ 0 & 5 & 1 \end{bmatrix}$

(b) $\begin{bmatrix} 2 & -1 & 0 \\ -1 & 1 & 0 \\ -15 & 5 & 1 \end{bmatrix}$ is the inverse of $\begin{bmatrix} 1 & 1 & 0 \\ 1 & 2 & 0 \\ 10 & 5 & 1 \end{bmatrix}$

10. **Inverses in Farmer Jones problem.** The entries in the columns of the slack variables in a tableau form the inverse of the matrix formed from the columns in the original tableau corresponding to the current set of basic variables. The order of the columns is determined by the order of the rows in which the variables are basic.

(a) Observing that in the final tableau for Example 3.2.1 x_2 is basic in row 1, x_1 is basic in row 2, and s_3 in row 3, demonstrate the inverse relationship for that tableau.

(b) Demonstrate the inverse relationship for the previous tableau.

11. In the simplex tableau below, several variables are candidates to become basic in the next solution.

x_1	x_2	x_3	s_1	s_2	s_3	s_4	
5	1	0	1	0	0	-3	40
2	0	0	$\frac{1}{2}$	1	0	2	18
$\frac{1}{2}$	0	0	$-\frac{4}{3}$	0	1	3	12
1	0	1	$\frac{2}{3}$	0	0	$\frac{1}{2}$	24
-5	0	0	-2	0	0	-6	245

Which variable should be made basic in the next solution if the goal is:

(a) For the new value of the objective function to be 285? Why?

(b) For the next solution to be degenerate? Why?

(c) To have s_3 be zero in the next solution? Why?

(d) To achieve the greatest increase in the value of the objective function? Why?

(e) To achieve the greatest increase in the objective function *per unit* increase in the new basic variable? Why?

12. Consider the following simplex tableau:

	x_1	x_2	x_3	s_1	s_2	s_3	s_4	
a_1	0	0	1	$\frac{1}{2}$	0	-2	84
a_2	1	0	0	-2	0	$\frac{5}{2}$	225
a_3	0	1	0	$\frac{3}{2}$	0	$\frac{1}{2}$	125
a_4	0	0	0	$-\frac{5}{2}$	1	$-\frac{3}{2}$	65
a_5	0	0	0	40	0	25	700

For each question below, give values $[a_1, \ldots, a_5]^T$ for the first column so that the tableau will satisfy the stated condition. If an entry need only be positive or negative, indicate by a "+" or a "−." Indicate that an entry that can be any number by an "A."

(a) The corresponding solution is optimal and unique.

(b) The corresponding solution is optimal but not unique, and $x_1 = 13$ in the alternative optimal basic solution.

(c) The corresponding solution is not optimal, and in the next solution $s_1 = 0$ and the value of the objective function is 742.

(d) The corresponding solution is not optimal, and in the next solution $x_3 = 0$ and $s_3 = 40$.

13. Solve the following linear program by the simplex algorithm and also draw the set of feasible solutions:

$$
\begin{array}{rrcl}
\text{Maximize}: & & x_2 & \\
\text{Subject to}: & -x_1 + x_2 & \leq & 20 \\
& x_2 & \leq & 40 \\
& x_1 \geq 0, \; x_2 \geq 0 &
\end{array}
$$

How do you interpret the situation?

3.4   Basic feasible solutions and extreme points

In the previous section we introduced the simplex algorithm as a means of moving through a succession of basic solutions, or more informally "corners," until an optimal solution was obtained. In this section we make the term "corner" precise and show that the corners correspond to basic feasible solutions. The discussion will justify the simplex algorithm.

To avoid certain technical complications, *we assume in this section that there are no redundant constraints in the linear program and that the solutions encountered are not degenerate.*

A subset S of R^m is *convex* if for any two points x and y of S the line segment joining x and y given by

$$z = tx + (1 - t)y \quad \text{for } 0 \leq t \leq 1$$

also belongs to S. The points $z = tx + (1 - t)y$ are called *convex combinations* of x and y.

The half-planes graphed in Section 1.4 are clearly convex. As the intersection of half-planes, the set of feasible solutions of a linear program is convex; that is, if x and y are feasible solutions, then all points on the line segment joining x and y are also feasible.

An *extreme point* of a convex set S is a point x such that if x is expressed as a convex combination of two points y and z of S, i.e., if

$$x = ty + (1-t)z \ \text{ for some } t, \ \ 0 < t < 1$$

then $y = z$. Thus, an extreme point of a convex set is one which does not lie in the interior of any line segment of the set. The corners which we referred to in solving linear programs graphically in Section 1.4 are instances of extreme points. Our goal here is to develop an algebraic characterization of extreme points allowing solution of linear programs with more variables which we cannot solve graphically. The algebraic characterization will relate basic solutions and linearly independent sets of vectors.

A *basic solution* to a problem of type (MLP) in which slack variables have been added is obtained by setting all but one variable for each constraint equal to zero and then solving the resulting system.

A *basic feasible solution* is a basic solution in which all coordinates are nonnegative and all constraints are satisfied. An *optimal basic solution* is a basic feasible solution which optimizes the objective function. The set of variables allowed to be nonzero in a basic solution is called the *basis*.

The terms "basic" and "basis" are suggested by the fact that the columns corresponding to the nonzero variables of the basic solutions that we will be considering form a linearly independent set of m vectors in R^m, and thus form a basis for R^m. Since a variable in a linear program usually represents an activity being performed, we will sometimes identify a column of the constraint matrix with the corresponding activity and speak of "interchanging activities" instead of interchanging columns of the matrix.

Before undertaking the theorems of the section, recall that a system of equations $Ax = b$ has a unique solution if and only if b is a linear combination of the columns of A and the columns of A form a linearly independent set. A key property of linear independence that will be needed is that a set which is not linearly independent can be reduced to one that is by eliminating vectors. Finally, recall that a square matrix A has an inverse if and only if the columns of A form a linearly independent set.

In the theorems, we assume that slack variables have been inserted into an n-variable and m-constraint problem of the type (MLP) so that the constraints can be written as equalities. Thus, the problem can be expressed in vector form as

$$\begin{aligned} \text{(LP)} \quad \text{Maximize}: & \quad z = c \cdot x \\ \text{Subject to}: & \quad Ax = b \\ & \quad x \geq 0 \end{aligned}$$

where $x \in R^{n+m}$, $b \in R^m$, and A is an $m \times (n + m)$ matrix. For notational convenience, here the slack variables are not designated by the letter s but are included among the x_i's.

The first theorem identifies basic solutions and extreme points.

Theorem 3.4.1. *A feasible solution $x^T = [x_1, x_2, \ldots, x_{n+m}]$ to the linear program (LP) is an extreme point of the set of feasible solutions if and only if the columns of A with $x_j > 0$ form a linearly independent set.*

Proof. By reindexing the columns and variables if necessary, we may assume that only the first r components of x are positive:

$$x_1 > 0, \ x_2 > 0, \ \ldots, \ x_r > 0, \ x_{r+1} = \cdots = x_{n+m} = 0.$$

We must show that x is an extreme point if and only if the corresponding set of columns $\{A_1, \ldots, A_r\}$ is linearly independent.

We first show that an extreme point satisfies the linear independence condition. We do this by proving the contrapositive:

Assume that this set of columns is not linearly independent, i.e., that there exist coefficients α_j not all zero such that

$$A_1\alpha_1 + A_2\alpha_2 + \cdots + A_r\alpha_r = 0.$$

Now let α be the vector $\alpha^T = [\alpha_1, \alpha_2, \ldots, \alpha_r, 0, 0, \ldots, 0]$ so that the previous equation becomes

$$A\alpha = 0.$$

Now let $w = x + \lambda\alpha$ and $\overline{w} = x - \lambda\alpha$, and choose λ small enough that $\lambda|\alpha_j| \leq x_j$ for each $j = 1, 2, \ldots, r$. Then both $w \geq 0$ and $\overline{w} \geq 0$. Thus, both w and $\overline{w}$ are feasible solutions, since

$$A(x + \lambda\alpha) = Ax + \lambda A\alpha = Ax + \lambda 0 = b$$

and similarly $A(x - \lambda\alpha) = b$.

However, $x = \frac{1}{2}w + \frac{1}{2}\overline{w}$ shows that x is not an extreme point. This vector calculation is illustrated in Figure 3.4.1.

Thus, we have proved the contrapositive and can conclude that if x is an extreme point, then the set of columns of A corresponding to the positive components of x is linearly independent.

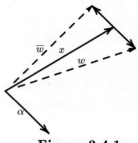

Figure 3.4.1

Conversely, suppose that $\{A_1, \ldots, A_r\}$ is a linearly independent set, and assume that

$$x = ty + (1-t)z, \ \ 0 < t < 1$$

for feasible solutions y and z. We show that $x = y = z$, i.e., that x is an extreme point of the set of feasible solutions. Expressed in terms of individual components,

$$x_j = ty_j + (1-t)z_j, \ \ j = 1, 2, \ldots, n+m.$$

Since $x_j = 0$ for $j > r$ and all components are nonnegative, we conclude that $y_j = 0$ and $z_j = 0$ for $j > r$. Therefore, because y and z are feasible solutions,

$$
\begin{aligned}
A_1 y_1 + A_2 y_2 + \cdots + A_r y_r &= Ay = b, \\
A_1 z_1 + A_2 z_2 + \cdots + A_r z_r &= Az = b
\end{aligned}
$$

and also

$$A_1 x_1 + A_2 x_2 + \cdots + A_r x_r = Ax = b.$$

But since the representation of a vector, here b, as a linear combination of a linearly independent set of vectors is unique, $x = y = z$, and x is an extreme point since y and z are not distinct. $\square$

Having characterized the extreme points among the feasible solutions, we conclude with a second theorem which shows that we need only consider basic feasible solutions in which the basic variables correspond to a linearly independent set of columns of A.

Theorem 3.4.2. *If x is any feasible solution to a bounded problem, then there exists a basic feasible solution x^b such that the columns corresponding to the positive coordinates of x^b form a linearly independent set and*

$$c \cdot x^b \geq c \cdot x.$$

Proof. If the columns corresponding to the nonzero coordinates of x form a linearly independent set, then there is nothing to prove.

Otherwise, let A' be the matrix formed from the columns of A corresponding to the positive components of x. Since the columns of A' are not linearly independent, there exists a nonzero vector y' such that $A'y' = 0$.

Inserting 0 as a component into y' for each column of A not in A', we obtain a nonzero vector y such that $x_i = 0$ implies that $y_i = 0$ and $Ay = 0$, i.e., $y \in N_A$. If y satisfies these properties, then so does $-y$, so that, by possibly exchanging y and $-y$, we may assume that $c \cdot y \geq 0$. Then for any scalar t,

$$A(x + ty) = Ax + tAy = b$$

so that $x + ty$ is also a solution.

There are three cases to consider:

Case 1. If some component of y, say y_i, is negative and $c \cdot y > 0$, then we must also have $x_i > 0$, since x is a feasible solution and $x_i = 0$ implies $y_i = 0$. Then solving $x_i - ty_i = 0$ yields $t = -\frac{x_i}{y_i}$ and causes the ith component of $x + ty$ to be zero for a positive value of t. Then increasing t from $t = 0$ to $t = -\frac{x_i}{y_i}$ causes the objective function to increase in value from $c \cdot x$ to $c \cdot x + \left(-\frac{x_i}{y_i}\right) c \cdot y$.

If more than one component of y is negative, then the maximum value of t which will preserve the nonnegativity of $x + ty$ is $\min\{-\frac{x_i}{y_i} : y_i < 0\}$. With this choice of t, $x + ty$ is a feasible solution of $Ax = b$, and

$$c \cdot (x + ty) \geq c \cdot x.$$

Further, $x + ty$ has one fewer nonzero coordinate than x, and if the set of columns corresponding to the nonzero coordinates is not linearly independent, the process can be continued until it is linearly independent without decreasing the value of the objective function.

Case 2. If $c \cdot y > 0$ and all components of y are nonnegative, then the vector $x + ty$ is a feasible solution for all positive t, so that

$$c \cdot (x + ty) = c \cdot x + t(c \cdot y)$$

can assume arbitrarily large values and the problem has no bounded maximum.

Case 3. If $c \cdot y = 0$, then we can use either a positive or negative value of t to eliminate one positive coordinate of x in the solution $x + ty$, as long as t is chosen to preserve the nonnegativity of coordinates of the new solution $x + ty$. This elimination can be continued until a solution is obtained for which the columns corresponding to the nonzero coordinates form a linearly independent set. $\square$

Recall that the columns of A belong to R^m, where m is the number of constraints. Then the theorem shows that the optimal solution can be assumed to have no more positive coordinates than there are constraints, and that the columns corresponding to the positive coordinates form a linearly independent set.

The example below will illustrate the key step in the proof of the theorem in the context of Farmer Jones' problem discussed in Example 3.2.1.

Example 3.4.3. Consider Farmer Jones' problem restated in the notation of Theorem 3.4.2. Slack variables have been inserted, making the constraints equalities, and the variables are x_j, $j = 1, \ldots, 5$, instead of indicating the slack variables by s_i's:

$$
\begin{array}{rlllll}
\text{Maximize}: & 80x_1 & + & 60x_2 & & \\
\text{Subject to}: & x_1 & + & x_2 & + & x_3 & & & & = & 100 \\
& 2x_1 & + & x_2 & & & + & x_4 & & = & 150 \\
& 5x_1 & + & 10x_2 & & & & & + & x_5 & = & 800 \\
\end{array}
$$
$$
x_i \geq 0, \ i = 1, 2, \ldots, 5
$$

The vector $x^T = [30, 65, 5, 25, 0]$ is a feasible solution, i.e., it satisfies the equations and has nonnegative components. However, it is not an extreme point of the set of feasible solutions illustrated in Figure 3.2.1. Instead of corresponding to a corner, it corresponds to a point on the line segment joining (0, 80) and (40, 60), as shown in Figure 3.4.2. It is easy to see that the point is on that particular edge of the set of feasible solutions since x_5, the slack variable representing unspent capital, is zero and that line segment lies on the edge of the half-plane determined by the restriction on capital.

Since the set of columns corresponding to the nonzero components of x includes four vectors in R^3, it is not a linearly independent set. Hence, the theorem guarantees the existence of a basic feasible solution x^b having at most three positive components and an objective function value at least as great as that of x.

Note that the objective function value of x is

$$c \cdot x = 80 \cdot 30 + 60 \cdot 65 = 6,300.$$

Using methods suggested by the proof of Theorem 3.4.2, we will determine a basic feasible solution which produces at least as great a value of the objective function.

According to Theorem 3.4.2, if we can determine a solution y to the associated homogeneous system below

$$
\begin{array}{rcrcrcrcrcl}
y_1 & + & y_2 & + & y_3 & & & & & = & 0 \\
2y_1 & + & y_2 & & & + & y_4 & & & = & 0 \\
5y_1 & + & 10y_2 & & & & & + & y_5 & = & 0
\end{array}
$$

such that $c \cdot y > 0$ and $x_j = 0$ implies that $y_j = 0$ for each j, then a basic feasible solution x^b can be found with $c \cdot x^b \geq 6300$. In this case, x^b can have at most three positive components. We start by setting $y_5 = 0$ since $x_5 = 0$. Then choose y_2 and determine y_1 to satisfy the resulting third equation:

$$
5y_1 + 10y_2 = 0.
$$

Choosing $y_2 = 1$, we must then have $y_1 = -2$. Substituting these values in turn into equations one and two yields

$$
y_3 = 1 \quad \text{and} \quad y_4 = 3.
$$

Thus, we have obtained the solution $y^T = [-2, 1, 1, 3, 0]$. Since a component is negative, this example falls under Case 1 of the proof. Since

$$
c \cdot y = 80 \cdot (-2) + 60 \cdot 1 = -100 < 0
$$

and to apply the method of the proof, $c \cdot y$ must be positive, we replace y with $-y$, so that

$$
y^T = [2, -1, -1, -3, 0]
$$

and $c \cdot y = 100 > 0$. Now we determine a scalar t such that $x + ty$ has at most three positive components, remains a feasible solution, and $c \cdot (x + ty) \geq c \cdot x$. Consider the vector

$$
(x + ty)^T = [30 + 2t, 65 - t, 5 - t, 25 - 3t, 0].
$$

Choosing the largest value of t that will make $x + ty$ nonnegative, we get

$$
t = \min \left\{ \frac{65}{1}, \frac{5}{1}, \frac{25}{3} \right\} = 5.
$$

Thus, the new candidate for a basic feasible solution is

$$
(x + 5y)^T = [40, 60, 0, 10, 0].
$$

We see that this solution, having only three positive components, is basic. Figure 3.4.2 shows the set of feasible solutions and illustrates the addition of a multiple of the vector y to x to obtain the basic solution. We also see that the solution obtained corresponds to the extreme point $(40, 60)$.

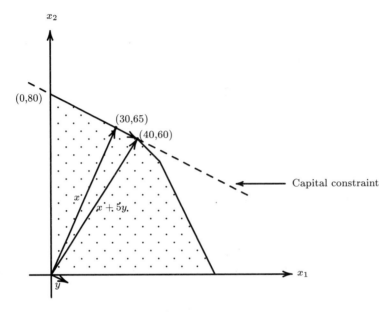

Figure 3.4.2

Finally, the value of the objective function

$$c \cdot (x + 5y) = 6,800$$

has increased. Hence this solution satisfies the requirements of Theorem 3.4.2 in that it has fewer positive components and the value of the objective function has not been decreased. Since this new solution is also basic, it is not necessary to continue eliminating positive components. ∎

The process of selecting the minimum of a set of quotients here is very similar to the method used to identify the row of the pivot in the simplex algorithm. The main difference is that there it was used to move from one basic feasible solution to another instead of from a feasible, but not basic, solution toward a basic feasible solution.

Theorem 3.4.1 showed that basic feasible solutions correspond to extreme points of the set of feasible solutions. Then Theorem 3.4.2 showed that for any feasible solution, there is a basic feasible solution with an objective function value at least as large. Thus, in the search for a solution producing the maximum value, we need only consider basic feasible solutions. Since this is the type of solution generated by the simplex algorithm, to show that the simplex algorithm produces the optimal solution we need only argue that it will reach the basic feasible solution corresponding to the largest value.

The only difficulty in establishing that the simplex algorithm will reach a solution is that there could be a zero replacement quantity that could cause the problem to become degenerate and cycle. As indicated in conjunction with Example 3.3.2, this is an extremely rare occurence. Thus, excluding this case in the next theorem is not a serious drawback.

Theorem 3.4.4. *If a maximum solution exists for a linear program, then the simplex algorithm locates a maximum solution in finitely many steps if no zero replacement quantities are encountered.*

Proof. Since there are only finitely many constraints, their intersections can produce only finitely many basic feasible solutions. By Theorem 3.4.2 the set of optimal solutions must include a basic feasible solution, so the simplex algorithm needs to check only finitely many points.

If each replacement quantity is positive, then the value of the objective function increases with each new basic solution. Thus, a new extreme point is examined for optimality at each iteration, and one producing the maximum value must be reached in finitely many steps. $\square$

Exercises

1. The special convex combination $tx + (1-t)y$ of points x and y, where $t = \frac{1}{2}$, is the *midpoint* of the line segment between x and y. Determine the midpoint of the line segment between $x^T = [2, -3, 4]$ and $y^T = [6, 5, 1]$.

2. A convex combination of three vectors x, y, and z is a vector of the form

$$t_1 x + t_2 y + t_3 z \quad \text{where} \quad t_i \geq 0 \quad \text{and} \quad t_1 + t_2 + t_3 = 1.$$

Every point in a triangle is a convex combination of the vertices of the triangle. Express $[3, 2]^T$ as a convex combination of $\{[1, 2]^T, [3, 4]^T, [5, 1]^T\}$.

3. In Example 3.4.3 replace the given feasible solution x by

$$x^T = [60, 30, 10, 0, 200].$$

Determine a vector y and a new solution as in Example 3.4.3.

4. Consider the linear program below:

$$
\begin{array}{llrrrrrrr}
\text{Maximize}: & 15x_1 & + & 3x_2 & + & 4x_3 & & & \\
\text{Subject to}: & 3x_1 & + & 2x_2 & - & x_3 & + & x_4 & & = & 55 \\
& 2x_1 & + & x_2 & + & x_3 & & & + & x_5 & = & 50 \\
\end{array}
$$
$$x_i \geq 0, \ i = 1, 2, \ldots, 5$$

and the vectors $y^1 = [-1, 0, 2, 5, 0]^T$, $y^2 = [2, 0, -4, -10, 0]^T$, and $x = [20, 0, 10, 5, 0]^T$.

(a) Show that x is a solution of the linear program. Is it a basic solution? Why or why not?

(b) What is the value of the objective function corresponding to x?

(c) Show that y^1 and y^2 are solutions to the system of homogeneous equations associated with this problem, i.e., the constraint equations with the right-hand-side replaced by $[0, 0, 0]^T$.

(d) Show that $y^1 + y^2$ and $4y^1$ are also solutions to the system of homogeneous equations.

(e) Determine a value of t so that $x + ty^1$ is a nonnegative solution and has only two positive coordinates, i.e., is a basic solution, and has an objective function value at least equal to that of x.

5. Consider Farmer Jones's problem from the previous section with slack variables inserted. The vector

$$x^T = [0, 50, 50, 100, 300]$$

is a nonbasic feasible solution. Determine a vector y and a basic feasible solution of the form $x + ty$.

6. Consider the following problem and the given nonbasic solution x:

$$
\begin{array}{llrrrrrrrrr}
\text{Maximize}: & 3x_1 & + & 2x_2 & + & 5x_3 & & & & & \\
\text{Subject to}: & -3x_1 & - & x_2 & + & x_3 & + & x_4 & & & = & 4 \\
& x_1 & + & x_2 & & & & & + & x_5 & - & x_6 & = & 10 \\
\end{array}
$$
$$x_i \geq 0, \ i = 1, 2, \ldots, 6$$

$$x^T = [0, 12, 0, 16, 0, 2]$$

Determine a vector y that indicates that the problem is unbounded.

7. Consider the following problem and the given nonbasic solution x:

$$
\begin{array}{llrrrrrrr}
\text{Maximize}: & 4x_1 & + & 5x_2 & + & 2x_3 & & & \\
\text{Subject to}: & x_1 & + & 2x_2 & + & x_3 & + & x_4 & & = & 10 \\
& x_1 & + & 3x_2 & + & 2x_3 & & & + & x_5 & = & 18 \\
\end{array}
$$
$$x_i \geq 0, \ i = 1, 2, \ldots, 5$$

$$x^T = [4, 0, 4, 2, 6]$$

Determine a basic solution which has a larger objective function value than x does by applying the technique of Theorem 3.4.2 twice.

8. Prove that the intersection of convex sets is a convex set.

9. Give an example to show that the union of two convex sets need not be convex.

3.5 Formulation examples

In this section we consider several examples which illustrate applications of linear programming, and we indicate the developments needed in the theory to be able to solve more general problems. We discuss the formulation of the linear programs to solve some of these problems and, in the process, present some basic "proverbs" to observe when developing linear programs.

Some of these problems as well as some from Chapter 1 are larger than one would care to solve by hand. See Appendices A and B for examples of software available for this purpose. Such software can be used profitably in conjunction with nearly all remaining topics.

Example 3.5.1. A bicycle manufacturer's product mix problem. A manufacturer of bicycles uses the same basic frame for both its 3-speed and 5-speed models. The plant can produce 100 frames a day. Tires, brakes and gearing mechanisms are purchased from a supplier. The final two stages of production are to apply the appropriate finish and then assemble and package for shipment. There are 40 hours of time available each day in the finishing shop and 50 hours in the assembly/packing shop. The profit is $12 for a 3-speed and $15 for a 5-speed.

The table below gives the number of hours required per bicycle in each of the final stages:

Table 3.5.1	x_1 3-speed	x_2 5-speed	
Finishing	$\frac{1}{3}$	$\frac{1}{2}$	$= 40$
Assembly/Packing	$\frac{1}{4}$	$\frac{2}{3}$	$= 50$

The manufacturer would like to determine how many of each model should be produced to maximize profit.

The objective function is simply the profit from the combination of x_1 3-speeds and x_2 5-speeds:

$$z = 12x_1 + 15x_2.$$

The number of hours required to finish x_1 3-speeds and x_2 5-speeds is

$$\frac{1}{3} \frac{\text{finishing hr}}{\text{3} - \text{speed}} \times x_1 \text{ 3-speeds} + \frac{1}{2} \frac{\text{finishing hr}}{\text{5} - \text{speed}} \times x_2 \text{ 5-speeds}$$

Note that we will be limiting the value of this expression by the number of hours available in the finishing shop. This suggests the

Formulation Proverb # 1: All terms in any constraint or the objective function must have the same units.

Incorporating the limit of 40 hours in the finishing shop, performing the analogous calculation for the assembly shop, and including the limit of 100 frames a day produces the following linear program:

$$
\begin{array}{rrcrcl}
\text{Maximize}: & 12x_1 & + & 15x_2 & & \\
\text{Subject to}: & \frac{1}{3}x_1 & + & \frac{1}{2}x_2 & \leq & 40 \\
& \frac{1}{4}x_1 & + & \frac{2}{3}x_2 & \leq & 50 \\
& x_1 & + & x_2 & \leq & 100 \\
& & & x_1 \geq 0, x_2 \geq 0 & &
\end{array}
$$

The set of feasible solutions is graphed in Figure 3.5.1.

We will solve this problem by the simplex algorithm in Section 3.7. The solution will be seen to occur at $(60, 40)$. Figure 3.5.1 shows that this solution can be reached in two iterations by first letting x_1 become positive, or in three iterations if x_2 is made positive first. We will take advantage of this observation when we solve the problem. ■

When we study duality theory, we will learn how to determine the relative value of the three resources: finishing shop time, assembly shop time, and number of frames. This information becomes of particular value when the manufacturer takes up problems such as are discussed in the next example.

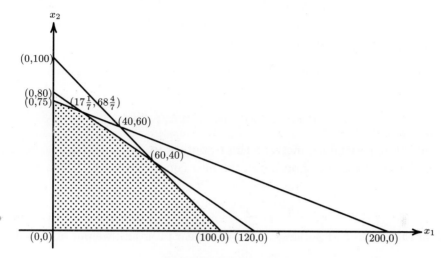

Figure 3.5.1

Example 3.5.2. The bicycle manufacturer in the previous example is considering an expansion in production capacity. The actual frame manufacture is proceeding at full capacity on two shifts, and the union contract does not permit a third shift. However, overtime is available in the other two shops. The incremental hourly overtime costs in shift differential and overhead are given in Table 3.5.2.

Table 3.5.2

	Hours available	Incremental cost
Finishing	16	$6.00
Assembly/Packaging	16	$4.50

The construction of up to 100 additional frames per day can be contracted out at a cost of $4 more per frame than if they were made in their own shop.

Under these conditions, how many additional frames should be ordered each day, and how should the overtime production be scheduled?

The addition of overtime and the contracted purchase of extra frames requires the addition of variables beyond the two used in the previous example:

x_3 = number of overtime hours in the finishing shop

x_4 = number of overtime hours in the assembly/packaging shop

x_5 = number of bicycle frames contracted out

The objective function is changed by subtracting from the profit the cost of overtime and of any contracted frames that are used:

$$z = 12x_1 + 15x_2 - 6x_3 - 4.5x_4 - 4x_5.$$

The additional variables increase the resources in the constraints. For instance, for the finishing shop hours the new constraint is:

$$\frac{1}{3}x_1 + \frac{1}{2}x_2 \le 40 + x_3.$$

For the purpose of putting this into a linear program, we put all variables on the left-hand side of the inequality:

$$\frac{1}{3}x_1 + \frac{1}{2}x_2 - x_3 \le 40.$$

When this has been done for all constraints, we obtain the following linear program:

Maximize :	$12x_1$	+	$15x_2$	−	$6x_3$	−	$4.5x_4$	−	$4x_5$		
Subject to :	$\frac{1}{3}x_1$	+	$\frac{1}{2}x_2$	−	x_3					$\le$	40
	$\frac{1}{4}x_1$	+	$\frac{2}{3}x_2$			−	x_4			$\le$	50
					x_3					$\le$	16
							x_4			$\le$	16
	x_1	+	x_2					−	x_5	$\le$	100
									x_5	$\le$	100

$$x_1 \ge 0, \ x_2 \ge 0, \ x_3 \ge 0, \ x_4 \ge 0, \ x_5 \ge 0$$

An alternative approach to incorporating overtime is suggested in Exercise 5 at the end of the section. A comparison of the two approaches will show the advantage of a careful choice of variables. ∎

When you have done the suggested exercise and solved the linear program above and the one in the exercise, the value of the following proverb will become apparent:

Formulation Proverb # 2: Choose variables so that the set of feasible solutions is as large as possible.

Example 3.5.3. A diet mix problem. Under the stress of finals, Eve has developed a nervous condition. She consulted a nutritionist who conducted a diet analysis and diagnosed a vitamin deficiency. The nutritionist prescribed a daily supplement of at least 600 units of vitamin A, 400 units of B, and 350 units of C. Two brands of vitamins are available from the nutritionist. Eve, being between work-study checks, determines the most economical combination to satisfy the requirements. Given the specifications below, what is the cheapest combination?

Table 3.5.3

	X_1 Pill 1	X_2 Pill 2
A content	50	20
B content	30	20
C content	50	10
Cost in cents	1.5	0.7

The formulation of this problem as a minimization problem of type (mLP) is given at the beginning of Section 3.7, where the solution method for such problems is presented. ∎

Example 3.5.4. Mixing with wrong way and equality constraints. The Slick Spread Paint Co. has a custom order for 5,000 gallons of red paint from a customer planning to paint the town. The paint must meet the following specifications.

For fire safety during application, the combustion point must be no lower than 225 degrees Fahrenheit. For proper application, the specific weight may be no more than 1.0. The customer is particularly concerned that the paint not fade, but retain its vivid hue. Thus, he has restricted the proportions of the common, but fugitive, pigments red-1 and red-3. The red-1 content may be no more than 10% by volume and the red-3 content no more than 1% by volume.

The paints approaching these specifications that are available to Slick Spread are riot red, alarm crimson, and racy rouge. Table 3.5.4 gives their costs and relevant characteristics. When the paints are mixed, these characteristics are assumed to combine linearly.

If the required paint can be mixed using these stock paints, determine their proportions to produce the minimum material cost.

Table 3.5.4

	Riot Red	Alarm Crimson	Racy Rouge
Combustion point	200°	240°	260°
Specific weight	0.95	1.06	0.99
Red-1 content	10.2%	9.5%	9.5%
Red-3 content	0.9%	0.8%	1.2%
Cost per gallon	$0.80	$1.00	$0.60

One approach we might take is to determine the lowest price for a single gallon of the required paint. Then the variables $x_i, i = 1, 2, 3$ represent the portion used of the corresponding paint. This leads to a new type of constraint – an equality:

$$x_1 + x_2 + x_3 = 1.$$

The requirement of a minimum combustion point of 225 degrees and the assumption that the paint characteristics combine linearly leads to a constraint with the direction of the inequality reversed from the usual for a maximization problem:

$$200x_1 + 240x_2 + 260x_3 \geq 225. \quad \blacksquare$$

We will learn how to adapt the simplex algorithm to handle these constraints in the next section. The other three constraints will all be of the $\leq$ type. Note that the equality constraint discussed above must be an equality to assure that a full gallon of paint is mixed. However, making any of the other constraints equalities may lead to a linear program without a feasible solution. Experimentation in this direction suggests

Formulation Proverb # 3: Do not over use equality constraints.

Example 3.5.5. An inventory planning problem. Laurie Squires, a furniture dealer, is preparing an order for floor lamps, end tables, and coffee tables. She has 60 square feet of space to store the new inventory and $4,584 budgeted for its purchase. Each lamp will cost $50, and a table of either kind $100. A floor lamp requires 1 square foot of floor space, an end table 4 square feet, and a coffee table 5 square feet. Since the tables can be stacked two high, she considers each to actually occupy half the floor space required. The overhead on her storage space is $1 per square foot.

Present stock and sales patterns indicate to Laurie that she should stock at least 16 end tables and at least 10 each of lamps and coffee tables. Beyond those requirements, she selects stock to maximize her potential profit. She figures her profit on each item as the selling price minus her expenses. She expects to sell the lamps for $120, the end tables for $236, and the coffee tables for $254.

Up to 100 square feet of storage space in a warehouse across town can be leased for $2 per square foot. The warehouser will charge her $4 per item to deliver each order. She is considering committing part of her capital to lease this space.

How many of each item should Laurie order, and should she lease the extra warehouse space? If she does lease extra space, which items should be stored there? ■

Example 3.5.6. Make versus buy analysis. XYZ, Inc., has recently put a new production line into service which has greatly expanded its capacity. The casting shop, which produces two needed subassemblies, has not yet been modernized to keep up. In order to fully utilize the new line in the interim, XYZ will need to purchase subassemblies. The two costs and production rates for the subassemblies are:

Table 3.5.5

	Subassembly A	Subassembly B
Make	$4.00/unit	$7.00/unit
Buy	$4.90/unit	$7.60/unit
Production rate	10 units/hour	20 units/hour

The company must have at least 700 of Subassembly A and 1400 of B each week. There are 80 hours of production time in the casting shop each week, and idle time in the shop costs XYZ $10/hour. Outside suppliers can provide at most 600 units of Subassembly B a week.

How many of each subassembly should XYZ make, and how many should it purchase to supply its new production line at minimum cost until the casting shop can be modernized? ■

Example 3.5.7. Gasoline blending. The Ace Refining Company produces two types of unleaded gasoline, regular and premium, which it sells to its chain of service stations for $36 and $42 per barrel, respectively. Both types are blended from Ace's inventories of refined domestic and refined foreign oil and must meet the following specifications:

Table 3.5.6

	Maximum vapor pressure	Minimum octane rating	Maximum demand, bbl/wk	Minimum deliveries, bbl/wk
Regular	23	88	100,000	50,000
Premium	23	93	20,000	5,000

The characteristics of the refined oils in inventory are:

Table 3.5.7

		Vapor pressure	Octane rating	Inventory, bbl	Cost, $/bbl
x_1	Domestic	25	87	40,000	16
x_2	Foreign	15	98	60,000	30

What quantities of the two oils should Ace blend into the two gasolines in order to maximize weekly profit?

The vapor pressure and octane rating constraints in this example introduce a type of constraint which requires some manipulation to place it into a linear form. As an illustration, we consider the restriction of the octane rating of regular gas.

Let x_1 and x_2 be the number of barrels of domestic oil and of foreign oil, respectively, used for regular gas. Then the resulting octane rating of the mixture – under the assumption that octane ratings combine linearly – is

$$\frac{87x_1 + 98x_2}{x_1 + x_2}$$

Thus, the requirement that the octane rating be at least 88 is

$$\frac{87x_1 + 98x_2}{x_1 + x_2} \geq 88$$

which is not linear. However, multiplying both sides by $x_1 + x_2$ and simplifying yields the linear constraint

$$-x_1 + 10x_2 \geq 0. \quad \blacksquare$$

The next section will discuss how to treat this constraint in the simplex algorithm.

The next example will illustrate the following proverb:

Formulation Proverb # 4: Use variable names that suggest the quantities that they represent.

Example 3.5.8. Product mix and labor allocation. The Home and Hearth Furniture Company divides its operations into three shops: fabricating, assembly, and finishing. The practice at H & H is to schedule production first to meet current orders and then to use any remaining worker time to produce a mix of chairs that would maximize their profit, assuming that all chairs sell.

In planning a week to be devoted to its three lines of chairs – Windsor, Early American, and Queen Anne – H & H finds that it has orders for 15, 12, and 8 chairs, respectively. The profit on each chair of the respective lines is $80, $48, and $100.

A Windsor requires 2 hours of fabricating and 1 of assembly; an Early American 1 hour of fabricating and 1 of assembly; and a Queen Anne 3 hours of fabricating and 2 of assembly. All three styles require 1 hour for finishing.

H & H has 9 workers – 3 who work in fabricating, 2 in assembly, and 1 in finishing. The other 3 can each work in any of the three shops. All workers work a 40-hour week.

Determine how H & H should allocate the time of the 3 employees who can work in any shop, and how many chairs of each line should be made during the week.

Using suggestive variable names, the constraints expressing the orders in this problem are

$$W \geq 15, \ EA \geq 12, \ QA \geq 8$$

where W, EA, and QA are the numbers of the respective lines of chair to be made. Lower bound constraints like these can be eliminated by changing variables:

$$T1 = W - 15, \quad T2 = EA - 12, \quad T3 = QA - 8,$$

and expressing the problem in terms of the Ti's. Then the objective function becomes:

$$
\begin{aligned}
z &= 80W + 48EA + 100QA \\
&= 80T1 + 48T2 + 100T3 + 2,576.
\end{aligned}
$$

The $2,576 represents the profit on the existing orders; it is placed in the lower right-hand corner of the simplex tableau as the initial value of the objective function. Alternatively, it can simply be added to the optimal value of the objective function. When the solution has been found, adding 15, 12, and 8 to the respective values of the Ti's yields the solution to the original problem. ∎

The problems discussed in this section, while very small as linear programs go, are generally too large for hand solution to be practical. For that reason, the solution of the Home and Hearth problem using the LINDO linear programming package is presented below. This serves as an introduction to the use of a computer to solve linear programs.

The formulation of the problem has been prepared in the file HH.DAT, which looks much like the listing in the output and is loaded into LINDO by the take command.

The descriptive names assigned to the variables make interpreting the output easy. Note that the last three constraints could have been eliminated by the means suggested in the discussion above.

In the output, the LINDO commands follow the : which is the LINDO prompt. Explanation of the REDUCED COST and DUAL PRICE values will be given in later sections. The question regarding RANGE ANALYSIS, which was answered in the negative here, will be discussed in Section 3.8. More detailed information on LINDO, including the preparation of data files, can be found in Appendix A.

Listing 3.5.1

```
:take HH.DAT
:look all

MAX      80 W + 48 EA + 100 QA
SUBJECT TO
        2)    2 W + EA + 3 QA - FBHR <=    120
        3)    W + EA + 2 QA - ASHR <=     80
        4)    W + EA + QA - FNHR <=    40
        5)    FBHR + ASHR + FNHR <=    120
        6)    W >=    15
        7)    EA >=    12
        8)    QA >=    8
    END
```

```
:go

LP OPTIMUM FOUND AT STEP       9

        OBJECTIVE FUNCTION VALUE
        1)     6896.00000

  VARIABLE          VALUE          REDUCED COST
         W       69.000000            0.000000
        EA       12.000000            0.000000
        QA        8.000000            0.000000
      FBHR       54.000000            0.000000
      ASHR       17.000000            0.000000
      FNHR       49.000000            0.000000


       ROW   SLACK OR SURPLUS      DUAL PRICES
        2)        0.000000         20.000000
        3)        0.000000         20.000000
        4)        0.000000         20.000000
        5)        0.000000         20.000000
        6)       54.000000          0.000000
        7)        0.000000        -12.000000
        8)        0.000000        -20.000000


  NO. ITERATIONS=         9

  DO RANGE(SENSITIVITY) ANALYSIS?
  ?n
  :quit
```

So we can conclude that Home and Hearth should make 69 Windsor chairs and only the numbers of Early American and Queen Anne chairs actually on order: 12 and 8, respectively. All 120 hours of flexible labor would be needed to achieve this level of production.

Note that in formulating this problem we suggested a change of variable that would avoid the three lower bound constraints but would put a constant in the objective function. Unfortunately, LINDO does not permit inclusion of a constant in the objective function. One work-around that incorporates a constant in the objective function is to include an additional variable and equality constraint assigning the constant value to the variable. With this done, our formulation would include:

Listing 3.5.2

```
MAX     80 T1   +   48 T2   +   100 T3   + CONST
SUBJECT TO
       2)   CONST = 2576
```

Example 3.5.9. Planning farming activities. The Miller family farm has 230 acres of land available and $12,000 in capital for investment. The family can generate 3,280 person-hours of labor during the winter months (mid-September to mid-May) and 4,200 person-hours during the summer. If any of their summer hours are not needed, the youngsters in the family can get work for $5 per hour during the summer at the nearby Dairy Barn.

The family has found that three crops, soybeans, corn, and potatoes, and two lines of livestock, dairy cows and sheep, are their most likely sources of income. In addition, the family has a chicken coop accommodating up to 100 hens that it uses some years and which does not compete for land with other activities. The family currently has eight dairy cows, which it expects to retain. In Table 3.5.9, the cost per additional cow ($600) is the allotted portion for the first year of the $1,400 purchase price. The Millers must pay $4,500 this year on the eight cows that they currently own.

The required resources per acre for crops and per animal for stock are shown in Tables 3.5.8 and 3.5.9 along with the expected annual income.

Table 3.5.8

	Soybeans	Corn	Potatoes
Initial cash investment	$8	$10	$14
Winter person-hours	15	10	10
Summer person-hours	35	25	30
Net income	$425	$300	$350

In order to continue their crop rotation program, the Millers must plant a total of at least 100 acres of corn and potatoes.

Table 3.5.9

	Dairy cow	Sheep	Chicken
Initial cash investment	$600	$85	$8
Winter person-hours	110	15	0.5
Summer person-hours	60	12	0.3
Land per animal	2	1	0
Net income	$1,030	$185	$5

Determine which activities the Millers should undertake in the coming year. ∎

Exercises

1. Formulate a linear program of type (mLP) for Example 3.5.3.

2. In Example 3.5.7, let x_3 and x_4 be the number of barrels of domestic and of foreign oil, respectively, used for premium gas. Formulate the constraints on vapor pressure.

3. The key to formulating the linear program for Example 3.5.8 is the allocation of the time of the three workers who can work in any of the three shops. This time is represented by three variables, which must have 120 as their sum – 40 hours for each worker. The variables represent the hours allocated to each of the respective shops and are added to the hours available from the other six workers in the respective shops.

Note that if the change of variable to t_j described in conjunction with the objective function of the example is made, then the same change of variable must also be made in the constraints. This will result in a reduction of the hours available by the hours which must be devoted to satisfying the orders.

Formulate the linear program for Example 3.5.8 using the suggested variables t_j.

4. Set up the linear program for Example 1.3.9.

5. The method used to add overtime in Example 3.5.2 is not the only approach. Develop an alternative formulation in which the variables are the number of 3-speeds made on regular time, the number of 3-speeds made on overtime, the number of 5-speeds made on regular time, the number of 5-speeds made on overtime, and the number of frames purchased.

Solve your linear program using this approach and the one given in Example 3.5.2 to decide which approach is better, and why.

6. Formulate the linear program to solve Example 3.5.5. Note that you will need to calculate profit for each item and determine how many of each item will be stored in her store and how many in the warehouse. Also note that a change of variable similar to that described for Example 3.5.8 could be used.

7. Formulate the linear program for Example 3.5.9.

8. Formulate the linear program to solve the following problem:

A metal producer wishes to make 500 tons of an alloy which must be 95% steel and 5% chromium. The producer can obtain unlimited quantities of three different alloys. Their compositions and costs are tabled below:

Table 3.5.10

	Alloy A	Alloy B	Alloy C
Steel	99%	90%	100%
Chromium	1%	10%	0%
Cost/ton	$40	$75	$30

How many tons of each alloy should the producer acquire in order to produce 500 tons of the required alloy at a minimum cost?

9. Formulate the linear program to solve the following problem:

The Mythic Forge & Steel Co. (MF&S) supplies castings to a variety of customers. It plans to devote the next week of production to just two, James Manufacturing and Woolcott Enterprises. MF&S uses a combination of pure steel and scrap metal to fulfill its orders and has 400 pounds of pure steel and 360 pounds of scrap metal in stock. The pure steel costs MF&S $6 per pound and the scrap $3 per pound. Pure steel requires 3 hours per pound to process into a casting, while scrap requires only 2 hours per pound. Total available processing time in the week is 2,000 hours.

The castings for James each require 5 pounds of metal, with a quality control restriction limiting the ratio of scrap to pure steel to a maximum of $\frac{5}{7}$. James has ordered 30 castings at a price of $50 each.

The castings for Woolcott each require 8 pounds of metal, with a quality restriction of a maximum scrap to pure steel ratio of $\frac{2}{3}$. Woolcott has ordered 40 castings at a price of $80 each.

Determine how MF&S should allocate their metal stocks to produce the castings ordered by these two customers if the objective is to maximize the value added to the metal, i.e., to maximize the selling price minus the cost of the metal.

10. Formulate the linear program to solve the following problem:

Leisure Furniture, Inc. (LFI) makes outdoor chairs, tables, lounges, and benches. The main resources required for production are plastic webbing, metal tubing, and wood. The number of units of each resource required per item and the per item profit are given below:

Table 3.5.11

		Tubing (feet)	Webbing (yards)	Wood (board feet)	Profit
x_1	Chair	18	28		$11
x_2	Table	18		10	$18
x_3	Lounge	24	35		$14
x_4	Bench	20		14	$ 9

(handwritten: $\geq 2x_2$; ≥ 100; ≤ 6000; $\leq 5,000$; ≤ 1000)

The main activities in production are tube bending and assembly. The number of hours of each activity required per unit of each product are tabled below:

Table 3.5.12

	Chairs	Tables	Lounges	Benches
Tube bending	$\frac{1}{3}$	$\frac{1}{8}$	$\frac{1}{4}$	$\frac{1}{8}$
Assembly	$\frac{1}{2}$	$\frac{1}{2}$	$\frac{1}{3}$	$\frac{1}{3}$

(handwritten: ≤ 120; ≤ 160)

LFI is planning its first week's production for spring. Available during that week are 120 hours of bending time, 160 hours of assembly time, 6,000 feet of tubing, 5,000 yards of webbing, and 1,000 board feet of wood. The lounge is the most popular product, so LFI wants to make at least 100 of them. Tables and chairs are commonly sold in sets of two chairs and a table, so they want to make at least twice as many chairs as tables. Otherwise they want to make the products that will maximize their profit if sold.

11. The Rolling Stock Company (RSC) produces three imaginative lines of childen's riding vehicles: ambulances, fire trucks, and roadsters. They sell exclusively by mail order and thus ship each vehicle individually.

The key activity in production is molding the plastic body. The molding equipment can produce four ambulance bodies an hour, three fire trucks an hour, and six roadsters an hour. After the vehicle body is made, the only other production step is "dressing," where any rough edges are smoothed and parts such as tires, steering wheels and insignia are added. The vehicles then move to the packing and shipping department. The times required in each of these departments are tabled below along with the per-unit profits:

Table 3.5.13

	Dressing	Packing & shipping	Profit
Ambulance	15 min	20 min	$70
Fire truck	20 min	10 min	$80
Roadster	10 min	10 min	$50

A small company, RSC prides itself on the versatility of its employees. Each of the four employees can work in any of the three jobs, and each of the four works 40 hours a week.

RSC is planning production for a 13-week quarter. Strangely enough, demand for their vehicles has shown a seasonal pattern, and they plan for the demand for fire trucks to be at least as great as the total demand for the other two lines. To maximize their profit during the period, using the assumption that they can sell all that they make, how should RSC allocate the time of their four employees, and how many of each vehicle should they make?

12. **Should Farmer Brown borrow?** Recall Farmer Brown's problem from Exmple 1.3.1:

   Farmer Brown is planning his planting for the coming year. He expects to raise potatoes and wheat. He has 100 acres of land available and will be able to devote 160 days of labor to his crops. He expects an acre of wheat to require four days of labor while an acre of potatoes requires only one day. He has $1,100 that he can use for the start-up costs of planting and cultivating. It costs $10 an acre to plant and cultivate potatoes, while the corresponding costs for an acre of wheat are $20. He expects a revenue of $40 per acre for potatoes and $120 an acre for wheat.

   As he is planning, he receives an offer of a loan for up to $1,500 at 5% for one year. It will cost him $1.02729 to repay the loan for each $1 borowed. This possibility adds two new issues to his planning: should he borrow, and if so, how should he use the money? He finds that he could rent land from his neighbor Farmer Jones for $20 an acre and that he could hire an additional farm hand for $25 a day. If he reduces his revenue by the amount needed to repay the loan, how many acres of each should he plant in order to achieve the maximum possible revenue, how much should he borrow, and how should he use the borrowed money?

13. Formulate the linear program for Example 1.3.3. Note that there are two approaches to accounting for the cost of the idle time. One is to make the resource constraints equalities by including the idle hours; the other is to express the idle hours in terms of the number of products, and adjust the profits accordingly. The latter method will require including a constant in the objective function.

14. Formulate the linear program for Example 1.3.4. Eliminate the lower bound constraints as in Example 3.5.8.

15. A retired NBA star has $2 million to invest. Since much of his other money is invested in rather risky ventures, his broker suggests bonds for this money. Table 3.5.14 provides the duration, the expected return, and an estimate of the return in the worst case.

Table 3.5.14

Bond	Expected return	Worst case	Maturity
Power & Light, Inc.	11%	6%	6
Municipal Sewage	8%	6%	7
Penn School District	9%	8%	3
Glenside Hospital	9%	4%	8

Formulate the linear program to determine how much should be invested in each bond if the objective is to maximize the expected return subject to the following restrictions:

- The worst-case scenario return should be at least 7%.

- The average maturity of the bonds in the portfolio must be at least 5 years.

- A maximum of 40% of the investment can be in any one bond.

3.6 General constraints and variables

Thus far, we have solved only maximizing linear programs, and all constraints have been of the form

$$a_{i1}x_1 + a_{i2}x_2 + \cdots + a_{in}x_n \le b_i$$

with $b_i \ge 0$.

In this section we extend the simplex algorithm to solve maximizing problems including equality constraints or constraints in which the inequalities are directed in the opposite direction. We also consider variables that are not restricted to be nonnegative. In the next section we will develop a method to solve minimizing linear programs.

General constraints

In Example 1.3.4 the company was required to produce a minimum number of units of each product. Such a constraint takes the form

$$a_{i1}x_1 + a_{i2}x_2 + \cdots + a_{in}x_n \geq b_i.$$

Since this usually represents a requirement, we will call it a *requirement constraint*.

The remaining type of constraint takes the form of an equality

$$a_{i1}x_1 + a_{i2}x_2 + \cdots + a_{in}x_n = b_i.$$

Such an *equality constraint* might occur in a blending problem, where the x_i's represent the percentages of different components which must add to 100% as in Example 3.5.4.

The first step in solving a linear program by the simplex algorithm is to express the constraints as equalities. With a problem containing only resource constraints, this is accomplished by inserting nonnegative slack variables. To understand how to properly express requirement and equality constraints for the simplex algorithm, it is helpful to recall the two roles played by slack variables in the solution process.

Within the context of an application, a slack variable accounts for unused resources. For instance, in Farmer Jones' problem, s_1 represented the number of acres not planted. Thus, the acreage resource constraint

$$x_1 + x_2 \leq 100,$$

was expressed as the equality

$$x_1 + x_2 + s_1 = 100.$$

In the initial simplex tableau each slack variable is isolated, i.e., has a coefficient of 1 in one equation and zero in the others. Thus, the initial basic feasible solution is easily obtained by setting each slack variable equal to the constant on the right-hand side of the equation.

Hence, a slack variable both has a role in the application representing an unused resource and also assists in the determination of the initial basic feasible solution. We next examine the need for a variable or variables in other types of constraints to serve these two purposes.

Requirement constraints

Consider first the requirement constraint

$$a_{i1}x_1 + a_{i2}x_2 + \cdots + a_{in}x_n \geq b_i.$$

Here possibly a solution may exceed the requirement. Adding a variable to represent the excess would not succeed, because all variables in the simplex algorithm must be nonnegative, and a variable added into the equation to fill this role would necessarily be nonpositive. However, the same purpose could be filled by subtracting a nonnegative variable to represent an excess over the minimum requirement:

$$a_{i1}x_1 + a_{i2}x_2 + \cdots + a_{in}x_n - s_i = b_i.$$

We will call such a variable s_i a *surplus variable*. While it will be the only variable having a nonzero coefficient in its column, the negative coefficient prevents a surplus variable from being used in an initial basic feasible solution consisting of nonnegative variables. To fill the second role played by a slack variable – that of obtaining an initial solution – we introduce a second nonnegative variable a_i with a coefficient of $+1$ called an *artificial variable*. Thus, the equation that is placed in the initial simplex tableau is

$$a_{i1}x_1 + a_{i2}x_2 + \cdots + a_{in}x_n - s_i + a_i = b_i.$$

The artificial variable in a requirement constraint will serve only to help determine an initial solution and has no significance in the actual solution. The simplex algorithm will be modified to ensure that any artificial variables introduced will be set to zero before the optimal solution is reached.

Equality constraints

In an equality constraint such as

$$a_{i1}x_1 + a_{i2}x_2 + \cdots + a_{in}x_n = b_i$$

there is no "surplus" or "slack" quantity that has significance within the problem. Hence, we need only introduce a nonnegative, artificial variable to facilitate obtaining an initial solution:

$$a_{i1}x_1 + a_{i2}x_2 + \cdots + a_{in}x_n + a_i = b_i.$$

The two-phase method

Once the slack, surplus, and artificial variables have been inserted into a linear program, in the first basic solution only slack and artificial variables will have positive values. The remaining new step will be to move from that solution – which is not feasible since artificial variables play no role in the actual context of the problem – to one that is feasible. This will be accomplished by means of the *two-phase method* which will require an extra objective function to "penalize" the artificial variables so that they will be forced to be zero.

To demonstrate the two-phase method, consider the following example:

Example 3.6.1. Solve the linear program:

$$
\begin{array}{rrcrcl}
\text{Maximize}: & 3x_1 & + & 4x_2 & & \\
\text{Subject to}: & -2x_1 & + & x_2 & \leq & 6 \\
& 2x_1 & + & 2x_2 & \geq & 24 \\
& x_1 & & & = & 8 \\
& \multicolumn{5}{c}{x_1 \geq 0, x_2 \geq 0}
\end{array}
$$

Restating the problem with slack, surplus, and artificial variables:

$$
\begin{array}{rrcrcrcrcrcl}
\text{Maximize}: & 3x_1 & + & 4x_2 & & & & & & & & \\
\text{Subject to}: & -2x_1 & + & x_2 & + & s_1 & & & & & = & 6 \\
& 2x_1 & + & 2x_2 & & & - & s_2 & + & a_2 & = & 24 \\
& x_1 & & & & & & & + & a_3 & = & 8 \\
\end{array}
$$
$$x_1 \geq 0, \ x_2 \geq 0, \ s_1 \geq 0, \ s_2 \geq 0, \ a_2 \geq 0, \ a_3 \geq 0$$

Here we have numbered the activity variables consecutively to associate them with the corresponding columns of the simplex tableau and have used s to designate slack and surplus variables and a to indicate artificial variables. The added variables are subscripted by the number of the constraint in which they are inserted.

The *two-phase method* uses a second objective function, called the *artificial objective function*, which forces the artificial variables to be zero when an optimal value is obtained. Since artificial variables are required to be nonnegative, we choose the negative of the sum of the artificial variables as the artificial objective function. Then the optimal value would be zero, and when achieved all artificial variables would necessarily be zero.

To be a basic variable, an artificial variable must have zero as its coefficient in the artificial objective function. We thus use the constraints to express the artificial variables in terms of the other variables. In the example, the artificial objective function then becomes:

$$\begin{aligned} -a_2 - a_3 &= -(24 - 2x_1 - 2x_2 + s_2) - (8 - x_1) \\ &= -32 + 3x_1 + 2x_2 - s_2 \end{aligned}$$

We set up the simplex tableau with the artificial objective function below the original objective function:

x_1	x_2	s_1	s_2	a_2	a_3	
-2	1	1	0	0	0	6
2	2	0	-1	1	0	24
1	0	0	0	0	1	8
-3	-4	0	0	0	0	0
-3	-2	0	1	0	0	-32

Notice that we have taken the negative of the coefficients of the artificial objective function just as with the actual objective function. Note also that the right-hand side of the artificial objective function is the negative of the sum of the values of the artificial variables in the initial solution below:

$$x_1 = 0, \ x_2 = 0, \ s_1 = 6, \ s_2 = 0, \ a_2 = 24, \ a_3 = 8.$$

This observation suggests a way to check the correctness of the artificial objective function: an entry in the row of the artificial objective function must be the negative of the sum of the entries in that column in the rows of the constraints requiring artificial variables, except for the columns of the artificial variables themselves, in which the entries must be zero. For example, in the column of x_1, $-3 = -(2 + 1)$. The entry -2 from row one is not included in the sum since the first constraint does not require an artificial variable. ∎

Before starting the solution process, we summarize how to set up a general maximization problem for the simplex algorithm:

- A nonnegative *slack variable* is inserted with a $+1$ coefficient into each resource constraint as before. Recall that a slack variable:

    – represents unused resources, and

  – has the same units as the constant on the right-hand side of the constraint.

- A *surplus variable* is a nonnegative variable inserted with a coefficient of -1 into a requirement constraint. A surplus variable:

  – represents the excess over the amount required, and

  – has the same units as the constant on the right-hand side of the constraint.

- An *artificial variable* is a nonnegative variable inserted with a coefficient of $+1$ into an equality or requirement constraint. An artificial variable:

  – is used only to obtain an initial basic solution,

  – cannot be positive in an optimal solution, and

  – has no significance in the applied context of the problem.

The *artificial objective function* is the negative sum of the artificial variables expressed in terms of the other variables in the problem. Applying the simplex algorithm to this objective function will cause the artificial variables to be set to zero and result in a basic feasible solution – if one exists – to the problem. A solution optimal for the artificial objective function in which one or more artificial variables remains positive indicates that no feasible solution exists.

Now we return to our example. The set of feasible solutions is shown in Figure 3.6.1. Because the constraints include an equality, the set of feasible solutions is a line segment which is represented by the heavy line joining the points $(8, 4)$ and $(8, 22)$.

Apply the simplex algorithm using the artificial objective function to decide on the variable to become positive and simply update the other objective function at each step. In the figure, the indicated points correspond to the basic solutions examined in our solution.

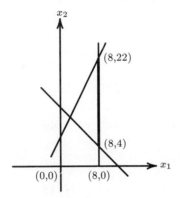

Figure 3.6.1

Thus, x_1 should become positive, and since the smallest replacement quantity, 8, occurs in the third row, a_3 becomes 0. Pivoting on the 1 in row 3 and column 1, we obtain:

x_1	x_2	s_1	s_2	a_2	a_3	
0	1	1	0	0	2	22
0	2	0	−1	1	−2	8
1	0	0	0	0	1	8
0	−4	0	0	0	3	24
0	−2	0	1	0	3	−8

The new solution lies on the x_1 axis and is not feasible since a_2 remains positive:
$$x_1 = 8, \ x_2 = 0, \ s_1 = 22, \ s_2 = 0, \ a_2 = 8, \ a_3 = 0.$$

The artificial objective function indicates that x_2 should become positive. The smallest replacement quantity, 4, occurs in the second row, so we pivot on the 2 in row 2 and column 2 to set $a_2 = 0$ to obtain:

x_1	x_2	s_1	s_2	a_2	a_3	
0	0	1	$\frac{1}{2}$	$-\frac{1}{2}$	3	18
0	1	0	$-\frac{1}{2}$	$\frac{1}{2}$	−1	4
1	0	0	0	0	1	8
0	0	0	−2	2	−1	40
0	0	0	0	1	1	0

Notice that the row of the artificial objective function indicates that the solution is optimal and has a value of zero. Hence, all of the artificial variables are zero, and the rest of the variables form a basic feasible solution corresponding to the point $(8, 4)$ at the lower end of the interval of feasible solutions in Figure 3.6.1.

The artificial variables have fulfilled their function, so we drop their columns and the row corresponding to the artificial objective function. This leaves the following tableau, to which we apply the simplex algorithm to obtain the final solution.

x_1	x_2	s_1	s_2	
0	0	1	$\frac{1}{2}$	18
0	1	0	$-\frac{1}{2}$	4
1	0	0	0	8
0	0	0	-2	40

Thus, the next basic solution is

$$x_1 = 8, \ x_2 = 4, \ s_1 = 18, \ s_2 = 0.$$

We clearly have only one option – to pivot on the $\frac{1}{2}$ in row 1, column 4, causing s_2 to become positive and s_1 to become 0:

x_1	x_2	s_1	s_2	
0	0	2	1	36
0	1	1	0	22
1	0	0	0	8
0	0	4	0	112

This is optimal, and the solution is

$$x_1 = 8, \ x_2 = 22, \ s_1 = 0, \ s_2 = 36$$

which lies at the other end of the interval of feasible solutions.

Note that in the example just concluded we dropped the columns of the artificial variables when no longer needed. However, these columns will be very important later to do sensitivity analysis. Thus, in Section 3.8 we will retain such columns and make use of them.

To summarize what has taken place in the example, we provide the two rules that we have added to the simplex algorithm as stated in Section 3.3.

They prepare the initial tableau for a problem having equality or requirement constraints.

Rule 0. To express the given constraints as equalities:

- Insert a **slack variable** with a coefficient of $+1$ in each **resource constraint**.

- Insert an **artificial variable** with a coefficient of $+1$ in each **equality constraint** and in each **requirement constraint**.

- Insert a **surplus variable** with a coefficient of -1 into each **requirement constraint**.

Rule 1A. Form the **artificial objective function** as the negative sum of the artificial variables. Obtain the **initial basic solution** by setting each slack variable and each artificial variable equal to the corresponding constant on the right-hand side of the constraint.

Rule 1B. There is no **feasible solution** if an artificial variable is positive in the optimal solution for the artificial objective function.

The flowchart in Figure 3.6.2 puts the general problem into the simplex algorithm context. Note that the procedure outlined in this flowchart calls on the one outlined in the flowchart in Figure 3.3.1 twice – once to optimize the artificial objective, and a second time to optimize the original objective function when a feasible solution has been reached.

Unrestricted variables

We now consider the steps necessary to solve problems containing unrestricted variables. While unrestricted variables seldom occur directly in a maximization, they do often arise in the dual of a minimization problem. This will be the case when we consider the transportation problem in the next chapter.

TWO-PHASE METHOD FLOWCHART

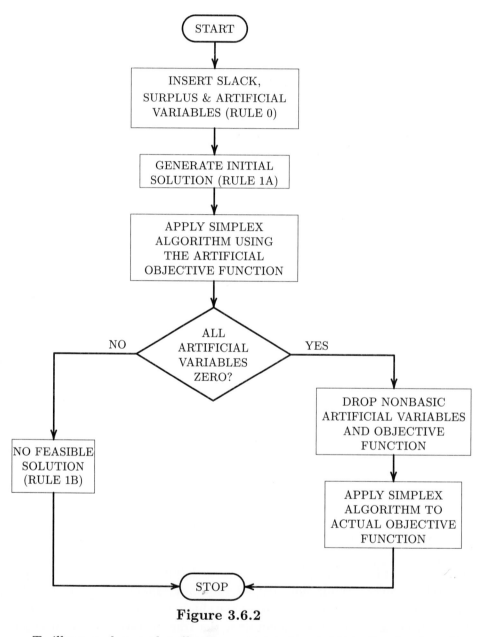

Figure 3.6.2

To illustrate how to handle an unrestricted variable in the simplex algorithm, consider the following example:

Example 3.6.2. Solve the linear program:

$$
\begin{array}{llrrrrrrr}
\text{Maximize}: & 3x_1 & + & 2x_2 & + & x_3 & & \\
\text{Subject to}: & x_1 & + & 2x_2 & + & 4x_3 & \leq & 24 \\
& 10x_1 & + & 4x_2 & - & 5x_3 & \leq & 100 \\
\end{array}
$$
$$
x_1 \geq 0, \ x_2 \text{ unrestricted}, \ x_3 \geq 0
$$

The simplex algorithm requires that all variables be nonnegative, so the procedure employed is to express the unrestricted variable x_2 as the difference of two nonnegative variables: $x_2 = w_1 - w_2$. The problem then becomes:

$$
\begin{array}{llrrrrrrr}
\text{Maximize}: & 3x_1 & + & 2w_1 & - & 2w_2 & + & x_3 & \\
\text{Subject to}: & x_1 & + & 2w_1 & - & 2w_2 & + & 4x_3 & \leq & 24 \\
& 10x_1 & + & 4w_1 & - & 4w_2 & - & 5x_3 & \leq & 100 \\
\end{array}
$$
$$
x_1 \geq 0, \ w_1 \geq 0, \ w_2 \geq 0, \ x_3 \geq 0
$$

The result is a problem in which the columns in the simplex tableau corresponding to w_1 and w_2 are negatives of each other. As a result, only one of the variables w_1 and w_2 can be basic at a time. If x_2 is negative in the optimal solution, then that will be indicated by $w_1 = 0$ and $w_2 > 0$, so that $x_2 = 0 - w_2$ is negative. Similarly, if x_2 is positive, the simplex algorithm will have $w_1 > 0$ and $w_2 = 0$. ∎

Exercises

1. Solve the linear program:

$$
\begin{array}{llrrrrr}
\text{Maximize}: & 4x_1 & + & 8x_2 & & \\
\text{Subject to}: & x_1 & + & x_2 & \leq & 10 \\
& -x_1 & + & x_2 & \geq & 4 \\
\end{array}
$$
$$
x_1 \geq 0, \ x_2 \geq 0
$$

2. Solve the linear program:

$$
\begin{array}{llrrrrrrr}
\text{Maximize}: & 2x_1 & + & 3x_2 & + & 4x_3 & & \\
\text{Subject to}: & x_1 & + & x_2 & + & x_3 & \leq & 60 \\
& 4x_1 & + & 2x_2 & + & x_3 & \geq & 24 \\
\end{array}
$$
$$
x_1 \geq 0, \ x_2 \geq 0, \ x_3 \geq 0
$$

3. Determine the initial simplex tableau for the linear program below:

$$
\begin{aligned}
\text{Maximize:} \quad & 4x_1 \;+\; 5x_2 \;+\; 3x_3 \\
\text{Subject to:} \quad & x_1 \;+\; 2x_2 \;+\; 3x_3 \;\le\; 40 \\
& 2x_1 \;+\; 4x_2 \;\ge\; 20 \\
& x_1 \;-\; x_2 \;+\; 2x_3 \;=\; 15 \\
& x_1 \ge 0,\; x_2 \ge 0,\; x_3 \ge 0
\end{aligned}
$$

4. Determine the initial simplex tableau for the linear program below:

$$
\begin{aligned}
\text{Maximize:} \quad & 4x_1 \;+\; 3x_2 \;-\; x_3 \\
\text{Subject to:} \quad & x_1 \;+\; x_2 \;+\; x_3 \;=\; 100 \\
& 2x_1 \;+\; 2x_2 \;+\; x_3 \;\le\; 200 \\
& 4x_2 \;+\; 3x_3 \;\ge\; 50 \\
& -5x_1 \;+\; 2x_2 \;\ge\; 40 \\
& x_1 \ge 0,\; x_2 \ge 0,\; x_3 \text{ unrestricted}
\end{aligned}
$$

5. Solve the linear program:

$$
\begin{aligned}
\text{Maximize:} \quad & 20x_1 \;+\; 50x_2 \\
\text{Subject to:} \quad & 5x_1 \;+\; 2x_2 \;\ge\; 10 \\
& -1.5x_1 \;+\; x_2 \;\le\; 11 \\
& 4x_1 \;+\; 5x_2 \;\le\; 40 \\
& 8x_1 \;+\; 5x_2 \;\le\; 60 \\
& x_1 \ge 0,\; x_2 \ge 0
\end{aligned}
$$

6. Solve the linear program:

$$
\begin{aligned}
\text{Maximize:} \quad & x_1 \;+\; 2x_2 \;+\; 3x_3 \\
\text{Subject to:} \quad & x_1 \;+\; 2x_2 \;+\; x_3 \;=\; 36 \\
& 2x_1 \;+\; x_2 \;+\; 4x_3 \;\ge\; 12 \\
& x_1 \ge 0,\; x_2 \ge 0,\; x_3 \ge 0
\end{aligned}
$$

7. Solve the linear program:

$$
\begin{aligned}
\text{Maximize:} \quad & 10x_1 \;+\; 20x_2 \\
\text{Subject to:} \quad & x_1 \;+\; x_2 \;\le\; 100 \\
& 3x_1 \;+\; x_2 \;\ge\; 28 \\
& x_1 \;+\; 2x_2 \;\ge\; 30 \\
& x_1 \;+\; 4x_2 \;\le\; 200 \\
& x_1 \ge 0,\; x_2 \ge 0
\end{aligned}
$$

8. Solve the linear program:

$$
\begin{array}{llrcrcrcrcl}
\text{Maximize}: & x_1 & + & x_2 & + & 2x_3 & + & 4x_4 \\
\text{Subject to}: & x_1 & + & 2x_2 & + & x_3 & + & x_4 & \leq & 400 \\
& x_1 & + & 2x_2 & & & + & x_4 & = & 200 \\
& & & x_2 & + & 2x_3 & & & = & 150 \\
\end{array}
$$
$$ x_1 \geq 0,\ x_2 \geq 0,\ x_3 \geq 0,\ x_4 \geq 0 $$

9. Solve the linear program for Example 1.3.9 that you formulated in Exercise 4 of Section 3.5.

10. Solve the linear program:

$$
\begin{array}{llrcrcrcrcl}
\text{Maximize}: & 10x_1 & + & 3x_2 & + & 5x_3 & + & 8x_4 \\
\text{Subject to}: & 2x_1 & + & 4x_2 & + & x_3 & & & \leq & 100 \\
& 3x_1 & + & x_2 & & & + & 4x_4 & \leq & 250 \\
& x_1 & + & x_2 & + & x_3 & + & x_4 & \geq & 25 \\
& x_1 & & & + & 3x_3 & + & 4x_4 & \leq & 120 \\
\end{array}
$$
$$ x_1 \geq 0,\ x_2 \geq 0,\ x_3 \geq 0,\ x_4 \geq 0 $$

11. If the column rank of the coefficient matrix of a linear program is less than the number of constraints, then one of the variables added in Rule 0 of the simplex algorithm must be basic in the optimal solution so that there is a basic variable in every row of the simplex tableau. This problem illustrates this case which occurs when there is a redundant constraint. When we consider transportation problems in the next chapter, we will see that this is quite common. Note that an active artificial variable must have the value zero if the problem has a feasible solution.

(a) Solve the linear program:

$$
\begin{array}{llrcrcrcl}
\text{Maximize}: & 10x_1 & + & 20x_2 & + & 5x_3 \\
\text{Subject to}: & 2x_1 & + & x_2 & + & 4x_3 & = & 30 \\
& x_1 & + & 2x_2 & + & 2x_3 & = & 45 \\
& -3x_1 & + & x_2 & - & 6x_3 & = & 5 \\
\end{array}
$$
$$ x_1 \geq 0,\ x_2 \geq 0,\ x_3 \geq 0 $$

(b) Show that the column rank of the matrix of coefficients is two.

12. Set up the initial simplex tableau for the following linear program:

$$
\begin{array}{llrcrcrcl}
\text{Maximize}: & 2x_1 & + & 3x_2 & + & 6x_3 \\
\text{Subject to}: & 2x_1 & + & x_2 & + & 4x_3 & \leq & 85 \\
& 3x_1 & + & 4x_2 & + & x_3 & \geq & 35 \\
& x_1 & + & x_2 & + & x_3 & = & 70 \\
& 5x_1 & - & 2x_2 & + & 3x_3 & \leq & 100 \\
\end{array}
$$
$$ x_1 \geq 0,\ x_2 \geq 0,\ x_3 \geq 0 $$

13. Solve the problem posed in Example 3.5.9.

14. Solve the problem posed in Example 3.5.4.

3.7   The dual and minimizing problems

Example 3.5.3 led to the following minimizing problem of type (mLP):

$$
\begin{array}{llrcrcl}
\text{Minimize}: & 1.5y_1 & + & 0.7y_2 & & \\
\text{Subject to}: & 50y_1 & + & 20y_2 & \geq & 600 \\
& 30y_1 & + & 20y_2 & \geq & 400 \\
& 50y_1 & + & 10y_2 & \geq & 350 \\
& & & y_1 \geq 0, \ y_2 \geq 0 & &
\end{array}
$$

The solution to such a problem may be obtained by solving an associated problem of type (MLP), called the *dual linear program*. In this section we will explore the relationship between a linear program and its dual. But before stating the rules for forming a dual linear program, we first consider an economic motivation for the dual.

Let us consider Example 1.3.1, Farmer Brown's problem, from an economic point of view.

Example 3.7.1. Farmer Brown is planning his planting for the coming year. He expects to raise two crops: potatoes and wheat. He has 100 acres of land available for planting, and will be able to devote 160 days of labor to his crops. He expects an acre of wheat to require four days of labor while an acre of potatoes requires only one day.

He has $1,100 that he can use for the start-up costs of planting and cultivating. It costs $10 an acre to plant and cultivate potatoes, while the corresponding costs for an acre of wheat are $20.

If Brown expects a revenue of $40 per acre for potatoes and $120 an acre for wheat, how many acres of each should he plant in order to achieve the maximum possible revenue?

For the purposes of examining this problem in an economic context, we now give Farmer Brown the ability to sell excess resources, i.e., acres of land, days of labor, or capital – or buy additional units of these resources if needed. We assign y_1, y_2, and y_3 as the buying or selling price per unit for the respective resources.

We now make the assumption that Brown operates in an economy characterized by *perfect competition*. In such an economy, if a firm makes a return in excess of the value of the resources needed, another firm enters the market at a lower level of return and drives prices down. The result is that the market seeks to force profits to zero. This situation is described as a *malevolent market*.

Since Brown can now generate revenue or incur costs by producing crops and buying or selling resources, his profit is given by the expression below, where x_1 is the number of acres of potatoes planted and x_2 is the number of acres of wheat:

$$40x_1 + 120x_2 + (100 - x_1 - x_2)y_1 + (160 - x_1 - 4x_2)y_2 + (1100 - 10x_1 - 20x_2)y_3.$$

Note that the three parenthetical quantities in the expression for profit represent the number of units of unused resources. Thus, depending upon whether these quantities are positive or negative, Brown sells his excess resources, or buys needed resources, at the respective unit prices of y_i, $i = 1, 2, 3$.

Since the market views any profit that Brown makes to be at the expense of others, the malevolent market reacts to minimize his profit. For instance, if Brown needs more labor than the 160 days he has available, e.g., if

$$160 - x_1 - 4x_2 < 0$$

then the market will set the price y_2 of labor very high, driving Brown into a loss. As a result, Brown will choose his levels of planting to keep from needing additional resources:

$$
\begin{aligned}
x_1 + x_2 &\le 100 \\
x_1 + 4x_2 &\le 160 \\
10x_1 + 20x_2 &\le 1,100.
\end{aligned}
$$

But conversely, for any resource in which Brown has an excess, e.g., if for labor

$$160 - x_1 - 4x_2 > 0$$

then the market will set the price of the resource to zero: $y_2 = 0$.

The result is that the last three terms of the expression for Brown's profit are all zero, and Brown's problem as a result is the linear program:

$$\begin{aligned}
\text{Maximize}: \quad & z = 40x_1 + 120x_2 \\
\text{Subject to}: \quad & x_1 + x_2 \le 100 \\
& x_1 + 4x_2 \le 160 \\
& 10x_1 + 20x_2 \le 1{,}100 \\
& x_1 \ge 0, \ x_2 \ge 0
\end{aligned}$$

We now rearrange Brown's profit function to examine it from the point of view of the market:

$$(40 - y_1 - y_2 - 10y_3)x_1 + (120 - y_1 - 4y_2 - 20y_3)x_2 + 100y_1 + 160y_2 + 1{,}100y_3$$

The coefficients of x_1 and x_2 represent opportunity costs for Brown to participate in the market by producing crops. If these quantities are positive, then Brown can make arbitrarily large profits by producing crops at any level he chooses. Therefore, the market will set its prices y_i so that these quantities are nonpositive:

$$\begin{aligned}
y_1 + y_2 + 10y_3 &\ge 40 \\
y_1 + 4y_2 + 20y_3 &\ge 120
\end{aligned}$$

Further, if the market sets the prices so that one of these inequalities is strict, then Brown will not produce the corresponding crop since that would mean operating at a loss. Thus, if

$$y_1 + y_2 + 10y_3 > 40$$

then Brown will not produce potatoes and will have $x_1 = 0$. In this way, the first two terms of the profit function viewed from the market viewpoint are zero, and the market's problem of minimizing profits becomes:

$$\begin{aligned}
\text{Minimize}: \quad & w = 100y_1 + 160y_2 + 1{,}100y_3 \\
\text{Subject to}: \quad & y_1 + y_2 + 10y_3 \ge 40 \\
& y_1 + 4y_2 + 20y_3 \ge 120 \\
& y_1 \ge 0, \ y_2 \ge 0, \ y_3 \ge 0
\end{aligned}$$

If we now compare Farmer Brown's linear program with that of the market, we will see that the two linear programs use the same parameters in different arrangements. For instance, the objective function coefficents of one are the right-hand-side constants of the other, the objective of one is maximization and of the other is minimization, and the matrix of coefficients of one is the transpose of the matrix of coefficients of the other. We will see shortly that these relationships are part of what makes the two linear programs duals of each other. ∎

Before formally examining the definition of the dual linear program, we first address the question of the existence of solutions to the two problems and the influence of the economic behavior of Brown and the market. We will use a "hat" as in $\hat{x}$ to indicate the optimal values of the variables.

The decision of the market to set the price of any resource in excess of supply to zero has the effect of making each of the following products equal to zero:

$$
\begin{aligned}
(100 - \hat{x}_1 - \hat{x}_2)\hat{y}_1 &= 0 \\
(160 - \hat{x}_1 - 4\hat{x}_2)\hat{y}_2 &= 0 \\
(1100 - 10\hat{x}_1 - 20\hat{x}_2)\hat{y}_3 &= 0
\end{aligned}
$$

since in each equation either the parenthetical quantity or y_i is zero.

Further, the decision of Farmer Brown not to produce a crop on which he will take a loss causes the following products to be zero

$$
\begin{aligned}
(40 - \hat{y}_1 - \hat{y}_2 - 10\hat{y}_3)\hat{x}_1 &= 0 \\
(120 - \hat{y}_1 - 4\hat{y}_2 - 20\hat{y}_3)\hat{x}_2 &= 0
\end{aligned}
$$

Together, these conditions are called *complementary slackness*. They will be established mathematically later in the section when we prove the key properties of duality theory.

Substituting these properties into the two expressions for profit above shows that the optimal values of the two objective functions are equal:

$$
z = 40\hat{x}_1 + 120\hat{x}_2 = 100\hat{y}_1 + 160\hat{y}_2 + 1100\hat{y}_3 = w
$$

Stated economically, this equation says that Farmer Brown's maximum revenue is equal to the market evaluation of the initial set of resources. Thus, it is an expression of perfect competition in that no excess profit is permitted.

The foregoing discussion has served to introduce aspects of duality theory that we will now investigate from a mathematical point of view.

If we follow the pattern suggested by a comparison between the linear programs above, and then consider a general minimization problem, the *dual* of the following minimizing linear program

$$\text{(P)} \quad \text{Minimize:} \quad w = c_1 y_1 + \cdots + c_m y_m$$
$$\text{Subject to:} \quad a_{11} y_1 + \cdots + a_{1m} y_m \geq b_1$$
$$\vdots$$
$$a_{n1} y_1 + \cdots + a_{nm} y_m \geq b_n$$
$$y_1 \geq 0, \ldots, y_m \geq 0$$

is the maximizing linear program:

$$\text{(D)} \quad \text{Maximize:} \quad z = b_1 x_1 + \cdots + b_n x_n$$
$$\text{Subject to:} \quad a_{11} x_1 + \cdots + a_{n1} x_n \leq c_1$$
$$\vdots$$
$$a_{1m} x_1 + \cdots + a_{nm} x_n \leq c_m$$
$$x_1 \geq 0, \ldots, x_n \geq 0$$

An examination of the relationships between the two problems illustrates how to form the dual of either a minimizing or a maximizing problem:

(a) Transpose the matrix of coefficients.

(b) The right-hand sides of the constraints become the coefficients in the objective function.

(c) The coefficients in the objective function become the right-hand sides of the constraints.

(d) The number of variables becomes the number of constraints, and vice versa.

(e) The directions of the inequalities are reversed.

(f) The objective of minimizing becomes one of maximizing, and vice versa.

(g) The variables of both problems are nonnegative.

Note that these rules are symmetric: they will provide a dual program for either a standard minimization problem or a standard maximization problem.

With this definition, the dual of the linear program stated at the beginning of this section is:

$$
\begin{aligned}
\text{Maximize}: \quad & 600x_1 \; + \; 400x_2 \; + \; 350x_3 \\
\text{Subject to}: \quad & 50x_1 \; + \; 30x_2 \; + \; 50x_3 \; \leq \; 1.5 \\
& 20x_1 \; + \; 20x_2 \; + \; 10x_3 \; \leq \; 0.7 \\
& x_1 \geq 0, \; x_2 \geq 0, \; x_3 \geq 0
\end{aligned}
$$

The following theorems develop the relationships between a linear program and its dual. The theorems are stated for "standard" linear programs, i.e., those with nonnegative variables and right-hand sides and with constraints of the $\geq$ type for a minimization problem and $\leq$ for a maximization problem. We will later state duality rules that include nonstandard problems.

Theorem 3.7.2. (The weak duality theorem) *For any feasible solutions y and x of* (P) *and* (D), *respectively,* $w \geq z$. *Further,* $w = z$ *if and only if*

$$
(b_j - \sum_{i=1}^{m} a_{ji} y_i) x_j = 0, \; j = 1, \ldots, n
$$

and

$$
(c_i - \sum_{j=1}^{n} a_{ji} x_j) y_i = 0, \; i = 1, \ldots, m.
$$

Proof. Introduce nonnegative "surplus" variables $y_{m+1}, \ldots, y_{m+n}$ into (P) to make the constraints equalities:

$$
\begin{aligned}
a_{11}y_1 + a_{12}y_2 + \cdots + a_{1m}y_m \quad - \; y_{m+1} \qquad\qquad\qquad &= \; b_1 \\
a_{21}y_1 + a_{22}y_2 + \cdots + a_{2m}y_m \qquad\qquad - \; y_{m+2} \qquad\quad &= \; b_2 \\
\vdots \qquad\qquad\qquad & \\
a_{n1}y_1 + a_{n2}y_2 + \cdots + a_{nm}y_m \qquad\qquad\qquad - \; y_{m+n} &= \; b_n
\end{aligned}
$$

Multiply each of these new equations by the corresponding dual variable x_i:

$$
\begin{aligned}
a_{11}y_1x_1 + \cdots + a_{1m}y_mx_1 - \; y_{m+1}x_1 \qquad\qquad\qquad &= \; b_1x_1 \\
a_{21}y_1x_2 + \cdots + a_{2m}y_mx_2 \qquad\qquad - \; y_{m+2}x_2 \qquad\quad &= \; b_2x_2 \\
\vdots \qquad\qquad\qquad & \\
a_{n1}y_1x_n + \cdots + a_{nm}y_mx_n \qquad\qquad\qquad - \; y_{m+n}x_n &= \; b_nx_n
\end{aligned}
$$

Now consider the difference between the two objective functions:

$$w - z = c_1 y_1 + c_2 y_2 + \cdots + c_m y_m - b_1 x_1 - b_2 x_2 - \cdots - b_n x_n.$$

Using the set of equations above, we can replace $b_i x_i$:

$$
\begin{aligned}
w - z \;=\; & c_1 y_1 + c_2 y_2 + \cdots + c_m y_m \\
& -(a_{11} y_1 + a_{12} y_2 + \cdots + a_{1m} y_m - y_{m+1}) x_1 \\
& -(a_{21} y_1 + a_{22} y_2 + \cdots + a_{2m} y_m - y_{m+2}) x_2 - \cdots \\
& -(a_{n1} y_1 + a_{n2} y_2 + \cdots + a_{nm} y_m - y_{m+n}) x_n.
\end{aligned}
$$

By collecting terms in the y_i's,

$$w - z = \left(c_1 - \sum_{j=1}^{n} a_{j1} x_j\right) y_1 + \cdots + \left(c_m - \sum_{j=1}^{n} a_{jm} x_j\right) y_m + \sum_{j=1}^{n} y_{m+j} x_j.$$

We must show that this quantity is nonnegative. Since x is a feasible solution to (D), we have for each $i = 1, \ldots, n$,

$$c_i - \sum_{j=1}^{n} a_{ji} x_j \geq 0.$$

That observation together with the fact that both y and x are nonnegative shows that each term in $w - z$ is nonnegative.

Thus, $w - z \geq 0$. Further, the two are equal if and only if

$$\left(c_i - \sum_{j=1}^{n} a_{ji} x_j\right) y_i = 0, \quad i = 1, \ldots, m.$$

and

$$y_{m+j} x_j = \left(b_j - \sum_{i=1}^{m} a_{ji} y_i\right) x_j = 0, \quad j = 1, \ldots, n. \;\square$$

We now can state three corollaries that follow from the theorem.

Corollary 3.7.3. (Unboundedness/infeasibility) *If the primal (respectively dual) linear program is unbounded, then the dual (respectively primal) linear program has no feasible solution.*

Since *any* value of the objective function of a minimizing linear program serves as an upper bound for *all* values of the objective function of the dual maximizing linear program, it is clear that if a maximizing problem is unbounded, then the dual minimization can have no feasible solution, since that would produce an upper bound. The situation is analogous for an unbounded minimization.

Corollary 3.7.4. (Optimality) *If the objective function values of z and w corresponding to feasible solutions x and y of* (D) *and* (P), *respectively, are equal, then x and y are optimal solutions to the respective problems.*

Since an objective function value of either problem is a bound for all solutions of the other problem, if the two values are equal, the objective function of neither can achieve any better value. Hence, both corresponding solutions are optimal.

Corollary 3.7.5. (Complementary Slackness) *Let x_j, $j = 1, \ldots, n$, and y_i, $i = 1, \ldots, m$, be feasible solutions to* (D) *and* (P), *respectively. Then both are optimal if and only if*

$$(b_j - \sum_{i=1}^{m} a_{ji} y_i) x_j = 0, \quad j = 1, \ldots, n$$

and

$$(c_i - \sum_{j=1}^{n} a_{ji} x_j) y_i = 0, \quad i = 1, \ldots, m.$$

The conditions in the corollary are those obtained in the calculation in the proof of Theorem 3.7.2 which are necessary for the values of the objective functions of the two problems to be equal. Note that they are also the conditions that follow from the decisions made by Farmer Brown and the malevolent market in the economic discussion of duality earlier in the section.

One use of complementary slackness is to obtain information about the solution of a linear program from the solution of its dual. This is illustrated in the next example.

Example 3.7.6. The solution to the following linear program from Exercise 1 of Section 3.3:

$$\begin{aligned}
\text{Maximize}: \quad & 20x_1 \;+\; 30x_2 \\
\text{Subject to}: \quad & x_1 \;+\; x_2 \;\le\; 4 \\
& -x_1 \;+\; x_2 \;\le\; 1 \\
& 2x_1 \;+\; 4x_2 \;\le\; 10 \\
& x_1 \ge 0, \; x_2 \ge 0
\end{aligned}$$

is

$$x_1 = 3, \; x_2 = 1, \; s_1 = 0, \; s_2 = 3, \; \text{and} \; s_3 = 0,$$

where s_i is the slack variable in the ith constraint. Determine the solution to the dual linear program by applying complementary slackness.

The constraints of the dual are

$$\begin{aligned}
y_1 \;-\; y_2 \;+\; 2y_3 \;&\ge\; 20 \\
y_1 \;+\; y_2 \;+\; 4y_3 \;&\ge\; 30
\end{aligned}$$

Because $x_1 > 0$ and $x_2 > 0$, from complementary slackness both dual constraints are tight, i.e., are equalities. Because the second constraint of the given linear program is slack, and complementary slackness requires that

$$y_2(1 + x_1 - x_2) = 0$$

we must have $y_2 = 0$. Thus, when these conclusions are included, the dual constraints become

$$\begin{aligned}
y_1 \;+\; 2y_3 \;&=\; 20 \\
y_1 \;+\; 4y_3 \;&=\; 30
\end{aligned}$$

which has the solution $y_1 = 10$ and $y_3 = 5$. We can confirm that this gives the optimal solution to the dual by evaluating the respective objective functions z for the given problem and w for the dual:

$$w = 4 \cdot 10 + 1 \cdot 0 + 10 \cdot 5 = 90 = 20 \cdot 3 + 30 \cdot 1 = z.$$

Since the two objective function values are equal, both solutions are optimal by Corollary 3.7.4. ■

Complementary slackness conditions are particularly useful in nonlinear programming, as we will see later in Chapter 6.

The solution of a minimizing problem can be accomplished by solving the associated dual maximizing problem. The next theorem provides the key relationship between the two problems. Then we will see how to identify the solution to the dual.

Theorem 3.7.7. (The Duality Theorem) *The objective function of a minimizing problem takes on a minimum value if and only if the objective function of the dual maximizing problem takes on a maximum value, and if they exist, the two optimal values are equal.*

We forego the proof of the duality theorem, and instead state a key rule. Note that it suggests the importance of retaining the columns of any artificial variables.

Rule 3.7.8 Identifying the solution to the dual Assuming that the simplex tableaux are set up as presented here, one can identify the solution of the dual minimizing problem as follows: *The optimal solution to the minimizing problem is given by the entries in the row of the objective function of the optimal tableau in the columns corresponding to the slack and artificial variables, and the successive values of the variables are read from left to right.*

To illustrate Rule 3.7.8 to determine the solution to a dual, consider the bicycle manufacturer's problem, Example 3.5.1. We will see that the solution of the dual contains potentially valuable managerial information.

Example 3.7.9. Managerial interpretation of the dual. When the linear program of Example 3.5.1 is rewritten and hours converted to minutes (to avoid fractions!), it becomes:

$$
\begin{array}{lrcrcll}
\text{Maximize}: & 12x_1 & + & 15x_2 & & & \\
\text{Subject to}: & 20x_1 & + & 30x_2 & \leq & 2,400 & \text{(finishing - shop time)} \\
& 15x_1 & + & 40x_2 & \leq & 3,000 & \text{(assembly - shop time)} \\
& x_1 & + & x_2 & \leq & 100 & \text{(bicycle frames)} \\
& \multicolumn{6}{l}{x_1 \geq 0,\ x_2 \geq 0.}
\end{array}
$$

The dual linear program is:

$$
\begin{array}{lrcrcrcl}
\text{Minimize}: & \multicolumn{7}{l}{2,400y_1 + 3,000y_2 + 100y_3} \\
\text{Subject to}: & 20y_1 & + & 15y_2 & + & y_3 & \geq & 12 \\
& 30y_1 & + & 40y_2 & + & y_3 & \geq & 15 \\
& \multicolumn{7}{l}{y_1 \geq 0,\ y_2 \geq 0,\ y_3 \geq 0.}
\end{array}
$$

According to Theorem 3.7.2, the optimal values of the two problems must be equal, and since the value of the objective function $z = 12x_1 + 15x_2$ is profit, the units assigned to the dual variables y_1, y_2, and y_3 must be chosen so that the minimum value of $w = 2,400y_1 + 3,000y_2 + 100y_3$ is also profit. Since the coefficients of the dual variables are the amounts of the respective resources available, the value of y_i must be the amount of profit attributable to a unit of resource i. To determine the solution to the dual, we solve the maximizing problem and then identify the dual solution in the objective row of the optimal tableau.

The initial simplex tableau is:

x_1	x_2	s_1	s_2	s_3	
20	30	1	0	0	2,400
15	40	0	1	0	3,000
1	1	0	0	1	100
−12	−15	0	0	0	0

Rule 2 of the simplex algorithm would make x_2 the entering variable. In Example 3.5.1, we claimed that the solution occurs at $(60, 40)$, and Figure 3.5.1 indicated that by letting x_1 enter instead, the optimal solution can be reached in two iterations of the algorithm going counterclockwise around the set of feasible solutions as opposed to three iterations in the clockwise direction. Thus, we let x_1 enter to save the iteration. Since the respective replacement quantities are

$$\frac{2,400}{20} = 120, \quad \frac{3,000}{15} = 200, \text{ and } \frac{100}{1} = 100$$

the slack variable in the last column is the departing variable. This produces the next simplex tableau:

x_1	x_2	s_1	s_2	s_3	
0	10	1	0	−20	400
0	25	0	1	−15	1,500
1	1	0	0	1	100
0	−3	0	0	12	1,200

Now x_2 enters, and the respective replacement quantities are

$$\frac{400}{10} = 40, \quad \frac{1,500}{25} = 60, \text{ and } \frac{100}{1} = 100$$

which indicates that the slack variable in column 3 should be the departing variable. The next tableau is:

x_1	x_2	s_1	s_2	s_3	
0	1	$\frac{1}{10}$	0	-2	40
0	0	$-\frac{5}{2}$	1	35	500
1	0	$-\frac{1}{10}$	0	3	60
0	0	$\frac{3}{10}$	0	6	1,320

This is the optimal tableau since there are no negatives in the objective row. Thus, in the optimal solution, $x_1 = 60$ 3-speeds and $x_2 = 40$ 5-speeds are produced with a resultant profit of

$$z = 12 \cdot 60 + 15 \cdot 40 = \$1,320.$$

All 2,400 minutes of finishing-shop time and all 100 bicycle frames are utilized while, 500 minutes of time in the assembly/packaging shop are unused.

From Rule 3.7.8, the values of the dual variables are located in the objective row in the last three columns and are read from left to right. The units assigned to the dual variables are profit per unit of resource. Thus, the solution to the dual is

$$\begin{aligned} y_1 &= \ \$\tfrac{3}{10} \text{ profit/finishing} - \text{shop minute} \\ y_2 &= \ \$0 \text{ profit/assembly} - \text{shop minute} \\ y_3 &= \ \$6 \text{ profit/bicycle frame} \end{aligned}$$

Hence, the dual variables indicate the additional profit that could be realized by having one more unit of an exhausted resource. However, we will see that these values are valid only if the solution resulting from an increase in the resource uses the same variables in the basis – here, x_1, x_2, and s_2. ∎

In Section 3.8 we will examine the question of how many additional units of a resource could be added without changing the basis of the optimal solution.

We now consider how to determine the dual of a nonstandard linear program, i.e., one in which the variables are not all nonnegative or in which the constraints are not all of the standard type. As in the case of standard problems, properties of the variables of one linear program are determined by the nature of the constraints of the other. Table 3.7.1 summarizes these relationships.

Table 3.7.1

Dual formation rules	
Maximization problem	Minimization problem
ith constraint $\leq$	ith variable ≥ 0
ith constraint $\geq$	ith variable ≤ 0
ith constraint $=$	ith variable unrestricted
jth variable ≥ 0	jth constraint $\geq$
jth variable ≤ 0	jth constraint $\leq$
jth variable unrestricted	jth constraint $=$

Note that the table indicates that some dual linear programs will involve unrestricted variables. Although unrestricted variables seldom occur in an applied problem, in the next chapter we will use the fact that an equality constraint in the minimizing problem corresponds to an unrestricted variable in the dual of the transportation problem.

The next example illustrates the use of Table 3.7.1 to determine the dual of a minimization problem having nonstandard constraints and an unrestricted variable. We will later determine the dual by first expressing the problem as a standard minimization and will use the rules for standard problems to suggest how to verify the rules in the table.

Example 3.7.10. Consider the linear program:

$$
\begin{array}{lrcrcrcr}
\text{Minimize}: & 8y_1 & + & 10y_2 & + & 4y_3 & & \\
\text{Subject to}: & 4y_1 & + & 2y_2 & - & 3y_3 & \geq & 20 \\
& 2y_1 & + & 3y_2 & + & 5y_3 & \leq & 150 \\
& 6y_1 & + & 2y_2 & + & 4y_3 & = & 40 \\
\end{array}
$$
$$y_1 \text{ unrestricted}, \ y_2 \geq 0, \ y_3 \geq 0$$

As for a standard problem, the coefficients of the right-hand side and the objective function are exchanged, and the matrix of constraint coefficients is transposed. We then use Table 3.7.1 to determine the nature of the constraints and of the variables.

From the last three lines of the table, because the constraints are of the types $\geq$, $\leq$, and $=$, the corresponding variables of the dual maximization problem are nonnegative, nonpositive, and unrestricted, respectively. Because the first variable is unrestricted, the first constraint of the dual is an equality. Because the other two variables of the given minimization problem are $\geq$, the other two constraints of the dual maximization problem are resource constraints of the $\leq$ type. Thus, the dual linear program is:

$$
\begin{array}{llrrrrrrr}
\text{Maximize:} & 20x_1 & + & 150x_2 & + & 40x_3 & & \\
\text{Subject to:} & 4x_1 & + & 2x_2 & + & 6x_3 & = & 8 \\
& 2x_1 & + & 3x_2 & + & 2x_3 & \leq & 10 \\
& -3x_1 & + & 5x_2 & + & 4x_3 & \leq & 4
\end{array}
$$

$$x_1 \geq 0, \; x_2 \leq 0, \; x_3 \text{ unrestricted.}$$

By making the following two changes of variable to obtain an equivalent problem with nonnegative variables,

$$
\begin{aligned}
x_2 &= -v_2 \\
x_3 &= v_3 - v_4
\end{aligned}
$$

we obtain a problem that can be submitted directly to the simplex tableau:

$$
\begin{array}{llrrrrrrrrr}
\text{Maximize:} & 20x_1 & - & 150v_2 & + & 40v_3 & - & 40v_4 & & \\
\text{Subject to:} & 4x_1 & - & 2v_2 & + & 6v_3 & - & 6v_4 & = & 8 \\
& 2x_1 & - & 3v_2 & + & 2v_3 & - & 2v_4 & \leq & 10 \\
& -3x_1 & - & 5v_2 & + & 4v_3 & - & 4v_4 & \leq & 4
\end{array}
$$

$$x_1 \geq 0, \; v_2 \geq 0, \; v_3 \geq 0, \; v_4 \geq 0$$

Setting up the initial tableau yields:

x_1	v_2	v_3	v_4	a_1	s_2	s_3	
4	−2	6	−6	1	0	0	8
2	−3	2	−2	0	1	0	10
−3	−5	4	−4	0	0	1	4
−20	150	−40	40	0	0	0	0
−4	2	−6	6	0	0	0	−8

After two iterations, we obtain an optimal tableau:

x_1	v_2	v_3	v_4	a_1	s_2	s_3	
1	0.647	0	0	0.118	0	−0.176	0.2353
0	−2.765	0	0	−0.412	1	0.118	7.1765
0	−0.765	1	−1	0.088	0	0.118	1.1765
0	132.353	0	0	5.882	0	1.176	51.7647

Thus, the solution to this version of the dual maximizing problem is

$$x_1 = 0.2353, \; v_2 = 0, \; v_3 = 1.1765, \text{ and } v_4 = 0.$$

Note that the columns for v_3 and v_4 remain negatives of each other and represent the unrestricted variable x_3. Thus,

$$x_3 = v_3 - v_4 = 1.1765.$$

Also, v_2 is the negative of the nonpositive variable x_2, so x_2 is also zero in the original dual maximizing problem.

Following the rule above for identifying the solution to a general dual, the values of the variables in the minimizing problem are the corresponding values in the columns of the slack and artificial variables in the objective row:

$$y_1 = 5.882, \ y_2 = 0, \ \text{and} \ y_3 = 1.176. \qquad \blacksquare$$

We now obtain this dual problem again by first rewriting the given problem as a standard minimization problem and then using the rules for forming the dual of a standard problem from early in the section. We thus first rewrite the problem with an equivalent set of constraints, all of the requirement type, and nonnegative variables.

Begin by letting $y_1 = u_1 - u_2$ with $u_1 \geq 0$ and $u_2 \geq 0$ so that all variables are nonnegative.

Then, to rewrite the second constraint as a requirement constraint, i.e., as a constraint of the $\geq$ type, we multiply through by -1 to reverse the direction of the inequality:

$$-2u_1 + 2u_2 - 3y_2 - 5y_3 \geq -150.$$

The third constraint, an equality constraint, is first expressed as a pair of opposing inequalities:

$$6u_1 - 6u_2 + 2y_2 + 4y_3 \geq 40$$
$$6u_1 - 6u_2 + 2y_2 + 4y_3 \leq 40$$

Then multiplying through the second of these inequalities by -1 gives a constraint of the standard minimization type, and the problem can be rewritten as

$$\begin{array}{lrrrrrr}
\text{Minimize}: & 8u_1 & - & 8u_2 & + & 10y_2 & + & 4y_3 \\
\text{Subject to}: & 4u_1 & - & 4u_2 & + & 2y_2 & - & 3y_3 & \geq & 20 \\
& -2u_1 & + & 2u_2 & - & 3y_2 & - & 5y_3 & \geq & -150 \\
& 6u_1 & - & 6u_2 & + & 2y_2 & + & 4y_3 & \geq & 40 \\
& -6u_1 & + & 6u_2 & - & 2y_2 & - & 4y_3 & \geq & -40 \\
\end{array}$$
$$u_1 \geq 0, \ u_2 \geq 0, \ y_2 \geq 0, \ y_3 \geq 0$$

The rules for forming a dual from the beginning of the section now apply and yield

$$\begin{array}{rrrrrrrrl}
\text{Maximize}: & 20x_1 & - & 150x_2 & + & 40x_3 & - & 40x_4 & \\
\text{Subject to}: & 4x_1 & - & 2x_2 & + & 6x_3 & - & 6x_4 & \le & 8 \\
& -4x_1 & + & 2x_2 & - & 6x_3 & + & 6x_4 & \le & -8 \\
& 2x_1 & - & 3x_2 & + & 2x_3 & - & 2x_4 & \le & 10 \\
& -3x_1 & - & 5x_2 & + & 4x_3 & - & 4x_4 & \le & 4 \\
\end{array}$$
$$x_1 \ge 0,\ x_2 \ge 0,\ x_3 \ge 0,\ x_4 \ge 0$$

This problem is obviously not the dual obtained by the table above: it has one too many variables, an extra constraint, and all variables are nonnegative. The process is completed by using changes of variables to reconcile the two problems.

First, we note that the columns for x_3 and x_4 are negatives of each other, so that they correspond to a single unrestricted variable. We put $w_3 = x_3 - x_4$ to obtain a single unrestricted variable. When we then observe that the first two constraints are opposing inequalities that can be expressed as an equality, the problem becomes:

$$\begin{array}{rrrrrrrl}
\text{Maximize}: & 20x_1 & - & 150x_2 & + & 40w_3 & & \\
\text{Subject to}: & 4x_1 & - & 2x_2 & + & 6w_3 & = & 8 \\
& 2x_1 & - & 3x_2 & + & 2w_3 & \le & 10 \\
& -3x_1 & - & 5x_2 & + & 4w_3 & \le & 4 \\
\end{array}$$
$$x_1 \ge 0,\ x_2 \ge 0,\ w_3 \text{ unrestricted}.$$

Finally, note that the column of coefficents of x_2 in this problem is the negative of the column in the originally obtained dual. By letting $w_2 = -x_2$, we obtain a nonpositive variable and the same column of coefficients as in the other problem:

$$\begin{array}{rrrrrrrl}
\text{Maximize}: & 20x_1 & + & 150w_2 & + & 40w_3 & & \\
\text{Subject to}: & 4x_1 & + & 2w_2 & + & 6w_3 & = & 8 \\
& 2x_1 & + & 3w_2 & + & 2x_3 & \le & 10 \\
& -3x_1 & + & 5w_2 & + & 4w_3 & \le & 4 \\
\end{array}$$
$$x_1 \ge 0,\ w_2 \le 0,\ w_3 \text{ unrestricted}.$$

This problem is now the same as the dual obtained from the table, except that the changes of variables used caused two of the variables to be w's instead of x's.

An alternative approach to solving a minimizing problem is to solve the maximizing problem obtained by taking the negative of the objective function and retaining the original constraints. For instance, Example 3.7.10 could be solved by solving the maximization problem below:

$$
\begin{array}{rrrrrrl}
\text{Maximize}: & -8x_1 & - & 10x_2 & - & 4x_3 & \\
\text{Subject to}: & 4x_1 & + & 2x_2 & - & 3x_3 & \geq & 20 \\
 & 2x_1 & + & 3x_2 & + & 5x_3 & \leq & 150 \\
 & 6x_1 & + & 2x_2 & + & 4x_3 & = & 40 \\
\end{array}
$$
$$x_1 \text{ unrestricted}, \ x_2 \geq 0, \ x_3 \geq 0$$

This method is most appropriate when the constraints of the problem are more similar to those of a maximization than of a standard minimization. Note that while this approach will yield the solution

$$x_1 = 5.882, \ x_2 = 0, \text{ and } x_3 = 1.176$$

as was obtained above by duality, there is no duality relationship between the original minimization and the maximization that will permit an interpretation such as that described in Theorem 3.7.2 and Example 3.7.9.

Exercises

1. Solve the following problem by applying the duality theorem. Check your solution by determining the solution geometrically.

$$
\begin{array}{rrrrrl}
\text{Minimize}: & 8y_1 & + & 6y_2 & \\
\text{Subject to}: & 2y_1 & + & y_2 & \geq & 3 \\
 & y_1 & + & y_2 & \geq & 2 \\
\end{array}
$$
$$y_1 \geq 0, \ y_2 \geq 0$$

2. Solve the following problem by the duality theorem:

$$
\begin{array}{rrrrrl}
\text{Minimize}: & 9y_1 & + & 15y_2 & \\
\text{Subject to}: & y_1 & + & 3y_2 & \geq & 1 \\
 & 2y_1 & + & 2y_2 & \geq & 9 \\
 & 3y_1 & + & 2y_2 & \geq & 1 \\
\end{array}
$$
$$y_1 \geq 0, \ y_2 \geq 0$$

3. Solve the following problem by the duality theorem:

$$
\begin{array}{rrrrrl}
\text{Minimize}: & 36y_1 & + & 18y_2 & \\
\text{Subject to}: & y_1 & + & y_2 & \geq & 6 \\
 & 2y_1 & + & 5y_2 & \geq & 10 \\
 & 4y_1 & + & y_2 & \geq & 8 \\
\end{array}
$$
$$y_1 \geq 0, \ y_2 \geq 0$$

4. The following tableau is optimal for a maximizing linear program with four $\leq$ constraints:

x_1	x_2	s_1	s_2	s_3	s_4	
0	0	-2	1	0	$\frac{3}{4}$	50
0	1	$\frac{1}{2}$	0	0	$-\frac{1}{4}$	40
1	0	-1	0	0	$\frac{7}{4}$	25
0	0	4	0	1	2	30
0	0	20	0	0	30	525

(a) Determine the optimal values for all variables.

(b) In which constraints are the resources used completely?

(c) What are the optimal values of the variables in the dual minimizing linear program?

(d) What would be the value of an additional unit of resource in each of the constraints where all resources are used?

5. Solve the linear program:

$$
\begin{aligned}
\text{Minimize}: \quad & 24y_1 + 48y_2 + 36y_3 \\
\text{Subject to}: \quad & y_1 + 3y_2 + 4y_3 \geq 10 \\
& 2y_1 + y_2 = 12 \\
& y_1 \geq 0,\ y_2 \geq 0,\ y_3 \geq 0
\end{aligned}
$$

6. Solve the linear program:

$$
\begin{aligned}
\text{Minimize}: \quad & 24y_1 + 18y_2 + 42y_3 \\
\text{Subject to}: \quad & y_1 + y_2 + 4y_3 \geq 12 \\
& 2y_1 + 3y_2 + 2y_3 \leq 28 \\
& 3y_1 + 2y_2 + 3y_3 \geq 24 \\
& y_1 \geq 0,\ y_2 \geq 0,\ y_3 \geq 0
\end{aligned}
$$

7. Solve the linear program of Exercise 6 by maximizing the negative of the objective function subject to the same set of constraints.

8. The solution to the linear program

$$
\begin{aligned}
\text{Maximize}: \quad & 2x_1 + x_2 + 4x_3 \\
\text{Subject to}: \quad & x_1 + x_2 + x_3 \leq 13 \\
& 2x_1 + 3x_2 + 2x_3 \leq 22 \\
& x_1 \geq 0,\ x_2 \geq 0,\ x_3 \geq 0
\end{aligned}
$$

is $x_1 = x_2 = 0, x_3 = 11, s_1 = 2$, and $s_2 = 0$. Using complementary slackness, determine the solution to the dual.

9. The solution to the linear program

$$
\begin{array}{lrcrcl}
\text{Maximize}: & 12x_1 & + & 20x_2 & & \\
\text{Subject to}: & 2x_1 & + & x_2 & \leq & 100 \\
 & -3x_1 & + & 5x_2 & \leq & 240 \\
 & x_1 & & & \leq & 40 \\
 & \multicolumn{5}{c}{x_1 \geq 0,\ x_2 \geq 0}
\end{array}
$$

is $x_1 = 20$, $x_2 = 60$, $s_1 = 0$, $s_2 = 0$, and $s_3 = 20$. Using complementary slackness, determine the solution to the dual.

10. Solve the linear program formulated in Exercise 8 of Section 3.5.

11. Determine the dual of the linear program:

$$
\begin{array}{lrcrcrcl}
\text{Minimize}: & 4y_1 & + & 3y_2 & + & 8y_3 & & \\
\text{Subject to}: & y_1 & + & y_2 & + & y_3 & \geq & 12 \\
 & 5y_1 & - & 2y_2 & + & 4y_3 & \leq & 20 \\
 & 2y_1 & + & 3y_2 & - & y_3 & = & 12 \\
 & \multicolumn{7}{c}{y_1 \geq 0,\ y_2 \geq 0,\ y_3 \text{ unrestricted}}
\end{array}
$$

12. Determine the dual of the linear program:

$$
\begin{array}{lrcrcrcl}
\text{Minimize}: & 24y_1 & + & 33y_2 & + & 60y_3 & & \\
\text{Subject to}: & 4y_1 & + & y_2 & + & 4y_3 & = & 85 \\
 & 3y_1 & + & 4y_2 & + & y_3 & \geq & 35 \\
 & y_1 & + & y_2 & + & y_3 & \geq & 70 \\
 & 5y_1 & - & 2y_2 & + & 3y_3 & \geq & 45 \\
 & \multicolumn{7}{c}{y_1 \geq 0,\ y_2 \text{ unrestricted},\ y_3 \geq 0}
\end{array}
$$

13. Consider the following linear program:

$$
\begin{array}{lrcrcl}
\text{Maximize}: & z = c_1x_1 + c_2x_2 & & & & \\
\text{Subject to}: & a_{11}x_1 & + & a_{12}x_2 & \leq & b_1 \\
 & a_{21}x_1 & + & a_{22}x_2 & \geq & b_2 \\
 & a_{31}x_1 & + & a_{32}x_2 & = & b_3 \\
 & \multicolumn{5}{c}{x_1 \geq 0,\ x_2 \text{ unrestricted}}
\end{array}
$$

(a) Determine the dual linear program.

(b) If z and w are the objective function values of the given linear program and its dual, respectively, corresponding to feasible solutions of the respective linear programs, prove that $w - z \geq 0$.

14. Solve the dual of the problem in Exercise 11 above.

15. The workload of a small company is such that the number of employees needed varies according to the day of the week. Work rules require that each employee work five consecutive days. Table 3.7.2 gives the number of employees needed each day.

Table 3.7.2

Day	Sun	Mon	Tue	Wed	Thu	Fri	Sat
Workers	6	11	10	12	14	15	13

(a) Formulate a linear program to determine a schedule that will meet the daily requirements for the number of workers while minimizing the total number of workers.

(b) Determine the dual for the linear program found in part (a).

3.8 Sensitivity analysis

Example 3.7.8 showed that in a maximization problem the dual variables indicate the values of an additional unit of resource in the corresponding constraint. Following the example we noted that there was a limit to the range over which those values of additional units are valid. In this section we investigate this limitation as well as limits on changes in the objective function coefficients.

Consider the following example:

Example 3.8.1. The Smith Company manufactures two products having respective profits of $40 and $10 and is planning production for a short period of time during which their inventory of two components has been allowed to reach very low levels. The two resources in short supply are a custom fastener used in assembly and paint. Product 1 requires 10 fasteners and product 2 requires only 2 fasteners, and there are only 400 in stock. The products require 15 and 10 units of paint, respectively, and there are 1,020 units in stock. In the brief period being planned, the company has 420 hours of labor available, and the products require 3 and 5 hours of labor, respectively.

Smith's goal during this period is to produce a mixture of its products that would yield a maximum profit if sold. Determine how many of each product should be made.

Letting x_1 and x_2 denote the number of units of the respective products produced, the following linear program will maximize the profit within the limits of Smith's resources:

$$
\begin{array}{rrcrcl}
\text{Maximize}: & 40x_1 & + & 10x_2 & & \\
\text{Subject to}: & 10x_1 & + & 2x_2 & \leq & 400 \\
 & 15x_1 & + & 10x_2 & \leq & 1,020 \\
 & 3x_1 & + & 5x_2 & \leq & 420 \\
 & \multicolumn{5}{c}{x_1 \geq 0,\ x_2 \geq 0}
\end{array}
$$

Since this problem has standard constraints, we proceed directly to the simplex algorithm:

x_1	x_2	s_1	s_2	s_3	
10	2	1	0	0	400
15	10	0	1	0	1,020
3	5	0	0	1	420
-40	-10	0	0	0	0

After two iterations we obtain the optimal tableau:

x_1	x_2	s_1	s_2	s_3	
1	0	$\frac{1}{7}$	$-\frac{1}{35}$	0	28
0	1	$-\frac{3}{14}$	$\frac{1}{7}$	0	60
0	0	$\frac{9}{14}$	$-\frac{22}{35}$	1	36
0	0	$\frac{25}{7}$	$\frac{2}{7}$	0	1,720

The optimal solution is

$$x_1 = 28,\ x_2 = 60,\ s_1 = 0,\ s_2 = 0,\ s_3 = 36$$

with the maximum value of the objective function equal to 1,720.

The set of feasible solutions is graphed in Figure 3.8.1.

Since both s_1 and s_2 are zero, the first and second constraints are *tight*, i.e., the corresponding resources are entirely used. Further, since the objective entries corresponding to both are positive, additional units of either resource would result in an increase in the optimal value of the objective function.

We therefore conduct an analysis of the sensitivity of the problem to a change in the amount of either resource. Examining the objective row, we see that the potential per-unit increase in the objective function is larger for the first constraint, $\frac{25}{7}$ versus $\frac{2}{7}$. Thus, we consider the first constraint first.

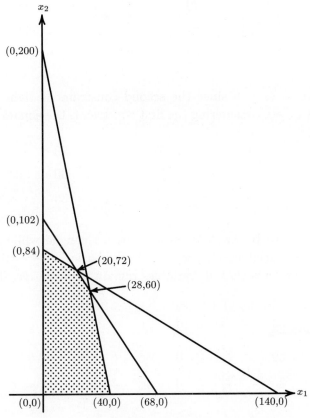

Figure 3.8.1

Let δ be a change in the resource of the first constraint, the limitation on fasteners. With this added quantity, the original first constraint becomes

$$10x_1 + 2x_2 + s_1 = 400 + \delta.$$

However, in the optimal tableau, $s_1 = 0$ and we have

$$10x_1 + 2x_2 = 400 + \delta.$$

But δ and s_1 each have the same units as the resource, so with $s_1 = -\delta$, we see that the change in the resource can be considered to be the slack variable s_1 (or the artificial variable depending on the nature of the constraint).

Expressing the constraints from the optimal tableau in equation form, we obtain:

$$
\begin{aligned}
x_1 \quad & + \frac{s_1}{7} - \frac{s_2}{35} & = 28 \\
x_2 & - \frac{3s_1}{14} + \frac{s_2}{7} & = 60 \\
& \frac{9s_1}{14} - \frac{22s_2}{35} + s_3 & = 36
\end{aligned}
$$

Then, setting $s_2 = 0$ since the second constraint is tight, and setting $s_1 = -\delta$ since we are considering the first constraint, the equations become:

$$
\begin{aligned}
x_1 \quad & - \frac{\delta}{7} & = 28 \\
x_2 & + \frac{3\delta}{14} & = 60 \\
& - \frac{9\delta}{14} + s_3 & = 36
\end{aligned}
$$

The question to be resolved is how large δ can be while allowing the same set of three variables $-\{x_1, x_2, s_3\}-$ to be basic. The restriction on any change in a resource is that all variables remain nonnegative. Thus, δ must satisfy:

$$
\begin{aligned}
x_1 &= 28 + \frac{\delta}{7} \geq 0 \quad \text{or} \quad \delta \geq -\frac{28}{\frac{1}{7}} = -196 \\
x_2 &= 60 - \frac{3\delta}{14} \geq 0 \quad \text{or} \quad \delta \leq \frac{60}{\frac{3}{14}} = 280 \\
s_3 &= 36 + \frac{9\delta}{14} \geq 0 \quad \text{or} \quad \delta \geq -\frac{36}{\frac{9}{14}} = -56
\end{aligned}
$$

Therefore, the resource can be increased by at most 280 units, and any increase beyond that would make x_2 negative. The calculations present two candidates for a limit on the maximum decrease of the resource. The maximum decrease is the smaller of the two candidates, since decreasing the resource by more than 56 units would result in a negative value for s_3.

Thus, the interval of values for the resource in the first constraint that would leave the optimal basis unchanged is

$$
344 = 400 - 56 \leq b_1 \leq 400 + 280 = 680.
$$

Figure 3.8.2 illustrates the changes in the set of feasible solutions that occur as a result of changes of the resource in the first constraint within the interval.

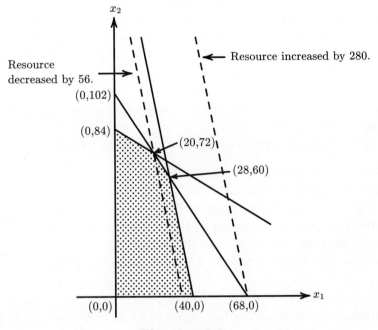

Figure 3.8.2

Choosing any value in this interval as the resource in the first constraint would result in an optimal solution in which the basic variables are the same as in the solution of the original problem: x_1, x_2, and s_3. In particular, for the maximum increase of $\delta = 280$ corresponding to a resource of 680 in the first constraint, the optimal solution and objective function value are calculated from the equations from the optimal tableau:

$$x_1 = 28 + \frac{280}{7} = 68$$

$$x_2 = 60 - \frac{3 \cdot 280}{14} = 0$$

$$s_3 = 36 + \frac{9 \cdot 280}{14} = 216$$

$$z = 1,720 + \frac{25 \cdot 280}{7} = 2,720.$$

The slack variables s_1 and s_2 remain zero. Note that while $x_2 = 0$, x_2 is considered a basic variable – we simply have chosen the maximum possible increase in the first resource and pushed the variable x_2 to the smallest possible feasible value, as seen in Figure 3.8.2.

Note that the increase of 1,000 in the objective function is an increase of $\frac{25}{7}$ for each unit in the 280 unit increase in the resource, as was indicated would occur in the discussion of Example 3.7.8 earlier. This means that it would be desirable for the Smith Company to acquire up to an additional 280 fasteners if it could obtain them at a cost less than $\$\frac{25}{7}$ per unit.

The graph shows that changing the resource b_1 moves the intersection of the lines

$$10x_1 + 2x_2 = b_1 \text{ and } 15x_1 + 10x_2 = 1{,}020$$

along the interval joining $(20, 72)$ and $(68, 0)$. The original value $b_1 = 400$ produces the optimal point $(28, 60)$. The maximum increase of 280 from 400 to 680 moves the intersection to $(68, 0)$, stopping when the x_1-axis is encountered to prevent violation of the constraint $x_2 \geq 0$. The result of including $(68, 0)$ in the set of feasible solutions is to increase the optimal value of the objective function to 2,720, an increase of $\frac{25}{7}$ for each unit of the 280 unit increase in b_1.

The maximum decrease of 56 to 344 moves the intersection to $(20, 72)$ and reduces the objective function value to 1520, a decrease of $\frac{25}{7}$ for each unit decrease in b_1. The movement of the intersection in that direction is stopped by the constraint

$$3x_1 + 5x_2 \leq 420$$

to prevent the slack variable s_3 from becoming negative.

Reviewing the last step in the calculations involving δ is helpful in light of this graphic interpretation. Note that the calculations that determine the limits of the increase or decrease of b_1 correspond to the lines that restrict the movement of the first constraint described in the graph.

In Figure 3.8.2, note that if the resource in the first constraint is increased by the maximum amount, the resulting optimal solution occurs at $(68, 0)$. Since this point is at the the intersection of three constraints, the corresponding basic solution is degenerate as discussed in Example 3.3.2. This happens by design. The maximum increase is obtained by setting a basic variable to zero, so that a degenerate solution will always result when a resource is raised or lowered by the maximum amount allowed by sensitivity analysis.

Finally, the equations used to determine the maximum increase and decrease in a resource can be used to determine the new optimal solution that results from the change. Suppose, for example, that an increase of $\delta = 140$ is made in the resource of the first constraint. Since a maximum increase of 280 is allowed, the equations used earlier remain valid. Substituting into those equations yields the new optimal, basic solution:

$$
\begin{aligned}
x_1 &= 28 + \frac{140}{7} = 48 \\
x_2 &= 60 - \frac{3 \cdot 140}{14} = 30 \\
s_3 &= 36 + \frac{9 \cdot 140}{14} = 126
\end{aligned}
$$

The new value of the objective function can be calculated in two ways:

- By using the $\frac{25}{7}$ per-unit change as for the basic variables:

$$
z = 1,720 + \frac{25}{7} \cdot 140 = 2,220.
$$

- By direct evaluation of the objective function:

$$
z = 40 \cdot 48 + 80 \cdot 30 = 2,220.
$$

Rules for right-hand-side sensitivity analysis

We now state the rule illustrated in these calculations. Let b'_i denote the respective entries in the column of the solution in the optimal tableau and a'_i represent the respective entries in the column of the slack or artificial variable associated with constraint k. Then:

The *maximum increase* in the resource (or requirement) for constraint k is

$$
\min \left\{ -\frac{b'_i}{a'_i} : a'_i < 0 \right\}.
$$

If $a'_i \geq 0$ for all i, then the resource (or requirement) can be increased without bound with no change in the optimal basis.

The *maximum decrease* in the resource (or requirement) for constraint k is

$$
\min \left\{ \frac{b'_i}{a'_i} : a'_i > 0 \right\}.
$$

If $a_i' \leq 0$ for all i, then the resource (or requirement) can be decreased without bound with no change in the optimal basis.

We can quickly determine the interval for the paint resource from the second constraint by applying the above rules:

Maximum increase:

$$\min \left\{ -\frac{28}{-\frac{1}{35}}, -\frac{36}{-\frac{22}{35}} \right\} = \min \{980, 57.27\} = 57.27$$

Maximum decrease:

$$\min \left\{ \frac{60}{\frac{1}{7}} \right\} = 420.$$

Thus, the interval for the resource in the second constraint is

$$600 = 1,020 - 420 \leq b_2 \leq 1,020 + 57.27 = 1,077.27.$$

Hence, the limitations on a resource may be calculated from selected quotients of the right-hand-side entries over entries from the column corresponding to the slack or artificial variable in the constraint. Within those limits the change in the objective function indicated by the entries in the objective row of the optimal tableau are valid. A change in the resource beyond those limits will change the set of variables in the optimal basis, and the objective function change per unit will no longer apply since the objective function entry would also change.

Rules for objective function coefficient sensitivity analysis

By a very similar reasoning, limits can be obtained for changes in the objective function coefficients of basic variables. We leave out the details and simply outline the process.

Let x_r be the variable that is basic in row k in the optimal solution. Let c_j' denote the objective row entries in the optimal tableau and let a_{kj}' denote the entries in row k in the optimal tableau, excluding the right-hand side and any columns of artificial variables. Let Δc_r denote a change in the original objective function coefficient of x_r.

Then by a parallel discussion to that for preserving the nonnegativity of the right-hand side given above, by considering the inequalities that preserve nonnegativity of the objective function coefficients, we obtain the following bounds for Δc_r:

The *maximum increase* in the objective function coefficient of x_r is

$$\min\left\{-\frac{c'_j}{a'_{kj}} : a'_{kj} < 0, j \neq r\right\}.$$

The *maximum decrease* in the objective function coefficient of x_r is

$$\min\left\{\frac{c'_j}{a'_{kj}} : a'_{kj} > 0, j \neq r\right\}.$$

Note that columns of any artificial variable are excluded in the above calculations, since objective row entries for artificial variables are permitted to be negative.

Thus, looking at x_1 in Example 3.8.1, for which the optimal tableau is reproduced below,

	x_1	x_2	s_1	s_2	s_3	
k	1	0	$\frac{1}{7}$	$-\frac{1}{35}$	0	28
	0	1	$-\frac{3}{14}$	$\frac{1}{7}$	0	60
	0	0	$\frac{9}{14}$	$-\frac{22}{35}$	1	36
c'_j	0	0	$\frac{25}{7}$	$\frac{2}{7}$	0	1,720

we get

$$-25 = -\min\left\{\frac{25}{7}\Big/\frac{1}{7}\right\} \leq \Delta c_1 \leq \min\left\{-\frac{2}{7}\Big/\left(-\frac{1}{35}\right)\right\} = 10.$$

Since the original objective function coefficent of x_1 in the problem was 40, this means that if

$$15 = 40 - 25 \leq c_1 \leq 40 + 10 = 50$$

then the set of basic variables will remain the same $-\{x_1, x_2, s_3\}$. Consider Figure 3.8.3 to interpret the geometric influence of these changes.

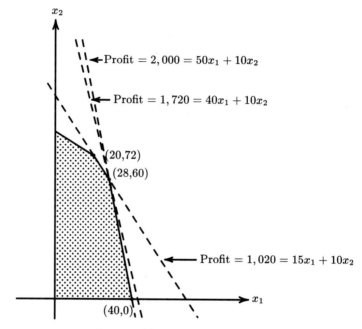

Figure 3.8.3

A change in an objective function coefficient affects the slope of the level curves of the objective function. To illustrate this, the figure shows the set of feasible solutions with three level curves of objective functions, drawn as broken lines, corresponding to optimal solutions. The one yielding a profit of $1,720 corresponds to the original objective function. The others, with profits of $2,000 and $1,020, respectively, correspond to the maximum increase and the maximum decrease in the coefficent of x_1. While $(28, 60)$ is optimal for all three objective functions, we see that the level curves of both changed objective functions are parallel to an edge of the set of feasible solutions and, thus, correspond to nonunique solutions.

To further emphasize the nonuniqueness, we examine the optimal tableaux obtained for the maximum increase and the maximum decrease.

For the objective function corresponding to the greatest decrease in the coefficient of x_1,

$$z = 15x_1 + 10x_2$$

the optimal tableau is

x_1	x_2	s_1	s_2	s_3	
1	0	0.143	−0.029	0	28
0	1	−0.214	0.143	0	60
0	0	0.643	−0.629	1	36
0	0	0.000	1.000	0	1,020

The zero in the objective row for the nonbasic variable s_1 indicates that the solution is not unique. Pivoting in the s_1 column yields the alternative solution:

x_1	x_2	s_1	s_2	s_3	
1	0	0	0.111	−0.222	20
0	1	0	−0.067	0.333	72
0	0	1	−0.978	1.556	56
0	0	0	1.000	0.000	1,020

For the objective function corresponding to the greatest increase in the coefficient of x_1,

$$z = 50x_1 + 10x_2$$

the optimal tableau is

x_1	x_2	s_1	s_2	s_3	
1	0	0.143	−0.029	0	28
0	1	−0.214	0.143	0	60
0	0	0.643	−0.629	1	36
0	0	5.000	0.000	0	2,000

The zero in the objective row for the nonbasic variable s_2 indicates that the solution is not unique. Pivoting in the s_2 column yields the alternative solution:

x_1	x_2	s_1	s_2	s_3	
1	0.2	0.1	0	0	40
0	7.0	−1.5	1	0	420
0	4.4	−0.3	0	1	300
0	0.0	5.0	0	0	2,000

Thus, at the extremes of the interval of values for an objective function coefficient, the solution is nonunique. This parallels the result for right-hand-side changes where at the extremes the solution is degenerate.

Analysis of a slack constraint or a nonbasic variable

In this section we have considered only changes affecting the right-hand-side
of tight constraints or the objective function coefficient of a basic variable.
Before concluding, some comment is appropriate on the cases of a slack
constraint or a nonbasic variable.

For a slack constraint, the value of the slack or surplus variable indicates
the number of units by which the corresponding right-hand side can be
changed without changing the basis. In the case of a $\leq$ constraint, the value
of the slack variable is the amount by which the corresponding resource can
be reduced; for a $\geq$ constraint, the value of the surplus variable is the amount
by which the corresponding requirement can be increased. In either case,
the size of the possible change is immediately available. There is no limit on
the change in the other direction.

For a nonbasic variable, the positive objective function coefficient indicates the amount by which the the value of the objective function would
decrease per unit if that variable were made positive. Thus, this entry indicates the minimum increase that would be required in the objective function
before the corresponding activity would make a positive contribution to the
value of the objective function if it were made basic.

The calculations of bounds on changes that preserve the optimal basis are
also provided by the LINDO package introduced in Section 3.5. The output
below for the solution to Example 3.8.1 includes these calculations by re-
ponding with a "y" to the question regarding sensitivity analysis. Note that
the solution to the dual is given under the column headed DUAL PRICES.
The column headed REDUCED COSTS gives the increase in objective function coefficients needed to make nonbasic activity variables basic. Here, they
are both zero, since both activity variables are basic.

Listing 3.8.1

```
:look all

 MAX      40 X1 + 10 X2
 SUBJECT TO
         2)    10 X1 + 2 X2 <=    400
         3)    15 X1 + 10 X2 <=   1020
         4)     3 X1 + 5 X2 <=    420
 END
```

```
:go

LP OPTIMUM FOUND  AT STEP     2

           OBJECTIVE FUNCTION VALUE

  1)         1720.00000

    VARIABLE        VALUE          REDUCED COST
         X1       28.000000           .000000
         X2       60.000000           .000000


        ROW    SLACK OR SURPLUS     DUAL PRICES
         2)          .000000         3.571429
         3)          .000000          .285714
         4)        35.999990          .000000


 NO. ITERATIONS=        2

  DO RANGE(SENSITIVITY) ANALYSIS?
?y

RANGES IN WHICH THE BASIS IS UNCHANGED:

                          OBJ COEFFICIENT RANGES
 VARIABLE        CURRENT        ALLOWABLE       ALLOWABLE
                  COEF          INCREASE        DECREASE
         X1     40.000000        9.999996       25.000000
         X2     10.000000       16.666670        2.000000

                     RIGHTHAND SIDE RANGES
     ROW         CURRENT        ALLOWABLE       ALLOWABLE
                  RHS           INCREASE        DECREASE
       2        400.000000      280.000000      55.999980
       3       1020.000000       57.272710     420.000000
       4        420.000000        INFINITY      35.999990
```

Exercises

1. Determine the maximum increase and decrease for the land and days of labor resources in Farmer Jones's problem as solved in Example 3.3.1.

2. Draw the set of feasible solutions for Example 3.6.1, and determine the maximum increase and decrease for the third constraint. Note that you will need to begin by calculating the a_3 column for the optimal tableau.

3. Determine the maximum increase and decrease in the resources of the tight constraints of the problem represented by the tableau in Exercise 4 of Section 3.7.

4. The following tableau is optimal for a problem involving four resource constraints:

x_1	x_2	x_3	s_1	s_2	s_3	s_4	
$\frac{1}{5}$	0	0	1	$\frac{1}{2}$	0	-2	84
-1	1	0	0	-2	0	$\frac{5}{2}$	225
0	0	1	0	$\frac{3}{2}$	0	$\frac{1}{2}$	125
2	0	0	0	$-\frac{5}{2}$	1	$-\frac{3}{2}$	65
12	0	0	0	40	0	25	700

   (a) The resources in the second and fourth constraints are exhausted. Increasing which of these two resources by the maximum amount possible without changing the basis would produce the greater increase in the objective function, and what would that increase be?

   (b) How many variables does the dual minimizing linear program have, and what are their optimal values?

   (c) Determine the limits on the change in the objective function coefficient of x_2 in order to preserve the same basis.

5. Draw the graph corresponding to Figure 3.8.2 to illustrate geometrically the changes that would result from the maximum increase and decrease in the second constraint of Example 3.8.1.

6. The optimal tableau for the following linear program

$$
\begin{array}{rlll}
\text{Maximize}: & 30x_1 + 100x_2 + 0.04x_3 - 0.06x_4 & & \\
\text{Subject to}: & x_1 + x_2 & \leq & 100 \\
& x_1 + 4x_2 & \leq & 160 \\
& 10x_1 + 20x_2 + x_3 - x_4 & \leq & 1,100 \\
& x_4 & \leq & 500 \\
\end{array}
$$
$$x_1 \geq 0,\ x_2 \geq 0,\ x_3 \geq 0,\ x_4 \geq 0$$

is given below:

x_1	x_2	x_3	x_4	s_1	s_2	s_3	s_4	
0	0	-1.00	1	6.667	3.333	-1.00	0	100
0	1	0.00	0	-0.333	0.333	0.00	0	20
1	0	0.00	0	1.333	-0.333	0.00	0	80
0	0	1.00	0	-6.667	-3.333	1.00	1	400
0	0	0.02	0	6.267	23.133	0.06	0	4,394

(a) Determine the range of values for the objective function coefficient of x_4 such that the optimal basis remains unchanged.

(b) Determine the new basic solution if the resource in the third constraint is increased by 50.

(c) Determine a value for the resource in the third constraint such that the new solution would be degenerate.

(d) What increase could be made in the objective function coefficient of x_3 such that the current solution would remain optimal?

7. In the linear program for Farmer Max below, x_1 is the number of acres of corn to be planted, x_2 is the number of acres of potatoes, and the objective function coefficents are the respective profits per acre. The units of the four resources are indicated below:

$$
\begin{array}{lrcrcll}
\text{Maximize}: & 50x_1 & + & 40x_2 & & & \\
\text{Subject to}: & x_1 & + & x_2 & \le & 50 & \text{Acres of land} \\
& 3x_1 & + & 2x_2 & \le & 120 & \text{Days of labor} \\
& 10x_1 & + & 60x_2 & \le & 1,200 & \text{Dollars of capital} \\
& 20x_1 & + & 10x_2 & \le & 800 & \text{Pounds of fertilizer} \\
& & x_1 \ge 0, x_2 \ge 0 & & & &
\end{array}
$$

In the optimal tableau below for the linear program, s_i is the slack variable for constraint i:

x_1	x_2	s_1	s_2	s_3	s_4	
0	0	1	$-\frac{5}{16}$	$-\frac{1}{160}$	0	5
0	1	0	$-\frac{1}{16}$	$\frac{3}{160}$	0	15
0	0	0	$-\frac{55}{8}$	$\frac{1}{16}$	1	50
1	0	0	$\frac{3}{8}$	$-\frac{1}{80}$	0	30
0	0	0	$\frac{65}{4}$	$\frac{1}{8}$	0	2,100

Answer each of the following:

(a) What are the optimal value and the units of each basic variable?

(b) What is the value of an additional day of labor?

(c) What are the maximum and the minimum amounts of capital that will permit Max to operate with the same set of basic variables?

(d) What is the new basic solution if the capital is increased by $160?

(e) Suppose that Max can hire additional days of labor for $25 a day. However, according to the optimal tableau above, all of his capital is needed for planting costs. Nevertheless, he is considering diverting up to $500 from planting to hiring additional labor. Complete the modification of the original linear program below by adding the variable x_3 and a constraint to determine how much capital it would be useful to divert.

$$
\begin{array}{rrcll}
\text{Maximize:} & 50x_1 + 40x_2 & & & \\
\text{Subject to:} & x_1 + x_2 & \leq & 50 & \text{Acres of land} \\
& 3x_1 + 2x_2 & \leq & 120 & \text{Days of labor} \\
& 10x_1 + 60x_2 & \leq & 1,200 & \text{Dollars of capital} \\
& & & & \text{New constraint} \\
& 20x_1 + 10x_2 & \leq & 800 & \text{Pounds of fertilizer} \\
\end{array}
$$

$$x_1 \geq 0, \ x_2 \geq 0, \ x_3 \geq 0$$

8. Grande Vision and Sound (GVS) makes electrical components. Four of their products depend heavily on a patented component which GVS purchases from the company with the rights to market it. An uncertain labor situation at that company has forced GVS to plan a year's production under the assumption that it can obtain only 10,000 of the component. Otherwise, they can devote 200 hours of production time per week to the four products for the 46 weeks that GVS expects to operate its production facility. The respective profits on an item of each of the four lines are $80, $120, $140, and $160. The number of production hours required and the number of components needed for a unit of each item are given in Table 3.8.1.

Table 3.8.1

	Item			
	1	2	3	4
Production (hr)	2	3	4	7
Components	3	4	5	6

The sales manager insists that a total of at least 700 of the two most profitable items be made. The linear program to maximize profit and the optimal tableau for the problem are:

$$\text{Maximize}: \quad 80x_1 + 120x_2 + 140x_3 + 160x_4 \quad \text{(Profit)}$$

$$\text{Subject to}: \qquad\qquad\qquad\qquad x_3 + x_4 \geq 700 \quad \text{(Items made)}$$

$$2x_1 + 3x_2 + 4x_3 + 7x_4 \leq 9{,}200 \quad \text{(hours)}$$

$$3x_1 + 4x_2 + 5x_3 + 6x_4 \leq 10{,}000 \quad \text{(components)}$$

$$x_1 \geq 0, \ x_2 \geq 0, \ x_3 \geq 0, \ x_4 \geq 0$$

The optimal tableau:

All we're making now
$x_2 = 1625$
$x_3 = 700$

	x_1	x_2	x_3	x_4	s_1	a_1	s_2	s_3	
Sales minimum	0	0	1	1	-1	1	0	0	700
Hours	$-\frac{1}{4}$	0	0	$\frac{9}{4}$	$\frac{1}{4}$	$-\frac{1}{4}$	1	$-\frac{3}{4}$	1,525
Components	$\frac{3}{4}$	1	0	$\frac{1}{4}$	$\frac{5}{4}$	$-\frac{5}{4}$	0	$\frac{1}{4}$	1,625
	10	0	0	10	10	-10	0	30	293,000

 # increase = RHS analysis w/ respect to constraint

obj. func.

(a) Suppose that another company is licensed to produce the key component. How much should GVS pay them per unit? How many should it consider buying? $\sim$RHS

(b) How would you advise the sales manager about his production requirement?

(c) Suppose that the quality assurance manager recommends a change in the method of production which would add an hour to the production time required for each unit of the third product line. What would you advise regarding the impact of this recommendation on production?

(d) What would the profit per unit on the fourth line need to be for it to be profitable to make?

9. Electra Manufacturing has decided to focus the next month of production on three related product lines. The per-unit profits on the lines are \$120, \$150, and \$90. The first line has been the most popular, so they plan to make at least as many of it as they make of the other two combined. They want to make a total of at least 3,000 items. The respective lines require 1, 0.5, and 0.75 hours of production time. In the month they anticipate having 2,420 hours of production available. A particular component is in short supply – they have access to only 7,000. Lines 1 and 3 require two of the component; line 2 requires three. Assuming that they can sell all they make, how many of each product line should they make to maximize their profit?

The linear programming formulation, initial tableau, and optimal tableau for the problem follow:

$$
\begin{array}{rrrrrll}
\text{Maximize}: & 120x_1 & + & 150x_2 & + & 90x_3 & \\
\text{Subject to}: & -x_1 & + & x_2 & + & x_3 & \leq & 0 \\
& x_1 & + & x_2 & + & x_3 & \geq & 3{,}000 & \text{Min. sales} \\
& x_1 & + & 0.5x_2 & + & 0.75x_3 & \leq & 2{,}420 & \text{Production hr} \\
& 2x_1 & + & 3x_2 & + & 2x_3 & \leq & 7{,}000 & \text{Comp. supply}
\end{array}
$$

$$x_1 \geq 0, x_2 \geq 0, x_3 \geq 0$$

The initial tableau:

x_1	x_2	x_3	s_1	s_2	a_2	s_3	s_4	
-1	1	1	1	0	0	0	0	0
1	1	1	0	-1	1	0	0	$3{,}000$
1	$\frac{1}{2}$	$\frac{3}{4}$	0	0	0	1	0	$2{,}420$
2	3	2	0	0	0	0	1	$7{,}000$
-120	-150	-90	0	0	0	0	0	0
-1	-1	-1	0	1	0	0	0	$-3{,}000$

The optimal tableau:

x_1	x_2	x_3	s_1	s_2	a_2	s_3	s_4	
0	0	1	0	-8	8	-4	-2	320
0	1	0	0	2	-2	0	1	$1{,}000$
1	0	0	0	5	-5	4	1	$1{,}680$
0	0	0	1	11	-11	8	2	360
0	0	0	0	180	-180	120	90	$380{,}400$

(a) If Electra could find another source of the component in short supply, how much should they pay for it?

(b) The sales manager would like to increase slightly the number of items made. How would you advise him?

(c) What range of production hours would result in the same set of basic variables?

(d) What would the new basic solution be if 100 fewer components were available?

(e) What would be the value an additional hour of production?

3.9 Summary and objectives

In this chapter we have developed the ability to identify, formulate, and solve linear programs for maximization and minimization problems.

Building on the intuitions gained from geometric solutions, we developed the simplex algorithm for solving larger problems algebraically in Section 3.3. The simplex algorithm employs the same row operations as Gauss-Jordan elimination to develop a sequence of solutions having increasing values of the objective function. Section 3.4 developed the background to show that the solutions generated by the simplex algorithm were the only solutions that we need to examine.

Sections 3.1 through 3.5 dealt only with problems in the two standard forms introduced at the beginning of the chapter:

$$\begin{array}{llll}
\text{(MLP)} & \text{Maximize}: & z = c \cdot x & \qquad \text{(mLP)} \quad \text{Minimize}: \quad w = d \cdot y \\
& \text{Subject to}: & Ax \leq b \quad \text{and} & \qquad \qquad \text{Subject to}: \quad Ey \geq d \\
& & x \geq 0 & \qquad \qquad \qquad \qquad \quad y \geq 0.
\end{array}$$

In Section 3.6 the simplex algorithm was extended to be able to solve problems having more general constraints. A method to circumvent the restriction of the simplex algorithm to nonnegative variables was introduced in which an unrestricted variable is written as the difference of two nonnegative variables.

We developed a theory of duality which relates a minimization problem to a dual maximization problem. The solution to the minimization problem is then determined from the solution to the dual maximization problem. Duality theory is summarized in Theorem 3.7.2 and its corollaries and Theorem 3.7.7. We found that determining the values of the dual variables provides information on the impact of changing the right-hand side of the problem.

Section 3.8 introduced sensitivity analysis, which allows analysis of the optimal simplex tableau to determine the effect of changes in the right-hand side of constraints or the objective function coefficients. This aspect of linear programming is of particular importance for the managerial value of the information it provides.

Objectives

The following objectives describe what the student should have mastered at the conclusion of the chapter. Note that the first few were introduced in Chapter 1. Examples and/or exercises that illustrate the objective are provided in most cases.

Be able to:

1. Identify problems for which a linear program is an appropriate means of solution and formulate the linear program. Examples 1–9 of Section 1.3. Exercises 1–10 of Section 3.5.

2. Solve a linear program in two variables graphically. Example 1.4.1. Exercises 4–6 of Section 1.4.

3. Draw the level curves of the objective function for a problem having two variables and being solved graphically, and identify the level curve corresponding to the optimal solution. Example 1.4.1. Exercises 8–9 of Section 1.4.

4. Recognize the correspondence between the extreme points of the set of feasible solutions and the basic solutions of a linear program having two variables. Example 3.2.1. Exercise 2 of Section 3.2.

5. Given a nonbasic feasible solution to a linear program, determine a basic solution with at least as great a value of the objective function by adding an element of the appropriate nullspace to the given nonbasic solution. Example 3.4.3. Exercise 4 of Section 3.4.

6. Solve a maximizing linear program using the simplex algorithm. Example 3.3.1. Exercises 1–3 of Section 3.3.

7. Demonstrate individual rules of the simplex algorithm as discussed in Section 3.3 using given simplex tableaus. Exercises 11 and 12 of Section 3.3.

8. Recognize a degenerate basic solution, and understand how a degenerate solution arises from a tie for the minimum replacement quantity. Example 3.3.2.

9. Solve a maximizing linear program having nonstandard constraints by the two-phase method. Example 3.6.1. Exercise 4 of Section 3.6.

10. Solve a linear program involving unrestricted variables by expressing each unrestricted variable as the difference of two nonnegative variables. Example 3.7.10. Exercises 11 and 14 of Section 3.7.

11. Form the dual of a linear program. Table 3.7.1. Example 3.7.10. Exercises 11 and 12 of Section 3.7.

12. Solve a minimizing linear program by solving its dual maximizing linear program by the simplex algorithm. Example 3.7.10. Exercise 3 of Section 3.7.

13. Interpret the values of the dual variables in a maximizing linear program in terms of the value of additional resources. Example 3.7.9. Exercise 4 of Section 3.7.

14. Solve a minimizing linear program by maximizing the negative of the objective function.

15. Use complementary slackness and the solution of a linear program to determine the solution of the dual linear program. Example 3.7.6. Exercises 8 and 9 of Section 3.7.

16. Determine the interval of values which a resource can assume in a maximization problem without changing the basis of the optimal solution. Example 3.8.1. Exercise 3 of Section 3.8.

17. Determine the interval of values which an objective function coefficient can assume in a maximization problem without changing the basis of the optimal solution. Example 3.8.1. Exercise 6 of Section 3.8.

18. Determine the new basic solution which results from a change in a resource within the bounds determined by sensitivity analysis. Example 3.8.1. Exercise 6 of Section 3.8.

19. Use LINDO or similar software to solve linear programming problems. Example 3.5.8, Example 3.8.1, and Appendix A.

Chapter 4

Network Models

4.1 Introduction

In certain linear problems the nature of the constraints makes it advisable to use an algorithm other than the simplex algorithm to solve the problem. We will consider four such special problems: the transportation problem, the critical path problem, the shortest path problem, and the minimal spannning tree problem.

Some of the problems have a large number of variables (many of which are zero), some have a large number of constraints, and some have variables restricted to be either 0 or 1. All these aspects of the problems contribute to the need to consider special algorithms for their solution. Ideally, when we use any algorithm, we should verify that it in fact leads to a correct solution and also address the issue of how effectively we can expect it to solve problems as their sizes increase. We will be able to address these issues in the case of the algorithms for the shortest path and the minimal spanning tree.

Because all these problems involve graphs, we first briefly consider graphs. Graphs will also be important in the branch-and-bound processes to be discussed in Chapter 7 since they involve a tree, a special type of graph.

A *graph* consists of two nonempty sets N and E having no common elements together with an assignment of two elements of N to each element of E. Elements of N are called *nodes* and elements of E are called *edges*. Each edge is said to "connect" the pair of nodes assigned to it. An edge is also said to be *incident* on the nodes assigned to it. Two examples are shown in Figure 4.1.1.

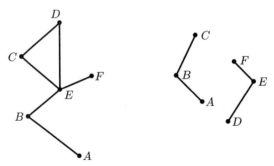

Figure 4.1.1

A *path* is a sequence

$$n_1, \ e_1, \ n_2, \ e_2, \ \ldots, \ n_{m-1}, \ e_{m-1}, \ n_m$$

consisting alternately of nodes and edges that are incident on the nodes before and after them. The nodes n_1 and n_m are called the *origin* and the *terminus* of the path, respectively, and we say that the path connects the origin and the terminus. Where the choice of edge incident on pairs of nodes in a path is unambigious, we will omit the edges in presenting a path.

A path in which the origin and the terminus are equal is called a *circuit*, or sometimes a *cycle*. The graph on the left in Figure 4.1.1 includes a cycle involving nodes D, C, and E. A graph is *connected* if any pair of vertices is connected by a path. Of the two examples in the figure, the one on the left is connected, the one on the right is not.

Networks

A *weighted graph* is one in which each edge is assigned a number, called a *weight*. We will also refer to a weighted graph as a *network*. Often these weights reflect an application such as distance, capacity, or a shipping cost. In the example below, the edges represent pipelines, and the edge weights are the costs of using the pipes.

With certain edge weights such as carrying capacities, there is often an accompanying assignment of a variable. For instance, in the next example the variable is the amount to be pumped through the pipeline.

Example 4.1.1. The Southsea Gas Company produces natural gas at three sites, labeled A, B, and C in the network in Figure 4.1.2, and supplies two markets located at X and Y. Intermediate pumping stations are located at P and Q. The edge weights indicate the cost of pumping a million cubic feet through that pipeline. Note that the lines representing edges have been replaced by arrows to indicate that movement is possible in only one direction.

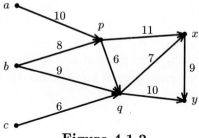

Figure 4.1.2

Southsea has 120, 180, and 140 million cubic feet of gas at a, b, and c, respectively, and their orders at x and y are for 200 and 210 million cubic feet, respectively. How should Southsea plan its pipeline use to meet its customers' needs at a minimum pumping cost?

We choose variables to indicate the pipeline with which they are associated. For example, ap denotes the number of million cubic feet flowing in the line joining a and p.

The following linear program to solve Southsea's problem indicates one source of structure in linear programs associated with networks. The first four constraints are *node-balance equations* which require that the amount of gas entering a node equals the amount leaving it.

Minimize : $10ap + 8bp + 9bq + 6cq + 6pq + 11px + 7qx + 10qy + 9xy$

Subject to :

$$
\begin{array}{rcl}
ap + bp \quad - pq - px & = & 0 \\
bq + cq + pq \quad - qx - qy & = & 0 \\
px + qx \quad - xy & = & 200 \\
qy + xy & = & 210 \\
ap & \leq & 120 \\
bp + bq & \leq & 180 \\
cq & \leq & 140
\end{array}
$$

All variables nonnegative.

∎

Trees

A *tree* is a graph in which a unique path joins any pair of nodes. Neither of the examples in Figure 4.1.1 is a tree. The first example fails because distinct paths can be found connecting E and D: one following the edge joining them and another going by way of C. In discussing minimal spanning trees later, we will use the distinct paths created from a cycle such as the one joining C, D, and E in the first example. The other example is not connected, and therefore not a tree, since several pairs of nodes, for example, A and D, are not joined by paths. Two examples of trees are given in Figure 4.1.3.

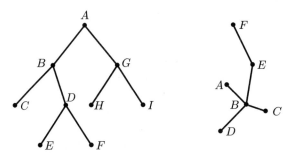

Figure 4.1.3

In Section 4.5 we will consider models requiring networks in which a tree having the minimal total edge weight is to be determined to represent an optimal set of connections in the network.

Because of the uniqueness of paths, trees are often used to record information. In Chapter 7 we will use trees to record the process of a search for a solution to traveling salesman and knapsack problems. The information storage application of trees will be explored in an exercise. The example on the left is the type that we will use because in choosing each path with origin at A there is a choice of two edges at each node. This type of tree fits the process of a search for a solution that involves selecting one of two choices at each step.

In Section 4.5 we will see that a tree is a graph with just enough edges to be connected but not enough for a cycle to exist. A graph with the maximum number of edges, i.e., an edge joining each pair of vertices, is called a *complete graph*.

Exercises

1. Given the tree in Figure 4.1.4, determine the unique path joining the indicated pairs of vertices:

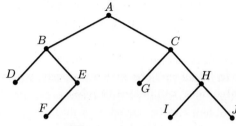

Figure 4.1.4

(a) D and G.

(b) E and H.

2. Draw the complete graphs having 2, 3, 4, and 5 vertices, and count the number of edges in each. Note that in the complete graph with n vertices the number of edges is $\dfrac{n(n-1)}{2}$.

3. Formulate and solve a linear program for the problem posed in Example 4.1.1 if the capacity of gas is restricted to 220 million cubic feet at each of the intermediate pumping stations.

4. The edge weights on the network in Figure 4.1.5 are maximum capacities, e.g., perhaps cubic feet of gas per hour or cars per minute. Determine the maximum total flow from the nodes a and b to the nodes f and g.

   A standard approach to this problem is to add a vertex o with unrestricted edges to a and b and a second vertex s having unrestricted edges leading to it from nodes f and g. Then maximize the total flow out of node o subject to the node-balance equations and the maximum capacities on individual edges.

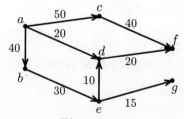

Figure 4.1.5

5. A company has 6 positions, a, b, ..., f, to fill, and has candidates, 1, 2, ..., 6. There is an experience requirement for each job, and Table 4.1.1 indicates which job, or jobs, each candidate could fill.

Table 4.1.1

Candidate	Job(s)
1	a, b
2	a, f
3	c, f
4	d, e
5	e
6	a, d

Is it possible to fill all the jobs with a properly experienced candidate? If so, provide a matching of candidates to jobs.

Hint: This problem can be solved as a maximum flow problem as above in which each edge has capacity 1.

6. A tree can be used to organize the key to encode, or decode, messages. Consider the tree in Figure 4.1.6 with the root indicated by 2 and 14 letters at the other nodes:

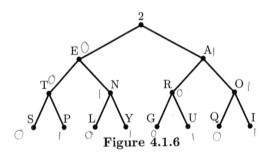

Figure 4.1.6

A letter is coded by the sequence of 0's and 1's which indicate the path from the root to its location on the tree. A 0 indicates a move to the left node on the next level down and a 1 indicates a move to the right node. A 2 indicates a return to the root to start a new letter and 22 indicates the beginning of a new word. For example, when encoded, "GO TARTANS" is "10021122002121020021201200".

(a) Encode the message "ONLY ONE PATH".

(b) Decode the message "002102020200022121020220120212000".

7. Examples of trees can be found in Figures 4.1.3, 4.1.4, and 4.1.6. For each example, count the edges and the vertices. Do you observe a pattern? This observation will be important in Section 4.5.

4.2 The transportation problem

The terminology of the transportation problem relies on two notions: origin and destination. In the following statement of the problem, it is helpful to think of an *origin* as a warehouse, a *destination* as a retail outlet, and of a specific commodity, such as a refrigerator, to be shipped.

Given the following information:

- m origins with the ith having a supply of a_i units, $i = 1, \ldots, m$;

- n destinations with the jth requiring b_j units, $j = 1, \ldots, n$; and

- $m \times n$ costs c_{ij} of shipping a unit of the commodity from origin i to destination j,

determine how to carry out the shipping to meet the requirements at minimum cost. As a linear program, the transportation problem takes the following form where the variable x_{ij}, $i = 1, \ldots, m$, $j = 1, \ldots, n$, is the number of units shipped from origin i to destination j:

$$\text{(TP)} \quad \text{Minimize}: \quad w = \sum_{i=1}^{m} \sum_{j=1}^{n} c_{ij} x_{ij}$$

$$\text{Subject to}: \quad \sum_{j=1}^{n} x_{ij} = a_i, \ i = 1, \ldots, m \quad \text{(supply constraints)}$$

$$\sum_{i=1}^{m} x_{ij} = b_j, \ j = 1, \ldots, n \quad \text{(demand constraints)}$$

a_i and b_j positive integers; x_{ij} nonnegative integers; and the c_{ij} are any constants.

For convenience, we add the assumption that

$$\sum_{i=1}^{m} a_i = \sum_{j=1}^{n} b_j$$

i.e., that the total supply equals the total demand. This assumption facilitates obtaining an initial basic solution. We will see later that problems not satisfying this assumption can be easily modified to satisfy it in a way that has a meaningful interpretation within the context of the problem.

The special structure of the problem is made more evident by looking at an example.

Example 4.2.1. The basic warehouse-retail outlet problem. Three warehouses with respective stocks of 10, 15, and 10 units supply four retail outlets with respective demands of 8, 12, 7, and 8 units. The matrix $[c_{ij}]$ of shipping costs in dollars is:

Table 4.2.1

		To j			
		1	2	3	4
	1	12	9	11	7
From i	2	15	8	10	9
	3	7	4	6	11

Determine the minimum shipping cost.

The graph in Figure 4.2.1 describing the problem includes a node for each warehouse and retail outlet, and an edge from each warehouse to each retail outlet.

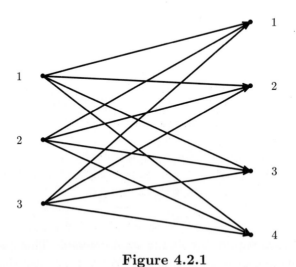

Figure 4.2.1

Writing the problem in the form of a linear program yields:

$$\text{Minimize}: w = 12x_{11} + 9x_{12} + 11x_{13} + 7x_{14} + 15x_{21} + 8x_{22} + 10x_{23}$$
$$+ 9x_{24} + 7x_{31} + 4x_{32} + 6x_{33} + 11x_{34}$$

Subject to :

$$
\begin{array}{llllll}
x_{11} + x_{12} + x_{13} + x_{14} & & & & = & 10 \\
 & x_{21} + x_{22} + x_{23} + x_{24} & & & = & 15 \\
 & & x_{31} + x_{32} + x_{33} + x_{34} & & = & 10 \\
x_{11} & +x_{21} & +x_{31} & & = & 8 \\
x_{12} & +x_{22} & +x_{32} & & = & 12 \\
x_{13} & +x_{23} & +x_{33} & & = & 7 \\
x_{14} & +x_{24} & +x_{34} & = & 8 \\
\end{array}
$$

$$x_{ij} \geq 0, \ i = 1, \ldots, 3; \ j = 1, \ldots, 4$$

Note that the sum of the first three constraints minus the sum of the next three constraints equals the last constraint. We will see that this can always be assumed to be the case, i.e., that the $m + n$ constraints give rise to a matrix of rank $m + n - 1$. This will prove useful in determining the solution.

The structure of the constraints in a transportation problem makes the use of a modeling language particularly appropriate. A LINGO model for this problem can be found in Appendix A.

The dual maximization problem will be important in the solution process. The structure of the transportation problem allows observations on the nature of the dual:

- Since each column contains only two nonzero coefficients, each constraint of the dual will involve only two dual variables.

- Since the variables of the transportation problem are nonnegative, the constraints of the dual will be $\leq$ inequalities.

- Since the constraints of the transportation problem are equalities, the variables of the dual will be unrestricted.

Now we examine the dual, letting the dual variables corresponding to the supply constraints be v_i's and those corresponding to the demand constraints be w_j's. The transportation algorithm will require that values be determined for the dual variables at each iteration. The special structure with only two variables in each constraint will make that an easy process.

$$\text{Maximize}: \quad z = 10v_1 + 15v_2 + 10v_3 + 8w_1 + 12w_2 + 7w_3 + 8w_4$$

$$
\begin{array}{llllll}
\text{Subject to}: & v_1 & + w_1 & & & \le & 12 \\
& v_1 & & + w_2 & & \le & 9 \\
& v_1 & & & + w_3 & \le & 11 \\
& v_1 & & & & + w_4 & \le & 7 \\
& v_2 & + w_1 & & & \le & 15 \\
& v_2 & & + w_2 & & \le & 8 \\
& v_2 & & & + w_3 & \le & 10 \\
& v_2 & & & & + w_4 & \le & 9 \\
& v_3 & + w_1 & & & \le & 7 \\
& v_3 & & + w_2 & & \le & 4 \\
& v_3 & & & + w_3 & \le & 6 \\
& v_3 & & & & + w_4 & \le & 11 \\
\end{array}
$$

$$v_i \text{ and } w_j \text{ unrestricted.}$$

Observe that if x_{ij} is positive then by complementary slackness the corresponding dual constraint is an equality, i.e., $v_i - w_j = c_{ij}$. The algorithm will take advantage of the fact that this equation involves only two variables to easily obtain a solution to the dual.

The Transportation Algorithm

The structure of transportation problems allows the simplex algorithm to be carried out in a more compact tableau than for the usual linear program. Before proving the theorem that justifies the algorithm, we first see how to set up the transportation tableau and determine the initial basic feasible solution.

Step I. Set up a tableau

The transportation tableau consists of an $m \times n$ array of rectangles, usually called *cells*, one for each variable. The rows correspond to supplies and the columns to demands. The costs are placed in boxes in the upper right-hand corners of the corresponding cells. The supplies are written to the left of the tableau and the demands across the top of the tableau. Values of the basic variables x_{ij} are placed in the lower left-hand corners of the cells.

Demands

		b_1		b_2	$\cdots$		b_n
			c_{11}		c_{12}		c_{1n}
a_1						$\cdots$	
		x_{11}		x_{12}		x_{1n}	

$$
\begin{array}{}
\text{Supplies}
\end{array}
$$

			c_{m1}		c_{m2}		c_{mn}
a_m		x_{m1}		x_{m2}	$\cdots$	x_{mn}	

Step II. Determine an initial basic solution

Beginning in the upper left-hand corner, assign values to the basic x_{ij}'s so that either demand j is satisfied or supply i is exhausted. Move to the next cell as follows:

- If a demand is satisfied by an assignment, move to the next cell to the right,

- If a supply is exhausted by an assignment, move to the cell below the one just assigned, or

- If both a demand and a supply are satisfied by an assignment, move diagonally to the cell down and to the right. In the event of a diagonal move, assign the value 0 to the variable in the cell below and to the left of the two involved in the diagonal move. This is essential to maintain the required $m + n - 1$ basic variables.

Because this method of determining the initial solution starts in the upper left-hand cell, it is called the *Northwest corner rule*.

Note that the diagonal move that occurs in the third case above produces a basic variable with value zero. As in the simplex algorithm, this then is a degenerate solution. Identification of any basic variables with the value zero is critical to being able to complete Step IV below to improve the solution. Thus we record the zero in the tableau, while nonbasic zeroes are not written.

The procedure above produces a first basic solution having the following two characteristics:

1. Since the problem has $m + n$ constraints, we would expect to have $m + n$ basic variables. However, there are only $m + n - 1$ basic variables because the rank of the matrix of the coefficients of the constraints is only $m + n - 1$. Thus, this is the maximum number of linearly independent columns, and only $m + n - 1$ variables are needed.

2. A basic variable occurs in each row and in each column of the transportation tableau.

Returning to Example 4.2.1, with the initial solution obtained by the Northwest corner rule the tableau is:

	8	12	7	8
10	12 8	9 2	11	7
15	15	8 10	10 5	9
10	7	4 2	6 8	11

Basic variables are indicated by the value of x_{ij} in the lower left corner of the cell. The absence of a value indicates that a value is not assigned in this process and that the variable equals 0 and is nonbasic. A value is shown for a basic variable that is zero.

The following theorem is the key to identifying an optimal solution and to improving a nonoptimal solution.

Theorem 4.2.2.

(a) *If $v_1, \ldots, v_m$ and $w_1, \ldots, w_n$ are any constants, then any solution to the $m \times n$ transportation problem with costs c_{ij} is also a solution to the problem with costs changed to $c_{ij} - v_i - w_j$ and with a constant subtracted from the objective function.*

(b) *A solution is optimal for one of the problems in* (a) *if and only if it is optimal for the other.*

(c) *If it is possible to determine values for the v_i's and w_j's such that $c_{ij} - v_i - w_j = 0$ whenever x_{ij} is basic and $c_{ij} - v_i - w_j \geq 0$ whenever x_{ij} is not basic, then the solution is optimal.*

Proof.

(a) We calculate the value of the objective function in the new problem and show that it equals that of the original function less a constant. Suppose that a solution to the original problem is given by x_{ij}, $i = 1, \ldots, m$, $j = 1, \ldots, n$. Then:

$$\sum_{i=1}^{m}\sum_{j=1}^{n}(c_{ij} - v_i - w_j)x_{ij} = \sum_{i=1}^{m}\sum_{j=1}^{n}c_{ij}x_{ij} - \sum_{i=1}^{m}\left(\sum_{j=1}^{n}x_{ij}\right)v_i - \sum_{j=1}^{n}\left(\sum_{i=1}^{m}x_{ij}\right)w_j$$

Since $\displaystyle\sum_{j=1}^{n}x_{ij} = a_i$ and $\displaystyle\sum_{i=1}^{m}x_{ij} = b_j$

$$\sum_{i=1}^{m}\sum_{j=1}^{n}(c_{ij} - v_i - w_j)x_{ij} = \sum_{i=1}^{m}\sum_{j=1}^{n}c_{ij}x_{ij} + \left(-\sum_{i=1}^{m}a_iv_i - \sum_{j=1}^{n}b_jw_j\right)$$

Observe that the quantity in parenthesis is a constant since the a_i's, b_j's, v_i's, and w_j's are constants.

(b) This is clear since the objective functions differ by a constant.

(c) If $c_{ij} - v_i - w_j < 0$ and $x_{ij} = 0$ for some i and j, then the cost can be lowered by a change of basis in which $x_{ij} > 0$. $\square$

Part (c) of the theorem indicates that the quantities $c_{ij} - v_i - w_j$ play a role analogous to the objective-row entries in the simplex tableau – a negative indicates which variable to make basic to improve the solution.

In the transportation algorithm, the v_i's and the w_j's will prove to be the dual variables. From examining the dual (DTP) below of the problem (TP), we see that (c) also implies that the solution to (TP) is optimal when the v_i's and the w_j's satisfy the constraints of the dual:

$$\text{(DTP)} \quad \text{Maximize}: \quad \sum_{i=1}^{m} a_i v_i + \sum_{j=1}^{n} b_j w_j$$

$$\text{Subject to}: \quad v_i + w_j \le c_{ij}; \; i = 1, \ldots, m, \; j = 1, \ldots, n$$

$$v_i \text{ and } w_j \text{ unrestricted.}$$

When x_{ij} is basic, complementary slackness dictates that the corresponding dual slack variable must be zero, which is equivalent to $c_{ij} - v_i - w_j = 0$. The requirement $c_{ij} - v_i - w_j \ge 0$ is simply the requirement that the ijth constraint of (DTP) be satisfied, i.e., that the solution to the dual (DTP) be feasible.

Returning to the description of the transportation algorithm, recall that we have determined an initial basic feasible solution having $m + n - 1$ basic variables and a basic variable in each row and each column.

Step III. Testing for optimality

(a) Determine values for the dual variables v_i and w_j by solving the system of equations

$$v_i + w_j = c_{ij}, \quad (i, j) \text{ such that } x_{ij} \text{ is basic.}$$

Since this is a system of $m+n-1$ equations in $m+n$ variables, we have a redundant linear system, and one of the variables can be arbitrarily set to 0. The others can be found by inspection since each equation involves only two variables. The v_i's are placed at the right side of the tableau and the w_j's at the bottom of the tableau for reference.

(b) Test the value of $c_{ij} - v_i - w_j$ for each (i, j) such that x_{ij} is not basic. Place these *test values* in the lower right corner of the corresponding nonbasic cells. If none of these values is negative, then the solution is optimal, and the algorithm terminates. If the test value is negative for some (r, s), then the solution can be improved by making $x_{rs} > 0$.

Step IV. Improving the solution

If one or more of the test values is negative, we improve the solution by the following procedure:

(a) Select a cell (r, s) such that $c_{rs} - v_r - w_s < 0$. Let $x_{rs} = t$. Determine a path of cells

$$(r, s), (r, u), (v, u), (v, w), (y, w), \ldots, (z, s)$$

such that $x_{ru}, \ldots, x_{zs}$ are basic variables. Alternately subtract t from and add t to the values of the variables in the cells along the path so that the constraints remain satisfied. At this point, the variables in the cells along the path are

$$t, \ x_{ru} - t, \ x_{vu} + t, \ x_{vw} - t, \ x_{yw} + t, \ldots, x_{zs} - t.$$

(b) Allocate to x_{rs} the minimum of the values from which t is subtracted in the path so that one variable is set to 0 and none become negative. If there is a tie for the minimum value, only one variable becomes nonbasic. The other(s), though having the value zero, remain basic variables and are recorded in the tableau. Note that a tie here corresponds to a tie for the small replacement quantity in the simplex algorithm and leads to a degenerate solution.

(c) Return to Step III.

The transportation algorithm is summarized in Figure 4.2.2.

We now look more closely at how to carry out Step III(a) to determine values for the v_i's and w_j's by applying the following complementary slackness condition:

$$x_{ij}(c_{ij} - v_i - w_j) = 0 \quad \text{for } x_{ij} \text{ basic.}$$

This leads to solving the system of equations obtained by making the dual constraints corresponding to the basic variables equalities:

$$
\begin{aligned}
v_1 &{}+ w_1 &&&&= 12 \\
v_1 &&{}+ w_2 &&&= 9 \\
v_2 &&{}+ w_2 &&&= 8 \\
v_2 &&&{}+ w_3 &&= 10 \\
v_3 &&&{}+ w_3 &&= 6 \\
v_3 &&&&{}+ w_4 &= 11
\end{aligned}
$$

As this system contains six equations in seven unknowns, we may choose one variable arbitrarily. For instance, choose $v_1 = 0$. Then we must have $w_1 = 12$ from the first equation and $w_2 = 9$ from the second equation. Knowing the value of w_2, we can now determine that $v_2 = -1$ from the third equation. From knowing that $v_2 = -1$, we then determine that $w_3 = 11$, and then from the next to last equation that $v_3 = -5$. Finally, we can conclude that $w_4 = 16$.

THE TRANSPORTATION ALGORITHM

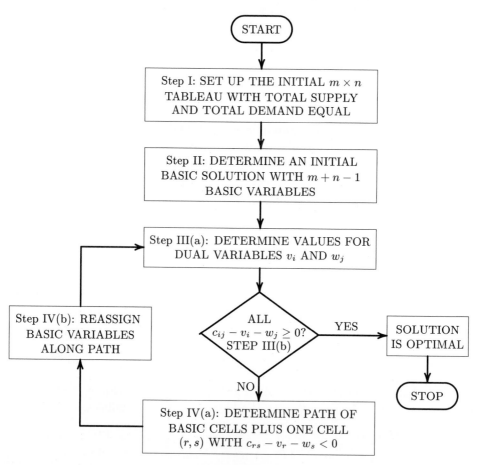

Figure 4.2.2

Writing these values to the right and below the tableau and placing the test quantities $c_{ij} - v_i - w_j$ in the lower right corner of each nonbasic cell yields the following tableau:

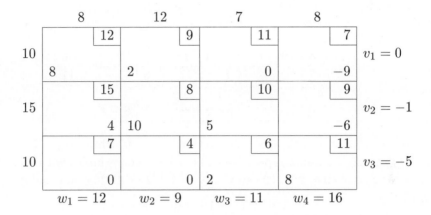

The two negative values of $c_{ij} - v_i - w_j$ obtained in the lower right corners indicate that the solution is not optimal, and that the cost can be lowered by shipping to outlet 4 from warehouse 1 or 2.

In the next solution, ship from warehouse 1 since it has the more negative test quantity. But shipping t units from warehouse 1 to outlet 4 requires compensation so that all constraints are satisfied by the new solution. This is illustrated in the next tableau. Following Step IV(a), we identify a path of cells along which to reassign the variable values. To allow values to change

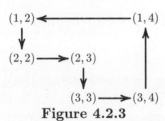

Figure 4.2.3

while satisfying all constraints, successive cells are alternately in the same column or row so that t is both added and subtracted in each affected constraint. To emphasize this, the subscripts of the cells are displayed on the left in their relative positions.

In the next tableau we alternately add and subtract t from the basic entries along the path of cells. Assign to t the minimum of the values of the x_{ij} from which it is subtracted. This creates a nonbasic zero while leaving the other variables whose values are changed nonnegative and basic.

	12	9	11	7	
8	2−t		0	t	−9
	15	8	10	9	
4	10+t	5−t			−6
	7	4	6	11	
0		0	2+t	8−t	

Here we set $t = \min\{2, 5, 8\} = 2$ so that $x_{12} = 0$, while $x_{23} = 5 - 2 = 3$ and $x_{34} = 8 - 2 = 6$ remain positive. The other two variables with changed values are $x_{22} = 10 + 2 = 12$ and $x_{33} = 2 + 2 = 4$. The new solution is shown below:

	12	9	11	7
8			2	
	15	8	10	9
	12	3		
	7	4	6	11
		4	6	

The value of the objective function for this new solution is given by

$$w = 12 \cdot 8 + 7 \cdot 2 + 8 \cdot 12 + 10 \cdot 3 + 6 \cdot 4 + 11 \cdot 6 = 326.$$

Now determine the v_i's and w_j's, starting again with the arbitrary choice of $v_1 = 0$. With $v_1 = 0$, because x_{11} and x_{14} are basic variables in the first row, we can determine values $w_1 = 12$ and $w_4 = 7$, respectively. From $w_4 = 7$, we can determine $v_3 = 4$ because x_{34} is a basic variable in the fourth column. From $v_3 = 4$, it is then possible to determine $w_3 = 2$ because x_{33} is a basic variable in the third row. Then v_2 can be determined to be 8 from the value $w_3 = 2$ and the fact that x_{23} is basic. Finally, from $v_2 = 8$ and the fact that x_{22} is basic, we can conclude that $w_2 = 0$.

When we include these values of the dual variables and the $c_{ij} - v_i - w_j$ test quantities, the resultant tableau is:

	$w_1 = 12$	$w_2 = 0$	$w_3 = 2$	$w_4 = 7$	
	[12] 8	[9] 9	[11] 9	[7] 2	$v_1 = 0$
	[15] -5	[8] 12	[10] 3	[9] -6	$v_2 = 8$
	[7] -9	[4] 0	[6] 4	[11] 6	$v_3 = 4$

The value of the objective function is:

$$w = 12 \cdot 8 + 7 \cdot 2 + 8 \cdot 12 + 10 \cdot 3 + 6 \cdot 4 + 11 \cdot 6 = 326.$$

We next make x_{31} basic since the corresponding test quantity -9 is the most negative. Like a negative entry in the objective row of a simplex tableau, the -9 is the per-unit change in the value of the objective function in the next solution. Letting $x_{31} = t$ and identifying a path of corrections for the values of the basic variables yields:

	$w_1 = 12$	$w_2 = 0$	$w_3 = 2$	$w_4 = 7$	
	[12] $8 - t$	[9] 9	[11] 9	[7] $2 + t$	$v_1 = 0$
	[15] -5	[8] 12	[10] 3	[9] -6	$v_2 = 8$
	[7] t -9	[4] 0	[6] 4	[11] $6 - t$	$v_3 = 4$

Letting $t = \min\{6, 8\} = 6$ yields the following new tableau. We have already calculated the dual variables and the test quantities:

	12	9	11	7	
2		0	0	8	$v_1 = 0$
	15	8	10	9	
	4	12	3	3	$v_2 = -1$
	7	4	6	11	
6		0	4	9	$v_3 = -5$
$w_1 = 12$		$w_2 = 9$	$w_3 = 11$	$w_4 = 7$	

The test quantities satisfy $c_{ij} - v_i - w_j \geq 0$ for all i and j. Hence, this solution is optimal. We calculate the value of the objective function:

$$w = 12 \cdot 2 + 7 \cdot 8 + 8 \cdot 12 + 10 \cdot 3 + 7 \cdot 6 + 6 \cdot 4 = 272.$$

As suggested above, the value of the objective function has decreased by $54, i.e., by $9 for each unit of the six unit increase in the new basic variable x_{31}.

Note that in three cells – (1,2), (1,3) and (3,2) – the test quantities are zero. Recall that a negative value for the test quantity $c_{ij} - v_i - w_j$ for a nonbasic variable is an indication that making that variable positive would lead to a reduction in the value of the objective function. Thus, a zero value for a test quantity indicates that making the corresponding variable positive would not change the value of the objective function. By analogy with Rule 6 of the simplex algorithm, we see that these zero values indicate a non-unique solution.

To demonstrate, we let one of the variables having a zero test quantity, x_{13}, become basic. Consider the path below reassigning variable values:

	12	9	11	7
$2 - t$		t	8	
	15	8	10	9
	12	3		
	7	4	6	11
$6 + t$		$4 - t$		

This leads to a value of $t = 2$ and the solution below, which is also optimal:

12		9		11		7
			2		8	
15		8		10		9
	12		3			
7		4		6		11
8			2			

Calculating the value of the objective function, we see that this solution leads to the same value:

$$w = 11 \cdot 2 + 7 \cdot 8 + 8 \cdot 12 + 10 \cdot 3 + 7 \cdot 8 + 6 \cdot 2 = 272.$$

In the exercises at the end of the section you will be asked to determine the other solutions.

Elimination of the restriction $\sum_{i=1}^{m} a_i = \sum_{j=1}^{n} b_j$

Having total supply equal to total demand has been built into the algorithm for solving a transportation problem. However, this condition will certainly not be satisfied in all such problems. Before undertaking the next example, we introduce a method of imposing this condition in a meaningful way by adding a "fictitious" origin or destination.

Excess supply: Introduce an $(n + 1)$st destination with demand

$$b_{n+1} = \sum_{i=1}^{m} a_i - \sum_{j=1}^{n} b_j > 0$$

to balance the excess supply. Let $c_{i,n+1} = 0$ for all i. If $x_{i,n+1} > 0$, then $x_{i,n+1}$ units are retained at origin i and not shipped.

Excess demand (rationing): Introduce an $(m + 1)$st origin with supply

$$a_{m+1} = \sum_{j=1}^{n} b_j - \sum_{i=1}^{m} a_i > 0$$

to balance the excess demand. Unless the problem indicates otherwise, let $c_{m+1,j} = 0$ for all j. If $x_{m+1,j} > 0$, then $x_{m+1,j}$ units of demand at destination j are not satisfied.

The following example indicates a case in which a nonzero cost is needed for an added supplier.

Example 4.2.3. Shipping for maximum profit. A manufacturing firm has three factories and serves five markets. It is able to practice price discrimination and would like to plan shipping to consider price, manufacturing costs, and varying shipping costs to maximize its profit. Its contracts with its customers include penalties if the product is not supplied on time. In markets 1 and 2, the penalty is $100 per unit; in the other three markets the penalty is only $80 per unit.

The following table gives the price structure and shipping costs:

Table 4.2.2

	Markets				
	1	2	3	4	5
Price	$64	$64	$61	$62	$60
Quantity demanded	76	52	68	65	54
Shipping cost from A	10	12	9	14	8
Shipping cost from B	8	9	13	11	10
Shipping cost from C	12	7	10	13	15

If the costs of making the product and the capacities of each of its three factories are:

Table 4.2.3

Cost	Capacity
$42 in A	120 units in A
$39 in B	145 units in B
$40 in C	40 units in C

determine a production and shipping schedule to maximize profit.

Here we use the device of adapting a minimizing technique to solve a maximization by using the negative of the profits as the costs c_{ij}.

Let the c_{ij} associated with x_{ij} be the negative of the difference between the selling price in market j and the sum of the cost in factory i and the appropriate shipping cost. For instance, for a product made in factory B for sale in the fourth market, the profit is $c_{24} = 62 - 11 - 39 = \$12$. Thus, -12 is entered in the tableau as the cost of shipping from B to the fourth market.

Introduce an extra "factory" with a capacity of 10 to balance the total supply and total demand. Let the costs c_{ij} associated with the added "factory" be the contractual penalty of \$100 or \$80. ∎

The next example involves "shipping" in time rather than between locations.

Example 4.2.4. The Ace Alloy Co. produces large material containers. It has orders for 26 in April, 31 in May, and 24 in June. At the beginning of April it will have three containers in inventory. Its production capacity is 20 containers a month at a cost of \$500 each on regular time. It can produce an additional five a month on overtime at a cost of \$650 each. If production for one month exceeds their needs, they can store a container at a cost of \$50 a month to meet future demand. Their contract does not permit back orders, i.e., they can not meet the demand for one month by production from a subsequent month. However, when they are unable to meet demand, they can borrow containers from another manufacturer for \$70 a month until they can replace them from their own production. Ace will shut down for vacation for the month of July and is willing to run its inventory to zero at the end of June.

How should Ace schedule production and delivery to minimize costs?

First we consider the problem of equalizing the total supply and the total demand. Using both regular time and overtime Ace can produce 25 containers a month or 75 during the three month period. That, together with the opening inventory of three and its willingness to use all that it can produce to satisfy the demands, gives it a total supply of 78. However, the total demand is for 81 containers. Thus, a fictitious supply of three must be added to balance the problem. Ace will provide these items by "borrowing" from another manufacturer.

The problem thus has eight origins: three months of regular time production, three months of overtime production, an initial inventory, and the borrowed containers. The destinations are the three demands.

The set-up of the initial tableau is then completed by calculating the 24 costs. The costs for the six origins involving production include the \$500 for regular production and the \$650 for overtime production. To this is added the storage cost of \$50 a month for production with delivery in a later month. For instance, the cost for regular production in the month of April for delivery two months later in June is $600 – the production cost plus two months storage at $50 a month.

The actual cost assigned for the three "borrowed" containers is not known since we are unable to determine when their production schedule will permit them to repay the other manufacturer with one of their own containers. However, it is clear that a container borrowed to meet April demand will cost $60 more – one month's charge – than one borrowed to meet May's demand or $120 more than one borrowed for June's demand. Note that if one assumes that the borrowed containers are replaced in the same month, then part (a) of Theorem 4.2.2 shows that the costs assigned need only reflect these relative differences rather than the actual costs since the actual cost calculation involves a v_i subtracted from all costs in the row representing borrowed containers.

The situation for the costs associated with the three units of inventory is similar.

Finally, since back orders are not permitted, the cost assigned to production in June for "shipment" to satisfy May's demand must prevent the inclusion of a positive variable in such a cell in the optimal solution. This is achieved by assigning a prohibitively high cost, say $10,000, to such cases.
■

Exercises

1. Consider the transportation problem having two origins and three destinations with the table of costs below:

Table 4.2.4

		To		
		1	2	3
From	1	5	8	6
	2	4	9	6

The supply at origin 1 is 12 and at origin 2 is 8. The respective demands at the destinations are 7, 6, and 7.

(a) Formulate the transportation problem (TP) and its dual (DTP) as linear programs.

(b) Solve the transportation problem.

(c) Show that the values of v_i and w_j determined in the optimal tableau are a feasible solution to the dual.

2. In a large city a number of city workers will have their jobs eliminated because their skills are no longer needed. The three categories to be eliminated include 20, 15, and 25 people, respectively. At the same time, the city finds itself needing an additional 30 electricians, 15 truck drivers, and 15 computer operators. The city decided to retain its employees from the categories being eliminated. The table below gives the retraining costs (in 100's of dollars) to move from the respective obsolete categories to the needed categories. Determine a reassignment plan and the minimal retraining cost.

Table 4.2.5

		To			
		1	2	3	
	1	8	6	4	20
From	2	5	4	5	15
	3	6	7	9	25
		30	15	15	

3. Solve the previous problem if the city needs 25 workers in each of the categories for which it will be retraining employees. Note that you will need to add a fictitious origin.

4. The Estes Pump Company has three weeks of production remaining before it closes for two weeks for plant maintenance. It is committed to meet shipping schedules during the entire five-week period. Shipping demands can be met by the current week's production or by production previously manufactured and stored.

Manufacturing each unit costs $500, and storing a unit for a week costs $20. The current inventory is 70 units, and Estes is willing to reduce its inventory to 10 units at the end of the period. The weekly demands and production capacities are tabled below:

Table 4.2.6

	1	2	3	4	5
Demand	50	70	80	25	40
Capacity	65	75	65	0	0

How should production be scheduled, and when should each unit produced be shipped to minimize costs?

5. Solve the following transportation problem:

	6	4	9	6
7	7	6	9	11
8	11	6	5	4
10	12	14	15	3

6. In Step IV of the algorithm, it is possible that more than one variable might be set to zero by the choice of t. However, each solution must contain $m+n-1$ basic variables because that is the rank of the constraint matrix. In carrying out the next iteration for the tableau below, x_{31} should become, basic and there is a choice of which variable should become nonbasic and which should remain basic, but be set to zero. Show that the optimal solution can be reached no matter which of the zeroes is declared to be basic.

	7	10	5	8
12	10 (7)	5 (5)	9	16
8	9	7 (5)	10	5 (3)
10	8	7	5 (5)	12 (5)

7. Determine the two other optimal solutions to Example 4.2.1 by letting x_{12} and x_{32} become a basic. Show that in each case the value of the objective function is unchanged.

8. A transportation problem has a nonunique solution when one of the test quantities $c_{ij} - v_i - w_j = 0$ in the optimal tableau. The corresponding variable can then be made positive without changing the value of the objective function. The following problem is an example of a transportation problem with a nonunique solution.

Find 2 solutions

	15	13	10	5
10	10	5	6	8
18	5	8	10	4
22	8	6	7	3

9. A manufacturer can ordinarily produce 300 units a month of his product and needs to schedule production for a three-month period in which the orders exceed this capacity. Inventory at the beginning of the first month is 120 units, and the demands for the successive three months are 420, 360, and 450 units. Monthly production capacity can be increased by up to 100 units at an additional cost of \$8 per unit. Holding costs to manufacture in one month and ship during a later month are \$2 per unit per month.

   Determine a production schedule that will minimize the total cost of exceeding the usual monthly capacity and holding costs.

10. Formulate and solve the problem posed in Example 1.3.7.

11. Formulate the initial tableau for the problem posed in Example 1.3.10.

12. If the constraint equations for an $m \times n$ transportation problem are denoted by $Tx = b$, then, as we have observed at the beginning of this section, T has mn columns and $m+n$ rows but its rank is only $m+n-1$. So, following the discussion of rank in Chapter 2, there must be a set S of $m+n-1$ columns such that all other columns are in the span of S. Returning to Example 4.2.1, let T_{ij} denote the column of T corresponding to the variable x_{ij}. Let S be the set of columns corresponding to the first basic solution obtained. Show that:

   (a) $T_{32} = T_{33} - T_{23} + T_{22}$.

   (b) $T_{14} = T_{12} - T_{22} + T_{23} - T_{33} + T_{34}$.

   (c) Note that the vectors in the linear combination for (b) above correspond to the basic variables associated with the path used to calculate the value of x_{14} in the next basic solution. Following that observation, determine T_{31} as a linear combination of vectors from S.

13. The ABC Co. manufactures its product in two plants, A and B, and sells its product in four markets. The capacity in Plant A is 300 units, in Plant B 350 units. The demands and shipping costs for the four markets are tabled below:

Table 4.2.7

	Markets			
	1	2	3	4
Demand	155	230	225	160
Shipping cost from A	10	20	15	25
Shipping cost from B	5	15	10	20

The usual per-unit labor cost is $95 in either plant. The other costs per-unit are $50 in plant A and $70 in plant B. Overtime labor can be hired only at Plant A at a per-unit cost of $140. If the capacity is not adequate to meet demand, additional items can be manufactured at Plant A using overtime labor.

Formulate the transportation problem to determine how ABC should schedule its production to meet all demand while minimizing its total costs.

14. The ABC Co. and DEF Inc. have merged to form a single company called ABCDEF Inc. The sites at J and H are to be closed and most of the employees reassigned to site K. The employees are divided into three job classifications. The number of each classification available for reassignment at J and H and the number needed at K are tabled below. The retraining costs in hundreds of dollars to move to a new classification are also provided.

Table 4.2.8

	Classification		
	1	2	3
Available at J	20	30	10
Available at H	15	20	14
Needed at K	25	55	20

Table 4.2.9

	Retraining costs			
		To		
		1	2	3
	1	0	5	8
From:	2	6	0	7
	3	4	2	0

Employees from J moving to K will be paid $1,500 for relocation expenses. Finally, any employee not needed at K can be laid off at a cost of $3,000 at J and $3,600 at H. How should the reassignment be carried out to minimize the cost? Determine the initial transportation tableau.

15. ABC Metals manufactures parts in two plants, A and B. They have orders from three customers for May and June as tabled below. The per-unit shipping costs to the customers are also provided.

Table 4.2.10

	Company		
	1	2	3
May	200	310	400
June	450	520	350

Table 4.2.11

	Shipping costs		
	1	2	3
A	$40	$28	$32
B	$36	$38	$24

The production capacity of ABC is 400 units a month at each of its two sites. It has 200 units in inventory at site A and 250 units at site B. ABC is willing to run its inventory to zero if necessary. Units can be delivered early, but not late. In case it cannot meet demand, it has a contract to buy the item from DEF Inc. for $700 which includes delivery to any of the three customers.

How should ABC schedule its production to meet all demands while minimizing the sum of the shipping costs and the possible cost of buying from DEF? Determine the initial transportation tableau.

16. Set up the initial transportation tableau and determine the initial basic solution for Example 4.2.4.

4.3   The critical path method

The administration of complex projects is an important managerial task. A big project often requires many activities, of which some may go forward simultaneously, and others must be completed in sequence. For instance, it is reasonable for the shingling of a house roof to take place at the same time as the exterior walls are being bricked. However, framing the walls must follow completion of the foundation.

The relationships among such activities and the lengths of time that they require invite description by a graph and, ultimately, analysis by a linear program. The resulting model is called the *critical path method,* abbreviated CPM.

We begin with an example, which involves new product development, and then introduce the required terminology and notation. In this example, effective management seeks to get the product on the market quickly to achieve maximum competitive advantage.

Example 4.3.1. Consider the problem of managing the design of a new product. The project consists of nine activities which produce a prototype, a marketing strategy, and a production capability. The activities, their estimated durations, and the relations among them are given in Table 4.3.1.

Table 4.3.1

	Activity	Duration (in months)	Immediate predecessors
A.	Design product	4	-
B.	Develop marketing strategy	3	-
C.	Design brochure	2	A
D.	Produce prototype	6	A
E.	Survey potential market	3	B, C
F.	Test prototype	3	D
G.	Develop pricing strategy	2	D, E
H.	Develop production capability	4	A
I.	Write implementation plan	1	F, G, H

To effectively administer the product development, the manager of the project would like to know the following:

- The minimum time to completion,

- The activities most crucial to on-time completion, and

- The flexibility, if any, in completing the activities.

The first step in the analysis is to form a CPM network from the list of activities and their predecessors. In the network, the node labeled 0 indicates the beginning of the project, and all others represent the time when an activity is completed and other activities may start. A directed edge will go from the node representing the starting time of an activity to the node representing the completion time. The following basic rules will produce a CPM network:

1. Node 0 indicates the start of the project. An edge should lead from node 0 for each activity that has no predecessor.

2. Number the nodes so that each terminal end has a higher number than the initial end. Thus the node representing completion of the project is assigned the highest number.

3. Each activity is represented by an edge.

4. Two nodes are connected by at most one edge, i.e., the graph has no parallel edges. This rule prevents two points in time from being joined by activities of possibly different durations.

The CPM network for our example is given in Figure 4.3.1.

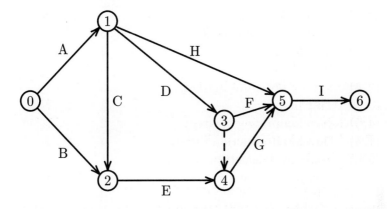

Figure 4.3.1

From the network in the figure, we see that edges represent activities, usually the tasks required in the project. The nodes represent events, i.e., points in time when an activity starts or ends. The dashed edge indicates that the development of the pricing strategy cannot start at t_4 until the prototype is developed at time t_3. This is not a constraint imposed by the process itself; it is a logical decision to wait to start one activity until another is concluded. We call such an activity a *dummy activity*.

The portion of a CPM network in Figure 4.3.2 illustrates the use of a dummy activity to eliminate parallel edges. Here it is used to prevent two predecessors of $9 \to 10$ from being forced to end at the same time.

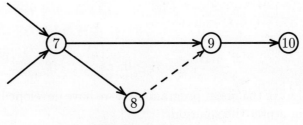

Figure 4.3.2

Returning to our example, when we assign an edge (i, j) to each activity and a time t_i to the ith node, the list of activities becomes:

Table 4.3.2

Edge	Activity	Duration	Start time
$(0,1)$	Design product	4	t_0
$(0,2)$	Develop marketing strategy	3	t_0
$(1,2)$	Design brochure	2	t_1
$(1,3)$	Produce prototype	6	t_1
$(2,4)$	Survey potential market	3	t_2
$(3,5)$	Test prototype	3	t_3
$(4,5)$	Develop pricing strategy	2	t_4
$(1,5)$	Develop production capability	4	t_1
$(5,6)$	Write implementation plan	1	t_5
	Completion time	-	t_6

With these variables and with the graph indicating the relationships among the activities, the minimum time to completion can be obtained by solving the linear program below. The objective function is clear – it is to minimize the time t_6 when the project ends. The constraints require that the time between the beginning and end of each activity is long enough to allow the activity to be completed.

$$
\begin{aligned}
\text{Minimize}: \quad & t_6 \\
\text{Subject to}: \quad -t_0 + t_1 & \geq 4 \\
-t_0 \qquad\quad + t_2 & \geq 3 \\
-t_1 + t_2 & \geq 2 \\
-t_1 \qquad\quad + t_3 & \geq 6 \\
-t_1 \qquad\qquad\quad + t_5 & \geq 4 \\
-t_2 \qquad\quad + t_4 & \geq 3 \\
-t_3 + t_4 & \geq 0 \\
-t_3 \qquad\quad + t_5 & \geq 3 \\
-t_4 + t_5 & \geq 2 \\
-t_5 + t_6 & \geq 1 \\
t_i \geq 0; \quad i = 1, \dots, 6
\end{aligned}
$$

We will solve the linear program after we have developed the terminology needed to interpret the solution.

Let $PR(j)$ denote the set of immediate predecessor events of j, i.e., the set of all events i such that an edge (i,j) exists. Let $D(i,j)$ denote the duration of activity (i,j). Then $D(i,j)$ is the weight of the edge (i,j) in the network.

One objective of CPM is to formulate a schedule for the project. The manager needs to know when each activity should start or finish, and where some flexibility might exist in the schedule. These needs are reflected in some of the terminology used in CPM.

The *earliest time*, $ET(i)$, for an event i is the time when the event will occur if the preceding activities are started as early as possible. The $ET(i)$'s are calculated as follows:

$$ET(0) \ = \ 0$$
$$ET(j) \ = \ \max\left\{ET(i) + D(i,j) : i \in PR(j)\right\}, \ j \geq 1.$$

Some of the calculations of earliest times in the example are:

$$
\begin{aligned}
ET(1) \ &= \ ET(0) + D(0,1) = 4 \\
ET(2) \ &= \ \max\left\{ET(0) + D(0,2), ET(1) + D(1,2)\right\} \\
&= \ \max\left\{0 + 3, 4 + 2\right\} \\
&= \ 6 \\
ET(5) \ &= \ \max\left\{ET(1) + D(1,5), ET(3) + D(3,5), ET(4) + D(4,5)\right\} \\
&= \ \max\left\{4 + 4, 10 + 3, 9 + 2\right\} \\
&= \ 13
\end{aligned}
$$

The *latest time*, $LT(i)$, for an event i is the last time at which the event can occur without delaying the project completion beyond its earliest time. If event N denotes the completion of the project, the $LT(i)$'s are calculated as follows, working backward from completion of the project:

$$LT(N) \ = \ ET(N)$$
$$LT(k) \ = \ \min\left\{LT(j) - D(k,j) : k \in PR(j)\right\}, \ k < N.$$

Some of the calculations of latest times in the example are:

$$
\begin{aligned}
LT(5) \ &= \ LT(6) - D(5,6) = 13 \\
LT(3) \ &= \ \min\left\{LT(4) - D(3,4), LT(5) - D(3,5)\right\} \\
&= \ \min\left\{11 - 0, 13 - 3\right\} \\
&= \ 10 \\
LT(1) \ &= \ \min\left\{LT(2) - D(1,2), LT(3) - D(1,3), LT(5) - D(1,5)\right\} \\
&= \ \min\left\{8 - 2, 10 - 6, 13 - 4\right\} \\
&= \ 4
\end{aligned}
$$

The *slack*, $SL(k)$, for an event k is the difference between its latest and earliest time:

$$SL(k) = LT(k) - ET(k)$$

The *float*, $FL(i, j)$, for an activity (i, j) is given by the following formula:

$$FL(i, j) = LT(j) - ET(i) - D(i, j).$$

Intuitively, the float of an activity is a measure of the amount of flexibility available in completing it. A *critical activity* is one with float equal to zero. A *critical path* is a path from the start of a project to its completion consisting entirely of critical activities.

We can now use these definitions to develop a schedule for the project that identifies when each event must occur to ensure an on-time completion.

Table 4.3.3

	Project schedule		
Event	Earliest	Latest	Slack
0	0	0	0
1	4	4	0
2	6	8	2
3	10	10	0
4	10	11	1
5	13	13	0
6	14	14	0

After calculating the floats for the activities we will be able to identify the critical path.

Table 4.3.4

	Activity float time	
Edge	Activity	Float
$(0, 1)$	Design product	0
$(0, 2)$	Develop marketing strategy	5
$(1, 2)$	Design brochure	2
$(1, 3)$	Produce prototype	0
$(2, 4)$	Survey potential market	2
$(3, 5)$	Test prototype	0
$(4, 5)$	Develop pricing strategy	1
$(1, 5)$	Develop production capability	5
$(5, 6)$	Write implementation plan	0

The critical path can now be identified as a path from beginning to completion including only activities with zero float. Here it is:

Figure 4.3.3

We now use LINDO to solve the linear program described previously and confirm our calculations. In Listing 4.3.1 the activities along the critical path can be identified as corresponding to the constraints having dual prices of -1. This indicates that any change in the duration of the corresponding activity will produce the same change in the length of the critical path.

Note that here we have used the feature of LINDO that allows the constraints to be identified by brief labels rather than just numbers.

Listing 4.3.1

```
MIN       T6
SUBJECT TO
        Des pro)    T1 - T0 >=    4
        Dev mkt)  - T0 + T2 >=    3
        Des bro)  - T1 + T2 >=    2
        Pro pro)  - T1 + T3 >=    6
        Pro cap)  - T1 + T5 >=    4
        Sur mkt)  - T2 + T4 >=    3
          Dummy)  - T3 + T4 >=    0
        Tst pro)  - T3 + T5 >=    3
        Dev pri)    T5 - T4 >=    2
        Wri pln)    T6 - T5 >=    1
    END


LP OPTIMUM FOUND AT STEP        7


            OBJECTIVE FUNCTION VALUE


        1)        14.00000


    VARIABLE         VALUE            REDUCED COST
```

T6	14.000000	0.000000
T1	4.000000	0.000000
T0	0.000000	1.000000
T2	8.000000	0.000000
T3	10.000000	0.000000
T5	13.000000	0.000000
T4	11.000000	0.000000

ROW	SLACK OR SURPLUS	DUAL PRICES
DES PRO)	0.000000	-1.000000
DEV MKT)	5.000000	0.000000
DES BRO)	2.000000	0.000000
PRO PRO)	0.000000	-1.000000
PRO CAP)	5.000000	0.000000
SUR MKT)	0.000000	0.000000
DUMMY)	1.000000	0.000000
TST PRO)	0.000000	-1.000000
DEV PRI)	0.000000	0.000000
WRI PLN)	0.000000	-1.000000

This ouput is summarized graphically in Figure 4.3.4.

The days of the project and the event times t_i range across the top of Figure 4.3.4. The activities are listed on the left side. A double line indicates when a critical activity is under way. A solid line indicates the duration of a noncritical activity and a broken line indicates float time for an activity. Note that for certain activities like E, for which the float is positive, no dashed line is shown. That is because the float for such activities is derived from completing predecessor tasks early. Vertical arrows connect the end of one activity with the beginning of an activity it must precede. The days of the project and the event times t_i range across the top of Figure 4.3.4. The activities are listed on the left side. A double line indicates when a critical activity is under way. A solid line indicates the duration of a noncritical activity and a broken line indicates float time for an activity. Note that for certain activities like E, for which the float is positive, no dashed line is shown. That is because the float for such activities is derived from completing predecessor tasks early. Vertical arrows connect the end of one activity with the beginning of an activity it must precede.

Project schedule

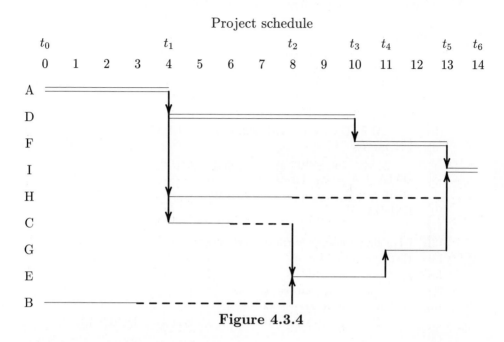

Figure 4.3.4

A LINGO model

While LINDO is useful in determining the critical path and minimal time to completion, LINGO can be employed for the calculation of the schedule. The LINGO model below calculates the earliest time, $ET(i)$; the latest time, $LT(i)$; the slack, $SL(i)$; and the floats, $FL(i, j)$, associated with the CPM problem discussed in this section. This model is adapted from [24]. While the values produced by this model are not in the same form as those generated from the linear program discussed previously, this approach has the advantage of proceeding directly from precedence and duration information found in Table 4.3.1. It is not necessary to first generate a CPM network.

The tasks are defined in the SET section and are associated with the letter names of the activities as subscripts. While the SET section indicates that activity labels are assigned as subscripts, note in line 13 that the first subscript is also automatically associated with the number 1. The durations of the tasks are then provided in the DATA section. Note that FIRST and LAST tasks have been added with zero durations. Finally, the precedence relations are defined in the SET section as a set PRED subscripted by ordered pairs of tasks taken from Table 4.3.1.

More information on the use of LINGO is given in Appendix A.

Listing 4.3.2

```
MODEL:
  1]  SETS:
  2]  TASK/ FIRST, A, B, C, D, E, F, G, H, I, LAST / : DUR, ET, LT, SL;
  3]
  4]  PRED( TASK, TASK)/ FIRST,A, FIRST,B, A,C, A,D, B,E C,E,
  5]      D,F, D,G, E,G, A,H, F,I, G,I, H,I, I,LAST /: FL;
  6]  ENDSETS
  7]
  8]  DATA: ! Activity durations;
  9]  DUR = 0, 4, 3, 2, 6, 3, 3, 2, 4, 1, 0;
 10]  ENDDATA
 11]
 12]  ! For first task the earliest start is 0;
 13]  ET( 1) = 0;
 14]
 15]  ! Compute other earliest times;
 16]  @FOR ( TASK( J)— J #GT# 1:
 17]      ET( J) = @MAX( PRED( I, J): ET( I) + DUR(I)););
 18]
 19]  ! For the last task, latest start = earliest start;
 20]  LTASK = @SIZE( TASK);
 21]  LT( LTASK) = ET( LTASK); SL( LTASK) = 0;
 22]
 23]  ! Compute other latest starts;
 24]  @FOR( TASK( I) — I #LT# LTASK:
 25]      LT( I) = @MIN( PRED( I, J): LT( J) - DUR( I));
 26]      SL( I) = LT( I) - ET( I););
 27]  @FOR(PRED(I,J):FL(I,J) = LT(J) - ET(I) - DUR(I));
END
```

VARIABLE	VALUE		
LTASK	11.00000	SL(A)	0.
ET(FIRST)	.0000000	SL(B)	5.000000
ET(A)	.0000000	SL(C)	2.000000
ET(B)	.0000000	SL(D)	0.
ET(C)	4.000000	SL(E)	2.000000
ET(D)	4.000000	SL(F)	0.
ET(E)	6.000000	SL(G)	1.000000
ET(F)	10.00000	SL(H)	5.000000
ET(G)	10.00000	SL(I)	0.
ET(H)	4.000000	FL(FIRST, A)	.0000000
ET(I)	13.00000	FL(FIRST, B)	5.000000

ET(LAST)	14.00000	FL(A, C)	2.000000
LT(FIRST)	.0000000	FL(A, D)	.0000000
LT(A)	.0000000	FL(A, H)	5.000000
LT(B)	5.000000	FL(B, E)	5.000000
LT(C)	6.000000	FL(C, E)	2.000000
LT(D)	4.000000	FL(D, F)	.0000000
LT(E)	8.000000	FL(D, G)	1.000000
LT(F)	10.00000	FL(E, G)	2.000000
LT(G)	11.00000	FL(F, I)	.0000000
LT(H)	9.000000	FL(G, I)	1.000000
LT(I)	13.00000	FL(H, I)	5.000000
LT(LAST)	14.00000	FL(I, LAST)	.0000000

In the solution in Listing 4.3.2, the given values of the durations of the tasks and the unnecessary slack values are not printed. The critical path can be identified from the zero values of the floats. Normally this output would be one list of variables and their values. Here they are shown in two columns to save space.

Other managerial models

So far we have assumed that the durations of tasks were fixed and have simply identified the critical path and activities and any flexibility that might exist for the noncritical activities. Now we consider problems of greater managerial significance. These models address issues beyond the determination of the critical path by incorporating costs and the allocation of resources to control the duration of the project. The discussion is inspired by [30]. The three models that we will consider are designed to answer the following questions:

- Given a deadline, how should the available resources be allocated to meet that deadline at minimum cost?

- Given a budget of B for additional resources, determine the earliest completion time within budget.

- What is the optimal completion time to minimize the total cost of the project?

To consider these problems, we must let the durations of activities be variable and must also have information on the cost of completing activities more rapidly. Let t_{ij} denote the time required to complete activity (i, j).

Suppose that for each edge (i, j) representing a task, we assume that we know:

u_{ij} The usual completion time,

c_{ij} The absolute minimum time required for (i, j), called the *crash time*, and

r_{ij} The cost to reduce time t_{ij} by one unit of time.

With this notation and these assumptions, Figure 4.3.5 shows the setting to allow a typical activity to have a variable duration.

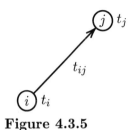

Figure 4.3.5

The constraints imposing a dependence relation between events i and j and the duration restrictions on the activity (i, j) are:

$$t_j - t_i \geq t_{ij} \quad \text{and} \quad c_{ij} \leq t_{ij} \leq u_{ij}.$$

Meeting a project deadline

With the notation introduced above, $r_{ij}(u_{ij} - t_{ij})$ is the cost of reducing the duration of activity (i, j) from the usual time u_{ij} to t_{ij}. Then if N indicates the event at the completion of the project, the following model minimizes the cost of meeting a project completion deadline of T units of time:

$$
\begin{aligned}
\text{Minimize:} \quad & \sum_{(i,j)} r_{ij}(u_{ij} - t_{ij}) \\
\text{Subject to:} \quad & t_j - t_i \geq t_{ij} \\
& t_{ij} \geq c_{ij} \\
& t_{ij} \leq u_{ij} \\
& t_N - t_0 \leq T \\
& t_i \geq 0; \ i = 1, \ldots, N \\
& t_{ij} \geq 0; \ i \in PR(j), \ j = 1, \ldots, N
\end{aligned}
$$

Solving this linear program for a succession of values of T produces an approximate graph for the cost of reducing the completion time as a function of time as in Figure 4.3.6.

Cost

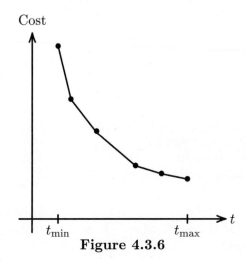

$t_{\min}$ $t_{\max}$

t

Figure 4.3.6

Staying within budget

A second problem is to determine the earliest completion time if a budget of $\$B$ is available to reduce the time required by committing extra resources to some of the activities. Note that this model is obtained from the previous one mainly by interchanging the objective function and the final constraint:

$$
\begin{aligned}
\text{Minimize}: \quad & t_N - t_0 \\
\text{Subject to}: \quad t_j - t_i \;\;&\geq\;\; t_{ij} \\
t_{ij} \;\;&\geq\;\; c_{ij} \\
t_{ij} \;\;&\leq\;\; u_{ij} \\
\textstyle\sum_{(i,j)} r_{ij}(u_{ij} - t_{ij}) \;\;&\leq\;\; B \\
t_i \geq 0; \;\; i &= 1,\ldots,N \\
t_{ij} \geq 0; \;\; i \in PR(j), \;\; j &= 1,\ldots,N
\end{aligned}
$$

We now return to Example 4.3.1 to consider a complication in the problem.

Example 4.3.2. Suppose that the CEO for the company in Example 4.3.1 decides that 14 months to be ready to market the new product is too long – he would like it to be ready by the annual stockholder's meeting in nine months. He reaches into his discretionary funds and produces $\$26{,}000$ in additional funding for the project.

In response, the project manager produces the following estimates of crash times and costs to reduce duration times:

Table 4.3.5

	Activity	Crash time	Cost per month
A.	Design product	2	$4,000
B.	Develop marketing strategy	1	$5,000
D.	Produce prototype	3	$4,000
F.	Test prototype	2	$3,000
H.	Develop production capability	2	$4,000

Can the project be completed in nine months if the $26,000 is allocated to reducing times for these activities? If not, what else might the project manager recommend?

The LINDO formulation of the linear program to see if a nine-month completion is possible is solved in Listing 4.3.3. The last constraint is the budget constraint. It is the algebraic simplification of the following constraint based on the model above with coefficients in units of $1,000:

$$4(4 - T01) + 5(3 - T02) + 4(6 - T13) + 3(3 - T35) + 4(4 - T15) \leq 26$$

The sensitivity analysis of the objective function coefficients and most right-hand sides have been omitted since they are not relevant. Note that the comments indicated by "!" may be included in a data file but do not appear within LINDO and are not written to the file using DIVERT and LOOK ALL.

Listing 4.3.3

```
MIN     T6
SUBJECT TO
    2)    T1 - T0 - T01 >=   0 ! Design product
    3) -  T0 + T2 - T02 >=   0 ! Marketing strategy
    4) -  T1 + T3 - T13 >=   0 ! Produce prototype
    5) -  T1 + T5 - T15 >=   0 ! Dev prod capacity
    6) -  T3 + T5 - T35 >=   0 ! Test prototype
    7) -  T1 + T2 >=   2       ! Design brochure
    8) -  T2 + T4 >=   3       ! Survey market
```

```
   9) - T3 + T4 >=   0          ! Dummy
  10)   T5 - T4 >=   2          ! Dev price strat
  11)   T6 - T5 >=   1          ! Write plan
  12)   T01 >=   2
  13)   T02 >=   1
  14)   T13 >=   3              ! Crash times
  15)   T15 >=   2
  16)   T35 >=   2
  17)   T01 <=   4
  18)   T02 <=   3
  19)   T13 <=   6              ! Usual times
  20)   T15 <=   4
  21)   T35 <=   3
  22)   4 T01 + 5 T02 + 4 T13 + 4 T15 + 3 T35 >=   54
END

LP OPTIMUM FOUND AT STEP      16

      OBJECTIVE FUNCTION VALUE

   1)      10.000000
```

VARIABLE	VALUE	REDUCED COST
T6	10.000000	.000000
T1	2.000000	.000000
T0	.000000	1.000000
T01	2.000000	.000000
T2	4.000000	.000000
T02	2.400000	.000000
T3	7.000000	.000000
T13	3.000000	.000000
T5	9.000000	.000000
T15	4.000000	.000000
T35	2.000000	.000000
T4	7.000000	.000000

ROW	SLACK OR SURPLUS	DUAL PRICES
2)	.000000	-1.000000
3)	1.600000	.000000

4)	2.000000	.000000
5)	3.000000	.000000
6)	.000000	.000000
7)	.000000	-1.000000
8)	.000000	-1.000000
9)	.000000	.000000
10)	.000000	-1.000000
11)	.000000	-1.000000
12)	.000000	-1.000000
13)	1.400000	.000000
14)	.000000	.000000
15)	2.000000	.000000
16)	.000000	.000000
17)	2.000000	.000000
18)	.600000	.000000
19)	3.000000	.000000
20)	.000000	.000000
21)	1.000000	.000000
22)	.000000	.000000

NO. ITERATIONS=   16

RANGES IN WHICH THE BASIS IS UNCHANGED:

		RIGHTHAND SIDE RANGES	
ROW	CURRENT RHS	ALLOWABLE INCREASE	ALLOWABLE DECREASE
7	2.000000	INFINITY	1.600000
8	3.000000	INFINITY	2.000000
9	.000000	1.000000	.000000
10	2.000000	1.000000	.000000
11	1.000000	INFINITY	10.000000
22	54.000000	3.000000	7.000000

The output shows a reduction to 10 months – not quite enough to satisfy the CEO.

The first question the project manager seeks to answer is whether a few thousand more dollars would do the trick. However, the DUAL PRICE for the budget constraint shows that within the current basis additional money has no value. The sensitivity analysis for that constraint shows that an increase of up to $3,000 or a decrease of up to $7,000 would leave the objective function unchanged. Note that since the original budget constraint was multiplied by -1 in forming the final LINDO constraint, an increase (resp. decrease) in the budget is a decrease (resp. increase) in the right-hand side of constraint 22.

So rather than trying to get more funding, the manager analyzes the tasks along the critical path. He identifies the activity of surveying the potential market as lying along the critical path and having the potential for time savings. He estimates that the time could be reduced by one month at a cost of $3,000. Whether or not this will work is left to an exercise.

Minimizing total project cost

As a final model, consider the problem of minimizing the total cost when all factors are considered. In the previous two models we considered only the direct costs associated with the project, i.e., the cost of carrying out the project itself. Most projects also involve costs which, while necessary, do not directly advance the project. Such costs are often lumped under the heading *overhead*, and include things like supervision, interest costs, and security on a job site.

To consider this model we add a final piece of data, $\$F$, the overhead cost per unit of time, and assume that it is constant over the duration of the project. Thus, the total overhead cost is given by $F(t_N - t_0)$, and the following model gives an approach to determining the optimimum completion time for the project:

$$
\begin{aligned}
\text{Minimize}: \quad & F(t_N - t_0) + \textstyle\sum_{(i,j)} r_{ij}(u_{ij} - t_{ij}) \\
\text{Subject to}: \quad & t_j - t_i \;\geq\; t_{ij} \\
& t_{ij} \;\geq\; c_{ij} \\
& t_{ij} \;\leq\; u_{ij} \\
& t_i \geq 0; \; i = 1, \ldots, N \\
& t_{ij} \geq 0; \; i \in PR(j), \; j = 1, \ldots, N
\end{aligned}
$$

When the direct cost obtained previously and the overhead cost are added together, we obtain a graph of the total project cost as a function of the duration (Figure 4.3.7).

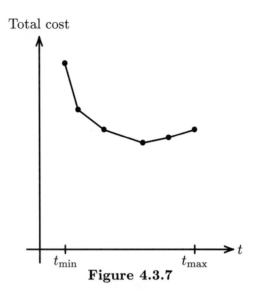

Figure 4.3.7

Exercises

1. Determine the critical path for the following project network:

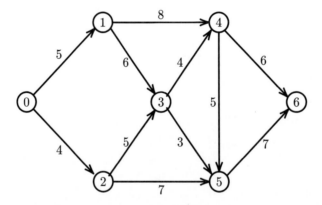

Figure 4.3.8

2. A software development firm has undertaken a project for the government. The systems analyst in charge of the project has decomposed the task into the following stages:

Table 4.3.6

	Activity	Duration (in months)	Immediate predecessors
A.	Requirement analysis	2	-
B.	Object design	3	A
C.	System design	4	A
D.	Coding	8	B, C
E.	Documentation	1	D
F.	Unit testing I	2	D
G.	Unit testing II	3	D
H.	System testing	4	F, G
I.	Deliverables	1	E, H

The project manager wants to know:

(a) Minimum time to completion of the project.

(b) Activities which are crucial to the on-time delivery of the system.

(c) Flexibility, if any, in completing the activities.

Determine a CPM network and obtain answers for the project manager.

3. You have negotiated a contract for the rock group Slash 'n Burn to appear in your town. Getting everything ready for the concert is quite complicated. The tasks, their durations, and the precedence relations among them are found in Table 4.3.7.

Table 4.3.7

	Task	Immediate predecessors	Time in days
A.	Rent concert hall	-	2
B.	Get sponsors	-	6
C.	Get program material	-	4
D.	Set ticket prices	A	1
E.	Plan advertising	A, B	3
F.	Get program ads	B	4
G.	Print tickets	D	2
H.	Print programs	C, F	3
I.	Advertise	E	10
J.	Sell tickets	E, G	10
K.	Hold concert	H, I, J	

(a) Draw a CPM network.

(b) How much time do you need between getting the contract and the concert?

(c) What are the critical tasks in preparing for the concert?

4. Consider the CPM project network below, where time is measured in days:

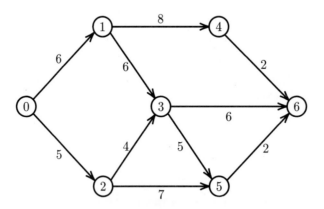

Figure 4.3.9

(a) Determine the earliest and latest times.

(b) Determine the floats for the activitities.

5. Consider the network in Figure 4.3.10 with times and costs in Table 4.3.8.

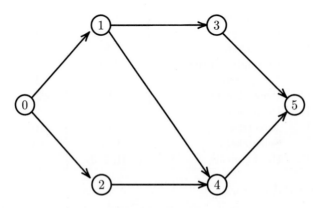

Figure 4.3.10

Table 4.3.8

Activity	Usual time	Crash time	Cost per unit time
(0, 1)	8	4	$600
(0, 2)	9	6	$800
(1, 3)	7	6	$750
(1, 4)	10	7	$650
(2, 4)	6	4	$900
(3, 5)	9	6	$400
(4, 5)	8	5	$600

(a) Determine the critical path using the usual times.

(b) Determine the least expensive way to reduce the length of the critical path by four time units.

(c) What is the shortest possible completion time if cost can be ignored?

6. Now suppose that some of the activities in the software development project of Exercise 2 above can be reduced in time. Suppose that system design (C) can be reduced to 3 months at a cost of $2,500 a month, coding (D) can be reduced to 5 months at a cost of $3,000 a month, and system testing (H) can be reduced to 2 months at a cost of $2,500 a month.

Formulate and solve a linear program to determine the cheapest way to reduce the project time to 18 months.

7. Consider the CPM project network in Figure 4.3.11, where time is measured in days.

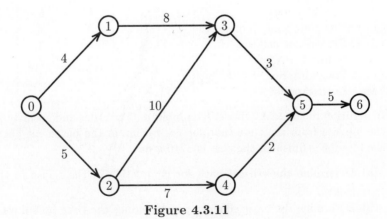

Figure 4.3.11

(a) Determine the earliest times and latest times for the events.

(b) Calculate the floats for the activities and determine the critical path.

(c) If the durations on the edges of the network are the usual times, and the crash times and the costs of a day's reduction for four of the activities are given in Figure 4.3.9, set up a linear program to determine how to reduce the length of the project to 19 days.

Table 4.3.9

Activity	Usual time	Crash time	Cost per day
(0, 1)	4	2	$500
(2, 3)	10	6	$700
(2, 4)	7	4	$600
(5, 6)	5	3	$300

8. Rural Residence, Inc. (RRI) manufactures and builds prefab log homes. The logs are cut at their plant and delivered to the site. All other materials such as roofing, doors, windows, etc. are purchased from other companies. The tasks involved in building one of their homes are shown in Table 4.3.10.

Table 4.3.10

	Activity	Immediate predecessor	Usual time	Crash time	Cost per day
A.	Prepare site	-	2	2	-
B.	Adjust design to site	A	2	1	$300
C.	Cut logs for house	A	3	2	$250
D.	Obtain other materials	B	7	7	-
E.	Excavate basement	B	2	1	$700
F.	Pour foundation	E	3	2	$350
G.	Ship logs	C	5	3	$125
H.	Assemble logs	F, G	8	5	$150
I.	Complete roof, doors, etc.	D, H	5	4	$250
J.	Prepare for utilities	D, H	5	3	$300
K.	Connect utilities	J	2	2	-
L.	Finish interior	J	7	4	$200
M.	Landscape lot	I, K	2	2	-

In addition to the tasks above, RRI maintains a trailer and security guard at the job site from the time that the excavation of the basement begins until the interior is finished; the cost is $210 a day.

(a) Determine the critical path for completion of the house in the usual time.

(b) Determine the most efficient way to reduce the time by 5 days.

(c) A realtor has a client very interested in the house as soon as possible and will pay $2,000 to speed up the building process. How large a time reduction can be made for that amount?

(d) Determine the completion time that would result in the least cost.

9. Consider the CPM project network in Figure 4.3.12, where the indicated times are the usual times measured in months.

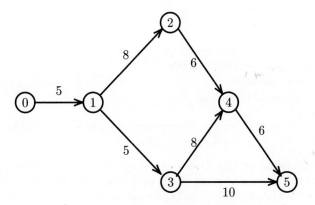

Figure 4.3.12

Suppose that three of the activities can be "crashed" if necessary as indicated in Table 4.3.11.

Table 4.3.11

Activity	Usual time	Crash time	Cost per month
(0,1)	5	3	$1,000
(1,2)	8	5	$800
(4,5)	6	3	$900

Formulate a linear program to determine the earliest that the project can be completed if $3,000 is available to reduce the times of the indicated activities.

10. Determine if crashing the activity of surveying the market in Example 4.3.2 in addition to the other reductions will permit the project to be completed in 9 months.

11. The Burnside Company has done the basic groundwork necessary to introduce a new product. Getting started will require preparing space, hiring and training workers, getting the necessary equipment, and procuring materials for production. Company policy requires that current employees have the first opportunity to fill the jobs created. The manager in charge has identified the following necessary activities, the dependencies among them, and their likely durations.

Table 4.3.12

	Activity	Duration (in weeks)	Immediate predecessors
A.	Prepare space	3	-
B.	Get bids on equipment	2	-
C.	Acquire equipment	3	A, B
D.	Hire from within	3	-
E.	Hire from outside	5	D
F.	Develop training program	4	C
G.	Acquire needed materials	4	C
H.	Train workers	6	E, F
I.	First production run	2	G, H

What are the critical path for the project and the minimum time needed for Burnside to complete the first production run?

12. Suppose that the Burnside Company in the exercise above detects a competitor for the market they are trying reach with their new product. To speed the new product to market, they decide to put additional resources into the process. They are not experts at training, so they contract a firm with extensive training experience in similar areas. The firm claims that for $3,000 a week it can reduce the development of a training program to two weeks, and for $4,000 a week it can reduce the training time to three weeks. Also, by engaging an employment agency for $2,500 a week to do the outside hiring, the time required can be reduced to three weeks. How much will these changes in plans reduce the time required if Burnside can commit $11,000 to the additional expense?

4.4   Shortest path models

The critical path obtained in the previous section is the longest path between the nodes representing the beginning and the ending of a project. Aside from that special application to a particular network, there is usually greater interest in determining shortest paths. In this section we consider a standard algorithm for that problem and examine applications where "shortest" has something other than the usual connotations of distance or time.

The efficiency and correctness of an algorithm are of vital importance if it is to be effectively employed. While most such considerations are beyond our scope, we discuss them in this section and the next to allow the interested reader to consider these issues in examples where the analysis is reasonably accessible. Those interested primarily in applications can simply master one of the algorithms or employ software such as LINGO or *Maple*.

Determination of the shortest path between two nodes can be formulated as a linear program with the variables restricted to assume only the values 0 or 1. For a network with edge weights d_{ij}, the following linear program will yield the shortest path between node 1 and node N. The variable x_{ij} is equal to 1 if edge (i, j) is part of the path; it is 0 otherwise.

$$\text{Minimize}: \quad \sum_{(i,j)} d_{ij} x_{ij}$$

$$\text{Subject to}: \quad \sum_{j=2}^{N} x_{1j} = 1$$

$$\sum_{j=1}^{N-1} x_{jN} = 1$$

$$\sum_{\substack{i \neq k}}^{N} x_{ik} = \sum_{\substack{j \neq k}}^{N} x_{kj}, \ 1 < k < N$$

$$x_{ij} \in \{0, 1\}$$

The first constraint above says that the path must include an edge going out of node 1 and the second requires that the path include an edge going into node N. The third enforces node balance, i.e., that the number of edges leaving any node other than 1 and N must equal the number entering the node.

While the shortest path can be obtained by a linear program, it is more commonly gotten by a specialized algorithm from [8], which we now consider.

Dijkstra's algorithm

Consider a connected weighted graph G with weights d_{ij}. To determine the shortest path from a vertex a to a second vertex z we will use a system of labels for the vertices. Labels assigned will be classified as "temporary" or "permanent," and the key to the algorithm is the rule for assigning the length of a path from a as the label of a vertex. All labels will start out temporary, and the label of a vertex will be made permanent when the label represents the shortest distance from a to the vertex.

Let T represent the set of vertices having temporary labels and let D denote the labeling function.

INIT: Set $D(a) := 0$, for $x \neq a$, set $D(x) := \infty$, and set $T := \{$all vertices$\}$.

TERMINATE?: If z is not in T, $D(z)$ is the length of shortest path. Stop. Do BACKTRACK.

REMOVE VERTEX: Choose v in T with $D(v) = \min\{D(x) : x \in T\}$ and set $T := T \setminus \{v\}$.

ADJUST LABELS: For x in T adjacent to v, reevaluate labels by $D(x) := \min\{D(x), D(v) + d_{vx}\}$. Do TERMINATE?

BACKTRACK: Beginning with $x = z$ until $x = a$, successively add to the path the edge (w, x) such that $D(x) = d_{wx} + D(w)$, and set $x := w$.

Example 4.4.1. Determine the shortest path from vertex 1 to vertex 7 in the graph in Figure 4.4.1.

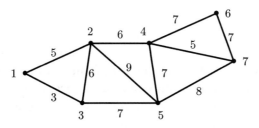

Figure 4.4.1

In the Table 4.4.1, the first column of labels is the result of the INIT step. Then the successive columns are the result of REMOVE VERTEX and ADJUST LABELS. When the label of a vertex is made permanent, it does not appear in the following columns.

Table 4.4.1

	Labels at iteration i						
Vertex	INIT	1	2	3	4	5	6
1	0						
2	∞	5	5				
3	∞	3					
4	∞	∞	∞	11	11		
5	∞	∞	10	10			
6	∞	∞	∞	∞	∞	18	18
7	∞	∞	∞	∞	18	16	

Note that vertex 7 is initially assigned a finite label, 18, at step 4 when the label on vertex 5 is made permanent. Then at the next step vertex 4 is permanently labeled and the label on vertex 7 is reduced to 16, becoming permanent when the algorithm terminates. Note that the label on vertex 6 remains temporary when the algorithm terminates.

The shortest path is shown by the solid edges in Figure 4.4.2.

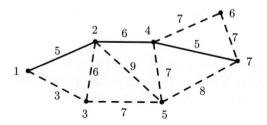

Figure 4.4.2

We now address the effectiveness of the algorithm. An algorithm is said to be *effective* for a type of problem if it can be shown to solve any problem of the type in such a way that the number of elementary computational steps can be bounded by a polynomial function of the problem size. Here we will measure problem size by the number of edges and the number of vertices in the graph under consideration.

Proposition 4.4.2. *Dijkstra's algorithm is effective, i.e., the total number of edges examined is at worst a polynomial function of the number of vertices.*

Proof. Let G be a connected graph without loops or parallel edges and having n nodes. There are two basic operations: comparisons and additions. We consider the number of these operations required in the worst case for each of the key steps of the algorithm.

[REMOVE VERTEX] At the ith step there are $n - i$ vertices in T, so $n - i$ comparisons are required. This step is repeated at most $n - 1$ times, so the maximum number of comparisons is

$$\sum_{i=1}^{n-1}(n - i) \ = \ (n - 1) + (n - 2) + \cdots + 2 + 1 \ = \ \frac{(n - 1)n}{2}$$

[ADJUST LABELS] In the worst case at the ith step there are $n - i$ vertices adjacent to r that must be relabeled, each requiring an addition and a comparison. Since there are at most $n - 1$ steps, as above there are $\frac{(n - 1)n}{2}$ comparisons required, and the same number of additions.

[BACKTRACK] In the worst case we may need to do $n - i$ comparisons and additions for each of $n - 1$ steps. So there are the same number of operations required as in [ADJUST LABELS].

So there are $\dfrac{3(n-1)n}{2}$ comparisons, and $\dfrac{2(n-1)n}{2} = n(n-1)$ additions required, and the number of basic operations is therefore at most $\dfrac{5(n-1)n}{2}$.

$\square$

An example showing how a graph is entered in *Maple* and the shortest path determined using Dijkstra's algorithm is given in Appendix A. The following examples indicate that shortest path problems can arise in unexpected contexts.

Example 4.4.3. Equipment replacement cost. A car has been purchased in year 0 for $12,000. Table 4.4.2 gives the trade-in value of the car and the maintenance costs in $1,000 units.

Table 4.4.2

Age	Trade-in	Maintenance
1	8	1
2	6	1
3	3	2
4	2	3
5	1	4
6	1	5

Determine a future time to purchase the next car at minimum cost if the price of the car remains at $12,000.

In the graph to determine the time of purchase that minimizes the total cost of owning a car, the nodes are the years involved starting with the purchase of the initial car at year 0. The edge weights are the total of the net cost of the next car and service costs accumulated during the life of the original car.

Example 4.4.4. Compact book storage. A collection of books has heights of the books $H_1, H_2, \ldots, H_n, H_i < H_{i+1}$, with the total thickness of the books of height H_i equal to L_i. H_i is measured in inches and L_i in feet. The owner of the collection seeks to design shelving at minimum cost to store the books and has obtained estimates of the cost for the shelves based upon their height. To build a shelf of height H_i will cost $\$C_i$ per foot plus a fixed cost of $\$K_i$. Determine how many feet of shelves of each height the owner should order.

In the graph to determine the minimal shelving cost for the collection there are $n+1$ nodes, one for each height of book, including books having "zero" height. The weight of the edge joining nodes i and j, where $i < j$, is the total cost of shelving all books having heights k, $i < k \le j$, on shelves of height H_j.

Exercises

1. Determine the shortest path from A to H in the network in Figure 4.4.3.

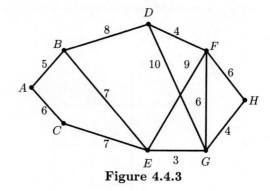

Figure 4.4.3

2. Determine the shortest path from node a to node i in Figure 4.4.4.

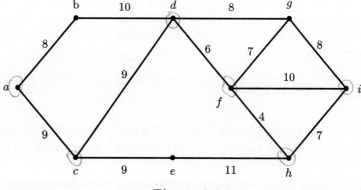

Figure 4.4.4

3. Determine the shortest path from node a to node i in the network in Figure 4.4.5.

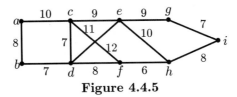

Figure 4.4.5

4. Solve the problem posed in Example 4.4.3.

5. A commuter lives at vertex h and works at vertex w on the city map shown in Figure 4.4.6. The edge weights are usual rush hour travel times in minutes. Each intersection adds a minute to the time on average because of the traffic light. If a left turn is required, the intersection is expected to add 2 minutes to the time. What route should the commuter take to work to minimize travel time?

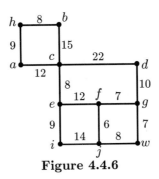

Figure 4.4.6

6. A machine shop is planning the purchase and maintenance of a piece of equipment that will cost them \$2,000. Their planning horizon is 5 years. The cost of the equipment is expected to increase by \$200 a year. Table 4.4.? shows the operating cost and year-end resale value of the equipment in the ith year of service.

Table 4.4.3

	Year of service				
	1	2	3	4	5
Operating cost	\$120	\$120	\$190	\$200	\$220
Resale value	\$1,400	\$1,000	\$700	\$400	\$100

If the shop should replace the equipment at some point during the five year period to minimize cost, determine when.

7. History of Art Professor Remington Sylvester has tired of having stacks of books all over his office. He has had them stacked according to their height. The stacks of books of height 9 inches and under total 15 feet, those between 9 and 10 inches total 24 feet, those between 10 and 11 inches total 18 feet, and those between 11 and 12 inches total 22 feet. To make efficient use of space, the shelves will be 10 feet long or 8 feet long, depending on which wall they are on. The respective costs of the shelves are given in Table 4.4.4.

Table 4.4.4

Maximum book height	8'	10'
9"	$40	$52
10"	$48	$57
11"	$55	$60
12"	$60	$66

Determine how to design shelves for Professor Sylvester at minimum cost.

4.5 Minimal spanning trees

The minimal spanning tree problem is chiefly found in areas such as connecting utilities, designing computer networks, and the secure communication of information. We will consider the algorithms of Kruskal and Prim as well as a LINGO model.

A *spanning tree* for a graph G is a subgraph which is a tree and includes all vertices of G. If the edges of G are weighted, a *minimal spanning tree* is a spanning tree of minimal total edge weight.

The following proposition, based on one in [17], characterizing trees will be useful in the discussion to follow. A *loop* in a graph is an edge that is incident on only one node, i.e., it departs from and returns to the same node. Two edges are said to be *parallel* if they are incident on the same pair of nodes. A *cycle* in a graph is a path that returns to its starting node. A key property of a cycle is that it provides two different paths between any two distinct vertices on the cycle.

Proposition 4.5.1. *The following are equivalent for a graph T having n vertices, no loops, and no parallel edges:*

(a) *T is a tree (i.e., has a unique path between each pair of vertices).*

(b) *T is connected and contains no cycles.*

(c) *T is connected and has $n - 1$ edges.*

(d) *T contains no cycles and has $n - 1$ edges.*

Proof.

(a) $\Rightarrow$ (b): T is clearly connected since there is a path between every pair of vertices. Suppose T contains a cycle. Since T contains no loops, the cycle includes distinct vertices a and b. But then the cycle contains two distinct paths between a and b, contradicting the fact that T is a tree.

(b) $\Rightarrow$ (c): Suppose T is connected and without cycles. We use induction on the number of vertices to show that T has $n - 1$ edges:

For $i = 1, T$ consists of a single vertex and no edges, so the result is true.

Now assume the result for k vertices, and let T be a connected graph without circuits and having $k + 1$ vertices.

Choose a path P of maximum length in T. Since P is not a circuit, it includes a vertex with only one edge incident on it. Remove that edge and vertex. The result is a connected graph with k vertices and no circuits. Hence, by the induction hypothesis, it has $k - 1$ edges. Thus, the original graph had k edges.

(c) $\Rightarrow$ (d): Let T be connected and have $n - 1$ edges. We must show that T contains no cycles. Suppose T contains a cycle. Then, because removing an edge from a cycle does not disconnect the graph, we can remove edges until the remaining graph has no cycles but is still connected.

But then by the proof of b) $\Rightarrow$ c), the resulting graph contains $n - 1$ edges. This contradicts the assumption that the graph contained a cycle.

(d) $\Rightarrow$ (a): Now suppose that T contains no cycles and has $n - 1$ edges.

We first show that T is connected. Suppose not, and let $T_1, T_2, \ldots, T_k$ be the components of T. Then $k > 1$ since T is not connected.

Each T_i is connected and has no circuits. Hence by (b) $\Rightarrow$ (c), if T_i has n_i vertices, then T_i has $n_i - 1$ edges. Now:

$$
\begin{aligned}
n - 1 &= (n_1 - 1) + (n_2 - 1) + \cdots + (n_k - 1) \\
&< (n_1 + n_2 + \cdots + n_k) - 1 \quad \text{since } k > 1 \\
&= n - 1
\end{aligned}
$$

which is a contradiction. Hence, T is connected.

Now suppose that there are distinct paths between vertices a and b. Then going from a to b on one, and returning to a on the other, creates a cycle in T, which is impossible. $\square$

The following two observations are useful when working with tree algorithms. They express the fact that a tree has as many edges as possible without containing a cycle and also has a few as possible to remain connected.

Lemma 4.5.2. *Adding an additional edge to a tree creates a unique cycle.*

Lemma 4.5.3. *Removing an edge that belongs to a cycle of a connected graph does not disconnect the graph.*

We now consider two algorithms to determine the minimal spanning tree of a graph. As the proposition above suggests, the algorithms consist of adding "short" edges to a graph in such a way that no cycle is formed until the graph contains one fewer edge than it does vertices.

Kruskal's algorithm

This algorithm appears in [22]. We assume that G is a weighted, connected graph without loops or parallel edges and having n vertices. The algorithm assumes the existence of a means to check that adding a specific edge will not create a cycle. For our small examples, this check is accomplished by inspection. The discussion of the LINGO model at the end of the section will give an indication of how this might be implemented in a program.

INIT: Set T equal to the set of vertices of G.

SORT: Sort the edges into nondecreasing edge-length order.

ADD EDGE: Add the next edge to T in order which does not create a cycle.

END?: Repeat ADD EDGE until $n-1$ edges have been added.

Example 4.5.4. Determine the minimal spanning tree for the network in Figure 4.5.1. To facilitate the use of Kruskal's algorithm, the edges are listed in nondecreasing order in Table 4.5.1.

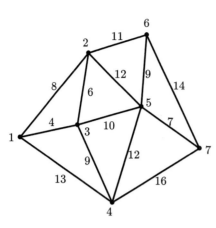

Figure 4.5.1

Table 4.5.1

Edge	Weight
$\{1,3\}$	4
$\{3,2\}$	6
$\{5,7\}$	7
$\{1,2\}$	8
$\{5,6\}$	9
$\{3,4\}$	9
$\{3,5\}$	10
$\{2,6\}$	11
$\{4,5\}$	12
$\{1,4\}$	13
$\{6,7\}$	13
$\{4,7\}$	16

We initialize the tree by setting it equal to the set of vertices. Then following the suggestion from (c) of Proposition 4.5.1, the algorithm repeats **ADD EDGE** until 6 edges have been added, i.e., one fewer edge than there are vertices.

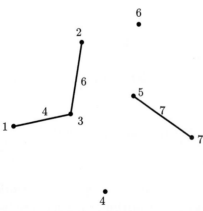

Figure 4.5.2

After putting in the three shortest edges and the corresponding vertices, we have the graph in Figure 4.5.2. The next edge in the ordering that should be added is $\{1,2\}$ with weight 8. However, together with the edges $\{1,3\}$ and $\{2,3\}$ this would create a cycle. So we skip edge $\{1,2\}$ and instead add $\{5,6\}$ and the next two edges in succession to complete the minimal spanning tree indicated by the solid edges in the graph in Figure 4.5.3.

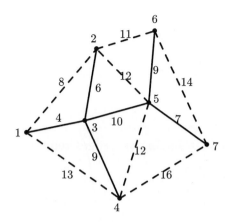

Figure 4.5.3

We now show that Kruskal's algorithm yields a minimal spanning tree.

Theorem 4.5.5. *Kruskal's algorithm is correct.*

Proof. Consider a graph G having n vertices and let T^* be the spanning tree created by Kruskal's algorithm. Let $\{e_1, e_2, \ldots, e_{n-1}\}$ be the edges of T^*, and for a tree T define $f(T)$ to be the smallest value of i such that e_i is not in T.

Now assume that T^* is not minimal and let T be a minimal spanning tree such that $f(T) = k$ is as large as possible. Then $e_1, \ldots, e_{k-1}$ belong to both T and T^*, but e_k is not in T. Then $T \cup \{e_k\}$ contains a unique cycle C. Let e'_k be an edge in C that is in T but not T^*. Since e'_k belongs to a cycle in $T \cup \{e_k\}$, $T' = (T \cup \{e_k\}) \setminus \{e'_k\}$ is connected and has $n - 1$ edges and hence is a spanning tree of G.

Now in Kruskal's algorithm, e_k was selected as the shortest edge so that the graph including the edges $\{e_1, e_2, \ldots, e_k\}$ has no cycle. Since the graph with edges $\{e_1, e_2, \ldots, e'_k\}$ is a subgraph of T, it also has no cycle. Hence, the weight of e'_k is at least as great as that of e_k.

Therefore, the weight of T' is no greater than that of T. So T is a minimal spanning tree. However, by construction, T' includes $\{e_1, e_2, \ldots, e_{k-1}, e_k\}$, so $f(T') > k = f(T)$. This contradicts the choice of T. Hence, $T = T^*$ and T^* is a minimal spanning tree. $\square$

Now that we know that the algorithm yields a minimum spanning tree, we address its efficiency.

A graph without cycles is called *acyclic*. Since it is a union of trees, it is also called a *forest*. The maximal trees in a forest are its components.

Theorem 4.5.6. *Kruskal's algorithm is effective.*

Proof. Let e denote the number of edges in the graph G and v the number of vertices.

It can be shown that sorting the edges requires approximately $e \ln(e)$ computations.

At each stage of the algorithm, the graph constructed to that point is a forest. To determine if the next edge to be added would create a cycle, it is sufficient to label all the vertices to record the component to which they belong.

An edge can then be added without creating a cycle provided the vertices at its ends have different labels. This takes e computations.

Finally, after each edge is added, the labels of the vertices must be checked, and changed as necessary. Each relabeling requires v computations, and, when repeated for each of the $v - 1$ edges necessary, this yields $v(v - 1)$ computations.

Hence, an upper bound for the number of computations required is $e \ln(e) + e + v(v - 1).\square$

Therefore, the number of operations depends chiefly on SORT. Typically, the number of interchanges required by a sorting algorithm is proportional to m^2 or $m \ln(m)$, where m is the number of edges.

Prim's algorithm

We will be able to study the next method, Prim's algorithm, more completely. Here a system of labels is used to assure that adding an edge does not create a cycle.

Let G be a graph with n vertices in a set V and with weight d_{ij} associated with edge ij. We define the minimal spanning tree by building up its set C of vertices and A of edges.

INIT: Determine the shortest edge ij and set $A = \{ij\}$ and $C = \{i, j\}$.

LABEL: For vertices i in $V \backslash C$ that are adjacent to a vertex in C, determine a vertex $k(i)$ in C such that $d_{ik(i)} = \min\{d_{ij} : j \in C\} = a_{k(i)}$ and label

i with $[k(i), a_{k(i)}]$. For i in $V \setminus C$ and not adjacent to a vertex in C, label i with $[0, \infty]$.

ADD: Identify I in $V \setminus C$ such that $a_{k(I)} = \min\{a_{k(i)} : i \in V \setminus C\}$. Add vertex I to C and add the edge $k(I), I$ to A.

STOP?: Terminate if C contains n nodes.

UPDATE LABELS: For j in $V \setminus C$, if $jk(I)$ is an edge in G and $a_{k(j)} > d_{jk(I)}$, make $[I, d_{jk(I)}]$ the new label for j. Do ADD.

We return to the graph of Example 4.5.4 to determine the minimal spanning tree for the graph in Figure 4.5.4 using Prim's algorithm.

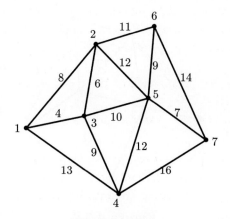

Figure 4.5.4

Because the shortest edge is $\{1,3\}$, we set $A = \{\{1,3\}\}$ and $C = \{1,3\}$ at the INIT step.

Figures 4.5.5 and 4.5.6 show the trees after steps 2 and 4, respectively. Table 4.5.2 then gives the labels on the other vertices for the remaining steps. The labels are removed as the edges are added to the tree.

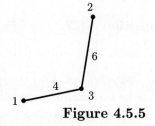

Figure 4.5.5

Table 4.5.2

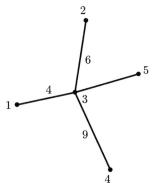

	Label at step				
Vertex	2	3	4	5	6
2	$[3,6]$				
4	$[3,9]$	$[3,9]$			
5	$[3,10]$	$[3,10]$	$[3,10]$		
6	$[0,\infty]$	$[2,11]$	$[2,11]$	$[5,9]$	$[5,9]$
7	$[0,\infty]$	$[0,\infty]$	$[4,16]$	$[5,7]$	

Figure 4.5.6

The result is the tree in Figure 4.5.7 and is the same tree we obtained earlier by Kruskal's algorithm.

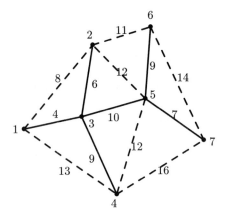

Figure 4.5.7

■

The following proposition confirms that starting to build a minimal spanning tree with the shortest edge is correct.

Proposition 4.5.7. *Any edge of the least weight belongs to a minimal spanning tree.*

Proof. Suppose not; i.e., suppose that edge ij has the minimal weight but belongs to no minimal spanning tree. Let T be a minimal spanning tree. Then $\{ij\} \cup T$ contains a cycle involving ij. Removing any edge from the cycle other than ij produces a spanning tree with total weight no larger than that of T, and hence a minimal spanning tree. Contradiction.□

Now we show that Prim's algorithm yields a minimal spanning tree.

Theorem 4.5.8. *Prim's algorithm is correct.*

Proof. We must show that the algorithm actually produces a minimal spanning tree. Letting T_i be the tree formed by the algorithm at step i, we proceed by induction.

Induction hypothesis: For each i, T_i is contained in some minimal spanning tree.

$i = 1$: This is clear from the proposition above since the shortest edge belongs to some minimal spanning tree.

Now assume $T_{i-1} \subset T$, T a minimal spanning tree. Let pq be the edge and q the node to be added to form T_i.

If $T_i \not\subset T$, we must show that T_i is contained in some minimal spanning tree. Consider the graph $H = T \cup \{pq\}$. H is not a tree since it contains the extra edge pq. Further, since pq joins a node not in T_{i-1} with one of T_{i-1}, H contains a cycle that involves another edge rs joining a node of T_{i-1} with a node not in T_{i-1}.

Removing rs from H produces a spanning tree T', and by Prim's algorithm, the weight of rs is at least as great as that of pq. Hence, the weight of T' is no greater than that of T, so T' is a minimal spanning tree containing T_i.□

Theorem 4.5.9. *Prim's algorithm is effective. The number of edges examined by the algorithm is at most a quadratic polynomial in the number of vertices.*

Proof. Let n be the number of vertices in the graph.

[INIT] requires examination of at most $\dfrac{n(n-1)}{2}$ edges, i.e., the number of edges in a complete graph with n vertices.

[LABEL] requires the examination of the number of edges joining the initial two vertices selected to the other $n - 2$ vertices – at most $2(n - 2)$ edges.

[ADD] requires no examination of edges.

If k is the number of nodes already in the tree, [UPDATE LABELS] requires the examination of $n - k$ edges each time it is executed. Thus, the number of examinations is:

$$\sum_{k=2}^{n-2}(n - k) = (n - 2) + (n - 3) + \cdots + 2 + 1 = \frac{(n - 2)(n - 1)}{2}.$$

So in the worst case the total number of edges examined is:

$$
\begin{aligned}
\frac{n(n - 1)}{2} + 2(n - 2) + \frac{(n - 2)(n - 1)}{2} &= \frac{(2n - 2)(n - 2) + 4n - 8}{2} \\
&= \frac{2n^2 - 2n - 2n + 2 + 4n - 8}{2} \\
&= \frac{2n^2 - 6}{2} \\
&= n^2 - 3. \quad \square
\end{aligned}
$$

The following application is from Prim's paper [29]. It relies on the notion of a symmetric function and the fact that a minimal spanning tree minimizes any symmetric function of the edge weights, not just their sum. A *symmetric function* of n variables is one whose value is not changed by interchanges of variable values.

Example 4.5.10. The following are examples of symmetric functions:

$$f(x_1, \ldots, x_n) = x_1 + x_2 + \cdots + x_n \quad \text{and} \quad g(x_1, \ldots, x_n) = x_1 x_2 \cdots x_n \qquad \blacksquare$$

Proposition 4.5.11. *A minimal spanning tree of a connected graph minimizes all increasing symmetric functions of the edge lengths and maximizes all decreasing symmetric functions.*

Before moving on to examine an application, we note that there is a dual result for maximal spanning trees.

Example 4.5.12. A message is to be passed to all members of an underground organization. Each member knows certain other members and has a means of contacting those that he or she knows. Associated with each contact i to j is a probability p_{ij} that the message will fall into hostile hands. Assuming that the probabilities of compromise are independent, how should the message be distributed to minimize the overall chance of compromise?

To express the problem as one involving a minimal spanning tree, define a graph as follows:

- The vertices are the members of the underground.

- Edges join underground members who know each other.

- The length of the edge joining members i and j is p_{ij}, the probability of compromise for the link.

Then the probability of compromise in the graph is given by

$$1 - \times (1 - p_{ij})$$

which is an increasing, symmetric function of the p_{ij}'s.

One could also interpret the p_{ij} as the probability of failure of a link in a computer network. In a similar application, permitted wiring patterns do not always follow straight lines, but the distance required is still minimized by the minimal spanning tree. ∎

In addition to the LINGO approach to determining a minimal spanning tree to be discussed below, the `spantree` command available in *Maple* as part of the `networks` package will determine a minimal spanning tree. The use of this command is introduced in Appendix B.

A LINGO approach

The modeling language LINGO can be employed to determine a minimal spanning tree. The model in Listing 4.5.1 includes the data to obtain the tree for Example 4.5.4 and is based on a sample model in [24].

Describing the graph requires three statements. Line 5 sets up the subscripts for seven nodes. Lines 7 and 8 establish that there will be two variables, DIST and X, defined for pairs of nodes. Finally, the lengths of the edges are entered beginning on line 13. A length of 999 is used to indicate that two nodes are not adjacent.

The statement beginning on line 31 represents the set of constraints that attempt to prevent the formation of a circuit. That line requires explanation.

The model designates node 1 as the *root* of the tree, i.e., the node from which all edges are considered to emanate. The choice of root can be made arbitrarily, but allows all nodes to be assigned a *level*, the number of edges between the node and the root. Thus, node 1 is assigned to the level 0, nodes adjacent to the root are on level 1, and all other nodes are assigned a level greater than 1. In the model, the level of node I is stored in U(I).

The other variable required to describe the tree is X(I,J). The model sets X(I,J) = 1 if the edge joining nodes I and J is in the tree and sets X(I,J) = 0 otherwise.

Note first that the statement beginning on line 31 produces a constraint for each ordered pair of vertices – in the case of our seven-node example this will be 42 constraints. These constraints prevent cycles in the tree.

Listing 4.5.1

```
MODEL:
 1]   ! Minimal spanning tree model;
 2]   ! Distance of 999 indicates that vertices are not adjacent;
 3]
 4]   SETS:
 5]   NODE / 1 .. 7/: U; ! U( I) = level of the node;
 6]   ! U( 1) = 0;
 7]   LINK( NODE, NODE):
 8]   DIST, ! The distance matrix;
 9]   X; ! X( I, J) = 1 if we use link I, J;
10]   ENDSETS
11]   DATA: ! Distance matrix, which need not be symmetric;
12]            ! Node 1 is the root of the tree;
13]   DIST = 0 8 4 13 999 999 999
14]          8 0 6 999 12 11 999
15]          4 6 0 9 10 999 999
16]          13 999 9 0 12 999 16
17]          999 12 10 12 0 9 7
18]          999 11 999 999 9 0 14
19]          999 999 999 16 7 14 0;
20]   ENDDATA
21]
22]   N = @SIZE( NODE);
23]   MIN = @SUM( LINK: DIST * X);
24]   @FOR( NODE( K)| K #GT# 1:
25]   ! It must be entered;
26]   @SUM( NODE( I)| I #NE# K: X( I, K)) = 1;
27]   ! U( K) must be at least 1;
```

```
28]   @BND( 1, U( K), 999999);
29]   ! Cycle breaking constraints;
30]   ! These are not very powerful for large problems;
31]   @FOR( NODE( J)| J #GT# 1 #AND# J #NE# K:
32]   U( J) > U( K) + X ( K, J) -
33]   ( N - 2) * ( 1 - X( K, J)) +
34]   ( N - 3) * X( J, K); );
35]   );
36]   ! Make the X's 0/1;
37]   @FOR( LINK: @BIN( X); );
38]   ! For a first level node we know...;
39]   @FOR( NODE( K)| K #GT# 1:
40]   U( K) < N - 1 - ( N - 2) * X( 1, K); );
41]   ! There must be an edge out of node 1;
42]   @SUM( NODE( J)| J #GT# 1: X( 1, J)) > 1;
END
```

The output provided by the model in Listing 4.5.1 is provided in edited form in Listing 4.5.2.

Listing 4.5.2

```
LP OPTIMUM FOUND AT STEP 16
OBJECTIVE VALUE = 45.0000000
ENUMERATION COMPLETE. BRANCHES= 0 PIVOTS= 16

LAST INTEGER SOLUTION IS THE BEST FOUND

RE-INSTALLING BEST SOLUTION...
```

VARIABLE	VALUE	REDUCED COST
N	7.000000	.0000000
U(1)	.0000000	.0000000
U(2)	2.000000	.0000000
U(3)	1.000000	.0000000
U(4)	2.000000	.0000000
U(5)	2.000000	.0000000
U(6)	3.000000	.0000000
U(7)	3.000000	.0000000
	Only nonzero X(I,J) are shown:	
X(1, 3)	1.000000	4.000000
X(3, 2)	1.000000	6.000000
X(3, 4)	1.000000	9.000000
X(3, 5)	1.000000	10.00000
X(5, 6)	1.000000	9.000000
X(5, 7)	1.000000	7.000000

Exercises

1. Determine the minimal spanning tree for the network in Figure 4.5.8.

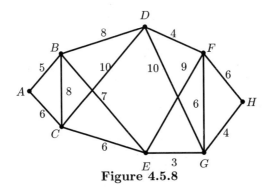

Figure 4.5.8

2. Determine a minimal spanning tree for the network in Figure 4.5.9.

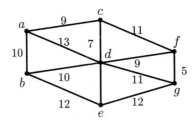

Figure 4.5.9

3. A utility is linking the communities in a new service area. It wants to make its connections with a minimal total distance between communties. Table 4.5.3 shows the distances in miles between pairs of communities for which a direct connection is feasible. Determine which links to include.

Table 4.5.3

	A	B	C	D	E	F	G
A	-	30		11	23		25
B	30	-	18	20		14	
C		18	-	25	20	12	
D	11	20	25	-			20
E	23		20		-		15
F		14	12			-	20
G	25			20	15	20	-

4. Bog County is unusually subject to flooding of streams and small rivers. It is not unusual for several of its roads between towns to be impassable at the same time as the need for emergency service is greatest. The county's emergency management team seeks to upgrade certain roads so that the probability that there will be a network of good roads available during periods of flooding is maximized. Toward this end they have compiled from historical records a table of probabilities that the links between towns are flooded (Table 4.5.4). Determine a set of roads to upgrade to produce the proposed network.

Table 4.5.4

	1	2	3	4	5	6
1	-	.3		.2	.1	.1
2	.3	-	.2	.1	.3	
3		.2	-	.3		.1
4	.2	.1	.3	-		
5	.1	.3			-	.2
6	.1		.1		.2	-

5. The minimal spanning tree of a network has the minimal total weight to connect all vertices. However, it may not include the minimal distances from any one vertex to each of the others. This may be the problem of greater interest if one of the vertices happens to represent a supply center for the network.

   The tree that contains the shortest path from a designated vertex to every other vertex can be found by modifying Dijkstra's algorithm. Note that the algorithm generates the shortest path from a designated vertex a to each vertex assigned a permanent label. By running the algorithm until every vertex has a permanent label, the shortest path from a to every other vertex is found.

   Show that the tree containing the shortest path from vertex 5 to each other vertex in the network of Example 4.5.4 has total weight 54, nine greater than that of the minimal spanning tree.

6. A local internet service provider is located at node n on the map in Figure 4.5.10. Distances are in miles. It needs to connect cable to each of the other nodes. How should it connect its cable to minimize the total amount of cable needed?

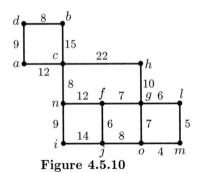

Figure 4.5.10

4.6   Summary and objectives

In this chapter we have considered several models based on networks. The structure of the constraints in these problems often makes it advantageous to use algorithms other than the simplex algorithm for their solutions.

Because the problems depend upon basic notions of graphs, the chapter began with a brief introduction to graphs. Among the graphs considered we looked most closely at trees. Because of the uniqueness of paths in trees they arise frequently in the organizing of information. We will use them in that context in Chapter 7.

The transportation problem is solved by an algorithm that parallels the simplex algorithm. The algorithm takes advantage of the known rank of the system of equality constraints to avoid the need for artificial variables. Each constraint of the dual problem involves only two variables, making it easy to generate a dual solution that allows a quick test for optimality and an easy determination of which variables could be made basic in the next solution.

Critical path models provide a tool for the manager to plan for the efficient scheduling of a complex project. The management of resources to shorten the time required for critical activities can be a key to meeting the deadline. Here the questions to be answered led to several linear programs designed to achieve differing managerial objectives. We also considered a LINGO model.

The shortest path problem was easily expressed as a linear program, but we solved it by an algorithm of Dijkstra that takes advantage of the structure of the problem. We considered applications in which the networks arose in unexpected contexts with edge weights other than those of time or distance which most readily come to mind.

A tree is a connected graph without cycles. A minimal spanning tree of a network is a subgraph that is a tree, includes all vertices of the original graph, and has the minimal total edge weight. The problem of determining a minimal spanning tree was approached by two algorithms, Kruskal's and Prim's. Before considering the two algorithms, it was necessary to explore the properties of trees. Key among them were that a tree has one fewer edge than it does nodes and adding an edge to a tree creates a cycle, while removing an edge disconnects the graph. Solution by a LINGO model was also discussed.

The algorithms for the shortest path and minimal spanning tree allowed consideration of two key properties of algorithms – effectiveness and correctness.

Objectives

After completing this chapter, the student should be able to:

1. Recognize a tree as a connected graph without cycles. Sections 4.1 and 4.5.

2. Identify problems which can be solved by these methods and formulate the problem for solution.

3. Solve a transportation problem using the transportation algorithm. Example 4.2.1. Exercise 5 of Section 4.2.

4. Identify parallels between the simplex algorithm and the transportation algorithm with regard to:

    (a) The number of variables in a basic solution,

    (b) Degenerate solutions in conjunction with Step III(b), and

    (c) A negative value of $c_{ij} - v_i - w_j$ as the per-unit decrease in the objective function in the next solution.

5. Set up a critical path (CPM) network. Example 4.3.1. Exercise 2 of Section 4.3.

6. Determine a critical path either by using a linear program or by identifying a path with all activities having a zero float. Example 4.3.1. Exercise 2 of Section 4.3.

7. Use linear programming models to determine how to efficiently reduce the time of a project. Example 4.3.2. Exercise 5 of Section 4.3.

8. Solve a shortest path problem using Dijkstra's algorithm. Example 4.4.1. Exercise 1 of Section 4.4.

9. Solve a minimal spanning tree problem using the algorithm of either Kruskal or Prim. Example 4.5.4. Exercise 1 of Section 4.5.

10. Use LINGO to solve network problems. See Appendix A and sample models in Section 4.3 and at the end of Section 4.5.

Chapter 5

Unconstrained Extrema

5.1 Introduction

This chapter is devoted to determining the maximum or minimum value of a function. Usually the objective is to determine a method of maximizing revenue or minimizing costs within a particular process or organization. The problem of maximizing profit is developed in the exercises.

The key theorem underlying the existence of maxima and minima follows.

Theorem 5.1.1. (The extreme value theorem) *A continuous function assumes both a maximum and a minimum value on a closed and bounded interval.*

A proof of this theorem is beyond the scope of this book. We will base the existence of extrema on the theorem and devote our efforts to methods of locating extrema. Unlike previous chapters, this one requires an understanding of differential calculus, and here the problems will involve nonlinear functions.

We first consider the single variable case and its application to inventory planning. The exercises following Section 5.3 introduce applications in a variety of settings.

Extension of the theory to the multiple variable setting will then allow a more sophisticated treatment of the inventory problem. The most important application will be to develop an essential statistical tool – least squares approximation – in Section 5.5. The chapter concludes with a brief look at the n-dimensional case.

5.2   Locating extrema

The extreme value theorem establishes the existence of extrema but provides
no information about their location. That is the central problem – to locate
the extrema of a function of a single independent variable defined on a closed
and bounded interval. The first step is to classify two types of extrema:
local and global. A *local maximum* (or *minimum*) value of a function f of
the variable x occurs at x_0 if there exists $\delta > 0$ such that $f(x_0) \geq f(x)$
(or $f(x_0) \leq f(x)$) for all x in the interval $(x_0 - \delta,\ x_0 + \delta)$ contained in the
domain of f. We call such an interval a *neighborhood* of the point x_0.

The definitions of global extrema require reference to a specific set, S, as the
domain. A *global maximum* (or *minimum*) value of a function f on a set S
occurs at x_0 in S if, for all x in S, $f(x_0) \geq f(x)$ (or $f(x_0) \leq f(x)$).

Example 5.2.1. Figure 5.2.1 illustrates the distinction between local and
global extrema.

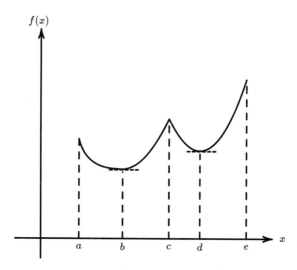

Figure 5.2.1

Here, the domain is the closed interval $[a, e]$. The global minimum
occurs at b and the global maximum at e. Local minima occur at b and
d and a local maximum occurs at c. The graph illustrates the three types
of points which are possible locations for extrema: points such as b and d
where the tangent line is horizontal, points such as c where the derivative

fails to exist, and end points such as e. The points b and e also show that a local extremum may or may not also be a global extremum. ■

A point, x_0, at which the tangent line to the graph of f is horizontal, i.e., at which $f'(x_0) = 0$, is called a *critical point*. The importance of critical points in locating extrema is established in

Proposition 5.2.2. (Fermat's theorem) *If a continuous function f has a local extremum at x_0 and if $f'(x_0)$ exists, then $f'(x_0) = 0$.*

Proof of the maximum case. Since f has a local maximum at x_0, there exists $\delta > 0$ such that $f(x_0) \geq f(x)$ for $x \in (x_0 - \delta, \, x_0 + \delta)$. To use this property to show that $f'(x_0) = 0$, we utilize the definition of $f'(x_0)$ as the limit of difference quotients.

If $0 < h < \delta$, then

$$f(x_0 + h) - f(x_0) \leq 0 \quad \text{and} \quad \frac{f(x_0 + h) - f(x_0)}{h} \leq 0$$

since $h > 0$. Then,

$$f'(x_0) = \lim_{h \to 0^+} \frac{f(x_0 + h) - f(x_0)}{h} \leq 0.$$

If $-\delta < h < 0$, then

$$f(x_0 + h) - f(x_0) \leq 0 \text{ and } \frac{f(x_0 + h) - f(x_0)}{h} \geq 0$$

since $h < 0$. Then

$$f'(x_0) = \lim_{h \to 0^-} \frac{f(x_0 + h) - f(x_0)}{h} \geq 0.$$

Since $f'(x_0)$ exists, these two limits must agree, and we have $f'(x_0) = 0$. □

Example 5.2.3. The condition $f'(x_0) = 0$ is a necessary condition for a differentiable function f to have a local extremum at x_0, but not a sufficient condition.

Consider $f(x) = (x - 1)^3$ and the point $(1,0)$ on its graph in Figure 5.2.2. Then $f'(x) = 3(x - 1)^2$ and $f'(1) = 0$. Thus, $x_0 = 1$ is a critical point. However, no $\delta > 0$ exists for which $f(1) = 0$ is the largest or the smallest value on the interval $(1 - \delta, 1 + \delta)$, since $f(x) < 0$ for $x < 1$ and $f(x) > 0$ for $x > 1$.

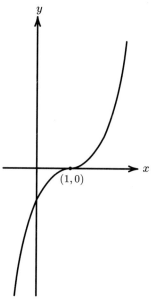

$(1,0)$

Figure 5.2.2

In the example, while the derivative is zero at $x = 1$, its sign does not change as x increases from less than 1 to greater than 1. With the added condition of a change in sign of the derivative, the necessary condition of $f'(x_0) = 0$ becomes sufficient. ∎

Proposition 5.2.4. (First derivative test) *A differentiable function, f, has a local maximum (or minimum) at a critical point, x_0, if $\delta > 0$ exists such that $f'(x) > 0$ (or $f'(x) < 0$) for $x_0 - \delta < x < x_0$ and $f'(x) < 0$ ($f'(x) > 0$) for $x_0 < x < x_0 + \delta$.*

Example 5.2.5. Locate all local extrema of $f(x) = x^3 + 6x^2 + 9x + 8$ and draw the graph.

Locate critical points by setting the derivative $f'(x) = 3x^2 + 12x + 9$ equal to 0 and solving for x:

$$3x^2 + 12x + 9 = 0$$
$$3(x + 3)(x + 1) = 0$$

Thus, $x = -3$ and $x = -1$ are critical points. To establish whether either is an extremum, determine the signs of $f'(x)$, summarizing them on the number line in Figure 5.2.3.

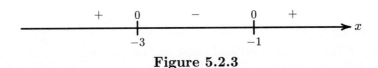

Figure 5.2.3

The sign of $f'(x)$ changes from positive to negative at $x = -3$, so a local maximum occurs there; and from negative to positive at $x = -1$, so a local minimum occurs there. The function is graphed in Figure 5.2.4. ∎

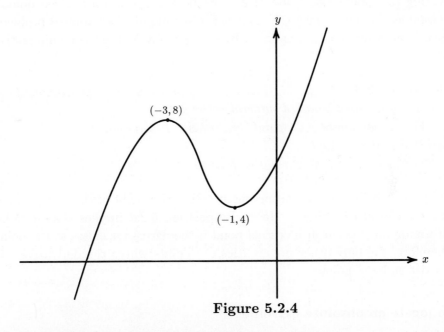

Figure 5.2.4

The change of sign condition is sufficient for an extremum to occur at a critical point, but has the drawback of requiring information about f at points other than the critical point. The next condition requires only information at the critical point and will later be generalized to functions having more than one independent variable.

Theorem 5.2.6. (Second derivative test) *If the function f has a continuous second derivative on a neighborhood of a critical point x_0, a sufficient* *condition for f to have a local maximum (or minimum) at x_0 is that $f''(x_0) < 0$ (or $f''(x_0) > 0$).*

Although this test is usually simpler to apply than the first derivative test, it can fail, as the next example shows.

Example 5.2.7. The test for extremum given in the preceding proposition can fail if $f''(x_0) = 0$ at a critical point x_0. For instance, if $f(x) = x^4$, then $f'(x) = 4x^3$, and $f''(x) = 12x^2$. The point $x_0 = 0$ is a critical point and is clearly a local minimum; however the second derivative vanishes and the proposition fails to apply. ∎

The theory of local extrema permits solution of the central problem of locating the global extremum of a continuous function on a given domain guaranteed by Theorem 5.1.1. This is the setting of most applied problems since often a domain is mandated by natural physical or economic restrictions.

Theorem 5.2.8. *The global maximum and minimum of a continuous function f on a closed bounded interval occur among:*
    (1) *Critical points, i.e., points x_0 where $f'(x_0) = 0$,*
    (2) *End points, and*
    (3) *Points where the derivative fails to exist.*

Proof. A global extremum occurring at an interior point of the domain must also be a local extremum. Hence Proposition 5.2.2 implies that a global extremum must occur at a critical point if the derivative exists at the point. Therefore, the only other possibilities are points where the derivative fails to exist and end points. □

To locate an absolute extreme

The theorem indicates the procedure for locating an absolute maximum or minimum on a closed and bounded interval:

    (a) Evaluate the function at points where the derivative fails to exist.

    (b) Evaluate the function at any critical points.

    (c) Evaluate the function at the end points.

(d) The maximum (minimum) occurs where the largest (smallest) value obtained above occurs.

Example 5.2.9. Determine the absolute extrema of

$$f(x) = \begin{cases} x^2 + 2, & x \le 2 \\ 8 - x, & x > 2 \end{cases}$$

on the interval $[-1, 7]$.

Differentiating f yields

$$f'(x) = \begin{cases} 2x, & x < 2 \\ -1, & x > 2 \end{cases}$$

and no derivative exists for $x = 2$. Since there is a critical point at $x = 0$, we must compare the values of f at the points $-1, 0, 2$, and 7. Since the largest value, 6, occurs at $x = 2$ and the smallest, 1, occurs at $x = 7$, they are the locations of the absolute maximum and minimum, respectively. The graph of f is provided in Figure 5.2.5. ■

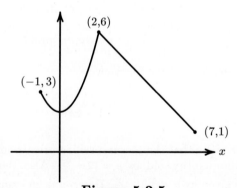

Figure 5.2.5

Exercises

1. Determine the derivative of each of the following functions:

(a) $f(x) = \dfrac{x^2}{x+1}$

(b) $g(x) = xe^x$

(c) $h(x) = \ln(x^2 + 1)$

2. Determine the values of x where the derivative $f'(x)$ is zero for the following functions:

(a) $f(x) = x^3 + x^2 - 8x - 1$

(b) $f(x) = x + \dfrac{16}{x}$

(c) $f(x) = x^4 - 4x^3 - 2x^2 + 12x + 1$

(d) $f(x) = \dfrac{x^3}{x^2 - 1}$

(e) $f(x) = xe^{-x^2}$

3. Carry out the proof of Theorem 5.2.2 for the minimum case.

4. Locate all local extrema of the function $f(x) = x^4 - 4x^3 + 1$ and draw the graph.

5. A small manufacturer has found that if p is the per-unit selling price of one of its products, then p is related to the quantity q that can be sold by $p(q) = 76 - 2q$. If the average cost per item of producing q items is $c(q) = 12 - \frac{2}{3q}$, then use the fact that the profit is $p(q)q - c(q)q$ to determine the quantity q that will produce the maximum profit.

6. Locate all local extrema of the function

$$f(x) = \frac{x}{1 + x^2}.$$

7. A firm has determined that the per-unit selling price, p, of one of its products is related to q, the quantity sold, by $p = 12 - \frac{9q}{q+8}$. Also, the average production cost per item is given by $c = 3.5 - \frac{1}{8q}$. Determine an expression for the firm's profit on q items, and the number of items that would maximize their profit.

8. A company has discovered that the per-unit selling price, p, of one of its products is related to the quantity sold, q, by the function $p = 10 - \frac{81q}{20q+125}$. Further, the average cost per item of the production of the product is given by $c = 6 - \frac{1}{2q}$. Determine an expression for the company's profit on q items, and the number of items that would maximize their profit.

5.3   The economic lot size model and convexity

The determination of the economic order quantity in inventory management is an example in which the minimum cost solution is a compromise between two costs – one of them is extremely high for small order quantities and the other extremely high for large quantitites.

Our first example is a function having the properties of the type of function that arises in the economic order quantity model.

Example 5.3.1. Determine any global extrema of $f(x) = x^2 + \dfrac{16}{x}$ over the set of positive values of x.

Taking the first derivative:

$$f'(x) = 2x - \frac{16}{x^2}.$$

Then, setting the derivative equal to zero and simplifying yields

$$2x^3 - 16 = 0$$

which leads to the critical point $x = 2$.

To determine if this critical point is an extreme, we take the second derivative:

$$f''(x) = 2 + \frac{32}{x^3}.$$

Since for all positive x, $f''(x) > 0$, $x = 2$ is a global minimum. ∎

The property exhibited by the function in the previous example – that the second derivative has the same sign at all points in the domain – can be seen to characterize an important set of functions. The latter part of this section will be devoted to an analysis of such functions. We first consider an important motivating example.

Example 5.3.2. A retailer is planning her yearly inventory strategy for a commodity which sells at a steady rate throughout the year and for which she anticipates a yearly demand of D units. Her objective is to minimize the inventory cost, which includes storage costs and the cost of placing the orders needed to maintain stock. The storage cost is \$$S$ per unit and the cost of placing an order is \$$C$. Assuming that orders may be placed so that an exhausted inventory is immediately replenished, determine how many orders of what size should be placed to minimize the total inventory cost.

Let x be the order size, i.e., the number of units in each order. Then, to fulfill a demand for D units, D/x orders must be placed during the year. Thus, the cost of placing the orders is $C(D/x)$.

The yearly inventory pattern is represented by the graph in Figure 5.3.1.

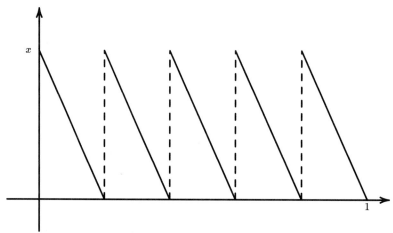

Figure 5.3.1

Since the average inventory in storage is $x/2$, the storage cost is given by $Sx/2$. Thus, the total inventory cost is given by

$$f(x) = \frac{Sx}{2} + \frac{CD}{x}$$

where x can theoretically assume any positive value. Taking derivatives yields

$$f'(x) = \frac{S}{2} - \frac{CD}{x^2} \quad \text{and} \quad f''(x) = \frac{2CD}{x^3}.$$

Solve $f'(x) = 0$ for x to locate any critical points:

$$\frac{S}{2} - \frac{CD}{x^2} = 0$$
$$Sx^2 = 2CD$$
$$x^2 = \frac{2CD}{S}$$
$$x = \sqrt{2CD/S}.$$

Since $f''(x) = \dfrac{2CD}{x^3}$ is positive for all positive values of x, by Theorem 5.2.6, this order quantity yields the required minimum inventory cost. The form of this expression for the optimal order quantity can be seen to confirm economic intuition. Note first that an increase in demand or ordering cost will tend to increase the order quantity since demand and ordering costs occur in the numerator. However, because storage cost is in the denominator, an increase in storage costs will tend to decrease the order size. ■

The graph of the ordering cost in Figure 5.3.2 shows that the solution represents the middle ground between high ordering costs associated with a large number of small orders and high storge costs resulting from a few very large orders.

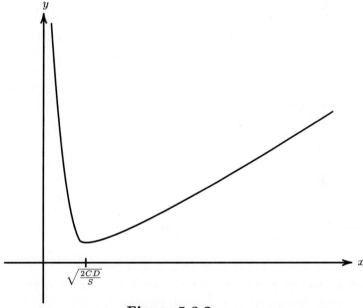

Figure 5.3.2

The function in the economic order quantity problem satisfies $f''(x) > 0$ for all positive values of x. Thus, the second derivative test guarantees that a local minimum occurs at any critical point. This useful property extends to functions of several independent variables, and we study such functions here to prepare for subsequent generalization.

To investigate such functions it is helpful to represent the points of an interval $[a, b]$ by

$$tb + (1 - t)a \quad \text{for} \quad 0 < t < 1.$$

Each point of the interval is thus expressed as a weighted average of the endpoints. For instance, the midpoint corresponds to $t = 1/2$:

$$\left(\frac{1}{2}\right) b + \left(1 - \frac{1}{2}\right) a = \frac{a+b}{2}$$

and the point two-thirds of the way from a to b corresponds to $t = \frac{2}{3}$:

$$\left(\frac{2}{3}\right) b + \left(1 - \frac{2}{3}\right) a = \left(\frac{2}{3}\right) b + \left(\frac{1}{3}\right) a.$$

A function f defined on $[a, b]$ is *convex* on $[a, b]$ if for any t, $0 < t < 1$, and any x and y in $[a, b]$, $f(tx + (1 - t)y) \le tf(x) + (1 - t)f(y)$. Geometrically, this says that the chord joining two points on the graph lies above the graph.

Example 5.3.3. By examining their graphs, it is easy to see that the following are convex functions on the indicated domains:

(a) $f(x) = x^2$; all x

(b) $f(x) = |x|$; all x

(c) $f(x) = 4x + \dfrac{3}{x^2}$, $x > 0$

(d) $f(x) = \dfrac{1}{x+2}$, $x > -2$.   ∎

We will see that convex functions include those satisfying $f''(x) > 0$ and share the property of having a local minimum at each critical point, but that $f''(x)$ need not exist for all convex functions.

Recall that the equation of the tangent line to the graph of $f(x)$ at the point $(x_0, f(x_0))$ is given by

$$y = f(x_0) + f'(x_0)(x - x_0).$$

Proposition 5.3.4. *The graph of a differentiable convex function lies above the tangent line.*

Proof. Let f be a differentiable convex function defined on the interval $[a, b]$. Let x_0 and x be distinct points in $[a, b]$. Then for any t, $0 \le t \le 1$,

$$f(tx + (1 - t)x_0) \le tf(x) + (1 - t)f(x_0).$$

We want to rewrite the inequality so that after taking a limit, the left-hand side will become the value of the tangent line. Begin by subtracting $(1 - t)f(x_0)$ from both sides and rearranging the terms on the left side:

$$tf(x_0) + f(tx + (1 - t)x_0) - f(x_0) \le tf(x).$$

Divide by t and rearrange the argument of f to begin formation of a difference quotient:

$$f(x_0) + \frac{f(x_0 + t(x - x_0)) - f(x_0)}{t} \le f(x).$$

To obtain the increment $t(x - x_0)$ of x_0 in the denominator, multiply and divide by $x - x_0$:

$$f(x_0) + \frac{f(x_0 + t(x - x_0)) - f(x_0)}{t(x - x_0)}(x - x_0) \le f(x).$$

Now letting $t \to 0$ causes $t(x - x_0) \to 0$, and the quotient approaches $f'(x_0)$:

$$f(x_0) + f'(x_0)(x - x_0) \le f(x).$$

Thus, the value of the function is greater than that of the tangent line. $\square$

If the second derivative of a function is positive, its graph "opens up" as in the graph in Figure 5.3.2 and therefore lies above the tangent line. Thus, we have

Proposition 5.3.5. *If the second derivative of f exists, is continuous, and satisfies $f''(x) \ge 0$ on $[a, b]$, then f is convex on $[a, b]$.*

Example 5.3.6. The definition of convex function includes functions which are not everywhere differentiable. Consider $f(x) = |x - 3|$ for all values of x. Then for any x and y and any t, $0 \le t \le 1$, if we add and subtract $3t$ and then use the triangle inequality we obtain the following:

$$
\begin{aligned}
f(tx + (1-t)y) &= |tx + (1-t)y - 3| \\
&= |tx - 3t + (1-t)y - 3 + 3t| \\
&\leq |tx - 3t| + |(1-t)y - 3 + 3t| \\
&= t|x-3| + (1-t)|y-3| \\
&= tf(x) + (1-t)f(y).
\end{aligned}
$$

The graph of f is shown in Figure 5.3.3. ∎

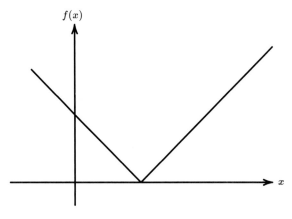

Figure 5.3.3

By examining the graphs of the examples and the one obtained in the economic order quantity problem, it appears that the convex functions are those whose graphs "open upward." If the function is differentiable, this is equivalent to the graph of the function lying above the tangent line and is the key to demonstrating that a minimum of a convex function occurs at a critical point.

The relationship between a convex function and its tangent line is the key to establishing the location of global minima of such functions.

Proposition 5.3.7. *If a differentiable convex function has a critical point within an interval, then its global minimum on the interval occurs at the critical point.*

Proof. Let f be differentiable and convex on the interval $[a, b]$ and suppose that $f'(x_0) = 0$ for some x_0 in $[a, b]$. By Proposition 5.3.4,

$$f(x_0) + f'(x_0)(x - x_0) \leq f(x)$$

for any other x in $[a, b]$. Since $f'(x_0) = 0$, this inequality becomes $f(x_0) \leq f(x)$, and the absolute minimum of f on $[a, b]$ occurs at x_0. $\square$

Application of the theory of convex functions is illustrated in the following two economic order size problems.

Example 5.3.8. A retailer anticipates an annual demand for 100 units of a commodity. If the unit storage cost is \$4 and it costs \$8 to place each order, what is the most economic order size?

Substituting these values into the inventory cost function from Example 5.3.2, we obtain

$$f(x) = 2x + 800x^{-1} \quad \text{and} \quad f'(x) = 2 - 800x^{-2}.$$

The critical point of f is $x_0 = 20$. Since f is convex on the set of all positive numbers, the global minimum occurs at $x_0 = 20$. Thus, 5 orders should be placed for 20 units each to achieve a minimum inventory cost of $f(20) = 2 \cdot 20 + 800 \cdot \left(\frac{1}{20}\right) = \$80.$ ∎

Example 5.3.9. Now suppose that the retailer in the previous example is confronted with limited storage facilities and can store at most 15 units of the commodity. The cost is still given by $f(x) = 2x + 800x^{-1}$, and $x_0 = 20$ remains a critical point. However, with the storage limitation, the problem now calls for the global minimum on the interval $[1, 15]$, since presumably no order can consist of fewer than a single unit. No critical point occurs in the interval and Theorem 5.2.8 implies that the global minimum must occur at an end point, since f is clearly differentiable. Since

$$f(1) = 2 \cdot 1 + 800 = \$802 \quad \text{and} \quad f(15) = 2 \cdot 15 + \frac{800}{15} = \$83\frac{1}{3}$$

we conclude that orders for 15 units should be placed at a rate of $6\frac{2}{3}$ per year. ∎

The two examples are illustrated in Figure 5.3.4.

The retailer's inventory minimization example earlier in the section clearly involved a single variable – the order quantity. The next example involves two variables, but we will be able to reduce it to a one variable problem by using a constraint on the solution to eliminate one variable.

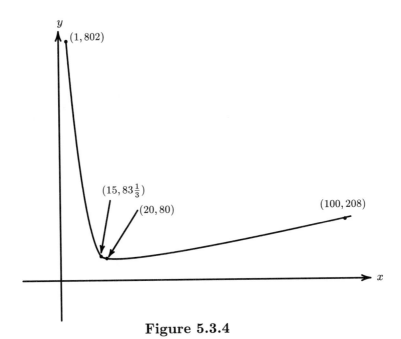

Figure 5.3.4

Example 5.3.10. A manufacturer needs to ship his products in cardboard boxes that have a capacity of 100 cubic inches. Because the boxes must be strong, the bottom will have a double thickness and the sides will be closed by a two-inch seam made by overlapping a tab two inches wide along one of the vertical corners of the box. The base of the boxes will be square to allow the bottom to be formed by folding in four pieces half the width of the base. To make the base with double thickness, four such rectangles will be required, while only two will be needed for the top. What should the dimensions of the box be to minimize the amount of cardboard required?

Letting x be the side of the base and y the height of the box, Figure 5.3.5 shows the piece of cardboard that is required. Solid lines indicate borders or where the cardboard is to be cut, while dotted lines indicate folds.

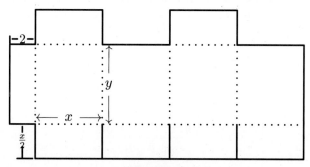

Figure 5.3.5

The equations for the volume and the surface area S then are

$$x^2 y = 100$$
$$S = 3x^2 + 4xy + 2y.$$

Using the volume equation – the constraint – to eliminate x from the surface area yields

$$S = 3\left(\frac{100}{y}\right) + 4y\left(\frac{10}{\sqrt{y}}\right) + 2y$$

$$= \frac{300}{y} + 40\sqrt{y} + 2y.$$

Differentiating, $S' = -\dfrac{300}{y^2} + \dfrac{20}{\sqrt{y}} + 2.$

Setting $S' = 0$ to determine any critical points leads to the equation

$$-300 + 20y^{\frac{3}{2}} + 2y^2 = 0.$$

Since there is no evident algebraic approach to solving this equation, we can quickly solve it with the symbolic mathematics package *Maple*:

Listing 5.3.1

```
> fsolve(-300+20*y^(3/2)+2*y^2,y);
```

$$5.297669594$$

An alternative is to apply Newton's method – which requires the derivative of the left-hand side of the above equation. Letting

$$f(y) = -300 + 20y^{\frac{3}{2}} + 2y^2 = 0$$

the function to calculate the iterations of Newton's method is

$$y_{i+1} = y_i - \frac{f(y_i)}{f'(y_i)}$$

$$= y_i - \frac{-300 + 20y_i^{\frac{3}{2}} + 2y_i^2}{30y_i^{\frac{1}{2}} + 4y_i}$$

$$= \frac{2y_i^2 + 10y_i^{\frac{3}{2}} + 300}{30y_i^{\frac{1}{2}} + 4y_i}$$

Now, taking a guess of $y_0 = 8$ to start Newton's method, we get

$$y_0 = 8$$
$$y_1 = 5.599131$$
$$y_2 = 5.302729$$
$$y_3 = 5.297671$$
$$y_4 = 5.297670$$

Considering the second derivative $S'' = 600/y^2 - 10/y^{\frac{3}{2}}$ shows that S is convex over the interval $(0,15)$, and thus $y = 5.29767$ is a minimum.

Using $y = 5.29767$, we get $x = 10/\sqrt{y} = 4.344678$, yielding a box with base about $4\frac{1}{3}$ inches square and 5.3 inches high that requires about 159.3 square inches of cardboard. ∎

Exercises

1. Show that the expression for the surface area of cylindrical can with volume 10,000 cm³ is a convex function of the radius of its base.

2. **Concave functions.** A function f defined on $[a, b]$ is *concave* on $[a, b]$ if for any t, $0 < t < 1$, and any x and y in $[a, b]$, $f(tx+(1-t)y) > tf(x)+(1-t)f(y)$. There are two approaches to establishing the properties of concave functions. One is to mimic proofs for convex functions and the other is to use the property in (d) below. Prove the properties in (a)–(c) below and then try the other approach suggested in (d) and (e).

   (a) If the second derivative of f exists, is continuous, and satisfies $f''(x) < 0$ on $[a, b]$, then f is concave on $[a, b]$. (Hint: Proof of Proposition 5.3.3.)

   (b) The graph of a differentiable concave function lies below the tangent line. (Hint: Proof of Proposition 5.3.4.)

(c) If a differentiable concave function has a critical point within an interval, then its global maximum on the interval occurs at the critical point. (Hint: Proof of Proposition 5.3.6.)

(d) If f is a concave function on $[a, b]$, then the function g defined by

$$g(x) = -f(x)$$

is convex on $[a, b]$.

(e) Prove (a)–(c) using (d) and the corresponding propositions for convexity.

3. Draw the graphs of each of the following functions and determine the intervals where each is convex or concave:

(a) $f(x) = x^3 - 3x^2 - 9x + 4$

(b) $g(x) = \dfrac{1}{x - 1}$

4. **Optimal operating capacity.** A firm is examining its pattern of profit to determine its optimal operating capacity. At 100% capacity, 750 units can be produced a month and production is a linear function of operating capacity. However, because operating at higher levels of capacity requires overtime and the utilization of more expensive secondary suppliers of materials, operating expense increases dramatically at high levels. The cost of operating appears to be inversely proportional to the unused capacity, i.e., inversely proportional to 100 minus the operating percentage of capacity. At a 70% level, the monthly operating cost is $40,000. If each unit sells at $400, what is the optimum level to produce the maximum profit, i.e., to maximize the difference between revenue and cost?

5. Solve the problem posed in Example 1.3.11.

6. **Inventory with limited storage.** A firm would like to improve its inventory policy for a commodity for which the annual demand is 375 units. If it costs $0.60 to store one unit for a unit of time and to initiate an order, $2, how many orders should the firm place for what quantity if the maximum number of units which they can store at one time is 40?

7. A farmer wishes to use the 800 yards of fencing material that he has available to fence a rectangular field of maximum area. If the field is to be divided by a fence parallel to one pair of sides, what should the dimensions of the field be?

8. The strength of a wooden beam of fixed length is directly proportional to its breadth and the square of its depth. Determine the cross-sectional dimensions of the strongest beam that can be cut from a log of radius 6 inches.

The next problem is considered in greater detail as a Case Study in Chapter 10.

9. **The minimal-surface cylinder.** Determine the ratio of the height to the radius of the base of the cylinder having a given volume and the minimal surface area.

10. **Soap bubbles.** The accompanying illustration shows the cross section of a soap film joining four rods at A, B, C, and D. The laws of physics dictate that the soap will arrange itself to minimize its surface area. Determine the angles α and β which result.

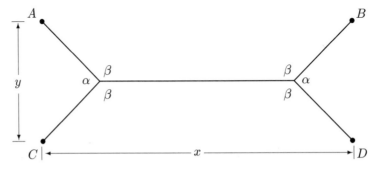

Figure 5.3.6

11. **Saving the World.** To save the Western World from destruction, Her Majesty's agent must reach a skiff 50 meters off shore from a point 100 meters away along a straight beach line, and then disarm a timing device. The agent can run along the shore at 5 meters per second, swim at 2 meters per second, and disarm a timing device in 30 seconds. Assuming that the device is set to trigger destruction in 2 minutes, is it possible for the agent to succeed?

12. **The previous exercise generalized.** A company wishes to lay a cable from a lighthouse one mile off a straight shoreline to a point P that is m miles up the shoreline from Q, the closest point to the lighthouse on the shore. It will cost c dollars per foot to lay the cable under water and k dollars per foot to lay the cable on shore.

   (a) Determine the point R at which the cable should come ashore in order to minimize the cost of laying the cable.

   (b) Determine the conditions which m, c, and k must satisfy in order that R lie properly between P and Q.

   (c) Determine the conditions which m, c, and k must satisfy in order that the cable should be run directly from the lighthouse to P.

5.4 Location of extrema in two variables

Extension of the theory of extrema to the multiple variable setting requires first the extension of the basic notions of interval, domain, and differentiation. The step from a single variable to two variables is the major one. From two variables to many variables, the main addition will be to express the sufficient condition in terms of matrices, which will be done in Section 5.8. The plane is denoted by R^2 and the set of all n-tuples by R^n.

The symmetric interval $(x_0 - \delta, \ x_0 + \delta)$ which is central in the single variable case, is replaced by the *ball of radius* δ around (x_0, y_0). In two dimensions, the ball is given by

$$B((x_0, y_0), \delta) = \{(x, y) : ((x - x_0)^2 + (y - y_0)^2)^{1/2} < \delta\}.$$

For more than two variables, additional terms are included in the sum of squared differences. Balls and symmetric intervals are collectively called *neighborhoods*.

A subset of R^n is *open* if every point in the set has a neighborhood contained in it. A set in R^n is *closed* if its complement is open. A set in R^n is *bounded* if it is contained in a ball of finite radius centered at the origin. Otherwise, a set is unbounded. A function, f, mapping a subset of R^2 is *continuous* at a point (x_0, y_0) if, for every $\epsilon > 0$ there exists a $\delta > 0$ such that for (x, y) in $B((x_0, y_0), \delta)$, $f(x, y)$ belongs to the interval

$$(f(x_0, y_0) - \epsilon, f(x_0, y_0) + \epsilon).$$

The main existence theorem is stated without proof as in the single variable case:

Theorem 5.4.1. *A function, f, continuous on a closed and bounded subset of R^n, assumes both a maximum and a minimum on the set.*

As in the single variable case, functions of several variables have both local and global extrema. A *local maximum* (*minimum*) of f occurs at (x_0, y_0) if $f(x_0, y_0)$ is the largest (smallest) value on some neighborhood of (x_0, y_0). A *global maximum* (*minimum*) of f on a set S occurs at (x_0, y_0), if $f(x_0, y_0)$ is the largest (smallest) value assumed by f on all of S.

Derivatives in the multiple variable setting are called *partial derivatives*, and the notation used must clearly indicate the variable with respect to which differentiation is being done. Higher order derivatives involving more than one variable are referred to as *mixed partial derivatives*.

Partial derivatives of f will be denoted by subscripts or by the ratio notation with "d" replaced by "∂". For example,

$$f_x(x,y) = \frac{\partial f}{\partial x} \quad \text{and} \quad f_{xy}(x,y) = (f_x)_y(x,y) = \frac{\partial^2 f}{\partial y \partial x}.$$

The second example indicates the order of differentiation: f_{xy} indicates differentiation with respect to x followed by differentiation with respect to y. Recall that if all partial derivatives up to and including a given order are continuous, then mixed partial derivatives of that order are equal, e.g.,

$$f_{xy} = f_{yx} \quad \text{and} \quad f_{xyx} = f_{yxx} = f_{xxy}.$$

A local extremum of a function of two independent variables is also an extremum for the two single variable functions obtained by holding one of the two variables constant. Thus, the derivatives of such a function must be zero at a local extremum. Since these are simply the partial derivatives, we have proven

Theorem 5.4.2. *If (x_0, y_0) is a local extremum of the differentiable function f, then $f_x(x_0, y_0) = 0$ and $f_y(x_0, y_0) = 0$.*

Such a point is called a *critical point*, as before, and corresponds geometrically to a point where the tangent plane is horizontal. We will see that the requirement that (x_0, y_0) be a critical point is necessary, but not sufficient.

Example 5.4.3. Locate all critical points of $f(x,y) = x^3 + x - 4xy - 2y^2$.

Differentiating yields $f_x(x,y) = 3x^2 + 1 - 4y$ and $f_y(x,y) = -4x - 4y$. To determine the critical points where both derivatives are zero, solve the following system of simultaneous equations:

$$\begin{aligned} 3x^2 + 1 - 4y &= 0 \\ -4x - 4y &= 0 \end{aligned}$$

The second equation leads to $y = -x$. When this is used to eliminate y from the first equation, we obtain $3x^2 + 4x + 1 = 0$. The roots of this equation are $x = -1$ and $x = -\frac{1}{3}$. Thus, the critical points of f are $(-1, 1)$ and $(-\frac{1}{3}, \frac{1}{3})$. ∎

Since multiple variable functions are more difficult to visualize graphically, the analogue of the second derivative test to distinguish which critical points lead to extrema is more important, as well as more complicated. The proof of the following theorem will be omitted.

Theorem 5.4.4. (Second derivative test) *Let f be a function of two variables whose second derivatives are all continuous on a neighborhood of a critical point (a, b) and $f_{xx}(a, b) \neq 0$. Then:*

(a) *If $f_{xx}(a, b) f_{yy}(a, b) - [f_{xy}(a, b)]^2 > 0$, then a local extremum occurs at (a, b) – a maximum if $f_{xx}(a, b) < 0$ and a minimum if $f_{xx}(a, b) > 0$.*

(b) *If $f_{xx}(a, b) f_{yy}(a, b) - [f_{xy}(a, b)]^2 < 0$, then no extremum occurs at (a, b).*

(c) *If $f_{xx}(a, b) f_{yy}(a, b) - [f_{xy}(a, b)]^2 = 0$, the test fails.*

A point (a, b) satisfying (b) is said to be the location of a *saddle point*. Every neighborhood of such a point contains a point (x_1, y_1) and a point (x_2, y_2) which satisfy $f(x_1, y_1) < f(a, b) < f(x_2, y_2)$ so that $f(a, b)$ can be an extreme value on no neighborhood of (a, b). The graph in Figure 5.4.1 provides the motivation for the term "saddle point."

Example 5.4.5. Consider the function $f(x, y) = y^2 - x^2$. The point $(0, 0)$ is easily seen to be a critical point and $f_{xx}(x, y) = -2$, $f_{yy}(x, y) = 2$, and $f_{xy}(x, y) = 0$. Thus,

$$f_{xx}(0, 0) f_{yy}(0, 0) - [f_{xy}(0, 0)]^2 = -4 < 0.$$

The graph in Figure 5.4.1 is reminiscent of a saddle and illustrates what occurs at a point where (b) of Theorem 5.4.4 holds.

Cutting the surface by the plane $y = b$ yields the parabola $z = b^2 - x^2$ opening downward. Cutting the surface by the plane $x = a$ yields the parabola $z = y^2 - a^2$ opening upward. Therefore, at the point $(0, 0, 0)$, the first type of parabola leads to points below the $z = 0$ plane and the second type to points above the $z = 0$ plane. Thus, the value $z = 0$ is neither a maximum nor a minimum.

Cutting the surface with the horizontal plane $z = c$ yields $y^2 - x^2 = c$, which is a hyperbola. These parabolic and hyperbolic cross sections lead to the name *hyperbolic paraboloid* for surfaces of this type. ∎

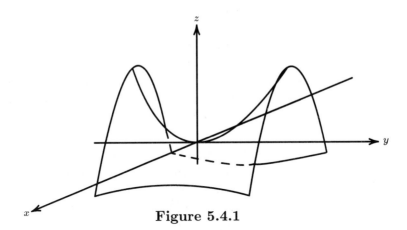

Figure 5.4.1

Example 5.4.6. Returning to the function $f(x, y) = x^3 + x - 4xy - 2y^2$ of Example 5.4.2, recall that critical points of f occur at $(-1, 1)$ and $(-\frac{1}{3}, \frac{1}{3})$. To test for extrema at these points, we must determine the second derivatives:

$$f_{xx}(x, y) = 6x, \quad f_{yy}(x, y) = -4, \quad \text{and} \quad f_{xy}(x, y) = -4.$$

Thus,

$$H(x, y) = f_{xx}(x, y) f_{yy}(x, y) - [f_{xy}(x, y)]^2 = -24x - 16.$$

Since

$$H(-1, 1) = 24 - 16 = 8 > 0$$

an extremum occurs at $(-1, 1)$ and since $f_{xx}(-1, 1) = -6$, the extremum is a local maximum. Since $H(-\frac{1}{3}, \frac{1}{3}) = 8 - 16 = -8 < 0$, a saddle point occurs at $(-\frac{1}{3}, \frac{1}{3})$. ∎

The ability to treat situations involving several independent variables makes possible more sophisticated models. The next example is a modification of our first model of inventory management.

Example 5.4.7. The retailer in Example 5.3.2 reordered immediately when her inventory was depleted. Now we consider the situation if she decides that her customers will accept shortages and that there could be an advantage to running shortages, provided the cost of maintaining a backorder list is smaller than the cost of maintaining the corresponding inventory.

Recall that in Example 5.3.2 the cost of placing an order was $\$C$, the cost of storage for one unit of inventory for one unit of time was $\$S$, and the estimated yearly demand was for D units. Now let $\$B$ denote the cost of maintaining an item on backorder for a unit of time. The problem now has two unknowns: the order size x and the shortage y that she will accept before ordering.

As before, $t = D/x$ is the interval between orders, but now $t = t_i + t_s$, where t_i represents the period of time when there is available inventory and t_s the time when there is a shortage. The assumption that the commodity sells steadily leads to the graph of the inventory pattern in Figure 5.4.2.

Her total inventory cost will have three parts: ordering cost, carrying or storage cost, and shortage cost. As before, the ordering cost is given by CD/x.

Calculation of the carrying and shortage costs is more complicated, since the period of time t between orders is now broken into two periods: one during which storage costs are incurred, represented by t_s, and one during which shortage costs are incurred, represented by t_i.

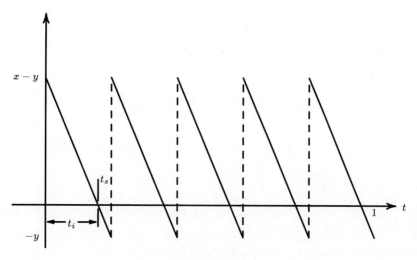

Figure 5.4.2

Calculation of the carrying cost:

The average inventory is $(x-y)/2$. This quantity must now be multiplied by S and the fraction t_i/t of time during which inventory costs are incurred. By similar triangles we have from Figure 5.4.2 that

$$\frac{t_i}{t} = \frac{x-y}{x}.$$

Thus, her carrying cost is

$$S\left(\frac{x-y}{2}\right)\left(\frac{x-y}{x}\right) = \frac{S(x-y)^2}{2x}.$$

Calculation of the shortage cost:

The average shortage is $y/2$, which must be multiplied by B and the fraction t_s/t of time during which shortages occur. Again using similar triangles we have

$$\frac{t_s}{t} = \frac{y}{x}.$$

Her shortage cost is therefore

$$B\left(\frac{y}{2}\right)\left(\frac{y}{x}\right) = \frac{By^2}{2x}.$$

Hence, her total cost is given by

$$g(x,y) = \frac{CD}{x} + \frac{S(x-y)^2}{2x} + \frac{By^2}{2x}$$

which becomes

$$g(x,y) = \frac{CD}{x} + \frac{Sx}{2} - Sy + \frac{Sy^2}{2x} + \frac{By^2}{2x}$$

upon expanding the middle term. Setting the first partial derivatives to zero yields the system of equations

$$g_x(x,y) = \frac{-CD}{x^2} + \frac{S}{2} - \frac{Sy^2}{2x^2} - \frac{By^2}{2x^2} = 0$$

$$g_y(x,y) = -S + \frac{(S+B)y}{x} = 0.$$

From the second equation we obtain,

$$\frac{y}{x} = \frac{S}{S+B}.$$

Multiplying the first equation by 2 and using the expression above to substitute for y/x produces

$$\frac{2CD}{x^2} = S - \frac{S^2}{S+B}$$

and solving for x yields the order quantity:

$$x = \sqrt{2CD} \cdot \sqrt{\frac{S+B}{BS}}.$$

Returning to (1) to determine y yields the shortage quantity

$$y = \sqrt{\frac{S}{S+B}} \cdot \sqrt{2CD} \cdot \frac{S+B}{BS} = \sqrt{\frac{2CD}{B}} \cdot \sqrt{\frac{S}{S+B}}.$$

We now compare the order quantity

$$x = \sqrt{\frac{2CD}{S}}$$

from Example 5.3.2 with the one just obtained. Note that for $0 < B < S$ the provision for a shortage will always increase the order quantity, since

$$\frac{S+B}{BS} > \frac{S}{BS} = \frac{1}{B} > \frac{1}{S}$$

implies that

$$\sqrt{\frac{2CD(S+B)}{BS}} > \sqrt{\frac{2CD}{S}}.$$

Further analysis of the two inventory models is left to the exercises. ∎

In the previous problem, the structure of the derivatives was helpful in the solution. Since this is not always the case, we re-solve the problem using *Maple* to illustrate how to use that symbolic mathematics package.

Note in Listing 5.4.1 that the *Maple* prompt is a > and that each command is ended by a semicolon. The first command defines the function g

as a function of two variables. The second line is a display of the function produced by *Maple* to indicate that it has accepted the definition. Exponentiation is indicated by a ˆ and multiplication by *, i.e., $3x^2$ is entered as 3*x^2.

The second command combines two operations to determine a critical point of g. It calculates the partial derivatives of g and also solves the system of equations obtained by setting both partial derivatives equal to zero.

Listing 5.4.1

```
> g := proc(x,y) C*D/x + S*x/2 - S*y + S*y^2/(2*x) + B*y^2/(2*x)
  end;
g := proc(x,y) C*D/x+1/2*S*x-S*y+1/2*S*y^2/x+1/2*B*y^2/x end

> solve({diff(g(x,y),x),diff(g(x,y),y)},{x,y});
             1/2  1/2  1/2  1/2            1/2  1/2  1/2           1/2
            2    C    D    S              2    C    D    (S + B)
   {y = - -------------------,  x = - --------------------------},
                1/2       1/2                      1/2  1/2
               B    (S + B)                       S    B


             1/2  1/2  1/2  1/2            1/2  1/2  1/2           1/2
            2    C    D    S              2    C    D    (S + B)
   {y = -------------------,  x = --------------------------}
                1/2       1/2                    1/2  1/2
               B    (S + B)                     S    B
```

Note that `solve` has returned two solutions. In the earlier solution we automatically excluded the first one, which has both x and y negative and therefore has no significance in the context of the inventory application.

Additional information on *Maple* can be found in Appendix B.

Exercises

1. Determine both partial derivatives of each function:

(a) $f(x,y) = 3x^2 - 2xy + x^2y - 6x + y$

(b) $z = \dfrac{x + y}{1 + x^2}$

2. Show that the mixed second partial derivatives of the following function are equal:

$$f(x, y) = x^2 e^{4x} - (x^2 + y)^2$$

3. Determine any local extrema or saddle points of the function

(a) $f(x, y) = x^2 + y^2 - 6x + 4y$

(b) $f(x, y) = x^2 + y^2 + xy^2 + 6$

(c) $f(x, y) = x^2 + 4y^2 - xy - 2y^3$

(d) $f(x, y) = x^2 + y^2 + xy - 3x$

4. Determine any local extrema or saddle points of $f(x, y) = xy(1 - x - y)$.

5. Show that the critical point of g determined in Example 5.4.7 yields a global minimum over the first quadrant by determining a general expression for $g_{xx}g_{yy} - (g_{xy})^2$ and applying Theorem 5.4.4.

6. Show that for $0 < B < S$, the order quantity always exceeds the shortage quantity in Example 5.4.7.

7. Show that as the backorder charge, B, approaches zero, both the optimal order quantity and the optimal shortage quantity increase without bound. Thus, if there were no backorder charge, it would be best to operate on a special-order basis and maintain no inventory. Alternatively, interpret the result as B increases without bound.

8. Determine the inventory savings achieved for a situation in which the ordering cost is \$5, the demand is 500 units, the storage cost is \$0.50, and the backorder cost is \$.20 by using the second model instead of the first.

9. The cost of diversifying. Suppose that the retailer in Example 5.3.2 is concerned that her supplier will be unable to meet her needs and so decides to divide her yearly demand equally among two suppliers. If the ordering cost is the same for each supplier, determine the ordering quantities from each and show that this diversification multiplies her inventory cost by $\sqrt{2}$.

10. A drug store carries two competing brands of multiple vitamins. They purchase brand A for \$3 a bottle and brand B for \$4 a bottle. The monthly demand in bottles sold for brands A and B, respectively, are

$$a = 22 - 16p_A + 18p_B$$
$$b = 20 + 15p_A - 20p_B$$

where p_A and p_B are the respective selling prices of brand A and brand B. How should the two brands be priced to achieve maximum profit?

11. A summer camp has decided to locate a new dining facility relative to three camping sites so that the sum of the squares of the distances to the camping sites is minimized. To this end they have established a coordinate system with units in 1,000's of feet. If the camping sites are at $(-1,7)$, $(6,9)$, and $(4,1)$, where should the new dining facility be located?

5.5   Least squares approximation

A principal concern of economic and managerial theory is the determination of relationships among variables. For instance, demand for a commodity depends on price, supply, and income; stock prices are linked to corporate earnings; and personal consumption is a function of disposable income. One method of establishing the coefficients in these relationships is the method of least squares.

The basic problem in least squares approximation – also called *simple regression* – is to determine constants a and b so that the straight line $y = ax + b$ in some sense "best approximates" the relationship between x and y based on the data available. Table 5.5.1 provides a sample set of data that will be used to illustrate the calculations.

Table 5.5.1

x	2	3	5	6	8
y	12	11	19	21	34

Before proceeding to the derivation of the formulas for a and b, we review the definition of arithmetic mean. Given numbers x_i, $i = 1, 2, \ldots, n$, their *arithmetic mean* is given by

$$\bar{x} = \frac{1}{n} \left(\sum_{i=1}^{n} x_i \right).$$

We will find it convenient to solve for a and b in terms of the means $\bar{x}$ and $\bar{y}$.

When a value x_i is substituted into $y = ax + b$, the resultant value $ax_i + b$ is called the *predicted value* of y and is to be compared with the corresponding *actual value* y_i. The predicted value is said to be the *least squares approximation* if a and b have been chosen to minimize the sum of the squares of the differences e_i between the actual and the predicted values. Thus, to obtain a and b we must determine the minimum value of the function

$$W = \sum_{i=1}^{n} e_i^2 = \sum_{i=1}^{n}(y_i - ax_i - b)^2.$$

The significance of the e_i can be seen graphically in Figure 5.5.1 at the end of this section.

To determine a and b, we set the first partial derivatives of W to zero and obtain the following system:

$$\begin{aligned} W_a &= 2 \cdot \sum_{i=1}^{n}(y_i - ax_i - b)(-x_i) = 0 \\ W_b &= -2 \cdot \sum_{i=1}^{n}(y_i - ax_i - b) = 0 \end{aligned}$$

Simplifying leads to the following system, called the *normal equations*:

$$\begin{aligned} \left(\sum x_i^2\right) a + \left(\sum x_i\right) b &= \sum x_i y_i \quad (1) \\ \left(\sum x_i\right) a + nb &= \sum y_i \quad (2) \end{aligned}$$

We solve this system under the assumption that we know the means $\bar{x}$ and $\bar{y}$. This is really not an additional assumption since we know $\sum x_i$ and $\sum y_i$ and need only divide by n to get the respective means. By dividing through (2) by n, we obtain the equation

$$a\bar{x} + b = \bar{y}. \qquad (3)$$

From (3), we see that the line will always pass through the point $(\bar{x}, \bar{y})$ and that b can easily be obtained once a has been found. Note that from the definition of $\bar{x}$, if we multiply (2) by $\bar{x}$ and subtract it from (1), b will be eliminated since $\sum x_i - n\bar{x} = 0$. The resulting equation

$$\left(\sum x_i^2 - \bar{x}\sum x_i\right) a = \sum x_i y_i - \bar{x}\sum y_i$$

then yields the value for a:

$$a = \frac{\sum x_i y_i - \bar{x}\sum y_i}{\sum x_i^2 - \bar{x}\sum x_i}$$

and from (3),

$$b = \bar{y} - a\bar{x}.$$

While the calculations in small examples like the one done next are not burdensome, in general, these calculations are best turned over to a machine. Use of a calculator to determine the least squares line and generate a plot similar to Figure 5.5.1 is discussed in Appendix C. There we also consider fitting a quadratic function to a set of data. Similar capabilities are demonstrated for *Maple* in Appendix B.

Example 5.5.1. To illustrate the calculation consider the data from Table 5.5.1. We first calculate the sums and means needed in the formulas for a and b (Table 5.5.2).

Table 5.5.2

x_i	y_i	$x_i y_i$	x_i^2
2	12	24	4
3	11	33	9
5	19	95	25
6	21	126	36
8	34	272	64
24	97	550	138

Since $n = 5$, $\bar{x} = 24/5 = 4.8$ and $\bar{y} = 97/5 = 19.4$.
Now substituting into the formulas for a and b:

$$a = \frac{550 - (4.8)(97)}{138 - (4.8)(24)} = 3.70$$
$$b = 19.4 - (3.70)(4.8) = 1.64$$

Thus, the least squares line for the data in Table 5.5.1 is $y = 3.70x + 1.64$. This line and the data are shown in Figure 5.5.1.

The dotted lines represent the errors e_i in the predictions. The predicted value corresponding to $x_3 = 5$ is

$$ax_3 + b = (3.70)(5) + 1.64 = 20.14$$

and the error is

$$e_3 = 19 - 20.14 = -1.14. \quad \blacksquare$$

Some relationships which are not expected to be linear can also be modeled by this technique. For instance, if one anticipates a relationship like $y = \sqrt{x} + b$, then the least squares technique can be applied with the the column of values x_i replaced by the values $\sqrt{x_i}$. Such a change is called a *data transformation*.

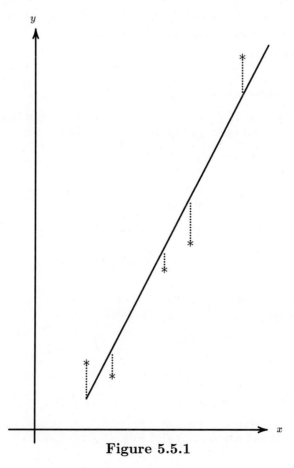

Figure 5.5.1

Exercises

1. Determine the least squares line for the data in Table 5.5.3.

Table 5.5.3

x	1	2	4	6	8
y	2	5	7	10	14

2. Determine the least squares line for the data in Table 5.5.4.

Table 5.5.4

x	−1	2	4	6	9	11
y	−6	−1	2	4	5	9

3. Given that $n = 10$, $\sum x_i = 451$, $\sum y_i = 76$, $\sum x_i y_i = 3,479$, and $\sum x^2 = 2456$, determine the least squares line.

4. Given that $n = 8$, $\sum x_i = 64$, $\sum y_i = 96$, $\sum x_i y_i = 1,041$, and $\sum x^2 = 716$, determine the least squares line.

5. Determine the predictions requested in Example 1.3.14.

6. Derive the system of equations corresponding to the normal equations for a quadratic least squares approximation of the form $y = ax^2 + bx + c$.

7. Time series. A special case of linear least squares, called time series, occurs when the independent variable x assumes the values

$$-m, -(m-1), \ldots, -1, 0, 1, \ldots, m-1, m$$

for some integer m. The simplified expressions for a and b which occur in this special case are derived in this exercise.

(a) Use mathematical induction to prove the formula

$$\sum_{i=1}^{n} i^2 = \frac{n(n+1)(2n+1)}{6}$$

(b) Using the result of part (a), show that

$$\sum_{i=-\frac{n-1}{2}}^{\frac{n-1}{2}} i^2 = \frac{(n-1)n(n+1)}{12}$$

(c) Use the result of part (b) and the fact that $\sum x_i = 0$ to show that for a time series,

$$a = \frac{\sum x_i y_i}{\sum x_i^2} \quad \text{and} \quad b = \bar{y}.$$

8. A foundry wishes to project its requirements for scrap-iron usage over the next two years based on past experience. Table 5.5.5 provides its scrap-iron usage (in thousands of pounds) for the previous seven years. Determine the appropriate time series and predict its needs for 1998 and 1999.

Table 5.5.5

Year	1991	1992	1993	1994	1995	1996	1997
Requirement	232	238	240	244	246	250	252

9. Sales versus interest rates. A firm wishing to correlate its sales figures to economic factors has gathered monthly sales figures (in 1,000's of dollars) and the prevailing prime interest rate for a six-month period. The information is contained in Table 5.5.6. Determine sales as a function of the interest rate.

Table 5.5.6

Sales	10	12	15	16	17
Prime rate	12.5	13.5	14.0	14.5	14.75

10. A company has analyzed the data from several production runs of one of its products. It seeks to set the price to charge retailers to maximize their profit.

   (a) The total cost and number of units from five production runs is in Table 5.5.7.

   Table 5.5.7

Units	80	89	93	105	116
Cost	$320	$355	$372	$421	$465

   Determine a linear function for the cost as a function of the number of units based on this data.

   (b) The company has offered the product on the wholesale market at several different prices and obtained the data on the resulting demands in Table 5.5.8.

   Table 5.5.8

Demand	85	91	101	104	115
Price	$57	$54	$49	$47	$42

   Determine a linear function for the wholesale price as a function of the number of units based on this data.

   (c) Based on the functions obtained in (a) and (b), determine a wholesale price that maximizes the company's profit.

11. **Maximization of profit.** A manufacturer of small boats has set its prices for the coming season at $3,400 for its luxury model (L) and $3,100 for its basic model (B). Its cost (in 1,000's of dollars) and production figures for the past five years are given in Table 5.5.9. Determine an expression for the cost in the form

$$C(L, B) = b_0 + b_1 L^2 + b_2 LB + b_3 B^2$$

and, presuming that all boats made can be sold at the stated prices, determine the optimum production levels to maximize profit.

Table 5.5.9

Cost	L	B
1965	303	500
1463	400	350
1254	506	205
2130	520	300
2272	532	316

12. A construction company has a contract to build a number of similar fast-food restaurants. One of the critical tasks involved, which normally requires eight days, can be "crashed," i.e., done more quickly, if more resources are allocated to it. The times in days and costs of the task for the first five such restaurants completed are given in Table 5.5.10. Based on this data, determine the cost of reducing the time of the task by one day.

Table 5.5.10

Days	Cost
3	$6,900
4	$5,800
6	$4,600
7	$4,000
8	$3,000

5.6   The n-variable case

Development of the n-variable case requires vector notation for the n-tuple of independent variables. Thus, we will let $x = (x_1, x_2, \ldots, x_n)$ denote an arbitrary point in R^n and $f(x)$ denote the value of a function of n-variables, i.e., $f(x) = f(x_1, x_2, x_3, \ldots, x_n)$. Notation for a particular point $a = (a_1, a_2, \ldots, a_n)$ and the differences from that point $h = (h_1, \ldots, h_n) = (x_1 - a_1, \ldots, x_n - a_n)$ are analogous.

Partial differentiation is indicated by subscripts, e.g., $f_{x_i}(x) = f_i(x)$ and, for second derivatives, $f_{x_i x_j}(x) = f_{ij}(x)$.

A critical point of a function of n-variables is a point a such that

$$f_i(a) = 0, \quad i = 1, \ldots, n.$$

Thus, a is obtained by solving a system of equations.

The key to identifying extrema among critical points is a general second derivative test. Previously we have used a single variable version of this test in Theorem 5.2.6 and a version for functions of two variables in Theorem 5.4.4.

When placed in a common context, we will see that all version of this test depend on the matrix of second derivatives called the *Hessian matrix* and given by

$$H(a) = \begin{bmatrix} f_{11}(a) & f_{12}(a) & \cdots & f_{1n}(a) \\ f_{21}(a) & f_{22}(a) & \cdots & f_{2n}(a) \\ & & \vdots & \\ f_{n1}(a) & f_{n2}(a) & \cdots & f_{nn}(a) \end{bmatrix}$$

In the single variable case $H(a)$ has only one entry, and we simply checked its sign. A positive indicated a minimum and a negative indicated a maximum.

In the two variable case we checked the sign of a quantity at the critical point (a, b) now seen to be the determinant of $H(a, b)$:

$$|H(a,b)| = \begin{vmatrix} f_{xx}(a,b) & f_{xy}(a,b) \\ f_{yx}(a,b) & f_{yy}(a,b) \end{vmatrix}$$

$$= f_{xx}(a,b)f_{yy}(a,b) - f_{yx}(a,b)f_{xy}(a,b)$$

and also the sign of the entry $f_{xx}(a, b)$ in the top left corner of $H(a, b)$.

Recalling that the continuity of the second derivatives of a function yields $f_{12}(a, b) = f_{21}(a, b)$, we have

$$\begin{aligned} |H(a,b)| &= f_{11}(a,b)f_{22}(a,b) - f_{12}(a,b)f_{21}(a,b) \\ &= f_{11}(a,b)f_{22}(a,b) - [f_{12}(a,b)]^2. \end{aligned}$$

Thus, the condition sufficient for a critical point to be an extremum is that the determinant of $H(a, b)$ is positive, and the choice of extremum is determined by the sign of the upper left-hand corner entry, $f_{11}(a, b)$, of $H(a, b)$.

We will see that the one and two variable examples indicate the general case: the sufficient condition for an extremum of a function of n variables will involve n sign requirements on determinants of an $n \times n$ matrix and its submatrices. The sign conditions for $n = 3$ are given below. Reference to the critical point is omitted.

For a maximum:

$$(1) \quad f_{11} < 0, \quad \begin{vmatrix} f_{11} & f_{12} \\ f_{21} & f_{22} \end{vmatrix} > 0, \quad \begin{vmatrix} f_{11} & f_{12} & f_{13} \\ f_{21} & f_{22} & f_{23} \\ f_{31} & f_{32} & f_{33} \end{vmatrix} < 0$$

For a minimum:

$$(2) \quad f_{11} > 0, \quad \begin{vmatrix} f_{11} & f_{12} \\ f_{21} & f_{22} \end{vmatrix} > 0, \quad \begin{vmatrix} f_{11} & f_{12} & f_{13} \\ f_{21} & f_{22} & f_{23} \\ f_{31} & f_{32} & f_{33} \end{vmatrix} > 0$$

A determinant of a submatrix located in the upper left-hand corner of a matrix is called a *principal minor*. A 3×3 matrix whose principal minors satisfy (1) is called *negative definite* and one satisfying (2) is called *positive definite*.

The definitions generalize to $n \times n$ matrices. A symmetric $n \times n$ matrix is *negative definite* if the determinants of the principal minors are alternately negative and positive, with those of even order being positive. A symmetric $n \times n$ matrix is *positive definite* if the determinants of all its principal minors are positive.

The definitions for $n \times n$ negative and positive definite matrices allow the statement of a general test for extrema.

Theorem 5.6.1. (The second derivative test) *If a function f has continuous second partial derivatives on a neighborhood of a critical point a, then f has:*

(a) *A local maximum at a if $H(a)$ is negative definite.*

(b) *A local minimum at a if $H(a)$ is positive definite.*

Example 5.6.2. Locate any local extrema of the function

$$f(x_1, x_2, x_3) = 4x_1^2 + 2x_2^2 + x_3^2 - x_1x_2 + x_2x_3 - 5x_1 - 9x_2 + x_3.$$

Setting the first partial derivatives equal to zero leads to the system of equations

$$\begin{aligned} f_1(x) &= 8x_1 - x_2 - 5 = 0 \\ f_2(x) &= -x_1 + 4x_2 + x_3 - 9 = 0 \\ f_3(x) &= x_2 + 2x_3 + 1 = 0 \end{aligned}$$

which has the solution $x_1 = 1$, $x_2 = 3$, and $x_3 = -2$. Thus, $a = (1, 3, -2)$ is a critical point. Taking second partial derivatives yields

$$f_{11}(x) = 8, \quad f_{22}(x) = 4, \quad \text{and} \quad f_{33}(x) = 2.$$

Thus, the Hessian matrix is

$$H(a) = \begin{bmatrix} 8 & -1 & 0 \\ -1 & 4 & 1 \\ 0 & 1 & 2 \end{bmatrix}.$$

Applying the second derivative test,

$$f_{11} = 8 > 0, \quad \begin{vmatrix} f_{11} & f_{12} \\ f_{21} & f_{22} \end{vmatrix} > 0, \quad \text{and} \quad |H(a)| = 54 > 0.$$

$H(a)$ is therefore a positive definite matrix, and a local minimum occurs at the point $a = (1, 3, -2)$. ∎

Because the computations in locating and testing for extrema can obviously be involved, we conclude the chapter with an example demonstrating how to use *Maple* to locate critical points and test for extrema.

Example 5.6.3. Determine any local extrema of the function for which all coordinates are nonnegative:

$$f(x, y, z) = -\frac{1}{2}x^2 - 5y^2 - 2z^2 - 2xy^2 - yz + 6x + 5y + 20z.$$

We begin by defining the function f and determining its critical points as in Example 5.47 where backorder costs were considered:

Listing 5.6.1

```
> f := proc(x,y,z) -(1/2)*x^2 - 5*y^2 - 2*z^2 - 2*x*y^2 - y*z
                + 6*x + 5*y + 20*z end;

f := proc(x,y,z) -1/2*x^2-5*y^2-2*z^2-2*x*y^2-y*z+6*x+5*y
                +20*z end;

> solve({diff(f(x,y,z),x),diff(f(x,y,z),y),diff(f(x,y,z),z)},
                {x,y,z});
    {y = 0, z = 5, x = 6},

         39                 1/2  1/2                     1/2 1/2
{x = - ----, z = 1/128 135    32    + 5, y = - 1/32 135    32  },
         16

           1/2   1/2               39                 1/2  1/2
{z = - 1/128 135    32    + 5, x = - ----, y = 1/32 135    32  }
                                     16
```

We need to test only the first of these critical points since the others each have negative coordinates.

We first load the `linalg` package because of the matrix operations involved with the Hessian matrix. The first command calculates the Hessian matrix, and then the next two test it for positive or negative definiteness.

In this case, the Hessian matrix depends on the values of x and y because of the term $-2xy^2$ in f. If definiteness of the matrix depends upon the values of one or more variables, *Maple* provides a set of equations or inequalities that the variables must satisfy for the matrix to be definite.

Listing 5.6.2

```
> with(linalg):

> H := hessian(f(x,y,z),[x,y,z]);
                      [   -1        - 4 y        0 ]
                      [                            ]
                 H := [ - 4 y   - 10 - 4 x     -1 ]
                      [                            ]
                      [    0         -1         -4 ]

> definite(H,'negative_def');
                   2                                        2
         - 5 - 2 x + 8 y  < 0 and - 39 - 16 x + 64 y  < 0

> definite(H,'positive_def');
                                 false

> A := subs({x=6,y=0,z=5},evalm(H));
                        [ -1    0     0 ]
                        [                ]
                   A := [  0   -34   -1 ]
                        [                ]
                        [  0    -1   -4 ]

> definite(A,'negative_def');
                                 true
```

Here, the tests indicate that H is not positive definite for any values of x and y, but is negative definite for points satisfying a system of two inequalities. Rather than check the inequalities by hand, we continue with

Maple. The `subs` command creates the matrix `A` by evaluating `H` at the critical point. We then test `A` for negative definiteness.

Since the Hessian matrix at the critical point is negative definite, the function f has a local maximum at the point by Theorem 5.6.1. ∎

Exercises

1. Determine any extrema of the following function:

$$f(x_1, x_2, x_3) = \frac{5}{2}x_1^2 + \frac{9}{2}x_2^2 + \frac{17}{2}x_3^2 - 6x_1x_2 + 7x_1x_3 - 12x_2x_3 - 37x_1 + 57x_2 + 77x_3.$$

2. Determine any extrema of the following function:

$$f(x_1, x_2, x_3) = 2x_1^2 + x_1x_3 + x_2^2 + x_2x_3 + x_3^2 - 6x_1 - 8x_2 - 7x_3 + 12.$$

3. Determine any local extrema of the following function:

$$f(x_1, x_2, x_3) = -\frac{1}{2}x_1^2 - 5x_2^2 - 2x_3^2 + 3x_1x_2 - x_2x_3 + 6x_1 + 5x_2 + 20x_3.$$

4. Determine if each of the following matrices is positive definite or negative definite:

(a)
$$\begin{bmatrix} 4 & -1 & 3 \\ -1 & 2 & 0 \\ 3 & 0 & 5 \end{bmatrix}$$

(b)
$$\begin{bmatrix} 3 & -4 & -1 \\ -4 & 2 & 3 \\ -1 & 3 & 5 \end{bmatrix}$$

5. For a symmetric $n \times n$ matrix Q, and vectors c and x in R^n, a *quadratic form* is a function of the form

$$f(x) = \frac{1}{2}x^T Q x + c \cdot x.$$

Show that the critical points of f are determined by solving the system of equations $Qx = -c$ and that the Hessian of f is Q.

6. Express each of the following quadratic expressions in the form of the previous exercise:

(a) $2x_1^2 + 6x_1x_2 + 4x_2^2 - x_1 + x_2$

(b) $x_1^2 - x_2^2 + 2x_3^2 - 2x_1x_2 + 6x_2x_3 + 2x_1x_3 + 4x_1 - 5x_2 + 3x_3$

Hint: $ax_ix_j = \frac{1}{2}ax_ix_j + \frac{1}{2}ax_jx_i.$

5.7   Summary and objectives

In this chapter we have considered methods of determining unconstrained extrema. Three important applications were presented: models of inventory cost minimization, of efficient box construction, and of least squares approximation.

The most important theorem developed was the second derivative test for local extrema. We considered versions for a function of a single variable (Theorem 5.2.6), for functions of two variables (Theorem 5.4.4), and for functions of n variables (Theorem 5.6.1).

Two important types of function were investigated – convex and concave. When such functions are twice-differentiable, we saw that they could be detected by the sign of the second derivative being always positive or always negative, respectively. Thus, a critical point of a twice differentiable convex function is always a global minimum; of a concave function always a global maximum.

Because the calculations involved can become burdensome, we introduced the use of *Maple*.

Objectives

Be able to:

1. Understand and use the definitions associated with unconstrained extrema. Theorem 5.2.8 and Example 5.2.9. Exercises 6 and 7 of Section 5.2.

2. Determine first and second derivatives of functions of one or several variables. Exercise 1 of Section 5.2 and Exercises 1 and 2 of Section 5.4.

3. Recognize convex and concave functions. Propositions 5.3.4 and 5.3.5. Exercise 3 of Section 5.3.

4. Determine critical points of functions of one or several variables. Examples 5.2.5 and 5.4.6. Exercises 2 and 6 of Section 5.2 and Exercise 3 of Section 5.4..

5. Determine if a matrix is positive or negative definite, or neither. Example 5.6.2. Exercise 4 of Section 5.6.

6. Identify local and global extrema of a function with one independent variable by applying first and second derivative tests. Example 5.2.9. Exercise 4 of Section 5.2.

7. Identify local and global extrema of a function with several independent variables by applying first and second derivative tests. Examples 5.4.3 and 5.6.2. Exercise 3 of Section 5.4 and Exercise 2 of Section 5.6.

8. Formulate and solve inventory cost minimization problems similar to those discussed in the chapter. Examples 5.3.2 and 5.4.7. Exercises 8 and 9 of Section 5.4.

9. Formulate and solve elementary unconstrained optimization problems. Example 5.3.10. Exercises 7, 8, and 9 of Section 5.3.

10. Determine the least squares line approximating a given set of ordered pairs. Example 5.5.1. Exercise 1 of Section 5.5.

11. Use *Maple* or other symbolic computing package for differential calculus computations. Example 5.6.3. Exercise 3 of Section 5.6. See also Appendices B and C.

Chapter 6

Constrained Extrema

6.1 Introduction

In Chapter 5 we considered the problem of determining extreme values of a function of several variables. No restrictions were placed on the variables. In most settings, however, restrictions are needed to express an economic or technical condition that a solution must satisfy. For instance, an organization seeks to maximize the use of funds within a given budgetary limitation or to minimize costs while still fulfilling commitments to customers and maintaining a quality product.

As before, such relationships among variables are called *constraints* and have the effect of reducing the domain of the objective function. The major change in this chapter is that the constraints are not required to be linear.

Constraints may be either equalities or inequalities. We will consider first an approach to problems with equality constraints which can later be extended to the inequality case. In some instances an equality constraint may be eliminated by substitution in the objective function. The following examples illustrate that approach and also indicate the need for another method.

Example 6.1.1. Determine the dimensions of the cylindrical can with volume one liter and the minimum possible surface area.

Let r be the radius of the base and h the height of the can. Both dimensions are measured in centimeters since the measure of a liter is 1,000 cubic centimeters. The equations for the volume, V, and surface area, S, of a cylinder then are

$$V = \pi r^2 h \quad \text{and} \quad S = 2\pi r^2 + 2\pi r h.$$

Since S is to be minimized while maintaining $V = 1,000 \text{ cm}^3$, the problem can be stated as

$$\text{Minimize}: \quad S = 2\pi r^2 + 2\pi r h$$
$$\text{Subject to}: \quad \pi r^2 h = 1,000.$$

One approach is to use the volume constraint to eliminate h from the objective function. Solving for h yields:

$$h = \left(\frac{1,000}{\pi}\right) r^{-2}.$$

Substituting this expression for h gives an expression for the surface area of a one-liter can as a function of its radius:

$$S = 2\pi r^2 + 2\pi r \left(\frac{1,000}{\pi}\right) r^{-2} = 2\pi r^2 + 2,000 r^{-1}.$$

Next we locate and test any critical points. Differentiating S gives

$$S' = 4\pi r - 2,000 r^{-2}.$$

Setting the derivative of the surface area to zero leads to $4\pi r^3 - 2,000 = 0$ and $r = \left(\dfrac{500}{\pi}\right)^{1/3}$. Since the second derivative

$$S'' = 4\pi + 4,000 r^{-3}$$

is positive for all positive values of r, the function is convex and the critical point yields a minimum value. The optimal value of h is determined by the expression derived from the constraint:

$$h = \left(\frac{1,000}{\pi}\right) \left(\frac{500}{\pi}\right)^{-\frac{2}{3}} = 2 \left(\frac{500}{\pi}\right)^{\frac{1}{3}}.$$

Thus, the can containing one liter and having the minimal surface area has its height equal to $2 \left(\dfrac{500}{\pi}\right)^{\frac{1}{3}} \approx 10.83 \text{ cm}$ and radius of its base equal to $\left(\dfrac{500}{\pi}\right)^{\frac{1}{3}} \approx 5.42 \text{ cm}$. ∎

The previous example demonstrated that, in some instances, a constrained optimization problem can be solved by using the constraint to eliminate a variable from the objective function.

This is not always the case, however, since an inequality constraint cannot be so used, and the next theorem indicates that it is not always possible to solve a constraint of the form $g(x, y) = c$ for either variable.

Theorem 6.1.2. (Implicit function theorem) *If the function g has continuous first partial derivatives on a neighborhood of (a, b), if $g(a, b) = c$, and if $g_y(a, b) \neq 0$, then there exists a differentiable function u such that $g(x, u(x)) = c$ on some neighborhood of (a, b), and*

$$u'(x) = -\frac{g_x(x, y)}{g_y(x, y)}.$$

Like the extreme value theorem from the previous chapter, the proof of the implicit function theorem is beyond our scope here and is omitted. However, the next example indicates its importance by highlighting one difficulty that may arise in selecting the variable to be eliminated by use of the constraint.

Example 6.1.3. Locate the point on the parabola $y = (x - 1)^2 + 3$ closest to the point (1,1).

The square of the distance from (x, y) to (1,1) is

$$f(x, y) = (x - 1)^2 + (y - 1)^2$$

and constraining (x, y) to the parabola leads to the problem

$$\begin{aligned} \text{Minimize}: \quad & f(x, y) = (x - 1)^2 + (y - 1)^2 \\ \text{Subject to}: \quad & g(x, y) = y - (x - 1)^2 = 3. \end{aligned}$$

Since the constraint can be written $(x - 1)^2 = y - 3$, it is natural to use it to eliminate x, reducing the problem to minimizing

$$F(y) = y - 3 + (y - 1)^2.$$

Thus, we locate and test any critical points of F. Differentiating, we get

$$F'(y) = 1 + 2y - 2 = 2y - 1.$$

Hence, $y = \frac{1}{2}$ is a critical point and, since $F''(\frac{1}{2}) = 2 > 0$, it yields a minimum. The corresponding value of x is obtained from

$$(x-1)^2 = \frac{1}{2} - 3 = -\frac{5}{2}.$$

However, this is clearly impossible, since $(x-1)^2 \geq 0$. Examination of Figure 6.1.1 reveals a geometric explanation for this failure – no point on the parabola $y = (x-1)^2 + 3$ can have its second coordinate equal to $\frac{1}{2}$. Thus, eliminating x leads to an impossible solution.

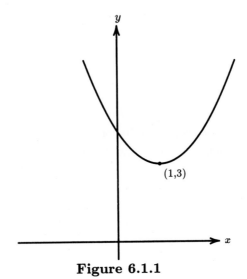

(1,3)

Figure 6.1.1

We will attempt to solve the problem again, this time by eliminating y, and then compare the two approaches to determine the source of the difficulty. Solving the constraint for y yields

$$y = (x-1)^2 + 3$$

or more conveniently,

$$y - 1 = (x-1)^2 + 2$$

from which

$$(y-1)^2 = (x-1)^4 + 4(x-1)^2 + 4.$$

With this substitution, the objective function becomes

$$F(x) = (x-1)^4 + 5(x-1)^2 + 4.$$

Differentiating,

$$F'(x) = 4(x-1)^3 + 10(x-1) = 2(x-1)(2x^2 - 4x + 7).$$

Since $2x^2 - 4x + 7$ is never 0, $x = 1$ is the only critical point. Testing it by the second derivative test,

$$F''(x) = 12(x-1) + 10 \quad \text{and} \quad F''(1) = 10 > 0$$

so that $x = 1$ yields a relative minimum. The corresponding value of y is $y = 0^2 + 3 = 3$, and the closest point to $(1,1)$ on the parabola is its vertex, $(1, 3)$. ∎

The difficulty in the first attempted solution which does not seem to have arisen in the second can be found by reviewing the implicit function theorem. To use a constraint of the form $g(x, y) = b$ to eliminate a variable, $g(x, y) = b$ must define that variable as a differentiable function of the remaining variables on a neighborhood of the optimal point. The hypotheses of the implicit function theorem then require that the partial derivative of g with respect to the variable to be eliminated be continuous and nonzero at the optimal point.

Returning to the example, we have

$$g(x, y) = y - (x-1)^2 = 3$$

with $g_x(x, y) = -2(x-1)$ and $g_y(x, y) = 1$. Thus, $g_x(1, 3) = 0$ and the required differentiable function of x in terms of y need not exist on a neighborhood of $(1, 3)$. Indeed, differentiating implicitly with respect to y, we have

$$1 - 2(x-1)\frac{dx}{dy} = 0$$

and

$$\frac{dx}{dy} = \frac{1}{2(x-1)}$$

so that the function has no derivative along the vertical line $x = 1$. However, differentiating with respect to x,

$$\frac{dy}{dx} - 2(x-1) = 0$$

which yields

$$\frac{dy}{dx} = 2(x - 1)$$

a derivative of y in terms of x that is defined throughout the plane.

A *level curve* of a function f is the graph of an equation of the form $f(x, y) = c$. By considering the graphs of several level curves for different values of the constant c, we can often learn about the graph of the function f. Here we will consider the relationship of the family of level curves of the objective function to the graph of the constraint as the value of c changes.

As shown in Figure 6.1.2, the family of level curves of the objective function $f(x, y) = (x-1)^2 + (y-1)^2$ is the set of concentric circles centered at $(1, 1)$. The value of the objective function at any point in the plane is the square of the radius of the member of the family of circles passing through the point. Thus, the solution lies on the circle of smallest radius which intersects the parabola. This occurs at the point found earlier, $(1, 3)$, and it is important to note that at that point the parabola and the circle have a common tangent line.

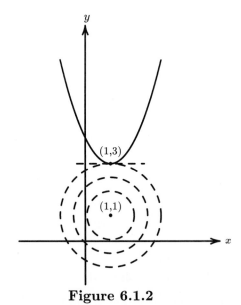

Figure 6.1.2

As the discussion of the graph indicates, level curves will be useful in describing geometrically what is taking place in constrained optimization problems.

Another useful tool is the *gradient*, which is the vector given by

$$\nabla f(x_0, y_0) = \left[\begin{array}{c} f_x(x_0, y_0) \\ f_y(x_0, y_0) \end{array} \right].$$

Geometrically, the gradient is perpendicular to the tangent line to the level curve of the function through the point (x_0, y_0) and points in the direction of maximum increase of f at the point.

Example 6.1.4. Consider the function $f(x, y) = x^2 - y^2$. Determine the gradient at $(2, 1)$ and show that it is perpendicular to the tangent line to the level curve at that point.

The partial derivatives are $f_x(x, y) = 2x$ and $f_y(x, y) = -2y$. Thus the gradient at $(2, 1)$ is

$$\nabla f(2, 1) = \left[\begin{array}{c} f_x(2, 1) \\ f_y(2, 1) \end{array} \right] = \left[\begin{array}{c} 4 \\ -2 \end{array} \right].$$

The level curve through $(2, 1)$ is the hyperbola $x^2 - y^2 = 3$. Along this curve $\frac{dy}{dx} = \frac{x}{y}$, so a vector tangent to the level curve at $(2, 1)$ is $T = [1, 2]^T$. T and the gradient are perpendicular since

$$\nabla f(2, 1) \cdot T = \left[\begin{array}{c} 4 \\ -2 \end{array} \right] \cdot \left[\begin{array}{c} 1 \\ 2 \end{array} \right] = 4 - 4 = 0.$$

■

We will find gradients and linear combinations of gradients useful later in describing geometrically what is happening at the optimal solution of problems. An alternative notation for the gradient is grad $f(x_0, y_0)$.

Exercises

1. Solve the problem in Example 6.1.1 by using the constraint to eliminate r instead of h.

2. Solve the problem

$$\begin{array}{ll} \text{Maximize}: & x^2 y \\ \text{Subject to}: & 2x^2 + 4xy = 25 \end{array}$$

3. Solve the problem

$$\begin{array}{ll} \text{Minimize}: & x^2 + y \\ \text{Subject to}: & x + y = 4 \end{array}$$

4. Consider the function $f(x_1, x_2) = x_1 + x_2^2$. Draw the level curve of f passing through the point $(0, -2)$. Determine $\nabla f(0, -2)$ and include it in the graph.

5. Consider the function $f(x_1, x_2) = x_1^2 + 4x_2^2$. Draw the level curve of f passing through the point $(2, 0)$. Determine $\nabla f(2, 0)$ and include it in the graph.

6. A graphic artist is designing a poster to contain 72 square inches of printed material. For visual appeal, she recommends 2 inch margins on the sides and top and a 3 inch margin on the bottom as suggested in Figure 6.1.3. The client agrees, but asks that the poster be of the minimum possible overall size. What should the overall dimensions be?

7. A commercial developer owns a piece of land that includes a 45° angle at one corner. He wants to build a building with a trapezoidal ground plan as shown in Figure 6.1.4. The building must have a ground floor area of 800 square feet. To minimize exterior finishing costs the perimeter of the building is to be as small as possible. What should its dimensions be?

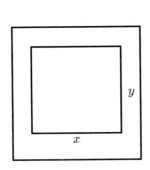

Figure 6.1.3

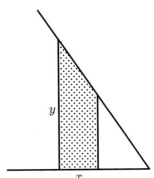

Figure 6.1.4

6.2   Two variable problems

The property of having a tangent line common to the constraint and to a level curve of the objective function in Example 6.1.3 will be seen to be necessary at the optimal point. It is equivalent to having the normals to the curves be parallel at the point. This latter condition is more convenient to express in terms of derivatives. For the problem

$$\text{Maximize}: \quad f(x, y)$$
$$\text{Subject to}: \quad g(x, y) = b$$

the requirement that the normals to f and g be parallel is

$$\begin{bmatrix} f_x(a, b) \\ f_y(a, b) \end{bmatrix} = \lambda \begin{bmatrix} g_x(a, b) \\ g_y(a, b) \end{bmatrix}$$

where λ is some constant.

The existence of such a proportionality constant is demonstrated in the following theorem. Based on the previous example, it is not surprising that the hypotheses on g are those of the implicit function theorem. The theory is developed only for the maximum case since to minimize an objective function it is sufficient to maximize its negative.

Theorem 6.2.1. *If (a, b) is a solution to the problem*

$$\text{Maximize}: \quad f(x, y)$$
$$\text{Subject to}: \quad g(x, y) = b_1$$

where f is differentiable and g has continuous first partial derivatives on a neighborhood of (a, b), one of which is nonzero at (a, b), then there exists a constant λ such that

$$\left[\begin{array}{c} f_x(a, b) \\ f_y(a, b) \end{array} \right] = \lambda \left[\begin{array}{c} g_x(a, b) \\ g_y(a, b) \end{array} \right].$$

The point (a, b) and the constant λ can often be efficiently located as the critical point of the associated function

$$L(x, y; \lambda) = f(x, y) + \lambda (b_1 - g(x, y))$$

called the *Lagrangian*. The constant λ is called a *Lagrange multiplier*. We use a semicolon in the list of variables to separate the variables of the problem from the multiplier. Note the conditions below that must be satisfied by a critical point $(a, b; \lambda)$ of L are those of the theorem plus the requirement that the constraint be satisfied:

$$\begin{array}{rcl} L_x(a, b; \lambda) & = & f_x(a, b) - \lambda g_x(a, b) = 0 \\ L_y(a, b; \lambda) & = & f_y(a, b) - \lambda g_y(a, b) = 0 \\ L_\lambda(a, b; \lambda) & = & b_1 - g(a, b) = 0. \end{array}$$

These conditions are necessary for the point (a, b) to be a solution to the problem

$$\text{Maximize}: \quad f(x, y)$$
$$\text{Subject to}: \quad g(x, y) = b_1.$$

As in the unconstrained case, the sufficient condition concerns signs of determinants of a matrix of second derivatives. An $m \times m$ *principal minor* of the Hessian matrix is the determinant of a matrix consisting of the entries from the first m rows and the first m columns of the matrix. Thus, a principal minor of a matrix is the determinant of a matrix formed by entries taken from a square upper left-hand corner of the matrix.

We first consider the Hessian for a constrained problem here, beginning the investigation of the principal minors in the next section.

Since $(a, b; \lambda)$ is a critical point of $L(x, y; \lambda)$ and $f(a, b) = L(a, b; \lambda)$ because for a feasible point (a, b) we have $b_1 - g(a, b) = 0$, the sufficient condition is simply that for an unconstrained extremum of L. The Hessian matrix for L at $(a, b; \lambda)$ is given below. $L_{\lambda\lambda}$ is placed in the upper left-hand corner for convenience:

$$H = \begin{bmatrix} L_{\lambda\lambda} & L_{\lambda x} & L_{\lambda y} \\ L_{x\lambda} & L_{xx} & L_{xy} \\ L_{y\lambda} & L_{yx} & L_{yy} \end{bmatrix}.$$

When the position of λ as the coefficient of g is considered, the matrix becomes

$$H = \begin{bmatrix} 0 & -g_x & -g_y \\ -g_x & f_{xx} - \lambda g_{xx} & f_{xy} - \lambda g_{xy} \\ -g_y & f_{yx} - \lambda g_{yx} & f_{yy} - \lambda g_{yy} \end{bmatrix}.$$

Such a matrix is called a *bordered Hessian*. It can be shown that because $g(x, y) = 0$, it is sufficient to test only the sign of $|H|$ to determine if a maximum occurs at (a, b). This discussion is summarized in

Theorem 6.2.2. *If the second derivatives of f and g are continuous at the point, a point (a, b) is the solution to*

$$\begin{aligned} \text{Maximize}: \quad & f(x, y) \\ \text{Subject to}: \quad & g(x, y) = b_1 \end{aligned}$$

if $(a, b; \lambda)$ is a critical point of $L(x, y; \lambda) = f(x, y) + \lambda(b_1 - g(x, y))$ such that $|H(a, b; \lambda)| > 0$.

Example 6.2.3. To illustrate the application of Lagrange multipliers in economics, consider the problem of a consumer seeking to maximize the utility derived from consumption of two commodities to be purchased under budgetary constraint. Suppose that the utility derived from the combination of x and y units of the respective commodities is

$$U(x, y) = (x + 5)(y + 3).$$

If the commodities cost \$6 and \$2, respectively, and the budget allocation is \$36, then the problem becomes

$$\text{Maximize}: \quad (x+5)(y+3)$$
$$\text{Subject to}: \quad 6x + 2y = 36.$$

We first rewrite the constraint so that its right-hand side is 0. In the next section we will see why we express the constraint with the budget, 36, having a positive coefficient. Then the Lagrangian is

$$L(x, y; \lambda) = (x+5)(y+3) + \lambda(36 - 6x - 2y).$$

Setting the first partial derivatives to zero to obtain a critical point yields the system of equations:

$$
\begin{aligned}
y + 3 - 6\lambda &= 0 \\
x + 5 - 2\lambda &= 0 \\
36 - 6x - 2y &= 0.
\end{aligned}
$$

Solving for x and y in terms of λ and substituting in the third equation yields

$$
\begin{aligned}
6(2\lambda - 5) + 2(6\lambda - 3) &= 36 \\
24\lambda &= 72 \\
\lambda &= 3.
\end{aligned}
$$

Then $x = 2\lambda - 5 = 1$ and $y = 6\lambda - 3 = 15$ are the quantities of the two commodities to be purchased. Taking second derivatives to test the bordered Hessian produces

$$
H(1, 15; 3) = \begin{bmatrix} 0 & -6 & -2 \\ -6 & 0 & 1 \\ -2 & 1 & 0 \end{bmatrix}
$$

and since $|H(1, 15; 3)| = 24 > 0$, the point $(1, 15)$ yields a maximum.

Level curves of the objective function are hyperbolas, of which only the portion in the first quadrant is economically meaningful. Since the utility is constant along each curve, the consumer is indifferent to which point is selected on a given curve. Thus, such level curves are called *indifference curves*.

Note in Figure 6.2.1 that the optimal point $(1, 15)$ is the point of tangency of the constraint to the curve representing the optimal $U = 108$ level.

Further, note that the gradient there points in the direction of indifference
curves corresponding to higher levels of utility.

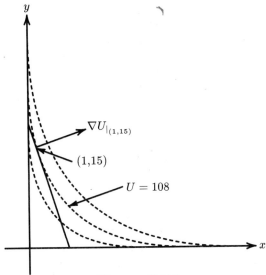

Figure 6.2.1

Finally, we evaluate the gradients of the objective function U and
the constraining budget function g at $(1, 15)$ to show that they are
proportional, with $\lambda = 3$ the constant of proportionality. Taking partial
derivatives,

$$U_x = y + 3 \quad \text{and} \quad U_y = x + 5$$

and

$$g_x(x, y) = 6 \quad \text{and} \quad g_y(x, y) = 2.$$

When we evaluate these derivatives at $(1, 15)$, we obtain

$$\nabla U_{|(1,15)} = \begin{bmatrix} 18 \\ 6 \end{bmatrix} = 3 \begin{bmatrix} 6 \\ 2 \end{bmatrix} = 3\nabla g_{|(1,15)}$$

so that the multiplier is the proportionality constant between the gradient
of the objective function and the gradient of the constraint at the point of
optimality. ∎

Exercises

1. **Lagrange multipliers.** Solve the following problem and sketch the constraint and level curves to illustrate the necessary conditions for a constrained extremum:

$$\text{Minimize}: \quad 4x^2 + 3y^2$$
$$\text{Subject to}: \quad 2x + 6y = 26.$$

2. **Distance from a point to a line.** The distance D from the point (x_0, y_0) to the graph of the line $Ax + By + C = 0$, where $AB \neq 0$, is given by

$$D = \frac{Ax_0 + By_0 + C}{\sqrt{A^2 + B^2}}.$$

Derive this formula by using the fact that this is the distance from (x_0, y_0) to the closest point on the straight line. Take advantage of symmetry. Illustrate by drawing level curves.

3. **Risk minimization.** A chemical plant making hazardous materials is to be located along a 10-mile line joining two communities of populations 10,000 and 25,000. In the event of a leak, the anticipated illnesses in a community are proportional to the population and inversely proportional to the square of the distance from the plant. Thus, the risk is proportional to

$$\frac{10,000}{x^2} + \frac{25,000}{y^2}$$

where x and y are the respective distances of the communities from the plant. Determine the location that would minimize the risk.

4. **Maximization of revenue.** A manufacturer produces two products having selling prices of \$144 and \$90, respectively. The products are in great demand, so that manufacturer need only be concerned with producing the combination which will yield the maximum revenue. If the cost in hundreds of dollars of producing x hundred units of the first product and y hundred units of the second product is

$$C(x, y) = 5x^2 + 2xy + y^2$$

determine the production that will maximize the manufacturer's revenue if the available capital is \$28,900.

5. Solve the problem:

$$\text{Minimize}: \quad \sqrt{x} + 3\sqrt{y}$$
$$\text{Subject to}: \quad x + 3y = 8.$$

6. Determine the point on the parabola $y = x^2$ closest to the point $(0, 2)$.

7. Solve the problem:

$$\text{Maximize}: \quad 4x + 2y$$
$$\text{Subject to}: \quad x^2 + y^2 = 16.$$

Draw a graph to illustrate the relationship between the objective function and the constraint at the point of optimality.

6.3   More variables; more constraints

The procedure involving n variables and m constraints, $n > m$, is similar. We will outline the key generalizations necessary before illustrating the method. The general problem is stated below with $x = (x_1, x_2, \ldots, x_n)$ in R^n :

$$\text{Maximize}: \quad f(x)$$
$$\text{Subject to}: \quad g^1(x) = b_1, \ g^2(x) = b_2, \ \ldots, g^m(x) = b_m.$$

The Lagrangian is set up as before, including a multiplier for each constraint:

$$
\begin{aligned}
L(x, \lambda) &= f(x) + \lambda_1(b_1 - g^1(x)) + \cdots + \lambda_m(b_m - g^m(x)) \\
&= f(x) + \sum_{i=1}^{m} \lambda_i(b_i - g^i(x)).
\end{aligned}
$$

As before, we require that f and the g^i be twice continuously differentiable on a neighborhood of the potential solution.

A key to the proof of Theorem 6.2.1 is that the constraint $g(x, y) = b$ satisfy the hypotheses of the implicit function theorem, namely that either g_x or g_y be nonzero at the critical point of $L(x, y; \lambda)$. Here, the constraint functions must satisfy a more general form of the implicit function theorem. Specifically, we require that the m rows of the matrix, called the *Jacobian matrix*,

$$
\begin{bmatrix}
g_{x_1}^1(a) & g_{x_2}^1(a) & \cdots & g_{x_n}^1(a) \\
g_{x_1}^2(a) & g_{x_2}^2(a) & \cdots & g_{x_n}^2(a) \\
& & \vdots & \\
g_{x_1}^m(a) & g_{x_2}^m(a) & \cdots & g_{x_n}^m(a)
\end{bmatrix}
$$

must be linearly independent for (a, λ) a critical point of $L(x; \lambda)$.

Theorem 6.3.1. *Let f and g^i, $i = 1, \ldots, m$, be twice continuously differentiable on a neighborhood of a where $(a_1, \ldots, a_n; \lambda_a, \ldots, \lambda_m)$ is a critical point of $L(x; \lambda)$ and let the Jacobian at a of g^i, $i = 1, \ldots, m$ have a row rank of m. Then $a = (a_1, \ldots, a_n)$ is a solution to*

$$\text{Maximize}: \quad f(x, y)$$
$$\text{Subject to}: \quad g^1(x) = b_1, \ldots, g^m(x) = b_m$$

if the last $n - m$ leading principal minors of the bordered Hessian $H(a)$ alternate in sign, with the sign of the first being that of $(-1)^{(m+1)}$.

Note that the theorem requires that only the largest $n - m$ principal minors have specific signs. In particular, if the number of variables is only one greater than the number of constraints, then only the determinant of $H(a)$ needs to be tested.

As we observed earlier in Example 6.2.3, in the two variable setting with a single constraint,

$$\text{Maximize}: \quad f(x, y)$$
$$\text{Subject to}: \quad g(x, y) = b_1$$

the Lagrange multiplier is the constant of proportionality between the gradients of f and g at the optimal point (a, b), i.e.,

$$\nabla f(a, b) = \lambda \nabla g(a, b).$$

With several constraints, the requirement that $(a; \lambda)$ be a critical point of

$$L(x; \lambda) = f(x) + \sum_{i=1}^{m} \lambda_i (b_i - g^i(x))$$

becomes

$$f_{x_j}(a) + \sum_{i=1}^{m} \lambda_i g^i_{x_j}(a) = 0, \quad j = 1, \ldots, n.$$

Since each of these equations involves a coordinate of the gradient, we see that the gradient of f at a is a linear combination of the gradients of the g^i, with the $-\lambda_i$ as the coefficients:

$$\nabla f(a) = - \sum_{i=1}^{m} \lambda_i \nabla g^i(a).$$

Although introduced as a geometrically inspired device to locate the optimal point, the multipliers also have a practical interpretation within the context of the problem. If we consider the constants $b_1, \ldots, b_m$ as variables in the Lagrangian,

$$L(x; \lambda, b) = f(x) + \sum_{i=1}^{m} \lambda_i(b_i - g^i(x))$$

note that

$$\frac{\partial L}{\partial b_i}(x; \lambda, b) = \lambda_i.$$

Since at the optimal point a the value of the objective function equals that of the Lagrangian, we have

$$\frac{\partial f}{\partial b_i}(a) = \frac{\partial L}{\partial b_i}(a; \lambda, b) = \lambda_i, \quad i = 1, \ldots, m$$

and we see that λ_i is a measure of the sensitivity of the solution to a change in the constant b_i. The following example and exercises illustrate this interpretation.

Example 6.3.2. Determine the point on the intersection of the planes

$$3x_1 - 2x_2 + 4x_3 = 9 \quad \text{and} \quad x_1 + 2x_2 = 3$$

which is closest to the point $(3, -1, 2)$.

As stated, the problem is a minimization problem. However, we can treat it as a maximization by maximizing the negative of the square of the distance. Thus, the problem is

$$\begin{aligned} \text{Maximize}: \quad & -(x_1 - 3)^2 - (x_2 + 1)^2 - (x_3 - 2)^2 \\ \text{Subject to}: \quad & 3x_1 - 2x_2 + 4x_3 = 9 \\ & x_1 + 2x_2 = 3. \end{aligned}$$

The Lagrangian is

$$\begin{aligned} L(x; \lambda) \;=\; & -(x_1 - 3)^2 - (x_2 + 1)^2 - (x_3 - 2)^2 + \lambda_1(9 - 3x_1 + 2x_2 - 4x_3) \\ & + \lambda_2(3 - x_1 - 2x_2) \end{aligned}$$

and setting the first partials of L to zero to locate a critical point leads to the equations

$$\begin{aligned} -2(x_1 - 3) - 3\lambda_1 - \lambda_2 &= 0 \\ -2(x_2 + 1) + 2\lambda_1 - 2\lambda_2 &= 0 \\ -2(x_3 - 2) - 4\lambda_1 &= 0 \\ 3x_1 - 2x_2 + 4x_3 &= 9 \\ x_1 + 2x_2 &= 3. \end{aligned}$$

Using the equation $x_1 = 3 - 2x_2$ from the second constraint to eliminate x_1 from the first constraint leads to $x_3 = 2x_2$. Now the first three equations can be reduced to equations in the variables x_2, λ_1, and λ_2 :

$$
\begin{aligned}
4x_2 &- 3\lambda_1 &- \lambda_2 &= 0 \\
-2x_2 &+ 2\lambda_1 &- 2\lambda_2 &= 2 \\
-4x_2 &- 4\lambda_1 & &= -4.
\end{aligned}
$$

Solving this system yields $\lambda_1 = \frac{2}{3}$, $\lambda_2 = -\frac{2}{3}$, and $x_2 = \frac{1}{3}$. Thus,

$$
x_3 = 2x_2 = \frac{2}{3} \quad \text{and} \quad x_1 = 3 - 2x_2 = \frac{7}{3}.
$$

The bordered Hessian that must be tested is

$$
H = \begin{bmatrix}
0 & 0 & -3 & 2 & -4 \\
0 & 0 & -1 & 2 & 0 \\
-3 & -1 & -2 & 0 & 0 \\
2 & 2 & -2 & 0 & 0 \\
4 & 0 & 0 & 0 & -2
\end{bmatrix},
$$

and since $|H| = -298 < 0$, $a = (\frac{7}{3}, \frac{1}{3}, \frac{2}{3})$ is the required point. The distance of a from the intersection is the square root of the negative of the objective function:

$$
\left[\left(\frac{7}{3} - 3 \right) 2 + \left(\frac{1}{3} + 1 \right) 2 + \left(\frac{2}{3} - 2 \right) 2 \right]^{\frac{1}{2}} = 2.
$$

The signs of the multipliers should indicate the influence of a change in the right-hand side of the corresponding constraints. Since $\lambda_1 = \frac{2}{3}$ is positive, an increase in the constant of the first constraint should increase the value of the objective function, i.e., move the solution closer to the intersection of the planes. Similarly, since $\lambda_2 = -\frac{2}{3}$ is negative, an increase of the second constraint constant should move the point away from the intersection. ∎

The preceding example illustrated the significance of the Lagrange multiplier as an indicator of the change that would be produced in the value of the objective function by a change in the constant in the corresponding constraint. In light of that discussion, the occurrence of a zero multiplier would seem to indicate that the corresponding constant could be changed without altering the value of the objective function. A zero multiplier is often an indication that the constraint is unnecessary, and simply omitting it would not alter the solution. This is illustrated in the following example.

Example 6.3.3. Determine the point in the intersection of the ellipsoid

$$2x_1^2 + x_2^2 + x_3^2 = 10$$

and the plane

$$8x_1 + 2x_2 + 2x_3 = 20$$

closest to the point $(10, 3, 3)$.

The problem is set up as:

$$\begin{aligned}
\text{Maximize}: \quad & -(x_1 - 10)^2 - (x_2 - 3)^2 - (x_3 - 3)^2 \\
\text{Subject to}: \quad & 2x_1^2 + x_2^2 + x_3^2 = 10 \\
& 8x_1 + 2x_2 + 2x_3 = 20.
\end{aligned}$$

The Lagrangian is

$$\begin{aligned}
L = \; & -(x_1 - 10)^2 - (x_2 - 3)^2 - (x_3 - 3)^2 + \lambda_1(10 - 2x_1^2 - x_2^2 - x_3^2)^2 \\
& + \lambda_2(20 - 8x_1 - 2x_2 - 2x_3)
\end{aligned}$$

and a critical point of L must satisfy

$$\begin{aligned}
-2(x_1 - 10) - 4x_1\lambda_1 - 8\lambda_2 &= 0 \\
-2(x_2 - 3) - 2x_2\lambda_1 - 2\lambda_2 &= 0 \\
-2(x_3 - 3) - 2x_3\lambda_1 - 2\lambda_2 &= 0 \\
2x_1^2 + x_2^2 + x_3^2 &= 10 \\
8x_1 + 2x_2 + 2x_3 &= 20.
\end{aligned}$$

The solution of this system is greatly simplified by the observation that the equations are symmetric in x_2 and x_3, so we may set $x_2 = x_3$ and drop one equation, say the third. The constraints then become

$$\begin{aligned}
2x_1^2 + 2x_2^2 &= 10 \\
8x_1 + 4x_2 &= 20.
\end{aligned}$$

The second constraint leads to $x_2 = 5 - 2x_1$, and when this is substituted into the first, we obtain

$$x_1^2 - 4x_1 - 4 = 0$$

so that $x_1 = 2$ and $x_2 = x_3 = 1$. Substituting these values into equations 1 and 2 to determine λ_1 and λ_2, we obtain

$$\begin{aligned}
-2(-8) - 8\lambda_1 - 8\lambda_2 &= 0 \\
-2(-2) - 2\lambda_1 - 2\lambda_2 &= 0
\end{aligned}$$

which is equivalent to the redundant system

$$\lambda_1 + \lambda_2 = 2$$
$$\lambda_1 + \lambda_2 = 2.$$

Thus, a value may be assigned arbitrarily to one of the variables and then the other determined. Thus, both $\lambda_1 = 2$, $\lambda_2 = 0$ and $\lambda_1 = 0$, $\lambda_2 = 2$ are accceptable solutions.

The bordered Hessian associated with the problem is

$$H(x_1, x_2, x_3) = \begin{bmatrix} 0 & 0 & -4x_1 & -2x_2 & -2x_3 \\ 0 & 0 & -8 & -2 & -2 \\ -4x_1 & -8 & -2 & 0 & 0 \\ -2x_2 & -2 & 0 & -2 & 0 \\ -2x_3 & -2 & 0 & 0 & 0 \end{bmatrix}.$$

When the point $a = (2, 1, 1)$ is substituted, the Hessian becomes

$$H(2,1,1,) = \begin{bmatrix} 0 & 0 & -8 & -2 & -2 \\ 0 & 0 & -8 & -2 & -2 \\ -8 & -8 & -2 & 0 & 0 \\ -2 & -2 & 0 & -2 & 0 \\ -2 & -2 & 0 & 0 & 0 \end{bmatrix}.$$

Since the first and second rows are identical, the matrix is singular and the test from Theorem 6.3.1 will fail since $|H(2,1,1)| = 0$. However, notice that the nonzero entries of the first two rows comprise the Jacobian of the constraints. Since the Jacobian must have rank 2 instead of 1, we see that the problem as stated does not satisfy the hypotheses of the theorem.

A geometric examination will reveal that the second constraint is the equation of the tangent plane to the graph of the first at the point $(2,1,1)$. Thus, the constraints have the same gradient at $(2,1,1)$ and have identical constraining effects, so that either can be dropped. This situation is illustrated in Figure 6.3.1.

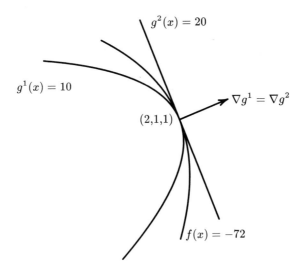

Figure 6.3.1

Dropping the second constraint yields the same critical point, and the bordered Hessian is

$$H(2,1,1) = \begin{bmatrix} 0 & -8 & -2 & -2 \\ -8 & -2 & 0 & 0 \\ -2 & 0 & -2 & 0 \\ -2 & 0 & 0 & -2 \end{bmatrix}.$$

Since we now have two more variables than constraints, we must test the last two principal minors of $H(2,1,1)$, and their signs must be positive and negative, in that order.

$$\begin{vmatrix} 0 & -8 & -2 \\ -8 & -2 & 0 \\ -2 & 0 & -2 \end{vmatrix} = -(-8)\begin{vmatrix} -8 & 0 \\ -2 & -2 \end{vmatrix} + (-2)\begin{vmatrix} -8 & -2 \\ -2 & 0 \end{vmatrix} = 136 > 0.$$

Since $|H(2,1,1)| = -288 < 0$, the point $(2,1,1)$ is the solution. ∎

Example 6.3.4. Equality constraints with three variables. A father has \$3000 to divide among his three children. His estimate of the "utility," in this case "happiness," derived from \$$x$ by each child is given by the following functions:

$$
\begin{array}{llcl}
\text{First child}: & u_1\,(x) & = & \ln x \\
\text{Second child}: & u_2\,(x) & = & 2\ln x \\
\text{Third child}: & u_3\,(x) & = & 3\ln x
\end{array}
$$

Note that the father has used some thought in devising the utility functions. Because $y = \ln x$ –shown in Figure 6.3.2–increases rapidly for small values of x and then levels off to increase very slowly, it often is used in utility functions. It expresses the fact that the first few dollars provide the greatest increase in utility, and then additional dollars provide decreasing utility as the amount increases.

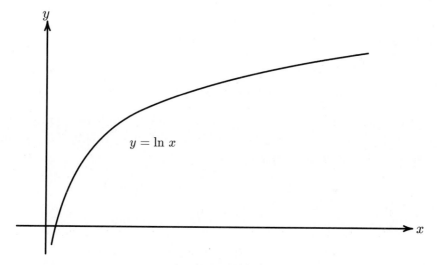

Figure 6.3.2

The father wants to give $\$x_1$ to his first child, $\$x_2$ to his second child, and $\$x_3$ to his third child and to maximize the sum of their utilities. His problem then is

$$
\begin{array}{ll}
\text{Maximize}: & f(x) = \ln x_1 + 2\ln x_2 + 3\ln x_3 \\
\text{Subject to}: & g(x) = x_1 + x_2 + x_3 = 3,000.
\end{array}
$$

The Lagrangian is

$$
L(x_1, x_2, x_3; \lambda) = \ln x_1 + 2\ln x_2 + 3\ln x_3 + \lambda(3,000 - x_1 - x_2 - x_3).
$$

Differentiating to locate a critical point leads to the system of equations

$$\lambda = \frac{1}{x_1}, \quad \lambda = \frac{2}{x_2}, \quad \lambda = \frac{3}{x_3}, \quad x_1 + x_2 + x_3 = 3,000.$$

Thus,

$$x_1 = \frac{1}{\lambda}, \quad x_2 = \frac{2}{\lambda}, \quad x_3 = \frac{3}{\lambda}.$$

and substituting for x_1, x_2, and x_3 in the last equation, we get

$$\frac{1}{\lambda} + \frac{2}{\lambda} + \frac{3}{\lambda} = 3,000$$

so $\dfrac{6}{\lambda} = 3,000$ and therefore $\lambda = \dfrac{6}{3,000} = \dfrac{1}{500}$.

Then we have

$$x_1 = 500, \quad x_2 = 1,000, \quad x_3 = 1,500.$$

We now interpret the multiplier to see a specific example of the multiplier property established following Theorem 6.3.1. When $x_1 = 500$, $x_2 = 1,000$, and $x_3 = 1,500$, the total utility is

$$\ln 500 + 2\ln 1,000 + 3\ln 1,500 = 41.9698.$$

If the father had $\$3,001$, then the optimal solution would be

$$x_1 = \$500.17, \quad x_2 = \$1,000.33, \quad x_3 = \$1,500.50.$$

Then the total utility would be

$$\ln 500.17 + 2\ln 1,000.33 + 3\ln 1,500.50 = 41.9718.$$

The change in the objective function would be $0.0020 = \frac{1}{500}$.

In general, if the father has $\$3,000 + \delta$, then

$$x_1 = 500 + \frac{1}{6}\delta, \quad x_2 = 1,000 + \frac{1}{3}\delta, \quad x_3 = 1,500 + \frac{1}{2}\delta,$$

and the total utility is

$$\ln\left(500 + \frac{1}{6}\delta\right) + 2\ln\left(1,000 + \frac{1}{3}\delta\right) + 3\ln\left(1,500 + \frac{1}{2}\delta\right).$$

We differentiate this with respect to δ and then set $\delta = 0$ to get

$$\left(\frac{\frac{1}{6}}{500 + \frac{1}{6}\delta} + \frac{(2)\left(\frac{1}{3}\right)}{1,000 + \frac{1}{3}\delta} + \frac{(3)\left(\frac{1}{2}\right)}{1,500 + \frac{1}{2}\delta} \right)\Bigg|_{\delta=0}$$

$$= \frac{\frac{1}{6}}{500} + \frac{\frac{2}{3}}{1,000} + \frac{\frac{3}{2}}{1,500}$$

$$= \frac{1}{3,000} + \frac{2}{3,000} + \frac{3}{3,000} = \frac{6}{3,000} = \frac{1}{500}.$$

The multiplier $\lambda = \dfrac{1}{500}$ is the rate of change of the objective function with respect to changes in the right-hand side of the constraint equation. Thus, we have confirmed our earlier conclusion. ∎

Exercises

1. Solve the problem of Example 6.3.2 with the first constraint changed to
$$3x_1 - 2x_2 + 4x_3 = 17.$$

2. Solve the problem of Example 6.3.2 with the first constraint changed to
$$x_1 + 2x_2 = 7.$$

3. Solve the following problem:
$$\begin{aligned} \text{Minimize}: \quad & 2x_1 + 2x_2 + x_3 \\ \text{Subject to}: \quad & 2x_1^2 + x_2^2 + 3x_3^2 = 48. \end{aligned}$$

4. Solve the following problem:
$$\begin{aligned} \text{Minimize}: \quad & x_1^2 + 2x_2^2 + 4x_3^2 \\ \text{Subject to}: \quad & 2x_1 + 2x_2 + x_3 = 8 \end{aligned}$$

5. Solve the following problem:
$$\begin{aligned} \text{Minimize}: \quad & 2x_1^2 + x_2^2 + 4x_3^2 \\ \text{Subject to}: \quad & x_1 + x_2 + x_3 = 6 \\ & -2x_2 + x_3 = 0. \end{aligned}$$

6. Determine the point(s) on the ellipsoid $x^2 + 2y^2 + 4z^2 = 8$ furthest from the point $(0, 0, 3)$.

7. Solve the following problem:
$$\begin{aligned} \text{Minimize}: \quad & x_1^2 + x_2^2 + (x_3 - 1)^2 \\ \text{Subject to}: \quad & x_1 + x_2 + x_3 = 2 \\ & 2x_1 + x_2 - 2x_3 = 4. \end{aligned}$$

6.4 Problems having inequality constraints

The addition of inequality constraints provides added flexibility by allowing for more constraints and for the possibility of unused resources. The method of Lagrange multipliers can be adapted to solve a problem with inequality constraints by reexpressing it as one having only equality constraints. We will find that additional variables must be introduced and that the signs of the multipliers will be more important.

To express the inequality $g(x) \leq b$ as an equality, introduce a non-negative variable s^2 to be the difference $s^2 = b - g(x)$ and write the constraint

$$g(x) + s^2 = b.$$

As with linear programming in Chapter 3, this new variable is called a *slack variable* and a constraint for which $b - g(x_0) > 0$ at a solution x_0 is said to be *slack* at x_0. A constraint for which $b - g(x_0) = 0$ is said to be *active* or *tight*. We will see that active constraints correspond to nonzero multipliers and slack ones to zero multipliers. We will also see that expressing the slack variable here as a square serves both to make it nonnegative and to give a convenient way to express complementary slackness conditions.

With the inequality constraints replaced by equalities through the introduction of slack variables s_j^2, the Lagrangian for the problem

$$\text{Maximize}: \quad f(x)$$
$$\text{Subject to}: \quad g^1(x) \leq b_1, g^2(x) \leq b_2, \ldots, g^m(x) \leq b_m$$

is formed much as for a problem having only equality constraints:

$$L(x; \lambda; s) = f(x) - \sum_{j=1}^{m} \lambda_i(g^j(x) + s_j^2 - b_j).$$

Note that we have changed to including the Lagrange multipliers with coefficients of -1. We do this because a critical proof using convexity will require that constraints be written $g^i(x) - b_i \leq 0$. This change allows us to retain the interpretation of λ_i as the rate of change with respect to b_i, i.e.,

$$\frac{\partial L}{\partial b_i} = \lambda_i.$$

A point satisfying the constraints of such a problem is called a *feasible point*. With equality constraints a necessary condition for a local extremum at x_0 is that the partial derivatives vanish, i.e.,

$$L_{x_i}(x_0; \lambda) = 0, \quad i = 1, 2, \ldots, n$$

or, equivalently, that the gradient of f is a linear combination of the gradients of the constraints, i.e.,

$$\nabla f(x_0) = \sum_{j=1}^{m} \lambda_j \nabla g^j(x_0).$$

With equality constraints no restriction was placed on the signs of the multipliers; however, with inequality constraints we will see that it is important that the signs be nonnegative.

To assure that a solution can be obtained with nonnegative multipliers, we make the following assumptions, traditionally called the *constraint qualifications*:

For every feasible point x, the following system of equations

$$
\begin{array}{llll}
L_{x_i}(x; \lambda, s) & = & 0, \quad i = 1, 2, \ldots, n & \qquad (1) \\
L_{s_j}(x; \lambda, s) & = & -2s_j \lambda_j = 0, \quad j = 1, 2, \ldots, m & \qquad (2)
\end{array}
$$

has a solution for nonnegative values of the Lagrange multipliers.

Geometrically, these assumptions prevent the active constraints from forming a cusp at a point x_0 as illustrated in Figure 6.4.1. Condition (1) is occasionally replaced by the requirement that the gradients of the active constraints form a linearly independent set at points which are candidates for a solution. Note that this is not the case in the figure, as each gradient is a negative multiple of the other. In the exercises we will outline an example for which the constraint qualifications fail.

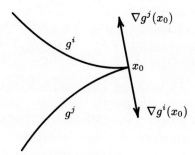

Figure 6.4.1

Having introduced additional variables of two types – Lagrange multipliers and slack variables – we will also need a term to refer to the original variables x_i. Since they often represent an action to be carried out in an applied setting, we will call them *activity variables*. In the theorem, the necessary conditions that the three types of partial derivative

L_{x_i} – the partial with respect to an activity variable
L_{λ_j} – the partial with respect to a Lagrange multiplier
L_{s_j} – the partial with respect to a slack variable

all vanish at a critical point are translated into conditions that will prove to be convenient in solving the problem. As before, discussion of sufficiency conditions will be delayed.

Theorem 6.4.1. *If the constraints $g^j(x) - b_j \le 0$, $j = 1, \ldots, m$, satisfy the constraint qualifications (1) and (2) above at a feasible point x_0 in R^n, then necessary conditions for a maximum of $f(x)$ to occur at x_0 subject to the constraints are*

$$L_{x_i}(x_0) = f_{x_i}(x_0) - \sum_{j=1}^{m} \lambda_j g^j_{x_i}(x_0) \;=\; 0; \quad i = 1, \ldots, n, \qquad (3)$$

$$\lambda_j(g^j(x_0) - b_j) \;=\; 0; \quad j = 1, \ldots, m, \qquad (4)$$

$$\lambda_j \;\ge\; 0; \quad j = 1, \ldots, m. \qquad (5)$$

Proof. The proof consists of demonstrating that the conditions of the theorem together with those of the constraint qualification imply that all first partial derivatives of the Lagrangian are zero at $(x_0; \lambda, s)$ and that the sign restriction (5) is necessary at a maximum. Condition (3) is simply a restatement of (1) from the constraint qualification. The requirement that the point x_0 be feasible is equivalent to $L_{\lambda_j} = 0$, since

$$L_{\lambda_j}(x_0) = g^j(x_0) - s_j^2 - b_j = 0$$

which is equivalent to $g^j(x_0) \le b_j$. Condition (2) of the constraint qualification is equivalent to (4), since $s_j^2 = b_j - g^j(x)$, so that $-2s_j\lambda_j = 0$ implies that

$$\lambda_j(g^j(x_0) - b_j) = 0.$$

To see the necessity for $\lambda_j \geq 0$, recall that a nonzero multiplier corresponds to an active constraint, i.e., one which has an effect on the location of x_0. For such a constraint,

$$g^j(x_0) = b_j$$

and increasing the value of b_j enlarges the set of feasible solutions, thus potentially increasing the value of f. Since

$$L_{b_j}(x_0) = f_{b_j}(x_0) = \lambda_j$$

this can only be the case if $\lambda_j \geq 0$. □

Since the only part of the proof specific to $f(x)$ assuming a maximum occurred in conjunction with the signs of the multipliers, we can state a version of the theorem for minimization problems.

Corollary 6.4.2. *If the constraints $g^j(x) - b_j \leq 0$, $j = 1, \ldots, m$, satisfy the constraint qualifications (1) and (2) at a feasible point x_0, then necessary conditions for a minimum of $f(x)$ to occur at x_0, subject to the constraints, are (3) and (4) of Theorem 6.4.1 and*

$$(5') \ \lambda_j \leq 0; \quad j = 1, \ldots, m.$$

The following example illustrates the use of condition (4) in locating a critical point which is also optimal. Note that since the equation in (4) is the requirement that the product of λ_j and a slack variable be zero, this is a complementary slackness condition as seen earlier in Section 3.7. In fact, we will later see that the λ_j's are dual variables.

Example 6.4.3. Geometrically, the following problem can be seen to be one of locating the point closest to $(2, 3)$ within the region defined by the constraints:

$$\begin{aligned} \text{Maximize}: \quad & -(x_1 - 2)^2 - (x_2 - 3)^2 \\ \text{Subject to}: \quad & x_1 + x_2 \leq 2 \\ & x_1^2 \quad\ \leq 4. \end{aligned}$$

When slack variables s and t have been introduced, the Lagrangian becomes

$$L = -(x_1 - 2)^2 - (x_2 - 3)^2 - \lambda_1(x_1 + x_2 + s^2 - 2) - \lambda_2(x_1^2 + t^2 - 4).$$

Setting the six partial derivatives equal to zero leads to the following system of equations:

$$
\begin{aligned}
L_{x_1} &= -2(x_1 - 2) - \lambda_1 - 2x_1\lambda_2 = 0 \\
L_{x_2} &= -2(x_2 - 3) - \lambda_1 = 0 \\
L_{\lambda_1} &= -(x_1 + x_2 + s^2 - 2) = 0 \\
L_{\lambda_2} &= -(x_1^2 + t^2 - 4) = 0 \\
L_s &= -2s\lambda_1 = 0 \\
L_t &= -2t\lambda_2 = 0.
\end{aligned}
$$

The third and fourth equations assure that the solution is feasible. The last two equations are the complementary slackness conditions expressed by (4) in Theorem 6.4.1.

There are four possible ways in which the last two conditions may be satisfied. The solution involves considering each in turn in light of the other four equations and the requirement that the multipliers be nonnegative.

Case 1: $\lambda_1 = \lambda_2 = 0$.

Substituting these values into the first two equations yields

$$-2(x_1 - 2) = 0 \quad \text{and} \quad -(x_2 - 3) = 0$$

which imply $x_0 = (2, 3)$. However, checking this point in the first constraint yields:

$$2 + 3 + s^2 = 2 \quad \text{or} \quad s^2 = -3$$

which is impossible. Thus, this point is not a solution since it is not feasible. Since multipliers that are zero correspond to slack constraints, this indicates that $(2, 3)$ is the location of the unconstrained maximum of the objective function.

Case 2: $\lambda_1 = t = 0$.

Substituting $t = 0$ in the second constraint yields $x_1^2 = 4$, so we have $x_1 = 2$ or $x_1 = -2$. Substituting $\lambda_1 = 0$ in the second equation yields $-2(x_2 - 3) = 0$ so $x_2 = 3$. Since $x_0 = (2, 3)$ was eliminated in the first case, we consider $x_0 = (-2, 3)$. Test this x_0 in the first constraint:

$$-2 + 3 + s^2 = 2, \quad \text{so} \quad s^2 = 1 > 0.$$

So the choices $\lambda_1 = t = 0$ lead to $x_1 = -2$ and $x_2 = 3$, which satisfy all six equations. It remains to check the nonnegativity of λ_2 by substituting into $L_{x_1} = 0$:

$$-2(-2-2) + 4\lambda_2 = 0, \quad \text{hence} \quad \lambda_2 = -2 < 0.$$

Thus, the choice $\lambda_1 = t = 0$ does not lead to a maximum.

Case 3: $\lambda_2 = s = 0$.

Substituting these values into $L_{x_1} = 0$, $L_{x_2} = 0$, and $L_{\lambda_1} = 0$ yields the following system:

$$
\begin{aligned}
-2x_1 + 4 - \lambda_1 &= 0 \\
-2x_2 + 6 - \lambda_1 &= 0 \\
x_1 + x_2 &= 2.
\end{aligned}
$$

Eliminating λ_1 from the first two of these equations yields

$$-2x_1 + 4 = -2x_2 + 6$$

which simplifies to $x_1 - x_2 = 1$. Solving the resulting system of equations

$$
\begin{aligned}
x_1 &+ x_2 &= 2 \\
x_1 &- x_2 &= -1
\end{aligned}
$$

yields $x_1 = \frac{1}{2}$ and $x_2 = \frac{3}{2}$. Since these values were obtained under the assumption that $s = 0$, the first constraint is necessarily satisfied, and we must check the second:

$$\left(\frac{1}{2}\right)^2 + t^2 = 4, \quad \text{hence} \quad t^2 = \frac{15}{4} > 0.$$

Thus, $x_0 = (\frac{1}{2}, \frac{3}{2})$ is feasible, and it remains to check the nonnegativity of λ_1. From $L_{x_2} = 0$ we have

$$-2\left(\frac{3}{2} - 3\right) - \lambda_1 = 0, \quad \text{so} \quad \lambda_1 = 3 > 0.$$

Hence, $x_0 = \left(\frac{1}{2}, \frac{3}{2}\right)$ satisfies all the required conditions, and the maximum value of

$$-\left(\frac{1}{2} - 2\right)^2 - \left(\frac{3}{2} - 3\right)^2 = -\frac{9}{4} - \frac{9}{4} = -\frac{9}{2}$$

occurs at x_0.

For completeness, we consider the fourth case:

Case 4: $s = t = 0$.

Since both slack variables are zero, this case will pick out any points of intersection of the constraints. Thus, we have the system of equations

$$\begin{aligned} x_1 \;+\; x_2 \;&=\; 2 \\ x_1^2 \qquad &=\; 4. \end{aligned}$$

The solutions $x_1 = 2$ and $x_1 = -2$ to the second equation lead to the pair of points $(2,0)$ and $(-2,4)$. To test for optimality, we must determine values for the multipliers. Substituting $x_0 = (2,0)$ in the first two equations, we get the system

$$\begin{aligned} -\lambda_1 - 4\lambda_2 \;&=\; 0 \\ 2 - \lambda_1 \;&=\; 0 \end{aligned}$$

so that $\lambda_1 = 2$ and $\lambda_2 = -\frac{1}{2} < 0$. Thus, $(2,0)$ is not a solution. Substituting $(-2,4)$, we get the system

$$\begin{aligned} 8 - \lambda_1 + 4\lambda_2 \;&=\; 0 \\ -2 - \lambda_1 \;&=\; 0 \end{aligned}$$

so that $\lambda_2 = -2 < 0$ and thus $(-2,4)$ is also not a solution.

Thus, the optimal value was found in Case 3, and the closest feasible point to $(2,3)$ is $x_0 = \left(\frac{1}{2}, \frac{3}{2}\right)$, which is $\frac{9}{2}$ units away. We have located this point without reference to graphs, which is important since the addition of more activity variables would make a solution relying on graphical techniques impossible.

The example is illustrated in Figure 6.4.2.

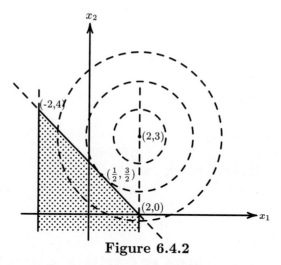

Figure 6.4.2

The shaded portion represents the set of feasible solutions. As in the case of equality constraints, we see that a level curve of the objective function is tangent to the set of solutions at the optimal point. The optimal point is on the edge formed by the constraint $x_1 + x_2 \leq 2$. The fact that the corresponding Lagrange multiplier $\lambda_1 = 3 > 0$ expresses the fact that this constraint is active, i.e., it affects the location of the solution.

Note that $(-2, 4)$ and $(2, 0)$ lie on intersections of constraints, as was indicated by the choice $s = t = 0$. ∎

Since such calculations can become complicated, in Listing 6.4.1 we illustrate how to solve these problems using LINGO. Except for entry of the problem, most aspects of using LINGO are similar to those of LINDO. The `model` command is used to enter the problem. The main differences from the entry of a problem in LINDO are that the objective – `max` or `min` – is followed by an equal sign and that each line ends with a semicolon. Note that in this listing we are using the command line version with a ";" and a prompt of :.

Listing 6.4.1

```
: model
? min =  (x1 - 2)^2 + (x2 - 3)^2;
? x1 + x2 < 2;
? x1^2 < 4;
end
```

```
: go

Rows =   3 Vars =   2 No. integer vars =   0
Nonlinear rows= 2 Nonlinear vars= 2 Nonlinear constraints= 1
Nonzeros =    8 Constraint nonz =   3 Density = 0.889


Optimal solution found at step:       4
Objective value:              4.500000
This releases CFA A6 for others
            Variable            Value        Reduced Cost
                  X1         0.5000000      -0.2024226E-06
                  X2         1.500000                 0.


            Row      Slack or Surplus      Dual Price
              1          4.500000           1.000000
              2          3.750000                 0.
              3               0.            3.000000
```

Note that the `Dual Price` column gives the Lagrange multipliers of the corresponding constraints from Case 3 above. More information on LINGO can be found in Appendix A.

Exercises

   1. Solve the following mathematical program:

$$\begin{aligned} \text{Maximize}: \quad & x_1 x_2 + x_3^2 \\ \text{Subject to}: \quad & x_1 \; + \; x_2 \; + \; x_3 \; \leq \; 10 \\ & 3x_1 \qquad\qquad + \; x_3 \; \leq \; 24. \end{aligned}$$

   2. Solve the following mathematical program:

$$\begin{aligned} \text{Maximize}: \quad & 5x_1 + 3x_2 - x_1^2 - x_2^2 \\ \text{Subject to}: \quad & 3x_1 \; + \; 2x_2 \; \leq \; 9 \\ & x_1 \; + \; 2x_2 \; \leq \; 6. \end{aligned}$$

   3. Consider the following mathematical program and follow the indicated steps to show that the constraint qualifications fail for this problem:

$$\begin{aligned} \text{Maximize}: \quad & x + y \\ \text{Subject to}: \quad & 2y - x \le 1 \\ & x - y^2 \le 0 \\ & -x \le 0. \end{aligned}$$

(a) By drawing the figure, show that the set of feasible solutions is a three sided figure – not all sides are straight lines – with "corners" at $(0,0)$, $(0, \frac{1}{2})$, and $(1,1)$.

(b) Add the graphs of several level curves of the objective function to your graph from part (a) and conclude geometrically that the solution occurs at $(1,1)$.

(c) Show that the gradients of the first and second constraints at $(1,1)$ are parallel and therefore do not form a linearly independent set. Also show that the gradient of the objective function at $(1,1)$ is not parallel to those of the constraints. Thus, the constraint qualifications are violated at $(1,1)$.

4. A furniture company is seeking to lower the cost of their desks. They must design a drawer to hold 2,500 cubic inches and be divided into three equal sections by partitions running from front to back. The maximum height of the drawer is 8 inches, the maximum width is 15 inches, and the maximum distance from front to back is 28 inches. If the material for the bottom costs $0.15 per square inch, for the front $0.20, for the back and sides $0.10, and for the partitions $0.05, what dimensions would yield the minimum cost?

5. A person is planning to divide her savings among three mutual funds having expected returns of 10%, 10%, and 15%. Her goal is a return of at least 12% while minimizing her risk. The risk function for an investment in this combination of funds is

$$200x_1^2 + 400x_2^2 + 100x_1x_2 + 800x_3^2 + 200x_2x_3$$

where x_1, x_2, and x_3 are the respective proportions of her savings in fund i. Determine the proportion invested in each fund.

6. A horse farmer is being forced to use a strip of land 180 feet wide along a busy highway to construct her new 30,000 square foot pasture. She plans a rectangular pasture divided into four equal parts by fences running perpendicular to the road. A special fence will be used for the side along the road that screens the view and costs $25 per foot. On the other three sides of the pasture the fence will cost $5 a foot, and the fence for the three partitions will cost only $4 per foot. To allow adequate room to exercise, no dimension of each of the four fenced areas can be smaller than 40 feet. What dimensions would minimize her fencing cost?

7. Farmer Descartes has decided to upgrade the electrical service to his farm. He plans to abandon the old sevice entry to his home, and erect a new service pole in his barnyard that would allow service to his large barn and silo in addition to his home. The electrical company will pay for the wire to the pole, but he will need to pay for the wire to the house, barn and silo. Of course, he wants to minimize this cost. To this end, he has diagramed his farmyard on a Cartesian plane with a corner of his home at the origin.

Given the diagram in Figure 6.4.3 below, what should the coordinates x and y of the sevice pole be?

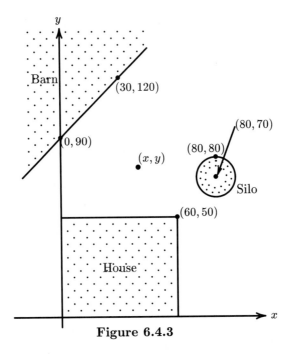

Figure 6.4.3

6.5 The convex programming problem

In Section 5.3 we briefly explored properties of convex functions and demonstrated that the necessary conditions for a minimum were also sufficient for such functions. Here we generalize the definition of convex to functions of several variables and prove the main theorem of convex programming.

The geometric view of convexity in Section 5.3 was stated in Proposition 5.3.4 and required that use of the tangent line to a graph. In higher dimensions, we use the tangent plane in an analogous manner. If f is a function of n variables and $z_0 = f(x_0)$, then the equation of the tangent plane to the graph of f at the point (x_0, z_0) in R^{n+1} is given by

$$z - f(x_0) = \nabla f(x_0) \cdot (x - x_0).$$

Example 6.5.1. Determine the equation of the tangent plane to the graph of

$$f(x, y) = x^2 + 5xy - 2y^2$$

at the point $(-2, 1, -8)$.

We first evaluate the partial derivatives at $(2, -1)$:

$$f_x(x, y) = 2x + 5y \qquad f_x(-2, 1) = -3$$
$$f_y(x, y) = 5x - 4y \qquad f_y(-2, 1) = -14.$$

Thus, the gradient is

$$\nabla f(-2, 1) = \begin{bmatrix} f_x(-2, 1) \\ f_y(-2, 1) \end{bmatrix} = \begin{bmatrix} -3 \\ -14 \end{bmatrix}$$

and the equation of the tangent plane is

$$z - (-8) = \begin{bmatrix} -3 \\ -14 \end{bmatrix} \cdot \begin{bmatrix} x + 2 \\ y - 1 \end{bmatrix}.$$

When the dot product is evaluated, the equation is

$$
\begin{aligned}
z + 8 &= -3(x + 2) - 14(y - 1) \\
z + 8 &= -3x - 14y + 8 \\
z &= -3x - 14y. \quad \blacksquare
\end{aligned}
$$

Since we will deal only with differentiable functions, we will take as our definition of convex function the direct generalization of Proposition 5.3.4. A function f of n variables is *convex* on a set D if for every x_0 in D the graph of f lies above the tangent to f at the point where $x = x_0$, i.e., if for all x in D,

$$f(x) \geq f(x_0) + \nabla f(x_0) \cdot (x - x_0).$$

A *convex programming problem* is a minimization problem in which both the objective function and the constraints are required to be convex. It is also convenient to consider the right-hand side of each constraint to be zero.

This may be accomplished by subtracting a nonzero right-hand side from both sides and including it as part of the constraint function. Thus, the typical convex programming problem is stated as

$$\text{(CXP)} \quad \text{Minimize}: \quad f(x)$$
$$\text{Subject to}: \quad g^1(x) \leq 0, \ldots, g^m(x) \leq 0$$

where f and the g^i are required to be convex.

By observing that the condition that x_0 be a critical point of f can be written as $\nabla f(x_0) = 0$, where 0 denotes the zero vector in R^n, the following proposition can be easily established by the method used to prove Proposition 5.3.7.

Proposition 6.5.2. *If a function is convex on a set D and has a critical point within D, then its global minimum on D occurs at the critical point.*

To solve the convex programming problem (CXP), we form the Lagrangian with slack variables as before:

$$L(x; \lambda, s) = f(x) - \sum_{j=1}^{m} \lambda_j (g^j(x) + s_j^2).$$

If the Lagrange multipliers are all nonpositive, as Corollary 6.4.2 indicates that they must be for a minimum to exist, then Exercise 3 at the end of the section will indicate that the Lagrangian is itself a convex function.

In the following theorem from [18] and [23], the conditions (1) – (4) of the constraint qualification and Theorem 6.4.1 have been replaced by the single requirement that $(\hat{x}, \hat{\lambda}, \hat{s})$ be a critical point of L.

Theorem 6.5.3. (Karush-Kuhn-Tucker theorem) *If the functions f and g^j, $j = 1, \ldots, m$, are all convex and $(\hat{x}, \hat{\lambda}, \hat{s})$ is a critical point of the Lagrangian L such that $\hat{\lambda}_j \leq 0$, $j = 1, \ldots, m$, then $\hat{x}$ is a global solution of the convex programming problem*

$$\text{(CXP)} \quad \text{Minimize}: \quad f(x)$$
$$\text{Subject to}: \quad g^1(x) \leq 0, \ldots, g^m(x) \leq 0.$$

Proof. Since $(\hat{x}, \hat{\lambda}, \hat{s})$ is a critical point of L, we have

$$L_{x_i} = f_{x_i}(\hat{x}) - \sum_{j=1}^{m} \hat{\lambda}_j g_{x_i}^j(\hat{x}) = 0, \ i = 1, \ldots, n$$

which can be rewritten as

$$\nabla f(\hat{x}) - \sum_{j=1}^{m} \hat{\lambda}_j \nabla g^j(\hat{x}) = 0. \qquad (1)$$

Also, we have

$$L_{\lambda_j} = g^j(\hat{x}) + \hat{s}_j^2 = 0, \quad j = 1, \ldots, m$$

so that $\hat{x}$ is a feasible solution.

Finally, from $L_{s_j} = -2s_j \hat{\lambda}_j = 0$ we have that for each $j = 1, \ldots, m$ either $\hat{\lambda}_j = 0$ or $g^j(\hat{x}) = 0$, so that

$$\hat{\lambda}_j g^j(\hat{x}) = 0, \ j = 1, \ldots, m. \qquad (2)$$

We now use (1) and (2) together with the convexity of all functions to establish that a global minimum occurs at $\hat{x}$. For feasible x, we have

$$f(x) \ \geq \ f(x) - \sum_{j=1}^{m} \hat{\lambda}_j g^j(x) \ \text{ since } \ \hat{\lambda}_j \leq 0 \text{ and } g^j(x) \leq 0$$

$$\geq \ f(\hat{x}) + \nabla f(\hat{x}) \cdot (x - \hat{x}) - \sum_{j=1}^{m} \hat{\lambda}_j (g^j(\hat{x}) + \nabla g^j(\hat{x}) \cdot (x - \hat{x}))$$

since f and each g^j are convex. We continue by collecting the coefficients of $x - \hat{x}$ on the right-hand side to allow the use of (1):

$$= \ f(\hat{x}) - \sum_{j=1}^{m} \hat{\lambda}_j g^j(\hat{x}) + [\nabla f(\hat{x}) - \sum_{j=1}^{m} \hat{\lambda} \nabla g^j(\hat{x})] \cdot (x - \hat{x})$$

$$= \ f(\hat{x}) + \sum_{j=1}^{m} \hat{\lambda}_j g^j(\hat{x}) \qquad \text{by (1)}$$

$$= \ f(\hat{x}) \qquad \qquad \text{by (2)}.$$

Thus, $f(x) \geq f(\hat{x})$ for all feasible x, and a global solution occurs at $\hat{x}$. $\square$

The theorem can now be applied to an equipment cost minimization.

Example 6.5.4. The deterioration of equipment represents various costs to industry, including repair costs and operating inferiority costs in comparison to more modern equipment. A minimum value for the total of costs due to deterioration and capital costs can be found by choosing the lifetimes of the equipment by convex programming. The objective function will be the average yearly cost. The constraint will be the requirement that the total of equipment lifetimes exceed a given limit so that replacement does not occur too frequently.

Suppose that Machine A costs $10,000 and Machine B $16,900. In addition, the operating inferiority costs of A are estimated to increase by $25 per year and to increase by $100 per year for B. If the capital to purchase them is borrowed at 12% annual interest, determine the useful lifetimes for each piece of equipment that will minimize their total cost. To avoid too frequent replacement, the sum of the lifetimes is required to be at least 20 years.

Let x_1 denote the lifetime of Machine A and x_2 that of Machine B. Then

$$\frac{10,000}{x_1} + \frac{16,900}{x_2}$$

represents the average yearly cost. If we assume that interest is paid on one-half of the purchase price each year, then we obtain

$$0.12\left(\frac{10,000}{2} + \frac{16,900}{2}\right) = \$1,614$$

for the annual interest cost.

The average operating inferiority cost for Machine A is

$$\frac{25 + 25 \cdot 2 + \cdots + 25x_1}{x_1} = \frac{25(1 + 2 + \cdots + x_1)}{x_1}$$

$$= \frac{25x_1(x_1 + 1)}{2x_1}$$

$$= \frac{25(x_1 + 1)}{2}.$$

Similarly, for Machine B the average operating inferiority cost is

$$\frac{100 + 100 \cdot 2 + \cdots + 100x_2}{x_2} = 50(x_2 + 1).$$

Adding the constraint on the sum of the lifetimes, we obtain the following problem:

$$\text{Minimize:} \quad \frac{25(x_1 + 1)}{2} + 50(x_2 + 1) + \frac{10,000}{x_1} + \frac{16,900}{x_2} + 1,614$$

$$\text{Subject to:} \quad 20 - x_1 - x_2 \leq 0.$$

The Lagrangian is

$$
\begin{aligned}
L(x; \lambda, s) \quad = \quad & \frac{25(x_1 + 1)}{2} + 50(x_2 + 1) + \frac{10,000}{x_1} + \frac{16,900}{x_2} + 1,614 \\
& -\lambda(20 - x_1 - x_2 + s^2).
\end{aligned}
$$

The conditions for a critical point of L are:

$$
\begin{aligned}
L_{x_1} \quad &= \quad \frac{25}{2} - \frac{10,000}{x_1^2} + \lambda = 0 \\
L_{x_2} \quad &= \quad 50 - \frac{16,900}{x_2^2} + \lambda = 0 \\
L_\lambda \quad &= \quad 20 - x_1 - x_2 + s^2 = 0 \\
L_s \quad &= \quad -2s\lambda = 0.
\end{aligned}
$$

Eliminating λ from the first two equations yields

$$\frac{25}{2} - \frac{10,000}{x_1^2} = 50 - \frac{16,900}{x_2^2}$$

which simplifies to

$$1,352x_1^2 - 3x_1^2 x_2^2 - 800x_2^2 = 0.$$

The equation $-2s\lambda = 0$ is satisfied with either $s = 0$ or $\lambda = 0$.

Case 1:

Assuming the case $s = 0$, we have $x_2 = 20 - x_1$ and the equation above becomes

$$1,352x_1^2 = 3x_1^2(20 - x_1)^2 + 800(20 - x_1)^2$$

which simplifies to the quartic equation

$$3x_1^4 - 120x_1^3 + 648x_1^2 - 32,000x_1 + 320,000 = 0.$$

This equation has the positive roots $x_1 = 9.4$ and $x_1 = 39.6$. We discard the latter root, since under the assumption $s = 0$ it leads to a negative value of

x_2. Since $x_2 = 20 - x_1$, we obtain $x_2 = 10.6$ from the first root. It remains to test the sign of λ. From the second equation,

$$\lambda = -50 + \frac{16,900}{(10.6)^2} = 100.4 > 0.$$

Hence, this cannot be the minimum and we must try the case with $\lambda = 0$.

Case 2:

The assumption $\lambda = 0$ leads to the equations

$$25x_1^2 = 20,000 \quad \text{and} \quad 50x_2^2 = 16,900$$

which yield $x_1 = 28.3$ and $x_2 = 18.4$. This is a feasible solution since $s^2 = 26.7 > 0$ and all conditions are satisfied. Thus, lifetimes of approximately 28.3 and 18.4 years for machines A and B, respectively, should lead to minimum costs. ■

For a practical situation with an inequality constraint, we return to the case of the manufacturer in Example 5.3.10.

Example 6.5.5. Now suppose that the manufacturer is further constrained to produce his boxes from cardboard stock that is 16 inches wide. By cutting the boxes from the stock in an interlocking pattern, as shown in Figure 6.5.1,

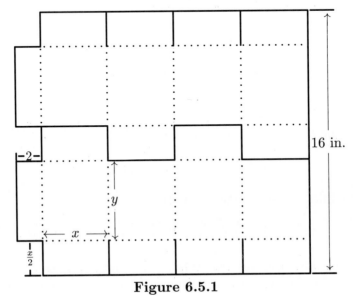

Figure 6.5.1

we see that the dimensions of the box are constrained by

$$2y + \frac{3}{2}x \le 16.$$

We also see that a rectangular piece of cardboard with area $3 \cdot \left(\frac{x}{2}\right) \cdot 2$ is wasted for each pair of boxes, and thus $\frac{3x}{2}$ must be added to the surface area of each individual box. With this change in the objective function and the added constraint, the problem becomes:

$$\begin{aligned} \text{Minimize}: \quad & 3x^2 + 4xy + \tfrac{3}{2}x + 2y \\ \text{Subject to}: \quad & x^2y = 100 \\ & 2y + \tfrac{3}{2}x \le 16. \end{aligned}$$

The Lagrangian is

$$L = 3x^2 + 4xy + \frac{3}{2}x + 2y - \lambda_1(x^2y - 100) - \lambda_2(2y + \frac{3}{2}x + s^2 - 16)$$

A critical point must satisfy

$$\begin{aligned} L_x &= 6x + 4y + \tfrac{3}{2} - 2xy\lambda_1 - \tfrac{3}{2}\lambda_2 = 0 \\ L_y &= 4x + 2y - x^2\lambda_1 - 2\lambda_2 = 0 \\ L_{\lambda_1} &= -(x^2y - 100) = 0 \\ L_{\lambda_2} &= -(2y + \tfrac{3}{2}x + s^2 - 16) = 0 \\ L_s &= -2s\lambda_2 = 0. \end{aligned}$$

Since the first constraint is an equality, we must have $100 = x^2y$. Further, since the second constraint is new and the solution to the earlier Example 5.3.10 does not satisfy it, we expect it to be tight, i.e., we expect to have $2y + \frac{3}{2}x = 16$.

Thus, $y = 8 - \frac{3}{4}x$, and eliminating y from the first constraint leads to the equation

$$8x^2 - \frac{3}{4}x^3 = 100$$

which simplifies to $f(x) = 3x^3 - 32x^2 + 400 = 0$.

We employ Newton's method to obtain the solution:

$$x_{i+1} = x_i - \frac{f(x_i)}{f'(x_i)}$$

$$= x_i - \frac{3x_i^3 - 32x_i^2 + 400}{9x_i^2 - 64x_i}$$

$$= \frac{9x_i^3 - 64x_i^2 - 3x_i^3 + 32x_i^2 - 400}{9x_i^2 - 64x_i}$$

$$= \frac{6x_i^3 - 32x_i^2 - 400}{9x_i^2 - 64x_i}.$$

Starting with $x_0 = 4.34$ from the solution to Example 5.3.10, we obtain:

$$x_1 = 4.7327$$
$$x_2 = 4.7452$$
$$x_3 = 4.7452.$$

This gives $y = 8 - \frac{3}{4}(4.7452) = 4.4411$. Thus the resulting box is slightly shorter when the additional constraint is imposed and the wasted cardboard considered. The Lagrange multipliers can be obtained from the complementary slackness conditions, which lead to the system of equations

$$\begin{cases} 42.147817\lambda_1 + 1.5\lambda_2 = 47.735602 \\ 22.516935\lambda_1 + 2\lambda_2 = 20.980805 \end{cases}$$

which has the solution $\lambda_1 = 1.266819$ and $\lambda_2 = -3.772040$. Since the first constraint was an equality, λ_1 is unrestricted in sign; and since the second constraint was a "$\leq$" constraint, λ_2 must be nonpositive. Hence, the multipliers we obtained meet the requirements of the Karush-Kuhn-Tucker theorem.

The signs of the multipliers can be interpreted in terms of the problem. Recall that the multipliers are the rate of change of the value of the objective function with respect to the right-hand side of the corresponding constraint. In the first constraint, if the required volume of the box were increased, the value of the objective function – the amount of cardboard – would increase, as is indicated by the positive λ_1. On the other hand, if the width of the cardboard stock from which the boxes are cut were increased, the second constraint would be relaxed and the value of the objective function would decrease, as indicated by the negative λ_2, and the amount of cardboard would go down. ∎

Listing 6.5.1 shows the result of submiting the model to LINGO to check the solution.

Listing 6.5.1

```
MODEL:
  1]min = 3*x^2 + 4*x*y + 1.5*x + 2*y;
  2]x^2*y = 100;
  3]1.5*x + 2*y < 16;
END
```

```
Rows =  3 Vars =  2 No. integer vars =  0
Nonlinear rows= 2 Nonlinear vars= 2 Nonlinear constraints= 1
Nonzeros =  8 Constraint nonz = 4 Density = 0.889

Optimal solution found at step:            9
Objective value:               167.8465
```

Variable	Value	Reduced Cost
X	4.745204	0.
Y	4.441097	0.

Row	Slack or Surplus	Dual Price
1	167.8465	1.000000
2	0.	-1.266820
3	0.	3.772057

The solutions agree to four places. Note that the negatives of the Lagrange multipliers of the our solution appear in the Dual Price column, indicating that LINGO is apparently employing a different approach to forming the Lagrangian.

Among the most important applications of nonlinear optimization is the optimization of investment strategy. The next example is an illustration.

Investments and the accuracy of calculations involving them depend upon unpredictable factors such as the economic climate and the whims of other investors. As a result, such activities are subject to seemingly random behavior. We need some terminology to discuss them.

A *probability experiment* is one involving random behavior which can be repeated under reasonably controlled conditions so that a historical record can be compiled. A simple example is to toss a coin five times. A *random variable* is an assignment of a numerical value to the result of such an experiment. In the coin-toss example, one random variable is the number of heads obtained. One can calculate an expected value, or *mean,* for such a variable as well as measures such as the variance and standard deviation indicating the degree to which the values of the random variable may vary.

In our example, the "experiment" is to invest in two stocks and wait a year to see what happens. While one can question the degree to which such an experiment can be repeated under controlled conditions, there is a substantial historical record, and appropriate measures of expectations and variances can be calculated. The goal in our example will be to maximize the return, which will be a random variable, while controlling the size of the risk, called the *variance.*

The numbers used in the example, .10, .12, .005, $-.006$, and .008, are computed for various stocks based on their history. They are tabulated and are available by subscription from financial service companies.

Example 6.5.6. Mean-variance investment. An agent can invest up to $1,000, distributing her investment between two stocks. Let x_1 denote the dollars she invests in the first stock, and x_2 the dollars in the second.

The mean return on the investment is $.10x_1 + .12x_2$, i.e., the first stock is expected to increase in value at an annual rate of 10% and the second at an annual rate of 12%. However, these rates are not guaranteed since the actual return is a random variable. An estimate of the variance expected for this combination of stocks is

$$.005x_1^2 - .006x_1x_2 + .008x_2^2.$$

For example, if the agent chooses $x_1 = 400$, $x_2 = 600$, then

$$
\begin{aligned}
\text{Expected return} &= (.10)(400) + (.12)(600) = 40 + 72 = \$112 \\
\text{Variance} &= (.005)(400)^2 - (.006)(400)(600) + (.008)(600)^2 \\
&= 800 - 1{,}440 + 2{,}880 = 2{,}240 \\
\text{Standard deviation} &= \sqrt{\text{variance}} = \sqrt{2{,}240} = \$47.33.
\end{aligned}
$$

Thus, with this portfolio the expected return is $112, but the actual return is random and has a standard deviation of $47.33. However, this variance seems an unhealthy risk.

Our agent wishes to choose x_1 and x_2 so as to maximize the mean return on her investment, subject to keeping the standard deviation at or below $25 (or equivalently, keeping the variance at or below 625). To apply the Karush-Kuhn-Tucker theorem, we formulate this problem as a minimization:

$$\text{Minimize}: \quad -.10x_1 - .12x_2$$
$$\text{Subject to}: \quad .005x_1^2 - .006x_1x_2 + .008x_2^2 \le 625 \qquad (1)$$
$$x_1 + x_2 \le 1,000 \qquad (2)$$

The Lagrangian is

$$L = -.10x_1 - .12x_2 - \lambda_1(.005x_1^2 - .006x_1x_2 + .008x_2^2 + s^2 - 625)$$
$$-\lambda_2(x_1 + x_2 + t^2 - 1,000).$$

The Karush-Kuhn-Tucker conditions for a critical point are:

$$\begin{aligned}
L_{x_1} &= -.10x_1 - .01x_1\lambda_1 + .006x_2\lambda_1 - \lambda_2 = 0 \\
L_{x_2} &= -.12x_2 + .006x_1\lambda_1 - .016x_2\lambda_1 - \lambda_2 = 0 \\
L_{\lambda_1} &= -(.005x_1^2 - .006x_1x_2 + .008x_2^2 + s^2 - 625) = 0 \\
L_{\lambda_2} &= -(x_1 + x_2 + t^2 - 1,000) = 0 \\
L_s &= -2s\lambda_1 = 0 \\
L_t &= -2t\lambda_2 = 0.
\end{aligned}$$

To solve this problem, we would divide the analysis into four cases:

Case 1: (1) and (2) are both tight.

Case 2: (1) is tight and (2) is slack.

Case 3: (1) is slack and (2) is tight.

Case 4: (1) and (2) are both slack.

We then look for Karush-Kuhn-Tucker points in each case. The solution comes from the second case. We leave the analysis of Cases 1 and 3 to the exercises, and the solution using LINGO appears in Listing 6.5.2.

Listing 6.5.2

```
: model
? max = .10*x1 + .12*x2;
? .005 *x1^2 - .006*x1*x2 + .008*x2^2 < 625;
? x1 + x2 < 1,000;
? end
```

```
: go

Rows=       3 Vars=      2 No. integer vars=        0
Nonlinear rows= 1 Nonlinear vars= 2 Nonlinear constraints= 1
Nonzeros=       8 Constraint nonz=    4 Density=0.889


Optimal solution found at step:         5
Objective value:               67.20215

    Variable           Value        Reduced Cost
       X1           348.0074        -0.6228539E-05
       X2           270.0117             0.

     Row      Slack or Surplus     Dual Price
      1           67.20215          1.000000
      2         -0.1100443E-07      0.5375998E-01
      3           381.9808               0.
```

Conclusion:

The optimal portfolio is $x_1 = \$348.01$, $x_2 = \$270.01$. This leads to

Expected return $= (.10)(348.01) + (.12)(270.01) = \$67.20$
Variance $= (.005)(348.01)^2 - (.006)(348.01)(270.01) + (.008)(270.01)^2$
$\qquad = 625.00092$
Standard deviation $= \$25.00002$
Dollars invested $= \$348.01 + \$270.01 = \$618.02$.

The agent presumably will put the remaining \$381.98 into a risk-free investment, such as a savings account. ∎

As a final example we add an inequality constraint to Example 6.3.4. Because the objective function involves $\ln x$ and the graph of this function in Figure 6.3.2 indicates that its graph lies below its tangent lines, this is not a convex programming problem. The objective function lies below its tangent plane, so it is actually what Exercise 4 will call a *concave function*. By analogy with Theorem 6.4.1 and Corollary 6.4.2, we expect to have a nonnegative multiplier at the optimal point, an observation which will be helpful in doing Exercise 6.

Example 6.5.7. The father in Example 6.3.4 is disappointed that his first child is only going to get \$500, so he stipulates that this child must receive at least \$750. The problem now is

$$\begin{aligned}\text{Maximize}: \quad & \ln x_1 + 2\ln x_2 + 3\ln x_3 \\ \text{Subject to}: \quad & x_1 + x_2 + x_3 = 3,000 \\ & x_1 \geq 750.\end{aligned}$$

The Lagrangian is

$$\begin{aligned}L \quad = \quad & \ln x_1 + 2\ln x_2 + 3\ln x_3 - \lambda_1(x_1 + x_2 + x_3 - 3,000) \\ & -\lambda_2(-x_1 + s^2 + 750).\end{aligned}$$

A critical point of the Lagrangian must satisfy

$$\begin{aligned}L_{x_1} \quad &= \quad \tfrac{1}{x_1} - \lambda_1 + \lambda_2 = 0 \\ L_{x_2} \quad &= \quad \tfrac{2}{x_2} - \lambda_1 = 0 \\ L_{x_3} \quad &= \quad \tfrac{3}{x_3} - \lambda_1 = 0 \\ L_{\lambda_1} \quad &= \quad -x_1 - x_2 - x_3 + 3,000 = 0 \\ L_{\lambda_2} \quad &= \quad x_1 + s^2 - 750 = 0 \\ L_s \quad &= \quad -2s\lambda_2 = 0.\end{aligned}$$

Case 1: The constraint $x_1 \geq 750$ is tight. Then $s = 0$ and therefore $x_1 = 750$. The equation $L_{\lambda_1} = 0$ becomes:

$$\begin{aligned}750 + \tfrac{2}{\lambda_1} + \tfrac{3}{\lambda_1} \quad &= \quad 3,000 \\ \tfrac{5}{\lambda_1} \quad &= \quad 2,250 \\ \lambda_1 \quad &= \quad \tfrac{1}{450}\end{aligned}$$

Then we obtain x_2 and x_3 as follows:

$$x_2 = \frac{2}{\lambda_1} = 900, \quad x_3 = \frac{3}{\lambda_1} = 1,350.$$

It remains to check the sign of λ_2.

$$\lambda_2 = -\frac{1}{x_1} + \lambda_1 = -\frac{1}{750} + \frac{1}{450} = -\frac{3-5}{2,250} = \frac{2}{2,250}$$

and $\lambda_2 \geq 0$ as required. We have found a critical point

$$x_1 = 750, \quad x_2 = 900, \quad x_3 = 1,350, \quad \lambda_1 = \frac{1}{450}, \quad \lambda_2 = \frac{2}{2,250}.$$

Case 2: The constraint $x_1 \geq 750$ is slack, i.e., $x_1 > 750$. Then $\lambda_2 = 0$, and the multiplier equations become

$$\lambda_1 = \frac{1}{x_1}, \quad \lambda_1 = \frac{2}{x_2}, \quad \lambda_1 = \frac{3}{x_3}.$$

These are the equations we had earlier in Example 6.3.4, and they lead to a solution

$$x_1 = 500, \quad x_2 = 1,000, \quad x_3 = 1,500, \quad \lambda_1 = \frac{1}{500}, \quad \lambda_2 = 0.$$

This is not a feasible solution since $x_1 \leq 750$.

Conclusion: The optimal solution $x_1 = 750$, $x_2 = 900$, $x_3 = 1,350$, and the associated multipliers are

$$\lambda_1 = \frac{1}{450} \approx 0.0022, \quad \lambda_2 = -\frac{2}{2,250} \approx -0.00089.$$

The optimal utility is $\ln 750 + 2 \ln 900 + 3 \ln 1,350 = 41.8484$. ∎

Exercises

1. Determine the equation of the tangent plane to the graph of

   $$f(x_1, x_2, x_3) = 3x_1^2 + 5x_1 x_2 + x_2^2 - 3x_2 x_3 - x_3^2$$

   at the point $(1, 2, -1, 22)$.

2. Prove Proposition 6.5.2.

3. Prove that a linear combination of convex functions in which the cofficients are nonnegative is convex.

4. **Concave functions.** Proceeding in a fashion analogous to that for convex functions, define concave function and prove that a global maximum of a concave function occurs at any critical point.

5. **Convex sets.** Define a *convex function* f to be one satisfying

   $$f(tx + (1-t)y) < tf(x) + (1-t)f(y)$$

for $0 \le t \le 1$ and any x and y in the domain of f contained in R^n. In this direct generalization of the definition given in Section 5.3, only the nature of the expression $tx + (1-t)y$ is changed, since it is now a convex combination of elements of R^n. A *convex set* S is a subset of R^n satisfying $tx + (1-t)y \in S$ for $0 \le t \le 1$ and any x and y in S.

(a) If f is a convex function and b a constant, show that $S = \{x : f(x) \le b\}$ is a convex set.

(b) Show that the intersection of convex sets is a convex set.

Thus, the set of feasible points in a convex program such as (CXP) is a convex set.

6. **Concave programming.** A *concave program* is a problem of the form

$$(\text{CCP}) \quad \begin{aligned} \text{Maximize}: &\quad f(x) \\ \text{Subject to}: &\quad g^1(x) \le 0, \ldots, g^m(x) \le 0 \end{aligned}$$

where f is concave and each g^i is convex. State and prove the theorem for the solution to a concave program analogous to Theorem 6.5.3.

7. Solve the following convex programming problem:

$$\begin{aligned} \text{Minimize}: &\quad (x_1 - 1) + x_2^2 \\ \text{Subject to}: &\quad x_1 + x_2 \le 2 \\ &\quad x_1 - 4 \le 0. \end{aligned}$$

8. Solve the following mathematical program after expressing it as a convex program:

$$\begin{aligned} \text{Maximize}: &\quad 4x_1 + x_2 + x_1^2 + 6x_1x_2 \\ \text{Subject to}: &\quad 2x_1 \;+\; x_2 \;\ge\; 6 \\ &\quad \;\;\; x_1 \;+\; 2x_2 \;\le\; 12 \\ &\quad \qquad\qquad x_2 \;\ge\; 0. \end{aligned}$$

9. Solve the following concave programming problem:

$$\begin{aligned} \text{Maximize}: &\quad 12x_1 + 24x_2 - x_1^2 - 3x_1x_2 - 4x_2^2 \\ \text{Subject to}: &\quad 2x_1 \;+\; x_2 \;\le\; 12 \\ &\quad -x_1 \;+\; x_2 \;\le\; 3. \end{aligned}$$

10. Solve the following mathematical programming problem:

$$\begin{aligned} \text{Maximize}: &\quad 20 - x_1^2 - 2x_1x_2 - 3x_2^2 \\ \text{Subject to}: &\quad x_1 \;+\; x_2 \;\ge\; 10 \\ &\quad 2x_1 \;-\; x_2 \;\le\; 2. \end{aligned}$$

11. By using the fact that λ_1 is zero, show that Case 3 in the solution of Example 6.5.6 leads to a contradiction – in particular, to two distinct values of λ_2 – and therefore that this case does not lead to a solution.

12. By using equality in the second constraint to eliminate x_1, show that Case 1 in the solution of Example 6.5.6 leads to a calculation for value for x_2 involving the square root of a negative number, and therefore that this case does not lead to a solution.

13. Example 6.5.6 explored determining the maximum return within acceptable risk. Here we essentially reverse the situation. Given the estimate of the variance from Example 6.5.6 on two investments of 10% and 12%, determine the allocation of $1,000 between the two investments that would yield an 11% return while minimizing the variance.

14. Consider a possible portfolio of three securities earning 12%, 8%, and 9% and having their variance given by the matrix product xAx^T where

$$
A = \begin{bmatrix}
.004 & .001 & -.002 \\
.001 & .002 & -.001 \\
-.002 & -.001 & .003
\end{bmatrix}.
$$

   (a) Determine the maximum return of an investment of $10,000 in a combination of these three securities subject to a maximum variance of 40,000.

   (b) Determine an allocation of $10,000 dollars among the three securities to earn a return of 9.5% while minimizing risk.

15. A company specializing in selling prefab storage buildings finds itself with an over supply of 8 foot pieces of lumber on hand and decides to use the supply to produce prefab houses for large dogs. To be certain that they can use the available lumber, they will require that the length plus the width of the doghouse be at most 8 feet. They will put a door – actually just an opening – measuring 2.5 feet high by 1.5 feet wide in one end. To allow a large dog to move about, the doghouse will be at least 2.75 feet wide and 3.5 feet long with walls at least 3 feet high. The roof will slope at a 45° angle, and will have a waterproof covering in addition to the wood. Finally, to allow adequate air circulation, the total volume is to be at least 35 cubic feet.

   If the lumber costs $0.20 per square foot and the water proof covering for the roof costs $0.10 per square foot, what should the dimensions of the doghouse be in order to minimize the material costs?

6.6 Linear programming revisited

Since linear functions are both convex and concave, the Karush-Kuhn-Tucker theorem can be applied to a linear program. In this section we work through a linear progam using this theorem. We will see that many of the ideas considered earlier in Chapter 3 can be revealed again.

For this illustration we return to Farmer Brown's problem:

$$
\begin{array}{llrcrcr}
\text{Maximize}: & 40x_1 & + & 120x_2 & & \\
\text{Subject to}: & x_1 & + & x_2 & \leq & 100 \\
 & x_1 & + & 4x_2 & \leq & 160 \\
 & 10x_1 & + & 20x_2 & \leq & 1,100 \\
 & \multicolumn{6}{c}{x_1 \geq 0, \; x_2 \geq 0.}
\end{array}
$$

Recall that x_1 and x_2 represent the numbers of acres of potatoes and wheat, respectively, and that the constraints are the resource limits on acres, days of labor, and capital, respectively.

When we move the resources to the left-hand side and form the Lagrangian, we obtain

$$
\begin{aligned}
L = \;& 40x_1 + 120x_2 - \lambda_1(x_1 + x_2 - 100 + s_1^2) \\
& - \lambda_2(x_1 + 4x_2 - 160 + s_2^2) - \lambda_3(10x_1 + 20x_2 - 1,100 + s_3^2) \\
& - \lambda_4(-x_1 + s_4^2) - \lambda_5(-x_2 + s_5^2).
\end{aligned}
$$

The conditions for a critical point of L are given below. All but the first two equations have been rewritten so that they will appear in a more familiar form.

$$
\begin{aligned}
L_{x_1} &= & 40 - \lambda_1 - \lambda_2 - 10\lambda_3 + \lambda_4 &= 0 \\
L_{x_2} &= & 120 - \lambda_1 - 4\lambda_2 - 20\lambda_3 + \lambda_5 &= 0 \\
L_{\lambda_1} &= & 0: \quad x_1 + x_2 + s_1^2 &= 100 \\
L_{\lambda_2} &= & 0: \quad x_1 + 4x_2 + s_2^2 &= 160 \\
L_{\lambda_3} &= & 0: 10x_1 + 20x_2 + s_3^2 &= 1,100 \\
L_{\lambda_4} &= & 0: -x_1 + s_4^2 &= 0 \\
L_{\lambda_5} &= & 0: - x_2 + s_5^2 &= 0 \\
L_{s_i} &= & -2s_i\lambda_i = 0, \; i = 1,2,\ldots,5.
\end{aligned}
$$

Now, by manipulating the equations $L_{x_j} = 0$ and the Lagrangian L, we can identify the dual of Farmer Brown's problem with the λ_i's as the variables. We can also verify that for an optimal solution $(\hat{x}, \hat{\lambda}, \hat{s})$ the objective function values of the linear program and its dual are equal. Finally, by differentiating L with respect to the right-hand side entries, we will see that the optimal values of the λ_i's are the shadow prices.

- Rewriting the equations $L_{x_j} = 0$, $j = 1, 2$, we obtain the dual constraints of Farmer Brown's problem with surplus variables, λ_4 and λ_5, included:

$$
\begin{aligned}
\lambda_1 + \lambda_2 + 10\lambda_3 - \lambda_4 &= 40 \\
\lambda_1 + 4\lambda_2 + 20\lambda_3 \qquad - \lambda_5 &= 120 \\
\lambda_i \geq 0, \ i = 1, 2, \ldots, 5.
\end{aligned}
$$

The nonnegativity of the λ_i's follows from the Karush-Kuhn-Tucker theorem, since this is a maximization problem with a concave objective function and the Lagrange multipliers are required to be nonnegative.

- Rewriting the Lagrangian reveals the objective function of the dual linear program:

$$
\begin{aligned}
L = \ &100\lambda_1 + 160\lambda_2 + 1,100\lambda_3 \\
&-x_1(\lambda_1 + \lambda_2 + 10\lambda_3 - \lambda_4 - 40) \\
&\quad -x_2(\lambda_1 + 4\lambda_2 + 20\lambda_3 - \lambda_5 - 120) \\
&\qquad -\lambda_1 s_1^2 - \lambda_2 s_2^2 - \lambda_3 s_3^2 - \lambda_4 s_4^2 - \lambda_5 s_5^2.
\end{aligned}
$$

For any feasible solution, all but the first three terms are zero – the parenthetical expressions are dual constraints with surplus variables included and thus must be zero, and the remaining terms must vanish by complementary slackness.

- Recall that all but the first three terms of the original expression for L vanish for a feasible solution. Then comparing the original expression for L with the one immediately above, we see that the optimal values of the primal and dual problems are equal:

$$
40\hat{x}_1 + 120\hat{x}_2 = 100\hat{\lambda}_1 + 160\hat{\lambda}_2 + 1,100\hat{\lambda}_3.
$$

Note that this equality reestablishes a central result of duality theory from Section 3.7.

- Suppose we consider the resources $b_1 = 100$, $b_2 = 160$, and $b_3 = 1,100$ as variables and differentiate the Lagrangian with respect to them. Note that

$$\frac{\partial L}{\partial b_i} = \lambda_i, \quad i = 1, 2, 3.$$

Since at a feasible point the objective function and the Lagrangian assume the same value, this demonstrates that the rate of change of the objective function with respect to the resource in a constraint is the corresponding dual variable. This confirms the use of the values of the dual variable in sensitivity analysis, as discussed in Example 3.7.8 and Section 3.8.

Thus, we see that the properties of linear programs investigated earlier fit into the more general context of convex or concave mathematical programs.

Exercises

1. Solve the following linear program by the Karush-Kuhn-Tucker theorem:

$$
\begin{array}{rrrcl}
\text{Maximize}: & 10x_1 & + & 12x_2 & \\
\text{Subject to}: & x_1 & + & x_2 & \leq & 150 \\
& x_1 & + & 2x_2 & \leq & 100 \\
& 8x_1 & + & 4x_2 & \leq & 320 \\
& \multicolumn{5}{c}{x_1 \geq 0, \ x_2 \geq 0.}
\end{array}
$$

2. Solve the following linear program by the Karush-Kuhn-Tucker theorem:

$$
\begin{array}{rrrcl}
\text{Minimize}: & 2y_1 & + & 8y_2 & \\
\text{Subject to}: & 3y_1 & + & 4y_2 & \geq & 15 \\
& 2y_1 & + & 5y_2 & \geq & 24 \\
& y_1 & + & 10y_2 & \geq & 27 \\
& \multicolumn{5}{c}{y_1 \geq 0, \ y_2 \geq 0.}
\end{array}
$$

3. Consider the transportation problem

$$\text{Minimize}: \quad \sum_{i=1}^{m} \sum_{j=1}^{n} c_{ij} x_{ij}$$

$$\text{Subject to}: \quad \sum_{j=1}^{n} x_{ij} = a_i, \quad i = 1, 2, \ldots, m$$

$$\sum_{i=1}^{m} x_{ij} = b_j, \quad j = 1, 2, \ldots, n$$

$$x_{ij} \geq 0.$$

If we choose the Lagrange multipliers to match the notation used in Section 4.2, the associated Lagrangian is

$$L = \sum_{i=1}^{m}\sum_{j=1}^{n} c_{ij}x_{ij} - \sum_{i=1}^{m} v_i(\sum_{j=1}^{n} x_{ij} - a_i) - \sum_{j=1}^{n} w_j(\sum_{i=1}^{m} x_{ij} - b_j).$$

Show that the dual constraints can be expressed as the nonnegativity of the partial derivatives with respect to the x_{ij}.

6.7 Summary and objectives

In this chapter we have considered constrained extrema problems in which the functions need not be linear. We considered four applications: maximizing the utility in a pattern of consumption, minimizing equipment replacement costs, maximizing investment return subject to variability restrictions, and building boxes economically from the available cardboard stock.

The solution to a general problem required the use of a matrix, called a bordered Hessian, to confirm the existence of extrema.

Example 6.4.3 is perhaps the best example in the section to illustrate the use of Lagrange multipliers and complementary slackness in the solution of a general mathematical programming problem. We also solved this problem using LINGO to illustrate the use of a computer package to solve a nonlinear optimization problem.

As in the case of unconstrained extrema in the previous chapter, we found that restricting the objective function and the constraints to be convex or concave functions eased the solution process. The most important result was the Karush-Kuhn-Tucker theorem for a convex programming problem. The corresponding theorem for a concave problem can be found in Appendix D as a partial solution to Exercise 6 of Section 6.5.

In the final section we considered linear programs from the standpoint of convex or concave programming. In the course of that investigation, we found that we could reconstruct many of the results of linear programming from Chapter 3.

Objectives

Be able to:

1. Determine the gradient of a function of several variables. Example 6.1.4. Exercise 4 of Section 6.1.

2. Draw level curves of a function of two variables. Exercise 5 of Section 6.1.

3. Solve a nonlinear mathematical program in two or three variables. Examples 6.3.4 and 6.4.3. Exercise 3 of Section 6.3 and Exercise 2 of Section 6.4.

4. Be able to use LINGO or *Maple* to aid in the solution of nonlinear mathematical programs. Example 6.5.6. Listings 6.4.1 and 6.5.2.

5. Take advantage of convexity and/or concavity in a mathematical program by applying the Karush-Kuhn-Tucker theorem. Example 6.5.4. Exercise 6.5.7.

6. Recognize the parallels between linear programming and the Karush-Kuhn-Tucker theorem. Section 6.6.

Chapter 7

Integer Programming

7.1   Introduction

An *integer program* is one in which the variables are constrained to assume only integer values. We will see that the use of integer variables greatly expands the range of problems that we can solve. Often the variables that prove most useful are restricted to the values 0 or 1. It is frequently useful to mix variables constrained to be integers with other variables in programs called *mixed-integer programs*.

Many of the problems that we have considered have had integer values in their solutions. In some cases, such as Farmer Brown's problem, this was planned by careful design of the constraints in advance. In others, like the transportation problem, the nature of the constraints guarantees integer solutions if the supplies and demands are integers.

In this chapter we consider problems where integer restrictions on the variables arise naturally in the problem and the solution process must be designed to produce integer solutions.

We begin with an example that shows that one cannot simply take a noninteger solution and round the values to integers.

Example 7.1.1. Rounding is not adequate. Consider the following integer program:

$$
\begin{aligned}
\text{Maximize}: \quad & 3x_1 \;+\; 13x_2 \\
\text{Subject to}: \quad & 2x_1 \;+\; 9x_2 \;\leq\; 40 \\
& 11x_1 \;-\; 8x_2 \;\leq\; 82 \\
& x_1 \text{ and } x_2 \text{ nonnegative integers}
\end{aligned}
$$

We first solve the problem ignoring the integer constraints. The resulting problem is called the *continuous relaxation* of the integer program. Here we quickly obtain the solution $x_1 = 9.2$ and $x_2 = 2.4$ which yields an objective function value of 58.8.

The set of feasible solutions is shown in Figure 7.1.1.

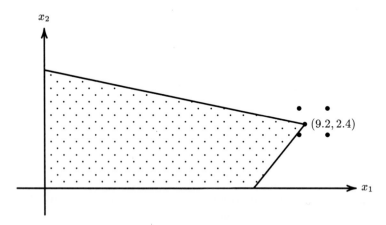

Figure 7.1.1

Note the four points closest – indicated by dots – to the continuous solution having both components integers. It can easily be seen that none of them is a feasible solution to the original problem. Thus, the integer solution cannot be obtained from the continuous one by rounding.

Now we use LINDO to solve the given problem. In the LINDO output below, the line `GIN 2` indicates that the two variables are restricted to be nonnegative integers.

Listing 7.1.1

```
MAX       3 X1 + 13 X2
SUBJECT TO
      2)    2 X1 + 9 X2 <=    40
      3)   11 X1 - 8 X2 <=    82
END
GIN      2


LP OPTIMUM FOUND AT STEP       6
OBJECTIVE VALUE =    58.7999992

NEW INTEGER SOLUTION OF    58.000000    AT BRANCH       0 PIVOT      8
```

```
            OBJECTIVE FUNCTION VALUE

      1)     58.000000

   VARIABLE        VALUE        REDUCED COST
      X1         2.000000         0.000000
      X2         4.000000         0.000000


     ROW    SLACK OR SURPLUS     DUAL PRICES
      2)         0.000000         1.000000
      3)        92.000000         0.000000
      4)         0.000000         1.000000


NO. ITERATIONS=       8
BRANCHES=     0 DETERM.=  1.000E    0
BOUND ON OPTIMUM:  58.00000
ENUMERATION COMPLETE. BRANCHES=       0 PIVOTS=        8


LAST INTEGER SOLUTION IS THE BEST FOUND
RE-INSTALLING BEST SOLUTION...
```

Clearly, the integer solution of $x_1 = 2$ and $x_2 = 4$ is not one that can be obtained from the continuous solution $x_1 = 9.2$ and $x_2 = 2.4$ by rounding. ∎

The references in the output to "branches" and "bounds" are indications of the procedure that LINDO uses to solve integer programs. Our strategy to developing the solution process suggested by LINDO is to first consider a special problem, the knapsack problem, in which the "branch-and-bound" solution process is clearly motivated by the constraints. We will then devote three sections to developing a branch-and-bound process that can be applied to any linear program with integer constraints.

The reader interested only in the applications of integer programming might want to skip ahead to Section 7.6 after the section on the knapsack problem. In Section 7.6 we will consider specific applications that require integer variables with an emphasis on formulating the integer programs. There we will rely on LINDO or an equivalent package to solve the problems.

Then in Section 7.7 we consider another branch-and-bound algorithm for the traveling salesman problem.

7.2   The knapsack problem

In this section we consider a mathematical programming problem with a structure leading to a natural introduction to the branch-and-bound approach referred to in the introduction. The general form of the *knapsack problem* involving a choice of n items is given below:

$$\text{(KP)} \quad \text{Maximize}: \quad v_1 x_1 + v_2 x_2 + \cdots + v_n x_n$$
$$\text{Subject to}: \quad w_1 x_1 + w_2 x_2 + \cdots + w_n x_n \leq W$$
$$x_j \in \{0, 1\}, \ j = 1, 2, \ldots, n.$$

The motivation for the name of the problem is planning for a hiking trip in which there is a limit to the weight that can be carried as well as a desire to take the most useful set of items. The v_j's are the *values* of the corresponding items, and the w_j's are their *weights* or *costs*. In the suggested setting of packing a knapsack, the value of an item is its estimated utility, and the cost is its weight, hence the use of the w_j's in the problem. The W in the right-hand side of the constraint represents the total weight that can be carried, or the total budget for a problem involving finances. The restriction of the value of x_j to zero or one indicates the use of x_j to reflect a decision: $x_j = 1$ means that item j is put into the knapsack; $x_j = 0$ means that it is not included.

The number of solutions to a knapsack problem increases rapidly with the number of items. Since a solution is determined by the subset of the n items that is included in the knapsack, the number of solutions – not necessarily all feasible – is 2^n, the number of subsets of an n-element set.

Hence, a problem with five items has $2^5 = 32$ possible solutions, while a problem with ten items has $2^{10} = 1,024$ possible solutions. An effective algorithm for the knapsack problem should obtain the optimal solution by examining only a small fraction of these solutions.

To introduce what we mean by a branch-and-bound algorithm, consider the graph in Figure 7.2.1.

In the tree associated with the solution of a problem by a branch-and-bound process, each node will correspond to a feasible solution, or partial solution, to the problem. A node in a tree is called a *terminal node* if only one edge is incident on the node. The edges indicate a relationship in which a choice between two alternatives has been made leading to two nodes closer to a complete solution. The process will begin at the node labeled R, for the *root* of the tree. We then devise a way to choose between alternatives, and a way to calculate a bound for the maximum (or minimum) value of all solutions further out on the tree. The process will end when a solution has been reached at a terminal node and the bounds indicate that all other solutions are less desirable.

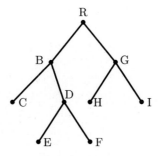

Figure 7.2.1

We will develop the solution process in the context of an example involving real estate.

Example 7.2.1. A real estate development firm is considering five projects for which it can raise an estimated \$100 million in capital. For each project, the firm's analysts have produced an estimate of the return of the project over the next 20 years. The estimated returns and project costs in millions of dollars are shown in Table 7.2.1.

Table 7.2.1

Project	Cost	Return
1	45	90
2	28	60
3	32	56
4	18	42
5	24	60

Before describing the algorithm to be used for the knapsack problem, we first consider what is necessary to define such an algorithm. Four things are needed in the description of a branch-and-bound algorithm:

- The order in which to consider the branches,

- The rule that terminates the search for the solution,

- The decision which forms the basis for a branch, and

- The formula for the calculation of the bound at each node of the search tree.

In our algorithm for the knapsack problem:

- The items will be considered in decreasing order by their *desirability*, i.e., the ratio of their value to their cost,

- The algorithm will terminate when all items have either been selected or eliminated to form a complete solution, and any other selection has been shown to have a value that is not greater,

- A branch will be determined by the decision to include or not include an item, and

- The bound will be the sum of the values of the items selected plus a high estimate of the value of those items that might still be selected.

Branch-and-bound algorithm for the knapsack problem

We first restate the problem and establish the notation for the algorithm:

$$
\begin{array}{ll}
\text{(KP)} \quad \text{Maximize}: & v_1 x_1 + v_2 x_2 + \cdots + v_n x_n \\
\text{Subject to}: & w_1 x_1 + w_2 x_2 + \cdots + w_n x_n \leq W \\
& x_j \in \{0,1\}, \; j = 1, 2, \ldots, n.
\end{array}
$$

In the statement of the algorithm, we will let S denote the set of all n items, B_i be the bound at node i, I_i be the set of items included at node i, E_i be the set of items excluded at node i, and n be the current number of nodes. The empty set is denoted by $\emptyset$.

We want the bound at a node corresponding to an infeasible solution to be an arbitrarily large negative number to be certain that any other bound is greater. For this purpose we use a convention called the "Big M." Here M denotes a positive number with the property that $M - a$ is positive no matter how large a may be. In this instance, since we want to express a large negative number, we will set the bound equal to $-M$. This same convention will be used in later branch-and-bound algorithms.

1. **Check feasibility:**

(a) Check that j exists such that $w_j \leq W$. If not, there is **no feasible solution** and the algorithm terminates.

(b) If $\displaystyle\sum_{j=1}^{n} w_j \leq W$, then all items can be loaded, and the problem is **trivially solved** by putting $I_1 = S$ and $E_1 = \emptyset$.

(c) If the algorithm did not terminate at (a) or (b), **sort** the items into decreasing order of desirability $\dfrac{v_i}{w_i}$.

(d) Establish **initial node:** Set $n = 1$ and for node n set $B_n = 0$, $I_n = \emptyset$, and $E_n = \emptyset$.

(e) Go to Step 2.

2. **Select the node for the next branch:**

(a) Select the terminal node k with B_k the largest existing bound for the next branching decision.

(b) If $I_k \cup E_k = S$, then an **optimal solution** is given by the items in I_k, so **stop**. Otherwise, form the next branch on the remaining item with index i' having the **largest desirability**

$$\frac{v_{i'}}{w_{i'}} = \max\left\{\frac{v_j}{w_j} : j \notin I_k \cup E_k\right\}.$$

(c) Go to Step 3.

3. **Form the next two nodes:**

(a) Set $n = n+1$, and index the **new left node** by n, and set $I_n = I_k$ and $E_n = E_k \cup \{i'\}$ to **exclude** item i'.

(b) Set $n = n + 1$, and index the **new right node** by n, and set $I_n = I_k \cup \{i'\}$ and $E_n = E_k$ to **include** item i'.

4. **Calculate the upper bounds of the new nodes:**

(a) If $\sum\{w_j : j \in I_k\} > W$, then the node corresponds to an **infeasible solution**, so set $B_k = -M$.

If $W - \sum\{w_j : j \in I_k\} < w_j$ for all $j \notin I_k \cup E_k$, then set $B_k = \sum\{v_j : j \in I_k\}$.

Otherwise, let B_k be $\sum\{v_j : j \in I_k\}$ plus the sum of the values v_j of all items in $S \backslash (I_k \cup E_k)$, taking them in order of decreasing desirability until the next item to be added would make the total of the weights greater than W. Add to B_k the proportional part of the next item considered if a fractional part of it can be included.

(b) When (a) has been applied for both new nodes, go to Step 2.

We now solve Example 7.2.1. Since there is at least one project that can be done within the budget, the problem has a feasible solution. Since the total of all the costs is more than the budget, there is no trivial solution.

We therefore sort the projects in decreasing order by desirability:

Table 7.2.2

Project	Cost	Return	Desirability
5	24	60	2.50
4	18	42	2.33
2	28	60	2.14
1	45	90	2.00
3	32	56	1.75

Because project 5 has the greatest desirability, we select it for the first branch. In the new left node, Node 2, we exclude project 5. We can include in the bound the costs of projects 4, 2, and 1 since the total of their costs is 91. When a fractional part of the return on project 3 is included to bring the total cost to 100, the bound is

$$B_2 = 42 + 60 + 90 + \frac{9}{32} \cdot 56 = 207.75.$$

In the new right node, Node 3, we include project 5. Since the total of the costs of projects 5, 4, and 2 is 70, we can include the total of their returns in the bound plus a proportional part of the return for project 1:

$$B_3 = 60 + 42 + 60 + \frac{30}{45} \cdot 90 = 222.$$

Note in the initial tree, shown in Figure 7.2.2, that we use an * to indicate an excluded project.

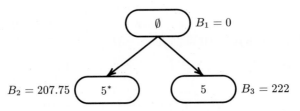

Figure 7.2.2

Since Node 3 is the terminal node with the highest bound, we branch from it to form the new nodes. We branch on the decision to include project 4 since it has the highest desirability of the nodes remaining to consider.

For the left node, Node 4, we exclude project 4. The sum of the costs of projects 5, 2, and 1 is 97, so the bound is:

$$B_4 = 60 + 60 + 90 + \frac{3}{32} \cdot 56 = 215.25.$$

The new right node includes project 4, and since the weights of projects 5, 4, and 2 sum to 70, the bound for Node 5 is:

$$B_5 = 60 + 42 + 60 + \frac{30}{45} \cdot 56 = 222.$$

Now branching from Node 5 with the decision based on project 2, we calculate the bounds as follows:

$$\begin{aligned} B_6 &= 60 + 42 + 90 + \frac{13}{32} \cdot 56 = 214.75 \\ B_7 &= 60 + 42 + 60 = 162. \end{aligned}$$

Note that the calculation of B_7 used the second alternative for bound calculation since the sum of the costs of the projects included, projects 2, 4 and 5, is 70 and no other project could be included since the smallest remaining one has a cost of 32.

The resulting tree is shown in Figure 7.2.3.

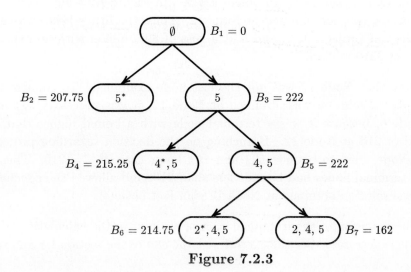

Figure 7.2.3

The largest bound on a terminal node is $B_4 = 215.25$. Since not all projects are included or excluded at Node 4, we have not reached a solution, but must continue branching from that node. We branch on the decision to include or exclude project 2, and continue with the calculations summarized below to achieve the final search tree:

$$
\begin{aligned}
I_8 &= \{5\}, & E_8 &= \{2, 4\}, & B_8 &= 60 + 90 + \tfrac{31}{32} \cdot 56 = 204.25 \\
I_9 &= \{2, 5\}, & E_9 &= \{4\}, & B_9 &= 60 + 60 + 90 + \tfrac{3}{32} \cdot 56 = 215.25 \\
I_{10} &= \{2, 5\}, & E_{10} &= \{1, 4\}, & B_{10} &= 60 + 60 + 56 = 176 \\
I_{11} &= \{1, 2, 5\}, & E_{11} &= \{4\}, & B_{11} &= 60 + 60 + 90 = 210 \\
I_{12} &= \{1, 2, 5\}, & E_{12} &= \{3, 4\}, & B_{12} &= 60 + 60 + 90 = 210 \\
I_{13} &= \{1, 2, 3, 5\}, & E_{13} &= \{4\}, & B_{13} &= -M \\
I_{14} &= \{4, 5\}, & E_{14} &= \{1, 2\}, & B_{14} &= 60 + 42 + 56 = 158 \\
I_{15} &= \{1, 4, 5\}, & E_{15} &= \{2\}, & B_{15} &= 90 + 42 + 60 = 192
\end{aligned}
$$

Note that for Node 13, projects 1, 2, 3, and 5 are included with a total cost of 132, more than the maximum of 100. Thus, it represents an infeasible solution, so $B_{13} = -M$.

The final graph for the problem is given in Figure 7.2.4 and shows that the optimal solution is found at Node 12. Thus, the firm's best strategy is to carry out projects 1, 2, and 5 at a cost of \$97 million with an expected return of \$210 million.

Note that Node 12 was not the last node examined. To confirm that the optimal solution was obtained at Node 12, it was necessary to return to Node 6, because it was a terminal node with a bound higher than the bound of 210 at Node 12. Branching on the decision regarding project 1 from Node 6 led to bounds B_{14} and B_{15} lower than $B_{12} = 210$. Then all other terminal nodes had bounds less than 210, and allowed the conclusion that the solution obtained at Node 12 is in fact optimal.

The inclusion of the fractional part of an item in the calculation of the bounds is necessary. See the exercises at the end of the section for an example.

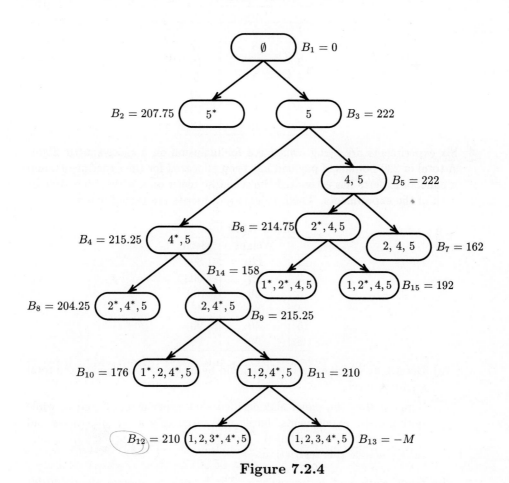

Figure 7.2.4

Exercises

1. Solve the knapsack problem if the maximum possible total weight is 40:

Table 7.2.3

	Weight	Value
1	15	20
2	12	24
3	9	15
4	8	14

2. If a budget is $45 and the possible purchases are tabled below, determine which to purchase:

Table 7.2.4

	Cost	Value
1	5	8 1,6
2	8	12 1,5
3	12	15 1,25
4	4	5 1,25
5	7	10 1,43
6	9	12 1,33
7	10	13 1,3

(3.) Six experiments are being considered for inclusion on a space-shuttle flight. A total of 220 pounds of payload has been allocated for the experiments, and a panel of experts has estimated the scientific merit on a scale of 0 to 100 for each of the experiments. Their weights and merits are tabled below:

Table 7.2.5

	Weight	Merit
1	120	80
2	70	60
3	50	100
4	85	40
5	40	90
6	90	70

(a) Determine which experiments should be included to maximize the total scientific merit.

(b) Suppose that the panel also decided that experiments 3 and 5, while both worthy experiments, have substantial overlap in objectives and should not both be included. Modify your solution process from part (a) to include this restriction.

4. **The fractional part is necessary.** The branch-and-bound algorithm for the knapsack problem involves including a fractional part of an item in the calculation of certain of the bounds. If this fractional part is never included, a nonoptimal solution may be identified as the solution. Show that in this example omitting the fractional part in the bound calculations leads to a nonoptimal solution. The maximum total weight is 41 pounds.

Table 7.2.6

Item	Weight	Value
A	11	8
B	18	10
C	4	4
D	9	6
E	8	4

5. James Lowtax is self-employed and operates a small business. True to his name he tries each year to minimize his taxes. This year he has identified five tax strategies that he could employ to reduce his taxes. Using them all would require that he have $16,650 of planning money available. He has only $10,200 available. Which combination of the five strategies should he employ to maximize his tax reduction?

Table 7.2.7

	Tax strategy	Cost	Tax reduction
1.	Start a Keough retirement plan	$7,500	$2,475
2.	Buy needed office equipment	$5,000	$2,700
3.	Take clients to the theatre	$650	$320
4.	Upgrade rental property	$2,000	$400
5.	Make contribution to church	$1,500	$495
		$16,650	

This problem is based on [13].

6. A small college has a budget of $150,000 for physical plant improvements over the summer. The possible projects have been rated according to their value. Which should they do to maximize the total value within their budget?

Table 7.2.8

Project	Cost	Value
1	$30,000	8
2	$45,000	9
3	$60,000	10
4	$40,000	7
5	$50,000	8

(handwritten annotations beside table:
2.6×10^{-4}
2×10^{-4}
1.67×10^{-4}
1.75×10^{-4}
1.6×10^{-4})

7.3   The Dual Simplex Algorithm

Our general approach to solving integer programs will be to first solve the continuous relaxation as we did in the introductory example and then to reimpose the integer constraints. The decisions made regarding which constraints to reimpose will form the basis for the branching process. This section and the next one develop the necessary ideas. The algorithm developed in this section will also allow us to reexamine some linear programs considered earlier.

Section 3.7 developed a method to solve minimizing linear programs by duality theory. Here, we develop an alternative approach that allows direct solution of a standard minimization problem in which all objective function coefficients are nonnegative. This algorithm is valuable not so much to solve such problems, but because of its usefulness in examining the effect of changes in a linear program after it has been solved.

Making changes in a linear program after it has been solved, for instance by changing the right-hand side of a constraint beyond the bounds provided by sensitivity analysis or by adding a constraint, often destroys the optimality of the final tableau. Determining the new solution then involves restoring the tableau to an optimal state. The dual simplex method facilitates the process of reoptimization.

At the end of this section we will see an example of the use of the dual simplex algorithm to analyze changes in the right-hand side. In the next section we consider the addition of a constraint.

The Dual Simplex Algorithm

Given a standard minimizing linear program with no negative coefficients in the objective function, prepare the problem for the dual simplex algorithm by:

- Inserting surplus variables to make the constraints equalities,

- Rephrasing the problem as a maximization by taking the negative of the objective function,

- Multiplying the constraints by -1 so that the surplus variables are isolated variables, and

- Setting up the initial simplex tableau.

Note that setting the surplus variables equal to the right-hand sides of the constraints produces a basic solution in which the variables have nonpositive values. However, the objective row has all nonnegative values. The dual simplex algorithm seeks to reach an optimal solution by making the values of the variables nonnegative. We will see that until an optimal solution is reached, all basic solutions generated by the algorithm will be infeasible because they violate nonnegativity.

Having prepared the problem, determine the solution by the following algorithm:

1. If a basic solution has all nonnegative values, the solution is **optimal**. Stop.

2. The **row of the pivot** is the row corresponding to the most negative right-hand-side value. The corresponding basic variable leaves the basis.

3. If all other entries in the selected row are nonnegative, there is **no feasible solution**. Stop.

4. The **column of the pivot** is the column producing the maximum negative quotient of the objective row entry over the pivot row entry. The corresponding variable enters the basis.

5. **Pivot** by applying Gauss-Jordan elimination and go to Step 1.

Example 7.3.1. Solve the following problem by the dual simplex algorithm:

$$
\begin{aligned}
\text{Minimize}: \quad & 5y_1 + 4y_2 \\
\text{Subject to}: \quad & y_1 + 2y_2 \geq 12 \\
& 5y_1 + y_2 \geq 31 \\
& 3y_1 + y_2 \geq 21 \\
& y_1 \geq 0, \ y_2 \geq 0
\end{aligned}
$$

With surplus variables s_1, s_2, and s_3 inserted, the constraints multiplied by -1, and the problem rephrased as a maximization, the problem becomes:

$$
\begin{aligned}
\text{Maximize}: \quad & -5y_1 - 4y_2 \\
\text{Subject to}: \quad & -y_1 - 2y_2 + s_1 = -12 \\
& -5y_1 - y_2 + s_2 = -31 \\
& -3y_1 - y_2 + s_3 = -21 \\
& y_1 \geq 0, \ y_2 \geq 0, \ s_1 \geq 0, \ s_2 \geq 0, \ s_3 \geq 0
\end{aligned}
$$

When this revised statement of the problem is placed into the simplex tableau, we have:

y_1	y_2	s_1	s_2	s_3	
-1	-2	1	0	0	-12
-5	-1	0	1	0	-31
-3	-1	0	0	1	-21
5	4	0	0	0	0

Since the entries in the right-hand side are negative, Step 1 indicates that the solution is not optimal. The -31 entry is the most negative, so using Step 2, we pivot in the second row. Examining the negative quotients formed from objective row entries over pivot row entries,

$$\max\left\{-\frac{5}{5}, -\frac{4}{1}\right\} = -1$$

so we pivot in the first column according to Step 4.

y_1	y_2	s_1	s_2	s_3	
0	$-\frac{9}{5}$	1	$-\frac{1}{5}$	0	$-\frac{29}{5}$
1	$\frac{1}{5}$	0	$-\frac{1}{5}$	0	$\frac{31}{5}$
0	$-\frac{2}{5}$	0	$-\frac{3}{5}$	1	$-\frac{12}{5}$
0	3	0	1	0	-31

The $-\frac{29}{5}$ entry is the most negative in the right-hand side, so we pivot in the first row. Examining the negative quotients of objective row entries over the pivot row entries according to Step 4, we get

$$\max\left\{-3/\frac{9}{5}, -1/\frac{1}{5}\right\} = -\frac{5}{3}$$

so we pivot in the y_2 column.

y_1	y_2	s_1	s_2	s_3	
0	1	$-\frac{5}{9}$	$\frac{1}{9}$	0	$\frac{29}{9}$
1	0	$\frac{1}{9}$	$-\frac{2}{9}$	0	$\frac{50}{9}$
0	0	$-\frac{2}{9}$	$-\frac{5}{9}$	1	$-\frac{10}{9}$
0	0	$\frac{15}{9}$	$\frac{2}{3}$	0	$-\frac{122}{3}$

The $-\frac{10}{9}$ entry is the most negative, so we pivot in the third row. Examining the negative quotients of objective row entries over the pivot row entries yields

$$\max\left\{-\frac{15}{9}/\frac{2}{9}, -\frac{2}{3}/\frac{5}{9}\right\} = -\frac{6}{5}$$

so we pivot in the s_2 column.

y_1	y_2	s_1	s_2	s_3	
0	1	$-\frac{3}{5}$	0	$\frac{1}{5}$	3
1	0	$\frac{1}{5}$	0	$-\frac{2}{5}$	6
0	0	$\frac{2}{5}$	1	$-\frac{9}{5}$	2
0	0	$\frac{7}{5}$	0	$\frac{6}{5}$	-42

Since the right-hand-side entries, except for the value of the objective function, are all nonnegative, this is the optimal solution:

$$y_1 = 6, \quad y_2 = 3, \quad s_1 = 0, \quad s_2 = 2, \quad s_3 = 0.$$

Recall that in preparing the problem for solution by the dual simplex algorithm we took the negative of the objective function. Thus, the actual value of the original objective function is

$$5y_1 + 4y_2 = 5 \cdot 6 + 4 \cdot 3 = 42.$$

To reiterate geometrically that the solutions generated by the dual simplex algorithm are infeasible until the optimal solution is reached, Figure 7.3.1 indicates the basic solutions found by the process until the optimal solution was reached at $(6, 3)$. ∎

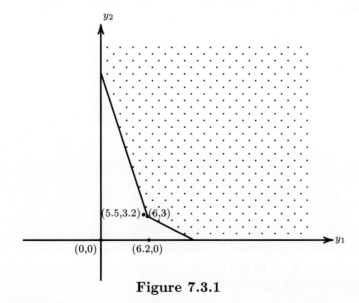

Figure 7.3.1

To demonstrate the use of the dual simplex algorithm in the analysis of changes in a linear program after it has been solved, we return to the problem from Example 3.8.1.

Example 7.3.2. Recall the linear program for the Smith Company first considered in the context of sensitivity analysis in Chapter 3:

$$
\begin{aligned}
\text{Maximize}: \quad & 40x_1 + 10x_2 \\
\text{Subject to}: \quad & 10x_1 + 2x_2 \leq 400 \\
& 15x_1 + 10x_2 \leq 1{,}020 \\
& 3x_1 + 5x_2 \leq 420 \\
& x_1 \geq 0, x_2 \geq 0
\end{aligned}
$$

Using the optimal tableau for this linear program, determine the optimal solution if the Smith Company had 750 fasteners in stock instead of 400.

The number of fasteners is the resource in the first constraint. So the problem seeks a new optimal solution with the first constraint increased to 750 without re-solving the linear program. This would be easy using sensitivity analysis as in Section 3.7, except that there we obtained an upper bound of 680 on the resource in the first constraint if the same basis were to be retained. Since 750 exceeds that limit, the set of basic variables must change, and the problem is more complicated.

Let us therefore recall the optimal tableau and see what must be done:

x_1	x_2	s_1	s_2	s_3	
1	0	$\frac{1}{7}$	$-\frac{1}{35}$	0	28
0	1	$-\frac{3}{14}$	$\frac{1}{7}$	0	60
0	0	$\frac{9}{14}$	$-\frac{22}{35}$	1	36
0	0	$\frac{25}{7}$	$\frac{2}{7}$	0	1,720

The optimal solution to the original problem was

$$x_1 = 28, \quad x_2 = 60, \quad s_1 = 0, \quad s_2 = 0, \quad s_3 = 36,$$

with the maximum value of the objective function equal to \$1,720.

The equations in Section 3.7 that allowed the new solution to be calculated for a change of δ in the resource of the first constraint remain valid. Here we express them in vector form:

$$\begin{bmatrix} x_1 \\ x_2 \\ s_3 \\ z \end{bmatrix} = \begin{bmatrix} 28 \\ 60 \\ 36 \\ 1,720 \end{bmatrix} + \delta \begin{bmatrix} \frac{1}{7} \\ -\frac{3}{14} \\ \frac{9}{14} \\ \frac{25}{7} \end{bmatrix}.$$

However, for a change beyond the limits indicated by sensitivity analysis, the solution produced will not be feasible. Here the bound for an increase in the number of fasteners was 280, and the problem calls for an increase of 350. Substituting $\delta = 350$, we obtain

$$\begin{bmatrix} x_1 \\ x_2 \\ s_3 \\ z \end{bmatrix} = \begin{bmatrix} 28 \\ 60 \\ 36 \\ 1,720 \end{bmatrix} + 350 \begin{bmatrix} \frac{1}{7} \\ -\frac{3}{14} \\ \frac{9}{14} \\ \frac{25}{7} \end{bmatrix} = \begin{bmatrix} 78 \\ -15 \\ 261 \\ 2,970 \end{bmatrix}.$$

which is not feasible because the value for x_2 is negative. Although not feasible, this solution is *algebraically* valid for the problem with the resource in the first constraint increased to 750. We can therefore consider the tableau obtained by using these values as a new right-hand side for the optimal tableau:

x_1	x_2	s_1	s_2	s_3	
1	0	$\frac{1}{7}$	$-\frac{1}{35}$	0	78
0	1	$-\frac{3}{14}$	$\frac{1}{7}$	0	-15
0	0	$\frac{9}{14}$	$-\frac{22}{35}$	1	261
0	0	$\frac{25}{7}$	$\frac{2}{7}$	0	2,970

This tableau misses being optimal only by the negative right-hand side-entry in the second row. This is an appropriate setting in which to apply the dual simplex algorithm to restore optimality. We pivot in the second row, and since the only negative constraint coefficient in that row is in the s_1 column, we pivot on that entry, yielding the following tableau:

x_1	x_2	s_1	s_2	s_3	
1	$\frac{2}{3}$	0	$\frac{1}{15}$	0	68
0	$\frac{-14}{3}$	1	$-\frac{2}{3}$	0	70
0	3	0	$-\frac{1}{5}$	1	216
0	$\frac{50}{3}$	0	$\frac{8}{3}$	0	2,720

As expected, the basis has changed, and the new optimal solution is

$$x_1 = 68, \quad x_2 = 0, \quad s_1 = 70, \quad s_2 = 0, \quad s_3 = 216$$

with the maximum value of the objective function equal to \$2,720.

The result of the increase in the number of fasteners available is easy to analyze. Since product 1 produces four times the profit as product 2, producing it is clearly preferable. However, with only 400 fasteners available and 10 fasteners required for each unit of product 1, production is very limited. The additional fasteners made it possible to produce product 1 exclusively. Since constraint 1 is slack, because excess fasteners are now available, the limitation on product 1 must come from another constraint. Indeed, we observe that the constraint for paint, the second constraint, is tight, and we note that the 68 units of product 1 produced is the maximum possible with 1,020 units of paint. ∎

This is the application of the dual simplex algorithm that we will find most fruitful – analyzing a change to a linear program that has been solved without re-solving the modified problem. When the modification is imposed on the optimal tableau and produces one or more negative entries in the right-hand side, then applying the dual simplex algorithm can restore the tableau to an optimal one that yields the solution to the modified linear program. This is most useful in adding a constraint, as we will see in the next section.

Exercises

1. Solve by the dual simplex algorithm:

$$\begin{array}{llllllll}
\text{Minimize}: & y_1 & + & 2y_2 & & & & \\
\text{Subject to}: & y_1 & - & 2y_2 & + & y_3 & \geq & 4 \\
& 2y_1 & + & y_2 & - & y_3 & \geq & 6 \\
& & & y_1 \geq 0,\ y_2 \geq 0,\ y_3 \geq 0 & & & &
\end{array}$$

2. Solve by the dual simplex algorithm:

$$\begin{array}{lllll}
\text{Minimize}: & 10y_1 & + & 18y_2 & \\
\text{Subject to}: & y_1 & + & y_2 & \geq 4 \\
& 2y_1 & + & 3y_2 & \geq 5 \\
& y_1 & + & 2y_2 & \geq 1 \\
& & y_1 \geq 0,\ y_2 \geq 0 &
\end{array}$$

3. Determine an optimal solution for the problem leading to the following tableau:

x_1	x_2	s_1	s_2	s_3	s_4	
0	0	-2	1	0	$\frac{3}{4}$	-10
0	1	$\frac{1}{2}$	0	0	$-\frac{1}{4}$	40
1	0	-1	0	0	$\frac{7}{4}$	25
0	0	4	0	1	2	30
0	0	20	0	0	30	525

4. Determine an optimal solution for the problem leading to the following tableau:

x_1	x_2	x_3	s_1	s_2	s_3	s_4	
0	0	1	0	-8	-4	-2	-8
0	1	0	0	2	0	1	100
1	0	0	0	5	4	1	168
0	0	0	1	11	8	2	36
0	0	0	0	32	12	9	38,040

5. A linear program and its optimal tableau are given below:

$$\begin{aligned}
\text{Maximize}: \quad & 80x_1 + 60x_2 \\
\text{Subject to}: \quad & x_1 + x_2 \le 100 \\
& 2x_1 + x_2 \le 150 \\
& 5x_1 + 10x_2 \le 800 \\
& x_1 \ge 0,\ x_2 \ge 0
\end{aligned}$$

x_1	x_2	s_1	s_2	s_3	
0	1	2	-1	0	50
1	0	-1	1	0	50
0	0	-15	5	1	50
0	0	40	20	0	7,000

Determine the new solution if the resource in the second constraint is increased by 60.

6. The linear program and the optimal tableau for the solution to Farmer Brown's problem, Example 1.3.1, are given below with x_1 the number of acres of potatoes and x_2 the number of acres of wheat.

$$\begin{aligned}
\text{Maximize}: \quad & 40x_1 + 120x_2 \\
\text{Subject to}: \quad & x_1 + x_2 \le 100 \\
& x_1 + 4x_2 \le 160 \\
& 10x_1 + 20x_2 \le 1,100 \\
& x_1 \ge 0, x_2 \ge 0
\end{aligned}$$

x_1	x_2	s_1	s_2	s_3	
0	0	1	$\frac{1}{2}$	$-\frac{3}{20}$	15
0	1	0	$\frac{1}{2}$	$-\frac{1}{20}$	25
1	0	0	-1	$\frac{1}{5}$	60
0	0	0	20	2	5,400

Determine the new solution if the number of days of labor – the resource in the second constraint – is increased by 70.

7.4 Adding a constraint

In this section we will consider a technique to add a constraint to a linear program after it has been solved. This is the key to reimposing integer constraints after the continuous relaxation has been solved.

Consider the following example:

Example 7.4.1. Amalgamated Chemical makes filters that are used in chemical manufacturing processes. Some of their filters can handle gases, and some cannot. Their filters also have varying capacities per unit time. Amalgamated has received an emergency order to be filled within one day. The order requires 35 filters with a total gas-filtering capacity of 50 cubic meters per hour.

Amalgamated believes that it can meet the needs of its customer with a combination made up from four of its filter models. The key factors that affect the way in which the order will be filled are the 150 hours of production time available before they must ship the filters and the 60 subassemblies that are in stock and are required by three of the filter models. Within these limitations, Amalgamated would like to maximize its profit.

The characteristics of the four models are given in Table 7.4.1.

Table 7.4.1

Model	Production hours per unit	Subassemblies needed	Gas capacity per hour	Profit per unit
1	2	0	2	$20
2	3	2	3	$30
3	6	1	0	$40
4	3	2	1	$20

Determine how many of each model of filter should be made to fill the order.

When formulated as a linear program with x_j representing the number of units of model j to be manufactured, the problem becomes:

$$\begin{array}{llllllllll}
\text{Maximize}: & 20x_1 & + & 30x_2 & + & 40x_3 & + & 20x_4 & & \\
\text{Subject to}: & 2x_1 & + & 3x_2 & + & 6x_3 & + & 3x_4 & \le & 150 \\
& x_1 & + & x_2 & + & x_3 & + & x_4 & = & 35 \\
& & & 2x_2 & + & x_3 & + & 2x_4 & \le & 60 \\
& 2x_1 & + & 3x_2 & & & + & x_4 & \ge & 50
\end{array}$$
$$x_1 \ge 0,\ x_2 \ge 0,\ x_3 \ge 0,\ x_4 \ge 0$$

The optimal tableau is:

x_1	x_2	x_3	x_4	s_1	a_2	s_3	s_4	a_4	
$-\frac{1}{3}$	0	1	0	$\frac{1}{3}$	-1	0	0	0	15
2	0	0	2	-1	6	0	1	-1	10
$-\frac{7}{3}$	0	0	0	$\frac{1}{3}$	-3	1	0	0	5
$\frac{4}{3}$	1	0	1	$-\frac{1}{3}$	2	0	0	0	20
$\frac{20}{3}$	0	0	10	$\frac{10}{3}$	20	0	0	0	1,200

This tableau indicates that an optimal solution has been reached. The solution is

$$x_1 = 0,\quad x_2 = 20,\quad x_3 = 15,\quad x_4 = 0,\quad s_1 = 0,\quad s_3 = 5,\quad s_4 = 10.$$

Thus, Amalgamated can fill the order with 20 filters of model 2 and 15 of model 3. It will have five subassemblies left in stock, and the customer will have an extra 10 cubic meters per hour of gas-filtering capacity. ∎

Example 7.4.2. Now suppose that as work on the order is beginning, the production manager realizes that only 100 units of the rechargeable filtering medium used in all the models are available. The four models require 3, 4, 2, and 2 units of the medium, respectively. From the optimal tableau above, determine a new solution that satisfies this added constraint.

When this new restriction is formulated as a constraint, it is

$$3x_1 + 4x_2 + 2x_3 + 2x_4 \le 100.$$

The process needed to add this new constraint to an optimal tableau is outlined below:

To add a constraint to an optimal simplex tableau

1. Test the current optimal solution in the constraint to be added. If it satisfies the new constraint, there is nothing to do, since the current solution remains optimal; otherwise move to Step 2.

2. Introduce an isolated variable into the added constraint and express it as an equality as follows:

   - If of the type $\leq$, introduce a slack variable with coefficient 1,

   - If an equality, introduce an artificial variable with coefficent 1, or

   - If of the type $\geq$, introduce a surplus variable with coefficient -1, then multiply the constraint by -1 so that the new variable is made isolated.

3. Include the equivalent row in the optimal simplex tableau.

4. If a nonzero coefficient in the new row occurs in the column of an otherwise basic variable, do a row operation to make the basic variable isolated again. Repeat until all previously basic variables are again isolated.

5. Apply the dual simplex algorithm to eliminate any negatives that have been produced in the right-hand side by the previous steps. Pivot to set any artificial variable that remains positive equal to zero. The resulting optimal solution satisfies all constraints.

The first thing to do is to check to see if the solution already obtained satisfies this constraint. When the original basic solution is substituted into the new filtering medium constraint,

$$3 \cdot 0 + 4 \cdot 20 + 2 \cdot 15 + 2 \cdot 0 = 110 \geq 100.$$

Thus, the new constraint is not satisfied by the old basic solution, and we must continue. Next, following Step 2, we introduce an isolated variable, here a slack variable, s_5, since this will become the fifth constraint:

$$3x_1 + 4x_2 + 2x_3 + 2x_4 + s_5 = 100.$$

When the corresponding row is added to the optimal tableau, we get:

x_1	x_2	x_3	x_4	s_1	a_2	s_3	s_4	a_4	s_5	
$-\frac{1}{3}$	0	1	0	$\frac{1}{3}$	-1	0	0	0	0	15
2	0	0	2	-1	6	0	1	-1	0	10
$-\frac{7}{3}$	0	0	0	$\frac{1}{3}$	-3	1	0	0	0	5
$\frac{4}{3}$	1	0	1	$-\frac{1}{3}$	2	0	0	0	0	20
3	4	2	2	0	0	0	0	0	1	100
$\frac{20}{3}$	0	0	10	$\frac{10}{3}$	20	0	0	0	0	1,200

Since the entries in the new row in the columns of the basic variables x_2 and x_3 are not zero, we must first do row operations to restore those columns to basic columns by making the entries in row five zero.

By subtracting four times row four from row five, we obtain the tableau:

x_1	x_2	x_3	x_4	s_1	a_2	s_3	s_4	a_4	s_5	
$-\frac{1}{3}$	0	1	0	$\frac{1}{3}$	-1	0	0	0	0	15
2	0	0	2	-1	6	0	1	-1	0	10
$-\frac{7}{3}$	0	0	0	$\frac{1}{3}$	-3	1	0	0	0	5
$\frac{4}{3}$	1	0	1	$-\frac{1}{3}$	2	0	0	0	0	20
$-\frac{7}{3}$	0	2	-2	$\frac{4}{3}$	-8	0	0	0	1	20
$\frac{20}{3}$	0	0	10	$\frac{10}{3}$	20	0	0	0	0	1,200

This returns the x_2 column to a basic column. Now we must subtract two times row 1 from row five to restore the x_3 column. That row operation yields:

x_1	x_2	x_3	x_4	s_1	a_2	s_3	s_4	a_4	s_5	
$-\frac{1}{3}$	0	1	0	$\frac{1}{3}$	-1	0	0	0	0	15
2	0	0	2	-1	6	0	1	-1	0	10
$-\frac{7}{3}$	0	0	0	$\frac{1}{3}$	-3	1	0	0	0	5
$\frac{4}{3}$	1	0	1	$-\frac{1}{3}$	2	0	0	0	0	20
$-\frac{5}{3}$	0	0	-2	$\frac{2}{3}$	-6	0	0	0	1	-10
$\frac{20}{3}$	0	0	10	$\frac{10}{3}$	20	0	0	0	0	1,200

In this tableau, only the -10 in the right-hand side of the fifth row keeps the solution from being optimal. We therefore apply the dual simple

algorithm to obtain the new optimal solution. There are two negatives in the
fifth row, but the -6 is in the column of an artificial variable which cannot
be made basic. Hence, we pivot in the x_4 column, yielding the tableau:

x_1	x_2	x_3	x_4	s_1	a_2	s_3	s_4	a_4	s_5	
$-\frac{1}{3}$	0	1	0	$\frac{1}{3}$	-1	0	0	0	0	15
$\frac{1}{3}$	0	0	0	$-\frac{1}{3}$	0	0	1	-1	1	0
$-\frac{7}{3}$	0	0	0	$\frac{1}{3}$	-3	1	0	0	0	5
$\frac{7}{6}$	1	0	0	0	-1	0	0	0	-1	15
$\frac{5}{6}$	0	0	1	$-\frac{1}{3}$	3	0	0	0	$-\frac{1}{2}$	5
$\frac{35}{3}$	0	0	0	$\frac{20}{3}$	-10	0	0	0	5	1,150

Thus, a new optimal solution has been reached:

$$x_1 = 0, \ x_2 = 15, \ x_3 = 15, \ x_4 = 5, \ s_1 = 0, \ s_3 = 5, \ s_4 = 0, \ s_5 = 0.$$

Hence, the added constraint has changed the combination of models
which Amalgmated should make. They should now make 15 each of models
2 and 3, and five of model 4. They will have five subassemblies left, and
their stock of filtering medium will be exhausted. With this combination,
their customer will get exactly the 50 cubic meters per hour of gas filtering
capacity that they require. Because the added constraint has reduced the
set of feasible solutions, we should expect the profit to drop, which it has by
$50.

We included the columns of the artificial variables because the a_2 column includes the value of the dual variable corresponding to the second
constraint. Note that since the second constraint is an equality, the dual
variable is unrestricted, and can be negative.

The reader should confirm that the following dual solution yields $1,150
as the optimal value of the dual linear program:

$$y_1 = \frac{20}{3}, \quad y_2 = -10, \quad y_3 = 0, \quad y_4 = 0, \quad y_5 = 5. \quad \blacksquare$$

In the next section we return to integer programming and develop the
general branch and bound technique.

Exercises

1. The optimal tableau for the linear program

$$\begin{aligned}
\text{Maximize}: \quad & 50x_1 + 40x_2 \\
\text{Subject to}: \quad & 3x_1 + 2x_2 \leq 120 \\
& x_1 + 6x_2 \leq 120 \\
& 2x_1 + x_2 \leq 80 \\
& x_1 \geq 0,\ x_2 \geq 0
\end{aligned}$$

is given below:

x_1	x_2	s_1	s_2	s_3	
0	1	$-\frac{1}{16}$	$\frac{3}{16}$	0	15
0	0	$-\frac{11}{16}$	$\frac{1}{16}$	1	5
1	0	$\frac{3}{8}$	$-\frac{1}{8}$	0	30
0	0	$\frac{65}{4}$	$\frac{5}{4}$	0	2,100

Starting from this tableau, determine the solution if x_2 is required to be at least 20.

2. The optimal tableau for the linear program

$$\begin{aligned}
\text{Maximize}: \quad & 4x_1 + 5x_2 \\
\text{Subject to}: \quad & x_1 + 2x_2 \leq 10 \\
& x_1 + 3x_2 \leq 18 \\
& x_1 \geq 0,\ x_2 \geq 0
\end{aligned}$$

is given below:

x_1	x_2	s_1	s_2	
1	2	1	0	10
0	1	-1	1	8
0	3	4	0	40

Solve the problem with the added constraint $2x_1 + x_2 \leq 12$.

3. The linear program and the optimal tableau for the solution to Farmer Brown's problem, Example 1.3.1, are given below with x_1 the number of acres of potatoes and x_2 the number of acres of wheat.

$$\begin{aligned}
\text{Maximize}: \quad & 40x_1 + 120x_2 \\
\text{Subject to}: \quad & x_1 + x_2 \leq 100 \\
& x_1 + 4x_2 \leq 160 \\
& 10x_1 + 20x_2 \leq 1,100 \\
& x_1 \geq 0,\ x_2 \geq 0
\end{aligned}$$

x_1	x_2	s_1	s_2	s_3	
0	0	1	$\frac{1}{2}$	$-\frac{3}{20}$	15
0	1	0	$\frac{1}{2}$	$-\frac{1}{20}$	25
1	0	0	-1	1	60
0	0	0	20	2	5,400

Suppose that Farmer Brown discovers that he will need 2 pounds of fertilizer per acre for each of his two crops. He has only 150 pounds on hand. Determine a new solution satisfying this added constraint by beginning with the optimal tableau above.

4. Consider the following linear program:

$$
\begin{aligned}
\text{Maximize}: \quad & 12x_1 + 15x_2 \\
\text{Subject to}: \quad & 20x_1 + 30x_2 \leq 2,400 \\
& 15x_1 + 40x_2 \leq 3,000 \\
& x_1 + x_2 \leq 100 \\
& x_1 \geq 0, \ x_2 \geq 0
\end{aligned}
$$

for which the optimal simplex tableau is:

x_1	x_2	s_1	s_2	s_3	
0	1	$\frac{1}{10}$	0	-2	40
0	0	$-\frac{5}{2}$	1	35	500
1	0	$-\frac{1}{10}$	0	3	60
0	0	$\frac{3}{10}$	0	6	1,320

Determine a new optimal solution in which s_3 is restricted to be at least 5.

5. Suppose that Electra manufacturing of Exercise 9 in Section 3.8 discovers that it has only 1,200 of a second component. One of this component is required for item 1 and item 2. How does this added constraint affect the solution?

The original linear program and the optimal tableau are given below.

$$
\begin{aligned}
\text{Maximize}: \quad & 120x_1 + 150x_2 + 90x_3 \\
\text{Subject to}: \quad & -x_1 + x_2 + x_3 \leq 0 \\
& x_1 + x_2 + x_3 \geq 3,000 \quad \text{Min. sales} \\
& x_1 + 0.5x_2 + 0.75x_3 \leq 2,420 \quad \text{Production hr} \\
& 2x_1 + 3x_2 + 2x_3 \leq 7,000 \quad \text{Comp. supply} \\
& x_1 \geq 0, x_2 \geq 0, x_3 \geq 0
\end{aligned}
$$

The optimal tableau:

x_1	x_2	x_3	s_1	s_2	a_2	s_3	s_4	
0	0	1	0	-8	8	-4	-2	320
0	1	0	0	2	-2	0	1	1,000
1	0	0	0	5	-5	4	1	1,680
0	0	0	1	11	-11	8	2	360
0	0	0	0	180	-180	120	90	380,400

7.5 Branch and bound for integer programs

The algorithm we discuss here is a standard one for solving integer programs and applies to programs containing general integer variables or $\{0, 1\}$ variables. We present the algorithm in the context of a maximization, but the adaptation for a minimizing problem will be clear. The procedure involves solving a set of problems derived from the original integer programming problem and arranging them in a tree structure as in the knapsack problem.

We refer to the first of these problems as the *continuous relaxation* of the given problem, and it is the linear program that results from dropping the integer restrictions of the original problem.

Let P denote the set of problems derived from the original integer program. Initially, P includes only the continuous relaxation. As we proceed toward the solution, P will include problems with added constraints as the integer restrictions are imposed.

Let p_0 denote the integer relaxation of the original problem. Let Z denote the current largest objective function value for an integer solution to the original problem. M will again denote the "Big M." Initializing Z to be $-M$ expresses the fact that as the algorithm starts no integer solution has been found. Let $[x]$ denote the greatest integer less than or equal to x.

Initialize: Set $Z = -M$ and $P = \{p_0\}$. Solve p_0. If the solution is integral, set Z equal to the optimal value and **Terminate**; or if there is no feasible solution, **Terminate**; else **Select problem.**

Select problem: Remove from P problem p having a solution that fails to satisfy some integer constraint and has an objective function value greater than or equal to Z and **Choose variable**; or if there is no such problem in P, **Terminate.**

Choose variable: Choose an integer constrained variable x_i having noninteger value b_i in the solution to problem p, and **Branch on x_i.**

Branch on x_i Add to P the problems p' and p'' formed by adding to p the constraints $x_i \leq [b_i]$ and $x_i \geq [b_i] + 1$, respectively. If an integer solution to p' or p'' is obtained with objective function value greater than Z, set Z equal to the new objective function value. **Select problem.**

Terminate: If $Z = -M$, then there is no feasible solution; otherwise, the solution corresponding to the current value of Z is optimal.

The **Branch on x_i** step produces two new problems for each problem selected. Thus, the problems generated may be arranged on a binary tree as we did the partial solutions in the knapsack problem. Because each branch adds constraints, the values of the objective function for the new branches cannot go up, and thus the objective function value of each problem is an upper bound for the set of problems that branch out from it.

The algorithm ends when all problems corresponding to terminal nodes of the tree yield integral solutions or have continuous solutions less than the best integral solution obtained so far, i.e., have corresponding objective function values less than Z.

To illustrate the algorithim, consider the following example:

Example 7.5.1. Solve the integer programming problem:

$$
\begin{array}{rrrrrrl}
\text{Maximize}: & 3x_1 & + & 2x_2 & + & 4x_3 & \\
\text{Subject to}: & 3x_1 & + & x_2 & + & x_3 & \leq 6 \\
& x_1 & + & 3x_2 & + & 2x_3 & \leq 5
\end{array}
$$
$x_i, \; i = 1, 2, 3$ nonnegative integers

The initial tableau for the continuous relaxation, denoted p_0 in the algorithm, is:

x_1	x_2	x_3	s_1	s_2	
3	1	1	1	0	6
1	3	2	0	1	5
-3	-2	-4	0	0	0

Pivoting on the 2 in the column of x_3 yields:

x_1	x_2	x_3	s_1	s_2	
$\frac{5}{2}$	$-\frac{1}{2}$	0	1	$-\frac{1}{2}$	$\frac{7}{2}$
$\frac{1}{2}$	$\frac{3}{2}$	1	0	$\frac{1}{2}$	$\frac{5}{2}$
-1	4	0	0	2	10

Now pivot on the $\frac{5}{2}$ in the x_1 column to obtain:

x_1	x_2	x_3	s_1	s_2	
1	$-\frac{1}{5}$	0	$\frac{2}{5}$	$-\frac{1}{5}$	$\frac{7}{5}$
0	$\frac{8}{5}$	1	$-\frac{1}{5}$	$\frac{3}{5}$	$\frac{9}{5}$
0	$\frac{19}{5}$	0	$\frac{2}{5}$	$\frac{9}{5}$	$\frac{57}{5}$

This indicates that $x_1 = \frac{7}{5}, x_2 = 0, x_3 = \frac{9}{5}$ is the optimal solution to the continuous relaxation. Since we have not yet obtained an integer solution, the bound corresponding to p_0 is $-M$, since it is the minimum of the empty set.

We now begin to impose the integer constraints by the branch-and-bound process. We could branch on either x_1 or x_3 since neither is an integer. Let's choose x_1. Since $x_1 = \frac{7}{5}$, we must solve the problem with the constraint $x_1 \leq 1 = \left[\frac{7}{5}\right]$ imposed – we'll call that problem p_1, and also the problem with the constraint $x_1 \geq 2 = \left[\frac{7}{5}\right] + 1$ imposed – we'll call it p_2.

To add the constraint $x_1 \leq 1$ we must include a slack variable s_3 so that we add a row for the equation

$$x_1 + s_3 = 1.$$

This yields the tableau:

x_1	x_2	x_3	s_1	s_2	s_3	
1	$-\frac{1}{5}$	0	$\frac{2}{5}$	$-\frac{1}{5}$	0	$\frac{7}{5}$
0	$\frac{8}{5}$	1	$-\frac{1}{5}$	$\frac{3}{5}$	0	$\frac{9}{5}$
1	0	0	0	0	1	1
0	$\frac{19}{5}$	0	$\frac{2}{5}$	$\frac{9}{5}$	0	$\frac{57}{5}$

This new tableau is not canonical, i.e., it does not have a basic variable for each of the three constraints. We must in effect pivot on the 1 in row 1 and column 1 to restore the column of x_1 to that of a basic variable. Note that this amounts to subtracting the first row from the new third row, and gives:

x_1	x_2	x_3	s_1	s_2	s_3	
1	$-\frac{1}{5}$	0	$\frac{2}{5}$	$-\frac{1}{5}$	0	$\frac{7}{5}$
0	$\frac{8}{5}$	1	$-\frac{1}{5}$	$\frac{3}{5}$	0	$\frac{9}{5}$
0	$\frac{1}{5}$	0	$-\frac{2}{5}$	$\frac{1}{5}$	1	$-\frac{2}{5}$
0	$\frac{19}{5}$	0	$\frac{2}{5}$	$\frac{9}{5}$	0	$\frac{57}{5}$

This produces a negative in the right-hand side. The negative indicates that with the added constraint the solution is no longer feasible. This should always occur if the addition of the constraint will change the solution. We now apply the dual simplex algorithm and pivot on the $-\frac{2}{5}$ in the third row. We obtain:

x_1	x_2	x_3	s_1	s_2	s_3	
1	0	0	0	0	$\frac{1}{2}$	1
0	$\frac{3}{2}$	1	0	$\frac{1}{2}$	$\frac{1}{2}$	2
0	$-\frac{1}{2}$	0	1	$-\frac{1}{2}$	$-\frac{5}{2}$	1
0	4	0	0	2	1	11

Thus $x_1 = 1, x_2 = 0, x_3 = 2$ is the optimal solution to problem p_1. As expected from the added constraint, x_1 is now equal to 1. The fact that x_2 and x_3 also have integer values is not expected, but since this is an integer solution, we assign the value $Z_1 = 11$ as the bound corresponding to the problem p_1.

Now we consider the problem p_2 in which the constraint $x_1 \geq 2$ is added. Here we must include a surplus variable s_3 and thus write the constraint

$$x_1 - s_3 = 2$$

which we rewrite as

$$-x_1 + s_3 = -2$$

so that s_3 will be added as a basic variable. When the corresponding row is added to the tableau, we get:

x_1	x_2	x_3	s_1	s_2	s_3	
1	$-\frac{1}{5}$	0	$\frac{2}{5}$	$-\frac{1}{5}$	0	$\frac{7}{5}$
0	$\frac{8}{5}$	1	$-\frac{1}{5}$	$\frac{3}{5}$	0	$\frac{9}{5}$
-1	0	0	0	0	1	-2
0	$\frac{19}{5}$	0	$\frac{2}{5}$	$\frac{9}{5}$	0	$\frac{57}{5}$

Again, we do not have three basic variables and must replace the third row by the sum of it and the first row to eliminate the -1 in column 1:

x_1	x_2	x_3	s_1	s_2	s_3	
1	$-\frac{1}{5}$	0	$\frac{2}{5}$	$-\frac{1}{5}$	0	$\frac{7}{5}$
0	$\frac{8}{5}$	1	$-\frac{1}{5}$	$\frac{3}{5}$	0	$\frac{9}{5}$
0	$-\frac{1}{5}$	0	$\frac{2}{5}$	$-\frac{1}{5}$	1	$-\frac{3}{5}$
0	$\frac{19}{5}$	0	$\frac{2}{5}$	$\frac{9}{5}$	0	$\frac{57}{5}$

The dual simplex algorithm now indicates that we pivot on the $-\frac{1}{5}$ in the s_2 column:

x_1	x_2	x_3	s_1	s_2	s_3	
1	0	0	0	0	-1	2
0	1	1	1	0	3	0
0	1	0	-2	1	5	3
0	2	0	4	0	9	6

As was the case above, x_1 has been constrained to the integer value 2, and x_2 and x_3 have integer values without additional restriction. Since this is an integer solution, we assign the bound $Z_2 = 6$ for the problem p_2.

The tree that summarizes the branch-and-bound process is shown in Figure 7.5.1.

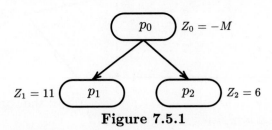

Figure 7.5.1

Since we have reached an integer solution on each branch, the algorithm terminates. We conclude that the the optimal solution was obtained at p_1 and is $x_1 = 1, x_2 = 0, x_3 = 2$ with an objective function value of 11. ∎

In small problems we can sometimes visualize the branch and bound process on a graph. Recall our first integer programming problem from Section 7.1.1. That problem was designed to show that the integer solution could not always be reached by simply rounding the values obtained for the continuous relaxation.

Example 7.5.2. Consider the following integer program:

$$
\begin{array}{rrrrcr}
\text{Maximize}: & 3x_1 & + & 13x_2 & & \\
\text{Subject to}: & 2x_1 & + & 9x_2 & \leq & 40 \\
 & 11x_1 & - & 8x_2 & \leq & 82 \\
\end{array}
$$
$$x_1 \text{ and } x_2 \text{ nonnegative integers}$$

In the introduction to this chapter we saw that the solution to the continuous relaxation of this problem occurred at the point $(9.2, 2.4)$, and that the integer constrained solution occurred at $(2, 4)$. The graph of the set of feasible solutions in Figure 7.5.2 shows the bounds used to move from $(9.2, 2.4)$ to the solution as dashed lines with arrows indicating the direction of the restriction. The constraints imposed, in order, are $x_2 \geq 3$, $x_1 \leq 6$, and $x_2 \geq 4$. The alternative branches, $x_2 \leq 2$, $x_1 \geq 7$, and $x_2 \leq 3$, are not shown. ∎

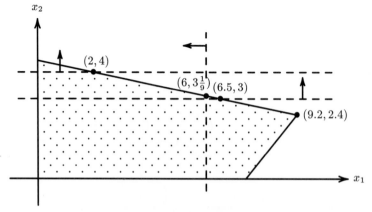

Figure 7.5.2

Exercises

Note that with first four problems which involve only two variables and one or two constraints the branch-and-bound process can be carried out graphically.

1. Solve the following integer program:

$$\begin{array}{rrrrr} \text{Maximize}: & 2x_1 & + & 7x_2 & \\ \text{Subject to}: & 5x_1 & + & 2x_2 & \leq & 11 \end{array}$$
$$x_1 \text{ and } x_2 \text{ nonnegative integers}$$

2. Solve the following integer program:

$$\begin{array}{rrrrr} \text{Maximize}: & 4x_1 & + & 3x_2 & \\ & 2x_1 & + & 3x_2 & \leq 7 \end{array}$$
$$x_1 \text{ and } x_2 \text{ nonnegative integers}$$

3. Solve the integer program

$$\begin{array}{rrrrr} \text{Maximize}: & 10x_1 & + & x_2 & \\ \text{Subject to}: & 2x_1 & + & 5x_2 & \leq & 11 \end{array}$$
$$x_1 \text{ and } x_2 \text{ nonnegative integers}$$

by the branch-and-bound method.

4. Solve the following integer program:

$$\begin{array}{rrrrr} \text{Maximize}: & 2x_1 & + & 3x_2 & \\ \text{Subject to}: & x_1 & + & x_2 & \leq & 6 \\ & 2x_1 & + & 4x_2 & \leq & 17 \end{array}$$
$$x_1 \text{ and } x_2 \text{ nonnegative integers}$$

5. The optimal tableau for the continuous relaxation of the integer program

$$\begin{array}{rrrrrrr} \text{Maximize}: & 2x_1 & + & x_2 & + & 4x_3 & \\ \text{Subject to}: & x_1 & + & x_2 & + & x_3 & \leq & 13 \\ & 2x_1 & + & 3x_2 & + & 2x_3 & \leq & 23 \end{array}$$
$$x_1, , x_2, \text{ and } x_3 \text{ nonnegative integers}$$

is

x_1	x_2	x_3	s_4	s_5	
0	$-\frac{1}{2}$	0	1	$-\frac{1}{2}$	$1\frac{1}{2}$
1	$\frac{3}{2}$	1	0	$\frac{1}{2}$	$11\frac{1}{2}$
2	5	0	0	2	46

Starting from this point, determine the solution to the integer programming problem.

6. The optimal tableau for the continuous relaxation of the mixed-integer program

$$
\begin{array}{llrrrrl}
\text{Maximize}: & & x_1 & + & 3x_2 & + & 3x_3 \\
\text{Subject to}: & & 2x_1 & + & x_2 & - & x_3 & \leq & 4 \\
& & 4x_1 & - & 3x_2 & & & \leq & 2 \\
& & -3x_1 & + & 2x_2 & + & x_3 & \leq & 3
\end{array}
$$
$$x_1 \geq 0,\ x_2 \text{ and } x_3 \text{ nonnegative integers}$$

is

x_1	x_2	x_3	s_1	s_2	s_3	
0	1	0	$\frac{4}{9}$	$\frac{1}{9}$	$\frac{4}{9}$	$3\frac{1}{3}$
1	0	0	$\frac{1}{3}$	$\frac{1}{3}$	$\frac{1}{3}$	3
0	0	1	$\frac{1}{9}$	$\frac{7}{9}$	$\frac{10}{9}$	$5\frac{1}{3}$
0	0	0	2	3	5	29

Starting from this point, determine the solution to the integer programming problem.

7. Solve Example 7.5.1 by initially branching on x_3 instead of x_1.

7.6 Basic integer programming models

In this section we consider problems that require integer variables. Thus, this is the key section in the chapter for the reader who is mainly interested in applications. Among the applications to be considered are scheduling problems, facility location problems, problems involving piecewise linear functions, and problems with go/no-go decisions.

We begin with a problem involving go/no-go decisions. It will illustrate the use of $\{0,1\}$ variables to decide which activities are to be done and to control which variables must be positive as a consequence. We will solve this problem completely before discussing other models and indicating the solution to the remaining problems in the section.

Example 7.6.1. Machine shop reopening. A small machine shop is reopening after a fire had forced it to close for extensive repairs. The shop has three product lines – plates, gears, and housings. Each product line requires specialized equipment, and because of inactivity and possible damage all equipment must be serviced before it is used.

The shop plans to open on a limited basis for the first two weeks, employing only three workers, each for 40 hours per week. It has available 2,800 units of metal and can purchase additional metal for $2 per unit. The labor, metal, overhead costs, and selling prices for their products are in Table 7.6.1.

Table 7.6.1

	Labor (minutes)	Metal (units)	Overhead ($)	Selling Price ($)
Plates	10	4	6	24
Gears	30	1	9	32
Housings	20	6	8	30

The existing backlog of orders for gears includes mostly orders for large quantities. Therefore, management does not believe that it would be useful to make gears during the first two weeks unless the shop can produce at least 200 of them.

The servicing costs are $600 for the plate equipment, $900 for the gear equipment, and $700 for the housing equipment. The shop does not expect to use all equipment in the first two weeks.

Management has $2,000 remaining from its fire insurance settlement, and plans to spend that sum on the necessary service and possibly additional metal stock. The large backlog of orders that accumulated while the shop was closed indicates that they can sell any products they make. The overhead is charged against the selling price.

Management's goal for the first two weeks is to maximize the profit so that they can afford to reopen full operations as quickly as possible.

We begin the formulation by choosing suggestive variable names. Let P, G, and H, respectively, denote the numbers of plates, gears, and housings to be produced and AM the number of additional units of metal to be purchased. When the selling prices have been reduced by the overhead and the available labor time has been converted to minutes, we get an objective function and two constraints that look like a problem that we could have solved in Chapter 3:

$$\text{Maximize}: \quad 18P + 23G + 22H$$
$$\text{Subject to}: \quad 10P + 30G + 20H \qquad\qquad \le 14,400$$
$$4P + G + 6H - AM \le 2,800$$

The need for integer variables arises in the issues that are not addressed in the constraints above: the need to service the equipment if a particular product line is to be produced and the stipulation that if gears are to be produced at all, then at least 200 of them must be made. To implement these aspects of the problem, we introduce three $\{0,1\}$ variables SP, SG, and SH to indicate the need to service the corresponding equipment. Since the $2,000 available is to be allocated to the service of equipment and the purchase of additional metal at $2 per unit, this leads to the constraint

$$600SP + 900SG + 700SH + 2AM \leq 2,000$$

in which an expenditure for service must be made if the corresponding variable takes the value 1.

Now it remains to connect the values of the servicing integer variables with those of the corresponding production variables. Here is where the effectiveness of integer variables becomes apparent. Consider the effect of the constraint

$$P \leq 500SP.$$

As long as P is positive and does not exceed 500, this constraint can be satisfied only if the $\{0,1\}$ variable SP is 1. In the context of our machine shop problem, this constraint then would force the $600 to be spent servicing the plate making equipment if any plates were made. Note, however, that if more than 500 plates were made, the constraint would prevent a solution, since the right-hand side can be no larger than 500.

Our formulation will require three such constraints, one for each product. The question is to choose an appropriately large coefficient in place of the 500 in the prototype above. One approach is to consider the relevant constraints and consider the greatest value that each variable could assume. In this case, if we assume in turn that all resources were devoted to a single product line and that the full $2,000 were put into additional metal – which is impossible, then an upper bound on all variables can be gotten by the following calculation:

$$3,800 = \max \left\{ \frac{14,400}{10}, \frac{14,400}{30}, \frac{14,400}{20}, \frac{3,800}{4}, \frac{3,800}{1}, \frac{3,800}{6} \right\}.$$

This leads to the following three constraints:

$$
\begin{array}{rcl}
P \quad\quad\quad - 3,800SP \quad\quad\quad\quad\quad\quad\quad\quad\quad\quad & \leq & 0 \\
G \quad\quad\quad\quad\quad\quad\quad - 3,800SG \quad\quad\quad\quad & \leq & 0 \\
H \quad\quad\quad\quad\quad\quad\quad\quad\quad\quad - 3,800SH & \leq & 0
\end{array}
$$

The requirement remains that if any gears are made, then at least 200 must be made. The constraint above for gears establishes that if any gears are made, then SG will be 1. Hence, the following constraint forces G to be at least 200 if it is positive:

$$200SG - G \leq 0.$$

The requirement that at least 200 gears be produced is called a *minimum batch size* constraint, a type that occurs commonly. When all the constraints are combined, one obtains a formulation in LINDO as below. Note that INTE SP – a shortened version of INTEGER SP – indicates that the variable SP is a $\{0,1\}$ variable. Note that the solution refers to a number of branches and bounds.

Listing 7.6.2

```
MAX      18 P + 23 G + 22 H
SUBJECT TO
       2)    600 SP + 900 SG + 700 SH + 2 AM <=    2000
       3)    10 P + 30 G + 20 H <=    14400
       4)    4 P + G + 6 H - AM <=    2800
       5) -  3800 SP + P <=    0
       6) -  3800 SG + G <=    0
       7) -  3800 SH + H <=    0
       8)    200 SG - G <=    0
END
INTE       SP
INTE       SG
INTE       SH


LP OPTIMUM FOUND AT STEP      24
OBJECTIVE VALUE =    20138.2200
FIX ALL VARS.(     1)  WITH RC >   975.858
SET    SG TO >= 1 AT  1, BND= .1896E+05 TWIN=  .1677E+05  27
SET    SP TO >= 1  AT  2, BND= .1828E+05 TWIN=  .1104E+05  31

NEW INTEGER SOLUTION OF   18282.73    AT BRANCH    5 PIVOT   31

       OBJECTIVE FUNCTION VALUE
```

```
         1)        18282.730

VARIABLE           VALUE            REDUCED COST
      SP          1.000000            845.454500
      SG          1.000000           1268.182000
      SH           .000000            986.363600
       P        700.909100              .000000
       G        246.363600              .000000
       H           .000000              8.363636
      AM        250.000000              .000000


      ROW     SLACK OR SURPLUS       DUAL PRICES
       2)           .000000           1.409091
       3)           .000000            .672727
       4)           .000000           2.818182
       5)       3099.091000            .000000
       6)       3553.636000            .000000
       7)           .000000            .000000
       8)         46.363640            .000000


NO. ITERATIONS=       31
BRANCHES=     5 DETERM.=  1.000E      0
BOUND ON OPTIMUM:  19162.37
DELETE        SP AT LEVEL      2
DELETE        SG AT LEVEL      1
RELEASE FIXED VARIABLES
SET   SG TO <=   0 AT  1, BND= .1522E+05 TWIN=  .1799E+05 40
DELETE        SG AT LEVEL      1
ENUMERATION COMPLETE. BRANCHES=      6 PIVOTS=       40

LAST INTEGER SOLUTION IS THE BEST FOUND
RE-INSTALLING BEST SOLUTION...
```

In this solution the numbers of items produced are left as nonnegative variables and not restricted to be integers. While we began the chapter with an example indicating that one could not necessarily round the solution to the continuous relaxation to get an integer solution, in this case it works. One might want to solve the problem with added lines in the formulation of the form GIN P to indicate that the variable P is a nonnegative integer. ∎

Before considering additional examples, we discuss areas in which integer variables are most useful. We have already encountered two aspects of models for which integer variables are particularly useful–fixed costs and minimum batch sizes. We consider those aspects of integer programming first.

Fixed costs

Often the purchase of a commodity involves a fixed cost, call it F, assessed in addition to the per-unit cost C. To express the cost $F + Cx$ of x units in a linear program, we need a safe upper bound M on the number of units to be purchased and a $\{0, 1\}$ decision variable d_i. Then we use $Fd_i + Cx$ wherever the cost is to occur and include the constraint $x \leq Md_i$ to force the variable d_i to be 1 if x is positive.

In the machine shop example we had fixed costs, the equipment servicing costs, associated with production levels. There we only needed a constraint to cause the fixed costs to be expended if the production levels were positive.

Minimum batch size

Also in the machine shop there was the requirement that if gears were to be produced, then at least 200 were to be made. Such a restriction is called a *minimum batch size* requirement. Imposing such a requirement requires the activity level variable x, the upper bound M, and the decision variable d_i as in the fixed cost case above. In addition, one needs the batch size B. Then the following two constraints are included with the indicated logical effects:

$$
\begin{array}{rcl}
x & \leq & Md_i \qquad \text{If } x \text{ is positive, then } d_i \text{ must be 1.} \\
Bd_i & \leq & x \qquad \text{If } d_i = 1, \text{ then } x \text{ is at least } B.
\end{array}
$$

Variables assuming only finitely many values

Occasionally a variable can assume only a value chosen from a finite set. For instance, suppose that a linear program involves selecting one investment from among m possible investments. Let the cost of investment i be c_i and its expected return be r_i. A constraint of the form

$$w_1 + w_2 + \cdots + w_m = 1, \quad w_i \in \{0, 1\}$$

where $w_i = 1$ indicates that the selection of investment i, is incorporated in the program formulation to specify that only one investment may be selected. Then the expression

$$r_1 w_1 + r_2 w_2 + \cdots + r_m w_m$$

is included wherever the return of the investment is needed, and the expression

$$c_1 w_1 + c_2 w_2 + \cdots + c_m w_m$$

is included wherever the cost of the investment is needed.

Piecewise linear functions

Above we considered fixed costs associated with production levels and also variables that can only assume values drawn from a finite set. Handling piecewise linear functions is in some ways a combination of these two processes. We illustrate with a specific example.

Suppose that a production process requires a part which the producer buys from an outside supplier. The terms of an order require a \$10 order charge. The first 10 parts cost \$5 each, the next 25 cost \$4 each, and any beyond that cost \$3 each. The maximum order that the producer ever places is 200.

We will calculate constants K_1, K_2, and K_3 so that the cost of the parts is expressed by the following piecewise linear function:

$$\text{cost} = \begin{cases} K_1 + 5x_1, & 1 \leq x_1 \leq 10 \\ K_2 + 4x_2, & 10 < x_2 \leq 35 \\ K_3 + 3x_3, & 35 < x_3 \leq 200 \end{cases}$$

K_1 is clearly the ordering cost, so $K_1 = 10$. The values of K_2 and K_3 must be calculated to also include the higher cost of the first 10 or the first 35 items purchased. Thus,

$$\begin{aligned} K_2 &= 10 + 5 \cdot 10 - 4 \cdot 10 \\ &= 20 \\ K_3 &= K_2 + 4 \cdot 35 - 3 \cdot 35 \\ &= 20 + 35 \\ &= 55 \end{aligned}$$

In the graph of the resulting function in Figure 7.6.1, the solid portion of each line is what is actually used, and the broken portion is the line extended to show the intercept with the vertical axis.

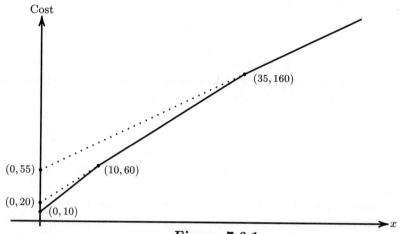

Figure 7.6.1

Now to implement the function in a linear program, we introduce three $\{0,1\}$ variables b_i to select the particular branch of the function that applies, variables x_i to be the corresponding numbers of parts, and the following constraints to choose exactly one branch:

$$
\begin{aligned}
x_1 && \leq && 10b_1 \\
x_2 && \leq && 35b_2 \\
x_3 &\leq& && 200b_3 \\
b_1 + b_2 + b_3 &\leq& && 1 \\
b_i \in \{0,1\}, \; i = 1,2,3
\end{aligned}
$$

Then in the program we use $10b_1 + 20b_2 + 55b_3 + 5x_1 + 4x_2 + 3x_3$ to denote the cost of the parts and $x_1 + x_2 + x_3$ to denote the number of parts.

Sample problems

Scheduling problems often fit into a model known as *set covering problems.* We first consider a basic covering problem and then look at some applications in the exercises. A set S is said to be *covered* by a family F of sets if each element of S belongs to at least one of the elements in F.

Example 7.6.2. Set covering. Consider the set $S = \{1, 2, 3, 4, 5, 6, 7\}$. Determine the minimal number of sets from the family F below needed to cover S.

$$F = \{\{1, 4, 6\}, \{2, 5, 7\}, \{1, 3, 5, 7\}, \{3, 5, 6\}\}.$$

To solve the set covering problem, assign a $\{0, 1\}$ variable u_i for each set, where $u_i = 1$ indicates that set i is included in the cover. To minimize the number of sets used, the objective function is the sum of the u_i's. A constraint is needed for each element of S to ensure that it is included in some set of the cover. For instance, since 3 belongs to only sets 3 and 4, the constraint requiring 3 to belong to some set in the cover is $u_3 + u_4 \geq 1$. Thus, either the third or fourth set must be in the cover to include 3. ∎

In a set covering model with an applied context, for instance the fire station location problem in the exercises or the paramedic basing problem below, the challenge is to generate the family of sets to fit the application.

Example 7.6.3. Scholarship allocation. The financial aid office at Hypothetical University is preparing awards for the coming academic year. It has selected n students to receive awards, and wants to grant at least N_i dollars to student i, $i = 1, \ldots, n$. The office has m scholarship awards available, and scholarship j is worth a_j dollars, $j = 1, \ldots, m$ to its recipient. Several awards may be given to the same student if necessary to meet his or her need of N_i. The amount of an award cannot be reduced below the level a_j. If the financial aid office does not give scholarship j in the coming year, the amount a_j earns interest and is available for the next year.

Determine how to grant the scholarships in such a way that student needs are met and the amount left invested for the next year is maximized. ∎

Example 7.6.4. Paramedic basing. An emergency planning team for a small urban area has identified five sites for basing paramedic teams and has broken the area into six demand regions. Their goals are to have paramedics based at most 5 minutes from the center of each demand region, and to have at least two bases at most 10 minutes from the centers of regions 2 and 4, the areas of the most critical expected need. Travel times in minutes from the sites, identified by A, B, C, D, and E, and the costs of the proposed bases in $1,000 units are shown in Table 7.6.2.

Table 7.6.2

		Travel times				
		A	B	C	D	E
	Costs	100	90	85	110	95
Demand region	1	5	14	7	4	8
	2	11	4	6	5	12
	3	7	6	4	15	5
	4	8	15	5	6	4
	5	4	9	11	5	8
	6	1	6	15	10	3

Using the letters of the sites as the variables, formulate an integer program to select the cities that will satisfy the team's goals at a minimum cost.

To solve this applied set covering model, we include a constraint for each city assuring that a paramedic team is based within 5 minutes. For instance, only sites A and D are within 5 minutes of region 5, so the constraint for region 5 is

$$A + D \geq 1.$$

To impose the additional condition that two bases are within 10 minutes of region 4, the constraint is

$$A + C + D + E \geq 2.$$

The objective function is the total cost of building the necessary bases. ■

In Example 7.2.1 we considered a knapsack problem in which a real estate firm chose among projects to maximize the return on a given investment. Here we extend the problem to consider projects over a multiyear planning horizon.

Example 7.6.5. Consider the capital budgeting problem where five projects are being considered for completion over the next three years. The expected returns for each project and the yearly expenditures (in thousands of dollars) are shown in Table 7.6.3.

Table 7.6.3

| | Expenditures for | | | |
Project	Year 1	Year 2	Year 3	Returns
1	5	1	8	20
2	4	7	10	40
3	3	9	2	20
4	7	4	1	15
5	8	6	10	30
Maximum available funds	25	25	25	

Formulate an integer program to choose the projects that will maximize the return.

To solve this problem, let x_i be a $\{0, 1\}$ variable expressing whether or not project i is to be done. Then there is a budget constraint for each year. For year two the budget constraint is

$$x_1 + 7x_2 + 9x_3 + 4x_4 + 6x_5 \le 25. \quad \blacksquare$$

Example 7.6.6. A company manufactures three products, each requiring a number of processes. The time requirements of each product for the processes are given in Table 7.6.4. The company has identified two of the processes and a storage capacity problem as areas where an improvement would be of great value. The directors have budgeted $35,000 for the upgrades.

The company has gotten four bids on equipment upgrades that would increase the time available for the two processes. For Process I, the minutes available can be increased 10% at a cost of $8,000 or 25% at a cost of $25,000. For Process II, the minutes can be increased 5% at a cost of $6,000 or 15% at a cost of $17,000. The company has identified an additional problem with a subcomponent required for Products 1 and 2. Each of these products requires one proprietary component. The components are delivered at the beginning of each production period and must be stored in a special secured area. The storage capacity can be increased from the current 400 to 600 at a cost of $5,000.

Table 7.6.4

	Minutes required			Minutes
	Product			
Process	1	2	3	available
I	3	5	4	20,000
II	5	3	3	24,000

If the profits per unit for products 1, 2, and 3 are $50, $70, and $60, respectively, which upgrades should be planned to maximize the profit?

To model this problem, let x_i be the number of units of product i produced, and UI_1, UI_2, UII_1, UII_2, and US be $\{0,1\}$ variables indicating whether or not the corresponding upgrades are to be done. The constraints for process I are

$$3x_1 + 5x_2 + 4x_3 - 2000UI_1 - 5000UI_2 \leq 20000$$
$$UI_1 + UI_2 \leq 1$$

where the second constraint prevents more than one upgrade from being done on process I.

There are analogous constraints on process II, a constraint on storage, and finally one restricting the total cost of the upgrades to be done to a maximum of $35,000. ∎

Example 7.6.7. Five major electrical consumers, e.g., manufacturing plants, hospitals, and housing developments, are to be added in a region served by three power plants. The connection costs to the new consumers (in $ million) and the unused capacities at the plants are given in Table 7.6.5. The unused capacity of the power plants is adequate to meet the additional demands. The objective is to connect the new consumers to the generating plants in the most economical way possible.

Table 7.6.5

		Consumer j					Unused
		1	2	3	4	5	Capacity
Plant i	1	2	2	3	1	8	40
	2	3	7	2	6	4	32
	3	5	4	4	3	6	30

12 10 15 16 15

The respective needs of the new consumers are 12, 10, 15, 16, and 15.

Two of the new consumers – numbers 1 and 2 in the list – are hospitals. To lessen the possibility that both hospitals could be without power simultaneously, they cannot both be connected to the same power plant.

Determine which new consumers should be connected to which power plant in order to minimize the connection costs. ∎

Example 7.6.8. At the H. M. O. Tight Budget Medical Pavilion, the basic emergency surgical procedures are classified into four types. Surgical residents are present around the clock in two 12 hour shifts, and each shift must include a surgeon capable of performing each type of surgery. The capabilities of the seven residents on staff are given in Table 7.6.6.

Table 7.6.6

	Surgical types			
	1	2	3	4
Resident 1	X	X		X
Resident 2			X	
Resident 3			X	
Resident 4	X			X
Resident 5	X	X		
Resident 6		X		X
Resident 7			X	X

Hospital rules prevent a resident from serving two consecutive shifts. Residents 2 and 3 have been known to throw scalpels at each other and thus cannot work on the same shift.

Formulate a {0, 1} integer program to assign surgeons to shifts for one 24-hour period if the objective is to minimize the number of surgeons used. ∎

Exercises

1. Consider a country where the coin denominations are 5, 10, 20, 25, and 50 cents. You work at the Beep 'n Buy convenience store and must give a customer 90 cents in change.

   Formulate an integer program, not necessarily using $\{0, 1\}$ variables, that can be used to minimize the number of coins needed to give the correct change.

2. **Fire station location.** The respective costs, in $1,000's, of building a fire station in each of the communities A, B, C, D, E, and F are 100, 130, 90, 140, 95, and 110. Given Table 7.6.7 of travel times, in minutes, determine the most economical locations for fire stations if service must be provided in 15 minutes or less. Assume that a fire station built in a community serves that community and that the distances are symmetric.

locations

Table 7.6.7

Communities

	B	C	D	E	F
A	5	25	10	15	20
B		20	5	20	10
C			25	10	15
D				30	20
E					10

3. Sure Power Fuels (SPF) produces regular and premium gasoline by refining and blending two types of crude oil: Texas and Offshore. Each gallon of regular must include at least 40% gasoline derived from Texas crude, and each gallon of premium must include at least 60% gasoline from Texas crude. Each gallon of regular can be sold for the wholesale price of 50 cents, while premium sells for 60 cents a gallon. SPF has 5,000 gallons of gasoline refined from Texas crude and 10,000 gallons of gasoline from Offshore oil in stock. Unusually large orders – at least for SPF – for 6,000 gallons of regular and 8,000 gallons of premium have just been received and must be satisfied quickly. SPF will not be able to get any additional Offshore crude, but if needed can obtain up to 15,000 gallons of Texas crude according to the following price schedule plus a $500 delivery fee:

First 5,000 gallons:	$0.40/gallon
Next 5,000 gallons:	$0.35/gallon
Next 5,000 gallons:	$0.30/gallon

   When refined, each gallon of Texas crude yields 0.7 gallons of gasoline. Under these constraints, determine if it will be possible for SPF to fill the two large orders. If it can, then determine how much of each brand of gasoline SPF should make if any gasoline made beyond the two orders is planned to maximize the the difference between the selling price and the cost of the addditional crude.

4. Consider the capital budgeting problem stated in Example 7.6.5.

   (a) Formulate and solve an integer program to solve the problem.

   (b) Revise your integer program, assuming that capital not spent in one year earns interest at 5% for a year and can then be used the next year. Use the fact that a sum of A deposited at 6% grows to $A(1.06)^k$ in k years.

   (c) Solve the formulations in (a) and (b) above using LINDO or other software and compare the solutions.

5. A small trucking company has a fleet of five trucks, and on a certain day has seven loads to deliver. In Tables 7.6.8 and 7.6.9 the capacities of the trucks and the sizes of the loads are both given in units of 1,000 pounds.

Table 7.6.8

Truck	Capacity	Daily cost
1	3	$200
2	6	$300
3	6	$400
4	8	$350
5	11	$500

Table 7.6.9

Load	Weight
A	1
B	2
C	3
D	4
E	4
F	5
G	8

Because of their locations, loads A and D cannot be delivered by the same truck, nor can loads B and E.

Determine which loads should be assigned to each truck to minimize the total daily cost.

6. Suppose in Example 7.6.7 that to make use of the extra capacity at the power plants it is necessary to upgrade the plants. The upgrade costs depend on the number of major new consumers connected. Table 7.6.10 provides these costs.

Table 7.6.10

		No. of new consumers		
		1	2	3
Plant i	1	2	2	3
	2	2	3	4
	3	1	2	2

Add this additional cost to the model for the example and determine the solution.

7. Suppose in the Rural Residence Inc. problem from the exercises for Section 4.3 that the activity of acquiring other materials can be completed in four days by asking for expedited delivery at a cost of $300. Determine whether it will further reduce the time of the project beyond the reduction obtained in part (d) of the problem.

8. **The assignment problem.** The special case of the transportation problem in which the number of supplies equals the number of demands and all supplies and demands are equal to 1 is called the *assignment problem*. The terminology comes from the application in which which each "supply" corresponds to a person to be assigned to a job and each "demand" corresponds to a job to be filled. The cost c_{ij} is the cost of assigning person i to job j.

   (a) Discuss why an assignment problem with at least two supplies will necessarily have a degenerate solution when solved as a transportation problem.

   (b) Solve the assignment problem in which Table 7.6.11 represents the cost of assigning the person corresponding to the row to the job corresponding to the column by treating it as an integer programming problem.

Table 7.6.11

	1	2	3	4	5
1	14	9	3	11	8
2	9	12	12	18	7
3	24	14	10	5	12
4	6	17	18	20	13
5	11	8	15	10	15

9. Pizza Express is planning to open restaurants in a city with several college campuses. They have found five possible locations, identified as A, B, C, D, and E. Pizza-hungry dormitory students are concentrated at locations $1, 2, \ldots, 7$. Table 7.6.12 gives the travel time in minutes between each of the potential store locations and the dormitories. Also included are the costs, in $1,000 units, of building at the possible store locations.

Table 7.6.12

	\multicolumn{7}{c	}{Travel time (minutes)}	Cost
	1	2	3	4	5	6	7	Cost
A	5	40	25	7	9	9	10	30
B	11	10	16	12	8	15	8	45
C	7	14	8	15	17	18	12	50
D	15	6	12	10	20	22	9	25
E	20	22	8	30	35	7	25	35

The goal of Pizza Express is to locate at least one outlet within 10 minutes of each dormitory concentration. Formulate an integer program to achieve this goal at minimum cost.

10. Esquire Products will produce four new lines in the next month. The respective profits on the lines are $200, $220, $185, and $190. They are basically testing the market and do not wish to produce more than 700 of any one line. The respective fixed start-up costs for the products are $4,000, $5,000, $3,000, and $3,500. Also included in the start-up costs is the purchase of a part, one of which is needed for every item produced. The supplier of the part charges according to the following schedule:

$$\left\{ \begin{array}{l} \$50 \text{ ordering charge} \\ \$9 \text{ each for the first } 100 \\ \$6 \text{ each for all additional} \end{array} \right.$$

Esquire has budgeted $20,500 for the start-up costs. Lines 1 and 2 require a half hour of production time per item while lines 3 and 4 require 0.4 hour per item. There will be 800 hours of production time available during the month. How many of each line should they produce to maximize their profit?

11. Dana and Robbie have just been given 20 minutes and 15 tickets each before leaving Funland. Having done some incidental learning while their father worked on this book, they devoted three of their minutes to generating the data in Table 7.6.13 and solving the problem to maximize their fun.

Table 7.6.13

Ride	Minutes required	Tickets	Fun value
Paratroopers	6	4	8
Teacups	4	3	6
Mini Himalayas	4	3	5
Whirling chairs	4	2	6
Helicopters	5	3	3
Merry-go-round	4	2	3
Jungle	5	3	5

Assume that they ride each ride at most once, and solve their problem.

12. A company makes three products. Each production run of product i involves a fixed cost F_i and a per-unit cost p_i so that the cost of x_i units is $F_i + p_i x_i$. These costs together with the per-unit revenue are given in Table 7.6.14.

Table 7.6.14

Product line	Fixed cost	Per-unit cost	Per-unit revenue
1	$1,500	$45	$240
2	$900	$38	$190
3	$1,000	$40	$210

There are two key production processes. The time requirements and availabilities for each line are given in Table 7.6.15.

Table 7.6.15

Process	Product 1	2	3	Hours available
I	0.25	0.20	0.30	300
II	0.40	0.50	0.20	400

The company will upgrade exactly one of the two processes. The upgrade to Process I will raise the number of effective hours by 20%; that to Process II will raise the number of effective hours by 10%.

Determine which process to upgrade and the production levels that will maximize the difference between revenue and cost.

13. An analytically minded basketball coach selects his starting lineup according to his ratings of his players, and of course, their position and height. His plan for the next game is to maximize the total shooting ability of the starting team while keeping the average height at 6'5" or more. He also wants to start at least two guards and a center.

The coach's data is shown in Table 7.6.16. Determine his starting 5.

Table 7.6.16

Player	Height	Position	Shooting
Bob	6'1"	Guard	9
Clyde	6'6"	Forward	8
Michael	6'4"	Guard	9
David	6'9"	Center	7
Scotty	6'6"	Forward	8
Bill	6'8"	Center	8
Dennis	6'6"	Forward	6
Earl	6'3"	Guard	10
Kareem	6'10"	Center	6
Sam	6'1"	Guard	8

7.7   The traveling salesman problem

Given n cities and the distances between them, the traveling salesman problem is that of determining the shortest circuit which will take a person to each city once and return to the starting city. Though phrased in terms of a circuit through cities, the model has other applications. Among the most important is determining the sequence in which several jobs should be performed on the same equipment with the objective of minimizing the total time.

Although we do not take a linear programming approach, the traveling salesman problem is a linear program. We first examine its structure to see why another approach is indicated.

For an n-city problem, let the variable x_{ij} be 1 if the link from city i to city j is included in a circuit; otherwise let x_{ij} be 0. Let c_{ij} be the cost of travel from city i to city j. Let D be a proper subset of the set of cities, i.e., any nonempty subset of the set of cities other than all of them. Then the linear programming formulation of the problem is:

$$\text{(TSP)}\quad \text{Minimize}:\quad w = \sum_{i=1}^{n}\sum_{j=1}^{n} c_{ij}x_{ij}$$

$$\text{Subject to}:\quad \sum_{j=1}^{n} x_{ij} = 1,\ i = 1,\ldots,n$$

$$\sum_{i=1}^{n} x_{ij} = 1,\ j = 1,\ldots,n$$

$$\sum_{i\in D, j\notin D} x_{ij} \geq 1,\ D \text{ a proper subset of cities}$$

$$x_{ij} \in \{0,1\},\ i = 1,\ldots,n,\ j = 1,\ldots,n$$

The first n constraints require that a circuit exit each city exactly once while the second n require that a circuit enter each city exactly once.

The last set of constraints ensures that a solution be a single, connected circuit reaching all cities. For instance, in a five city problem, the "solution"

$$x_{12} = x_{23} = x_{31} = 1 \quad \text{and} \quad x_{45} = x_{54} = 1$$

with all other $x_{ij} = 0$ corresponds to two partial circuits in which each city is entered and exited exactly once. However, as Figure 7.7.1 indicates, there is no connection between the two partial circuits:

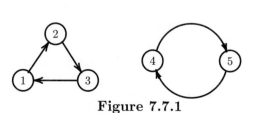

Figure 7.7.1

The constraint of the last type above with $D = \{1, 2, 3\}$ would prevent this problem. It would require a connection between one of the first three cities and one of the last two; i.e., at least one of the following variables would necessarily equal 1:

$$x_{ij} \text{ with } i \in \{1, 2, 3\} \text{ and } j \in \{4, 5\}.$$

Since the set of all constraints of this type includes all $2^n - 2$ such subsets of cities, the linear programming representation of a traveling salesman problem has a large number of constraints. For $n = 5$, there are the first 10 constraints concerning entering and leaving each city plus $2^5 - 2 = 30$ others, one for each subset. The problem thus has 40 constraints and 25 variables.

There are also a large number of possible solutions to a traveling salesman problem. Since a circuit returns to the city of origin, the optimal circuit does not depend on the starting point. Basic combinatorics thus indicates that for n cities there are $(n-1)!$ possible circuits if there are direct links between all pairs of cities. The number of possible circuits grows rapidly – for five cities there are only 24 circuits, for ten cities there are 362,880 circuits.

Recall that in the branch-and-bound process for the knapsack problem in an earlier section, the branches were made on the decision to include (or not include) a particular item in the knapsack. There the order in which we considered including the items was based on the ratio of their values to their costs, and the bounds were estimates of the maximum total value with the items selected to that point.

The branch-and-bound algorithm to solve the traveling salesman problem must identify an order in which to consider the links to efficiently sift through the large number of possible circuits to produce the optimal one. The algorithm discussed here will not yield an optimal solution to all traveling salesman problems in an acceptable amount of time. However, it will produce an optimal solution for many smaller problems. We will consider a dynamic programming approach to this problem in Chapter 8, and there we will be able to analyze the computational challenge of solving a larger traveling salesman problem.

The branch-and-bound algorithm will construct the circuit one link at a time. Prospective links for inclusion in the circuit will be identified by constructing an opportunity matrix that indicates the desirable link to add at each step.

A problem is described by expressing the distances in matrix form as below:

Example 7.7.1. Determine the shortest routing among five cities with the distances given in Table 7.7.1.

Table 7.7.1

		To				
		1	2	3	4	5
	1	M	23	12	18	13
	2	16	M	16	22	24
From	3	5	17	M	19	12
	4	16	17	18	M	32
	5	12	15	20	9	M

The M's along the diagonal are treated as arbitrarily large positive numbers, and are included to indicate that it is impossible to go from a city to itself. Previously in the context of the knapsack problem we ascribed to this "Big M" the property that no matter how large a number is subtracted from it, the difference is positive. For convenience, we will simply write M instead of $M - a$ when we subtract from M.

M's will also be used in the algorithm to prevent completion of a circuit before all cities have been visited.

Note that the distances involved in the example are not symmetric; i.e., we do not have $d_{ij} = d_{ji}$ for all i and j. Symmetry is often expected of distances, but it has purposely been omitted from the example to illustrate that the algorithm makes no assumption of symmetry.

The example will be solved following the description of the algorithm.

Branch-and-bound traveling salesman algorithm

Let L denote the lower bound for a circuit and begin with $L = 0$. The algorithm will successively increment L until it reaches the length of the optimal circuit. Lower bounds will also be formed for the set of circuits not including the link of the circuit added at each step.

1. Form an **opportunity matrix**: When this step is completed, each column and each row should contain at least one zero.

    (a) For each column, add to L the minimum entry in the column and subtract the minimum entry from each entry in the column.

    (b) For each row in the new matrix that contains no zero, add the minimum entry in the row to L and subtract the minimum entry from all entries in the row.

2. **Complete the circuit** (if possible):

    (a) If the new matrix is a 2×2, complete the circuit by adding the links corresponding to the two zeros; otherwise go to Step 3.

    (b) If there exists a terminal node with a bound lower than the node corresponding to the new circuit, return to explore that branch. Continue until a circuit is obtained with a bound lower than all terminal nodes. That circuit is optimal.

3. **Calculate regrets** to identify a link to include in the circuit: For each zero in the matrix, calculate the sum of the smallest other entry in the row and the smallest other entry in the column. This number is a measure of the regret for not including the corresponding link in the circuit and represents the cheapest alternative "in" and "out."

4. **Add a link and update the lower bound**:

    (a) Select the zero with the largest regret and include the corresponding link in the circuit. If two or more links have the same regret, choose the one corresponding to the smallest cost in the original matrix. If the original costs are also equal, choose the one in the earlier row, and if the rows are also tied, the earlier column. The lower bound for the set of circuits including all links identified so far is L.

    (b) The lower bound for the set of circuits including all links previously added but not including the one just added in Step (a) is L plus the regret.

5. **Reduce the matrix**: Form a new matrix by dropping the row and the column of the link just added to the circuit. Determine the row and column containing no M and replace their common element by an M. Go to Step 1.

The algorithm is summarized in the Figure 7.7.2.

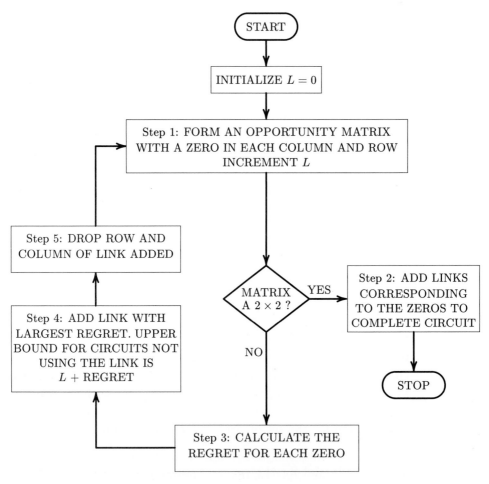

BRANCH-AND-BOUND ALGORITHM FOR
THE TRAVELING SALESMAN PROBLEM

Figure 7.7.2

We now return to the example. Step 1(a) produces the following matrix and calculation of L:

	1	2	3	4	5
1	M	8	0	9	1
2	11	M	④	13	12
3	0	2	M	10	0
4	11	②	6	M	20
5	7	0	8	0	M

$$L = 5 + 15 + 12 + 9 + 12 = 53$$

Rows 2 and 4 contain no zero, and their smallest entries must be subtracted and added to L in Step 1(b):

	1	2	3	4	5
1	M	8	0	9	1
2	7	M	0	9	8
3	0	2	M	10	0
4	9	0	4	M	18
5	7	0	8	0	M

$$L = 53 + 4 + 2 = 59$$

Since the matrix is not a 2×2, we proceed to Step 3. The regrets are calculated for the zero entries and recorded in the lower left hand of the corresponding square in the next array.

Recall that the regret represents the cost of not including the link in the circuit. Thus we select the link from 5 to 4 to start the circuit, since its regret is the largest.

$L = 59$ is the lower bound both for all circuits and for circuits including the link from 5 to 4. The lower bound for circuits not including the 5 to 4 link is 68, which is obtained by adding the regret to L. This information is summarized graphically in Figure 7.7.3.

	1	2	3	4	5
1	M	8	0 ₁	9	1
2	7	M	0 ₇	9	8
3	0 ₇	2	M	10 ₁	0
4	9 ₄	0	4	M	18
5	7	0 ₀	8	0 ₉	M

The link from 5 to 4 is indicated by $5 \to 4$ and the absence of that link by $\sim 5 \to 4$. Each oval represents the set of circuits containing (or excluding) the link indicated as well as all previously identified links. The lower bounds are indicated to the right of the oval.

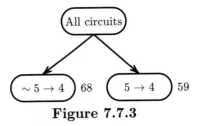

Figure 7.7.3

The reduced matrix is now formed according to Step 5 by eliminating row 5 and column 4. The 18 in row 4 and column 5 is replaced by an M to prevent including the link from 4 to 5 later and prematurely concluding the circuit. This enforces the final set of constraints in the linear programming formulation of the problem at the beginning of the section. The new regrets are also calculated.

	1	2	3	5
1	M	8	0 (1)	1
2	7	M (7)	0	8
3	0 (7)	2	M (1)	0
4	9	0 (6)	4	M

The two maximum regrets of 7 indicate that either the link from 3 to 1 or that from 2 to 3 should be added to the circuit. We choose $3 \to 1$ because it corresponds to the smaller initial-cost entry, as suggested in Step 4(a). When the regret is added to form the bound for circuits including $5 \to 4$ but not $3 \to 1$, the new tree is as shown in Figure 7.7.4.

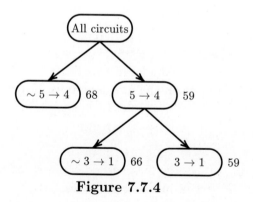

Figure 7.7.4

When row 3 and column 1 are removed and the required M inserted in row 1 and column 3, we have:

	2	3	5
1	8	M	1
2	M	0	8
4	0	4	M

Because there is no zero in the column corresponding to 5, we must increase L at Step 1 and form a new opportunity matrix. Doing that and calculating the regrets yields:

	2	3	5
1	8	M	0 (15)
2	M (11)	0	7
4	0 (12)	4	M

$$L = 59 + 1 = 60$$

We see that the link with the largest regret is $1 \to 5$, hence it should be added to the circuit, and when the new matrix is formed, it is a 2×2:

	2	3
2	M	0
4	0	M

The circuit can now be completed at Step 2 by including links $2 \to 3$ and $4 \to 2$. The final tree in Figure 7.7.5 summarizes all steps in the formation of the circuit.

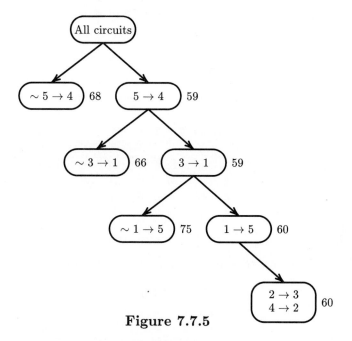

Figure 7.7.5

We now represent the optimal circuit by a diagram in Figure 7.7.6 and note that the sum of the distances is 60.

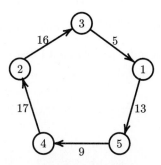

Figure 7.7.6

In the example considered above and in the exercises below, the length of the path found is lower than any of the bounds found for the alternatives. Thus, there is no need to consider alternative paths. There are examples for which it will be necessary to investigate other paths, but we will not consider such examples here.

If one of the bounds were lower than the length of the circuit produced by the algorithm, it would be necessary to repeat the algorithm and make an alternative choice to follow the path leading to a possible shorter circuit.

Exercises

1. Solve the five-city traveling salesman problem with distances as in Table 7.7.2.

Table 7.7.2

	1	2	3	4	5
1	M	18	16	12	9
2	15	M	8	16	2
3	12	4	M	8	11
4	7	11	9	M	8
5	5	4	12	7	M

2. Solve the four-city traveling salesman problem with distances as in Table 7.7.3.

Table 7.7.3

	1	2	3	4
1	M	20	15	35
2	20	M	18	40
3	28	15	M	25
4	25	10	20	M

3. Formulate and solve the traveling salesman problem from Example 1.3.8.

4. Formulate and solve the traveling salesman problem from Example 1.3.6.

5. Solve the traveling salesman problem with distances as in Table 7.7.4.

Table 7.7.4

	1	2	3	4
1	M	15	22	18
2	9	M	11	14
3	12	17	M	20
4	14	8	7	M

6. Using the costs from the assignment problem – after inserting the appropriate M's – from the exercises of Section 7.6, solve the corresponding traveling salesman problem. Compare the constraints of the assignment problem with those of the traveling salesman problem and discuss why the objective value of the traveling salesman problem is greater than that of the assignment problem.

In the introduction to the traveling salesman problem we noted that the numbers of constraints and of possible circuits grew quickly with the size of the problem. For this reason, in practice *heuristic* methods of solution are often used. Such a method usually is more simply implemented than one leading to an optimal solution, but leads to an acceptable solution that is not likely to be optimal. The remaining exercises consider two such heuristic methods.

7. In the *nearest-neighbor heuristic* one chooses a starting city and then forms a circuit by successively moving to the closest city that does not prematurely close the circuit. Generate a solution to Example 7.7.1 by generating a nearest-neighbor circuit starting at each of the cities and then choosing the best one.

8. If c_{ij} denotes the cost of travel from i to j and the link $i \to j$ belongs to a circuit, then the cost of inserting k between i and j is given by $c_{ik} + c_{kj} - c_{ij}$. A second heuristic approach to the traveling salesman problem, the *closest-insertion heuristic* (CIN), is to start with a partial circuit $i \to j \to i$ consisting of going from one city to another and then returning. The costs of all insertions into the circuit of a city not yet visited are calculated. The cheapest one is chosen and added to the circuit. The insertion process continues until a full circuit is obtained.

Apply the CIH to determine a circuit for Example 7.7.1.

7.8 Summary and objectives

After introducing the need for special procedures to solve an integer program, we solved the knapsack problem by a branch-and-bound algorithm. Since the branch-and-bound approach for the knapsack problem is reasonably intuitive, it served to introduce the technique to be developed in the next three sections.

Branch-and-bound algorithms were then used throughout the chapter. The problems were solvable by this technique for two main reasons:

- Their solutions can be described by binary decisions that partition the set of possible solutions.

- An upper bound can be calculated for the set of solutions identified by a partition.

In Section 7.3 we considered the dual simplex algorithm, which provides an alternative approach to the solution of minimization problems of the form (mLP). More importantly, it provides a tool to reoptimize a simplex tableau after the introduction of a new constraint. We examined that reoptimization process in Section 7.4.

In Section 7.5 we saw how the reoptimization process could be employed to develop a branch-and-bound algorithm for any integer program. Then in Section 7.6 we considered specific formulation techniques employed in integer programming applications. This is the most critical section from an applications standpoint. Specifically, we developed techniques to deal with piecewise linear functions, go/no-go decisions, and variables assuming only finitely many values.

Finally, the traveling salesman problem was solved by a branch-and-bound algorithm that provides an efficient way to search the possible circuits for the optimal circuit. While the algorithm presented does not always produce an optimal solution, it is practical for use with small problems and will usually yield a useful, if not optimal, solution.

Objectives

After completing this chapter, the student should be able to:

1. Solve a standard minimization problem by the dual simplex algorithm. Example 7.3.1. Exercise 2 of Section 7.3.

2. Using the dual simplex algorithm, determine the new basic solution which results from a change in a right-hand-side constant beyond the bounds determined by sensitivity analysis. Example 7.3.2. Exercise 5 of Section 7.3.

3. Given a linear program and the optimal tableau, determine a new optimal tableau when a constraint has been added. Example 7.4.2. Exercise 2 of Section 7.4.

4. Solve a knapsack problem using a branch-and-bound algorithm. Example 7.2.1. Exercise 3 of Section 7.2.

5. Solve small integer programs using the branch-and-bound method. Example 7.5.1. Exercise 2 of Section 7.5.

6. Formulate the program and use LINDO to solve linear programs requiring integer variables. Example 7.6.1 and Appendix A. Exercise 5 of Section 7.6.

7. Solve a traveling salesman problem using a branch-and-bound algorithm. Example 7.7.1. Exercise 2 of Section 7.7.

Chapter 8

Introduction to Dynamic Programming

8.1 Introduction to recursion

Unlike the simplex algorithm or the transportation algorithm, the method of dynamic programming does not presume a standard structure for the problems that it can be used to solve. Instead it uses a general approach that requires only a few basic characteristics in the problem to be applicable. Many of the problems that we consider will be variations on ones considered earlier that are approachable by dynamic programming.

A problem for which the dynamic programming method is appropriate is one in which the identification of a solution – not necessarily an optimal one – can be achieved by viewing the solution as consisting of several independent decisions, usually called *stages,* which can be considered individually. The range of decisions for each stage is called the set of *states* for the stage. For example, in a traveling salesman problem the decision of whether or not to include a particular link can be viewed as a stage having two states – a 0 to indicate that the link is not in the circuit under consideration, or a 1 to indicate that it is.

The key step in the solution process will be to define a function, called a recursion, that connects decisions in successive stages. We devote this section to introducing such functions and to deriving related ideas needed to count the operations involved in some problem solutions.

A *recurrence relation* for a sequence is a function that relates the nth term to one or more of its predecessors. The example given below is probably the most familiar and basic one.

Example 8.1.1. The Fibonacci sequence is defined as follows:

$$\begin{cases} F_0 &=& 1 \\ F_1 &=& 1 \\ F_n &=& F_{n-1} + F_{n-2}, \ n \geq 2. \end{cases}$$

This definition produces the sequence which Leonardo of Pisa introduced in terms of breeding pairs of rather special immortal rabbits:

$$1, \ 1, \ 2, \ 3, \ 5, \ 8, \ 13, \ 21, \ \ldots .$$

However unbelievable his rabbits may seem, the terms of Fibonacci's sequence can be found in many areas of nature and clearly are associated with patterns of growth. See, for instance, [27]. ∎

A recursion more similar to those we will use in dynamic programming can be found in the problem of the Towers of Hanoi.

Example 8.1.2. According to legend, monks in Hanoi were presented with three pegs in a row, with 64 disks of different sizes stacked on one of the end pegs ranging from the largest at the bottom to the smallest on the top, as illustrated in Figure 8.1.1.

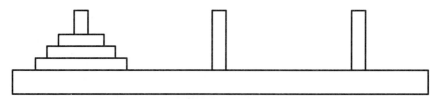

Figure 8.1.7

They were told to move the disks to the peg at the other end according to the following rules:

- Only one disk could be moved at a time, and

- No disk could ever be placed on top of a smaller disk.

They were told that when their task was completed the world would end.

With this weighty significance attached to the completion of the task, the computation of the length of time required becomes a matter of interest. We start with a calculation of the number H_n of disk moves that would be necessary as a function of the number n of disks.

Obviously if there were only one disk, the task could be completed with a single move, so $H_1 = 1$.

Of greatest interest is that the recursion can be determined without knowing the actual mechanism to move the disks, only how to relate H_n to H_{n-1}. We will see that this may also be the case when we consider recursions in the context of dynamic programming.

The key to the recurrence is the observation that to move n disks from one end peg to the other, we first need to move $n - 1$ disks to the center peg, then move disk n, the largest disk, to the other end and then move the first $n - 1$ disks from the center to the end peg on top of the largest disk. Thus, we first do H_{n-1} moves to get the $n - 1$ disks to the middle, then move the largest disk to the other end, then another H_{n-1} moves to put the $n-1$ disks atop the largest one. Hence, the recurrence is $H_n = 2 \cdot H_{n-1} + 1$.

In the exercises we derive an expression to evaluate H_n. One can then make an assumption about how long it takes to move a disk, and go on to forecast the end of the world according to the legend. ∎

In the foregoing examples we have seen that the recurrence may depend upon only the preceding term, as in the case of the Towers of Hanoi, or upon more than one preceding term, as in the Fibonacci sequence. In dynamic programming we will see that the recurrence depends upon all preceding terms.

We now consider special recurrences that occur frequently and lead to ideas that are critical in many applications.

Factorials and permutations

Consider the factorial function defined as follows:

$$\begin{cases} \text{Fact}(0) & = & 1 \\ \text{Fact}(n) & = & n \cdot \text{Fact}(n-1), \ n \geq 1. \end{cases}$$

Evaluating the function by repeatedly applying the recursion shows that

Fact (n) is just the product of the first n integers:

$$
\begin{aligned}
\text{Fact}\,(n) &= n \cdot \text{Fact}\,(n-1) \\
&= n \cdot (n-1) \cdot \text{Fact}\,(n-2) \\
&= \cdots \\
&= n \cdot (n-1) \cdot (n-2) \cdot \, \cdots \, \cdot 3 \cdot \text{Fact}\,(2) \\
&= n \cdot (n-1) \cdot (n-2) \cdot \, \cdots \, \cdot 3 \cdot 2 \cdot 1
\end{aligned}
$$

Factorials are also written

$$
\text{Fact}\,(n) = n! = n(n-1)(n-2) \cdot \, \cdots \, \cdot 3 \cdot 2 \cdot 1.
$$

One characteristic of the factorial function is that it increases rapidly. A few sample values:

$$
3! = 6, \qquad 6! = 720, \qquad 10! = 3,628,800, \qquad 15! = 1,307,674,368,000.
$$

An important use of factorials is in counting. Here we examine only the ideas necessary to count the number of operations involved in the solution of some dynamic programming problems.

Proposition 8.1.3. (First principle of counting) *If two actions can occur in* n *and* m *ways, respectively, then the number of ways in which the two can occur is* $n \cdot m$ *ways.*

An arrangement of distinct items in order is called a *permutation* of the items. One application of factorials is in counting permutations. The next proposition follows from the first principle of counting by observing that the first item can be selected in n ways, the second in $n-1$ ways, etc.

Proposition 8.1.4. *The number of permutations of* n *items is* $n!$.

Often we do not want to order all items of a set, so the following more general proposition is more useful:

Proposition 8.1.5. *The number of permutations of* n *items taken* r *at a time,* $0 \le r \le n$, *is* $P(n,r) = \dfrac{n!}{(n-r)!} = n(n-1) \cdot \, \cdots \, \cdot (n-r+1)$.

As a quick application, consider

Example 8.1.6. In how many ways may the first four horses finish in an 11 horse race?

This is simply the number of permutations of 11 things taken four at a time: $P(11,4) = 11 \cdot 10 \cdot 9 \cdot 8 = 7,920.$ ∎

Recursion, subsets, and binomial expansions

The remainder of this section will be devoted to a two-variable recursion and its connection to the binomial expansion. This material will be used later to calculate the number of operations required by the dynamic programming solution to the traveling salesman problem. Otherwise, the reader can omit the remainder of this section.

Consider the following two-variable recurrence relation:

$$\begin{cases} C(0,0) & = & 1 \\ C(1,0) & = & 1 \\ C(1,1) & = & 1 \\ C(n+1,k) & = & C(n,k) + C(n,k-1), \ n \geq k \geq 1. \end{cases}$$

Note that for each value n of the first variable the recurrence generates $n+1$ values as the second variable runs through the values $\{0, 1, \ldots, n\}$.

Applying this recurrence for values up to $n = 5$ generates the following triangular array, called Pascal's triangle.

$$\begin{array}{ccccccccccc} & & & & & 1 & & & & & \\ & & & & 1 & & 1 & & & & \\ & & & 1 & & 2 & & 1 & & & \\ & & 1 & & 3 & & 3 & & 1 & & \\ & 1 & & 4 & & 6 & & 4 & & 1 & \\ 1 & & 5 & & 10 & & 10 & & 5 & & 1 \end{array}$$

This triangle can be regarded as consisting of the nonzero entries in an array with zero entries in each row extending indefinitely in either direction. That view allows the recursion to be used to generate subsequent rows by simply adding the two entries from the previous row immediately above and to the right and left of the the new entry.

The third row of the triangle, and possibly the fourth and more, might well seem familar. They are the coefficients of the two most common binomial expansions:

$$(a+b)^2 = (a+b)(a+b) = a^2 + 2ab + b^2$$

and

$$
\begin{aligned}
(a+b)^3 &= (a+b)(a+b)(a+b) \\
&= a^3 + 3a^2b + 3ab^2 + b^3.
\end{aligned}
$$

An observation about such expansions helps us discover a counting significance of the terms $C(n,k)$ of the recursion. The expansion of $(a+b)^3$ includes all products that can be formed by choosing an a or a b from each of the three factors. For instance, to obtain ab^2 an a is chosen from one of the three factors and a b is chosen from each of the other two. The coefficient 3 indicates that there are exactly three ways to do this: choose an a from the first, second, or third factor and a b from each of the other two.

Thus, the expansion can be written

$$
\begin{aligned}
(a+b)^3 &= C(3,0)a^3 + C(3,1)a^2b + C(3,2)ab^2 + C(3,3)b^3 \\
&= a^3 + 3a^2b + 3ab^2 + b^3.
\end{aligned}
$$

Note that the exponent of b is always the value of the second variable in the coefficient.

In general, for any positive integer n, the binomial expansion can be written as

$$
\begin{aligned}
(a+b)^n &= \sum_{i=0}^{n} C(n,i)a^{n-i}b^i \\
&= C(n,0)a^n + C(n,1)a^{n-1}b + C(n,2)a^{n-2}b^2 + \cdots \\
&\quad + C(n,n-1)ab^{n-1} + C(n,n)b^n \\
&= a^n + na^{n-1}b + \frac{n(n-1)}{2\cdot 1}a^{n-2}b^2 + \cdots + nab^{n-1} + b^n.
\end{aligned}
$$

So $C(n,i)$ is the number of ways in which b can be chosen from exactly i of the n factors $(a+b)$. Since the choice of i factors is the same as identifying a subset of an n element set having exactly i elements, such a subset is called a *combination* of n elements taken i at a time. A combination differs from the permutations discussed above in that no order is involved with combinations.

The calculation of $C(n,r)$ in terms of factorials depends upon the value of $P(n,r)$ and the first principle of counting:

Proposition 8.1.7. The number of combinations of n items taken r at a time is $C(n,r) = \dfrac{n!}{(n-r)!r!}$.

Proof. Note that we can break the formation of an ordering of r elements of an n-element set into two steps. First, we select the r-element subset, which can be done in $C(n,r)$ ways, and then we place the r-element subset in order which can be done in $r!$ ways. Applying the first principle of counting, we get

$$P(n,r) = C(n,r) \cdot r!$$

and then this is solved for $C(n,r)$ to yield

$$C(n,r) = \frac{n!}{(n-r)!r!} \qquad \square$$

Example 8.1.8. Poker is a card game played with five card hands dealt from a standard deck of 52 cards. A flush is a hand with all cards belonging to the same suit, i.e., all clubs, all diamonds, all hearts, or all spades. Determine the number of flushes.

Since there are 13 cards in each suit, the number of flushes of any one suit is $C(13,5)$. Using the first principle of counting, we must multiply the number of flushes in one suit by the number of suits. Thus, the total number of flushes is

$$4 \cdot C(13,5) = 4 \cdot \frac{13!}{8!5!} = 4 \cdot 1,287 = 5,148. \qquad \blacksquare$$

The key step in the calculation of the number of operations involved in solving the traveling salesman problem will be a connection between the binomial expansion and the number of elements of a subset. This connection is revealed in the proof of the next proposition.

Proposition 8.1.9. *The number of subsets of an n element set is 2^n.*

Proof. We need to add up the numbers of subsets of all sizes, beginning with the empty set and ending with the set consisting of all n elements. But these are just the binomial coefficients $C(n,r)$ as r goes from 0 to n. We complete the proof by observing that the required sum is the result of the binomial expansion of the sum of two 1's:

$$\begin{aligned}
(1+1)^n &= C(n,0)1^n + C(n,1)1^{n-1}1 + C(n,2)1^{n-2}1^2 + \cdots + C(n,n)1^n \\
&= C(n,0) + C(n,1) + C(n,2) + \cdots + C(n,n) \\
&= 2^n \qquad \square
\end{aligned}$$

Exercises

1. Consider the Towers of Hanoi recurrence obtained above:

$$\begin{cases} H_1 &= 1 \\ H_n &= 2 \cdot H_{n-1} + 1, \ n \geq 2. \end{cases}$$

By using this formula in succession from n down to 1, express H_n as the sum of a geometric sequence with ratio 2 and then use the fact that the sum of the first n terms of a geometric series is given by

$$\sum_{i=1}^{n} ar^{i-1} = a + ar + ar^2 + \cdots + ar^{n-1} = \frac{a(1-r^n)}{1-r}, \quad r \neq 1.$$

to show that $H_n = 2^n - 1$.

2. Determine the number of five card poker hands from a standard deck of 52.

3. A *straight* in poker is a hand having five cards in sequence. Assuming that an ace is always high, apply the first principle of counting to calculate the number of straights.

4. Determine the expansion of $(2x^3 + 3)^4$.

5. Determine the expansion of $(2 - x^2)^5$.

6. If p is the probability of success in an activity that is repeated independently n times, then the term in the expansion of $(p + (1-p))^n$ in which the exponent of p is k, $0 \leq k \leq n$, represents the probability of k successes and $n - k$ failures in n repetitions.

   (a) If a baseball player is hitting .300, determine the probability of exactly two hits in five at bats.

   (b) Suppose that a sample of computer chips contains 2% that are defective. A quality control officer chooses a chip from the sample at random, tests it, and then replaces it. If he does this 10 times, what is the probability that at most two of the chips tested are defective?

7. An exercise in Section 2.4 provides a formula for the determinant of an $n \times n$ matrix in terms of the determinants of n $(n-1) \times (n-1)$ submatrices. If the number of multiplications required to evaluate the determinant of an $n \times n$ matrix is denoted by D_n, determine a recursion to evaluate D_n, and, initializing it by $D_2 = 2$, evaluate D_5 and D_6.

8.2 The longest path

In Section 4.4 we considered Dijkstra's algorithm for determining the shortest path between two nodes in a network. Here we consider the reverse problem – that of determining the longest such path – as our first dynamic programming example. We have seen this before in the context of a CPM network and done a similar process to determine the earliest time of events.

For our example, we return to the network of Example 4.3.1.

Example 8.2.1. Determine the longest path from node 0 to node 6 in the network in Figure 8.2.1.

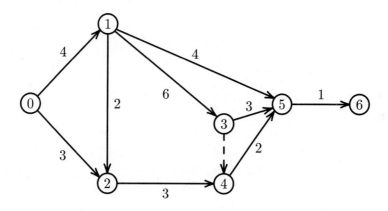

Figure 8.2.1

Before beginning the solution, let us first review the characteristics of the problem that make a solution by dynamic programming appropriate. They are:

1. The identification of a solution can be divided into stages. Here a stage will be reaching a node on the way from node 0 to node 6. The decision to make at each stage is the next node to choose in the longest path going through the current node.

2. Each stage has a number of states associated with it – in this case the choice of the next node.

3. The longest path through a given node depends upon the longest path from each adjacent node that is closer to node 6.

4. A recursion can be defined relating the length of the longest path through one node to those through nodes previously examined.

To begin to define the recursion, let d_{ij} denote the length of the link between nodes i and j and let L_i denote the length of the longest path from node i to node 6. Assume that L_i is defined for $i = k+1, k+2, \ldots, 6$ Then L_k is defined by

$$L_k = \max\{L_i + d_{ki} : d_{ki} \text{ is defined and } i > k\}.$$

This is essentially the same as the calculation of the earliest times for CPM networks, except that here we will start at node 6 and work back to node 0. Of course, for node 6, we have $L_6 = 0$. In the calculations below we record for each node the node which yields the maximum so that the longest path can be easily identified.

$$
\begin{aligned}
L_5 &= L_6 + d_{56} = 0 + 1 = 1, \quad \{6\} \\
L_4 &= L_5 + d_{45} = 1 + 2 = 3, \quad \{4\} \\
L_3 &= \max\{L_4 + d_{34}, L_5 + d_{35}\} \\
&= \max\{3 + 0, 1 + 3\} = 4, \quad \{5\} \\
L_2 &= L_4 + 3 = 3 + 3 = 6, \quad \{4\} \\
L_1 &= \max\{L_2 + d_{12}, L_3 + d_{13}, L_5 + d_{15}\} \\
&= \max\{6 + 2, 4 + 6, 1 + 4\} = 10, \quad \{3\} \\
L_0 &= \max\{L_1 + d_{01}, L_2 + d_{02}\} \\
&= \max\{10 + 4, 6 + 3\} = 14, \quad \{1\}
\end{aligned}
$$

Starting with node 0 and examining the path produced quickly yields the longest path, shown in Figure 8.2.2, which has length 14 as indicated by the calculation of L_0.

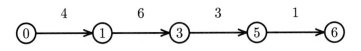

Figure 8.2.2

∎

Exercises

1. Determine the longest path from A to H in the network in Figure 8.2.3.

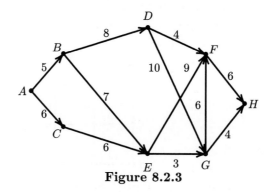

Figure 8.2.3

2. Determine the longest path from node a to node i in Figure 8.2.4.

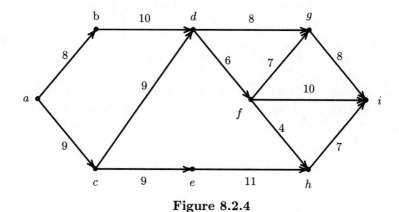

Figure 8.2.4

3. Determine the longest path from node a to node i in the network in Figure 8.2.5.

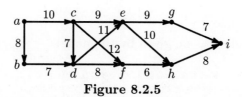

Figure 8.2.5

4. A new colleague has just called you at vertex w to say that he is leaving his home at h to come in for work at w as shown in Figure 8.2.6. The edge weights are the usual rush hour travel times in minutes. Each intersection adds a minute to the time on average because of the traffic light. If a left turn is required, the intersection is expected to add 2 minutes to the time. Assuming that the new colleague will make the worst possible choice of route, how long should it take him to get to w?

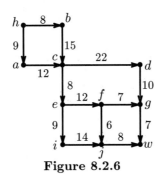

Figure 8.2.6

8.3 A fixed-cost transportation problem

We now consider a less familiar example based on one in [28]. It extends the transportation model from Chapter 4 by adding fixed costs.

Example 8.3.1. Fixed-cost transportation problem. Two warehouses have 8 and 10 units, respectively, of an item in stock. Four retail outlets demand 5, 6, 4, and 3 units, respectively. The means of shipping this commodity requires a fixed cost if any item is shipped. Thus, the cost of shipping a positive number x_{ij} of units from warehouse i to retail outlet j is given by

$$c_{ij}x_{ij} + f_{ij}, \quad i = 1,2, \ j = 1,2,3,4.$$

Let the variable costs c_{ij} be given by the matrix

$$C = \begin{bmatrix} 10 & 8 & 5 & 3 \\ 7 & 9 & 4 & 6 \end{bmatrix}$$

and the fixed costs f_{ij} be given by the matrix

$$F = \begin{bmatrix} 2 & 2 & 2 & 3 \\ 4 & 1 & 3 & 4 \end{bmatrix}.$$

Determine a shipping schedule to meet the demands at a minimum total cost.

Before considering a solution to the problem, we discuss the aspects of a problem suggested in the previous section that make it appropriate for solution by dynamic programming. They are:

1. The identification of a solution can be divided into *stages* with a decision to be made at each stage. Here, a stage is the decision of how to satisfy the demand at one of the retail outlets.

2. Each stage has a number of *states* associated with it. Here a state will be the number of items going to a retail outlet from warehouse 1. Thus, there are five states for outlet 3: $\{0, 1, 2, 3, 4\}$. Any remaining demand is then automatically filled from warehouse 2.

3. The optimal decision at any stage can be made as a continuation of decisions made at prior stages.

4. If there are N stages for the problem, a recursion can be found relating the cost (or the return in a maximization) during stage k to that of stages $k+1, k+2, \ldots, N$.

We begin the solution by first establishing some notation and then considering what happens at the individual stages – here, retail outlets.

Denote the respective demands by d_i, i.e., $d^T = [5, 6, 4, 3]$. We first consider as an example the function giving the cost of fulfilling the demand of 6 at outlet 2. Since the six units must come from either warehouse 1 or 2, we can write the cost g_2 as a function of the number of units coming from warehouse 1:

$$
g_2(x) = \begin{cases}
8 \cdot 6 + 2 & \text{if } x = 6 \\
8x + 2 + 9(6 - x) + 1 & \text{if } 1 \le x \le 5 \\
9 \cdot 6 + 1 & \text{if } x = 0.
\end{cases}
$$

In the general calculation of the cost of satisfying the demand at retail outlet j, we subscript the variable as x_{1j} to indicate the number of units coming from warehouse 1 to retail outlet j. The cost then is

$$
g_j(x_{1j}) = \begin{cases}
c_{1j}d_j + f_{1j} & \text{if } x_{1j} = d_j \\
c_{1j}x_{1j} + f_{1j} + c_{2j}(d_j - x_{1j}) + f_{2j} & \text{if } 0 < x_{1j} < d_j \\
c_{2j}d_j + f_{2j} & \text{if } x_{1j} = 0
\end{cases}
$$

for $j = 1, \ldots, 4$.

As the first step toward defining the required recursion among the g_j's we first calculate the values of the g_j's and display them in Table 8.3.1. Note that the domains of the g_j's vary according to the demand at each outlet. Thus the columns do not all have the same number of entries.

Table 8.3.1

	j			
x_{1j}	1	2	3	4
0	39	55	19	22
1	44	56	22	22
2	47	55	23	19
3	50	54	24	12
4	53	53	22	
5	52	52		
6		50		

We now can define the recurence relation

$$F_k(y) = \min\{g_k(x) + F_{k+1}(y - x) : x \le y, x \le d_k\}$$

where y is the total number of units shipped from warehouse 1 to retail outlets $k, \ldots, 4$. The domain of F_k is the set

$$\{0, \ldots, \min\{8, \sum_{i=k}^{4} d_i\}\}$$

where 8 is the supply at warehouse 1 and $\sum_{i=k}^{4} d_i$ is the total demand at retail outlets $k, \ldots, 4$.

Thus, the first step in the recurrence is $F_4 = g_4$. Since the total demand at retail outlets 3 and 4 is 7 and the supply at warehouse 1 is 8, the domain of F_3 is $\{0, 1, \ldots, 7\}$, and

$$F_3(y) = \min\{g_3(x) + g_4(y - x) : x \le y, x \le 4\}.$$

Table 8.3.2 defines F_3 using values of g_3 and g_4 from Table 8.3.1. In the table, x_{13} is the number of units shipped from warehouse 1 to retail outlet 3.

Table 8.3.2

y	x_{13}	$F_3(y)$
0	0	41
1	0	41
2	0	38
3	0	31
4	1	34
5	2	35
6	3	36
7	4	34

Observe that this process also serves to define x_{13} as a function of y. For instance, for $y = 4$,

$$
\begin{aligned}
F_3(4) &= \min\{22 + 12, 23 + 19, 24 + 22, 22 + 22\} \\
&= \min\{34, 42, 46, 44\} \\
&= 34
\end{aligned}
$$

where the successive terms correspond, respectively, to the values 1, 2, 3, and 4 of x_{13}. Since the minimum occurs when $x_{13} = 1$, the value 1 appears in the x_{13} column. We acknowledge this dependence on y by heading the column with $x_{1j}(y)$ in the subsequent tables.

In Table 8.3.3 we calculate $F_2(y)$, which has domain $\{0, 1, \ldots, 8\}$, since there is only a supply of 8 items at warehouse 1 and the total demand at outlets 2, 3, and 4 is 13.

Table 8.3.3

y	$x_{12}(y)$	$F_2(y)$
0	0	96
1	0	96
2	0	93
3	0	86
4	1	87
5	2	86
6	3	86
7	4	84
8	5	83

Finally, we calculate

$$
F_1(y) = \min\{g_1(x) + F_2(y - x) : x \leq y, x \leq 5\}.
$$

Since F_1 is the total cost of supplying all outlets, the minimum value of this function is the cost of the optimal shipping schedule. The value of y yielding the minimum will be the starting point for determining the solution.

Table 8.3.4

y	$x_{11}(y)$	$F_1(y)$
0	0	135
1	0	135
2	0	132
3	0	125
4	0	126
5	0	125
6	0	125
7	0	123
8	0	122

Since the minimum of 122 occurs for $y = 8$ and $x_{11} = 0$ (Table 8.3.4), we conclude that the first retail outlet is supplied entirely from warehouse 2, i.e., that $x_{21} = 5$. Since that leaves 8 items to be shipped from warehouse 1 to the outlets 2 through 4, we look back to row 8 of Table 8.3.3. From that row we conclude the $x_{12} = 5$ and therefore that $x_{22} = 6 - 5 = 1$. This leaves a total of 3 items to be shipped from warehouse 1 to outlets 3 and 4. So we look next at row 3 of Table 8.3.2 and find that $x_{13} = 0$ and therefore that $x_{23} = 4$. This leaves $x_{14} = 3$ and $x_{24} = 0$, and the solution is complete.

Exercises

1. Solve the fixed-cost transportation problem with two warehouses and three retail outlets if the warehouse supplies are 7 and 9, respectively, the demands are 5, 7, and 4, respectively, the variable costs are

$$C = \begin{bmatrix} 8 & 5 & 4 \\ 4 & 7 & 6 \end{bmatrix}$$

and the fixed costs are

$$F = \begin{bmatrix} 2 & 3 & 2 \\ 3 & 3 & 1 \end{bmatrix}.$$

2. Using LINDO or other software, solve Example 8.1.1 as an integer programming problem by using the approach to linear functions suggested in Section 7.6.

3. A regional production manager has gotten careless with his ordering and now faces obtaining 7 of a key part needed at three plants by expedited – hence expensive – means of shipping. He has located the parts, combined their prices with the variable shipping costs, and priced the fixed shipping penalities. Ajax Equipment has 4 of the parts and Excelsior Supplies has 3. The results of his search are given in Tables 8.3.5 and 8.3.6.

Table 8.3.5

Variable costs			
	Plant		
	1	2	3
Ajax	20	30	25
Excelsior	15	35	20

Table 8.3.6

Fixed penalties			
	Plant		
	1	2	3
Ajax	30	40	35
Excelsior	25	55	40

How should the manager place the orders to minimize the cost of acquiring the parts if he needs 2 at the first plant, 3 at the second, and 2 at the third?

4. Jim of Timely Construction must move 6 earth movers from jobs just finishing at Akron and Berea to 3 just starting. Because earth movers are oversized loads, their movement requires paying a fee. The fee does not depend on the number of loads moved as long as they are moved together and identified as over-sized loads by leading and following vehicles. He has totaled the fees accompanying vehicle costs required for each route from an ending to a beginning job, and also the gasoline and personnel costs for each earth mover for each trip. This information is in Tables 8.3.7 and 8.3.8.

Table 8.3.7

Cost per earth mover			
	Opening site		
	1	2	3
Akron	180	130	90
Berea	190	120	140

Table 8.3.8

Fees, etc.			
	Opening site		
	1	2	3
Akron	300	350	225
Berea	200	150	300

How should Jim route the earth movers if 4 are starting from the site at Akron and 2 at Berea while 2 are needed at each of the opening sites?

8.4   More examples

We begin with the cargo loading problem which is a variation of the knapsack problem discussed in Section 7.2. The approach used is based on [9]. The difference between the problems is that in the knapsack problem we had only one of each item to consider, whereas in the cargo loading problem we can load several of each item to achieve the maximum value.

Example 8.4.1. Table 8.4.1 gives the weight w_i and the value v_i for each of four items. How many of each should we load if the total weight may not exceed 15?

Table 8.4.1

	w_i	v_i
1	5	15
2	7	12
3	4	16
4	3	11

We will use a single recursion function. The stage variable will be the weight loaded. To develop the recursion, imagine that the optimal loading of items for all total weights less than w has been obtained, and now we need to determine the maximal loading for total weight w. We must consider adding any of the four possible items. So the incremental value of each item j is evaluated by adding v_j to $F(w - w_j)$, and then the maximum of the four values obtained is selected.

Writing this as a recursion, we obtain

$$F(w) = \max \{v_i + F(w - w_i) : 1 \leq i \leq 4\}.$$

To allow for all possible values of $F(w - w_i)$, to initialize the recursion we must assign values to F for w less than the smallest w_i. In this example, we must establish values for F up to $w = 2$. As before, we use a "Big M" to indicate a large positive number and set $F(w) = -M$ for $w < 0$. We set $F(w) = 0$ for $0 \leq w \leq 2$.

The next three values are easily found because for them only one item can be loaded. The first calculations are shown in detail to indicate how the values just assigned are used:

$$\begin{aligned} F(3) &= \max \{15 + F(3 - 5), 12 + F(3 - 7), 16 + F(3 - 4), 11 + F(3 - 3)\} \\ &= \max \{15 - M, 12 - M, 16 - M, 11 + 0\} = 11 \\ F(4) &= \max \{15 + F(4 - 5), 12 + F(4 - 7), 16 + F(4 - 4), 11 + F(4 - 3)\} \\ &= \max \{15 - M, 12 - M, 16 + 0, 11 + 0\} = 16 \\ F(5) &= \max \{15 + 0, 12 - M, 16 + 0, 11 + 0\} = 16 \end{aligned}$$

Ultimately to identify the optimal solution we will want to know not only the values of $F(w)$, but also the item loaded at stage w. Therefore in the calculations below, the item – or items in the case of a tie – that yield the maximum is recorded.

$$
\begin{aligned}
F(6) &= \max\{15 + F(6-5), 12 + F(6-7), 16 + F(6-4), 11 + F(6-3)\} \\
&= \max\{15 + 0, 12 - M, 16 + 0, 11 + 11\} = 22, \ \{4\} \\
F(7) &= \max\{15 + 0, 12 + 0, 16 + 11, 11 + 16\} = 27, \ \{4, 3\} \\
F(8) &= \max\{15 + 11, 12 + 0, 16 + 16, 11 + 16\} = 32, \ \{3\} \\
F(9) &= \max\{15 + 16, 12 + 0, 16 + 16, 11 + 22\} = 33, \ \{4\} \\
F(10) &= \max\{15 + 16, 12 + 11, 16 + 22, 11 + 27\} = 38, \ \{3, 4\} \\
F(11) &= \max\{15 + 22, 12 + 16, 16 + 27, 11 + 32\} = 43, \ \{4, 3\} \\
F(12) &= \max\{15 + 27, 12 + 16, 16 + 32, 11 + 33\} = 48, \ \{3\} \\
F(13) &= \max\{15 + 32, 12 + 22, 16 + 33, 11 + 38\} = 49, \ \{3, 4\} \\
F(14) &= \max\{15 + 33, 12 + 27, 16 + 38, 11 + 43\} = 54, \ \{3, 4\} \\
F(15) &= \max\{15 + 38, 12 + 32, 16 + 43, 11 + 49\} = 59, \ \{3, 4\}
\end{aligned}
$$

The final calculation above shows that the optimal value is 59, and that the last item loaded could be either item 3 or item 4. This choice can lead to multiple ways to reach the same solution, depending upon which of the two we choose. Let's assume that it was item 4 that we added last. Since $w_4 = 3$, the previous item was added when we calculated $F(15-3) = F(12)$. Reviewing that calculation reveals that at that stage we added item 3. Since $w_3 = 4$, we go back to the calculation of $F(8)$ and find that we also added item 3 there. So we reduce w by 4 again and go to the calculation of $F(4)$ to find that we also added item 3 at that stage. Reducing w by 4 yields zero, so a complete solution has been found.

Expressing the solution in terms of x_i, $1 \le i \le 4$, the number of each of the items loaded, we get the solution $x_1 = x_2 = 0, x_3 = 3, x_4 = 1$. Checking our answer with $F(15) = 59$,

$$
15 \cdot 0 + 12 \cdot 0 + 16 \cdot 3 + 11 \cdot 1 = 59.
$$

Since we had a choice of item based on the calculation of $F(15)$, there are alternative ways to generate a solution. We leave their exploration to the exercises.

A solution to this problem using the TI-92 calculator is discussed in Appendix C.

For our next example we return to the traveling salesman problem previously discussed in Section 7.7. The branch-and-bound method we used there obscured the number of computations required, but we observed that it could become too computationally intensive for a large problem. Here the computational demands of the problem will be made apparent following the solution.

The dynamic programming approach is again based on [9]. The example is from Section 7.7.

Example 8.4.2. Determine the shortest routing among five cities with the distances given in Table 8.4.2.

Table 8.4.2

		To				
		1	2	3	4	5
	1	M	23	12	18	13
	2	16	M	16	22	24
From	3	5	17	M	19	12
	4	16	17	18	M	32
	5	12	15	20	9	M

The stages in the problem are the inclusions of links as we build up to a complete circuit. Since a circuit visits each city once and returns to its starting point, to simplify matters any city can be considered as the starting point. We choose to start at city 1.

To develop the recurrence, consider what is needed to describe a partial circuit beginning at 1 and ending at j. In addition to the beginning and ending cities, we must know the set S of intermediate stops. For example, we will indicate the calculation of the minimal length of a path ending at 4 and going through 2 and 5 by $F_3(4, \{2, 5\})$. The subscript is the stage reached, i.e., the number of links required.

The recursion must add the distance d_{ij} from the city i visited just before j to the cost of reaching city i through a set of intermediate cities not including i. The number of intermediate cities visited increases by one. This yields

$$F_{k+1}(j, S) = \min \{F_k(i, S \setminus \{i\}) + d_{ij} : i \in S\}, \quad k = 1, 2, \ldots, n.$$

The recursion is initialized by the case where there are no intermediate stops, i.e., where $S = \emptyset$. These values are read directly from the top row of Table 8.4.2, since they are distances from city 1:

$$F_1(2, \emptyset) = 23, \ F_1(3, \emptyset) = 12, \ F_1(4, \emptyset) = 18, \ F_1(5, \emptyset) = 13.$$

The next stage involves a single intermediate city and so can be immediately calculated:

$$F_2(j, \{i\}) = d_{1i} + d_{ij}.$$

Since in our five-city example there are four ways to choose the city j that is reached and then three ways to choose the intermediate city i, from the first principle of counting there are $4 \cdot 3 = 12$ evaluations of F_2 to make:

$$
\begin{aligned}
F_2(2, \{3\}) &= 12 + 17 = 29 & F_2(4, \{2\}) &= 18 + 17 = 35 \\
F_2(2, \{4\}) &= 18 + 17 = 35 & F_2(4, \{3\}) &= 12 + 19 = 31 \\
F_2(2, \{5\}) &= 13 + 15 = 28 & F_2(4, \{5\}) &= 13 + 9 = 22 \\
F_2(3, \{2\}) &= 23 + 16 = 39 & F_2(5, \{2\}) &= 23 + 24 = 47 \\
F_2(3, \{4\}) &= 18 + 18 = 36 & F_2(5, \{3\}) &= 12 + 12 = 24 \\
F_2(3, \{5\}) &= 13 + 20 = 33 & F_2(5, \{4\}) &= 18 + 32 = 50
\end{aligned}
$$

In the calculations for F_3 there two ways to choose the intervening city, so a minimization is necessary. Again 12 evaluations are required, since there are four ways to choose the ending city, and for each ending city there are three sets of two intervening cities. Following the calculation we indicate in brackets the choice of the intervening city that yielded the minimum to help in the identification of the optimal circuit when the calculations are complete. The details are shown for the first calculation.

$$
\begin{aligned}
F_3(2, \{3, 4\}) &= \min\{F_2(3, \{4\}) + d_{32}, F_2(4, \{3\}) + d_{42}\} \\
&= \min\{36 + 17, 31 + 17\} = 48, \quad \{4\} \\
F_3(2, \{3, 5\}) &= \min\{33 + 17, 24 + 15\} = 39, \quad \{3\} \\
F_3(2, \{4, 5\}) &= \min\{22 + 17, 40 + 15\} = 39, \quad \{4\} \\
F_3(3, \{2, 4\}) &= \min\{35 + 17, 35 + 16\} = 51, \quad \{4\} \\
F_3(3, \{2, 5\}) &= \min\{28 + 16, 47 + 20\} = 44, \quad \{5\} \\
F_3(3, \{4, 5\}) &= \min\{22 + 18, 40 + 20\} = 40, \quad \{5\} \\
F_3(4, \{3, 5\}) &= \min\{33 + 19, 24 + 9\} = 33, \quad \{5\} \\
F_3(4, \{2, 3\}) &= \min\{29 + 22, 39 + 19\} = 53, \quad \{3\} \\
F_3(4, \{2, 5\}) &= \min\{28 + 22, 47 + 9\} = 50, \quad \{5\} \\
F_3(5, \{3, 4\}) &= \min\{36 + 12, 31 + 32\} = 48, \quad \{3\} \\
F_3(5, \{2, 3\}) &= \min\{29 + 24, 39 + 12\} = 51, \quad \{2\} \\
F_3(5, \{2, 4\}) &= \min\{35 + 24, 35 + 32\} = 59, \quad \{4\}
\end{aligned}
$$

In the next stage there is only a single set of three intervening cities between 1 and the ending city. Thus there is a single calculation for each ending city, but the minimization is over three choices of the city immediately preceding the ending city.

$$F_4(2, \{3,4,5\}) = \min\{F_3(3, \{4,5\}) + d_{32}, F_3(4, \{3,5\}) + d_{42},$$
$$F_3(5, \{3,4\}) + d_{52}\}$$
$$= \min\{40 + 17, 33 + 17, 48 + 15\} = 50, \quad \{4\}$$
$$F_4(3, \{2,4,5\}) = \min\{39 + 16, 50 + 18, 59 + 20\} = 55, \quad \{2\}$$
$$F_4(4, \{2,3,5\}) = \min\{39 + 22, 44 + 19, 51 + 9\} = 60, \quad \{5\}$$
$$F_4(5, \{2,3,4\}) = \min\{48 + 24, 51 + 12, 53 + 32\} = 63, \quad \{3\}$$

The values of F_4 are for partial tours that start at 1 and enter each of the other four cities. Thus it remains only to return to city 1. This requires a single minimization over the four possibilities for the last city visited before completing the circuit.

$$F_5(1, \{2,3,4,5\}) = \min\{F_4(j, \{2,3,4,5\} \setminus \{j\}) + d_{j1} : j = 2,3,4,5\}$$
$$= \min\{50 + 16, 55 + 5, 60 + 16, 63 + 12\}$$
$$= 60, \quad \{3\}$$

So we return to 1 from 3. Looking back to the calculation of $F_4(3, \{2,4,5\})$, we see that before 3 we visited 2. Since 3 cannot precede 2, we examine $F_3(2, \{4,5\})$, which reveals that before 2 we visited 4. Since the circuit started at 1, by process of elimination, we must have first gone to 5. Figure 8.4.5 shows the optimal tour of length 60.

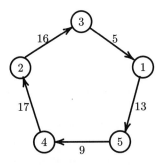

Figure 8.4.7

We now use Proposition 9.1.9 to calculate the number of additions required to solve an n-city traveling salesman problem by this method. At any stage, there are $n-1$ ways to choose the ending city of the partial circuit. If there are i intervening cities, since cities j and 1 are not candidates for intermediate stops, there are $C(n-2, i)$ ways to choose the set of i intervening cities. There is an addition for each intervening city.

Thus, using the first principle of counting, this yields $(n-1)iC(n-i,i)$ additions at stage i. Summing this quantity over i,

$$(n-1)\sum_{i=1}^{n-2} iC(n-2,i) = (n-1)\sum_{i=1}^{n-2} i\frac{(n-2)!}{i!(n-2-i)!}$$

Now by canceling the i's and factoring out $n-2$,

$$= (n-1)(n-2)\sum_{i=1}^{n-2} \frac{(n-3)!}{(i-1)!(n-2-i)!}$$

and by letting $j = i - 1$,

$$= (n-1)(n-2)\sum_{j=0}^{n-3} \frac{(n-3)!}{j!(n-3-j)!}$$

we obtain by Proposition 9.1.9:

$$= (n-1)(n-2)2^{n-3}.$$

So, unlike the graph algorithms analyzed in Chapter 4, this dynamic programming approach to the traveling salesman problem is not effective, i.e., the number of elementary operations is not bounded by a polynomial expression in the size of the problem. With the factor 2^{n-3} in the expression for the number of additions, the number needed can be expected to double with the addition of each city to the problem. Our formula gives 48 additions for our example above. For a 10-city problem – not at all large by practical considerations – the number is 9,216, and for 20 cities it is 44,826,624.

Exercises

1. By making alternative choices of the item loaded, generate the solution to Example 8.3.1 by two other sequences of loadings.

2. A candidate for a county office is planning her advertising campaign. Her advisors suggest three kinds of advertising: radio, newspaper, and billboards. The proposed ads cost $250, $300, and $600, respectively. Estimates are that a radio ad would reach 3,000 people, a newspaper ad 7,000, and a billboard 10,000. Her advertising budget is $2,800. How many ads of each type should she buy to reach the most people?

3. A county adminstrator needs to invest $20,000 of county funds. By statute his choices are limited to certain funds which happen to accept investments only in several thousand dollar increments. The increments and expected returns are shown in Table 8.4.3.

Table 8.4.3

Very Secure Bond Fund	$3,000	8%
Risky Venture Fund	$3,500	10%
Stodgy Blue Chip Fund	$2,000	7%
Aggressive Growth Fund	$1,000	9%
Gold & Oil Hedge Fund	$4,000	9%

How many increments of each fund should he purchase to maximize the expected return?

4. Solve Exercise 2 in Section 7.7 by dynamic progamming.

5. Solve Exercise 1 in Section 7.7 by dynamic progamming.

6. Solve Exercise 5 in Section 7.7 by dynamic progamming.

8.5 Summary and objectives

Dynamic programming is a general problem solving technique that applies to problems for which

1. A solution can be generated by a sequence of stages, and

2. At each stage there is a choice to be made among several states.

For example, in applying dynamic programming to a network problem such as the longest path problem or the traveling salesman problem, the stages are the nodes which are reached, and the states are the choices for the next node.

Because dynamic programming requires recursive functions, the chapter began with an introduction to recursion. The examples of the Fibonacci sequence, the Towers of Hanoi, and the binomial coefficients were introduced. These examples have in common the fact that each term after the first can be determined in terms of a function of one or more preceding terms.

We first considered the longest path problem, which provided a familiar place to start because of its similarity to the calculations of earliest times in critical path networks in Section 4.3. We then considered the fixed-cost transportation model, the cargo loading problem, and revisited the traveling salesman problem.

Objectives

Having read this chapter, the reader should be able to:

1. Construct a basic recurrence relation to solve a problem.

2. Recognize a problem appropriate for solution by dynamic programming.

3. Determine the longest path joining two nodes in a network. Example 8.2.1. Exercise 1 in Section 8.2.

4. Solve a two supplier fixed-cost transportation problem by dynamic programming. Example 8.3.1. Exercise 1 in Section 8.3.

5. Solve a cargo loading problem by dynamic programming. Example 8.4.1. Exercise 2 in Section 8.4.

6. Solve a small traveling salesman problem by dynamic programming. Example 8.4.2. Exercise 3 in Section 8.4.

Chapter 9

Case Studies

The goal of this chapter is to present a more challenging problem solving experience. Appropriate software is assumed to be available.

The first case – the Widget Incorporated production problem – is solved in its entirety as an example. The solution of the basic product mix problem can be done without integer variables. Approaching the planning issues posed by the management of Widget involves incorporating additional flexibility in the model. One of the issues is best considered using integer variables.

Some of the problems can lead to extensive discussion of the solution. For instance, the problem for American Oak, Inc., is to allocate the time of the senior employees and to determine the number of parts to be purchased. However, the student may also wish to discuss how to schedule time on the machines in order to implement the solution.

The problem involving the design of storage lockers involves nonlinear optimization to decide how many lockers can be built with the available space and budget. Since the number of lockers must be an integer, an integer variable is required.

The McIntire family must decide how to use its resources for the coming year. As is common with farms, borrowing money to obtain start-up capital for the season is an issue.

A fraction of a cent saved in the production of a beverage container means a major savings over the course of a large production run. The problem on cylinders investigates several aspects of this optimization problem.

The Books 'n Pastry case involves management of a construction project and the options of employing additional workers that might arise. Decisions among the options are likely to involve integer variables.

The blind trust case requires that a portfolio of four stocks be redistributed to maximize the return for a year based on a broker's prediction. Integer variables are required to trigger commission charges.

The case involving Max's efforts to reduce his taxes involves integer variables to control the application of the amounts in the tax reduction strategies between deductions and tax credits.

Supplying goods to a network of customers is a common network problem. The case discussed here leads to a combination of shortest path questions with a transportation problem.

9.1 Tweaking Widget's production

Widget Incorporated (WI) is planning the production of three of its key products for a four week period. The products they are considering sell for prices of $430, $520, and $380, respectively. Four of the component parts needed are made by the company. The number of each of the four parts needed for each product is provided in Table 9.1.1.

Table 9.1.1

		Parts			
		1	2	3	4
	1	2	1	1	1
Products	2	1	1	2	1
	3	0	1	2	1

Two types of worker are employed by WI in both the production of parts as well as in the production of the three products. The number of minutes of each kind of worker time required for each part appear in Table 9.1.2. The table also provides the other costs in terms of materials and overhead needed for each part and product.

Table 9.1.2

	Parts				Products		
	1	2	3	4	1	2	3
Work 1 time	5	0	8	0	8	12	0
Work 2 time	0	9	0	10	0	5	12
Other costs	$8	$4	$6	$5	$55	$70	$45

Each worker generates 38 hours a week of useful production time. The company employs three workers of type one and four of type two. An hour of work of type one costs $25 and of type two costs $20.

Basing their recommendations on past sales for the time of year the sales staff recommends that a minimum of 400 of Product 2 and 500 of Product 3 be produced. The basic problem is to plan Widget's production of the three products to maximize their profit.

Management has also asked analysts to consider four other questions which they believe have the potential to strengthen their bottom line. Their questions are:

1. Production of part 3 can be outsourced to Elcheapo Manufacturing at a cost of $8 per unit. At that price would it be advantageous to stop their production of part 3 at WI and use the parts produced by Elcheapo?

2. The company has found a market for part 1 as an independent product. Would it be profitable to sell it for $19?

3. Would any re-assignment of workers from one work type to the other be effective in enhancing their profit?

4. Are the recommendations of the sales staff effective in generating the maximum profit?

The basic model

Analysis of the problem begins with a model of the current situation. It can then be altered to consider the four planning questions asked by management. We use $X1$, $X2$, and $X3$ to represent the number of each of the three products produced, $W1$ and $W2$ to represent the number of minutes of the two types of work involved, and $P1$ to $P4$ to represent the respective number of each of the four parts produced.

The objective function coefficients of the Xi are the selling prices reduced by the other costs from Table 9.1.2.

The coefficients of the Pi are the negatives of the corresponding other costs from Table 9.1.2.

Because the production times are given in minutes, we convert the cost of the two types of work to the cost per minute. The negatives of those costs are the objective function coefficients of $W1$ and $W2$.

Turning to the constraints, note that each has a label in the LINDO model that indicates something about the constraint.

The first two constraints are the sales requirements. The next four each come from a column in Table 9.1.1 and serve to determine the number of each part needed to make a mix of the three products. The next two constraints each come from a row in Table 9.1.2 and serve to determine the number of minutes of each work type needed. The final two constraints limit the number of minutes available. Their right-hand sides are the product of the number of workers, 38 hours per week, four weeks, and 60 minutes per hour.

This model and its solution appear in Listing 9.1.1.

Listing 9.1.3

```
   MAX      385 X1 + 450 X2 + 335 X3 - 0.417 W1 - 0.333 W2
            - 8 P1 - 4 P2 - 6 P3 - 5 P4
   SUBJECT TO
           Prod 2)   X2 >=    400
           Prod 3)   X3 >=    500
           Part 1)   2 X1 + X2 - P1 =    0
           Part 2)   X1 + X2 + X3 - P2 =    0
           Part 3)   X1 + 2 X2 + 2 X3 - P3 =    0
           Part 4)   1 X1 + X2 + X3 - P4 =    0
           Work 1)   8 X1 + 12 X2 - W1 + 5 P1 + 8 P3 =    0
           Work 2)   5 X2 + 12 X3 - W2 + 9 P2 + 10 P4 =    0
           W1 avl)   W1 <=    27360
           W2 avl)   W2 <=    36480
   END


LP OPTIMUM FOUND AT STEP        5

        OBJECTIVE FUNCTION VALUE

        1)        419969.1

   VARIABLE         VALUE          REDUCED COST
         X1       17.689243           0.000000
         X2      400.000000           0.000000
         X3      856.255005           0.000000
         W1    27360.000000           0.000000
         W2    36480.000000           0.000000
```

P1	435.378479	0.000000
P2	1273.944214	0.000000
P3	2530.199219	0.000000
P4	1273.944214	0.000000

ROW	SLACK OR SURPLUS	DUAL PRICES
PROD 2)	0.000000	-27.733068
PROD 3)	356.254974	0.000000
PART 1)	0.000000	57.880478
PART 2)	0.000000	48.820717
PART 3)	0.000000	85.808762
PART 4)	0.000000	54.800797
WORK 1)	0.000000	9.976095
WORK 2)	0.000000	4.980080
W1 AVL)	0.000000	9.559095
W2 AVL)	0.000000	4.647079

RANGES IN WHICH THE BASIS IS UNCHANGED:

OBJ COEFFICIENT RANGES

VARIABLE	CURRENT COEF	ALLOWABLE INCREASE	ALLOWABLE DECREASE
X1	385.000000	145.802109	21.787169
X2	450.000000	27.733068	INFINITY
X3	335.000000	252.561356	89.724380
W1	-0.417000	INFINITY	9.559095
W2	-0.333000	INFINITY	4.647079
P1	-8.000000	72.901054	17.940722
P2	-4.000000	INFINITY	103.895523
P3	-6.000000	37.525608	64.800941
P4	-5.000000	INFINITY	103.895523

RIGHTHAND SIDE RANGES

ROW	CURRENT RHS	ALLOWABLE INCREASE	ALLOWABLE DECREASE
PROD 2	400.000000	13.896714	400.000000
PROD 3	500.000000	356.254974	INFINITY
PART 1	0.000000	1138.333252	57.290325
PART 2	0.000000	61.666664	764.273499

PART 3	0.000000	1176.578857	35.806450
PART 4	0.000000	55.500000	687.846130
WORK 1	0.000000	9412.630859	286.451599
WORK 2	0.000000	555.000000	6878.461426
W1 AVL	27360.000000	9412.630859	286.451599
W2 AVL	36480.000000	555.000000	6878.461426

Thus, if Widgets ignores the questions raised by management, its profit of nearly $420,000 would be attained by producing only a token number of the first product, the minimum recommended number of the second, and well over the minimum number of the third.

Of the issues raised by management, only the question regarding the recommendations of the sales staff can be clearly addressed by the solution to the basic model. Note that the dual price associated with the first constraint that requires at least 400 of the second product be made is negative. This indicates that increasing the right hand side would lower the profit, decreasing it would increase the profit. It follows that the requirement that the 400 level should be reduced to increase profit. So whatever the motivation of the sales staff in recommending this level of production is, it is above the optimal level. This, together with the sensitivity analysis report indicates that elimination of this constraint entirely would increase the profit.

Recommendations to management

We now consider the other three questions. Since they are essentially unrelated, we will make three separate modifications to the model in Listing 9.1.1 to address them.

Considering first the outsourcing of part 3, we need to modify the model to allow a choice between buying the part or making it. We let OSP3 denote the number of units outsourced and include it in the Part 3 constraint, and also in the objective function with a coefficient of -8 to indicate that we are buying it. We then need to follow the procedures used in Section 7.6 to make certain that at most one of P3 and OSP3 is positive. We introduce two $\{0,1\}$ variables, DP3 and DOSP3, to impose this restriction. In constraints Lim P3 and Lim OSP3 the 99,000 is just a number much larger than any value that we could expect for either P3 or OSP3. Together with these constraints, constraint Just 1 guarantees that at most one of P3 and OSP3 is positive.

To allow part 1 to be treated as an independent product, we denote the number sold by SP1. This new variable is inserted in the objective function

with a coefficient of 11, the selling price minus other costs; and in the `Work`
1 constraint to allow work to be allocated to its production.

Finally, to consider the possibility of re-assigning workers from work 1
to work 2, we introduce two new variables, `W1TO2` and `W2TO1`, to represent
the number of minutes moved from work 1 to work 2 or moved from work
2 to work 1, respectively. Then inserting + `W1TO2` − `W2TO1` into the `Work`
1 constraint and − `W1TO2` + `W2TO1` into the `Work 2` constraint allocates the
shifted minutes appropriately. The difference in cost of a minute of time is
$0.084. Putting the two new variables in the objective function with the
appropriate sign on the 0.084 completes the modification. Note that we
expect at most one of these new variables to be positive, but that adding
constraints as for `P3` and `OSP3` is not necessary. The columns of `W1TO2` and
`W2TO1` are negatives of each other, so at most one of them can be positive.
This is essentially expressing an unrestricted variable as the difference of two
nonnegative variables as discussed in Section 3.6.

Listing 9.1.2 contains the new model and its solution.

Listing 9.1.4

```
    MAX     385 X1 + 450 X2 + 335 X3 - 0.417 W1 - 0.333 W2
          - 8 P1 - 4 P2 - 6 P3 - 5 P4 + 0.084 W1TO2 - 0.084 W2TO1
          - 8 OSP3 + 11 SP1
    SUBJECT TO
            Prod 2)    X2 >=    400
            Prod 3)    X3 >=    500
            Part 1)    2 X1 + X2 - P1 =     0
            Part 2)    X1 + X2 + X3 - P2 =     0
            Part 3)    X1 + 2 X2 + 2 X3 - P3 - OSP3 =      0
            Part 4)    1 X1 + X2 + X3 - P4 =     0
            Work 1)    8 X1 + 12 X2 - W1 + 5 P1 + 8 P3   + W1TO2
                    - W2TO1 + 5 SP1 =     0
            Work 2)    5 X2 + 12 X3 - W2 + 9 P2 + 10 P4   - W1TO2
                    + W2TO1 =      0
            W1 avl)    W1 <=    27360
            W2 avl)    W2 <=    36480
            Lim P3) - 99000 DP3 + P3 <=    0
            Lim OSP3) - 99000 DOSP3 + OSP3 <=     0
            Just 1)    DP3 + DOSP3 <=    1
    END
    INTE    DP3
```

```
INTE    DOSP3
```

NEW INTEGER SOLUTION OF   623710.812 AT BRANCH 1 PIVOT   36
BOUND ON OPTIMUM: 623710.8

OBJECTIVE FUNCTION VALUE

1)   623710.8

VARIABLE	VALUE	REDUCED COST
DP3	0.000000	0.000000
DOSP3	1.000000	0.000000
X1	0.000000	24.540390
X2	1179.024414	0.000000
X3	500.000000	0.000000
W1	27360.000000	0.000000
W2	36480.000000	0.000000
P1	1179.024414	0.000000
P2	1679.024414	0.000000
P3	0.000000	79.759216
P4	1679.024414	0.000000
W1TO2	7316.585449	0.000000
W2TO1	0.000000	0.000000
OSP3	3358.048828	0.000000
SP1	0.000000	40.099514

ROW	SLACK OR SURPLUS	DUAL PRICES
PROD 2)	779.024414	0.000000
PROD 3)	0.000000	-4.212976
PART 1)	0.000000	59.099514
PART 2)	0.000000	95.223122
PART 3)	0.000000	8.000000
PART 4)	0.000000	106.359024
WORK 1)	0.000000	10.219902
WORK 2)	0.000000	10.135902
W1 AVL)	0.000000	9.802902
W2 AVL)	0.000000	9.802902
LIM P3)	0.000000	0.000000
LIM OSP3)	95641.953125	0.000000

JUST 1)   0.000000   0.000000

The first thing we note is that the profit is up about \$200,000 or just under 50%. At least one of management's ideas can be effective.

Since SP1 is zero, that part shouldn't become a product. Its reduced cost indicates that WI would need to charge at least \$40 more per part for it to be a profitable venture.

But outsourcing part 3 seems to be a major success, and since W1T02 is over 7,300 minutes, one worker should be moved from work 1 to work 2 for about three of the four weeks. Since this would result in a loss of pay for that worker, management will need to resolve any work rules issues that might arise.

Finally, note that production of product 3 is at its minimum required level. The dual price is negative, but much less than that corresponding to product 2 in the solution of the basic model. So in this model the suggestions from the sales staff seem more appropriate.

9.2 A furniture sales opportunity

American Oak, Inc., manufactures furniture, both finished and unfinished. One of their sales staff, perhaps over anxious to obtain a significant order in bad economic times and not as aware as he should have been of the company's limitations, has taken an order that requires the company to produce 1,000 unfinished oak tables. The catch is that the order must be fulfilled in one week.

Each table requires a base, four shafts, and a top. These parts are produced using three types of machines: a lathe, a saw, and a sander. The company has four machines of each type available. The time required on each machine for each part and the current parts inventory are given in Table 9.2.1.

Table 9.2.1

	Minutes per part			Parts
	Lathe	Saw	Sander	inventory
Base	6.0	10.0	7.00	60
Shaft	3.0	0.2	0.25	80
Top	0.0	5.0	7.50	20

In addition, each table is shipped unassembled and requires 10 minutes to package for shipment.

A base requires 2 board feet of lumber, a top requires 8. American Oak has 9,000 board feet of lumber in stock and could purchase more for $1.35 per board foot. The linear stock needed for the table shafts is used in many other products, and supply of it is not expected to be a factor in planning the week's production.

American Oak has thirteen production employees. Two can operate only a lathe, two only a saw, and two only a sander. Four work only in packaging. The remaining three are senior employees and can operate all three types of equipment, as well as work in packing. All production employees work 40 hours each week.

Because of the exceptional opportunity presented by this large order, American Oak is willing to devote all the week's labor to it and to run its inventory of table parts to zero if necessary. Because it does not seem likely that the company can make all the necessary parts itself, American Oak has investigated other sources for parts. The best prices that it has found from another supplier are $10.50 for a base, $0.65 for a shaft, and $24.50 for a top.

How should American Oak allocate the time of the three senior employees to minimize the cost of the parts and/or lumber, if any, that must be bought?

9.3   Building storage lockers

After years of indecision, McGeorge Landowner has finally decided what to do with a parcel of land he owns. The biggest level rectangular part of the land measures 85 feet by 42 feet, just big enough to put in some rental storage lockers. He has $8,000 available for this enterprise, and has done some research to guide his planning.

He plans to build the lockers in two rows backing on each other with the roof line running above the wall separating the two rows of storage lockers. A plan of the end view of the building is shown in Figure 9.3.1.

McGeorge has found that the smallest useful size for a storage locker is a rectangualar solid of volume 400 cubic feet. For all the space to be useful, the exterior wall will be no higher than 6 and half feet. Thus, the 400 cubic feet does not include any additional space beneath the sloping roof. He has obtained quotes for the interior walls separating the compartments of $0.45

per square foot, of $0.65 per square foot for exterior walls, and $0.75 per square foot for the roof. To allow fairly large items to be stored he will install a door 6 feet high and 3 and a half feet wide in each locker. Such a door will cost him $45. The building will sit on a concrete pad that will cost $2 per square foot.

Because of the relatively great expense of the roof, he has decided to go with a roof that slopes at only 30° and has no overhang. He is also planning to omit gutters. The concrete pad will extend 3 feet from the front of the lockers and two feet from each end of the building.

Determine the maximum number of storage lockers that he can build.

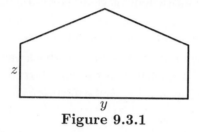

Figure 9.3.1

9.4 The McIntire farm

Angus McIntire and his family are part-time farmers who are making plans for the coming growing season. They are considering three crops: potatoes, soybeans, and corn. The family has also previously raised pigs and sheep. However, there is an old chicken coop on the property that they bought three years ago. It has the capacity for 600 chickens and can be prepared for use at a cost of $500.

Their farm has 200 acres for crops and a 3,000-square-foot pen for their livestock. A neighbor has made an offer to rent all or part of one 50-acre section of their land for $60 per acre.

The family can commit 200 days of labor to their farm, and they have $1,500 for start-up costs. Additional labor can be hired for $30 per day, but in the McIntire's experience a hired hand is only 80% as effective as a family member. Table 9.4.1 gives the time requirement, input cost, income per bushel, and yield per acre for each of the three crops.

Each pig requires two days of labor, 20 bushels of corn, and 120 square feet of pasture space. A sheep requires 200 square feet of pasture, 15 bushels of corn, and three days of labor. Each roost of 100 chickens requires 15 bushels of corn, 200 square feet of space, and two days of labor.

Table 9.4.1

	Income per bushel	Days per acre	Bushels per acre	Input cost per acre
Corn	$4.50	3	25	$60
Soybeans	$7.00	4	20	$80
Potatoes	$5.00	2	30	$40

Input costs for a pig, a sheep, and a roost of 100 chickens are $20, $25, and $50, respectively. Their respective net revenues are $80, $90, and $120. Angus has 150 bushels of corn in storage for use early in the season, but he needs to store corn from this year's crop for the next season. His plan is to store a supply equal to half of their needs for livestock this year. If necessary, additional corn to feed livestock can be bought for $6 per bushel.

The McIntires can borrow up to $2,000 at 8% annual interest compounded monthly. It will cost $1.0439 to pay back each dollar borrowed.

Determine how much of each crop to plant and the number of each type of livestock to raise to maximize their farm revenue.

9.5   Cylinders for beverages

In this case we consider several settings of the problem of producing a cylinder – most likely a can for a food or beverage product – in an optimal manner. We start out by posing the purely geometric problem first considered as an exercise in Section 5.3.

The minimal-surface cylinder. Determine the ratio of the height to the radius of the base of the cylinder having a given volume and the minimal surface area.

In the case of a beverage can, the process of filling it under pressure makes it necessary to leave space at the top. We consider the effect of that requirement on the shape of the can.

The empty-space effect. Determine the ratio of the height to the radius of the base of a cylindrical can to hold 200 cc of a fluid if the top centimeter of the can must be empty. How does the ratio change from that of the abstract cylinder considered above?

But if one were to actually manufacture a cylinder, some material might be lost in the production process, and that might make a change in the shape of the cylinder requiring the least material. Here we consider a rather primitive approach to making a can from a sheet of tin.

The problem considering waste. The curved sides of a cylindrical can are made from a single rectangle, and we can assume that no waste is involved in cutting it from a sheet of tin. But in making the circular ends, one approach would be to cut each end from a hexagonal piece of material, as illustrated in Figure 9.5.1. This process does involve wasted material from each end. Allowing for this waste, what proportions for a cylindrical tin can of a given volume will require the smallest amount of tin?

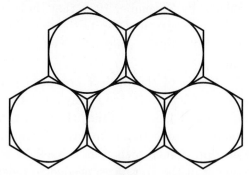

Figure 9.5.1

Because the curved lateral surface of a can resists pressure from the contents better, there may be an advantage to using different materials in the ends and in the sides. Then we might want to consider minimizing the cost of the material. When this complication is added, a numerical method of solving polynomial equations becomes very helpful. The solve(command on a TI-82 would do, as would `fsolve` in *Maple*.

Introducing prices. A purveyor of canned vegetables is modifying can production to employ metric units. It wishes to manufacture cylindrical cans holding 1/5 liter (200 cc) keeping the material cost to a minimum. The metal in the ends of the can costs 0.1 cent/cm^2, and the metal in the sides costs 0.05 cent/cm^2. Soldering is necessary around both ends and along the straight seam from top to bottom. Soldering costs 0.02 cent/cm. Determine the dimensions of the cheapest can and the ratio of its height to the radius of its base.

The next version of the problem combines the issues of the waste involved in the ends with the costs of material.

A model with waste and prices. Determine the most economical tin can for the purveyor in the previous exercise allowing for waste as above.

9.6   Books by the holidays

On August 20 the Timely Construction Company (TCC) learns that it has submitted the successful bid to be the major contractor on the construction of a new superstore in the Books 'n Pastry chain. An important part of its successful bid was a commitment to meeting deadlines. Books 'n Pastry wants the store completed by November 10 so that they can take full advantage of the holiday shopping season. Despite their confidence in TCC, they have placed a $3,000 penalty in the contract for each day that the opening of the store is delayed.

For this reason planning of the project has been placed in the hands of Jim Timely – JT to his friends – the company's most experienced project supervisor. As a first step, JT has determined the activities involved, the dependencies among them, and an estimate in days on some of their durations. The activities without durations provided in Table 9.6.1 will have durations based on JT's assessment of the crew sizes needed to finish on time.

Note that in his planning JT allows for adding additional workers on some of the tasks. These workers must be taken from other job sites. Since pulling workers off a project affects its schedule, he strongly prefers not to add workers unless he must in order to avoid the contractual penalty.

The building site is level, so the only excavation required is for water access and for pouring footers. Different crews will work on these projects, so they can proceed at the same time. The footers can be dug in four days with one backhoe, or in two days with two backhoes.

The footers for the walls can be poured in four days with one concrete truck and crew or in two days with a second truck and crew. In either case an additional day is required for the concrete to cure before concrete block walls can be laid on them or the floor of the building can be poured.

JT estimates that 4,800 concrete blocks will be needed, of which 1,200 are for the front. A bricklayer typically can lay 200 blocks a day. The estimated number of bricks required is 20,700, of which 1,800 will go on the store front. A bricklayer can lay an estimated 450 bricks a day. Timely plans to have two bricklayers working on the walls and to add a third while the front is being bricked. A third bricklayer could be added for the walls if necessary.

The concrete floor can be poured in four days with one concrete mixer and crew, or in two days with two mixers and crews. The floor must cure a day before workers can walk on it.

A crew of four can put up the roofing trusses in six days. Assigning two more workers to the task will reduce it to four days.

Table 9.6.1

	Activity	Immediate predecessors	Duration
A.	Prepare site	–	2
B.	Get initial supplies	–	2
C.	Excavate for footers	A	
D.	Install water access	B	4
E.	Pour concrete footers	C, D	
F.	Lay block walls	E	
G.	Pour concrete floor	E	
H.	Brick side walls	F	
I.	Block and brick store front	E	
J.	Frame interior walls	G	
K.	Install roof trusses	F	
L.	Install doors and store front	I	3
M.	Pave parking lot	K	2
N.	Build roof	M	
O.	Wire interior	J, N	
P.	Finish interior	O	
Q.	Landscape lot	H, I, M	2

JT finds that the building will require 600 square yards of roofing. A two-person team of roofers can build 60 square yards of roofing in a day. Adding two more workers to the team will increase the building rate to 100 square yards a day.

Another crew of four can frame the interior walls in five days. The addition of two more workers will reduce the task to three days. JT is gambling that the weather will permit interior framing to proceed before the roof is complete.

Wiring the interior is estimated to require four days for a crew of three electricians. The addition of another electrician will reduce that time by a day.

Finishing the interior to a point where the building can be turned over to Books 'n Pastries to stock the shelves will take the crew of four eight days.

Up to three more workers can be added to this task, and each worker added will reduce the time required by a day.

Determine if Timely can complete the project on time using a five-day work week, and if so, determine a schedule for its completion that will minimize the use of added labor. Also analyze how to respond if JT's gamble on the weather appears to be failing and framing of the interior walls must be delayed until the roof has been completed.

9.7   Into a blind trust

You have just accepted a sensitive government assignment on Wall Street for a year. One of the conditions is to avoid conflict of interest issues your stock portfolio must be placed into a blind trust. You are permitted to reapportion your investments among currently held stocks, but you may not purchase any new stocks whose fortune you might be in a position to know, or perhaps even to affect, during your government service.

Currently, your portfolio consists of four stocks: 300 shares of Robo Maid, a fast-growing company manufacturing and selling androids capable of performing an ever-increasing list of household tasks with shares now trading at $46; Air Flit, a passenger airline specializing in quick overseas flights, whose shares, of which you own 400, sell for $72; 200 shares of Zen Net, a recent start-up devoted to teaching Zen meditation over the Internet, which you bought as an initial product offering (IPO) and now is selling for $5 a share; and the big item in your portfolio, Grande Vision and Sound, an established consumer electronics manufacturer of which you hold 700 shares now selling for $54.

To establish your trust you consult your broker, Merrill Hunter, whose firm handled the Zen Net IPO. He consults his charts and economic indicators and provides the predictions in Table 9.7.1 for the value of your stocks a year from now, together with an estimate of their dividends for the year.

Table 9.7.1

Stock	Predicted price	Estimated dividend
Robo Maid	$52	$2
Air Flit	$60	$3
Zen Net	$6	0
Grande Vision and Sound	$58	$4

Merrill recommends that for diversification at least 30% of the current value of the portfolio remain in a combination of the more established companies Air Flit and Grande Vision and Sound.

The terms of the trust provide for a one-time reallocation among the stocks. Each transaction from one stock to another triggers a $50 commission for Merrill. Fractional shares are permitted. If you follow your broker's advice, how should you reallocate your portfolio to have the maximum total value at the end of your year of government service? Assuming that Merrill's predictions are correct, how much does following his advice on diversification reduce the year-end value of your portfolio?

9.8 Max's taxes

The principality of Upper Tropical Haven (UTH) has tax policies that are quite friendly to individual proprietorships. Indeed, many of the leading citizens are tax exiles from much larger, better-known states.

The principality allows a tax deduction for both the central and local taxes on a number of business expenses. The central tax rate is 22%; local rates vary. But the neat feature is that some expenses qualify for a tax credit; i.e., the full amount of the expense is subtracted from the tax due. But there is a limit – this tax credit is capped at 15% of the previous year's central tax liability. Of course, an expense cannot be applied to both a deduction and a credit, nor can it be split between a deduction and a credit.

Fitzhugh (Max) Maxworth is one of the individual proprietors who came to UTH to enjoy the tax laws as well as the splendid weather. Last year he paid $108,000 in central taxes, and at mid-year this year he anticipates a central tax liability of $140,000 before any business deductions or tax credits. His local tax rate as a resident of Palm Plantation is 4%.

Max wants to take steps in the second half of the year to reduce his tax burden. He figures that he can allocate $30,000 among several tax reduction strategies as listed in Table 9.8.1. The table indicates the amount Max is planning, the taxes the category is subject to, and whether the item qualifies as a tax credit.

Of these amounts, the retirement contribution and the church pledge are maximum amounts – the actual amounts can vary. The other items are all fixed amounts.

Table 9.8.1

Strategy	Amount	Tax liability Central	Local	Tax credit
Retirement plan contribution	$4,000	Yes	No	No
Hire his son	$8,000	Yes	Yes	Yes
Repair roof	$5,000	Yes	Yes	Yes
Entertain clients	$1,400	Yes	No	No
Prepay church pledge	$2,500	Yes	Yes	Yes
Prepay rent	$3,200	Yes	Yes	Yes
Buy office equipment	$4,100	Yes	Yes	No
Expand staff health plan	$3,500	Yes	No	Yes
Buy car for business	$15,000	Yes	No	Yes

Determine which options Max should take, which ones should be deductions, and which should be applied to tax credits for the maximum tax reduction.

9.9 A supply network

The network in Figure 9.9.1 shows the marketing region for an organization with three warehouses – located at A, B and C – that supply retail outlets at nodes $1, 2, \ldots, 8$. The edge weights are the costs of shipping one unit over the corresponding link.

Tables 9.9.1 and 9.9.2 give the supplies and demands in the system for one shipping period. The contracts between the supplier and the retailers call for a penalty per unit for orders not fulfilled, and the penalties are also provided.

Table 9.9.1

Supplies	
A	200
B	170
C	160

Table 9.9.2

	Demand	Penalty
1	75	$10
2	60	$8
3	35	$5
4	70	$10
5	100	$10
6	40	$8
7	90	$5
8	80	$8

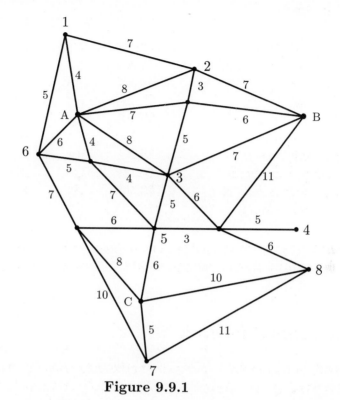

Figure 9.9.1

Determine how many items should be shipped from each warehouse to each retail outlet to minimize the total shipping and penalty costs.

Appendix A

Brief Introductions to LINDO and LINGO

A.1 LINDO

The linear programming software LINDO runs on a variety of platforms: DOS, Windows, *Macintosh*, and unix. Here we will discuss the Windows platform.

LINDO can be used in either of two modes – one uses a Windows based editor and toolbar as its user interface and the other, called a **Command window**, is much less flexible and will not be discussed here. For most purposes taking advantage of the Windows features is preferable. However, one can see the use of command line features in many of the examples where LINDO has been used. See for instance Listing 3.5.1 where the commands `take`, `look`, `go`, and `quit` are illustrated.

As an example for solving a linear program using LINDO, we consider Exercise 5 from Section 3.5. We restate it here.

Example A.1.1. The Mythic Forge & Steel Co. (MF&S) supplies castings to a variety of customers, but plans to devote the next week of production to just two customers, James Manufacturing and Woolcott Enterprises. MF&S uses a combination of pure steel and scrap metal to fulfill it's orders, and has 400 pounds of pure steel and 360 pounds of scrap metal in stock. The pure steel costs MF&S $6 per pound and the scrap $3 per pound. Pure steel requires 3 hours per pound to process into a casting, while scrap requires only 2 hours per pound. Total available processing time in the week is 2,000 hours.

The castings for James each require five pounds of metal, with a quality control restriction limiting the ratio of scrap to pure steel to a maximum of $\frac{5}{7}$. James has ordered 30 castings at a price of $50 each.

The castings for Woolcott each require eight pounds of metal, with a quality restriction of a maximum scrap to pure steel ratio of $\frac{2}{3}$. Woolcott has ordered 40 castings at a price of $80 each.

Determine how MF&S should allocate their metal stocks to produce the castings ordered by these two customers if the objective is to maximize the value added to the metal, i.e., to maximize the selling price minus the cost of the metal. ■

The model shown in Listing A.1.1 could either be entered with any editor as a file with a .LTX extension or typed directly into the LINDO editor. When initiated, LINDO provides an edit window with the file name untitled for problem entry.

Descriptive variable names are used. By letting P stand for Pure steel, S for Scrap, J for James, and W for Woolcott, the four variables can easily be interpreted in the context of the problem. For instance, PJ indicates the number of pounds of Pure steel used for the castings for James. Variable names in LINDO may include from one to eight alphanumeric characters but must begin with a letter. Note that unless otherwise indicated, LINDO automatically considers all variables to be nonnegative.

Listing A.1.1

```
TITLE   Mythic Forge and Steel Example
MAX      4 PJ + 4 PW + 7 SJ + 7 SW   ! Value added
SUBJECT TO
   JaMet)   PJ + SJ =     150     ! Metal for James
   WoMet)   PW + SW =     320     ! Metal for Woolcott
   Time )   3 PJ + 3 PW + 2 SJ + 2 SW <=   2000    ! Time
   Scrap)   SJ + SW <=   360     ! Scrap available
   Steel)   PJ + PW <=   400     ! Pure steel available
   JaQua)  - 5 PJ + 7 SJ <=   0 ! James quality control
   WoQua)  - 2 PW + 3 SW <=   0 ! Woolcott quality control
END
```

The model shows three features of LINDO that allow for documentation. First, there is the TITLE of the model on the first line. Second, there are brief identifiers assigned to each constraint. They are optional, but are particularly helpful in identifying the slack variables and solution to the dual. If they are omitted, LINDO will assign numbers to the constraints beginning with 2. Finally, comments at the end of each line follow the !.

Once entered, the model is solved by selecting **Solve** from the menu item of the same name. A dialog window will open indicating the status of the solution, and if solved successfully, you will be asked if want sensitivity analysis. A reports window containing the solution opens.

Listing A.1.2 shows the solution of the example with sensitivity analysis requested.

Listing A.1.2

```
LP OPTIMUM FOUND AT STEP        2

          OBJECTIVE FUNCTION VALUE

      1)        2451.500

  VARIABLE          VALUE         REDUCED COST
        PJ       87.500000          0.000000
        PW      192.000000          0.000000
        SJ       62.500000          0.000000
        SW      128.000000          0.000000



       ROW    SLACK OR SURPLUS      DUAL PRICES
    JAMET)         0.000000          5.250000
    WOMET)         0.000000          5.200000
     TIME)       780.500000          0.000000
    SCRAP)       169.500000          0.000000
    STEEL)       120.500000          0.000000
    JAQUA)         0.000000          0.250000
    WOQUA)         0.000000          0.600000

  NO. ITERATIONS=        2



RANGES IN WHICH THE BASIS IS UNCHANGED:
```

OBJ COEFFICIENT RANGES

VARIABLE	CURRENT COEF	ALLOWABLE INCREASE	ALLOWABLE DECREASE
PJ	4.000000	3.000000	INFINITY
PW	4.000000	3.000000	INFINITY
SJ	7.000000	INFINITY	3.000000
SW	7.000000	INFINITY	3.000000

RIGHTHAND SIDE RANGES

ROW	CURRENT RHS	ALLOWABLE INCREASE	ALLOWABLE DECREASE
JAMET	150.000000	206.571442	150.000000
WOMET	320.000000	200.833328	320.000000
TIME	2000.000000	INFINITY	780.500000
SCRAP	360.000000	INFINITY	169.500000
STEEL	400.000000	INFINITY	120.500000
JAQUA	0.000000	1050.000000	750.000000
WOQUA	0.000000	847.500000	602.500000

When the problem has been solved and the window containing the formulation is highlighted, a Reports menu is active. Listing A.1.3 contains the Formulation report. Note that it contains the TITLE and the constraint identifiers, but not the comments. One can use copy and paste from the toolbar to copy a model containing comments into the reports window.

Listing A.1.3

```
TITLE   MYTHIC FORGE AND STEEL EXAMPLE
MAX     4 PJ + 4 PW + 7 SJ + 7 SW
SUBJECT TO
    JAMET)   PJ + SJ =     150
    WOMET)   PW + SW =     320
     TIME)   3 PJ + 3 PW + 2 SJ + 2 SW <=    2000
    SCRAP)   SJ + SW <=    360
    STEEL)   PJ + PW <=    400
    JAQUA) - 5 PJ + 7 SJ <=   0
    WOQUA) - 2 PW + 3 SW <=   0
END
```

The Tableau report displays the current tableau. The optimal tableau is shown in Listing A.1.4. Note that the objective row appears first and is identified by ART. The constraint identifier and the variable that is basic appear to the left of each row. Note that slack variables are indicated by SLK I where I is the row number of the corresponding constraint in the LINDO formulation of the problem.

Listing A.1.4

THE TABLEAU

ROW	(BASIS)		PJ	PW	SJ	SW	SLK	4
1	ART		0.000	0.000	0.000	0.000	0.000	
JAMET		PJ	1.000	0.000	0.000	0.000	0.000	
WOMET		PW	0.000	1.000	0.000	0.000	0.000	
TIME	SLK	4	0.000	0.000	0.000	0.000	1.000	
SCRAP	SLK	5	0.000	0.000	0.000	0.000	0.000	
STEEL	SLK	6	0.000	0.000	0.000	0.000	0.000	
JAQUA		SJ	0.000	0.000	1.000	0.000	0.000	
WOQUA		SW	0.000	0.000	0.000	1.000	0.000	

ROW	SLK	5	SLK	6	SLK	7	SLK	8	
1	0.000		0.000		0.250		0.600		2451.500
JAMET	0.000		0.000		-0.083		0.000		87.500
WOMET	0.000		0.000		0.000		-0.200		192.000
TIME	0.000		0.000		0.083		0.200		780.500
SCRAP	1.000		0.000		-0.083		-0.200		169.500
STEEL	0.000		1.000		0.083		0.200		120.500
JAQUA	0.000		0.000		0.083		0.000		62.500
WOQUA	0.000		0.000		0.000		0.200		128.000

The optional statements providing for integer variables are included following the END in the model. The statement INT X1 declares the variable X1 to be a $\{0, 1\}$ variable. The statement GIN X1 declares X1 to be a general integer variable. There are alternative version of these statements that declare several variables to be interger variables. For instance, INT 5 declares 5 variables as integer variables, but the variables so declared must appear as the first 5 variables in the formulation of the problem.

Finally, the statement **FREE X1** identifies **X1** as an unrestricted variable allowed to assume a negative value.

The ease of editing a model, including adding constraints, and the fact that the solutions generated appear successivly in the **Reports Window** make it feasible to manually step through the branching required for a small integer program to implement the algorithm from Section 7.5.

Help on LINDO is accessed by clicking on an icon. It provides for a topic search and also includes several sample models.

Much more detailed information about LINDO and its applications is available in [32].

A.2   LINGO

The LINGO package is a modeling language with an interface similar to that of LINDO and sharing some of its basic commands. However, LINGO can solve nonlinear problems and also problems that do not involve optimization. For instance, Listing 4.3.2 gives such a model for determining a CPM schedule.

As a modeling language LINGO allows repetitive constraints to be entered with a single command when the appropriate data is provided. That capability will be illustrated later with a transportation problem. Additional information is available in [24] and [33].

To illustrate the use of LINGO to solve a nonlinear model, we consider Section 6.4 Exercise 4. We first restate it here.

Example A.2.1. A furniture company is seeking to lower the cost of their desks. They must design a drawer to hold 2,500 cubic inches and be divided into three equal sections by partitions running from front to back. The maximum height of the drawer is 8 inches, the maximum width is 15 inches, and the maximum distance from front to back is 28 inches. If the material for the bottom costs $0.15 per square inch, for the front $0.20, for the back and sides $0.10, and for the partitions $0.05, what dimensions would yield the minimum cost? ■

The **model** command initiates input of a model. Constraints in the model are terminated with a semicolon; a model may have an objective of the form

"MIN = expression"   or   "MAX = expression."

The end of a model is signified with the word "END." Because LINGO must handle nonlinear functions, the notation for such functions is required. Among the most useful symbols are:

- Relations: > < =

- To establish the order of operations: ( )

- Arithmetic operations within expressions: + - / * ^

Note in Listing A.2.1 that comments are included beginning with a ! and ending with a ;. Whether entered in the LINGO editor or through another text editor, the file extension for a model is LNG.

Listing A.2.1

```
model:
TITLE Section 6.4 no.  4 Optimal drawer;
min = 15*x*y + 30*x*z + 30*y*z;
! Required volume;
x*y*z=2500 ;
! Maximum width;
x < 15 ;
! Maximum front to back;
y < 28 ;
! Maximum height;
 z < 8;
end
```

Selecting Solve from the toolbar generates the following solution which appears in the reports window. The extension for a report file is LGR.

Listing A.2.2

```
Rows=      5 Vars=       3 No. integer vars=      0
Nonlinear rows= 2 Nonlinear vars= 3 Nonlinear constraints= 1
Nonzeros=     13 Constraint nonz=     6 Density=0.650
No. < :   3 No. =:   1 No. > :   0, Obj=MIN Single cols=      0

Optimal solution found at step:          5
Objective value:                   13287.50
```

```
Model Title: SECTION 6.4 NO. 4 OPTIMAL DRAWER
```

Variable	Value	Reduced Cost
X	15.00000	0.0000000
Y	20.83333	0.0000000
Z	8.000000	0.0000000

Row	Slack or Surplus	Dual Price
1	13287.50	1.000000
2	-0.1992476E-07	-3.875000
3	0.0000000	93.33334
4	7.166667	0.0000000
5	0.0000000	135.9375

We now consider the use of LINGO for a transportation problem to illustrate how it can be made to handle repetitive constraints.

The data to be used in a model are provided in two sections – the **SETS** section in which the structure of the data is described and the **DATA** section in which the actual data is provided.

The following set functions are very useful in developing models. In the syntax below, **SET** is the name of the set, **COND** is a logical condition to choose only certain members of the set, and **EXP** is an expression involving elements of a set.

The last three functions in the list return, respectively, the number of elements in the set, the maximum value of the expression, and minimum value of the expression.

```
@SUM( SET | COND: EXP)
@FOR( SET | COND: EXP)
@SIZE( SET)
@MAX( SET | COND: EXP)
@MIN( SET | COND: EXP)
```

Note in Listing A.2.3 that a single **FOR** statement is needed for the entire set of demand constraints and a second for the supply constraints. Note also that the **DATA** section and the lines defining the **ORIGIN** and **DESTIN** sets are all that one needs to change the problem.

Listing A.2.3

```
MODEL:
  1]  ! The 3 warehouse, 4 retail outlet transportation;
  2]  ! problem from Section 4.2 Example 4.2.1;
  3]  SETS:
  4]  ! Inclusion of W1, W2, W3 causes them to print;
  5]  ! instead of 1, 2, and 3. Likewise for the Ri.;
  6]  ! No. of entries on next two lines specify nos. of;
  7]  ! origins and no. of destinations.;
  8]      ORIGIN / W1, W2, W3/      : SUPPLY;
  9]      DESTIN / R1, R2, R3, R4/  : DEMAND;
 10]      LINKS( ORIGIN, DESTIN)    : COST, X;
 11]  ! Lines 8-10 specify SUPPLY subscripted by ORIGIN, DEMAND;
 12]  ! by DESTIN, and COST and X subscripted by both.;
 13]  ENDSETS
 14]
 15]  ! Objective function;
 16]  ! Note that the double sum is accomplished by using a;
 17]  ! doubly subscripted variable - here LINKS - rather;
 18]  ! than by "nesting" @SUM commands.;
 19]      MIN = @SUM( LINKS: COST * X);
 20]
 21]  ! Demand constraints;
 22]      @FOR( DESTIN( J):
 23]          @SUM( ORIGIN( I): X( I, J)) = DEMAND( J));
 24]
 25]  ! Supply constraints;
 26]      @FOR( ORIGIN( I):
 27]          @SUM( DESTIN( J): X( I, J)) = SUPPLY( I));
 28]
 29]  DATA:
 30]      SUPPLY =    10, 15, 10 ;
 31]      DEMAND =     8, 12, 7, 8 ;
 32]      COST   =    12, 9, 11,  7,
 33]                  15, 8, 10,  9,
 34]                   7, 4,  6, 11 ;
 35]  ENDDATA
END
```

As with LINDO, all variables are assumed to be nonnegative. The statement @FREE(X1) makes X1 an unrestrictd variable. There are optional statements providing for integer variables. The statement @INT(X1) declares the variable X1 to be a $\{0, 1\}$ variable. The statement @GIN(X1) declares X1 to be a general integer variable.

While integer variables are not used in any of the nonlinear models solved in the text, one will be useful in the storage locker case in Chapter 9.

Appendix B

A Brief Introduction to Maple

Maple is a symbolic computation package that is available on a variety of platforms, including PCs running Windows, *Macintoshs,* and unix systems. Some of the sample output here was produced on a unix workstation using Release 2 of *Maple* V and some using a Windows based version of *Maple*.

On a *Macintosh* or Windows system, a *Maple* session is initiated by clicking on the appropriate icon or item in a program list. On a machine running X-windows, *Maple* is used by typing **xmaple** in a typescript or Xterm window. Note that this will prevent other use of your typescript or Xterm window until the *Maple* session is ended. Adding a & to the command by typing **xmaple &** will allow access to the window while *Maple* is running.

The *Maple* window features pull down menus, including File, Edit, View, Options and Help. For many basic operations, mainly the File menu is needed. A discussion of using the File menus to save your session will conclude this appendix. A *Maple* session is ended by entering the `quit;` command or by selecting Exit from the *Maple* File menu.

B.1   The basics

Here we briefly illustrate the power of *Maple* to treat expressions symbolically and provide a few basics of graphing. In Listing B.1.1 we differentiate an expression containing an unspecified constant and then determine its critical points. The final x in the `diff` command indicates the variable of differentiation.

Listing B.1.1

```
> diff(x^4 - A*x^3 + B,x);
```

$$4 x^3 - 3 A x^2$$

```
> solve(%,{x});
```

$$\{x = 0\}, \ \{x = 0\}, \ \{x = 3/4 \ A\}$$

Note that the *Maple* prompt is a > and that each command is terminated by a semicolon. The `solve` command assumes that you are solving the equation obtained by setting the included expression equal to zero. The % refers to the output from the previous command; in this case, the derivative above. Note that this usage of % is correct in *Maple* V Release 5. Earlier releases used a " to refer to the previous expression. Since it could also solve for A, the option {x} is included to explicitly specify the variable for which we are solving.

In Listing B.1.2 we consider the function with the parameters specified – here, A = 4 and B = 5. The first command defines $f(x)$ as a function which can be referred to in subsequent commands. The second line is a display of the function produced by *Maple* to indicate that it has accepted the definition.

We then differentiate the function just defined, and then solve the equation $f'(x) = 0$. Note that this time we explicitly set the previous expression equal to zero. Since there is only one candidate for the variable, we do not need to explicitly state the variable for which we are solving.

Listing B.1.2

```
> f := proc(x) x^4 - 4*x^3 + 5 end;
f := proc(x) x^4-4*x^3+5 end

> diff(f(x),x);
```

$$4 x^3 - 12 x^2$$

```
> solve(% = 0);
```

$$0, \ 0, \ 3$$

The double root indicates that the function will have fewer than the maximum possible number of extrema. Viewing the graph should confirm that.

The first command in Listing B.1.3 will produce a plot of f over the interval $[-3, 6]$ with the range restricted to $[-30, 80]$. Depending on the current setting of the variable `plotdevice`, the plot will appear in a separate window or directly below the command in your *Maple* session. Once the domain and range intervals have been selected to yield a useful plot, output parameters can be set to send the plot to a file formatted for the proper printer. The middle two commands in Listing B.1.3 produce a plot for a postscript printer in the file `quartic`.

Listing B.1.3

```
> plot(f(x), x=-3..6,y=-30..80);

> interface(plotdevice=postscript,plotoutput=quartic);

> plot(f(x), x=-3..6,y=-30..80);

> interface(plotdevice=x11);
```

The file `quartic` can now be printed.

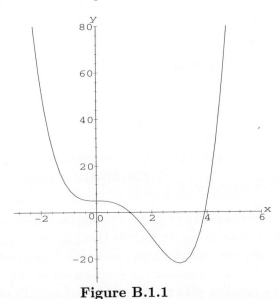

Figure B.1.1

Note that all subsequent plots will be sent to this file until the `interface` command changes the setup. The last command in Listing B.1.3 returns subsequent plots to their own windows in a unix system. Replacing `x11` by `window` would do the same for a Windows system; replacing it by `inline` would return the plots to appearing in your *Maple* session.

Classical optimization

Maple can reduce the use of the Karush-Kuhn-Tucker Theorem to an exercise in careful typing. As the next example, we solve the following problem:

$$
\begin{aligned}
\text{Maximize}: &\quad 12 - x_1^2 - x_2^2 \\
\text{Subject to}: &\quad 5x_1 + 2x_2 \geq 10 \\
&\quad x_1^2 - 2x_1 + x_2 \leq 8
\end{aligned}
$$

Note in Listing B.1.4 that to ease the typing, we use shorter variable names than usual—x_1 and x_2 are replaced by x and y, the Lagrange multipliers are u and v, and the slack variables are s and t.

The Lagrangian is entered using a `proc` command. The solution is obtained using `fsolve` which yields a floating point solution. The `solve` command used previously solves the equation symbolically.

Listing B.1.4

```
> L := proc(x,y,u,v,s,t) 12-x^2-y^2-u*(-5*x-2*y+10+s^2)
>                  -v*(x^2-2*x+y-8+t^2) end;
L := proc(x,y,u,v,s,t) 12-x^2-y^2-u*(-5*x-2*y+10+s^2)
              -v*(x^2-2*x+y-8+t^2) end

> fsolve({diff(L(x,y,u,v,s,t),x),diff(L(x,y,u,v,s,t),y),
   diff(L(x,y,u,v,s,t),u),diff(L(x,y,u,v,s,t),v),
diff(L(x,y,u,v,s,t),s), diff(L(x,y,u,v,s,t),t)},{x,y,u,v,s,t});
> > {v = 0, u = .689655172, y = .689655172, t = 2.790334941,
              x = 1.724137931, s = 0}
```

Note that if nonnegativity constraints had been included in the problem, it would have been necessary to include them in the Lagrangian.

Note that the `proc` command, and some other long ones, use two lines to enter a single command. Pressing the **Return** key at the end of the first line simply causes a new line with a > prompt to appear. Typing then continued until the command was completed. The inclusion of the ; at the end of the command then caused *Maple* to process the command.

Errors do happen, and *Maple* tries to be helpful when it detects a syntax error. Listing B.1.5 shows a sample error message indicating that an * for multiplication has been omitted. The error can be corrected by placing the cursor between the 5 and the x and entering the *. Then hitting **Return** will execute the corrected command.

Listing B.1.5

```
>
syntax error:
L := proc(x,y,u,v,s,t) 12-x^2-y^2-u*(-5x-2*y+10+s^2)
                                        ^

              -v*(x^2-2x+y-8+t^2) end;
```

In entering a command as complicated as the `fsolve` in Listing B.1.4, it is helpful to take advantage of some interface features. One approach is to type `diff(L(x,y,u,v,s,t),x)`, and then copy it to form the other five derivatives. This is done by depressing the mouse button at the beginning of the expression to be copied, dragging it over the expression, then releasing it at the end. Then clicking the copy icon causes the expression to be copied. Finally, clicking on Paste causes the item to be copied at the current cursor location. In this case, one then need only change the variable of differentiation in each derivative.

Getting help

The Help menu gives a convenient way to explore *Maple*. The Help Browser option gives access to a hierarchical list of commands and features. To cause a help window to be displayed for a command or term without using the browser, type ? followed by the name of the item and a **Return**.

File operations

To save your session, select Save from the File menu. A window will open suggesting that the file be saved with an mws extension for *Maple* worksheet. You can change the directory, the file name, or the disk by making the appropriate choices indicated in the window. The format of the file can be changed by selecting Export as from the File menu. You will need to select a format, then a window smilar to the Save window, will open.

To print your session, select Print ... from the File menu. This will cause a Print window to open asking for confirmation of the printer and the number of copies. The option Print Preview will open a window that will show how the print-out should look.

B.2   Using packages

Maple provides a variety of capabilities the require additional commands to be loaded by using the with command. Here we briefly look at the packages for linear algebra, the simplex algorithm, curve fitting, and networks.

Matrix operations

To use the linear algebra capabilities of *Maple*, one must first load a package called linalg containing the linear algebra functions. In Listing B.2.1 we load that package and solve a system of equations from Section 2.6. Normally the command loading linalg would produce a lengthy list of linear algebra functions as well as warnings about redefinitions of commands as a result of the package. However, here we have ended the with command with a : instead of a ; to suppress the printing of this list.

Listing B.2.1

```
> with(linalg):

> S:={3*x1-2*x2+x3=-3,x1+2*x2+2*x3=10,4*x1-x2-x3=12};
    S := {3 x1 - 2 x2 + x3 = -3, x1 + 2 x2 + 2 x3 = 10,
            4 x1 - x2 - x3 = 12}


> solve(S,{x1,x2,x3});
                            157              73
              {x1 = 34/9, x2 = ---, x3 = - ----}
                             27              27
```

The system is entered as a set of equations, and then we call the same `solve` command as above, giving it the name of the set of equations and indicating the variables for which we wish to solve.

Now we explore how to enter and modify a matrix.

A bracketed sequence of entries, $[\cdots]$, is called a *list* in *Maple*. Thus, the command in Listing B.2.2 in which a matrix is entered shows that a matrix is a list of lists, with each individual list forming a row of the matrix. *Maple* prints the matrix in response to confirm that it has been entered.

The matrix is the optimal tableau for Exercise 13 of Section 1.4 shown below:

$$
\begin{aligned}
\text{Maximize}: \quad & 30x + 15y \\
\text{Subject to}: \quad & 2x + y \leq 20 \\
& x \quad\quad\quad \leq 8 \\
& -x + y \leq 10 \\
& x \geq 0, y \geq 0
\end{aligned}
$$

The first two columns of the matrix correspond to activity variables, the next three to slack variables, and the final column to the values of the basic variables. The last row is the objective row with the value of the objective function as the final entry.

Note that it has a typo in row 2 column 1 since the only nonzero entry in the column of a basic variable must be a 1. We assign the correct value, and then revaluate the matrix to check that the correction has been made:

Listing B.2.2

```
> OT:=matrix([[0,1,1,-2,0,4], [2,0,0,1,0,8], [0,0,-1,3,1,14],
    [0,0,15,0,0,300]]);
```

$$
OT := \begin{bmatrix}
0 & 1 & 1 & -2 & 0 & 4 \\
2 & 0 & 0 & 1 & 0 & 8 \\
0 & 0 & -1 & 3 & 1 & 14 \\
0 & 0 & 15 & 0 & 0 & 300
\end{bmatrix}
$$

```
> OT[2,1]:=1;
```

$$
OT[2, 1] := 1
$$

```
> evalm(OT);
```

```
[ 0   1    1   -2   0    4   ]
[                            ]
[ 1   0    0    1   0    8   ]
[                            ]
[ 0   0   -1    3   1   14   ]
[                            ]
[ 0   0   15    0   0  300   ]
```

Note that the slack variable in the second constraint is not basic, but has a 0 coefficient in the objective row. Thus, this tableau corresponds to a nonunique solution, and by pivoting in the column of s_2, column 4, we should obtain an alternative optimal solution which also has 300 as its objective function value. The commands in Listing B.2.3 carry out the pivot. The first multiplies the pivot row by $\frac{1}{3}$ to make the coefficient of s_2 equal to 1, and then the second operation forces the other coefficients in the column to be 0 by pivoting in row 3 and column 4.

Listing B.2.3

```
> OT2:=mulrow(OT,3,1/3);
```

```
              [ 0   1    1    -2   0     4   ]
              [                             ]
              [ 1   0    0     1   0     8   ]
       OT2 := [                             ]
              [ 0   0  -1/3    1  1/3  14/3  ]
              [                             ]
              [ 0   0   15     0   0   300   ]
```

```
> OT3:=pivot(OT2,3,4);
```

```
              [ 0   1   1/3   0   2/3  40/3  ]
              [                             ]
              [ 1   0   1/3   0  -1/3  10/3  ]
       OT3 := [                             ]
              [ 0   0  -1/3   1   1/3  14/3  ]
              [                             ]
              [ 0   0   15    0    0   300   ]
```

The result is that s_3 has been replaced by s_2 as a basic variable, and a new solution has been obtained with the objective function still equal to 300.

By entering the matrix corresponding to the original simplex tableau and making the selection of pivot row and column on one's own, the simplex algorithm could be carried out within *Maple* by this means. Once the optimal tableau of a problem is in *Maple*, the commands `vector`, `augment`, `stack`, `swaprow`, and `swapcol` are very useful for manipulating the tableau to carry out computations such as adding a constraint or a variable.

The command `vector` can be used to enter a vector into *Maple*. Then `augment` can be used to add a vector as a new column or `stack` to add it as a new row. These comands place the added row or column on one edge of the matrix representing the tableau. The command `swaprow` or `swapcol` can be used to move the new row or column into its proper position.

The simplex package

Maple includes a `simplex` package which provides an alternative way to solve a linear program. In Listing B.2.4 below, `simplex` is loaded, and the following linear program is solved:

$$\begin{array}{lrcrcrcr}
\text{Maximize}: & 3x_1 & + & 4x_2 & + & x_3 & & \\
\text{Subject to}: & x_1 & + & x_2 & + & x_3 & \geq & 10 \\
& 2x_1 & + & x_2 & + & x_3 & \leq & 16 \\
& & & x_2 & + & x_3 & = & 6
\end{array}$$

$$x_1 \geq 0, \ x_2 \text{ unrestricted}, \ x_3 \geq 0$$

Note that this example includes all three types of constraints and an unrestricted variable.

Listing B.2.4

```
> with (simplex);
Warning, new definition for maximize
Warning, new definition for minimize

[basis, convexhull, cterm, define_zero, display, dual,
    feasible, maximize, minimize, pivot, pivoteqn, pivotvar,
    ratio, setup, standardize]
```

```
> consts := {x1+x2+x3 >=10,2*x1+x2+x3<=16,x2+x3=6}:
> obj := 3*x1+4*x2+2*x3:
> maximize(obj,consts union {x1>=0,x3>=0});
```

$$\{x3 = 0, \ x1 = 5, \ x2 = 6\}$$

Curve fitting

The `stats` package adds curve fitting and other statistical capabilities to *Maple*. We will consider two examples to illustrate its use.

The example in Listing B.2.5 determines a least square fit expressing z as a function of x and y. The variables are first identified in a `list` and then the data is provided in the form of three lists, one for each variable, contained within parentheses in an order corresponding to that of the variables. The : ending the command loading the `stats` package suppresses the listing of the functions loaded.

Listing B.2.5

```
> with(stats):
> fit[leastsquare[[x,y,z]]]([[1,2,3,6],[2,5,6,9],[4,9,12,13]]);
```

$$z = 8/13 - \frac{22}{13} x + \frac{33}{13} y$$

The `fit` command allows one to specify the nature of the function. In the example shown in Listing B.2.6, a quadratic fit is specified. In the example we first load the `plots` package so that we can conclude with a plot of the quadratic obtained together with the data. The data is entered by defining lists and the nature of the function is specified along with the variables in the `fit` command. Most of the commands are terminated with a : to surpress intermediate output.

Following calculation of the quadratic fit, the data is stored in a sequence of ordered pairs and then a plot of the data is stored as `plt1`. The quadratic, having been copied into a `plot` command by using the editing features of *Maple*, is then graphed in `plt2`. The `display` command is then used to graph the two plots on the same axes. Note that `display` requires the `plots` package. The resulting graph is shown in Figure B.2.2.

Listing B.2.6

```
> with(plots):
> with(stats):
> Xvals:=[1,2,3,4]:
> Yvals:=[3,5,11,23]:
> fit[leastsquare[[x,y], y=a*x^2+b*x+c, {a,b,c}]]([Xvals,Yvals]);
```

$$y = 5/2\ x^2 - \frac{59}{10}\ x + 13/2$$

```
> points := seq([Xvals[i],Yvals[i]],i=1..4):
> plt1 := plot([points],style=POINT, symbol=BOX):
> plt2 := plot(5/2*x^2-59/10*x+13/2,x=0..4.5):
> display([plt1,plt2]);
```

As suggested in the definition of `plt1` the data points are indicated by small boxes in Figure B.2.2.

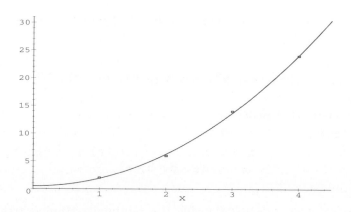

Figure B.2.2

Networks

The **networks** package contains implementations of the network algorithims discussed in Chapter 4. Listing B.2.7 shows a network **G** initialized, and then its vertices and edges entered by the commands **addvertex** and **addedge**. This example is an undirected network and the edges are entered as two element sets, i.e., enclosed in curly brackets { , }. The edges of a directed network would be entered as ordered pairs of vertices contained in square brackets [,]. Note that the list of vertices omits **e** because it is used elsewhere and not legal for a vertex.

As indicated by its name, the output of **shortpathtree** is the tree which contains the shortest path to each of the vertices of **G**. Recall that in Dijkstra's algorithm the shortest path was obtained by backtracking from last vertex reached. Here, the shortest path is available as the path back to **a** from the vertex reached.

Listing B.2.7

```
> with(networks):
> new(G):
> addvertex({a,b,c,d,f,g},G);
```

$$a, f, b, c, d, g$$

```
> addedge([{a,b},{a,c},{b,d},{b,f},{c,d},{c,f},{d,f},{d,g},
    {f,g}],weights=[3,2,5,6,8,7,2,5,4],G);
```

$$e1, e2, e3, e4, e5, e6, e7, e8, e9$$

```
> T := shortpathtree(G,a):
> path([g,a],T);
```

$$[g, d, b, a]$$

The command **spantree(G)** yields the minimal spanning tree of the graph G. Finally, the ecommand **draw(G)** will draw the graph.

Appendix C

Introduction to Texas Instruments Calculators

C.1   A brief introduction to the TI-82

The basics

Here we present the basics for novice users – things like turning the TI-82 on and off, the key modes, the main graphing keys, and how the TI-82 approaches calculus. Non-beginnners will probably skip this section.

The page references are to the TI-82 GUIDEBOOK [35] which comes with the calculator.

Turning on (and off)

The calculator is turned on by pushing the $\boxed{\text{ON}}$ key at the lower left. Turn it off by pushing first the blue $\boxed{\text{2nd}}$ key near the top left followed by the $\boxed{\text{ON}}$ key which, as the blue letters above it indicate, is OFF when preceeded by $\boxed{\text{2nd}}$.

Key modes

Most keys on the TI-82 have two or even three functions, depending on the prior use of the blue $\boxed{\text{2nd}}$ key or the gray $\boxed{\text{ALPHA}}$ key. If $\boxed{\text{2nd}}$ has just been pushed, the result of pushing a key is indicated by the blue item, if any, to the left above the key. The $\boxed{\text{2nd}}$ mode is indicated on the display by an up arrow in the flashing block cursor. If the $\boxed{\text{ALPHA}}$ key has just been pressed,

493

or the sequence 2nd A-LOCK has been entered, then pressing a key with a white character to the right above it produces that character. The ALPHA mode is indicated by an A in the block cursor.

ALPHA

applies only to the next key pressed. A-LOCK leaves alphabetic mode on until ALPHA is pressed again or a key without significance in ALPHA mode is pressed.

The first time TI-82 user of a is sometimes confused by the presence of minus signs on two different keys. The gray (-) key in the bottom row is for *negation*, i.e., to indicate a negative number. The dark blue key with the − on it in the right most column is for *subtraction*. The difference is discussed on p. 1-21.

Basic graphing

The five most important keys for graphing are the black keys just below the display:

- Entering a function - the Y= key. (pp. 3-5 - 3-7.) The X,T, θ key is used to produce the independent variable X when graphing a function in rectangular coordinates. The same key will produce the variable T or θ if the graphing mode has been set to parametric, Par, or polar, Pol, respectively, by means of the MODE key. (p. 3-5.)

- Graphing a function - the GRAPH key. (pp. 3-11 - 3-12.)

- Zooming in or out on a graph - the ZOOM key. (pp. 3-16 - 3-18.)

- Traveling along a graph to display the coordinates of points on the graph–the TRACE key. (pp. 3-13 - 3-15.)

- Changing the size of a graphing window - the WINDOW key. Note also that the ZStandard option under ZOOM can also be used to restore the window to its default state: $-10 \leq X \leq 10$, $-10 \leq Y \leq 10$. (pp. 3-8 - 3-10.)

If an error is made, for instance if you use the wrong minus sign key as discussed above, an error indication appears. The error conditions are discussed on p. 1-22.

Calculus operations

Numerical versions of differentiation and integration are found among the options in the menu obtained by the $\boxed{\text{MATH}}$ key. They are nDeriv((p. 2-7.) for the numerical value of a derivative and fnInt((p. 2-7.) for the approximate numerical value of an integral. If a function has been defined as Y1, then defining another of the Yi variables as nDerive(Y1,X,X) will allow you to draw the graph of the derivative of Y1. Alternative implementations of differentiation and integration for a function whose graph is displayed can be found in the menu accessed by the sequence $\boxed{\text{2nd}}$ $\boxed{\text{CALC}}$. In these functions, the parameters are entered by moving the point along the graph and pushing $\boxed{\text{ENTER}}$ when the desired point is reached.

Occasionally the TI-82 does not produce what is expected, or what is correct. One instance of this occurs with nDeriv(.

nDeriv(, found under $\boxed{\text{MATH}}$,calculates the numerical derivative by approximating the value of the following limit

$$\lim_{h \to 0} \frac{f(x+h) - f(x-h)}{2h}.$$

This limit is discussed in Problem 20 of the Problems Plus section following Chapter 2 of [34]. That problem shows that this limit may exist even though the derivative does not. This is born out by using nDeriv(to calculate the derivative of $|x|$ at $x = 0$. This calculation looks like nDeriv(abs X,X,0) and, as suggested in Stewart's problem, it yields a value of 0 for the derivative which, of course, fails to exist. Drawing a graph to illustrate the problem will reveal how this limit fails to identify the non-existence of the derivative at this point.

More on graphing

Of the keys introduced above, $\boxed{\text{ZOOM}}$ and $\boxed{\text{WINDOW}}$ are the most complicated and powerful.

The $\boxed{\text{WINDOW}}$ key allows you to set the screen variables and display characteristics. The roles of four of the variables are evident from their names: Xmin, Xmax, Ymin, and Ymax. The remaining two–Xscl and Yscl–indicate the increments in which the respective axes are marked. Other aspects of the display, such as choosing not to display the axes, are set from the FORMAT menu accessed by $\boxed{\text{WINDOW}}$ ▷.

The $\boxed{\text{ZOOM}}$ key causes a graph to be redisplayed with the WINDOW variables changed. Most of the options under $\boxed{\text{ZOOM}}$ have special uses, which here are merely indicated. For detailed documentation, see pages 3-16 - 3-20. They are:

1 : ZBox Permits the user to select the region to zoom to by using the four cursor keys.

2 : Zoom In Zooms to the region centered around the cursor with the rate of magnification dependent on the parameters XFact and YFact. ZOOM MEMORY 4 allows the user to set these factors.

3 : Zoom Out This is Zoom In reversed.

4 : ZDecimal Replots the screen with each pixel assigned to one decimal. Useful for observing removeable discontinuities in functions.

5 : ZSquare Replots the screen with one variable adjusted so that the graph of a circle will actually be circular.

6 : ZStandard Replots the screen with $-10 \leq X \leq 10$ and $-10 \leq Y \leq 10$ and the axes marked in increments of 1.

7 : ZTrig Replots the screen with a WINDOW for plotting trigonometric functions: $-6.15 \leq X \leq 6.15$, $Xscl = \frac{\pi}{2}$, and $-4 \leq Y \leq 4$.

8 : ZInteger Similar to ZStandard except that you first must position the cursor to the position that you want centered in the new graph.

9 : ZoomStat Redefines the WINDOW to display the data set identified by STATPLOT.

If a zooming operation does not produce the expected result, the previous graph can be recalled by using the MEMORY option accessed by the sequence ZOOM $\triangleright$ 1. MEMORY also permits a set of WINDOW variables to be stored for later recall, and to change the XFact and YFact variables that govern the rate of zooming.

The options selected with the MODE key are also important in the display of a graph. Aside from setting the graphic mode, MODE lets one split the screen, set the number of digits of a number displayed, and choose whether lines are drawn connecting the points calculated–the Connected mode, or whether only the calculated points are displayed–the Dot mode. The difference can be dramatic. The graph in Figure C.1.2 is the greatest integer function–found as int under the NUM menu of MATH –drawn in Connected mode and the graph in Figure C.1.3 is the same graph in Dot mode.

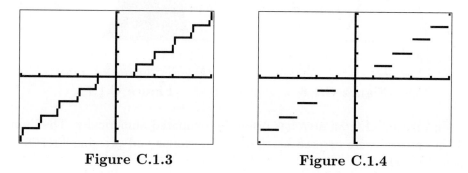

Figure C.1.3   **Figure C.1.4**

You might want to investigate the difference in the case of $y = \tan(x)$.

Solving equations and other operations

Various computational tools for functions which are defined for graphing by Y = are accessed by MATH or by 2nd CALC . The options from 2nd CALC are shown in Figure C.1.4.

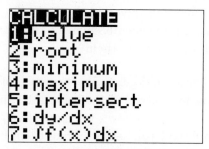

Figure C.1.5

In Figure C.1.5, the TI-82 is being set up to determine the root of an equation. The "6" in the upper right indicates that the function graphed is defined as Y6. The two triangles at the top of the display indicate the interval over which the search for the root will be carried out. Those values were determined by moving the cursor, appearing here as a small square near the root, along the graph and pressing ENTER when an appropriate value has been found. It remains to press ENTER one more time to enter a guess for the root.

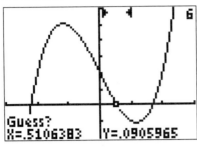

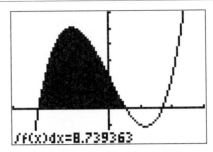

Figure C.1.6   Figure C.1.7

In Figure C.1.6, an area has been approximated numerically. The limits of the integral were entered by moving the cursor and pressing ENTER as mentioned above.

The interface for the other CALC operations is similiar.

The operations accessed by the MATH key are not graphical, and all parameters are entered in the home screen. Two of these operations–nDeriv(and fnInt(–provide numerical differentiation and integration capability, respectively. They can be used to generate graphs of the derivative or antiderivative of a function.

Curve fitting

The TI-82 can analyze functions given in the form of a table as discussed in Section 5.5. On a TI-82, a table is entered as a pair of lists. Such data might be obtained in several ways, among them

- You can simply enter the data. The sequence of comands STAT Edit will cause the first few entries of the lists L1, L2 and L3 to be displayed. The list editing window is shown in Figure C.1.7. A maximum of six lists can be stored, and you select among them by the ▷ and ◁ keys. The bottom line initially displays the value of L1(1). By moving the cursor to the label above an empty list, you can calculate a new list from old. Manipulation of lists is indicated in the GUIDEBOOK example discussed beginning on page 12-2.

- A program or a command in the home screen can generate a list. The name of a list is entered by preceding the corresponding number with 2nd. For instance, the command

$$\text{seq}(1/(2\text{I}-1),\text{I},1,10,1) \quad \boxed{\text{STO} \ \triangleright} \quad \text{L2}$$

will store the reciprocals of the first 10 odd integers in L2.

- The data can be captured by a Calculator Based Laboratory and down loaded to the calculator for analysis.

There are graphing options to view data stored in lists. Before using them, turn off any functions that may be selected by the key sequence $\boxed{\text{2nd}}$ Y-VARS 5 2. Then $\boxed{\text{2nd}}$ STAT PLOT will allow the graph of the data to be defined. Move the cursor to the number of one of the three plots and press $\boxed{\text{ENTER}}$ to select that plot. Selecting ON and pushing $\boxed{\text{ENTER}}$ turns the desired plot on. Figure C.1.7 shows lists L4 and L5 set up by $\boxed{\text{STAT}}$ Edit to be edited. The STAT PLOT screen is shown in Figure C.1.8.

Figure C.1.8   Figure C.1.9

After turning the plot on, choose the Type of plot, the Xlist and Ylist, and the Mark to be used in the plot. Then display the plot by $\boxed{\text{ZOOM}}$ 9. This gives the ZoomStat option which automatically selects the correct window variables.

Once the graph is viewed to give an indication of the nature of any functional relationship, the data can be fit with a variety of curves, e.g., straight line, quadratic function, or exponential function. The following key sequence will produce a quadratic fit with the independent variable in L4 and the dependent variable in L5. Note that the lists in this command are gotten by pressing $\boxed{\text{2nd}}$ followed by the corresponding number between 1 and 6:

$$\boxed{\text{STAT}} \text{ CALC 6 L4,L5}$$

which will produce

QuadReg
$y=ax^2+bx+c$
$a=.1877441131$
$b=-.3783479574$
$c=1.850675363$

To graph the equation obtained, you can copy the equation for the fit into a Yi function. First press [Y=], move the cursor to the desired Yi, and press CLEAR to erase a previous function if necessary. Then the key sequence [VARS] 5 EQ 7 will enter the equation.

This will cause the curve to be plotted with the data the next time [GRAPH] is pressed. The plot of the data and the quadratic curve are shown in Figure C.1.9.

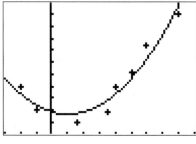

Figure C.1.10

Replacing the 6 by a 5 in the displayed key sequence above will produce a linear fit as discussed in Section 5.5.

Odds and ends

Occasionally you might want to store a constant. The [STO▷] key provides for storing constants. Just enter the desired value, followed by [STO▷] and the name of the variable you want to use–A through Z and θ are allowed. Don't forget the [ALPHA] to get into alphabetic mode. Avoid X, Y, R, T, and θ since the TI-82 graphing routines reassign their values.

The [DEL] key deletes the item under the cursor. The function of [DEL] is reversed by [2nd]–this allows you to insert characters into the line. The presence of the INS mode is indicated by a flashing character instead of the usual cursor. Typing a ▷ to move ahead in the line will turn off INS. This mode is particularly useful when an error has occurred and you are given a chance to correct a line.

You may want to use the result of one calculation in the next. It is available as ANS and is accessed by 2nd (-) . If you simply want to add, subtract, multiply, or divide the previous answer by some quantity, just hit the corresponding operation key, and you will get ANS followed by the opperation, e.g., ANS+.

The combination 2nd ENTER recalls the previous command. The command can then be modified using the cursor keys, DEL and INS, and over-striking before pushing ENTER to execute it. Repeating 2nd ENTER allows going back several commands.

Hardware basics

A TI-82 calculator has a port for communicating, and an included cable allows two calculators to exchange data and programs. The communication process uses the LINK key discussed on pp. 16-2 - 16-8.

The contrast on the display is adjusted by first pressing the 2nd key and then holding the △ key to increase the contrast or ▽ to decrease the contrast. An indication that your batteries might need to be replaced is that the screen is dim and you need to increase the contrast.

A TI-82 is powered by two kinds of batteries: four AAA alkaline batteries and a CR1616 or CR1620 lithium battery. If the calculator is turned off during the process, you should be able to change either the AAA batteries or the lithium battery without losing stored information. Keep the cover on the calculator while changing batteries to assure that ON is not accidentally pressed. See page B-2 for more details.

C.2   A brief introduction to the TI-92.

The TI-92 has many more capabilities than the TI-82. For instance, it does differentation and integration symbolically rather than numerically, it can graph functions of two independent variables, has a more powerful programming language, and has a text editor. In this section we can only begin to suggest its potential for solving mathematical programming problems.

Like the TI-82 there are several modes for some of the keys. The modes are indicated by three keys - a 2nd key associated with the yellow entries, a ◇ key associated with the green items, and a conventional up arrow shift key to get upper case letters. The letters all have hidden second meanings associated with the 2nd mode. To view this "hidden keyboard," press ◇ k.

Choice among items in a menu, or movement of the cursor in some applications, is accomplished by the round blue key in the upper right corner. Pushing on the appropriate part of the key produces movement in any of four directions. Pressing any of the three blue ENTER keys chooses the indicated item on a menu.

The default mode when entering commands or other text is for characters to be inserted where entered. The ⭠ key deletes the character preceding the cursor in the usual way. But when preceded by ◇, it deletes the character to the right of the cursor. When preceded by 2nd, it puts the calculator into an overwrite mode. Repeating 2nd ⭠ puts it back into insertion mode.

By using primarily the green Y=, WINDOW, GRAPH, and TABLE options found above the top row of keys one can operate the TI-92 much like a TI-82. These options are obtained by first pressing the ◇ key at the lower left.

Access to most of the other applications is gotten through the APPS key. It provides a menu of nine applications. In Figure C.2.1, the Data/Matrix Editor has been selected and the cursor moved to the right to allow the choice of file to open. The Current choice elects the most recent item edited, even if the power has been off.

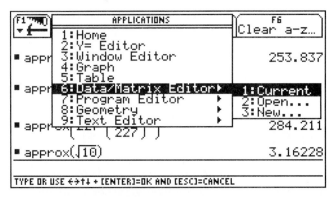

Figure C.2.1

The TI-92 has five graphing modes including a 3D mode for functions of two independent variables. The selection of graphing mode is the first item when MODE is pressed. The behaviors of the Y=, WINDOW, and GRAPH are altered accordingly. The graph of $f(x,y) = x^3 + x - 4xy - 2y^2$ from Example 5.4.6 is shown in Figure C.2.2. It shows a local maximum to the right and a saddle point near the origin.

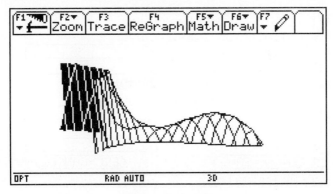

Figure C.2.2

Curve fitting

The data for curve fitting is entered by selecting the Data/Matrix Editor option by the keys APPS 6. Of the two formats offered, choose Data. Figure C.2.3 shows this editor.

	c1	c2	c3	c4	c5
1	-2	undef			
2	1	5			
3	3	7			
4	6	10			
5	7	14			
6	10	15			
7	11	21			

r1c1=-2

Figure C.2.3

When the data to be fit have been entered as two columns, F5 accesses the dialog box in Figure C.2.4. A choice of several curve fitting models is available, the columns used are entered, and the yi(x) in which to store the regression equation is indicated. Note that options not currently available appear very faint.

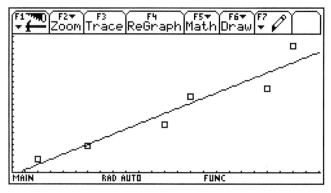

Figure C.2.4

The ◇ Y= combination allows definition of the plot. Here any functions other than the one selected in the dialog box above can be turned off. The plots are located above the yi(x) choices, and pressing ENTER selects one. The type of plot, the columns, and the symbol to indicate a point are chosen.

The data and the regression line are then displayed by ◇ GRAPH followed by F2 and Zoomdata to adjust the screen coordinates for the data. Figure C.2.5 shows a set of data points and the corresponding straight line fit.

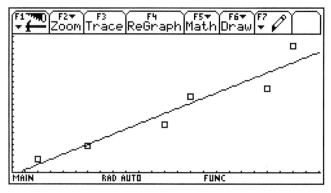

Figure C.2.5

A programming example

All the commands for a program can be accessed by 2nd CATALOG which produces an alphabetical list of all commands. Pressing any letter then moves the cursor to the first command beginning with that letter and the cursor control allows scrolling up or down the list. Pressing ENTER causes the selected command to be inserted at the current position in a program or the command line on the home screen.

The program below solves the cargo loading problem from Example 8.4.1 using the same recursion as the dynamic programming solution from Chapter 8. The recursion is defined in the function load which is called by this program and is listed next.

The solution is generated in much the same way as the earlier one – the item loaded last is determined by evaluating load(15), its weight is subtracted, and then load is successively reevaluated until all items loaded are determined.

Listing C.2.1

```
:cargo(t)
:Prgm
:Local y,l,w,r
:{5,7,4,3}→w          © Store weights in item order
:t→y                  © Store maximum weight
:While y>0
:       load(y,1)→r   © Store load result
:       Disp r
:       y-w[r[2]]→y   © Reduce weight
:EndWhile
:EndPrgm
```

Note that the output of load below is a two element set where the first element is the value of the load and the second is the number of the item loaded. If the set is denoted by r, then the respective entries are r[1] and r[2].

Listing C.2.2

```
:load(y,l)
:Func
:Local vl,x,i,j
:©   First few cases initialize the recursion
:©   Second variable l is not used in the calculation
:©   but is the item loaded when output by Return.
:If y<0 Then
:       Return {-100,0}
:ElseIf 0≤y and y≤2 Then
:       Return {0,0}
:ElseIf y=3 Then
:       Return {11,4}
:ElseIf y=4 Then
:       Return {16,3}
:ElseIf y=5 Then
:       Return {16,3}
:©   The recursive step. Possible values are
:©   first stored in a list, then the maximum
:©   is calculated.
:Else
:       {15+load(y-5,1)[1],12+load(y-7,2)[1],16+load(y-4,3)[1],
   11+load(y-3,4)[1]}→vl
:          max(vl)→x
:© Loop decides which item was loaded.
:          1→j
:          Loop
:              If x=vl[j] Then
:                   j→i
:                   Goto fnd
:              EndIf
:              j+1→j
:          EndLoop
:          Lbl fnd
:          Return {x,i}
:EndIf
:EndFunc
```

Various calculations

The TI-92 can do symbolic calculus operations. The home screen shown in Figure C.2.6 shows a differentiation and an antidifferentiation. Note that the differentiation is a partial derivative.

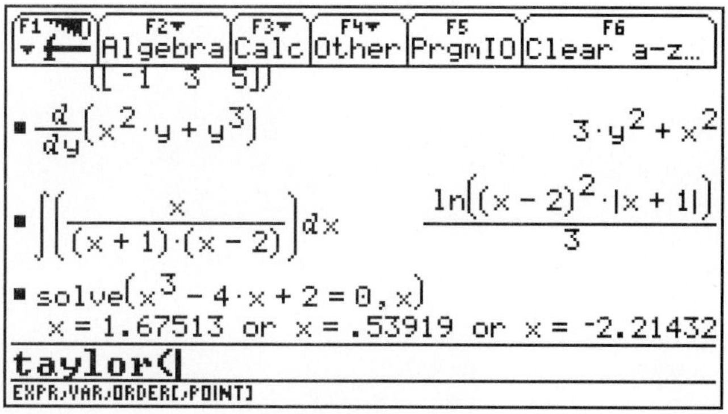

Figure C.2.6

The calculus commands are accessed by using [F3] to open the pull-down Calc menu at the top of the screen, or by [2nd] MATH, or by [2nd] CATALOG. An advantage of using CATALOG is shown in the command line. There taylor(indicates the beginning of the calculation of a Taylor polynomial. Note that the arguments for the command–EXPR,VAR,ORDER[,POINT]–are shown below the command line. This occurs only when CATALOG is used.

As a final example, an equation is solved just above the command line.

Appendix D

Selected Answers and Hints

D.1 Chapter 1

Section 1.3

1. Look ahead to Example 3.2.1 for a similar model.

3. Changing the case costs \$400, the plate \$900, and the caps \$500 for a total of \$1,800.

4. Constraint for the blanking shop: $x_1 + x_2 + 2x_3 + .5x_5 \leq 120$.

5. $120 - x_1 - x_2 - 2x_3 - .5x_5$.

7. Some sample cost calculations:
   From 30S to 48S-SE: \$600 + \$300 + \$500 = \$1,400
   From 48L to 30L: \$500
   From 48L-SE to 48S: \$400 + \$300 + \$400 = \$1,100

9. Objective function: $60x_1 + 70x_2 + 80x_3 + 90x_4 + 50x_5$
   Constraint: $35x_1 + 45x_2 + 55x_3 + 42x_4 + 35x_5 \leq 140$

Section 1.4

1. $10x_1 + 20x_2 \leq 1,100$. The graph includes the line through $(110, 0)$ and $(0, 55)$ and the half of the plane that includes the origin.

3. The graph is the triangle with corners at $(6, 0, 0), (0, 8, 0)$, and $(0, 0, 4)$.

5. $x_1 = 3, x_2 = 10$.

7. $x = 7, y = 2$.

8. $y_1 = 6, y_2 = 3$. In part (b), the line corresponding to $w_0 = 340$ should cut across the set of feasible solutions, the line corresponding to $w_1 = 310$ should intersect the set of feasible solutions only at the point $(6, 3)$, and the line corresponding to $w_2 = 250$ should not intersect the set of feasible solutions.

11. With the numbers of respective products indicated by R, F, and C, the linear program is:

$$
\begin{array}{rrrrrr}
\text{Maximize}: & 150R & + & 100F & + & 90C \\
\text{Subject to}: & 3R & + & 2F & + & 2C & \leq & 45 \\
& 725R & + & 675F & + & 525C & \leq & 9,000 \\
& & & & & C & \leq & 3 \\
& -R & + & F & + & C & \leq & 0 \\
\end{array}
$$
$$R \geq 0,\ F \geq 0,\ C \geq 0$$

13. The level curves of the objective function, shown dashed, are parallel to the side of the set of feasible solutions imposed by $2x + y \leq 20$. Therefore $\left(\frac{10}{3}, \frac{40}{3}\right)$ and $(8,4)$ both lie on the level curve corresponding to the optimal value of 300. The point $(6,8)$ is not at a corner and also produces the value 300.

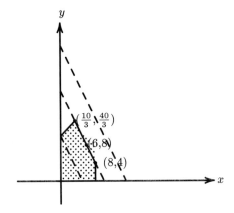

15. $x_1 = 28, x_2 = 16, s_1 = 0, s_2 = 0, s_3 = 20; z = 760$.

D.2   Chapter 2

Section 2.2

1. Both associations should give $[6, 8, 18]^T$.

3. $[17, 8, 31]^T$.

5.

$$x - y = \begin{bmatrix} -2 \\ 6 \end{bmatrix}$$

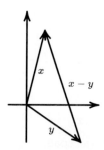

7. $8x_1 + 10x_2 + 12x_3 + 7x_4$.

Section 2.3

1. From $\begin{bmatrix} 5 \\ a \end{bmatrix} = c \begin{bmatrix} 2 \\ -3 \end{bmatrix}$ we get $c = \dfrac{5}{2}$, hence $a = -\dfrac{15}{2}$.

3. $c_1 = \frac{1}{2}, c_2 = \frac{3}{2}$.

5. $[1.56, 6.48, 4.44, 2.28, 5.40]^T$.

7. Between years 1 and 2 their profit declined by \$8,300.

Section 2.4

1.(b)

$$\begin{bmatrix} 10 & 20 & -6 \\ 18 & 16 & 16 \end{bmatrix}$$

3.(b) Can be multiplied in both orders. Given order yields

$$\begin{bmatrix} 4 & 26 \\ 23 & 7 \end{bmatrix},$$

the other

$$\begin{bmatrix} 26 & 18 \\ 10 & -15 \end{bmatrix}.$$

4. 80 acres, 230 days of labor, and \$1,300 will be required.

5. $x = -1, y = \dfrac{3}{2}$.

7. Calculate $C = AB$ and $D = B^{-1}A^{-1}$. Then show that $CD = I$.

Section 2.5

1.(a) There is at least one equation in one unknown which has no solution.

2.(c) Only the given statement is true. The equation has no solution, which satisfies "at most one."

3.(a) The converse: If n is a multiple of 2, then n is a multiple of 4. The given statement is true. Its converse is false: Consider $n = 6$.

3.(c) If $a \neq b$, then $a^2 \neq b^2$. Both are false.

7. $[-2, 4, -1]^T = \frac{1}{2}[2, 4, -4]^T + [-3, 2, 1]^T$.

Section 2.6

1.(a) $x_1 = \frac{7}{5}, x_2 = \frac{6}{5}, x_3 = \frac{1}{5}$.

3. The vector is in the span.

5.

$$
\begin{bmatrix} x_1 \\ x_2 \\ x_3 \\ x_4 \end{bmatrix} = \begin{bmatrix} -\frac{21}{5} \\ \frac{32}{5} \\ 0 \\ -\frac{39}{5} \end{bmatrix} + a \begin{bmatrix} \frac{23}{5} \\ -\frac{21}{5} \\ 1 \\ \frac{32}{5} \end{bmatrix}
$$

Note that standard application of Gaussian elimination would yield a solution in which the choice of x_4 is arbitrary, but leaving x_3 arbitary appeared to simplify the arithmetic in this case.

6.(a) Rank $= 3$, nullity $= 1$.

$$
\begin{bmatrix} x_1 \\ x_2 \\ x_3 \\ x_4 \end{bmatrix} = \begin{bmatrix} \frac{1}{4} \\ -\frac{3}{4} \\ 0 \\ 1 \end{bmatrix} + a \begin{bmatrix} -\frac{7}{4} \\ \frac{1}{4} \\ 1 \\ 0 \end{bmatrix}
$$

8.(a) $x_1 = 2, x_2 = -1, x_3 = 3$.

8.(c) $[\frac{7}{3}, -\frac{5}{9}, 0, 0]^T + a[-\frac{2}{3}, \frac{4}{9}, 1, 0]^T + b[\frac{2}{3}, \frac{2}{9}, 0, 1]^T$.

9. $y_1 + 3y_2 - 5y_3 = 0$.

10. $-10y_1 + 8y_2 + 7y_3 = 0$.

11. The plane flies 180 mph and the wind blows 20 mph.

13. The man earns \$15, his older son \$12, and his younger son \$9.

15. They can make 28 of the first part and 13 of the second.

17. All four subsets containing three vectors are linearly dependent. Every two vector subset is linearly independent.

Section 2.7

1. $x^T = [1, 2, -1]$.

2.(b)

$$\begin{bmatrix} -\frac{8}{13} & \frac{5}{13} & \frac{5}{13} \\ \frac{2}{13} & -\frac{9}{26} & \frac{2}{13} \\ \frac{1}{13} & \frac{1}{13} & \frac{1}{13} \end{bmatrix}$$

2.(c) No inverse exists.

3. Solve the system of equations $Ax = e_3$.

D.3 Chapter 3

Section 3.2

1.

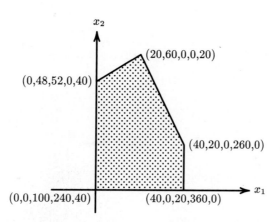

3.

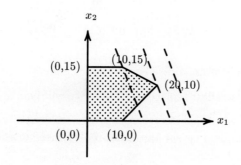

5. $x_1 = 7, x_2 = 0, s_1 = 36, s_2 = 0, s_3 = 8.$

7. The matrix obtained by pivoting on $\frac{15}{2}$ is

x_1	x_2	s_1	s_2	s_3	
0	0	1	$-\frac{1}{3}$	$-\frac{1}{15}$	$-\frac{10}{3}$
1	0	0	$\frac{2}{3}$	$-\frac{1}{15}$	$\frac{140}{3}$
0	1	0	$-\frac{1}{3}$	$\frac{2}{15}$	$\frac{170}{3}$

Section 3.3

1. $x_1 = 3, x_2 = 1$. The slack variable in the second constraint has the value 3. The optimal value of the objective function is 90.

3. $x_1 = 27.5, x_2 = 30, x_3 = 40$.

5.(b) If x_1 is made basic, the new tableau is

x_1	x_2	x_3	s_1	s_2	s_3	
0	1	6	$-\frac{1}{2}$	$\frac{2}{3}$	0	30
1	0	1	$-\frac{1}{2}$	$\frac{1}{3}$	0	3
0	0	-3	0	$-\frac{2}{3}$	1	2
0	0	-1	1	$\frac{4}{3}$	0	76

7. $x_1 = 10, x_2 = 0, x_3 = 0$.

8. The formulation for this problem is

$$
\begin{array}{llll}
\text{Minimize}: & 40x_1 + 75x_2 + 30x_3 & \\
\text{Subject to}: & 0.99x_1 + 0.9x_2 + x_3 & = & 475 \\
& 0.01x_1 + 0.1x_2 & = & 25 \\
& x_1 \geq 0, x_2 \geq 0, x_3 \geq 0
\end{array}
$$

where x_1 =amount of Alloy A, x_2 =amount of Alloy B, x_3 =amount of Alloy C.

9. Multiplying each pair of matrices should yield the identity matrix.

11.(a) x_1 because the smallest replacement quantity will be 8 and the new objective value will be $245 + 5 \cdot 8 = 285$.

11.(b) s_1 because there is a tie for the small replacement quantity between rows 2 and 4.

11.(c) s_1 because the increase will be $2 \cdot 36 = 72$ which is larger than the increases for x_1 and s_4.

11.(d) s_4 because s_4 has the most negative coefficient in the objective row.

13. The optimal tableau below indicates a nonunique solution and an unbounded set of feasible solutions:

x_1	x_2	s_3	s_4	
0	1	0	1	40
1	0	-1	1	20
0	0	0	1	40

Section 3.4

1. $[4, 1, \frac{5}{2}]^T$.

3. If we choose $y = [1, 1, -2, 0, -15]^T$, then setting $t = 5$ in $x + ty$ yields the basic solution $x^b = [65, 35, 0, 0, 125]^T$.

5. If we choose $y = [0, 1, -1, -1, -10]^T$, then setting $t = 30$ in $x + ty$ yields the basic solution $x^b = [0, 80, 20, 70, 0]^T$.

7. The successive choices $y = [1, 0, 1, -2, -3]^T$ with $t = 1$ and then $y = [1, 0, -1, 0, 1]^T$ with $t = 5$ lead to the basic solution $x^b = [10, 0, 0, 0, 8]^T$.

9. Try a distinct pair of lines that intersect in a single point.

Section 3.5

1. Example 3.5.3 leads to the following minimization problem where y_1 is the number of Pill 1 and y_2 the number of Pill 2.

$$
\begin{array}{llrll}
\text{Minimize}: & 1.5y_1 & + & 0.7y_2 & \\
\text{Subject to}: & 50y_1 & + & 20y_2 & \geq 600 \\
& 30y_1 & + & 20y_2 & \geq 400 \\
& 50y_1 & + & 10y_2 & \geq 350 \\
& \multicolumn{4}{l}{y_1 \geq 0, \ y_2 \geq 0}
\end{array}
$$

3. With the change of variables suggested in the Exercise and Example 3.5.8, the linear program is

$$
\begin{array}{ll}
\text{Maximize}: & 80T1 + 48T2 + 100T3 + 2,576 \\
\text{Subject to}: & 2T1 + T2 + 3T3 - FA \leq 54 \\
& T1 + T2 + 2T3 - AS \leq 37 \\
& T1 + T2 + T3 - FI \leq 5 \\
& FA + AS + FI \leq 120 \\
& \text{All variables nonnegative.}
\end{array}
$$

4. The objective function shows how to allow for discounts for a percentage of the

cars:

Maximize :

$$[.9 + (.1)(.9)]14500x_1 + [.9 + (.1)(.9)]19000x_2 + [.8 + (.2)(.8)]23000x_3$$

$$
\begin{array}{rcrcrcr}
\text{Subject to :} & x_1 &+& x_2 &+& x_3 &\geq& 100,000 \\
& -7x_1 &+& x_2 &+& 8x_3 &\leq& 0 \\
& & & & & x_3 &\geq& 20,000 \\
& x_1 &+& x_2 & & &\leq& 90,000 \\
\end{array}
$$

$$x_1 \geq 0,\ x_2 \geq 0,\ x_3 \geq 0$$

5. Let x_1 and x_2 be the numbers of 3- and 5-speeds made on regular time, x_3 and x_4 the respective numbers made on overtime, and x_5 the number of frames bought.

Maximize :

$$x_1 + x_2 + (12 - \tfrac{1}{3} \cdot 6 - \tfrac{1}{4} \cdot 4.50)x_3 + (15 - \tfrac{1}{2} \cdot 6 - \tfrac{2}{3} \cdot 4.5)x_4 - 4x_5$$

$$
\begin{array}{rcrcrcrcrcr}
\text{Subject to :} & x_1 &+& x_2 &+& x_3 & & & & &\geq& 100,000 \\
& \tfrac{1}{3}x_1 &+& \tfrac{1}{2}x_2 & & & & & & &\leq& 40 \\
& \tfrac{1}{4}x_1 &+& \tfrac{2}{3}x_2 & & & & & & &\leq& 50 \\
& & & & & \tfrac{1}{3}x_3 &+& \tfrac{1}{2}x_4 & & &\leq& 16 \\
& & & & & \tfrac{1}{4}x_3 &+& \tfrac{2}{3}x_4 & & &\leq& 16 \\
& x_1 &+& x_2 &+& x_3 &+& x_4 &-& x_5 &\leq& 100 \\
\end{array}
$$

$$x_i \geq 0,\ i = 1, \ldots, 5$$

7. The formulation and solution can be found in the answer to Exercise 13 of Section 3.6.

9. The LINDO formulation of the linear program to solve this problem is an example in Appendix A1 on LINDO.

11. With $A, F,$ and R representing the numbers of ambulances, fire trucks, and roadsters, respectively, the formulation is

$$
\begin{array}{lll}
\text{Maximize :} & 70A + 80F + 50R & \\
\text{Subject to :} & \frac{A}{4} + \frac{F}{3} + \frac{R}{6} - MH \leq 0 & \\
& \frac{A}{4} + \frac{F}{3} + \frac{R}{6} - DH \leq 0 & \text{Dressing} \\
& \frac{A}{3} + \frac{F}{6} + \frac{R}{6} - PH \leq 0 & \text{Pack/Ship} \\
& MH + DH + PH \leq 4 \cdot 40 \cdot 13 & \text{Hours} \\
& A - F + R \leq 0 & \text{Demand} \\
\end{array}
$$

All variables nonnegative.

13. The formulation below includes equality constraints with the "slack" variables in the objective function to account for the idle hours:

$$\begin{aligned}
\text{Maximize:} \quad & 64v + 72w + 104x + 120y + 56z - 12s_1 - 8s_2 - 9s_3 - 12s_4 \\
\text{Subject to:} \quad & v + w + 2x && + .5z + s_1 && = 120 \\
& v && + 3x + 2y + z + s_2 && = 120 \\
& .5v + .25w + && y + .5z + s_3 && = 80 \\
& v + 2w + x + 2y + z + s_4 && = 160
\end{aligned}$$

All variables nonnegative.

15. Letting x_i be the amount invested in bond i:

$$\begin{aligned}
\text{Maximize:} \quad & 11x_1 + 8x_2 + 9x_3 + 9x_4 \\
\text{Subject to:} \quad & x_1 + x_2 + x_3 + x_4 = 2{,}000{,}000 \\
& -x_1 - x_2 + x_3 - 3x_4 \ge 0 \\
& x_1 + 2x_2 - 2x_3 + 3x_4 \ge 0 \\
& x_i \le 800{,}000, \ i = 1, \dots, 4 \\
& x_1 \ge 0, \ x_2 \ge 0, \ x_3 \ge 0, \ x_4 \ge 0
\end{aligned}$$

Note that constraints 2 and 3 are obtained as in Example 3.5.7.

Section 3.6

1. $x_1 = 0, x_2 = 10$.

2. $x_1 = 0, x_2 = 0, x_3 = 60$.

3. The initial tableau:

x_1	x_2	x_3	s_1	s_2	a_2	a_3	
1	2	3	1	0	0	0	40
2	4	0	0	−1	1	0	20
1	−1	2	0	0	0	1	15
−4	−5	−3	0	0	0	0	0
−3	−3	−2	0	1	0	0	−35

5. $x_1 = 0, x_2 = 8$.

7. $x_1 = 66\frac{2}{3}, x_2 = 33\frac{1}{3}$.

9. The optimal tableau, not including artificial variables:

x_1	x_2	x_3	s_1	s_2	s_3	s_4	
0	1	0	0	.1	1	.9	58,750
0	1	1	0	.1	0	.9	78,750
1	1	0	0	0	0	1	90,000
0	1	0	1	.1	0	1.9	68,750
0	17625	0	0	2760	0	33675	3,030,750,000

11. $x_1 = 5, x_2 = 20, x_3 = 0, a_2 = 0$ with a_2 an active variable.

13. The LINDO formulation and solution. Note that the CASH right-hand side takes into consideration the 8 existing cows.

```
MAX       425 SY + 300 CN + 350 P + 1030 D + 185 SH + 5 CH + 5 DB
  SUBJECT TO
    LAND)    SY + CN + P + 2 D + SH <=    230
    CASH)    8 SY + 10 CN + 14 P + 600 D + 85 SH + 8 CH <= 12300
    WNHR)    15 SY + 10 CN + 10 P + 110 D + 15 SH + 0.5 CH <= 3280
    SMHR)    35 SY + 25 CN + 30 P + 60 D + 12 SH + 0.3 CH + DB = 4200
    MCOW)    D >=    8
    COOP)    CH <=    100
    ROTA)    CN + P >=    100
  END


OBJECTIVE FUNCTION VALUE: 56226.48

VARIABLE VALUES: SY = 15.771231, CN = 100, P = 0, D = 17.383511,
       SH = 8.749690, CH = 0, DB = 0
```

Section 3.7

1. $y_1 = 1, y_2 = 1$.

3. $y_1 = \frac{2}{3}, y_2 = \frac{16}{3}$.

4.(b) The resources are used completely in the first and the fourth constraints since the corresponding slack variables, s_3 and s_6, are not basic and are therefore zero.

5. $y_1 = 6, y_2 = 0, y_3 = \frac{4}{3}$.

7. $y_1 = 6\frac{2}{3}, y_2 = 0, y_3 = \frac{4}{3}$.

9. The dual is

$$
\begin{aligned}
\text{Minimize}: \quad & 100y_1 + 240y_2 + 40y_3 \\
\text{Subject to}: \quad & 2y_1 - 3y_2 + y_3 \geq 12 \\
& y_1 + 5y_2 \qquad\;\; \geq 20 \\
& y_1 \geq 0,\; y_2 \geq 0,\; y_3 \geq 0
\end{aligned}
$$

Because $x_1 > 0$ and $x_2 > 0$, both constraints are tight. Because the third constraint of the primal problem is slack, $y_3 = 0$. Hence, solve

$$
\begin{aligned}
2y_1 - 3y_2 &= 12 \\
y_1 + 5y_2 &= 20
\end{aligned}
$$

which has the solution $y_1 = 9\frac{3}{13}, y_2 = 2\frac{2}{13}$.

11. The dual is

$$
\begin{aligned}
\text{Maximize:} \quad & 12x_1 \;+\; 20x_2 \;+\; 12x_3 \\
\text{Subject to:} \quad & x_1 \;+\; 5x_2 \;+\; 2x_3 \;\le\; 4 \\
& x_1 \;-\; 2x_2 \;+\; 3x_3 \;\le\; 3 \\
& x_1 \;-\; 4x_2 \;-\; x_3 \;=\; 8 \\
& x_1 \ge 0, \; x_2 \le 0, \; x_3 \text{ unrestricted}
\end{aligned}
$$

13. The dual is

$$
\begin{aligned}
\text{Minimize:} \quad & w = b_1 y_1 + b_2 y_2 + b_3 y_3 \\
\text{Subject to:} \quad & a_{11}y_1 \;+\; a_{21}y_2 \;+\; a_{31}y_3 \;\ge\; c_1 \\
& a_{12}y_1 \;+\; a_{22}y_2 \;+\; a_{32}y_{32} \;=\; c_2 \\
& y_1 \ge 0, \; y_2 \le 0, \; y_3 \text{ unrestricted}
\end{aligned}
$$

Following the process of Theorem 3.7.2, express the difference $w - z$ as

$$
(b_1 - a_{11}x_1 - a_{12}x_2)y_1 + (b_2 - a_{21}x_1 - a_{22}x_2)y_2 + (b_3 - a_{31}x_1 - a_{32}x_2)y_3 + x_1 y_4
$$

Note that y_4 is a nonnegative surplus variable that is inserted in the first constraint of the dual. The third term is zero because the third primal constraint is an equality; the others can be easily seen as the products of two factors of the same sign.

15. Letting y_i be the number of people starting work on day i of the week, the minimization problem is

$$
\begin{aligned}
\text{Minimize:} \quad & y_1 \;+\; y_2 \;+\; y_3 \;+\; y_4 \;+\; y_5 \;+\; y_6 \;+\; y_7 \\
\text{Subject to:} \quad & y_1 \phantom{{}+{}y_2+{}y_3} + y_4 \;+\; y_5 \;+\; y_6 \;+\; y_7 \;\ge\; 6 \\
& y_1 \;+\; y_2 \phantom{{}+{}y_3} + y_5 \;+\; y_6 \;+\; y_7 \;\ge\; 11 \\
& y_1 \;+\; y_2 \;+\; y_3 \phantom{{}+{}y_4} + y_6 \;+\; y_7 \;\ge\; 10 \\
& y_1 \;+\; y_2 \;+\; y_3 \;+\; y_4 \phantom{{}+{}y_5+{}y_6} + y_7 \;\ge\; 12 \\
& y_1 \;+\; y_2 \;+\; y_3 \;+\; y_4 \;+\; y_5 \;\ge\; 14 \\
& y_2 \;+\; y_3 \;+\; y_4 \;+\; y_5 \;+\; y_6 \;\ge\; 15 \\
& y_3 \;+\; y_4 \;+\; y_5 \;+\; y_6 \;+\; y_7 \;\ge\; 13 \\
& y_i \ge 0, \; i = 1,\ldots,7
\end{aligned}
$$

The dual is

$$
\begin{aligned}
\text{Maximize:} \quad & 6x_1 + 11x_2 + 10x_3 + 12x_4 + 14x_5 + 15x_6 + 13x_7 \\
\text{Subject to:} \quad & x_1 \;+\; x_2 \;+\; x_3 \;+\; x_4 \;+\; x_5 \;\le\; 1 \\
& x_2 \;+\; x_3 \;+\; x_4 \;+\; x_5 \;+\; x_6 \;\le\; 1 \\
& x_3 \;+\; x_4 \;+\; x_5 \;+\; x_6 \;+\; x_7 \;\le\; 1 \\
& x_1 \phantom{{}+{}x_2+{}x_3} + x_4 \;+\; x_5 \;+\; x_6 \;+\; x_7 \;\le\; 1 \\
& x_1 \;+\; x_2 \phantom{{}+{}x_3+{}x_4} + x_5 \;+\; x_6 \;+\; x_7 \;\le\; 1 \\
& x_1 \;+\; x_2 \;+\; x_3 \phantom{{}+{}x_4+{}x_5} + x_6 \;+\; x_7 \;\le\; 1 \\
& x_1 \;+\; x_2 \;+\; x_3 \;+\; x_4 \phantom{{}+{}x_5+{}x_6} + x_7 \;\le\; 1 \\
& x_i \ge 0, \; i = 1,\ldots,7
\end{aligned}
$$

Section 3.8

1. Land can be increased by $3\frac{1}{3}$ acres or decreased by 25. Labor can be increased by 5 days or decreased by 10 days.

2. The set of feasible solutions is a line segment because of the equality constraint. The right hand side can be increased without bound; the maximum decrease is 6.

3. For the first constraint, the maximum increase is 25 and the maximum decrease is 7.5. For the fourth constraint, the maximum increase is 160 and the maximum decrease is 14.29.

5. When the maximum increase and decrease for the second constraint are calculated the new constraints are shown dashed in the figure below.

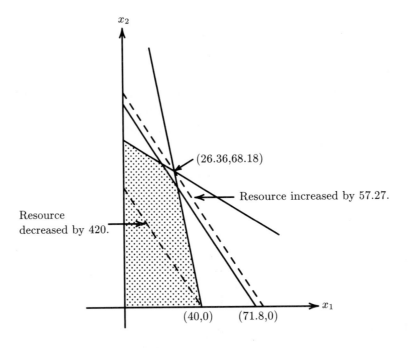

7.(b) An additonal day of labor is worth \$16.25.

7.(d) If the capital is increased by \$160, the new values of the basic variables are

$$
\begin{aligned}
x_1 &= 30 - \tfrac{1}{80} \cdot 160 = 28 \\
x_2 &= 15 + \tfrac{3}{160} \cdot 160 = 18 \\
s_1 &= 5 - \tfrac{1}{160} \cdot 160 = 4 \\
s_4 &= 50 + \tfrac{1}{16} \cdot 160 = 60
\end{aligned}
$$

7.(e) If the new variable is the number of dollars diverted to hiring additional labor, its column of coefficients is $[0, -\frac{1}{25}, 1, 1, 0]^T$.

9.(a) They should pay no more than $90 for an additional component.

9.(b) The -180 as the objective row coefficient of a_2 indicates that increasing the number of items made would be a bad idea.

9.(c) The number of production hours could range from 2,375 to 2,500 and retain the same set of basic variables.

D.4 Chapter 4

Section 4.1

1.(a) The path is D, B, A, C, H.

3. When the constraints $ap + bp \le 220$ and $bq + cq \le 220$ are added to the formulation in Example 4.1.1, the solution is $ap = 90, bp = 100, bq = 80, cq = 140, pq = 0, px = 190, qx = 10, qy = 210, xy = 0$.

5. The assignments of applicants to jobs is 1 to b, 2 to f, 3 to c, 4 to d, 5 to e, 6 to a.

7. There is one more vertex than there are edges.

Section 4.2

1.(a) When formulated as a linear program, the problem is:

$$\text{Minimize: } 5x_{12} + 8x_{12} + 6x_{13} + 4x_{21} + 9x_{22} + 6x_{23}$$

Subject to:
$$x_{11} + x_{12} + x_{13} = 12$$
$$x_{21} + x_{22} + x_{23} = 8$$
$$x_{11} + x_{21} = 7$$
$$x_{12} + x_{22} = 6$$
$$x_{13} + x_{23} = 7$$

1.(b) The positive variables in the solution are $x_{12} = 6, x_{13} = 6, x_{21} = 7, x_{23} = 1$.

3. With the total demand of 75 exceeding the total supply by 15, a fourth origin is added with supply 15. The positive variables in the solution are $x_{13} = 20, x_{22} = 15, x_{31} = 25, x_{42} = 10$, and $x_{43} = 5$. Thus, 10 truckdriver and 5 computer operator positions are unfilled.

5. Values of positive variables: $x_{11} = 2, x_{12} = 4, x_{13} = 1, x_{23} = 8, x_{31} = 4, x_{34} = 6$.

7. Letting x_{12} become basic leads to a solution with positive variables $x_{12} = 2, x_{14} = 8, x_{22} = 10, x_{23} = 5, x_{31} = 8$, and $x_{33} = 2$. Letting x_{32} become basic leads to a solution with positive variables $x_{11} = 2, x_{14} = 8, x_{22} = 8, x_{23} = 7, x_{31} = 6$, and $x_{32} = 4$.

9. The matrix of costs is below. Supplies are in chronological order down the first column, demands left to right across the top. The last column is a fictitious demand to balance the problem. The $6 charge in the first row of the fictitious demand represents existing inventory that has not been shipped. The other costs are zero under the assumption that the items they represent will not be built. The M's represent impossible situations since there is no provision for back ordering.

	420	360	450	90
120	0	2	4	6
300	0	2	4	0
100	8	10	12	0
300	M	0	2	0
100	M	8	10	0
300	M	M	0	0
100	M	M	8	0

11. The matrix of costs for the initial tableau is shown below. Each column is headed by the demand, month, and dealer; each row by the supply, month and plant. A fictitious demand of 11 is added to achieve balance. The calculations involve shipping cost, the $100 additional cost at plant B, the $80 a month late fee, and the $55 a month storage cost for building ahead. The supplies are gotten by dividing the number of hours available by the hours per motor.

| | 12 | 10 | 8 | 9 | 12 | 11 | 11 | 8 | 12 | 11 |
| | 1 | 2 | 3 | 1 | 2 | 3 | 1 | 2 | 3 | |
	Apr	Apr	Apr	May	May	May	Jun	Jun	Jun	
20 Apr A	45	50	75	100	105	130	155	160	185	0
17 Apr B	160	170	140	215	225	195	270	280	250	0
18 May A	125	130	155	45	50	75	100	105	130	0
14 May B	240	250	220	160	170	140	215	225	195	0
18 Jun A	205	210	235	125	130	155	45	50	75	0
17 Jun B	320	330	300	240	250	220	160	170	140	0

13. The table of costs is shown below. Each column is headed by the market and the demand; each row by the plant and the capacity. The O indicates the use of overtime at plant A and the supply of 120 is calculated to balance supply and demand. Costs include labor, other, and shipping.

| | 1 | 2 | 3 | 4 |
	155	230	225	160
A 300	155	165	160	170
O 120	190	210	205	215
B 350	170	180	175	185

15. The table of costs is given below. Each column is headed by the customer, month, and demand; each row by the plant, month, and capacity. The beginning inventories are included in the capacities for May. The capacity of 180 is assigned to DEF to balance supply and demand. Costs are for shipping or the contractual amount to DEF.

	1 May 200	2 May 310	3 May 400	1 Jun 450	2 Jun 520	3 Jun 350
A May 600	40	28	32	40	28	32
B May 650	36	38	24	36	38	24
A Jun 400	M	M	M	40	28	32
B Jun 400	M	M	M	36	38	24
DEF 180	700	700	700	700	700	700

Section 4.3

1. The critical path is $0 \to 1 \to 3 \to 4 \to 5 \to 6$.

3. The CPM network is:

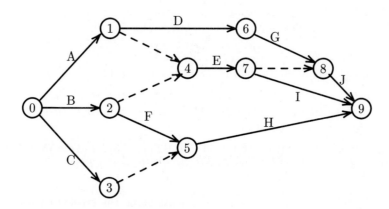

The critical path is 19 days long and is $0 \to 2 \to 4 \to 7 \to 9$. The critical tasks are getting sponsors, planning advertising, and advertising.

5.(a) The critical path is $0 \to 1 \to 4 \to 5$.

5.(b) A LINDO formulation to reduce the length of the critical path to 22 at minimum cost. The constant F is the amount $\sum r_{ij} u_{ij}$ from the project deadline model.

```
MIN     F - 600 T01 - 800 T02 - 750 T13 - 650 T14 - 900 T24 - 400 T35
            - 600 T45
    SUBJECT TO
            2) - T01 + T1 - T0 >=   0
```

```
 3)     T01 >=    4
 4)     T01 <=    8
 5)  -  T02 -  T0 + T2 >=    0
 6)     T02 >=    6
 7)     T02 <=    9
 8)  -  T13 -  T1 + T3 >=    0
 9)     T13 >=    6
10)     T13 <=    7
11)  -  T14 -  T1 + T4 >=    0
12)     T14 >=    7
13)     T14 <=    10
14)  -  T2 + T4 -  T26 >=    0
15)     T24 >=    4
16)     T24 <=    6
17)  -  T35 -  T3 + T5 >=    0
18)     T35 >=    6
19)     T35 <=    9
20)  -  T45 -  T4 + T5 >=    0
21)     T45 >=    5
22)     T45 <=    8
23)  -  T0 + T5 <=    22
24)     F =       37550
   END
```

The time reduction is accomplished by crashing $(0,1)$ from 8 to 4 at a cost of $2,400.

5.(c) The completion time can be reduced to 16 by by reducing $(0,1)$ to 4, $(1,3)$ to 6, $(1,4)$ to 7, $(3,5)$ to 6, and $(4,5)$ to 5.

7.(a) The earliest times are: $ET(0) = 0, ET(1) = 4, ET(2) = 5, ET(3) = 15, ET(4) = 12, ET(5) = 18, ET(6) = 23$. The latest times are: $LT(0) = 0, LT(1) = 7, LT(2) = 5, LT(3) = 15, LT(4) = 16, LT(5) = 18, LT(6) = 23$.

7.(b) The critical path is $0 \to 2 \to 3 \to 5 \to 6$. Floats along the critical path are 0. The others are $F(0,1) = 3, F(1,3) = 3, F(2,4) = 4, F(4,5) = 4$.

7.(c) The cheapest way to complete the project in 19 days is to reduce $(2,3)$ from 10 days to 8, and $(5,6)$ from 5 days to 3 at a cost of $2,000.

9. In the LINDO formulation below the last constraint is

$$1,000(5 - t_{01}) + 800(8 - t_{12}) + 900(6 - t_{45}) \le 3,000$$

revised so that LINDO will accept it.

```
MIN      T5
   SUBJECT TO
```

```
 2)    T1 - T0 - T01 >=    0
 3)    T01 >=    3
 4)    T01 <=    5
 5) -  T0 + T2 - T12 >=    0
 6)    T12 >=    5
 7)    T12 <=    8
 8) -  T1 + T3 >=    5
 9) -  T3 + T4 >=    8
10) -  T2 + T4 >=    6
11)    T5 - T4 - T45 >=    0
12)    T45 >=    3
13)    T45 <=    6
14)    T5 - T3 >=    10
15)    1000 T01 + 800 T12 + 900 T45 >=    13800
END
```

11. The critical path includes activities D, E, H, and I and is 16 weeks long.

Section 4.4

1. Shortest path from A to H is A, B, E, G, H.

3. Shortest path from a to i is a, c, f, h, i.

5. The commuter should follow the path h, a, c, e, f, g, w.

7. Put the books 9″ or under on 2 shelves on the 8′ wall; those between 9″ and 10″ on 3 shelves on the 8′ wall; and those between 10″ and 12″ on 4 shelves on the 10′ wall at a total cost of $486.

Section 4.5

1. The minimal spanning tree includes the links $B \to A, A \to C, C \to E, E \to G, G \to H, H \to F, F \to D$.

3. The minimal spanning tree includes the links $A \to D, D \to G, G \to F, F \to B, G \to E$, and $F \to C$.

5. The resulting tree is shown below. Compare it with the minimal spanning tree in Figure 4.5.7.

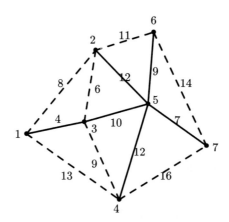

D.5   Chapter 5

Section 5.2

1.(a) $f'(x) = \dfrac{x^2 + 2x}{(x+1)^2}$

1.(c) $h'(x) = \dfrac{2x}{x^2 + 1}$

3. Since f has a local minimum at x_0, there exists $\delta > 0$ such that $f(x_0) \le f(x)$ for $x \in (x_0 - \delta, x_0 + \delta)$. If $0 < h < \delta$, then

$$f(x_0 + h) - f(x_0) \ge 0 \quad \text{and} \quad \frac{f(x_0 + h) - f(x_0)}{h} \ge 0$$

since $h > 0$. Then,

$$f'(x_0) = \lim_{h \to 0^+} \frac{f(x_0 + h) - f(x_0)}{h} \ge 0.$$

If $-\delta < h < 0$, then

$$f(x_0 + h) - f(x_0) \ge 0 \text{ and } \frac{f(x_0 + h) - f(x_0)}{h} \le 0$$

since $h < 0$. Then

$$f'(x_0) = \lim_{h \to 0^-} \frac{f(x_0 + h) - f(x_0)}{h} \le 0.$$

Since $f'(x_0)$ exists, these two limits must agree, and we have $f'(x_0) = 0$.

5. $q = 32$.

7. $q \approx 25.9$.

8. $q = 50$.

Section 5.3

1. The expression for the surface area of such a can is $S = 2\pi r^2 + \dfrac{20,000}{r}$. The second derivative is $S'' = 4\pi + \dfrac{40,000}{r^3}$ which is positive for positive r. Hence, the function is convex.

3. Order ≈ 115.47 items at a time.

5. Order 200 at a time.

7. The field should be $\frac{400}{3}$ by 200, and should be divided in the short direction.

9. $\dfrac{h}{r} = 2$.

11. Yes, with just under 48.1 seconds to spare.

Section 5.4

1.(b) $z_x = \dfrac{1 - x^2 - 2xy}{(1 + x^2)^2}$, $z_y = \dfrac{1}{1 + x^2}$.

3.(a) A minimum occurs at $(3, -2)$.

3.(c) A minimum occurs at $(0, 0)$.

7. $g_{xx} = \dfrac{2CD}{x^3} + \dfrac{Sy^2}{x^3} + \dfrac{By^2}{x^3}$ which is positive in the first quadrant, and the determinant $g_{xx}g_{yy} - (g_{xy})^2 = \dfrac{2(S + B)CD}{x^4}$ which is also positive.

9. When the orders x and y are divided equally between the two suppliers, the cost is $h(x, y) = \dfrac{S(x + y)}{2} + \dfrac{CD}{2x} + \dfrac{CD}{2y}$. The minimum of h occurs at $(\sqrt{\frac{CD}{S}}, \sqrt{\frac{CD}{S}})$. Evaluating h at this point yields $2\sqrt{CDS}$. The cost from Example 5.3.2 is $\sqrt{2CDS}$.

11. The dining center should be at $(3, 5.66667)$.

Section 5.5

1. $y = 1.5976x + .8902$.

3. $y = -.002874x + 7.47038$.

5. The prediction for year 6 is $16\frac{1}{5}$ and for year 7 is $18\frac{2}{5}$.

9. $y = -30.3632815 + 3.203125x$.

11. To generate the required cost function using *Maple*, make 3 new variables, i.e., calculate $x = L^2, y = LB$, and $z = B^2$. Then the 4-variable analog of the procedure shown in Listing B.2.5 with Cost as the dependent variable will yield the result

$$w = -1433.069 + .006277L^2 + .007844LB + .006528B^2.$$

The coefficients here have been changed from the original rational numbers given by *Maple*. The profit function is then $p = 3,400L + 3,100B - w$. This function has a maximum at $L \approx 119,634.7, B \approx 196,079.8$.

Section 5.6

1. No extrema.

3. A maximum occurs at $(78, 24, -1)$.

5. Note that $f_{x_i}(x) = \sum_{j=1}^{n} q_{ij}x_j + c_i$.

6.(a) $2x_1^2 + 6x_1x_2 + 4x_2^2 - x_1 + x_2 = [x_1, x_2] \begin{bmatrix} 2 & 3 \\ 3 & 4 \end{bmatrix} \begin{bmatrix} x_1 \\ x_2 \end{bmatrix} + \begin{bmatrix} -1 \\ 1 \end{bmatrix} \cdot \begin{bmatrix} x_1 \\ x_2 \end{bmatrix}$

D.6   Chapter 6

Section 6.1

1. Solving the constraint for r gives $r = \sqrt{\frac{1000}{\pi h}}$. Substituting in the objective function gives $S = \dfrac{2000}{h} + 2\sqrt{\pi}1000^{1/2}h^{1/2}$ and solving for h yields $h = \left(\frac{4,000}{\pi}\right)^{1/3} \approx 10.83$.

3. $(x, y) = (.5, 3.5)$.

5. The level curve is the ellipse $x_1^2 + 4x_2^2 = 4$ and $\nabla f(2, 0) = [4, 0]^T$.

7. $x = 25.74, y = 43.95$. It is helpful to know that if one of the short sides of a $45° - 45° - 90°$ triangle is x, then the other sides are x and $\sqrt{2}x$.

Section 6.2

1. The solution occurs at $(1, 4)$. The line $2x + 6y = 26$ is tangent to the ellipse $4x^2 + 3y^2 = 52$ at that point.

3. $x \approx 5.090, y \approx 6.909$.

5. $x = 0, y = 2\frac{2}{3}$.

7. $x \approx 3.577715, y \approx 1.788841$. The value of the objective function is ≈ 17.88854 and the line $4x + 2y = 17.88854$ is a level curve of the objective function and is tangent to the circle $x^2 + y^2 = 16$ at the point of solution.

Section 6.3

1. $x_1 = 0, x_2 = 1.5, x_3 = 5$.

3. $x_1 = 0, x_2 = 0, x_3 = 4$.

5. $x_1 = 2.914286, x_2 = 1.028571, x_3 = 2.057143$.

7. $x_1 = 2, x_2 = 0, x_3 = 0$.

Section 6.4

1. $x_1 = 4, x_2 = 4, x_3 = 2$.

3. (a) and (b)

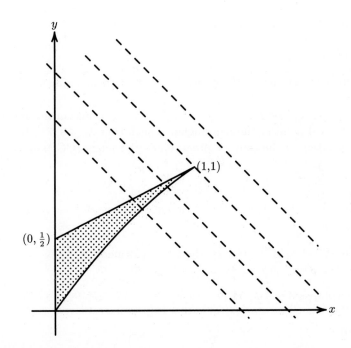

5. $x_1 = 0.5, x_2 = 0.1, x_3 = 0.4$.

7. Locate the service pole at $(43.46, 79.72)$.

Section 6.5

1. The equation of the tangent plane is $w - w_0 = \nabla f(x_0) \cdot (x - x_0)$. Here that yields $w = 16x_1 + 15x_2 - 4x_3 - 28$.

3. If f and g both lie above their tangent planes, i.e.,

$$f(x) \geq f(x_0) + \nabla f(x_0) \cdot (x - x_0) \text{ and } g(x) \geq g(x_0) + \nabla g(x_0) \cdot (x - x_0)$$

and a and b are both nonnegative constants, then

$$
\begin{aligned}
af(x) + bg(x) &\geq a\left(f(x_0) + \nabla f(x_0) \cdot (x - x_0)\right) + b\left(g(x_0) + \nabla g(x_0) \cdot (x - x_0)\right) \\
&= (af + bg)(x_0) + \nabla(af + bg)(x_0) \cdot (x - x_)
\end{aligned}
$$

so $af + bg$ is convex.

5.(a) Let f be convex and x_1 and x_2 both belong to $S = \{x : f(x) \leq b\}$ and $c = tx_1 + (1 - t)x_2$ for $0 \leq t \leq 1$. Then

$$f(c) \leq tf(x_1) + (1 - t)f(x_2) \leq tb + (1 - t)b = b.$$

Thus, S is convex.

6. The theorem for a concave mathematical program corresponding to Theorem 6.5.3 is:

    If f is a concave function and g^i, $i = 1, \ldots, m$ are all convex functions and $(\hat{x}, \hat{\lambda}, \hat{s})$ is a critical point of the Lagrangian L such that $\hat{\lambda}_i \geq 0$, $i = 1, \ldots, m$, then $\hat{x}$ is a global solution of the concave programming problem (CCP).

8. $x_1 = \frac{19}{11}, x_2 = \frac{28}{11}$.

9. $x_1 = \frac{24}{7}, x_2 = \frac{12}{7}$.

10. $x_1 = 4, x_2 = 6$.

13. Divide the \$1,000 equally between the two investments.

15. A doghouse should be 3.5 feet long, 2.75 feet wide, with walls 3.3863 feet high, and having a total cost of \$48.55.

Section 6.6

1. The Lagrangian is

$$
\begin{aligned}
L &= 10x_1 + 12x_2 - \lambda_1(x_1 + x_2 + s_1^2 - 150) - \lambda_2(x_1 + 2x_2 + s_2^2 - 100) \\
&\quad - \lambda_3(8x_1 + 4x_2 + s_3^2 - 320) - \lambda_4(-x_1 + s_4^2) - \lambda_5(-x_2 + s_5^2)
\end{aligned}
$$

The solution is $x_1 = 20$, $x_2 = 40$.

3. $L_{x_{ij}} = c_{ij} - v_i - w_j \geq 0$.

D.7 Chapter 7

Section 7.2

1. Take items 1, 2, and 3 for a maximum value of 59.

3.(a) Include experiments 1, 3, and 5 for a total merit of 170.

3.(b) Include experiments 2, 3, and 6 for a total merit of 230.

5. James should employ strategies 2, 3, 4, and 5 for a tax savings of $3,915.

Section 7.3

1. $y_1 = 3\frac{1}{3}, y_2 = 0, y_3 = \frac{2}{3}$.

3. $x_1 = 30, x_2 = \frac{75}{2}, x_3 = 5$.

5. $x_1 = 100, x_2 = 0, s_1 = 0, s_2 = 10, s_3 = 300$.

Section 7.4

1. The new solution is $x_1 = 0$ and $x_2 = 20$.

3. The final *Maple* tableau for the new solution, with the new constraint in the fourth row, is

$$
M8 := \begin{bmatrix}
0 & 0 & 1 & 0 & 0 & -1/2 & 25 \\
0 & 1 & 0 & 1/3 & 0 & -1/6 & 85/3 \\
1 & 0 & 0 & -1/3 & 0 & 2/3 & 140/3 \\
0 & 0 & 0 & -10/3 & 1 & -10/3 & 200/3 \\
0 & 0 & 0 & 80/3 & 0 & 20/3 & 15800/3
\end{bmatrix}
$$

5. The final *Maple* tableau for the new solution, with the new constraint in the fifth row, is

$$
M6 := \begin{bmatrix}
0 & 0 & 1 & 1/4 & 0 & 0 & 1 & 0 & -3/4 & 620 \\
0 & 1 & 0 & 3/8 & 0 & 0 & -1/2 & 0 & 7/8 & 890 \\
1 & 0 & 0 & -3/8 & 0 & 0 & 1/2 & 0 & 1/8 & 1510 \\
0 & 0 & 0 & -7/8 & 0 & 0 & -3/2 & 1 & -11/8 & 70 \\
0 & 0 & 0 & 1/4 & 1 & -1 & 1 & 0 & 1/4 & 20 \\
0 & 0 & 0 & 135/4 & 0 & 0 & 75 & 0 & 315/4 & 370500
\end{bmatrix}
$$

Section 7.5

1. $x_1 = 0, x_2 = 5$.
3. $x_1 = 5, x_2 = 0$.
5. $x_1 = 0, x_2 = 0, x_3 = 11$.

Section 7.6

1. A LINDO formulation:

```
MIN     X1 + X2 + X3 + X4 + X5
  SUBJECT TO
       2)   5 X1 + 10 X2 + 20 X3 + 25 X4 + 50 X5 =      90
  END
  GIN     5
```

3. A LINDO formulation:

```
TITLE Section 7.6 no. 3:
max .50 tr + .50 or + .60 tp + .60 op - .40 t1 - .35 t2 - .30 t3
  - 500 d1 - 750 d2 - 1250 d3
st
  texas) tp + tr - .7 t1 - .7 t2 - .7 t3 < 5000   ! Texas supply
  offsh) op + or < 10000      ! Offshore supply
  premi) tp + op > 8000       ! Premium demand
  regul) tr + or > 6000       ! Regular demand
  40%re) .6 tr - .4 or > 0    ! Regular 40% Texas
  60%pr) .4 tp - .6 op > 0    ! Premium 60% Texas
  most1) d1 + d2 + d3 < 1     ! At most one di = 1
  setf1) t1 - 15000 d1 < 0    ! Force spending
  setf2) t2 - 15000 d2 < 0    ! the fixed cost
  setf3) t3 - 15000 d3 < 0    ! if needed.
end
int d1
int d2
int d3
```

5. Letting all variables be $\{0,1\}$, let t_i represent the decision to use truck i and Ai, Bi, etc., represent the decisions to assign the respective loads to truck i. Then the objective function is

$$\text{Minimize}: 200t_1 + 300t_2 + 400t_3 + 350t_4 + 500t_5$$

Then there are four constraints for each truck – a capacity constraint, a constraint to force $t_i = 1$ if the truck is assigned a load, and constraints to prevent loads A and D and loads B and E from going on the same truck. Here are the constraints for truck 3:

$$A3 + 2B3 + 3C3 + 4D3 + 4E3 + 5F3 + 8G3 \leq 6$$
$$A3 + B3 + C3 + D3 + E3 + F3 + G3 \leq 7t_3$$
$$A3 + D3 \leq 1$$
$$B3 + E3 \leq 1$$

7. If $t_6 - t_2 \geq 7$ is the constraint for "D. Obtain other materials," introduce a $\{0, 1\}$ variable d into the linear program with a coefficient of 300 in the objective function and change the constraint to

$$t_6 - t_2 + 3d \geq 7.$$

9. Let each variable represent the decision to build at the corresponding site:

Minimize:	$30A$	$+$	$45B$	$+$	$50C$	$+$	$25D$	$+$	$35E$		
Subject to :	A			$+$	C					$\geq$	1
			B			$+$	D			$\geq$	1
					C			$+$	E	$\geq$	1
	A					$+$	D			$\geq$	1
	A	$+$	B							$\geq$	1
	A							$+$	E	$\geq$	1
	A	$+$	B			$+$	D			$\geq$	1

All variables $\{0, 1\}$

11. Robbie and Dana will ride the Teacups, Mini Himilayas, Whirling Chairs, and the Jungle.

13. Clyde, Michael, Scotty, Bill, and Earl should start.

Section 7.7

1. The shortest cycle goes from 2 to 5 to 1 to 4 to 3 to 2 and has length 32.

3. The matrix of costs is

M	11	9	21.6	9
12	M	11	4	15
8	11	M	8.4	28.8
21.6	4	8.4	M	5
10	16	28.8	6	M

The solution has a cost of \$38 and is $4 \to 2 \to 3 \to 1 \to 5 \to 4$.

5. The shortest cycle goes from 1 to 2 to 4 to 3 to 1 and has length 48.

6. The solution to the assignment problem does not need to form a cycle, thus it has a larger set of feasible solutions.

7. The lengths of the 5 cycles generated range from 60 – the optimal one found by starting with city 3 – to 78 for the one starting with city 5. The example below starting with city 2 is one of two with length 66.

$$2 \rightarrow 1 \rightarrow 3 \rightarrow 5 \rightarrow 4 \rightarrow 2$$

D.8   Chapter 8

Section 8.1

1.

$$
\begin{aligned}
H_n &= 2H_{n-1} + 1 \\
&= 2(2H_{n-2} + 1) + 1 \\
&= 2(2(2H_{n-3} + 1) + 1) + 1 \\
&= 2^3 H_{n-3} + 2^2 + 2 + 1 \\
&= \cdots \\
&= 2^{n-1} H_{n-(n-1)} + 2^{n-2} + \cdots + 2^2 + 2 + 1 \\
&= 2^{n-1} + 2^{n-2} + \cdots + 2^2 + 2 + 1 \\
&= 2^n - 1.
\end{aligned}
$$

   since $H_{n-(n-1)} = H_1 = 1$.

3. With ace high, there are 9 ways to choose the rank of the high card, then 4^5 ways to choose the actual cards, so the number of straights is $9 \cdot 4^5 = 9,216$.

5. $(2 - x^2)^5 = -x^{10} + 10x^8 - 40x^6 + 80x^4 - 80x^2 = 32$

7. The recursion is $D_n = n(1 + D_{n-1})$. $D_5 = 205$. $D_6 = 1,236$.

Section 8.2

1. The longest path goes from A to B to D to G to F to H and has length 35.

3. The longest path goes from a to c to d to e to h to i and has length 46.

Section 8.3

1. Ship all 7 from warehouse 1 to retail outlet 2, ship 5 from warehouse 2 to retail outlet 1, and the other 4 to outlet 3 with a total cost of 86.

3. At plant 1 get one part each from Ajax and Excelsior, all the parts at plant 2 should come from Ajax, and all parts at plant 3 should come from Excesior at a cost of 300.

Section 8.4

3. Buy 4 of Risky Venture, 2 of Aggressive Growth, and 1 of Gold & Oil Hedge.

5. The shortest cycle goes from 2 to 5 to 1 to 4 to 3 to 2 and has length 32.

References

[1] Austin, L. M., " 'Project EOQ': A Success Story in Implementing Academic Research," *Interfaces,* vol. 7 no. 4, 1977, pp. 1–14.

[2] Beale, E. M. L., "Cycling in the Dual Simplex Algorithm," *Naval Res. Logist. Quart.,* vol. 2 no. 4, December, 1955, pp. 269–276.

[3] Bradley, Stephen P., and Arnoldo C. Hax, and Thomas L. Magnanti, *Applied Mathematical Programming,* Addison-Wesley Publishing Company, 1977.

[4] Byrd, Jack, Jr., and L. Ted Moore, "The Application of a Product Mix Linear Programming Model in Corporate policy Making," *Management Science,* vol. 24 no. 13. Also reprinted in [11].

[5] Charnes, A. W., W. W. Cooper, and B. Mellon, "Blending Aviation Gasolines–A Study in Programming Interdependent Activities in an Integrated Oil Company," *Econometrica,* vol. 20 no. 2, 1952, pp. 135–159.

[6] Dantzig, George B., "Maximization of a Linear Form Whose Variables are Subject to a System of Linear Inequalities," Headquarters, USAAF, Nov. 1, 1949. Also reprinted in [21].

[7] Dantzig, George B., *Linear Programming and Extensions,* Princeton University Press, 1963.

[8] Dijkstra, E. W., "A note on two problems in connexion with graphs," *Numer. Math.,* vol. 1, 1959, pp. 269–271.

[9] Dreyfus, Stuart E., and Averill M. Law, *The Art and Theory of Dynamic Programming,* Academic Press, 1977.

[10] Duffin, Richard J., Elmor L. Peterson, and Clarence Zener, *Geometric Programming–Theory and Application,* John Wiley & Sons, 1967.

[11] Dyer, James S., and Roy D. Shapiro, *Management Science/Operations Research,* John Wiley & Sons, 1982.

[12] Gale, David, *The Theory of Linear Economic Models*, McGraw-Hill, 1960.

[13] Gibley, Raymond A., and Janet R. Gibley, "Sheltering Your Profits," *National Public Accountant,* vol. 37, 1992, pp. 20–22.

[14] Glover, Fred, Gene Jones, David Karney, Darwin Klingman, and John Mote, "An Integrated Production, Distribution and Inventory Planning System," *Interfaces,* vol. 9 no. 5, 1979, pp. 21–35. Also reprinted in [11].

[15] Grötschel, M., M. Jünger and G. Reinelt, "Optimal Control of Plotting and Drilling Machines: A Case Study," *Zeitschrift für Operations Research–Methods and Models of Operations Research,* 35, pp. 61–84.

[16] Hillier, Frederick S., and Gerald J. Lieberman, *Introduction to Mathematical Programming*, McGraw-Hill, Inc., 1990.

[17] Johnsonbaugh, Richard, *Discrete Mathematics*, Macmillan Publishing Company, 1984.

[18] Karush, W., "Minima of Functions of Several Variables with Inequalities as Side Conditions," M.S. Thesis, Department of Mathematics, University of Chicago, 1939.

[19] King, R. A., C. E. Bishop, and J. G. Sutherland, "Programming Resource Use and Capital Investment in Agriculture," *Management Science,* vol. 3 no. 2, 1957, pp. 173–184.

[20] Kolesar, Peter J., "A Branch and Bound Algorithm for the Knapsack Problem," *Management Science,* vol. 13 no. 9, 1967, pp. 723–735.

[21] Koopmans, T. C., ed., *Activity Analysis of Production and Allocation*, Cowles Commission Monograph no. 13, John Wiley & Sons, 1951.

[22] Kruskal, J. B. Jr., "On the shortest spanning subtree of a graph and the traveling salesman problem," *Proc. Amer. Math. Soc.,* vol. 7, 1956, pp. 48–50.

[23] Kuhn, H. W., and A. W. Tucker, "Nonlinear Programming," pp. 481-492 in *Proceedings of the Second Berkeley Symposium on Mathematical*

Statistics and Probability, Jerzy Neyman, ed., University of California Press, 1950.

[24] *LINGO User's Guide,* LINDO Systems Inc., 1995.

[25] Little, J. D. C., K. G. Murty, D. W. Sweeney, and C. Karel, "An algorithm for the traveling salesman problem," *Operations Research,* 11, 1963, pp. 979–983.

[26] Love, Robert R., Jr., and James M. Hoey, "Management Science Improves Fast-Food Operations," *Interfaces,* vol. 20, no. 2, 1990, pp. 21–29.

[27] Niven, Ivan, *Mathematics of Choice,* The Mathematical Association of America, 1965.

[28] Owen, G., *Finite Mathematics,* W. B. Saunders Company, 1970.

[29] Prim, R. G., "Shortest Connection Networks and Some Generalizations," *Bell Systems Technical Journal,* 36, 1957, pp. 1389–1401.

[30] Ravindran, A., Don Phillips, and James Solberg, *Operations Research: Principles and Practice,* Second Edition, John Wiley & Sons, 1987.

[31] Roberts, Stephen M., and Karen J. Mask, "Shutdown Management– Five Years of Learning," *American Association of Cost Engineers Transactions,* vol. 2, 1992, pp. U.3.1–U.3.7.

[32] Schrage, Linus, *Linear, Integer and Quadratic Programming with LINDO,* The Scientific Press, 1986.

[33] Schrage, Linus, *Optimization Modeling with LINGO,* LINDO Systems, Inc, 1998.

[34] Stewart, James, *Calculus, Early Transcendentals,* Third Edition, Brooks/Cole Publishing Company, 1995.

[35] TI-82 *GRAPHICS CALCULATOR GUIDEBOOK,* Texas Instruments Incorporated, 1993.

[36] *TI-92 GUIDEBOOK,* Texas Instruments Incorporated, 1995.

[37] Totten, Louise, and Noha Tohamy, "Home for the Holidays," *ORMS Today,* vol. 22, no. 6, 1995, pp. 24–29.

[38] Wagner, Harvey M., *Principles of Operations Research*, Second Edition, Prentice-Hall, Inc., 1975.

[39] Winston, Wayne L., *Inroduction to Mathematical Programming: Applications and Algorithms*, PWS-KENT Publishing Company, 1991.

Index